ARCHAEOLOGY OF ATLANTIC AFRICA AND THE AFRICAN DIASPORA

Archaeology of Atlantic Africa and the African Diaspora

edited by
Akinwumi Ogundiran and Toyin Falola

Indiana University Press

Bloomington and Indianapolis

Publication of this book is made possible in part with the assistance of a
Challenge Grant from the National Endowment for the Humanities,
a federal agency that supports research, education, and public programming
in the humanities. Any views, findings, conclusions, or recommendations
expressed in this publication do not necessarily reflect those of the
National Endowment for the Humanities.

This book is a publication of

Indiana University Press
601 North Morton Street
Bloomington, IN 47404-3797 USA

http://iupress.indiana.edu

Telephone orders   800-842-6796
Fax orders   812-855-7931
Orders by e-mail   iuporder@indiana.edu

© 2007 by Indiana University Press

All rights reserved

The paper used in this publication meets the minimum requirements of
American National Standard for Information Sciences—Permanence of
Paper for Printed Library Materials, ANSI Z39.48-1984.

Manufactured in the United States of America

Library of Congress Cataloging-in-Publication Data

Archaeology of Atlantic Africa and the African diaspora /
edited by Akinwumi Ogundiran and Toyin Falola.
p. cm.—(Blacks in the diaspora)
Includes bibliographical references and index.
ISBN 978-0-253-34919-4 (cl : alk. paper)
1. Blacks—Africa, West—Antiquities. 2. Blacks—America—Antiquities.
3. Africans—America—Antiquities. 4. Slave-trade—Africa, West—History.
5. Slave-trade—America—History. 6. African diaspora. 7. Archaeology and
history—Africa, West. 8. Archaeology and history—America. 9. Africa, West—
Antiquities. 10. America—Antiquities. I. Ogundiran, Akinwumi. II. Falola, Toyin.
DT473.A73 2007
966'.02—dc22
2007004655

1 2 3 4 5 12 11 10 09 08 07

Contents

Figures

Tables

Preface

This is the first book devoted to the archaeology of Africans on both sides of the Atlantic. Previous anthologies have provided discrete though informative perspectives on African lives in the United States, western Africa, and the Caribbean in the early modern era (DeCorse 2001a; Haviser 1999; Singleton 1999a). This anthology brings the diverse and textured African experiences in the Atlantic basin during the era of Atlantic slavery together into one volume. The book is inspired by the ongoing efforts of historians, archaeologists, and cultural anthropologists to account for the unity in African experience and the impacts of the European-dominated modern economic system on the African world. The goal is to demonstrate the possibilities of a transcontinental African archaeology, highlight the potentials of comparative transatlantic African archaeology, and make archaeologists familiar with the themes and paradigms of the archaeology of the African world on both sides of the Atlantic. In addition, the book fills some of the conceptual gaps between Atlantic African and African Diaspora archaeologies and demonstrates the possibilities of a comparative understanding of the archaeology of African communities in the Atlantic. This book is aimed at a broad readership, and it provides an accessible scholarly introduction to the archaeology of Africa and the African Diaspora since 1500 for both specialists and nonspecialists.

We have assembled papers that are based on original research and that address a wide range of topics, such as the incorporation of Africa into the Atlantic economy; the impacts of Atlantic slavery and merchant capitalism on African societies; the dynamics of African resistance to Atlantic slavery on both sides of the Atlantic; the quotidian lives of Africans during the era of the Atlantic trade, under slavery, and after emancipation; African cultural production and the shaping of African identities in the Americas; African skills and knowledge in the making of American economic systems; the intergroup relations between Africans, on the one hand, and Europeans and Native Americans, on the other; and the social practice of archaeology of Atlantic Africa and African Diaspora, among others.

The contributors are students of material culture and professional archaeologists with extensive experience and common interest in interdisciplinary approaches to archaeology. By bringing together both senior and junior scholars, multigenerational ideas are foregrounded in the volume. The diverse backgrounds of the authors—Africans, North Americans, and South Americans—are also significant in bringing the vision and dynamics of their national, academic, and cultural traditions to bear on the diversity of perspectives represented in the following pages. The editors would like to thank all the contributors for their enthusiasm for this project.

This collection of essays celebrates the visions of W. E. B. Du Bois, Melville Herskovits, and Merrick Posnansky. Du Bois wrote the first scholarly transatlantic African history, a feat that laid the foundations for his later pan-African political movement. Herskovits pioneered a truly transatlantic anthropology of Africa that links the cultural historical experience of African Diaspora to its African background. Posnansky recognized the emancipatory role of transatlantic African archaeology and worked hard to achieve that vision through the training of students, many of whom are now senior scholars in their respective fields. It is to these three men of pioneering spirits that we dedicate this volume.

Toyin Falola, Austin, 2006
Akinwumi Ogundiran, Miami, 2006

Acknowledgments

The editors would like to thank all those who offered comments on the manuscript, especially Babatunde Agbaje-Williams, James Sidbury, anonymous readers, and our graduate students in Austin and Miami. Our deep gratitude also goes to the following: Darden A. Pyron (aka southern son) offered useful guidance at the conceptual stages of the project through friendship and intellectual exchanges; David Lewis of Florida International University's Technology Services generously assisted us with the illustrations; and Elaine Durham Otto gave us remarkable eagle-eyed editorial assistance. We are also grateful to Bisi Falola and Lea Koonce Ogundiran who, despite very busy schedules, provided us with the conducive space and tolerance that made the execution of the project possible.

I

INTRODUCTION

CHAPTER ONE

Pathways in the Archaeology of Transatlantic Africa

Akinwumi Ogundiran and Toyin Falola

This book is a contribution to the archaeology of the modern world, with a focus on the African experience on two sides of the Atlantic—in Africa and the Americas—from about 1500 to the 1800s. The advent of the early modern world system was heralded by division of labor and production on three continents—Africa, the Americas, and Europe (Fig. 1.1). Whereas Europe seeded the initial capital that launched this early modern system, the Americas became its center of production and Africa supplied the labor (Inikori 2002; E. Williams 1944). Given the silence of African voices and transcripts in the traditional historical archives, historical archaeology, with its emphasis on the combination of material records and words, both written and oral, is invaluable in formulating new questions and answers not only on how Africans contributed to the foundation of the modern era but also on its impact on their daily lives, cultural development, and the shaping of "African character" in the past five hundred years. This collection of essays is aimed at demonstrating that a transatlantic perspective provides a truly global dimension of African experiences in the Atlantic basin and has potential for bringing about a fuller understanding of the present socioeconomic and political conditions of Africa and its diaspora in the Atlantic world (see Franklin and McKee 2004, 1).

Since the 1980s, historiography has been turning to transatlantic perspectives in explaining the role of Africans in the development of the modern world (e.g., Eltis 2000; Inikori 2002; J. C. Miller 1988; Thornton 1992). These comparative, transnational, and transatlantic perspectives challenge nationalist historiography in conceiving and explaining the state, class, race, ethnicity and identities, cultural transformation, gender, power, colonialism, domination and resistance, nation building, consumption and production, and material life.

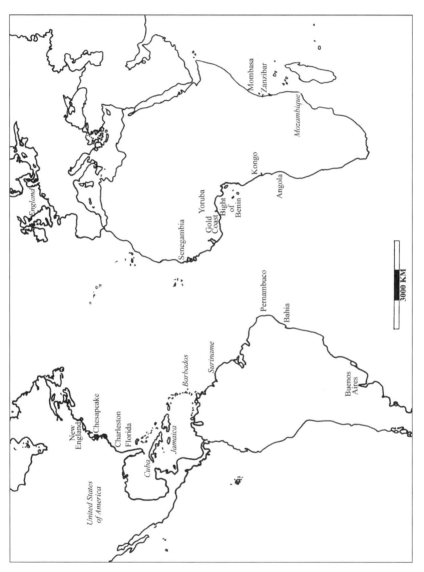

Fig. 1.1. Atlantic basin.

Archaeologists have also been attuned to establishing transatlantic dialogues, although with primary interest in establishing cultural continuities between Africa and the Americas (DeCorse 1998; Posnansky 1984, 1999; Singleton 2001a). This book continues this dialogue but with emphasis on the comparative, empirical, and conceptual nature of Atlantic perspectives in African and African Diaspora archaeology.

We have defined Atlantic Africa in this volume to include not only the coastal regions and the hinterlands of western Africa but also the eastern and southern African coasts and their hinterlands. Although western Africa, from Senegambia to Angola, was the primary region in which Europeans set up their trading posts and docked their ships, and the region from which 98 percent of captives were forced into the Middle Passage (Eltis et al. 1999), enslaved "Moçambiques" from East Africa also arrived in significant numbers in Brazil during the late eighteenth and nineteenth centuries (Alpers 2005). Even more important, the Indian Ocean and East African coast as well as southern Africa constituted early frontiers of European expansion in the fifteenth century, and those African regions made the unprecedented volume of the Atlantic commerce possible. Given the wide range of Asian commodities included in the European imports to Africa (e.g., Alpern 1995; Richardson 1979), without the integration of the Indian Ocean trade into transatlantic commerce, the extent of the volume and success of the European trade with western Africa would not have been achieved and the scale of forced migration of more than twelve million Africans to the Americas might not have occurred.

Although there were many African diasporas before 1500 (Palmer 1998a, 21), we are concerned in this volume with the diaspora of Africans in the Americas. This is the one which developed as a consequence of the integration of Atlantic Africa into the early modern global economy through the Middle Passage, the largest emigration before the nineteenth century, transporting between twelve and fifteen million Africans to the Americas and Europe in about four hundred years (Curtin 1969; Inikori 1976; Lovejoy 1982; Solow 2001). This migration made Africans the majorities in much of Brazil, all of the Caribbean, and most of the southern United States, and it infused a significant African presence into the rest of the Americas before 1800 (M. Klein 1978; J. C. Miller 1988).

Revisionist Thesis and the Archaeology of Transatlantic Africa

This volume is guided by the vision that not only do we have historical continuity between Atlantic Africa and African Diaspora but we also have come to a point where both should be integrated into one unit of analysis (Law and Lovejoy 1997). This vision is not new. It was first articulated in academic and scholarly circles by African American scholars, especially Carter G. Woodson

(1936) and W. E. B. Du Bois (1939), and it has been the mainstay of the conceptual framework proposed by the Africa-centered scholars who maintain that Africa must be at the center of the study of African Diaspora experience (Holloway 1990, 16; Oyebade 1990, 233; Palmer 1998a, 25). Historians of the cultures of enslaved Africans in the Americas (e.g., Gomez 1998; G. Hall 1992; Karasch 1987; Reis 1993; Schuler 1970) have sought "to better understand the impact of African history and culture on the world the slaves made" (Mann and Bay 2001, 6). To these scholars, Africa is not limited to a bounded landmass or a racial category. It is a living cultural expression, a concrete idea, and a historical spirit that link continental Africa to the Americas through the Middle Passage. Although the view that African Diaspora history is an integral part of continental African history has remained at the conceptual or even ideological level for a long time, it is only recently that empirical historical research is demonstrating its feasibilities and realities due to improved understanding of the transatlantic nature of enslaved Africans' biographies, the demography of the transatlantic slave trade, and the continuities of African ethnicities in the Americas (e.g., Eltis et al. 1999; Falola and Childs 2004; G. Hall 2005; Mann and Bay 2001; Law and Mann 1999; Law and Lovejoy 2001).

Paul Lovejoy argues that African history is incomplete without the history of its diaspora in the Americas, and that African history holds the key to the comprehension of the diaspora. Lovejoy's revisionist thesis, also known as "continuous historical experience thesis," has implications for the archaeological understanding of the diaspora. This revisionist thesis is justified on three grounds. First, instead of looking for quaint and symbolic African cultural survivals in the diaspora, the revisionist thesis asks us to holistically view enslaved and free Africans in diaspora as people who "interpreted their conditions in the Americas" with "the political issues and live interpretations" they brought from Africa. In other words, enslaved and freed Africans in the Americas lived their lives as Africans, recognized themselves as such, and "interpreted their American experience in terms of the contemporary world of Africa" and their African intellectual and cultural backgrounds. Second, "in most parts of the Americas, slaves tended to perceive of themselves in terms of communities and identities that had roots in Africa," such as the Akan in Jamaica; Yoruba in Cuba, Brazil, and Trinidad and Tobago; Kongo and Angola in the U.S. eastern seaboard, Brazil, Haiti, and Cuba; Fon in Haiti; and the Bambara in New Orleans, to mention the most obvious (Lovejoy 1997). Third, since the forced movement of identifiable groups of Africans was often tied to specific historical events and processes in Africa, the displaced Africans often carried over such events and processes to the Americas, with significant consequences for the slave economies that received them (e.g., Lovejoy 1994; Reis 1993; Thornton 1993). In emphasizing continuities between Africa and the African Diaspora, however, we need not overlook the disjuncture between the two. But, according to Lovejoy, "these disjunctures must be analyzed in terms of the continuities that have been largely overlooked." In fact, the revisionist thesis recognizes that the experience of enslaved and freed Africans needs to be studied and interpreted in the contexts of the colonial, imperial, and nation-states in which they lived. It is also cognizant of the milieu of cultural heterogeneity and fluidity in which forced immigrants from Africa reconstituted their lives in the Americas. The crux of the revisionist thesis is that the specific African backgrounds of these diasporic African experiences must be incorporated into the collection of data and the study and analysis of African experience, and that the culture of enslaved Africans was not more American than they were African.

Archaeology of Atlantic Africa developed almost parallel to the archaeology of the African Diaspora. A number of scholars have long realized the possibilities and advantages of a transatlantic archaeology of Africa and have offered programmatic outlines on how the archaeology of Atlantic Africa can benefit from that of the African Diaspora and vice versa (DeCorse 1998; Posnansky 1984, 1999; Posnansky and DeCorse 1986; Singleton 2001a). Only a few have designed and executed archaeological research projects that are truly transatlantic in problem and objective. Such few studies that exist serve, for example, to understand the continuities between Africa and its diaspora in the matters of technology and settlement patterns (e.g., Agorsah 1999; Armstrong and Kelly 2000; see Goucher, this volume). The stimulation for the possibilities of a transatlantic African archaeology has come, to a large extent, from the historical archaeologists in the Americas who are interested in interpreting the material records of the enslaved and free Africa Diaspora sites and their cultural transcripts with reference to the African cultural contexts (e.g., Ferguson 1992). The possibilities, problems, and challenges involved in these interpretations have been raised by Africanist and Americanist archaeologists. Africanist archaeologists have argued that many archaeologists of the African Diaspora have been poorly equipped with the knowledge of African material records, history, and culture, and as a result, generalized, ahistorical, and presentist African cultural practices are sometimes superimposed on the African Diaspora material records (DeCorse 1998, 1999; Kelly 2004; Posnansky 1984, 1999). According to Christopher DeCorse (1998, 133), the problem also derives in part from "the paucity of comparative data from many of the relevant parts of Africa." Indeed, the pace and sophistication of research in Atlantic Africa have not matched that of the African Diaspora, prompting Kelly (2004, 220) to warn that "it is imperative to know something about the Africa that was contemporary to the populations contributing to the African Diaspora" if we hope to be able to explain the formation processes and characteristics of the African Diaspora culture and its contributions to the cultures of the Americas (also see Singleton 2001a, 183).

Yet the archaeology of transatlantic Africa should not be reduced to the one-way interest in how Africa influenced its diaspora. We also need to explore the possibilities of uncovering cultural practices and forms of African origins that survived in the Americas but that are no longer present in Africa due to the intense and multiple dislocations that the continent and its peoples have experienced in the past five hundred years.

As an integral part of the archaeology of the modern world (Orser 1996), the primary goal of transatlantic African archaeology lies in contributing to the understanding of the global dimensions of African cultural transformations and innovations in the modern era. This goal includes using material records, written accounts/sources, oral traditions, and ethnography to understand the entanglement of Africa and Africans in the Atlantic economy, especially slavery (e.g., DeCorse 1991), and the consequences of Atlantic slavery on the peoples, societies, and institutions in Africa and the world of the enslaved and free Africans in the Americas. Its strategic mission is to understand the impacts of this entanglement and the advent of the modern world system on transformations in quotidian lives, institutions, cultural production, production of goods and consumption, market economies, colonialism, religion and belief systems, ideas of liberty, freedom and resistance, economic opportunities and marginalization, migration, identity and ethnicity, racial ideology and racism, class structures, and gender relations on both sides of the Atlantic.

Organization of the Book

This collection of essays is aimed at filling some of the conceptual gaps between Atlantic African and African Diaspora archaeologies, to showcase the types of research themes and questions that the two archaeologies have been addressing, demonstrate the possibilities of a comparative understanding of the archaeology of African communities on both sides of the Atlantic, and highlight the possible areas of collaboration in the future.

The book is divided into three parts. Part 1 (this introduction) summarizes its organization. The second and third parts focus on Atlantic Africa and the African Diaspora, respectively.

The seven chapters in part 2 examine the impact of the Atlantic economy in shaping African quotidian lives—consumption, production, slavery, households, settlement patterns, sociocultural practices and defensive mechanisms, political institutions, and sociopolitical organizations. Whereas one of the chapters deals with East Africa, the rest concentrate on West Africa. Four chapters in this section, on the Middle Senegal Valley, Gold Coast Hinterlands, northern Yorubaland, and the Swahili coast, take longitudinal approaches to understanding the nature of culture change and sociopolitical transformations and the intersections of African societies in pre–Atlantic world systems through the trans-Saharan and the Indian Ocean commercial networks. This *longue durée* perspective allows us to understand how the Atlantic encounters benefited from these preexisting economic systems and how they were transformed by the Eurocentric Atlantic economy, facilitates the understanding of the nature of impact of the Atlantic encounters on African societies, and shows the dynamism and complexity of African cultural institutions.

Ann Brower Stahl examines the transformations in the daily lives of Banda people in a Gold Coast hinterland as a result of five hundred years of entanglements in transcontinental and regional economies. This is followed by a study of household and material life in a Yoruba hinterland township in the seventeenth and eighteenth centuries by Ogundiran. Cameron Monroe analyzes the political transformations in Dahomey, one of the most influential kingdoms of Atlantic Africa, with a view to demonstrating how this seventeenth-century polity adjusted its politics to its socioeconomic interests. The impacts of slaving and the slave trade on sociopolitical development and devolution, regional settlement patterns, population movement, and social relations in the Middle Senegal Valley and northern Yorubaland, respectively, are the focus of chapters 5 and 6. Chapurukha Kusimba then foregrounds the rise of East African coastal city-states in the Indian Ocean trade networks and attributes the collapse of these states to the development of the Atlantic economy and Portuguese colonialism. He illustrates the importance of the Indian Ocean trade networks to the Atlantic commercial development. Lastly, Brempong Osei-Tutu examines contemporary transatlantic politics and contestation of social memory of the Atlantic slave trade, especially between Ghanaian government officials and the African Diaspora activists, over the strategies of protecting and presenting the European forts in Ghana for public education and international tourism.

Part 3 deals with the archaeology of the African Diaspora. The major themes addressed are the racial, ethnic, and symbolic constructions of African identity; archaeology of social differences focusing on race and racism, class and social differences; technology, exchange, and market economy; cultural interactions, cultural change, identity, resistance, freedom fighting, and marooning; and the implications of maritime archaeology for transatlantic African archaeology. Chapters on the archaeology of Nantucket's African Baptist Society Meeting House and the ongoing work at Buenos Aires demonstrate the importance of port towns for the development of the African Diaspora cultures. The social practice and relevance of African Diaspora archaeology is the focus of the last chapter. Three conceptual metaphors—power, agency, and race—are central to the themes covered in part 3, and methodologically all the chapters emphasize the need to combine rigorous behavioral analysis of material records with landscape approaches. The theme of quotidian lives and cultural production in slavery and plantation contexts dominates the African Diaspora section.

The primary focus of the African Diaspora archaeology has been on slavery, and rightfully so. After all, it was as a result of this demand for bonded labor that Africans were forced into the Middle Passage. The development of African Diaspora identities is therefore rooted in enslavement. This volume examines not only the living conditions and identity formations under slavery and post-emancipation but also the resistance against slavery and the dynamics of African interactions with Europeans and Native Americans. Four primary themes have dominated the archaeology of the African Diaspora, and these are reflected in the chapters that follow: the formation and maintenance of African cultural identity; the daily lives of enslaved Africans; the resistance by Africans against slavery; and African interactions with other ethnic and racial groups in the diaspora. These themes are not mutually exclusive; in fact, they reinforce one another in many ways. Since the primary methodological approach of the archaeologist is to use material records to explain the experiences of African presence in the diaspora, the same materials that inform us about African cultural identities are inescapably also germane to understanding the aspects of African daily lives including burial traditions, beliefs, religion and worldview, food customs, architecture and domestic use of space, and work-related activities. Likewise, it has been demonstrated that interethnic/interracial resistance took place in the contexts of identity formation and daily lives.

Pathways

The remainder of this introduction discusses the relevance of each chapter to some of the major themes in the archaeology of Atlantic Africa and the African Diaspora, identifies pertinent gaps, and proposes new lines of inquiry.

Atlantic Entanglement in Western Africa

Western Africa constitutes the starting point for the archaeology of transatlantic Africa because it was there that a truly Atlantic commerce between Europe and Africa began in the mid-fifteenth century (e.g., Northrup 2002). The incorporation of the Americas into this economic system in the early sixteenth century substantially transformed the place of Africa in the Atlantic exchanges (Inikori 2001). The post-1500 archaeological records of western Africa show that this Atlantic-oriented commerce significantly added to the repertoire of western African material life, initially more in the coastal regions than in the hinterlands. However, by the seventeenth century, the material signature of the Atlantic economy had become ubiquitous across the region (e.g., Connah 1975; see relevant chapters in DeCorse 2001b; Stahl 2001a; and Ogundiran 2002a). This material signature includes cowries, beads, bottles and other glass objects, objects of copper and its alloys, imported iron objects, including bars and tools, smoking pipes (local and imported), chinaware, and firearms paraphernalia. There are also perishable objects—cloth, alcoholic beverages, and gunpowder—that have not survived in the archaeological records but that are abundantly referenced in the historical accounts (Alpern 1995).

The Atlantic pull not only increased commercial activities in the hinterland but it also intensified craft specialization. The European demands for African cloth, dyestuffs, and ivory transformed the organization of production and consumption patterns, affected the methods of labor recruitment, transformed the social valuation of labor, and reshaped social relations across gender and age. The increasing involvement of some parts of Atlantic Africa in the new transcontinental commerce impacted local production activities. The dramatic increase in the volume of trade impacted social relations, intensified political formations, created new towns, mostly on trading routes, and thereby increased the process of urbanization in some areas. Likewise, the European demands for enslaved cargo unleashed violence that decimated populations and destroyed villages and towns in other parts of the region (Déme and Guèye, this volume; Lovejoy 1989).

It was not only imported commodities that transformed the material and daily lives of Atlantic Africa but also the introduction of American food crops—maize, cassava, tomato, papaya, and varieties of beans. The understanding of the impact of these American cultigens on African populations remains rudimentary partly because the evidence of these products is tenuous in the archaeological record. The crop that played the most critical role in the daily lives of western Africans since the sixteenth century was maize (Miracle 1966). The ubiquity of maize cob impressions on ceramics in the archaeological deposits of western Africa shows that farmers were experimenting with the American crops by the mid-sixteenth through the seventeenth centuries in the hinterlands. The fact that maize cultivation required less labor than other western African crops, especially yams, rice, and peas, may have made this crop a prime food item in the seventeenth century, especially during several droughts of the period (G. Brooks 2003, 102–103; J. C. Miller 1982).

Archaeologists have yet to critically engage the study of agroecological transformations in western Africa as different groups and individuals jockeyed to mitigate the effects of drought episodes of the seventeenth and eighteenth centuries, to meet the European demands for cloth, dyestuff, ivory, and slaves, and to provide the increasingly mobile traders and travelers—Africans and Europeans—with food and commodities. Such investigations will decidedly take a landscape approach such as the one alluded to by Kenneth Kelly, who suggests that the abandonment of agricultural terraces constructed for yam cultivation in the seventeenth-century Danyi plateau in southern Togo is an indication of the adoption of low-impact maize cultivation in the region (Kelly 2004, 226). The essays in part 2 address how the entanglement of western Africa in the Atlantic economies affected settlement and domestic household formations as well as consumption and production patterns.

Chapter 2 offers a longitudinal study, using the changes in intrasettlement and household production/consumption dynamics to assess the nature of entanglements of an African hinterland in panregional political economic systems over six centuries. Here Stahl demonstrates how the Banda area was entangled in the networks of commerce and exchanges that linked the area of modern central Ghana to the Mediterranean world between the eleventh and seventeenth centuries and to the Atlantic economy from the seventeenth to nineteenth centuries. Studying a political and cultural frontier region like Banda is important in the archaeology of Atlantic Africa and African Diaspora because it was in such frontier zones that significant numbers of Africans became victims of Atlantic slavery (Inikori 2003, 192). Stahl writes that incessant attacks from imperial Asante depopulated the Banda area and increased the risk of enslavement in the eighteenth century. Those who fell victim to enslavement would have brought their skills as farmers and as specialists in metal, pottery, and ivory to the Americas. On their arrival, they probably identified themselves with the major ethnolinguistic group in the region, the Akan.

Similar themes of daily lives are addressed in chapter 3 focusing exclusively on the critical period of the seventeenth and eighteenth centuries in the Bight of Benin hinterland. Here the intersection of local history with regional political and economic processes is underscored, showing how the material life in Okun township was shaped by "the expanding regional economic system that was tied to the Atlantic trade." Although the daily lives in Okun were not predetermined by the new-age Atlantic commerce, Ogundiran shows that the foundation and the growth of the settlement were directly shaped by the networks of trading contacts between the coast and the hinterland. Like Banda region, Okun represents a typical community from which the majority of enslaved Africans would have originated. Hence the discussion of the nature of domestic architecture and the associated material life, as well as the transformation in the consumption pattern during those centuries, could give insights into the understanding of material life among the enslaved Africans in the Americas, such as the relationship between linear simple module houses in the Bight of Benin and shotgun houses from the Carolinas to the Caribbean, and the transatlantic relationships in the manufacture, style, and use of objects of African origins whose forms widely circulated in the Atlantic world.

The differential impacts of the Atlantic entanglements on different parts of Atlantic Africa are noted in this volume. The coastal areas were certainly more enmeshed in the European-dominated modern economic system than the hinterlands, and it is in the coastal areas that one tends to find vestiges of the Atlantic encounters (e.g., Bredwa-Mensah, 2004; DeCorse 2001a; Kelly 1995). But the effect of the Atlantic economy on the hinterlands, though without direct Africa-European contact, was a significant factor in shaping regional economic, sociopolitical, and cultural institutions, especially starting from the end of the seventeenth century (e.g., Ogundiran 2003; Stahl 1999). Archaeologists committed to the study of the entanglement of Africa in the Atlantic world tend to dispense with the world systems theory in preference for a loosely described model of "global encounters" and the related "culture contact." Whereas the classic version of the world systems theory focuses on the agency of Europeans in creating a Europe-centered world system and the peripherization of Atlantic Africa (Wallerstein 1974, 1980, 1986), the global encounters proponents seek to focus on African agencies and internal African dynamics (Stahl 1999, 2001a). But the quest to understand the role of colonialism, capitalism, and European-dominated economy in constraining and enabling different kinds of historical agents in the making of the Atlantic African world and cultures may move the world systems and global encounters proponents closer in formulating compatible theoretical frameworks.

Impacts of Atlantic Slavery in Atlantic Africa

There are two major ways in which the impacts of Atlantic slavery on Atlantic Africa are being investigated: the impact on those enslaved within Africa in European plantation regimes, and the impact on communities and polities whose members were raided for enslavement. Atlantic slavery, the engine of economic growth in the Atlantic basin, began in Africa, first off the African coast on the Portuguese-colonized Atlantic islands of São Tomé and Cape Verde in the fifteenth century and later on the coastal African mainland, continuing as late as the nineteenth century. The study of European plantation enclaves in mainland coastal Africa has focused on the "social world of the enslaved people," especially how they manipulated the material world around them to forge new living conditions on European-owned plantations. One study was conducted at the nineteenth-century Danish Frederiksgave plantation in coastal Ghana (Bredwa-Mensah, 2004, 208). The excavation of the refuse mound and living quarters of the plantation's slaves, who were mostly from the Gold Coast (modern Ghana), reveals a rich diversity of artifacts, including locally manufactured pottery, beads, lithics, cowry shells, kaolin smoking pipes, firearms, stone and glass beads, metal and glass buttons, metal nails, door locks and hinges, and faunal remains. These artifacts give insights into the everyday lives of the slaves at Frederiksgave: housing, drinking, smoking, clothing, and body adornment. These materials of everyday life are not different from those that have been found on American plantations: they demonstrate how the global circulation of Asian- and European-derived commodities affected even slaves. The Frederiksgave materials and contexts offer a pertinent database for comparative investigation of Atlantic slavery and the culture of the enslaved Africans living directly within the ambit of the European economic system. They are relevant to understanding the nature of cultural and behavioral changes, in socioeconomic contexts associated with bondage, in Atlantic Africa. The studies like that of Frederiksgave plantation have many implications for understanding the formation of enslaved African cultures in the Americas.

Whereas ship logs, correspondence among slavers, and oral accounts give us a broad macro-scale understanding of the aftermath of Atlantic-related slaving in Africa, archaeological data are better placed, when used with other sources, to inform us of the specific impacts of Atlantic slavery on the communities who experienced wholesale raiding and destruction in the hands of individual vagabonds as well as state-sponsored banditry. To this end, Alioune Déme, Ndèye Sokhna Guèye, and Aribidesi Usman apply archaeological data to demonstrate the debilitating impacts of slavery in the Senegambian valley and north-central Yorubaland. Both chapters provide us with some of the turbulent historical backgrounds in Africa from which the African Diaspora emerged. Citing Walter Rodney (1966, 1970, 1981), Déme and Guèye argue that the Atlantic slave trade and direct European intervention transformed the character of the class system, social hierarchy, and state structure in the Senegambia region, paving the way for the warrior class to dominate the region's political institutions from the sixteenth century onward. As the European factors intensified their demands on the warrior-political agents for human cargo, insecurity of lives and property became a daily concern, and autocracy and exploitation by the warrior-rulers increased. Déme and Guèye's chapter is also a longitudinal study of how the Atlantic slave trade was an expansion of the trans-Saharan slave trade in some areas and a new experience in other parts of the Senegambian region. The ecological and settlement pattern approaches adopted in the essay demonstrate how the landscape was utilized for defensive purposes against the slave trade–motivated wars of the sixteenth through nineteenth centuries and how different ecological zones were deployed in the face of the uncertainties of drought and famine to pursue flexible economic strategies, such as fishing, farming, and pastoralism.

By the early nineteenth century, the effects of the slave trade—warfare, displacement, and famine—had left the people of Senegambia so mobile that they were unable to exercise elaborate acquisition and creativity in material culture as their ancestors had done. In fact, the region experienced poverty, technological decline, and minimalism in ceramic decorations. Most of the pots belonging to this period were poorly fired and bore very simple decorations, if any. Déme and Guèye conclude that the Senegambian societies were impoverished by the Atlantic slave trade, rendered perpetually mobile by war and slave raiding, and straining under the loss and weakening of the institutions that had held the societies together. The impoverishment of the material record and the scanty ceramic decoration grammar in eighteenth- and nineteenth-century Senegambia could provide insights into how we can interpret similar occurrences in the Americas.

Since pottery is the most prevalent class of artifacts in the archaeological contexts of the African Diaspora, it has become the most important locus for understanding food customs and African ethnic identity in the Americas (see Weik and also Hauser, this volume). The potteries identified with African manufacture and sites in the Americas, from the Carolinas to the Caribbean and Brazil, such as colonoware and yabbas, share many characteristics. Above all, they are low-fired earthenware, undecorated and of little variability in form (Hauser and Armstrong 1999, 69). These potteries are a subject of intense disputations among archaeologists (e.g., Ferguson 1992). Hill (1987) has argued that these earthenware could not have been inspired by African ceramic traditions because pots are always highly decorated in western Africa. Kelly (2004, 224), on the other hand, has speculated that because more than 90 percent of archaeologically recovered ceramics from the late seventeenth and early eighteenth centuries at Savi (Bight of Benin) "exhibit little or no decoration," the makers of the colonoware might have originated from Savi. Both Hill's and Kelly's arguments are problematic because they are based on the assumption that the surface patterns, manufacturing techniques, and formal properties of ceramics are idiosyncratic cultural practices that must be replicated at all times and in all situations. This assumption overlooks the instrumental purposes that objects and styles often serve in daily lives, especially in the context of weak institutions.

We would argue that the grammar of ceramic decoration is not always a reflection of idiosyncratic cultural practices; rather, ceramic production, including the level of complexity of surface decoration patterns, often reflects the political economy, institutional variability, and sociopolitical relations of a community or polity at any given time. The predominantly low-fired plain ceramics across the western African region during the turbulent nineteenth century indicate that the production of certain items such as pottery became attuned to utilitarian purposes rather than social signification due to the weakening of institutions that mediated social relationships. Likewise, coming from traditions where ceramic decoration patterns were a means by which group identities and aesthetic values were linked to class, status, group identity, honor, and therefore a complex repertoire of meanings, enslaved peoples found themselves in the historical conditions of slavery where such identities and meanings were no longer in existence or were weakened and less relevant. The result is that the grammar of ceramic decoration or ceramic complex from a cultural zone in Atlantic Africa often became fragmented in the Americas. It is not surprising, therefore, that Americanist archaeologists have been at a loss to match the repertoire of decorations and forms of pottery in the New World African sites with those from pre-Atlantic and even Atlantic Africa. The foregoing challenges us to consider ceramic decorations, like ethnic identities, as historically conditioned, not necessarily derived from ingrained extrasomatic cognitive qualities. Such qualities would be perpetuated and replicated in material forms only when the social relations and cultural systems that could support them existed.

Political Formation and Transformation

The impact of Atlantic trade on sociopolitical formation and devolution in western Africa has been a subject of intense debate in the historiography. At the core of this debate is the degree to which the Atlantic slave trade affected political traditions in Africa's subregion (Barry 1988; Curtin 1975; Fage 1969; Rodney 1970). Large-scale political centralization was achieved in only a few parts of Atlantic Africa before the advent of the Atlantic economy, and hegemonic and imperial ambitions were at their nascent stages in the Bight of Benin (e.g., Benin), West Central Africa (e.g., Kongo), and Senegambia during the fifteenth century (Inikori 2003, 179). For the most part, the majority of western Africans south of the Sudanic belt, from Senegambia to the Kalahari Desert, lived in independent small-scale polities organized on the basis of lineages, clans, and villages in the fifteenth century (Wondji 1992, 368). Although this pattern continued throughout the Atlantic age, there were also major political changes. The gradual specialization of European imports in human captives at the end of the sixteenth century and throughout the seventeenth century altered the direction of political development in Atlantic Africa. Seventeenth-century Atlantic Africa not only had a very few centralized states strong enough to protect their people from the banditry of outside raiders, but the institutions and politico-military organizations of even the larger ones, such as the Kongo, were too weak to check the destabilization unleashed by the European demands for captives (see Hilton 1985). Within a few decades, between the late seventeenth and early eighteenth centuries, polities whose economic survival rested on specializing in slave raiding and slave trading developed in Atlantic Africa, such as the Arochukwu of the Bight of Biafra (Okpoko and Obi-Ani 2005), Efik city-states of the Old Calabar (Lovejoy and Richardson 1999), and the Akwamu, Akyem, Kwaku, and Krepi of the Gold Coast (see Daaku 1970, 31). The result was that peer-polity rivalry and conflict bitterly intensified, and the old cleavages of regional hierarchies began to give way to new political configurations characterized by militarism, imperialism, and hegemonic ideology (Ogundiran 2003, 62–65). What forms of transformations in political culture made these Atlantic hegemonies such as Oyo, Asante, Benin, and Dahomey possible? What were the courses of political centralization that these new hegemonies took? How were they able to establish and maintain dominance in their respective regions? What role did the Atlantic economy play in the rise of these hegemonies? Cameron Monroe responds to these questions in chapter 4 by zeroing in on the impact of Atlantic economy on political transformations in Dahomey.

Many polities in western Africa, especially in the coastal Bight of Benin, collapsed as a result of sustained European contact and primary interest in human cargo imports (Law 1992). Yet a few were also able to develop and even expand their spheres of influence. Dahomey was one of the most successful of the latter, and there have been sustained debates about why. Whereas some historians have argued that Dahomey succeeded where others failed because it radically altered its political organization—the *political transformation* thesis—others have argued for the *political continuity* thesis, that Dahomey did not break radically away from the political traditions of the past. Monroe resorts to archaeological methods to settle the debate, using innovative

16

approaches that combine archaeological survey, aerial photography, oral interviews, documentary sources, European witness accounts, and test excavations to identify the distribution and internal layout of Dahomean royal structures (palaces) between the late seventeenth and nineteenth centuries. By analyzing the distribution of palaces in Dahomey, mainly on the Abomey plateau, and the activity specialization within these palaces, Monroe concludes that Dahomey restructured its political organization in response to the conditions of the Atlantic slave trade through bureaucratization and centralization of its political system.

The general indirect-intervention approach by the Europeans, for the most part, in the political affairs of West Africa, contrasts the experience of West Central and East Africa where the Portuguese in both cases sought and established colonies as early as the sixteenth century. In chapter 7, Chap Kusimba provides a longitudinal study that examines not only the entanglement of East Africa in the Indian Ocean commerce and the resultant creation of Swahili culture but also the origins of European colonization in East Africa and the consequent destruction of the autonomy of the Swahili city-states in the sixteenth century. Challenging the prevailing idea that environmental factors caused the decline of Swahili city-states in the early modern era, Kusimba blames the demise of these coastal trading polities on Portuguese imperial and merchant mercantile ambitions. Through the analysis of settlement patterns and the integration of material records with documentary sources, he demonstrates that the armed incursion of the Portuguese, beginning in the sixteenth century, caused a mass exodus of coastal peoples to the hinterland, so that "out of the more than four hundred coastal settlements, only a handful were inhabited by the seventeenth century; the rest vanished." Under the Portuguese colonial rule, Kusimba writes, quality of life deteriorated, indigenous industries collapsed, and "the unique qualities of the coastal civilization faded away, replaced by a new set of ideals and attitudes." Of course, factional conflicts among the coastal states also accelerated the Portuguese conquest of the region (see also Fleisher 2004, 119). Kusimba shows that the Portuguese and later the Dutch, as well as the British access to the East African coast between the sixteenth and mid-nineteenth centuries, and the impacts on the Swahili states and peoples of East Africa, are an integral part of the Atlantic history.

Cultural Change, Continuity, Contacts, and Identities

African cultural identities and ethnicities in the Americas have received substantial archaeological attention. These studies have been framed by the tension between the Africanism and Creole Schools, especially by the debate between Melville Herskovits and E. Franklin Frazier (for a summary, see Gershenhorn 2004). Based on his multisite and transatlantic anthropological studies, Herskovits concluded that many aspects of West African culture survive in the

Americas. Frazier argued to the contrary that due to the devastating impact of the Middle Passage and slavery, African cultures have not survived in the United States. Sidney Mintz and Richard Price intervened in this debate in 1976 with the publication of *An Anthropological Approach to the Afro-American Past: A Caribbean Perspective*. The book has since become the fountain of the Creole School in the study of New World African identities. A sophisticated aspect of the Mintz-Price thesis is that distinct African Diaspora cultures immediately developed in the Americas and that these cultures have been subjected to an intensive process of creolization over time. The thesis moves us to the center of the Herskovits-Frazier debate by arguing that the African Diaspora cultures that developed during slavery were not carbon copies of the continental African cultures. This could not have been otherwise. After all, cultures are always in motion, since they are not fully autonomous of the ever-changing political and economic conditions of everyday life, a perspective well developed in 1985 by Sidney Mintz. The emphasis of the Creole School on syncretism, heterogeneity, fluidity, and hybridity of the African Diaspora culture has been a useful and popular framework for conceptualizing and interpreting the African Diaspora cultures and identities since the 1970s (see the essays in Morgan 1998; Singleton 1999a). As the lines of arguments blur in the intersecting exchanges among scholars, though, it seems that the Creole School has become a theoretically elegant umbrella for almost everyone who professes different things, including acculturationists and catastrophist theorists.

There are, however, a number of problems with the Mintz-Price thesis that continue to divide members of the Creole School (for archaeological perspective, see the articles in the journal *Historical Archaeology*, vol. 34, no. 3). First, the thesis argues in opposition to Herskovits's Africanism that there was no significant impact of particular African regions or ethnicities on the African Diaspora. Mintz and Price assume (incorrectly) that enslaved Africans came from diverse "tribal" enclaves and formed an incoherent crowd in the Middle Passage. Such diversity, they reason, made the survival of specific African regional culture and ethnicity impossible in the Americas. The Mintz-Price thesis suggestively argues further that African Diaspora cultures were unlike anything that the captives left behind in Africa, and therefore scholars should focus on the transformations of Afro-Creole culture and not worry about their African origins. Cumulative empirical historical research since the 1980s has shown that indeed Africans from particular regions and ethnicities did cluster in specific regions in the Americas (Hall 2005) and that the cultures from those specific African regions served as the foundations and sometimes mainstream of African Diaspora cultures (e.g., Geggus 2001).

In its insistence on setting up creolization as an opposite of Africanism, and in treating the African origins as insignificant to the formation of the African Diaspora, the Creole School is conceptually weak for dealing with the transatlantic dynamics of African Diaspora cultures, and it falls into the ahistorical pit it claims to avoid (see Mintz 1984; Mintz and Price 1976, 1992; Morgan

1998). The transatlantic vision of the Africanist School and its rootedness in empirical historical research fills some of the conceptual gaps in the Creole School and offers the opportunity to understand the transatlantic dimensions and contexts of African Diaspora cultures (e.g., Gomez 2006; Law and Lovejoy 1997). For sure, Africans participated in the cultural syncretism that became the defining characteristic of all American cultures after 1500, but neither was this a simplistic process of the enslaved or free Africans merely blending with the cultures they encountered, European and Indian, etc., in the Americas, nor was African Diaspora culture abstractly invented without African roots. Indeed, the process of creolization and syncretism did not begin in the Americas for members of the African Diaspora. Islamic and Christian traditions, regional intermixing of diverse African cultures, and European expansion in the early modern world were already shaping the lives of most Africans and their cultures before they were enslaved. All these show that (1) it is not in the Americas that Africans discovered cosmopolitanism and multiple cultural encounters, (2) the process of cultural syncretism began in Africa, and (3) some of the African cultures that arrived with the enslaved in the Americas also brought explicit and discursive universal ethics and "values of justice, equity, and solidarity" that influenced African struggles for freedom, human dignity, and independence in the Americas (Yai 2001, 353). It might therefore be more conceptually rewarding to examine the formation of African Diaspora cultures and identities in the context of the Africanization of the Americas (e.g., Philips 2005).

In order to bridge the theoretical divides between the Africanist and Creole Schools, attempts have been made to bring Africa-centered history and agency into the conceptualization of creolization or cultural syncretism using what has been labeled a "transformation" or "historical creolization" thesis (Armstrong 1999, 178–80; Chambers 1992). This thesis argues that the African components in an African Diaspora culture were transformed not merely because of contacts with other cultures in the Americas but because Africans had negotiated their own creative solutions to the challenges of daily life under slavery, emancipation, and racism, from slavery to peasantry, from plantation isolation to urban intermixing. The "transformation thesis" offers an open framework for the long-term study of the process of identity and cultural formation, not only among the peoples of African Diaspora but also among those of Atlantic Africa who became part of the machinations of modern economic systems from the sixteenth century onward. By according African agency a prime place in continuity and change, the transformation thesis situates African culture as the major ingredient in the identity formation of the African Diaspora (see I. Miller 2004), not a marginal component as the classic Creole School has suggested. In this respect, the transformation thesis has more in common with the revisionist thesis.

The archaeological quest to identify African ethnic identities and cultural continuities in the diaspora based on the outdated anthropological notion of "bounded culture" has been seriously challenged by the fact that discrete packages of neatly bounded cultural and ethnic attributes did not and do not exist anywhere in Africa, and Africans in the Americas did not occupy cultural enclaves where they reproduced isolated "tribal" ethnic identities. We are now beginning to understand that the current African ethnic categories that form the basis of almost all anthropological research and writings are themselves products of long-term history and transformations. Moreover, some of the ethnic terminologies that were used to describe enslaved Africans in the Americas were not always congruent with the deployment of ethnic labels in Africa. Whereas anyone from the nineteenth-century Sokoto caliphate in central Sudan could be referred to as "Hausa" in Brazil, that person might have come from one of the non-Hausa communities conquered by the Sokoto jihadists. Likewise, although Nago is one of the subgroups of the Yoruba in West Africa, the name "Nago" was extended to include all Yoruba speakers in Bahia in the early nineteenth century, and the term *Kongo*, which refers to the people and their state in Central Africa, was adopted to refer to almost all African Diaspora groups who originated from West Central Africa, including Angola. For the most part, the use of "cultural zones" rather than narrow ethnolinguistic identities is closer to understanding the cultural backgrounds of the African Diaspora (Thornton 1992). And it is more feasible to identify diagnostic markers of these cultural zones rather than ethnolinguistic units in the archaeological records (e.g., Ogundiran 2003).

Reworking Melville Herskovits's concept of "cultural zones" (Herskovits 1958, 295), John Thornton (1992) has suggested that the peoples of the Atlantic coast of Africa can be divided into three cultural zones: Upper Guinea, Lower Guinea, and the Angolan group. He further classifies these zones into seven subgroups using linguistic criteria. There are archaeological potentials for refining and expanding these divisions for the coastal areas and the hinterlands of western Africa. Thornton reasons that not only the people who share closely related languages but also those who occupy contiguous areas but speak different languages will have lower variations in cultural practices:

> In many parts of western and central Africa people of diverse language groups interacted with each other from day to day as a result of residential proximity or commerce. In the course of these interactions they might exchange many cultural ideas even if they did not exchange languages. Thus, they might share religious ideas or aesthetic principles to such a degree that they possessed a common religious or artistic heritage despite their linguistic diversity. (Thornton 1992, 186)

For example, versions of Yoruba were spoken in the eighteenth century throughout the non-Yoruba eastern section of the Bight of Benin (S. Greene 2000), where the language was considered "noble" (Law 1991, 24). Likewise, Yoruba religious practices and beliefs were adopted in the Bight of Benin beyond the Yoruba-speaking areas during the eighteenth and nineteenth centuries, such as among the Anlo and the Fon. Thus many western Africans, especially those in the margins of larger cultural zones and powerful polities, arrived in the Americas having been exposed to two or more cultures and languages (Greene 2000, 98). Without any evidence of the way these multilingual individuals identified themselves, we are better off not imposing modern anachronistic sensibilities of ethnicity on the archaeological record of the Diaspora or of Africa during the era of the slave trade. For archaeological purposes, cultural zones may be more useful in some situations than a narrow ethnolinguistic identifier in defining the African backgrounds of the enslaved. Meanwhile, the systematic collation and analyses of the slave ship records, census data, and court/police records have shown that cohorts or groups of enslaved Africans who were relocated to specific regions in the Americas often originated from specific ethnolinguistic and cultural regions of Africa, and most identified themselves with specific African ethnicities and were able to transmit their African identities to subsequent generations (Hall 2005, 45; also see Eltis et al. 1999). These empirical studies show that the slave trade was not as random as the Creolists initially thought. It is now realized that the cultural history of the enslaved peoples originated in known cultural areas of Africa, not on the ships of the Middle Passage. Advances in bioanthropological research are also shedding light on the question of demography and origins of diasporic Africans. For example, the mitochondrial DNA sequences from thirty-two individuals in the New York African Burial Ground show that they shared maternal ancestors with the living populations in present-day Benin, Niger, Nigeria, and Senegal (Mack and Blakey 2004, 11). The DNA sequencing and comparisons with living African populations are still at the preliminary stages, but such bioanthropological studies may expand the frontiers of our knowledge of the roots and routes of the Middle Passage.

However, as much as the demography of African ethnicities, age, and gender is important in the study of the historical development of the various African Diaspora cultures, the ongoing practice of collapsing cultural history with demographic trends and patterns can only give us inaccurate assessments of how and why certain African cultural institutions and practices gained more ground than others in the Americas. As Colleen Kriger (2005, 262) observes in a conceptual essay on the cultural history of the Atlantic basin, "one should not expect that there will be a clear and consistent correlation between the numbers of people and the degree of their cultural impact in a new social environment." Evidence abounds, for example, that some African cultural institutions survive and continue to be reproduced as a result of their universal ethics and values, not so much because their carriers were in the majority of those forced into the Middle Passage (e.g., Falola and Childs 2004).

The archaeology of cultural history in Atlantic Africa has focused for the most part on European-African interactions, especially in the coastal area, at "sites of early Portuguese, French, Dutch, English, Swedish, Danish, and Brandenberger" presence, as well as the African settlements adjacent to the European ones (DeCorse 2001b, 7). These studies are predicated on the assumption that cultural contacts are prime movers of cultural change.

The archaeological fieldworks in Elmina, Savi, and Whydah serve as the best examples of such studies (DeCorse 1992, 2001a; Kelly 1997a, 2004). At Elmina, over 100,000 artifacts have been recovered from more than thirty structures, and the imported artifacts—ceramic, glass, metal goods, beads, buttons, buckles, slate pencils, and writing slates, among others—far outnumber the locally produced items. The excavator argues that the mere presence of these commodities does not indicate creolization, since the ways these objects were deployed was to maintain African cultural institutions, and that what has changed is not a whole culture but behavioral patterns. DeCorse (1998, 369) unequivocally concludes that "how the Elmina people thought about the trade materials they used, viewed the buildings they occupied (though using the European method of stone construction), and conceived their religious life . . . suggests resilience rather than sequaciousness, continuity rather than change in African beliefs and identity." This Africanist perspective also challenges our conceptualization of material goods and culture in the African Diaspora archaeology.

The results of archaeological investigations across western Africa during the era of the slave trade show that most Africans who entered slavery were already aware of some of the commodities that were circulating in the Atlantic world or were inspired by the Atlantic encounters before their capture, and many had owned and used some of these commodities (such as beads, cowries, copper/brass products, pipes, tobacco, rum, European and Asian ware and cloth) in their daily lives. These objects played important roles in the production of African symbols, aesthetics, and tastes in the Americas, just as they were shaping cultural sensibilities in Atlantic Africa. Thus the mere fact that we have a few or even substantial trade goods at a site does not mean that a society or a group forsook its cultural autonomy to imitate a culture implicitly or explicitly regarded as superior by the contemporary scholar (Kent 1998, 16). Likewise, as Anna Agbe-Davies points out in this volume, that Africans in the Americas adopted mass-produced objects does not mean Africans and their descendants internalized the meanings accepted by those who controlled the design, production, and distribution of those objects. In fact, a careful study of artifact assemblages and their contexts often reveals that the acquisition of European manufactures in both slavery and post-emancipation contexts was based on African-driven consumer choices (Wilkie 1999), sometimes aimed at subverting white authority and hierarchies (White and White 1995, 162). Material records, like words, have the intrinsic quality of ambiguity and multivalence of dialogues and meanings (M. Hall 2000, 16). The task before the archaeologists is to identify the meanings that the different African Diaspora groups gave these mass-produced commodities in their daily lives. However, as we pursue this task, it is important to be cognizant of the fact that it is neither in artifacts nor in people that meanings intrinsically reside but in the moments or contexts of interaction between the two. By setting our interpretations of material records in the contexts of the history of power relations girding, enabling, and constraining identity and cultural formations in Atlantic Africa and its diaspora, we will come closer to grasping some of the meanings of material life in the African and the diasporic African world.

Inasmuch as the focus of research is on the archaeology of the African Diaspora, it will be necessary to identify Africanism in the archaeological-material complex whether as object, style, symbol, assemblages, or even the built landscape. But this pursuit of Africanism must not be divorced from the African cultural systems and the colonial American histories that created them. This study of Africanism, as Perry and Paynter (1999, 300) have noted, must not be limited to proving the establishment of an African presence in the Americas, but must fundamentally deal "with the character of that presence," "the level and domains of cultural autonomy and creativity, the degree of suppression and censorship, [and] the forgotten or unacknowledged sources of the [American] colonial life." In other words, we need to grapple with the specific historical contexts that shaped the African cultural production in the Americas. It is therefore important that our search for Africanism deploys suitable conceptual frameworks that will enable us to use the material life, contexts, and the landscape to study "the effect of African captivity and the Middle Passage on the place of Africa and African Americans in American culture" (Perry and Paynter 1999, 300). Moreover, as Kristin Mann and Edna Bay (2001, 6–7) have suggested, our attention should also turn to the study of how, when, and why enslaved Africans "were able to draw on material, social, ideological, and other resources from one or other traditions to fashion communities for themselves and cope with the demands of bondage." The essays in this volume critically engage these challenges.

Christopher Fennell addresses the character of African identity, focusing on the symbolic representations of BaKongo identity in the Americas. At once conceptual, theoretical, and empirical, his chapter challenges both the classical Creole School and Herskovits's Africanism by arguing that the presence of emblematic and instrumental expressions of BaKongo core symbols across the Americas shows that the artifacts and symbols of African Diaspora religious practices found in American sites represent neither the shreds and tatters of past African religions nor vague pan-African Diaspora religious beliefs. He argues that BaKongo religion is a reservoir of core cultural symbols that were used in a broad spectrum of expressive modes across the Americas. In an extensive survey of the archaeological records of West Central African symbolic representations from North to South America, informed comparison of the West Central African and African Diaspora religious/symbolic expressions, and a careful reading of ethnographic analogies, Fennell contrasts the use of private, instrumental symbolism of BaKongo religious beliefs at African-American sites in North America with the public, emblematic, communicative, and embellished symbolism that blends elements of diverse African cultures, including the BaKongo, Yoruba, and Dahomean belief systems in Central and South Americas. The author accounts for regional differences and diachronic

23

variability in the expressions of the BaKongo core symbols throughout the Americas and establishes that there is continuity in ritual undertakings between the BaKongo in West Central Africa and their descendants in the Americas. The conceptual and methodological approaches applied in the chapter offer the opportunity to understand how the African Diaspora social-group memberships were formed and transformed over the past four hundred years. This innovative analysis also moves us beyond the whole-culture assumption of the classical Creole School, makes a case for the transplantation of core African cultural forms in the Americas, projects the importance of interactions among core African cultures in the making of African Diaspora identities, rather than just between African and non-African core cultures, and demonstrates the historical conditionings that served as the crucible for the forging of BaKongo culture in North America, the Caribbean, and South America between the late seventeenth and nineteenth centuries.

The discussion of the dynamics of African cultural continuities, adaptation, and changes in the Americas is often related to African-European interactions, yet as both Christopher Fennell and Terrance Weik argue in this volume, we get different and refreshing perspectives when we consider other forms of cultural interactions among African ethnicities and cultural groups and between African groups and the Native American cultural entities. Weik examines the interactions between Africans and Native Americans in the context of resistance against racial domination and slavery. His chapter illustrates cultural interactions in the borderlands of the dominant/hegemonic spaces, contested by the Spanish, the English, and later Euro-, and addresses some of the ways in which Africans and Seminole Indians interacted during the Euro-American colonial expansion in central Florida (also see Cusick 2000, 49). Noting that the study of African Diaspora ethnicity has not widened our view beyond the recognition of its African roots, Weik challenges us to redefine our conceptualization of the African Diaspora in the Americas in ways that capture the multiple experiences and the cultural and interaction dynamics that identify other roots and routes of African Diaspora identity formation. To this end, he focuses his study on the African-Indian identity—black Seminole Maroons—at a nineteenth-century site called Pilaklikaha in central Florida. Weik argues that the formation of African-Indian identity in this border area involved the daily challenges of living in uncertainty, of intense mobility, of resistance against slavery, and of alliances and conflicts between the Seminoles and Africans.

Technology, Exchange, and Market Networks

The archaeology of African identities and African cultural production in the Americas has long been pursued out of the contexts of the political economies and economic relationships that sustained the colonial American societies, especially the plantation systems. This is partly a result of the fixation on the ahistorical extrasomatic conception of culture and the now discredited assumption that enslaved Africans were dependent at all times on the planters for all their material needs or at best were engaging only in self-sufficient subsistence gardening. Recent historiography and archaeological studies have demonstrated that enslaved men and women indeed engaged in production activities to meet their dietary and material needs (McKee 1999), and also participated in exchange economies, openly and clandestinely, sometimes with the encouragement of their owners, especially in the Caribbean (e.g., Hauser and Armstrong 1999; Mintz 1974; Wilkie 1999). The ongoing archaeological interest in the nature of the market economy that enslaved Africans participated in is showing that colonoware, yabbas, and colonopipes were not produced solely to serve subsistence needs but were part of plantation-based cottage industries that responded to regional demand and supply (Heath 1999a; Orser 1996, 117–29). Indeed, many enslaved communities and households acquired these earthenwares as a result of informal and institutionalized exchanges, and the plantation regimes encouraged and supervised the production of commodities that catered to the tastes and needs of enslaved Africans (Heath 1999b).

The focus on production centers and exchange networks in the colonial economy may aid in understanding the dynamics of integration of Africans as slaves and later as peasants into the colonial economies across the Americas, as well as the multiple meanings associated with the consumption patterns of Africans in the Americas. Likewise, the understanding of the organization of production and distribution of African commodities has implications for understanding the construction of identities and how we interpret the correlations between objects and African identities. Mark Hauser examines the organization of production and distribution of yabbas, locally produced coarse earthenware found in the Caribbean and associated primarily with African Diaspora sites. The organization of the production and distribution of these commodities can be used to determine the scale and extent of social relations forged through the internal market economy and the dynamics of interactions between the plantations/rural areas and the urban centers in the Caribbean. Hauser argues that despite the variability in the surface patterns and forms of yabbas, the aplastic inclusions show that the pottery was produced in a few sites within the same region for three centuries in Jamaica. Similarly, in another context, Monroe and Mallios (2004, 80) conclude that colonopipes were products of a cottage industry in Jamestown, Virginia, in which both Africans and Europeans participated, and that, as with the case in Jamaica, the production, distribution, and consumption of colonopipes were sustained by a colonial market system that facilitated the distribution of those pipes across the James River Valley during the seventeenth century. These studies have implications for our understanding of the production and distribution of colonoware in the Carolinas. Likewise, they demonstrate that plantation economies were not self-sufficient and that enslaved Africans were not isolated and monotonous producers of tobacco, rice, cotton, and sugarcane. Rather, they participated in the chains of production and consumption of manufactured goods (Hauser and Armstrong 1999, 66). These insights serve as a critique of the preoccupation of archaeologists with searching for "Africanisms" in the archaeological records without taking into consideration the complex social, economic, and historical contexts in which colonowares, yabbas, colonopipes, and other classes of objects associated with the material culture of Africans in the Americas were produced, distributed, and consumed.

Several of the features of market economies, technologies, and organization of production that had roots in Africa continued in the Americas, especially in the Caribbean and South America. Objects of daily lives, produced for and by Africans in the diaspora, such as colonoware, colonopipes, and yabbas, not only objectified cultural identities but also articulated gender and generational discourses. Pottery remained the domain of women, as it had been in Africa, whereas men produced colonopipes in Virginia and metal items in the Caribbean, as their forebears in Africa had done. Here, the broad sweep of gendered division of labor in African cultures coincided with the European traditions, yet capitalist mass production often changed the course of these traditions as a result of global transformations in production and consumption patterns and the development of new material bases for social distinction (Stahl and Cruz 1998).

Scholars have identified some of the important areas in which African skills enriched the economic foundations of colonies and nation-states in the Americas (e.g., Carney 1996, 2001). Candice Goucher has shown the possibilities of a transatlantic archaeology of African metallurgy, an archaeology that is not only about how the European raw and manufactured iron objects influenced metallurgical traditions in Africa, but also about how African skills and knowledge impacted metallurgical technology in the Americas, especially in the Caribbean. The insights from Goucher's studies have helped dispel the misconception that African technologies declined as a result of the encounters with European iron technologies (see also Anozie 1998; Pole 1982). Instead, African iron technologies improved.

Iron tools became part of the English and Dutch imports to the Bight of Benin in the seventeenth century (Richardson 1979). The archaeological evidence that these iron imports were traded as far as 150 km inland was found recently in central Yorubaland where imported tools were present in a 1600–1750 context. European imports of iron bars not only supplemented the local production but also required new skills for transforming some of the semifinished iron imports into finished goods. The impact of these imports on indigenous iron production, and on the local agricultural production and craft specialization, is not well understood for most parts of western Africa.

It is also likely that the insecurity brought by slaving activities in the hinterlands impacted the collapse of iron smelting in some parts of western

Africa, although the availability of slave labor may also have contributed to the expansion of smelting in other areas (MacEachern 2001). A regionwide study of the political economy of iron production during the Atlantic period would improve our understanding of the development of iron technology as related to the organized militarism and forms of warfare during the Atlantic period. Excavations of iron forges and sources of ores, and the application of archaeometallurgical analyses to the study of the technologies of iron produc-tion would help in discerning the forms of change and continuity that charac-terized metallurgical traditions in Atlantic Africa.

In the light of the archaeological excavations and historical research at Reeder's Foundry in Morant Bay, Jamaica, Goucher's chapter shows that the foundry workers in the Caribbean were predominantly of African origin, vari-ously referred to as slaves, Maroons, and free colored (also see Goucher 1999). Since African skills are so critical to understanding the history of Caribbean metal technology during the eighteenth century, we need to scrutinize the modes in which African metallurgical skills were transferred to the Caribbean in order to better understand the complexity of the African-European technol-ogy transfer. Certainly, technology was one of the sites of cultural negotiation between Africans and Europeans in the Americas. Enslaved Africans used their skills to develop the rice plantation systems in the Carolinas (see Carney 1996, 2001), and they participated in cottage industries, manufacturing textiles, pot-tery, and so forth (Heath 1999a, 199b; Monroe and Mallios 2004). They also contributed in no small measure to the technological transformations of the Americas and the sustenance of the American colonial economies.

Landscape and Archaeology of Social Difference

Archaeologists have been exploring the social spaces in which Africans produced their cultures in the Americas, especially in a post-sixteenth-century world in which Africans lived in bondage and in demarcated spaces between freedom and slavery, white and black, rich and poor (e.g., Armstrong and Kelly 2000; Delle 1998; Upton 1988). In North America, the use of the landscape and architecture for spatial separation of masters from laborers, of the rich planters from the poor planters, of Europeans and Africans, and of indentured European servants from the enslaved Africans was achieved by the last dec-ades of the seventeenth century in Chesapeake, Virginia (Epperson 1999a; Upton 1990). Thus the very process by which plantation slavery's division of labor was being specialized was also one in which race ideologies, racial rela-tions, and class divisions were being defined in colonial America.

The yardscape, an "area of land, bounded and . . . enclosed, which imme-diately surrounds a domestic structure and is considered an extension of that dwelling," is a significant crucible for the forging of African cultures in the Americas (Heath and Bennett 2000, 38; also see Mintz 1974, 225–50). As a place for work, leisure, performance of aesthetics, social reproduction, and community interactions, the yard is an important site for studying culture formation and change (see Armstrong 1990a; Gundaker 1993; Mintz 1974; Westmacott 1992). Based on the empirical archaeological data from her recent studies at the Hermitage Plantation of Andrew Jackson (seventh president of the United States) in Tennessee, Whitney Battle-Baptiste evokes the powers of African story and narrative, of memory and orality, of literature and ethnography, and of material life to show how enslaved Africans actively shaped and manipulated the plantation landscapes for autonomous cultural production. Battle-Baptiste suggests that by understanding the place of yard-scapes in the daily African lives, it is possible to accurately account for how enslaved Africans living in different house units on a plantation forged social networks and how they created group identities and cultural autonomies by manipulating the landscape in ways that challenged the authorities of the plantation system. Blurring the division between the domestic/private/household and outside/public/landscape and reexamining the material records associated with this holistic view of the landscape open new ways for understanding that the African conceptions of family and gender roles as well as space played important roles in the ways African communities were created under slavery.

The yardscape served as what Battle-Baptiste calls "a bridge connecting several individual families" on an American plantation or linking several individuals in an African compound or community. It also served as a bridge connecting enslaved Africans to virtually all parts of western Africa where yardspaces served as the arena of socialization, religious worship, cooking, burial, playing, working, family deliberations, etc. (e.g., Walsh 1997). Indeed, the yard or courtyard was the communal space where people conducted their daily lives in full view of the other members of the household in precolonial West Africa (Vlach 1976, 51). Given the many activities that women performed outdoors—food processing, cooking, soap making, weaving and dyeing, sewing, laundry, and socializing children, African women profoundly influenced the yard spaces (M. Franklin 2001, 113–14). Careful excavations of the yard spaces and systematic analysis of the yard material records would provide immense opportunities for understanding the gendered character of the yard and how free and enslaved women, in Africa and in the Americas, contributed to the socioeconomic reproduction of the family, village, compound, and plantation system (also see Edwards 1998; Gundaker 1993). Such a gendered archaeology of the yardscape must grapple with the sociopolitical institutions, economic regimes, and politics of social differences of the context being studied. This gendered analysis of the yard space should also be responsive to the changing gender roles in Africa in the course of the integration of Atlantic Africa into the production, distribution, and consumption networks of the transatlantic systems (Stahl and Cruz 1998; Ogbomo 1997) and the sociopolitical transformations in the Americas.

Although the creation of the African yardscapes as cultural spaces across the Americas was partly a result of the partitioning of the landscapes for the purpose of encoding and enforcing racial and class differences, the planters immediately recognized them as spaces of cultural autonomy that enslaved Africans could use to plan and execute resistance against their enslavement. African yardscapes therefore became an unsettling source of potential danger for European planters and colonial authority, and they made efforts to control and monitor the activities on African yardscapes through a series of laws that sought to Europeanize or de-Africanize the yardscape (Epperson 1990, 1999a). In Cuba, for example, slaveholders sought to destroy African yardscapes by housing slaves in prisons, regimenting the spatial order of plantations, and establishing strict surveillance techniques. But these measures did not deter slaves from running away, planning rebellions, and sometimes killing those they identified as their oppressors (Singleton 2001b, 110).

There is perhaps no other domain in the archaeological record of the Americas where group identity, race, power, and class intersect and are most succinctly expressed as the landscape (Kelso and Most 1990). As a spatial manifestation of relations between humans and their physical, social, economic, and political environments, landscape has been an active focus of archaeological research (Crumley and Marquardt 1990; Thomas 2001). This is much the case in the archaeology of the modern world where the accentuation of social inequality based on race and mercantile/industrial capitalism has constituted significant aspects of everyday lives for the past four hundred years (e.g., Delle 1998, 1999; Fitts 1996; McGuire 1991; Mrozowski 1991; Perry 1999). One of the central debates in American historical archaeology is the extent to which the planters and gentry of colonial America succeeded in using the built space to establish order, control, social hierarchy, and freeman-slave dichotomies. Did slaves share the same perception of landscape as the planters and the middling Europeans? Were Africans part of the intended audience of the grandiose colonial architecture and gardens that enacted social differences in colonial Americas (e.g., Epperson 1999a; Leone 1984, 1988; Upton 1990)?

The metaphor of the landscape as an experiential space has been useful in answering these questions (M. Hall 2000; Pulsipher and Goodwin 1999; Walter 1988) and in mapping and interpreting African expressions and experience of the landscape built and dominated by the European elite. The inherent ambiguity of the landscape and its multivalent meanings imply that although enslaved Africans may have accommodated the patriarchy of the master's spatial authority, they possibly resisted the master's interpretations and meanings based on racism. Some of these issues are addressed in chapter 11, where Alexandra Chan examines the ways the Royalls of Medford, Massachusetts, created a landscape intended to project and accentuate their class and status, to define themselves in relation to others, to create a physical separation between themselves and the enslaved members of their household, and to dispense rules that would reinforce the ideology of white superiority and black inferiority. Yet

Chan shows that the slaves resisted the hegemonic expectations of the European elite by creating different readings and meanings of the landscape and alternative uses of the space surrounding the Royalls' mansion and the slave quarters.

The cultural landscape was therefore a contested space, a theater of domination, resistance, and accommodation. However, rather than assuming a single African response or a uniform African reading, Chan combines the documentary sources with archaeological data to locate the different personalities of enslaved Africans, the nature of their duties in the Royalls' household, and how these differences may have affected their divergent responses to the rigidity and controlling nature of the landscape. In other words, the positioning of each enslaved African in the socioeconomic and labor systems of slavery influenced who was excluded from or incorporated into the most social and intimate architectural spaces of power, authority, grandeur, and status of the master. We need to pay attention to these nuances of power relations, hierarchies, and social differences that cut across race and ethnicity. To this end, an attempt has been made to use class—based on economic power—as an analytical category to account for the social structures at different periods and contexts in the Americas (see Orser 1988a). This attempt was initially inspired by the need to account for the economic divisions of the plantation system (Otto 1984; Delle 1998, 1999). It has been argued that the basic division on the plantations in the United States was between the planters and their overseers and slaves (Handler and Lange 1978, 28). Whereas this planter-overseer-slave division captures the dynamics of power relations in the plantation system on a macro scale, it may not account for micro-scale analysis of hierarchies in specific plantations or explain the evolution of such social divisions. For this reason, we should avoid the planter-overseer-slave model being overly determinative of our interpretations of specific plantation archaeological records. It would be useful, for instance, to examine how social differences among Africans in the diaspora affected the ways that identities and cultural productions were achieved among Maroons and slaves, between Maroons and free blacks, and between free, propertied blacks and whites. It is in these lines of inquiry that we may be able to understand "the material manifestations that integrate African American identity with social class" (Singleton 1999a, 4). Moreover, by combining class and race in the study of the development of plantation social hierarchies and differences, we will come closer to the understanding of the interplay between those who use structural asymmetrics of resources and ideology in exercising power and domination over others and those who resisted this domination through the deployment of materials, symbols, and practices of social and cultural opposition from below (Paynter and McGuire 1991, 1; also see G. Hall 1992; McKee 1992; Singleton 1995).

Most enslaved Africans came from societies with strong social hierarchies and elaborate symbols of social status and systems of lateral and vertical social differences (McIntosh 1999c; see Déme and Guèye, Monroe, Stahl, and Usman, this volume). In the Yoruba-Edo region, for example, different lineages and family groups maintained discrete spatial units. Likewise, palaces and other elite residences were often demarcated from the rest of the town or city-scape with walls and/or ditches (Ojo 1966). In the coastal town of Savi, the elite used a ditch system to distinguish themselves spatially from the rest of the population in the seventeenth century (Kelly 1996, 689). At the domestic level, architectural features and spatial organization reveal distinct social hierarchies. It would be useful, therefore, to assess how enslaved Africans deployed their traditions of social hierarchy and hierarchization of space to challenge and accommodate the Eurocentric institutions and practices of social differences. We cannot take it for granted that enslaved Africans generally conformed to the plantation sense of hierarchies and power and did not develop parallel authorities. Such authorities may have been based on the African sensibilities of occult, religious, and medicinal knowledge, as well as administrative, arbitration, and occupational skills, age, family status, and gender. We should move beyond the Eurocentric models of power and status by taking the archaeological contexts of spatial layout of slave quarters and the associated activity, the spatial distribution of artifacts, as well as specific ritual contexts among the enslaved through a closer reading of the historical records, including oral narratives and historical ethnography, in order to address questions of status, hierarchies, and social differences among the diasporic Africans. Likewise, the advances in the African Diaspora and American historical archaeology offer some possibilities in understanding how race, class, and power were deployed in western Africa as a result of the socioeconomic changes of the era, especially in the coastal areas where Europeans had a sustained presence (Bredwa-Mensah 2004; Brooks 2003, DeCorse 2001a; Lovejoy and Richardson 1999). We think the archaeologists of western Africa who are interested in African-European interactions would benefit from the "critical race" and "critical materialism" theories that scholars of American historical archaeology and those of southern Africa have applied to understanding the place of enslaved and free Africans in the political economies of the early modern world (Epperson 1999b; M. Hall 2000; Orser and Fagan 1995, 194).

Archaeology of Resistance

One area of intense archaeological interest is the African resistance to slavery. The creation of autonomous cultural spaces, articulation of distinct cultural identities, defiance of the legal and ideological basis of slavery, and the sabotage of slavery economies through destruction of machinery and crops and through feigning ignorance and illness to reduce and avoid work formed part of the daily resistance to slavery. But more work is needed on how diasporic Africans used their autonomous cultural spaces to articulate ideas that challenged the slavery institution and its attendant oppression. The excavations of

31

African burial grounds, especially in the United States and the Caribbean, offer rich opportunities to explore burial practices, funerary rites, and the beliefs associated with death, afterlife, and the spirit world (Handler 1997; Jamieson 1995). It will be rewarding to know how burial practices and beliefs were organized, especially in the eighteenth and nineteenth centuries, to shape quintessential African moral idioms that challenged and transcended the dominant mores of the planters and colonial society. In Jamaica, like other parts of the Caribbean, where Africans had a very high mortality rate (Vasconcellos 2004), funerary rites that attuned the enslaved to their African ancestry became the sites of social communion, of affirming their African kinship and solidarity, and of espousing African moral codes that challenged the European Christian moral order. Contemporary observers in Jamaica recognized African funerary rites not only as "the principal festivals" and sacred African practices and beliefs of the Negroes "upon which occasions they call forth all their magnificence and display all their taste" (Beckford 1790, 388), but also as offensive and sometimes subversive to the European sensibilities (Leslie 1739; Phillippo 1843). As archaeological excavations have shown, sacrifices defined the character of African burial practices from the seventeenth century through the early nineteenth century. It is here that archaeologists may hope to capture not only African burial traditions but also the moral and political discourses that these sacrifices of foodstuff, animals, beads, mirrors, cowries, coins, etc., articulated vis-à-vis the material conditions of enslaved Africans in the colonial world of the plantation systems and racism.

An important area of research that archaeologists have explored in the past twenty years is maroonage and material records of violent resistance (Agorsah 1993a, 1994a, 2001; Orser and Funari 2001; Weik 1997). These studies are demonstrating the African origins of the antislavery movements in the diaspora (Diouf 2003; McGowan 1990; Rathbone 1986), especially that Africans were among the very first groups in the Americas to articulate demands for freedom and social justice. These studies therefore challenge the master narrative of antislavery movements that privileges the Enlightenment ideals of liberty, freedom, and self-determination as the core intellectual groundwork responsible for the awareness of abolitionist and antislavery dispositions among Africans, including the monumental slave revolt in Saint Domingue and the consequent revolution (Genovese 1979; James 1963; M. Klein 1994).

The relevant chapters in this volume show that both in Africa and in the Americas, Africans formed their own ideological arguments for their resistance against slavery different from Enlightenment ideas. In fact, whereas the European-centered abolition movement in the late eighteenth and nineteenth centuries focused only on abolishing the institution of slavery, antislavery Africans sought socioeconomic freedom and opportunity for self-determination (Beckles 1990). Likewise, the ideas of antislavery and ideology of resistance that Africans espoused in the diaspora have been traced to their African roots. In the Sudan, for example, Islamic-based institutions sought to end the disruptive effects of the slave trade, moved in part by nationalist interests and their opposition to the European Christian slavers. The masses aligned with these Islamic leaders to mount one of the most powerful ideological resistances to Atlantic slavery, but this Islamic alternative failed to put an end to the slave trade. Rather, it "was soon caught up in the vicious circle of the forces it sought to control and ended up depending on slaving for survival" (Inikori and Engerman 1992, 4). There is surely a connection between the antislavery jihads in Sudan and the Male/Nago uprisings in Brazil; between the political turmoil and civil unrest against slavery in Kongo during the seventeenth century and the Haitian revolution and Stono rebellion in the eighteenth and nineteenth centuries; between the ethos of resistance and freedom in Yoruba *Orisa* ontology and the Lucumi/Nago/Fon rebellions in Cuba and Brazil; and between the Senegambian antislavery Islamic brotherhood and the "Bambara" revolts against slavery in New Orleans and other parts of the Americas (see Apter 2002; Campbell 1997; Lovejoy 1994; I. Miller 2004; Reis 1993; Schuler 1970; Thornton 1993). Archaeological approaches that are informed by historical sensibilities provide possibilities for understanding the multiple dimensions of African resistance against slavery, colonialism, and oppression in the Atlantic world.

Several studies have discussed how West Africans used earthen fortifications, trenches, stone walls, and stockades of living trees and thorn bushes to deter attacks and kidnappings. They defended themselves by living in the mountains, caves, hilltops, and marshes, swamps, and rivers (see chapters in Diouf 2003; Swanepoel 2003). These strategies of resistance to slavery and enslavement continued in the Americas, where runaways found refuge in remote hilltop settlements and inhospitable swamps and marshes.

The literature on the archaeology of the Maroons has been growing since the early 1990s (e.g., Agorsah 1993a, 1994a; Deagan and McMahon 1995; Funari 1995a; Orser and Funari 2001; Weik 1997, 2004). Chapters 14–16 in this volume demonstrate the potentials of archaeology for restoring Africans to the center of narratives on abolition and independence in the Americas beyond interest in the "romantic notion of African rebels openly defying the slave regime" (Orser 1998, 69). Agorsah (2001) argues that the Maroons should be the starting point of the narratives of freedom and liberty in the Americas because they not only fought against the slavery plantation systems but were the first to fight against colonialism in the Americas. Archaeology of the Maroons opens a window into the world of African freedom fighters, their defense strategies, including the use of the environment for defensive and offensive purposes, the social and communicative networks they established with other groups, especially Native Americans, and marginal European groups as was the case in Brazil, and the ways of life that they developed in order to maintain their freedom. Archaeologists have identified at several Maroon sites the distinctive patterns of subsistence, culinary self-sufficiency, and local manufacturing activities (pottery and tobacco pipes), some of which bear Native American as well as African stylistic motifs (Weik 2004, 36). Yet we also know that these Maroon sites shared intensely in the everyday material life of colonial America as evident in the presence of imported pipes, buttons, pharmaceutical bottles, ceramic bowls, plates, cups, buckles, iron nails, gunflints, fragments of gun barrel, and musket balls. All these show that the Maroons participated in the colonial economy of their respective regions. These finds have complicated the quest to understand the processes of African cultural formation in these fugitive enclaves. The initial expectation that Maroon sites will necessarily preserve pristine and whole African material culture has given way to a more constructive quest to understand the dynamic nature of cultural interactions and syncretism that sustained the Maroon communities (Orser 1998, 69).

Kofi Agorsah and Pedro Funari, in their respective chapters, demonstrate the usefulness of landscape approaches to the archaeology of the Maroons. The focus on the spatial distribution of fortifications, footpaths, and trails will give us insights into the guerrilla lifestyle and social networks that sustained the Maroon settlements, as well as the art of African militancy and warfare. The combination of landscape and material culture analysis will also enlighten us about the frantic offensive efforts that colonial regimes mounted to destroy Maroon settlements, in awareness of the dangers that these islands of freedom posed to the slavery economy. The spatial arrangement of structures and artifacts in Maroon settlements may also reveal the nature of hierarchy and power relations (e.g., Orser and Funari 2001) and the formation and transformation processes that these communities underwent during the struggle against slavery and colonialism. Although most Maroon settlements eventually succumbed to the superior weaponry of the colonial states (Agorsah 2001, 5), archaeological records at sites like Seaman's Valley in Jamaica and Palmares in Brazil also testify to the casualties that the Portuguese and British soldiers sometimes suffered at the hands of people whose only motivation to fight was their "devotion to the idea of liberty at any price" (Rashid 2003).

Maritime Archaeology and the Making of African Diaspora

As a subfield concerned with the study of humans and their interactions with the sea, with the sites related to maritime activities such as lighthouses, port constructions, or shore-based whaling stations, and with the vessels that transported goods and people across the waters, maritime archaeology holds immense possibilities for understanding the development of African Diaspora culture and sociopolitical actions before the late nineteenth century. In this volume, Fred McGhee demonstrates the potential contributions of maritime archaeology to the archaeology of the Atlantic African world, especially the archaeology of African Diaspora. He raises a number of conceptual issues about the ship, the most important artifact and instrument in the making of the modern era. The ship is vital to the creation of the Atlantic world and the modern economy (Gibbins and Adams 2001). Central to McGhee's argument is that ships are geographies unto themselves and that they traverse geographic boundaries. The ship blurs continental boundaries and restructures our mental geographies of space, place, time, culture, and history (Rice 2003). As a facilitator and product of global capitalist economy, the study of the materials associated with the ship affords us new perspectives to understand the dispersal of Africans not only across the Atlantic to the Americas but also to non-Atlantic zones that were contemporaneous with and facilitated by the Atlantic crossings. This perspective charges us to move beyond the fragmented view of the landmasses of the Atlantic basin and to recognize that metaphorically the Atlantic may have been a "lake" bounded by Africa, Europe, and the Americas but that the "lake" merges into other "lakes"—the Pacific and Indian oceans. And as these oceans merged, so did people, culture, ideas, and goods of the Atlantic enter the Pacific and Indian oceans, and vice versa. This conceptualization of the ship and the Atlantic not only emphasizes the multiple consciousness and dynamism of black identity formation under complicated geographies in motion but also turns our attention to the ship and its contents as an important artifact in the study of the Middle Passage (including living conditions, ship designs, and onboard African revolts), the African Diaspora identities, and the socioeconomic niches that Africans carved for themselves in the Americas by taking to seamanship (Bolster 1997, 45). Moreover, the study of shipwrecks affords us the opportunity to gather information about the types of commodities that were involved in the transatlantic trade and the dynamics of consumption in the Atlantic African world.

Maritime archaeology of the African Diaspora is, however, not just about the ship and the Middle Passage crossings. Canoes, lighters, schooners, and pettiaugers (flatboats) sustained the plantation system in the New World because these vessels were used for the transportation of sugar, rice, and tobacco bound for local and regional markets (Bolster 1997, 117). As captains and pilots of boats, canoes, and pettiaugers between the Caribbean surf and Carolinian rivers, Africans' maritime skills mostly "kept the plantation system afloat" (Bolster 1997, 45). African boating skills benefited the New World transportation systems. After all, in Western Africa, myriad waterways constituted important highways for commerce, transportation, warfare, and communication with the use of dugout canoes, some being over seventy feet long and seven to eight feet wide (Osiruemu 2005; R. Smith 1970). Unlike any other occupation, seamanship was the most racially integrated labor force in the Americas before the nineteenth century, and the promises of freedom that seamanship offered the enslaved Africans also make the material culture of sea/river vessels amenable to understanding the processes involved in the African struggle for their human rights. On the whole, through maritime archaeology we have the prospects of having an enriched understanding of how the forces of capitalism were interlinked with the construction of race and racism, ethnicity and identity, organization of labor, and production and consumption as well as the idea and achievement of liberty, freedom, and independence in the African Atlantic world.

It was through ports that Africans were rudely introduced into slavery. Many remained attached to these ports for the rest of their lives, because the ports were the nerve centers of colonial and Atlantic commerce. One of these seventeenth- and eighteenth-century ports was Buenos Aires, as Daniel Schávelzon discusses in this volume. The excavations taking place at that city's African sites have immense potential for revealing the conditions of life (disease, diet, working conditions) as well as the nature of race relations, ethnicities, identities, cultural contacts, and the forms of tolerance and resistance that Africans developed there. Through research in urban centers such as Buenos Aires, we have the possibility of comparing and contrasting the lifeways of Africans in the urban settings with those on the plantations in colonial America.

"Emancipated" African Diaspora and Colonized Africa

If seafaring, despite its associated dangers and paltry remuneration, gave a few Africans/blacks in the Americas some measure of respite from the grueling life on the plantations, the seaports or port towns/cities associated with sea life are central to understanding how freedom was transformed from an idea into reality. Nowhere in the Americas was this transition from slavery into freedom, and from dependent bondsmen into freedmen, better demonstrated than in New England, where between the American Revolution and the Civil War free black men sought jobs as whalers, pilots, captains, deckhands, and riggers and established connections to the seaports. By the early nineteenth century, many African seamen in the northern United States were using their meager wages to support antislavery movements and churches, schools, and other public institutions devoted to uplifting their downtrodden brethren and sisters (Bolster 1997). During those decades, the echoes of freedom from the ocean surf merged with the increasingly loud march of the antislavery movement on land. The effect shook the very foundations of the modern economy and the young republic.

The New England seaports were abolition centers at the dawn of the nineteenth century. Along with New London, Connecticut; Portsmouth, New Hampshire; and Boston, Nantucket was a preeminent center of the whaling industry and a port where black mariners began to coalesce. They were joined there by other freed and fugitive Africans from the South, a trend that lasted until the outbreak of the Civil War. Although the abolition of slavery at Nantucket in 1770 had made the island a haven for refugee slaves and free blacks (Hayden and Hayden 1999, 219), the racially segregated landscape of Nantucket throughout the nineteenth century forced the free African community to establish institutions that paralleled the white organizations. Africans maintained their own stores, churches, schools, and cemetery. Those churches were testimonies to the post-emancipation quest of blacks to achieve self-determination in a world that was segregationist and hostile to their independence. Robert Hayden (1987), for example, calls the African Meeting House on Beacon Hill, Boston, built in 1806, the black community's "political, social, educational, and religious epicenter." In alliance with the white antislavery sympathizers and organizations, the meetings at these sanctuaries focused on abolishing slavery, reducing racial prejudices, providing havens for runaway slaves, and educating black children.

Focusing on the African Meeting House, a building and lot that simultaneously served as a church, a school, and a civic community center for the black Nantucketers, Mary Beaudry and Ellen Berkland use the transformations in the racial landscape and material life during the rapid sociopolitical currents of the century to reconstruct the postslavery emergence of African American culture. All the knickknack items found in the African Meeting House originated from the Euro-American industries, and they point to a community celebrating freedom while also struggling to transform that freedom into economic independence, self-determination, and better living conditions. In the only chapter devoted to the material life of free blacks in the nineteenth-century antebellum United States, Beaudry and Berkland introduce readers to the emerging consumer culture in African Diaspora communities in the very beginnings of post-emancipation and the Industrial Age. The numerous fragments of earthenware plates, pearlware vessels for brewing and drinking tea, creamware plates, and lead-glazed redwares (crocks and bowls), as well as perfume, alcohol, and medicine bottles, apparel and personal adornment objects, toys, and harmonica fragments, indicate that "emancipated" blacks were actively integrating themselves into the capitalist marketplace through hard work and increasing purchasing power. By participating in the consumption of objects that signify and symbolize the American sense of abundance, nationalism, and democracy, blacks were able to challenge the racial caricatures that America had constructed for them and to articulate their quest for full citizenship (Mullins 1999). The material life in the nineteenth-century Nantucket African Meeting House illustrates the changing African American consumer culture and the importance of common daily objects in understanding the intersection of desire, consumerism, race, ethnicity, freedom, citizenship, and nationalism in the lives of Africans in the post-emancipation United States (Mullins 1999).

As blacks in the Americas were being "emancipated," only to face another century of Jim Crow laws and racial segregation, especially in the United States, it is of interest that continental Africa was simultaneously being colonized. By the close of the nineteenth century, the whole continent had been colonized by a few European nations. Thus, whereas emancipation meant the beginning of struggle for diasporic Africans to acquire citizenship in their respective nations and to fight discrimination, continental Africans were being balkanized into new political configurations that denied them autonomy and full citizenship. Moreover, as the seaports on the American side were being restructured by the abolitionist movements, those on the African side were also experiencing tremendous changes. Very early in the century, the ports of Badagry, Lagos, Freetown, Ouidah, Calavi, Grand Popo, Agoue, Lome, Allada, Savi, Cotonou, and Porto-Novo became arenas for staging European Enlightenment: Christianity, Western education, abolition of slavery, and European colonialism. Commerce, not excluding slave trading for the first half of the century, remained the engine on which these ports were propelled. Simultaneously, they became centers of European colonial ambitions as well as arenas for anticolonial struggles. The Africans returning from the Americas, first-generation post-emancipation Africans of the diaspora, as well as those rescued on the high seas by the British antislavery squadrons, had an immense impact on the cultural history of Atlantic Africa in the nineteenth century.

In similar ways that the western African coast mediated the relationship between the hinterlands and the merchant capitalism of the Atlantic basin between 1500 and 1800, the African port towns and cities became, once again, the gateway for funneling Industrial Age material culture into the African hinterlands during the nineteenth century, reinforcing and seemingly completing the long road to the marginalization of Africa in the global capitalist economy. At the micro levels, the archaeologists can assess not only how this changed the monetary culture and taste of the subcontinent but also how it reconfigured social relations and power across gender, age, and class (Guyer 2004). In some parts of the hinterlands, archaeological studies show that imported objects were playing a larger role in daily lives than objects of local production in the second half of the nineteenth century. In Makala, Central Ghana, for example, Ann Stahl recovered a wider range and greater quantity of imports in nineteenth-century contexts than from the earlier centuries. These imports included beads, ball-clay smoking pipes, glass bottles, imported ceramics, gunflints, and metal objects. The trend in the archaeological records of the mid- to late nineteenth century was toward reduced diversity and increasing quantity in material records, especially of objects that were applied to bodily adornment (Mullins 1999; Stahl 2002, 839). These changes in the material records were taking place across western Africa in the contexts of the European political economic hegemony: industrial capitalism/colonization/ "legitimate trade" nexus. These Industrial Age objects were put to similar uses with various local flavors in different parts of the world. The implications of these everyday objects for structuring social relationships, defining aspirations and identities, and articulating multiple discourses at the local levels should therefore be examined with an eye for inferring global dimensions of culture, power, knowledge, group identity, individual aspirations, domination, and resistance at the local levels. Comparative study of material life in nineteenth-century Africa and the African Diaspora may give us insights into the integration of these peoples into the Industrial Age, an age that transformed diasporic and continental Africans into wage and tenant laborers and that, more than ever before, bound continental Africans to the European political economic systems.

It is in southern Africa that the archaeology of Industrial Age European colonialism is best illustrated, partly because of the similarities of experience in the Americas and southern Africa where we have cases of European settlements, displacement and enslavement of African populations, and the establishment of European plantations and mining operations (M. Hall 1993, 2000). In South Africa, archaeologists are studying the effects of industrialization and colonialism on the African domestic economy, foodways, building technology, settlement patterns, migrations, gender relations and family, consciousness, and consumption (Behrens 1999; M. Hall 1993, 1997; Lane 1999). The archaeological study of the impact of the Industrial Revolution, European colonization, and industrialization has been driven by the quest to access the lives and experience of the subalterns—the women, blacks, underclasses, and slaves—who are not represented in the traditional archives. The powerful story that archaeology and high-powered scientific analyses are able to uncover about the daily lives of these subalterns is a true testimony to the importance of archaeology of the modern world. For example, the stable carbon and nitrogen isotopic analyses of individuals from an underclass cemetery in colonial Cape of Good Hope provide tantalizing information on the "roots of the working class in the old colonial world" (Cox et al. 2001, 91). These analyses reveal how merchant capital forced people from different parts of the world—enslaved and free Africans and Muslims from Asia—into underclass working conditions in the Cape and how these individuals participated in the consumption of goods—trade beads, tobacco pipes, clothing, buttons, sewing and cutting tools—that demonstrate their incorporation into the European material world.

In Nigeria, an archaeological study into the foundations of British colonization in the late nineteenth century has also begun by focusing on how colonial institutions modified the landscape through the building of barracks, prisons, hospitals, schools, residences, and cemeteries, and the impacts on obliterating the precolonial settlements in Zungeru (Ogedengbe 1998), a gateway to the colonization of what became northern Nigeria. Limited excavations in and around the colonial settlement yielded glass bottles, plastic containers, and metal objects. The abundance of military artifacts, such as bullets and gun fragments, in the archaeological deposits show the coercive nature of the British colonial enterprise in Nigeria. The Zungeru project reveals the "mundane brutalities of colonial dispossession and resistance" at the local levels and how objects of everyday life and the imposing architecture of colonial authority created new material, cognitive, and ideological references for the colonized (see M. Hall 2000, 15).

Archaeology, Power, and Social Practice

Practitioners of African and African Diaspora archaeology have frequently reflected on the significance and consequences of their work for people of African descent and the public at large (e.g., Andah 1995; Chappell 1999; M. Franklin 1997a; Ogundiran 2002b; Shepherd 2002; Wilkie 2004; also see contributions on the politics, methods, theories, presentation, logistics, and social relevance of practicing African archaeology in *African Archaeological Review*, vol. 13, no. 1, 5–34). Within the context of archaeological practice in the United States, Anna Agbe-Davies assesses the research themes and approaches in African American archaeology, especially themes of Africanism, consumption, agency, and power; how these are related to the interpretation of African living experience in relation to slavery, racism, and disenfranchisement; and how these historical experiences are related to poverty, ghettoism, and social marginalization in the United States. In her chapter, Agbe-Davies addresses the power differentials that have mediated the expressions of African identities in the Americas, configured the practice and research agenda of African Diaspora archaeology, and defined the struggle over the control of the scripts of African experience.

The injustices of the past and the often defective or malfunctioning social justice of the present, defined along the contours of race, class, ethnicity, and gender, have impacted the ways the past is constructed and have shaped the struggle over the intellectual power aimed at a research agenda that is more responsive to the needs and concerns of African-descent communities and the various interest groups among them (Austen 2001; Dubin 1999, 38; Epperson 1999b; Franklin 1997a, 1997b). Whether it is the African Burial Ground in New York City (Harrington 1996; LaRoche and Blakey 1997) or the African Meeting House in Boston, the Maroon sites in Jamaica (Agorsah 1994a) or the slave forts on the coastlands of West Africa (Osei-Tutu, this volume), the monuments and sites of African entanglements in Atlantic slavery, racism, and modern world systems are apt to challenge the scientific goals of archaeology (Agbe-Davies, this volume). This must be resolved in favor of empowering Africans and the African Diaspora while making the archaeology of transatlantic Africa a better science (e.g., Mack and Blakey 2004). Such empowerment recognizes the potentials of transatlantic African archaeology in providing alternative scripts that can challenge, and even undermine, the hegemonic discourses on the rise of the modern world and that can be deployed in the struggles for equality (Schmidt and Patterson 1995). Yet, as Stahl (2004a, 61–62) reminds us, we should also pay attention to the diversity and complexity of power relations among the dominated peoples — in this case, African communities on both sides of the Atlantic (Osei-Tutu, this volume). As the struggle for control of the transcripts of Africans' Atlantic past continues, it is important to avoid according a single agency to all Africans: African slavers and brigands must be separated from the victims and survivors of brigandage, kidnapping, the Middle Passage, and enslaved labor. Likewise, the powers of the marginal gainers must be separated from those who appropriated the profits of slavery in dominating the modern world (Inikori 2002). Even as we celebrate the contributions of African technologies and skills to the making of the Atlantic world (e.g., Carney 2001), we need to account for both the achievements and the limitations of African agencies in relation to the power relations of the modern world. Otherwise, as Rosalind Shaw (2002, 19) warns, "we risk collapsing distinctions among contrasting kinds of agency that are associated with contrasting kinds of power. The agency of those who deploy 'weapons of the weak' and of those who creatively appropriate signs and processes of domination 'from below' . . . are each very different from the agency of those whose authority allows them to act upon the world through control of an apparatus of domination."

Further Directions: Material Life and Archaeology of Transatlantic Africa

The ultimate goal of the archaeology of transatlantic Africa, like other branches of historical archaeology, is to explain the intersection of the local with the global, how the local shaped the global, and, conversely, how the global has acted on local practices, based on the understanding that local culture is a determined part of the global world system (Ulin 2001, 222). The sources that form the basis of archaeological interpretations—material records—are contextually local. It is from these local sources that archaeologists must, however, make interpretations about global historical and cultural processes. Although material record is the heart and soul of archaeology, the archaeology of Atlantic Africa and the African Diaspora recognizes the symbiotic relationship of things and words (written and oral). To this end, each author in this volume has creatively mined spoken words, written words, and objects (including the landscape) to understand different facets of the African past on both sides of the Atlantic. Each chapter demonstrates a clear understanding that objects must be analyzed and interpreted within the context of a specific culture and the dynamics of intergroup relations at a given time.

As part of the archaeology of the modern world, the archaeology of Atlantic Africa and the African Diaspora must grapple with how the global expansion of new products and the commoditization of objects, facilitated by the globalization of production and consumption and worldwide penetration of capitalism, have impacted cultural, political, economic, and social relations at the local levels in the African world. Ceramics, tobacco pipes, beads, cowries, buttons, metal objects, and alcoholic and medicinal beverage containers are some of the ubiquitous artifacts in the archaeological contexts of Atlantic Africa and the African Diaspora. It is important to understand how these artifacts were deployed in the African constructions of power, dominance and resistance, work and production, gender and age relations, and recreation in different sociopolitical and economic settings. This question recognizes artifacts as "active voices" not only in identity formation but also in communicating and negotiating status and aspirations at individual and group levels (Beaudry, Cook, and Mrozowski 1991). The archaeology of transatlantic Africa will move us closer to the realization of the commitment of historical

41

archaeology to understanding the roles of Africans in the making of the modern world and the impact on the African world. This quest should move beyond the focus on colonialism and capitalism as the programmatic agenda of historical archaeology (e.g., Orser 1996). Rather, we should critically probe those other settings of cultural production, especially in continental Africa, where Africans were drawn into the Atlantic economy without being colonized and without swallowing the pill of European capitalism hook, line, and sinker. In this regard, understanding the material life in Atlantic Africa would be a prerequisite for meaningful interpretations of the material records in the African Diaspora sites.

Approaches to the study of material life are varied among archaeologists of the African world. The most prevalent approach often adopts a functional-formal analysis that catalogues archaeological finds, uses them as type-fossils for deducting age/dates of archaeological levels, analyzes their formal properties, and interprets them as indicators of social variation, material wealth, and trade goods/consumption patterns (e.g., Calvocoressi 1968, 1977; DeCorse 1989; Effah-Gyamfi 1981; Ozanne 1962; York 1972). Functional-formal analysis often gives very little attention, if any, to the doers, thinkers, and users of the artifacts. Archaeologists, especially in Atlantic Africa, have veered more to the side of functionalist interpretation of material records than on attempting to understand the meanings of material records as a way of capturing how Africans made sense of their changing world due to the penetration of European imports and capitalism.

Borrowing from Pierre Bourdieu's conceptualization of distinction as an embodied practice (Bourdieu 1984), Stahl has eloquently advocated taste as the most amenable theme for archaeological probing of material records. As a form of embodied practice, taste focuses our attention on production and consumption and on "socially conditioned preference and choices." Although she recognizes that taste making is symbolic and endowed with meanings, she is convinced that these meanings are beyond the reach of archaeologists, especially "in contexts where language-based sources are few or absent" (Stahl 2001a, 35–36). The focus on taste for interpreting material records privileges sensorial factors in constituting sociocultural practices through the object worlds (Stahl 2002, 832–35), seeks to connect artifacts to the regional and global/political/economic relationships that structured their production, distribution, and consumption, and helps in understanding the production and market forces that gave birth to commodities that eventually became archaeological artifacts—tobacco pipes, beads, metal imports, cowries, chinaware, etc. (Stahl 2004b). Placing taste at the center of production, circulation, importation, and consumption of goods provides an avenue for understanding how Africans entangled themselves in the Atlantic economy and developed new sets of relationships as a result of the shifts in global/political economy. This perspective transcends the dominance/resistance paradigm and avoids the one-sided view that avaricious capitalism overwhelmed Africans in all situations and led to the loss of authentic African culture. Rather, it enables us to understand how objects, both locally produced and imported, were used to constitute local African cultures and the nuances of relationships in which these objects and cultures were created and transformed through the articulation of African practices with global historical processes on both sides of the Atlantic.

Yet, inasmuch as objects are part of the signs and symbols that make living possible, archaeologists cannot afford to shy away from uncovering the symbolic meanings that are embedded in objects. Symbolic representations in artifact attributes, iconography, and space not only served as instruments of communication to accomplish or contest power, domination, and self/group determination (Wobst 1977). They also constituted and structured the mental and social world. It was possible for African cultures to be transported to the Americas and be adapted to a new sociophysical environment because of the intrinsic quality of symbols as "mental building blocks" that allowed humans to "orient themselves in the world, think, and act through learned, culturally specific structures" (Robb 1998, 335). Like myths and legends, objects, whether locally or externally derived, are critical to generating, transforming, and transmitting ideas and values into physical reality. In fact, they constitute a cognitive system that shapes the perception of reality and provides insights about the world and the new experience. The explanation of the meanings and social valuation of an object is always a prerequisite for a firm understanding of the range of functions of the object and why the object was desired or out of favor at a particular point in time (W. Smith 2002, 9). The understanding of what an object or an association of objects meant to the people who used them, however, "requires knowing [the] beliefs and perceptions that are external to the object itself," often with the help of comparative ethnography, oral, and written sources (Lubar and Kingery 1993, xii; also see Guyer 1993). The quest for meanings in objects is an attempt to identify some of the symbolically constructive acts that humans have invested in the material world. These acts are central to understanding the power and social relations in which Africans lived their daily lives for the past five hundred years. Since objects are cultural, and there is hardly anything cultural that is not symbolic, and given the elaborate cultural dimensions of power relations in the Atlantic world, it is important that the archaeology of transatlantic Africa be attentive to the different sites in which symbols were made as instruments of domination, as tools of resistance, and as constitutive blocks for building cultural lives of distinctive African characters.

It is therefore important to transcend the dichotomies between the study of taste and meanings, and of political economy and symbolism, in material life in order to holistically assess not only the role of objects and the landscape in constituting African cultures in the Atlantic world, but also how objects and the landscape were used by Africans to recontextualize and transform their cultural world. This will help to integrate ideas with objects, and mentality with materiality. It will also move us closer to the deep recesses of African agencies in the Atlantic world, especially as we seek to understand why

Africans sought and acquired certain commodities to the exclusion of others, and the transformative roles of these objects on institutions, cognitive references, belief systems and religion, power relations, political formations, and social relationships, including gender relations, ethnic formations and identities, and domination and resistance.

This taste/meaning-oriented analysis recognizes that the social valuations and meanings of objects are subjected to changes according to time, place, and context (e.g., Ogundiran 2002c); they are culturally emergent, mutable, and contestable, rather than fixed and physically embedded in objects (Robb 1998, 337; see also Gosden 1994; Tilley 1999); and these changes are always politically and culturally mediated (Appadurai 1986; Kopytoff 1986). Hence our interpretation of material records on both sides of the Atlantic must grapple with the roles that politics of knowledge and power play in assigning or constructing an object's value and meaning (e.g., W. Smith 2002), the competing discourses of social valuation and meaning across gender, class, ethnicity, and race (e.g., Gregory 1996), and how these discourses changed over time (e.g., Gosden and Marshall 1999). In other words, we must locate the validation of certain functions, tastes, and meanings to the exclusion of other possibilities in the context of power structures and social and political economic relations in which the objects functioned. The swinging tides of these structures and relations should also be assessed in relation to how they transformed the meanings of objects and altered the taste and functional values associated with them.

Likewise, our interpretative lenses of material life in transatlantic African archaeology should consider how the forces of capitalist production and distribution affected the supply-demand nexus of objects in the Atlantic world of Africans, probe the meanings that these objects evoke in the sensibilities of the African users, and examine the relationships between the use-value and social valuation of similar types or categories of objects in Atlantic Africa and the African Diaspora. The longitudinal study of the variability of meanings and values associated with Atlantic imports and local products of different forms in western Africa, in the context of their cultural settings as well as the power and political economic relations and the production/exchange systems that underlie their distribution, may provide insights into the social valuation of these objects among diasporic Africans. The contexts in which these objects functioned and the choices the owners had in their procurement are important to assessing the taste and cultural meanings of material life among the African Diaspora populations.

Concluding Remarks

On the whole, this collection of essays demonstrates how compelling interdisciplinary approaches are in the archaeology of transatlantic Africa, especially in the understanding of Africans' entanglements in the Atlantic world, through cultural contacts, economic relationships, migrations, and slavery, and the impacts on sociopolitical, economic, and cultural transformations as well as identity formations and cultural productions. This volume challenges the epistemological practice of separating African archaeology from the archaeology of its diaspora, and it highlights the possibilities for collaboration with archaeologists across the Atlantic in the onerous task of understanding the place of Africa and Africans in the development of the modern world. Although the essays are divided between Atlantic Africa and the African Diaspora, this introduction is intended to help readers see the connections. Each chapter can be read alone, but many address related themes that offer opportunities for comparative reading and assessment. The topics explored in this volume are not exhaustive of the themes in the archaeology of transatlantic Africa. This is only a contribution to what we hope will be an exciting future of archaeological collaboration across the Atlantic.

II

ATLANTIC AFRICA

Entangled Lives: The Archaeology of Daily Life in the Gold Coast Hinterlands, AD 1400–1900

Ann Brower Stahl

Western perceptions of Africa are underwritten by the assumption that Africa only recently "joined" the modern world. Media portrayals of Africa as a violent, disease-ridden continent share with documentary images of exotic "tribal" societies a view of African villages as enmeshed in a world of timeless tradition characterized by life "as it ever was" (Achebe 1978; Ebron 2002, 2–5; Hammond and Jablow 1970; Mudimbe 1988, 1994). Perceived as a world of constant rhythms rooted in the seasonal demands of a subsistence economy, the seemingly traditional quality of African village life provides a seductive portal to the past for academics and tourists alike (see Ebron 2002, viii–xi, 189–212). Thick descriptions of contemporary or historic village life enrich our imaginings of past village life in Africa and elsewhere. Larkin (1988, xv), for example, invokes third world villages in an effort to conjure the sensory character of everyday life in America at the close of the eighteenth century, while scholars of Africa's past often emphasize the dynamism of urban contexts while assuming a fixity of rural life (see LaViolette and Fleisher 2005 for a discussion). Such views long obviated the need to study ancient African village life (e.g., Clark 1990, 193). Why pursue archaeological studies of ancient villages when village life could be so much more fully studied in the (ethnographic) present?

Whereas popular imaginings of Africa continue to be animated by these views, academic perspectives over the past quarter-century have emphasized long-standing connections and broader political economic contexts that conditioned life in Africa for at least the last millennium (e.g., Piot 1999; Wallerstein 1986; Wolf 1982, 195–231). In West Africa these connections developed first in the context of the trans-Saharan trade and later transformed and expanded with the developing Atlantic trade (MacEachern 2005). Academic perspectives on culture have similarly shifted from a view of culture as a product—fixed and finished, inherited and more or less faithfully reproduced by its constituents—to a process shaped by convention yet subject to refashioning as cultural actors confront new circumstances, something constantly and actively fashioned and refashioned (e.g., Bourdieu 1977; Giddens 1979; Sahlins 1981; Thompson 1963). Today it is an academic commonplace to assert that African cultures and rural village life have long been dynamic, that the contours and rhythms of daily life have been reshaped—not once or twice but continuously—by broader geopolitical contexts and weblike exchange networks. It becomes a verity to suggest that Africans have long led entangled lives, just as have Europeans, Asians, and Americans. Just as commonplace is the insistence that local responses to global forces were neither homogeneous nor dictated by the global "core" (Ortner 1984, 142–43). Yet this commonplace knowledge runs the same risk as did the emperor who had no clothes, for in many parts of the world the hard work of empirically documenting the character and effects of these connections, the specific ways in which lives were entangled, remains to be accomplished (cf. Cusick 1998; M. Hall 2000; Pauketat 2001; Paynter 2000a, 2000b; Schrire 1995). We require empirically robust case studies that draw on a variety of evidential sources (documentary, oral, and archaeological) to comparatively assess patterns of continuity and change in African village life through time. Only then will we be able to clothe our conceptual emperor with spatially and temporally specific understandings of the entangled lives of African peoples in past centuries. The resulting knowledge has relevance beyond the culture history of specific African peoples, for it contributes to a broader comparative study of the African Diaspora and global encounters more generally.

In what follows, I summarize what we have learned from an ongoing case study focused on the Banda area of west central Ghana. Since 1986, the Banda Research Project has undertaken oral historical, documentary, and archaeological research directed toward understanding how changing geopolitical economic conditions affected daily life in Banda. We have explored patterns of change and continuity in ethnicity, political organization, settlement, exchange, craft, and subsistence production in the period ca. AD 1000 to the present (Cruz 2003; L. Smith 2007; Stahl 1991, 1994a, 1999, 2001a, 2001b, 2002; Stahl and Cruz 1998; Stahl and Stahl 2004). Here I focus on what we have learned from archaeological investigations about daily life from about AD 1400 to 1900, considered against a backdrop of life in the early second millennium AD.

The Banda Area in Historical Context

The Banda area comprises the lands of the Banda chieftaincy, one among a large number of traditional chieftaincies represented in the National House of Chiefs in the contemporary nation-state of Ghana. Located just north of the tropical forest in a savanna woodland setting bounded on the north by the

Black Volta River (Fig. 2.1), Banda encompasses two dozen villages occupied by a mix of ethnic-linguistic groups, most of whom immigrated into the area over the course of recent centuries (Stahl 1991, 2001a, 51–60). Oral and documentary sources suggest that the chieftaincy was founded in the early eighteenth century by Nafana, who came to Banda from an area in what is today northeastern Côte d'Ivoire (Stahl 2001a, 151). Within decades of its founding, the Banda chieftaincy became subject to Asante overrule, an expansionist Akan state centered in the forested region of present-day Ghana. Incorporated by military siege in the dry season of 1773/74 (Yarak 1979), Banda later became one of a handful of non-Akan internal provinces of Asante (Wilks 1975, 54–55) and adopted Asante political regalia (Bravmann 1972). The Asante-style chieftaincy that characterizes the area today appears to have been a product of later colonial efforts to implement indirect rule in the British Gold Coast Colony (Stahl 2001a, 153–55). Effective British colonization occurred in the early twentieth century, when Banda gained a measure of autonomy vis-à-vis Asante. In recent decades the area has been plagued by a chieftaincy dispute with significant implications for the study of Banda history (see Stahl 2001a).

Historically, Banda lay at the crossroads of trade routes that linked the gold-rich forested region to the south with trade emporia along the Niger River to the north (Posnansky 1987; Wilks 1993); however, in the late nineteenth century and through six decades of British colonial rule, Banda became peripheralized and remains so within the contemporary Ghanaian nation-state. Its peripheral character is underscored by the state of its infrastructure. Banda has been slated since the early independence period (from 1957) for the construction of a hydroelectric dam (at Bui); however, the dam has yet to be constructed, and the electrical grid was extended to Banda only in the twenty-first century. Historically, one of the Asante Great Roads passed through Banda (Wilks 1975, 1–18), yet contemporary motor roads are rudimentary affairs that dead-end at the Volta River, making Banda a "one-way" destination. The few lorries that make the daily trip to the nearest market center (40 miles distant) depart Banda in the morning and return in the evening. Although Banda farmers produce some cash crops (yams, calabash, and tobacco), Banda families subsist primarily on what they grow. Although more houses are being built with cement walls and metal roofing sheets (particularly in the main town of Banda-Ahenkro), earthen-walled construction and grass thatch roofs predominate in the villages. Potting is actively pursued in several villages on Banda's western margins, while crafts like cloth production ceased within living memory. It is therefore easy and seductive to imagine that, although political crosscurrents may have wrought changes in the Banda polity and affected the lives and fortunes of its leaders, the daily lives of ordinary people differed little from life in the recent past. Archaeological and oral historical research conducted over the past eighteen years suggests otherwise, and I turn now to a brief overview of what we have learned about the patterns of daily life in the Banda area. Opening sections focus on the forging of northern connections and their effects in the

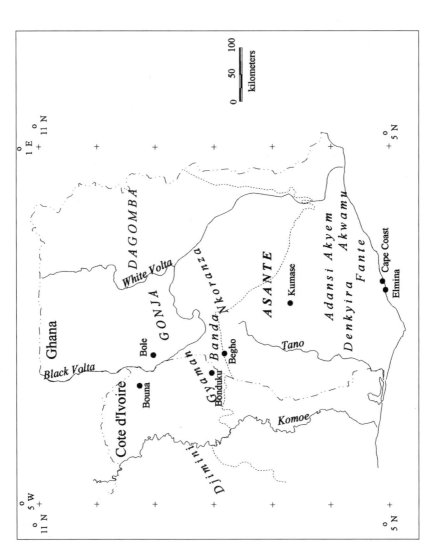

Fig. 2.1. Historic polities and towns.

period AD 1000–1400 as a backdrop against which to consider transformations in daily life with the forging of Atlantic connections from the fifteen century.

The Antiquity of Northern Connections

The archaeology of the central Volta basin in the first millennium AD is poorly known (Posnansky 1979, 32; Stahl 1994b). Smith's (2007) systematic regional site survey of the Banda area has identified sites that promise to fill the gap between the Kintampo Complex occupation of the second millennium BC and the better-known early second millennium AD occupation of sites like Begho (Crossland 1989; Posnansky 1979, 1987), Buipe (York 1973), Bono Manso (Effah-Gyamfi 1985), and Ahwene-Koko (Boachi-Ansah 1986). Preliminary results from a recent Banda Research Project regional testing program suggest that highly eroded soft paste pottery, which occurs in small quantities in the basal levels of many sites, may be associated with an early first millennium AD occupation of the area. Most of the highly fragmented pottery is undecorated; however, eroded red paint and dentate/comb impressions appear diagnostic of this early pottery (cf. Mathewson's [1968] Krachi type). A single associated AMS date on charcoal in the lower levels of Mound 7 at site A-212 in the western Banda area (Fig. 2.2) yielded a calibrated radiocarbon age estimation of AD 80–340 (A-12606; Table 2.1).[1] Yet our knowledge of this early occupation is rudimentary, and we know little of associated settlement, technology, or subsistence. Iron fragments indicate that these were iron-using peoples; however, we have not as yet located any early first millennium AD smelting sites in the Banda area, though such sites have been documented farther south (Goucher 1981). Neither have we recovered exotics in association with these ceramics, which stands in contrast to both earlier (Kintampo complex; mid-second to early first millennium BC; Casey 2005) and later occupations of the Banda area.

In a preliminary chronology of the Banda area, all red-painted pottery sites were grouped together as "Iron Age 3" (IA3; Stahl 1985, 127–32); however, recent research results suggest that we can distinguish an early second millennium AD subset tentatively referred to as the Volta Phase (Table 2.2). Volta Phase pottery is red-painted, though characterized by harder pastes and geometric designs rather than overall red paint. Similar pottery has long been known in the Volta Basin and referred to by a variety of names, including design-painted ware, Gonja painted pottery (Davies 1964), Silima Ware (York 1973), or Deber type (Mathewson 1968). Seven dates from sites with geometric painted pottery (Banda 13 and Banda 27) cluster in the calibrated range of ca. AD 1000–1300 (A-12610–12616; Table 2.1). For decades, researchers assumed that red-painted pottery signaled the beginning of Sudanic connections in the Volta basin (Davies 1964, 11; Posnansky 1987, 17), a view shaped by the presumption that the Sudanic belt was the source of innovations adopted by peoples of the wooded savanna and forested regions to the south (e.g., Murdock 1959). Yet

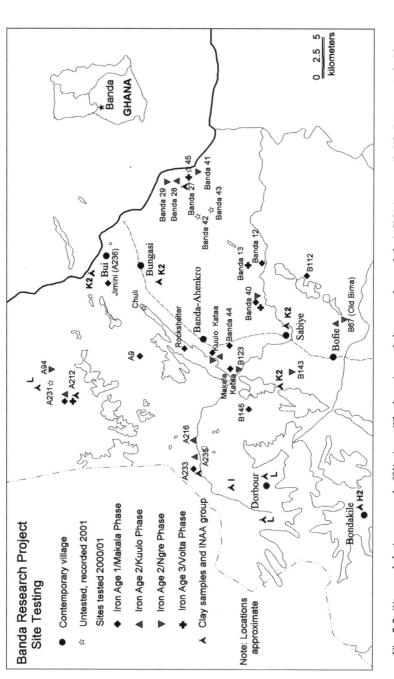

Fig. 2.2. Sites and their temporal affiliations. The locations of clay samples and their INAA group (I, K2, L) are noted. Clay samples with no affiliation are those that could not be assigned to any group in the INAA study.

Table 2.1. Radiocarbon Dates

Site	Lab #	BP	CALIB AD (95.4%)	Provenience (mound; level; cm bd[*])
A212	A-12606	1815 ± 40	AD 80–110 (2.8%)	M7; L10; 90–100
			AD 120–340 (92.6%)	
Banda 13	A-12610	985 ± 40	AD 980–1160	M2; L7; 60–70
Banda 27	A-12611	765 ± 45	AD 1180–1300	M2; L9; 90–100
	A-12612	825 ± 60	AD 1030–1290	M2; L10; 100–110
	A-12613	725 ± 45	AD 1210–1310 (81.8%)	M2; L12; 120–130
			AD 1350–1390 (13.6%)	
	A-12614	870 ± 50	AD 1030–1270	M2; L13; 130–140
	A-12615	805 ± 50	AD 1060–1090 (2.5%)	M2; L14; 140–150
			AD 1120–1140 (2.2%)	
			AD 1150–1300 (90.7%)	
	A-12616	815 ± 45	AD 1060–1090 (2.5%)	M?; L19; 190–200
			AD 1120–1140 (2.3%)	
			AD 1150–1290 (90.6%)	
Banda 40	A-12618	630 ± 40	AD 1290–1410	M4; L7; 60–70
	A-12619	715 ± 45	AD 1220–1330 (75.5%)	M4; L10; 90–100
			AD 1350–1400 (19.9%)	
	A-12620	595 ± 45	AD 1290–1420	M4; L17; 160–170
	A-12621	595 ± 50	AD 1290–1430	M4; L25; 240–250
	A-12622	635 ± 40	AD 1280–1410	M4; L26; 250–260
	A-12623	750 ± 40	AD 1210–1310 (93.9%)	M4; L27; 260–270
			AD 1370–1380 (1.5%)	
Banda 41	A-12624	605 ± 45	AD 1290–1420	M1; L6; 50–60
	A-12625	600 ± 50	AD 1290–1420	M1; L7; 60–70
	A-12626	685 ± 50	AD 1250–1410	M1; L16; 160–170
	A-12627	700 ± 45	AD 1240–1330 (63.7%)	M1; L19; 190–200
			AD 1340–1400 (31.7%)	
	A-12628	710 ± 50	AD 1220–1330 (70.3%)	M1; L20; 200–210
			AD 1340–1400 (25.1%)	
A-94	A-12598	680 ± 50	AD 1260–1410	M1; L5; 40–50
	A-12599	750 ± 50	AD 1160–1310 (90.7%)	M1; L6; 50–60
			AD 1350–1390 (4.7%)	
	A-12600	795 ± 45	AD 1160–1300	M1; L7; 60–70
	A-12601A	760 ± 50	AD 1160–1310 (93.1%)	M2; L6; 50–60
			AD 1360–1390 (2.3%)	
B-123	A-12683	735 ± 55	AD 1180–1330 (82.5%)	M1; L8; 70–80
			AD 1340–1400 (12.9%)	

continued

Table 2.1. *(continued)*

Site	Lab #	BP	CALIB AD (95.4%)	Provenience (mound; level; cm bd*)
	A-12684	720 ± 45	AD 1210–1320 (79%) AD 1350–1390 (16.4%)	M1; L10; 90–100
	A-12685	730 ± 70	AD 1160–1410	M1; L11; 100–110
	A-12686	700 ± 40	AD 1240–1330 (65.1%) AD 1340–1400 (30.3%)	M1; L12; 110–120

*cm bd = centimeters below datum.

Table 2.2. Working Chronology of the Banda Area

1985 Groupings	Phases	Period	Sites	Comments
Iron Age 3		1st–4th centuries AD	A212, M7, L7-10	Poorly defined early occupation. Eroded pottery with overall red paint, some dentate stamp.
	Volta Phase	AD 1000–1300	Banda 13 Banda 27	Pottery painted red with geometric motifs, occasional dentate stamp. Deep, hollow pedestal bases.
Iron Age 2	Ngre Phase	AD 1250–1400	Banda 29 Banda 40, M4 Banda 41 A-94 B-123 B-143 Kuulo Kataa	Wider variety of decorative treatments including mica slip, wavy line roulette, and ridged bands. Carinated vessels common, as is overall surface treatment (cord herringbone roulette). Distinctive jar forms with incurving rims.

Table 2.2. (*continued*)
Working chronology of the Banda area

1985 Groupings	Phases	Period	Sites	Comments
	Kuulo Phase	AD 1400–1650	A-212, M7, L1-6 A-216 A-235 Kuulo Kataa	Red paint/slip becomes rare; mica slip persists but is less common. Alternating bands of wavy-line roulette and dentate stamp/roulette are common. Carinated forms are common, as is surface treatment (cord, herringbone roulette). Distinctive, profusely decorated globular jar forms.
Iron Age 1	Makala Phase	mid to late 1700s–1820s	Banda 12 Banda 40, M1 A212, M1 A233 A 236 B112 B145 Early Makala Kuulo Kataa	Maize cob roulette surface treatment is common. Typical Iron Age 2 decorative treatments (wavy line, dentate) are rare, while punctates (circular and later triangular), crisscross, and diagonal incision become common. Pedestaled bowl forms are typical. Globular jars disappear from ceramic repertoire.

the stratigraphic ubiquity of red-painted pottery at the base of later occupations throughout the Banda area, combined with the single date from A-212, implies a deeper chronology in the central Volta basin than previously suspected. Moreover, we have conducted instrumental neutron activation analysis (INAA) of two dozen pottery samples from two painted-pottery sites (Banda 13 and Banda 27). INAA is a technique that assesses the bulk chemical composition (i.e., both ceramic paste and tempering material) of ceramic samples. These chemical

Table 2.3. Instrumental Neutron Activation Analysis (INAA) Results on Pottery from Banda Area Sites by Temporal Phase in Relation to Five Clay Sources (L, K1, K2, H1, and Unassigned): Number of Samples (% in Parentheses) by Site Location (East or West of the Banda Hills). Boldfaced Figures Are Totals for Each Phase.

Group	Phase	Site Location[1]	L (West)	K1 (East?)	K2 (East)	H1 (East?)	Unassigned	Total
IA3	**Volta**	East (3 sites)	**6 (11)**	–	**41 (78)**	–	**6 (11)**	**53 (100)**
IA2	Ngre	East (4 sites)	23 (35)	14 (21)	19 (29)	–	10 (15)	66
		West (1 site)	4 (40)	4 (40)	1 (10)	–	1 (10)	10
			27 (36)	**18 (24)**	**20 (26)**	–	**11 (14)**	**76 (100)**
	Kuulo	East (1 site)	–	68 (79)	–	–	18 (21)	86
		West (3 sites)	2 (9)	4 (18)	–	–	16 (73)	22
			2 (2)	**72 (67)**	–	–	**34 (31)**	**108 (100)**
IA1	**Makala** (Early)	East (3 sites)	33 (45)	3 (4)	13 (18)	15 (21)	9 (12)	73
		West (3 sites)	3 (11)	21 (75)	–	–	4 (14)	28
			36 (35)	**24 (24)**	**13 (13)**	**15 (15)**	**13 (13)**	**101 (100)**
	Makala (Late)	East (1 site)	**11 (42)**	–	**10 (38)**	–	**5 (20)**	**26 (100)**

[1]Site placement relative to main chain of Banda hills.

signatures are compared to clay samples from known clay pits in order to identify the clay sources used in pottery making. We have had good success with
INAA because clay sources east and west of the Banda hills have distinct chemical signatures (Cruz 1996, 2003, 527–47; Stahl 1999, 23–26). Forty-one of the
53 pottery samples from Volta Phase sites analyzed to date were made from K2
clays found in clay pits east of the Banda hills (see Table 2.3). Six samples from
Banda 13 yielded chemical signatures consistent with "L" group clays associated
with sources west of the Banda hills, while six samples were unassigned. Even
though the unassigned samples could not be linked to a specific clay group, they
fall within the general range of Banda clays (Neff and Glascock 1997).

Thus red-painted pottery was locally produced in the Banda area in the
early second millennium AD and cannot be assumed to indicate northern
connections. Neither have we found evidence of long-distance connections
in materials recovered from small test units excavated at IA3 sites (limited
to two 1 × 2-m soundings of midden deposits at two sites; Stahl and Smith,
n.d.). Imported beads (DeCorse et al. 2003; Magnavita 2003; Robertshaw
et al. 2003) and copper alloys are early indicators of long-distance connections
in West Africa. Because there are few indigenous West African copper sources
(Craddock et al. 1989), the presence of copper alloy artifacts signals extra-
regional exchange in either raw materials or finished products (Childs and
Herbert 2005). However, neither beads nor copper alloys have been recovered
from painted-pottery sites in the Banda area to date.

The earliest indications of long-distance connections in the Banda area are
associated with sites (Banda 40, Banda 41, A94 and B123) that have yielded
occasional glass beads and small copper alloy artifacts and have been dated to
AD 1250–1400 (CALIB; A-12618–12623; A-12624–12628; A-12598–12601A;
A-12683–12686; see Table 2.1). These dates are consistent with preliminary
reports of excavations at Begho (Posnansky 1987). Begho, located immediately
south of the Banda area, was an entrepôt known to Arab geographers where
forest products including gold were transferred to caravans that plied the route
between the Niger River and the West African forest. Banda area sites dating to AD 1250–1400 have yielded small quantities of copper alloy ornaments,
imported glass beads, and marine shells (including cowries) that signal involvement in long-distance exchange; however, its scale and effects on daily life are
only beginning to be understood through archaeological investigations.

Involvement in the Northern Trade

From AD 1250 to 1650, occupants of the Banda area participated in the
northern trade. Ceramics of this period show broad similarities and were
grouped as "Iron Age 2" (IA2) in an initial survey of the area (Stahl 1985,
100–102, 120–27). However, calibrated radiocarbon dates and ceramic evidence from recently excavated sites suggest that there is sufficient temporal

variation to merit division into two phases (see Tables 2.1, 2.2), tentatively an early Ngre Phase (AD 1250–1400) and a later Kuulo Phase (AD 1400–1650). Ngre Phase occupations of the area yielded evidence of northern trade, while Kuulo Phase occupations were involved in both the northern and Atlantic trades. The phases are tentative and overlapping, and the boundary at AD 1400 should be taken as a somewhat arbitrary one based on the upper and lower extent of radiocarbon dates. Although there is variation between Ngre and Kuulo Phase ceramics, the ceramics associated with these phases are more similar to one another than they are to the preceding IA3 (Volta Phase painted pottery) or succeeding IA1 (Makala Phase) ceramic assemblages.

Although red-painted pottery persists at IA2 sites, IA2 ceramics are characterized by a wider variety of decorative treatments and vessel shapes than IA3 assemblages. Mica paint or slip, though never abundant, is diagnostic, as is wavy line stamp/roulette and surface treatment with herringbone roulette (elsewhere referred to as "mat," Stahl 1999, 23). Cord roulette impression is common, though not diagnostic, for it continues into the subsequent IA1. The decorative grammar of IA2 pottery is characterized by alternating horizontal bands of grooves, wavy lines, and dentate stamp/roulette. Both unrestricted (bowls) and restricted orifice vessels (jars) are commonly carinated (characterized by an angular shoulder). The area below the carination on jars is often surface treated with cord or carved herringbone roulette. Distinctive jar forms appear to be associated with earlier Ngre Phase occupations compared to later Kuulo Phase occupations. Ngre Phase contexts are associated with everted jars with incurving rims (i.e., the rim curves outward above the neck constriction and inward at the lip). These forms are uncommon in Kuulo Phase contexts. Kuulo Phase contexts are instead commonly associated with a constricted orifice jar form that lacks a clear neck area. These globular jars are characterized by a carinated shoulder area that angles inward to a constricted orifice. In contrast to the everted-rimmed jars common to all IA2 contexts, the entire surface of most globular jars is decorated or surface treated. The interior surface of these constricted orifice vessels often shows pitting consistent with having held a fermented beverage such as beer (Leith Smith, pers. comm. 1995).

Because we have conducted small test excavations at Ngre Phase sites (1 × 2-m probes into midden deposits), our understanding of daily life in the period AD 1250–1400 (CALIB) is limited. Nonetheless, these excavations provide a window into the character of local life before the advent of the Atlantic exchange. Sites of this period are characterized by clusters of irregularly shaped mounds ranging from ovoid to subrectangular, although one site (B-143) was characterized by linear/curvilinear mounds similar to those associated with earlier IA3 occupations (Banda 27). Although most mounds are presumably the remains of collapsed structures, we have little insight into the characteristic architecture of this period as yet. Ngre Phase sites are notable for evidence of iron smelting on living sites. Most were characterized by slag heaps visible from the surface, and slag was recovered from midden contexts. In addition, one site (B-143) yielded fragments of what appeared to be crucibles—small ceramic vessels, some of which are encrusted with what appears to be metallurgical residue. Small numbers of cop-per alloy objects, including wire fragments, have been recovered from two Ngre Phase sites (Banda 40 and Banda 41), though we do not know whether these were imported as finished products or alloys that were subsequently cast by Ngre Phase inhabitants of the Banda area. In contrast to subsequent Kuulo Phase contexts, we have encountered no evidence for ivory working in Ngre Phase contexts.

INAA results on pottery samples from Ngre Phase sites (n=76) suggest local exchange of ceramics, though without apparent specialization in terms of vessel forms or sizes. Sites east of the Banda hills (Banda 40, Banda 41, B-123 and B-143) yielded vessels made from both western clay (L-group) and from clays east of the hills (K2 source; see Table 2.3). The K1 source was represented at all Ngre phase sites except Banda 41; this source is known only from archaeo-logical specimens and remains unprovenienced but has a chemical signature similar to sources east of the Banda hills (Stahl 1999, 25). The Ngre Phase site west of the Banda hills (A94) yielded pottery made from sources both east (K1 and K2) and west (L) of the Banda hills. Eleven Ngre phase samples remained unassigned; however, their chemical composition did fall completely outside the range of Banda area sources. These data suggest that Ngre Phase villagers consumed pottery produced both east and west of the Banda hills.

Although fine-grained analysis of faunal remains is ongoing, IA2 faunas (combined Ngre and Kuulo Phases) include a considerable number of wild spe-cies, indicating that hunting played an important role in subsistence pursuits. The wild fauna included carnivores, fish, turtles, tortoise, and large rodents. Although bovid bones account for a considerable proportion of the identifiable remains, the degree of fragmentation precluded more specific identification, and no domestic species were identified. A distinctive characteristic of the IA2 faunas was the abundance of dog (canid) remains showing evidence of butch-ery and/or burning, and in one Kuulo Phase context, a cluster of five domestic dog mandibles suggests ritual treatment (Stahl 2001a, 131–32; Stahl 2007). Canid remains are notably less common in later Makala Phase assemblages, where there is no evidence of butchery, perhaps suggesting discontinuity in belief systems between Kuulo and Makala Phase contexts.

In sum, our limited knowledge of Ngre Phase sites indicates the presence of substantial settlements. Their inhabitants produced iron, engaged in regional exchange in/for pottery, and obtained items necessary for household reproduction from within the region. Although some objects were obtained from long-distance trade, available evidence suggests that for the first century or two of the northern trade, international exchange did not dramatically alter the daily lives of villagers.

Emerging Atlantic Connections

From the late fifteenth century, maritime trade routes plied by Europeans began to compete with the centuries-old caravan trade with Arab North Africa.

Ultimately this caused a southward shift in the gravity of trade, yet robust northern trade continued into the early centuries of the maritime trade. Merchant centers like Jenné-jeno on the Niger River flourished in the fifteenth and sixteenth centuries (McIntosh, Gallagher, and McIntosh 2003, 174), and market centers on the northern margins of the forest were not brought under southern control until the early eighteenth century. There was certainly strife in this period. Jenné-jeno and other Sudanic centers came under attack in the late sixteenth century as North African rulers attempted to reestablish the northward flow of gold and other commodities (McIntosh, Gallagher, and McIntosh 2003, 174), and the forested regions of contemporary Ghana were characterized by struggle between small polities endeavoring to capture control of the southern trade. But it appears that the central Volta basin was sufficiently distant from centers of conflict that it was spared the disruptions that affected areas farther north and south in this period. Situated on the forest/wooded savanna boundary, the western Volta basin was home to transit markets where forest products (gold, kola) were transferred to northbound caravans and through which northern products (salt, copper alloys) flowed south (Arhin 1970, 1987, 52–53, 1989). The region prospered from its involvement in both the northern and southern trades through the end of the seventeenth century (Posnansky 1987, 17), after which prosperity declined following attacks by Asante, an expansionist forest polity.

Excavations at Kuulo Kataa, on the east side of the Banda hills, provide our best insight into village life in the period AD 1400–1650 (CALIB; for details on radiocarbon and thermoluminescence dates, see Stahl 1999, 12–16). Kuulo Phase villages are relatively large and show evidence of periodic rebuilding of durably constructed rectangular earthen-walled structures. The pattern of reconstruction is consistent with routine maintenance in which house floors were periodically renewed, and collapsed walls repaired/reconstructed. Two large deep midden mounds built up on the site as the Kuulo Phase occupants of Kuulo Kataa discarded their refuse, and test excavations in these mounds combined with areal excavations of house mounds provide good insight into daily life in this period.

A variety of crafts were produced at Kuulo Kataa during the Kuulo Phase occupation. Thick layers of iron slag, a by-product of reducing iron ore to a useable metal, were encountered in midden contexts across the site, although slag was more concentrated in some areas than in others. Two furnace features were exposed by our excavations, one of which was positioned in close proximity to a complex of floors and domestic hearth features. The lack of evidence for a furnace superstructure suggests that these were forging rather than smelting features. There is some evidence that copper alloys were worked on the site as well. We recovered small quantities of greenish-colored slags suggestive of copper alloys (Bachmann 1982, 4) as well as the outer shell of a likely casting mold. A small number of copper alloy objects were recovered from Kuulo Phase contexts at Kuulo Kataa, including some wire fragments, several ornaments (ring, probable bracelet), several cast objects of unknown use, and miscellaneous fragments. Three figurative cast objects, similar in size to objects used historically as gold weights (Garrard

1980), came from Kuulo Phase contexts. One was recovered during our 1995 excavations, appeared unique in design, and represented one of the few (and perhaps oldest) securely provenienced gold weight from an archaeological context (Stahl 2001a, plate 9, 138–39; see Schaedler 1997, 137, plates 226 and 228 for remarkably similar but unprovenienced specimens in private collections). During our 2000 excavations, we recovered two more figurative copper alloy objects. Although smaller than the 1995 specimen, they are remarkably similar stylistically. One is a dual-headed seated figure, while the other has a single head. Both have knees drawn up and arms clasped around the knees. The feet are indistinct, spatulate (platelike), and outflaring. The head of the 1995 figure is triangular with knoblike ears and bulging eyes. The heads on the 2000 specimens are more elongated but also have knoblike projections for ears and in one instance bulging eyes. The presence of three such similar figures combined with evidence of forges and a casting mold suggests on-site manufacture. Assuming they represent figurative gold weights, they signal local involvement in the gold trade.

Ivory also appears to have been worked on the site (Stahl and Stahl 2004). We recovered small numbers of ivory blanks, bangles, and combs/pins. Several of the bangles and pins appear unfinished and may represent specimens that broke during manufacture. Although most of the 36 bangles recovered from Kuulo Kataa were made from elephant ivory (n = 23), a small number were fashioned from hippo ivory (n = 6; the remaining 7 were of indeterminate source; Stahl and Stahl 2004, 91). The precision craftsmanship represented by these objects suggests a level of skill consistent with a degree of specialization. The Banda ivories also suggest that at least some ivory in the period AD 1400–1650 was locally fashioned into objects of personal adornment and perhaps combs (see also T. Shaw 1961, 94), a pattern that contrasts to later periods of the Atlantic exchange when ivory was exported in significant quantities as whole tusks (Feinberg and Johnson 1982; Johnson 1978a). Locally manufactured ivory objects like those found at Kuulo Kataa, Begho (Posnansky 1987, 17), or Dawu in southern Ghana (Shaw 1961) may have circulated in regional trade alongside trade in unworked ivory destined for foreign markets (Insoll 1995). This pattern stands in contrast to later periods when ivory became a royal prerogative at the same time as international demand for ivory increased.

Another product that was probably produced on site by Kuulo Phase villagers at Kuulo Kataa was pottery (Stahl 1999, 23–26). INAA data hint at changes in regional ceramic production from the Ngre to Kuulo Phases. Whereas pottery derived from various sources in the Ngre Phase, a narrower range of sources is represented in the Kuulo Phase samples (see Table 2.3). The INAA data set for the Kuulo Phase is dominated by samples from Kuulo Kataa (86 of the 108 specimens), where there was significant reliance on the as yet unprovenienced K1 source. Almost 80 percent of the sherds sampled from Kuulo Kataa derived from this source. The K2 source that is commonly represented at Ngre Phase sites was not present in Kuulo Phase samples. The small sample of sherds tested from sites west of the Banda hills shows that K1 source ceramics appear there as well, alongside some "L" group sources (sources west of the Banda hills). Most of the samples from Kuulo Phase sites west of the Banda hills could not be assigned to any group (73 percent), though again they fell within the general range of Banda clays. Two patterns are notable in relation to earlier Ngre Phase samples: the absence of K2 sources in the Kuulo Phase samples in contrast to their ubiquity in Ngre Phase contexts, and the absence of L group sources at Kuulo Kataa (east of the hills) in contrast to their importance in Ngre Phase contexts east of the Banda hills. These discontinuities, combined with the focus on K1 sources, suggest changes in pottery production from the Ngre to Kuulo Phases and suggest greater specialization of ceramic production during the Kuulo Phase.

Available data thus indicate that Kuulo Phase villagers produced a variety of crafts alongside subsistence pursuits. Hunting, trapping, and collecting activities contributed to a diverse faunal assemblage that included large dangerous fauna that were probably pursued by skilled hunters. The large fish present at Kuulo Kataa were likely obtained through regional exchange with villages situated closer to the Volta River. The importance of domestic animals to Kuulo Phase villagers is probably masked by bone fragmentation (making the presence of domestic species difficult to determine); however, the wide variety of wild species makes clear that these were an important dietary component for Kuulo Phase villagers (see Stahl 2001a, 131–35). Plant remains suggest that Kuulo villagers were experimenting with new crops in the sixteenth and seventeenth centuries. Maize phytoliths from both cob bodies and leaves have been identified in soils associated with Kuulo Phase contexts at Kuulo Kataa (Stahl 2001a, 134–35). Phytoliths are durable silica bodies that form in plant cells and map the distinctive shape of diverse species (Pearsall 1989, 341). The presence of maize phytoliths in sixteenth- and seventeenth-century contexts suggests that domesticates from the Americas diffused into the West African interior well ahead of the frontiers of European contact. Adding maize to the roster of African domesticates grown in the area (which historically included yams and sorghum) had important implications for nutritional ecology. Maize is harvested during the hungry months between the yam and sorghum harvests and presumably had demographic implications by closing the gap of the hungry season.

Tobacco is another nonindigenous crop for which we have indirect evidence in Kuulo Phase contexts. Researchers have long assumed that the appearance of smoking pipes signals the diffusion of tobacco across West Africa (J. E. Philips 1983; T. Shaw 1960; see McIntosh, Gallagher, and McIntosh 2003, 172–74 for a summary of debates), a view consistent with the post-Columbian age of smoking pipes across the subcontinent. Smoking pipes first appear in Kuulo Phase contexts in the Banda area. Our 1995 excavations yielded twenty-one pipe fragments, while our comparably sized 2000 excavations yielded slightly more than two hundred pipe fragments. The difference is accounted for by the fact that our 2000 excavations included mounds with later Makala Phase occupations stratified above the Kuulo Phase component. Although we are still working through detailed contextual information for the pipes from 2000, the fact that over half of the pipes were recovered from the top five excavation levels of their respective contexts indicates that most are associated with either Makala Phase or late Kuulo Phase contexts. INAA data from a small collection of smoking pipes from Kuulo Phase contexts suggests that, by contrast to the pattern of specialized pottery production, pipes were produced in a variety of locations throughout the region (Table 2.4).

It is thus clear that Kuulo Phase villagers lived in a world of connections, the most immediate of which were probably with regional centers and entrepôts like Begho and Old Bima (Bravmann and Mathewson 1970). Begho, located a short distance south of the Banda area, was the site of extensive excavations in the 1970s, the results of which have not as yet been fully reported (Posnansky 1979, 1987). Old Bima is located in the southern reaches of contemporary Banda chieftaincy lands and was subject to survey in the 1960s and small test excavations by Smith in 1997 (Smith 2007). IA2 ceramics from the Banda area are consistent with Begho ware pottery described by Crossland (1989) and with pottery recovered from Old Bima. Both sites were occupied through the Ngre and Kuulo Phase occupations of the larger Banda area, though Posnansky suggests that the period AD 1400–1700 saw intensified contact with the Middle Niger, coinciding with the florescence of Begho (Posnansky 1976, 51; Posnansky and McIntosh 1976, 189). Although Kuulo phase villagers lived some distance from apparent centers of exchange (Begho, Old Bima), small quantities of exotic goods made their way into village settings. Fewer than a dozen imported beads have been recovered from Kuulo Phase contexts at Kuulo Kataa while hundreds of beads were reportedly recovered from Begho (Crossland 1976, 87; Posnansky, 1979, 29). The few monochrome glass beads and imported stone (e.g., carnelian) beads at Kuulo Kataa occurred alongside a more substantial collection of locally produced ceramic and stone beads. Kuulo Phase villagers at

Table 2.4. Instrumental Neutron Activation Analysis (INAA) Results on Smoking Pipes from Banda Area Sites by Temporal Phase in Relation to Five Clay Sources (L, K1, K2, H1, and Unassigned): Number of Samples (% in Parentheses) by Site Location (East or West of the Banda Hills). Boldfaced Figures Are Totals for Makala Phase Sites East and West of Hills.

Group	Phase	Site Location[1]	L (West)	K1 (East?)	K2 (East)	H1 (East?)	Unassigned	Total
IA2	**Kuulo**	East (1)	4 (33)	2 (17)	3 (25)	–	3 (25)	12 (100)
IA1	**Makala**	East (2)	2	2	6	–	2	12
	(Early)	West (3)	3	9	–	–	2	14
			5 (19)	**11 (42)**	**6 (23)**		**4 (16)**	**26 (100)**

[1]Site placement relative to main chain of Banda hills.

sites like Kuulo Kataa probably accessed imports by producing goods like iron and pottery in excess of immediate needs and exchanging these and perhaps ivory for copper alloys and beads. Cloth and salt may also have been sought after by Kuulo villagers, although of course there are no durable residues. The presence of spindle whorls at Begho combined with documentary evidence suggests that cloth was produced at Begho; however, we have not recovered spindle whorls from IA2 contexts in the Banda area. Thus cloth may have been an item of exchange if Kuulo villagers consumed cloth at all; however, woven cloth may have been a prestige good in this period that remained unavailable to villagers.

In sum, the daily rhythms of Kuulo Phase villages were presumably shaped in part by the seasonal demands of agriculture. Farmers experimented with new crops (maize certainly, tobacco possibly), with implications for the seasonal availability of foodstuffs. The addition of maize would have required experimentation in the kitchen as well as in the fields, although we can imagine that cooks were guided in their experimentation by their familiarity with indigenous starchy grains (sorghum, millet). At the same time, Kuulo villagers produced crafts that were vital to the household economies of their neighbors (iron, pottery) as well as ornaments that appealed to regional tastes (ivory, copper alloys). Increased involvement in craft production implies adjustments in the allocation of labor—raw materials (ore, clay) must be mined, transported, and processed. Transformative technologies like smelting and ceramic firing require collection of fuels (in significant amounts in the case of iron smelting). And finished goods had to be distributed. In light of available evidence, we can only speculate on whether finished goods were transported to markets, goods were exchanged on an itinerant basis, or consumers traveled to production centers to obtain desired goods. All three models are historically documented for the area (Cruz 2003; Stahl and Cruz 1998). We can also assume that the technological and spiritual/ritual knowledge involved in the production of metals implies a degree of specialization, and the transferal of specialized knowledge between generations likely involved apprenticelike relationships. Precision working of ivory occupied some villagers, the working of which implies the use of specialized tools including double-cut saws, three-pronged drill bits probably powered by a bow drill, and scribing implements (Stahl and Stahl 2004, 97–98).

The Era of Atlantic Trade

Although gold brought Europeans to the West African coast, slaves kept them there. The influence of Atlantic trade grew as European powers expanded plantation production in the Western Hemisphere and industrial production took hold at home. These developments invoked thoroughgoing transformations at home and abroad, altering the rhythms of life alongside sensibilities and tastes and creating new desires for products that originated a world away (Mintz 1985; Thompson 1963). West Africa increasingly became bound up in the slave trade but also served as a market for industrial products including cloth (see Steiner 1985). Although trade in slaves was a long-standing practice—slaves had long been traded across the Sahara to the Mediterranean (Lovejoy 1983)—new demands for slaves on the Atlantic coast led to political economic realignments as the small polities that initially controlled trade with the coast (e.g., Adansi, Denkyira, Akwamu) were conquered by expansionist polities that dominated the eighteenth-century landscape (Daaku 1966). Along the Gold Coast, the forest polity of Asante emerged as the primary power through a series of military campaigns directed against their southern neighbors and then their northern neighbors (Wilks 1975, 1993). Imported firearms played a key role in these struggles (Inikori 1977; Kea 1971). Begho was the target of several Asante campaigns in the early eighteenth century, and the movement of artisans from there to the Asante capital at Kumase further eroded Begho's role as a prominent market center. Oral histories are replete with stories of population dispersal, although the site shows some evidence of continued occupation (Garrard 1980, 45–46; Posnansky 1987, 20). Asante did not exercise direct control over the area following Begho's defeat, so it seems likely that the demise of centers like Begho left a political economic vacuum in this part of the Volta basin in the early eighteenth century.

Although we have no evidence for rapid abandonment or destruction, the Kuulo Phase occupation of Kuulo Kataa appears to end toward the late seventeenth century. Portions of the site were later occupied by people using Makala Phase ceramics; however, our fullest evidence for the Makala Phase occupation of the Banda area comes from the site of Makala Kataa, located a short distance down the same low ridge on which Kuulo Kataa is situated. Oral sources help create a context for the Makala Phase occupation of the Banda area (Stahl 1991, 2001a, 148–58). In brief, both archaeological and oral historical evidence points to discontinuities in occupation consistent with a view of Banda as a frontier in the eighteenth century (sensu Kopytoff 1987). Oral histories suggest a period of uncertainty in which power relations were being negotiated between people who claimed autochthonous status in the area and immigrants from the west who had fled unrest at home. The historic Banda chieftaincy emerged out of this conjuncture of people from diverse ethnic-linguistic backgrounds. The historic chieftaincy was dominated by Nafaanra-speaking peoples who had immigrated from the west. However, Nafana dominance masks a complex history of immigration in which people of diverse backgrounds—many seeking refuge—settled in Banda and embraced Nafana identity, at the same time as Nafana cultural practices were transformed (Stahl 1991). Banda presents a prime example of what Amselle (1993, 15) termed "hybrid systems…with crossbred forms of logic (*logiques métisses*)." In other words, this was a society being actively forged by members of diverse ethnic-linguistic groups drawing on different modalities of kinship, political organization, religious practices, and so on in the process. Such societies, of which there are many (Amselle 1998; Kopytoff 1987, 1999), fly in the face of anthropological assumptions of cultural (or structural) coherency and raise serious questions about the practice of modeling earlier societies in the image of supposedly later "traditional" ones, the forms of which represent the endpoints of intensely negotiated processes (Stahl 2001a, 5–8, 154–55, 215–24).

The Banda chieftaincy was forcibly incorporated into Asante within roughly five decades of its founding (Stahl 2001a, 149–50, 155–58). The Asante campaign against Banda yielded many captives (Yarak 1979), some destined for the Middle Passage and, if they survived, to live as enslaved plantation workers. This raises the issue of the source societies of enslaved Africans. In a provocatively titled paper, Kelly (2004) makes the case that the African Diaspora began in coastal West Africa. Yet we must recall that the societies from which slaves originated were typically those on the losing end of battles, on the tributary side of power relations, and/or members of smaller-scale societies subject to raiding by their neighbors. And characteristically, most of these societies were located well into the interior. Yet as Van Dantzig (1982) cogently argued over two decades ago, there was no long-term stability in the role that societies played in the slave trade. A society might be a source of slaves in one period and play a middleman role in the exchange of slaves in a later period. The same society might become a consumer of slaves in the internal trade that continued into the twentieth century in some areas. Evidence suggests that the Banda chieftaincy played multiple roles in the slave trade through the eighteenth and nineteenth centuries (see Stahl 2001b). Although empirical evidence is wanting, it seems likely that the disruptions to the regional economy caused by Asante's attacks on Begho and neighboring polities diminished local security and that the risk of enslavement probably increased for people in this newly created frontier. Traumatic as oral traditions suggest it was, Banda's incorporation into Asante probably reduced the long-term threat of enslavement for those who survived.

The period following the expansion of Asante hegemony over Banda appears to coincide with the earliest occupation of Makala Kataa (Early Makala). The pottery recovered from Early Makala shows certain continuities of decorative grammar with the earlier Kuulo Phase, but is marked by the disappearance of characteristic Kuulo Phase decorative treatments (wavy line stamp/roulette and dentate stamp/roulette) and an increase in the use of punctate decorations (circular and triangular). Carved herringbone roulette–treated surfaces disappear, and surface treatment is accomplished by either a cord-wrapped stick roulette or, increasingly with time, a maize cob stripped of its kernels. The globular jars of the Kuulo Phase disappear, while a form of pedestaled bowl is typical of Makala Phase assemblages (Stahl 1999, 47–49). Such ceramics were grouped as Iron Age 1 (IA1) in the initial Banda survey (Stahl 1985, 103–17), and later differentiated into Makala Phase 1 (Late Makala; late nineteenth to early twentieth century) and Makala Phase 2 groups

(Early Makala; late eighteenth to early nineteenth century; Stahl 1999, 12–13; 2001a, 159–61).

Our excavations at Early and Late Makala have documented a number of changes in daily life through the nineteenth century. Although settlement was disrupted in the period following Begho's demise, by the late eighteenth century we once again see village sites characterized by substantial, often L-shaped structures. Exposed residential complexes at Early Makala suggest that compounds were accretionary, coursed earthen-walled structures (i.e., rooms added as needed) oriented around a central, open-air kitchen. Evidence for rebuilding is consistent with routine maintenance of structures as floors and walls were refurbished. There is substantially less refuse at Makala Kataa compared with Kuulo Kataa, a pattern that is accounted for in part by changing patterns of craft production. Whereas Kuulo Phase villagers produced iron and probably pottery on site, Makala Phase inhabitants of Early Makala did not. Although there were occasional pieces of iron slag, there is no substantive evidence for iron smelting at Makala Kataa. Nor is there evidence for the working of copper alloys. We recovered a small number of finished copper alloy objects, including several personal ornaments, but no crucible fragments or casting molds (Stahl 2001a, 184–85). INAA results from Early Makala show that ceramic jars were made from L-group clays (sources west of the Banda hills) while bowls were disproportionately made from H1 clays, a source that is as yet unprovenienced but with a signature consistent with an origin east of the Banda hills (Cruz 2003, 542–43; Stahl 2001a, 174–76). The K1 clays that so predominated the Kuulo Phase samples had a minor presence in samples from Makala Kataa. An expanded INAA study incorporating sites from our regional testing program complicates the pattern somewhat, in that the K1 source appears in Makala Phase samples from sites west of the Banda Hills (Table 2.3). The combined results nonetheless suggest a more dispersed pattern of ceramic production during the Makala Phase compared to the preceding Kuulo Phase occupation. In the case of Makala Kataa, consumers seem to have selected jars from one source and bowls from another, but they clearly relied on extra-village production for household needs including pottery and iron tools.

We have recovered no evidence for either the production or consumption of ivory in Makala Phase contexts in the Banda area. This is not to say that ivory did not pass through the hands of Banda peoples. Hippo and elephant were locally available, but it may be that any tusks acquired through hunting or scavenging were passed along whole. Ivory was, by this time, a royal prerogative and was also in demand in the international market (see McCaskie 1983, 29–32 on elephant symbolism in Asante). Regardless, it was no longer finding its way into the refuse left behind by Makala villagers. At the same time, new crafts were being practiced in the household context. Although we found no credible evidence for textile production in earlier Kuulo Phase contexts, small numbers of spindles have been recovered from Early Makala Phase contexts (Makala Phase 2). These occurred in a variety of contexts across both Early and Late Makala in a pattern consistent with the household production of textiles described by early colonial officials (Stahl and Cruz 1998).

Locally produced clay pipes are ubiquitous in Early Makala Phase contexts, attesting to the widespread practice of smoking, presumably of tobacco, probably locally or regionally grown by this point. The stylistically diverse pipes contrast with Makala Phase ceramics, which are homogeneous in both form and decorative treatment. The pipes were well made, clearly the product of skilled potters, and their diversity suggests that they served as a medium for social display. INAA data indicate that pipes were produced from a diverse range of ceramic sources, a pattern consistent with that of pottery production in this period (see Table 2.4). These combined ceramic data attest to regional exchange, while the presence of modest numbers of exotics indicates some involvement in international exchange as well.

Our knowledge of imports in this period comes from both archaeological and documentary sources. Dupuis, British emissary to the Asante capital of Kumase in 1820, described the gifting of cloth, rum, and gunpowder by the Asantehene in reward for the Banda chief's service in a war with neighboring Gyaman (Dupuis 1966, 164). Each of these gifts drew the Banda chief and his subjects deeper into the Atlantic trade. The cloth created anew the Banda chief's prestige in a period when the local strip woven cloth that had been an object of exchange was becoming an item of household production (Stahl 2002, 836–38). The imported drink objectified the triangle of trade that now linked Europe, Africa, and the Western Hemisphere, produced as it was by enslaved Africans in the diaspora. The gunpowder signaled an altered access to weaponry. The knives, javelins, bows, and arrows carried by the Banda chief's entourage in 1820 represented democratic weaponry: "Every man knows how to construct one; the materials are readily available, the techniques uncomplicated, the missiles easy to replace" (Goody 1971, 43). But the new means of destruction to which Banda armies had only recently gained access depended on a supply of gunpowder, access to which was affected by Asante's strategic concerns. Archaeological evidence confirms a still minor yet increased consumption of imports, including diverse glass and stone beads, small quantities of exotic ceramics, and gunflints. Elsewhere I have argued that, although some of these objects may be seen as substitutes for locally produced ones, the use of imported goods, particularly those linked to prestige, altered Banda people's relationship to socially powerful objects (Stahl 2001a, 184; 2002). By removing production from the local/regional sphere, continued access to these prestige-making and -maintaining goods depended on continued access to external networks.

Subsistence at Early Makala indicates the continued importance of wild fauna in the diet. Species that frequent open settings and cleared areas were particularly common and suggest a pattern of garden hunting, collecting, and trapping strategies. A variety of domestic animals were present (chicken, guinea fowl, dog, sheep/goat, and cattle), although the small number of dog remains contrasted with Kuulo Kataa, where they were considerably more common (Stahl 2001a, 177–79; Stahl 2007). The diminished importance of dog hints at discontinuities in ritual practice given the specialized treatment of canid remains at Kuulo Kataa. Archaeobotanical evidence documents a range of plant foods including maize and sorghum. Yams are difficult to detect archaeologically, but were probably grown by Early Makala villagers as well.

In sum, we know that local involvement in the broader political economy continued, though in altered circumstances. Now subject to Asante, Banda people's access to imports was shaped by Asante trade policies. Although incorporation as an inner province of Asante may have offered a measure of protection against enslavement, it meant that Banda villagers were drawn into Asante's wars, both near and far. Family histories recount substantial losses through warfare that were in some cases offset by the incorporation of captives (Stahl 2001b). The routines of domestic life, which appear to have focused primarily on subsistence rather than craft production in the case of Makala Kataa, would thus have been periodically disrupted by the demands of warfare. In the end, warfare accounts for the widespread signature of abrupt abandonment of Early Makala Phase settlements throughout the Banda area. At Makala Kataa, the early-nineteenth-century occupation appears to have ended abruptly. Kitchens were abandoned with useable vessels and equipment intact, a pattern that we would not expect if people relocated nearby. Abrupt abandonment is consistent with oral histories that describe Banda people fleeing the area under attack by neighboring Gyaman, and it is a pattern that we see repeated at Makala Phase 2 (Early Makala) sites across the region.

The period following abandonment of Early Makala (middle to late nineteenth century) was one of considerable instability in the central Volta basin. Asante's provinces periodically rebelled, and warfare among provinces was common (Stahl 2001a, 190–95). According to oral histories, Banda peoples lived in exile from the Banda area for much of this period. Not until the end of the nineteenth century, as the British became increasingly involved in Asante's hinterland, did Banda peoples reoccupy their former lands. At the same time, the central Volta basin came under pressure from the troops of the Imam Samori who were being driven eastward by French colonial pressure. Bonduku, an important trade town to the west of Banda and center of the Gyaman state, succumbed to Samori in 1895, and Bonduku became a staging ground for Samori's move into Gonja and Wa, north and east of the Black Volta River (Stahl 2001a, 97). Samori's troops lived off the land, raiding for food and slaves and causing significant dislocation in the western Volta basin. British troops entered the Banda area in 1896–97, determined to drive Samori's troops from lands that they claimed in the wake of the 1884–85 Berlin Conference where Africa was divided up among colonizing nations (Wallerstein 1986, 16). Anxious to solidify their paper claims, the British nervously monitored the movements of Samori (Stahl 2001a, 96–98). Britain formally annexed Asante's hinterland in 1897, and Samori's troops were driven northward and out of British-claimed territory by 1898 (Stahl 2001a, 194).

The upheavals of the mid- to late nineteenth century resulted in food short-ages and settlement dislocation in many areas of the western and central Volta basin. Many people were hungry and homeless and seeking refuge in areas that had been spared the worst of Samori's scorched earth campaigns. Banda was one such area, and the Banda chieftaincy grew by continuing to absorb immi-grants. British troops garrisoned at Lawra (Bui) on the south bank of the Black Volta River received food from Banda, and Banda provisions were sent north to supply British troops in Bona. Banda peoples had congregated at this riverside settlement during the 1890s, but moved out from it after 1898 as the threat from Samori's forces subsided and British demands increased. Oral histories relate that Banda people reoccupied their former settlements, which is consis-tent with a series of late-nineteenth- and early-twentieth-century occupations adjacent to modern villages. These archaeological sites represent short-lived occupations—perhaps two decades—that were abandoned when British colo-nial officials "encouraged" resettlement in villages laid out on a grid plan. Vil-lage relocation was promoted as part of a broader sanitation initiative but was clearly motivated by British visions of order as well. Sometime between 1926 and 1931, virtually all Banda villages relocated a short distance to "laid out" areas that form the core of contemporary villages (Stahl 2001a, 194–200).

Excavations at Late Makala, one such abandoned village, provide insight into daily life as Samori was driven out of western Volta basin. By contrast with the L-shaped mounds characteristic of Early Makala, the house mounds at Late Makala were small and circular. Refuse was deposited in sheet middens around the site or in pits rather than confined to midden mounds. Excavations suggest that the houses at Late Makala were likely post-and-daga construction, a building technique that is still used to construct temporary farm or kitchen shelters. This stands in contrast to the more labor-intensive coursed earthen-wall construction technique documented at Early Makala and in Kuulo Phase contexts at Kuulo Kataa. Our interpretation is that these represented minimal residential units (one or two rooms); they may represent structures that were raised rapidly as Banda peoples reoccupied their former sites. Coming on the heels of several decades of disruption, people may have been reluctant to invest in more permanent structures until they gauged whether the peace imposed by the British was lasting. Or the "provisional" quality of Late Makala housing may represent a stage in the life cycle of a village. British village planning may have interrupted a longer-term process of compound construction in which minimal residential units were augmented by additional rooms (Stahl 2001a, 203). In any case, the houses at Late Makala were abandoned gradually, as indicated by the lack of useable items left behind.

As we might anticipate, given the disruptions of the nineteenth century, pat-terns of regional exchange at Late Makala differed from those at Early Makala. The pottery at Late Makala is more homogeneous in decorative treatment and vessel morphology, and INAA data indicate that the sources used in pottery production had changed in the intervening decades. The K1 and H1 sources are not represented among Late Makala ceramics, and there is a proportionate increase in the representation of K2 sources that suggests a reconfiguration of ceramic exchange in this period (Table. 2.3). This pattern differs in turn from contemporary potting—all contemporary potting villages in Banda are west of the hills and exploit L-group sources. Pottery is routinely traded across the hills (Cruz 2003). Although it is difficult to pinpoint the precise cause of this shift, it seems likely that regional political economic developments influenced productive practice—it may be that travel through the Banda hills remained risky or that potters were among the immigrants who joined the Banda peoples and took up potting on an expanded scale in eastern villages. Although there is no evidence for smelting at Late Makala, Makala villagers probably accessed iron tools through networks of regional production. Thus Makala villagers relied on extrahousehold production for the tools necessary for household reproduction—the pottery in which to prepare food as well as the iron tools required to cultivate, hunt, and protect their families. At the same time, local/regional production of smoking pipes stopped altogether as Banda peoples embraced an imported alternative—European ball-clay pipes, which were ubiquitous at Late Makala. Yet cloth, a commodity by this time vital to rites of passage and household reproduction (Stahl and Cruz 1998), was still produced at the household level as indicated by the presence of small numbers of spindle whorls across the site.

Although evidence for it is illusory, we need to consider the effect of nineteenth-century upheavals on the reproduction of social and technological knowledge among Volta basin societies. Oral histories give the impression that Banda peoples moved frequently through the middle and late decades of the nineteenth century, that losses of personnel to warfare were considerable, and that many people became members of Banda society as they sought refuge from difficult circumstances at home. All of this has implications for social transmission of practices. We might imagine that apprenticeships were disrupted or perhaps truncated. Dangerous times may have resulted in the loss of knowledgeable practitioners, at the same time as the incorporation of immigrants brought new forms of knowledge to Banda society (e.g., Guyer and Belinga 1995). Although archaeological evidence provides a dim window into these dimensions of cultural process, we need to keep them in view, for they underscore the fact that village life did not consist of an unvarying script but was instead actively made and remade, at times under conditions of considerable duress.

Although there is general continuity in subsistence practices, we need to factor into our reconstructions the ecological effects of political economic upheavals in the western Volta basin. Early British officials reported that Samori's troops had nearly exterminated large game (an observation prompted by the interest of colonial officials in hunting large game themselves!), and the "post-Samori" profile of wild fauna exploited by Late Makala villagers suggests intensified garden hunting and collecting. The wild fauna includes considerable numbers of hares/rabbits, large rodents, and lizards. But before we attribute this pattern to the effects of overhunting, we need to consider issues of labor allocation in relation to subsistence activities. The early colonial period was marked by demands from colonial officials for labor and foodstuffs. Male labor was periodically siphoned off to colonial district centers, while young men were drawn from the area by migrant work on expanding cocoa plantations in the south. Migration was prompted in part by British demands that newly levied taxes be paid in coin, a demand that may have led to expanded cash crop cultivation as well (e.g., cotton and tobacco, both of which were grown in Banda in the colonial period). Opportunistic garden hunting/trapping may reflect a response to labor shortages, as wives and elder men simultaneously engaged in agricultural tasks and worked to provision their families with animal protein. At the same time, continued insecurity in the hills and areas to the west may have inhibited hunting activities. Whatever the cause, the range of wild fauna narrowed in comparison with earlier occupations and focused increasingly on small packages of meat that could be accessed opportunistically. Adoption of cassava (manioc), another New World domesticate, may have spread through the Volta basin during the nineteenth century. Cassava is today an important hungry-season crop in Banda, but it spread slowly through West Africa, in part because knowledge of processing techniques were required to render bitter varieties nontoxic (Lancaster et al. 1982). Ohadike (1981) has argued that a taste for cassava developed primarily in the context of crises when labor shortages meant that more labor-intensive crops like yams were in short supply. Cassava requires few labor inputs and can be grown on exhausted soils, factors that may have encouraged its incorporation into local cuisines during the nineteenth century.

By the end of the nineteenth century, imported objects had come to play a larger role in the lives of Makala villagers. A wider range and greater quantity of imports were recovered from Late Makala, including beads, ball-clay smoking pipes, bottle glass, small amounts of imported ceramics, a few gunflints, and a small number of imported metal objects (Stahl 2001a, 209–12). The increased involvement in interregional trade contrasts with the apparent constriction in regional trade. I have argued that continued insecurity may have contributed to the more localized pattern of pottery trade across the Banda hills. Would not the same conditions inhibit the interregional trade? It may be that major roads were more secure than the footpaths crossing the Banda hills, or perhaps commodity trading was in the hands of men while trade in pottery was conducted by women (the contemporary pattern in the area today). We cannot know for certain why regional trade appears to have contracted at the same time that interregional trade expanded; however, the pattern undercuts assumptions that the two necessarily covary (Stahl 2001a, 212).

Monetary transactions were likely involved in the acquisition of at least some of the imported objects recovered from Late Makala, many of which were involved in individual bodily practice rather than the routines of household reproduction which still depended on goods and tools produced locally/ regionally (pottery, iron tools). This pattern is consistent with the hopes of colonial officials who worked to pioneer British-dominated commerce and cultivate a taste for British imports (Stahl 2001a, 195–96). A primary motivation for British expansion at the end of the nineteenth century was to cultivate protected markets for homeland manufactures. Yet a single modest find from Late Makala belies the pen-and-ink boundaries through which the British intended to constrain the flow of people and products. Painstakingly reconstructed by a Binghamton University undergraduate (Krista Feichtinger), a clear glass Vaseline jar embossed with the name of the Chesebrough Company, New York, dating to 1908 attests the circulation of non-British manufactures and speaks to the experimentation of villagers with products that were simultaneously familiar (akin to locally produced pomades made from shea nut) yet strange in appearance and derivation.

The twentieth century witnessed a variety of changes in political organization and the gendered organization of production. Though these cannot be detailed here (see Stahl 1991, 2001a; Stahl and Cruz 1998), the practices that characterize "ethnographic" Banda are the culmination of a long history—a history of choices made in relation to changing political economic circumstances such that "Banda culture" was not merely reproduced but rather made and remade through the practices of daily living. Village life today is thus an inheritance, but one with a complex genealogy, the contours of which can only be known through detailed case studies that draw on a variety of evidential sources.

Conclusion

The work of archaeology is painstaking and slow, its results often frustratingly partial. Yet it is our primary means to gain insight into the entangled lives of the men, women, and children who forged the contemporary world order(s). Its results belie simplistic assumptions about the dreary sameness of village life through the centuries and generate an appreciation of how the entangled world in which we live came to be. Village life is not a time capsule—it does not provide a window into the ancient societies from which African descendants in the diaspora were drawn. But neither is village life today an invention of the recent past. It is, like life everywhere, rooted in the past but not constrained to its earlier forms. The challenge is to give substance to the commonplace academic claim that life everywhere is entangled—to clothe our conceptual emperor in a rich, empirically grounded tapestry that captures the varied responses of villagers to the broader political economic circumstances that conditioned their lives.

Acknowledgments

Funding for the Banda Research Project has been provided by the U.S. National Science Foundation (1994–97, SBR-9410726; 2000–2003,

SBR-9911690), the National Geographic Society (1990, Grant #4313-90), and the Wenner-Gren Foundation for Anthropological Research (1989, Grant #5133). The research was licensed by the Ghana Museums and Monuments Board, and I am grateful to the Ghana Museums staff for their support. Leith Smith conducted regional survey and test excavations on which this chapter draws as part of the 2000–2001 Banda Research Project regional testing phase, and I grateful to him for his considerable efforts in documenting these often remote sites. Maria Cruz's initial work with INAA analysis is also gratefully acknowledged. Hector Neff, Michael Glascock, and Jeff Speakman of the Missouri Research Reactor conducted the INAA analysis in a timely fashion and were of considerable help in sorting out the patterning of the Banda samples. Finally, the success of our project has depended on Banda peoples—the workmen who have assisted us, members of the Banda Traditional Council who have supported our work, and the families among whom we have lived. We are very grateful.

Note

1. All calibrated radiocarbon dates are expressed at the 95-percent confidence level. Dates were calibrated using OxCal Program, v. 3.8 (Bronk-Ramsey 2002), which is available as a free download from the Oxford University Archaeological Research Laboratory (http://www.rlaha.ox.ac.uk/orau/oxcal.html).

CHAPTER THREE

Living in the Shadow of the Atlantic World: History and Material Life in a Yoruba-Edo Hinterland, ca. 1600–1750

Akinwumi Ogundiran

Sometime in the early seventeenth century, a group of people who identified themselves as Alare descendants began to coalesce in the Okun area of Ilare district in central Yorubaland (Ijesa-Yoruba subgroup), 24 km north of Ilesa, and 50 km northeast of Ile-Ife (Fig. 3.1).[1] They were determined to repossess their lost glory and their territory. One or two generations earlier, their ancestors had been forcibly ejected from the first Ilare town (Ilare I, also known as Iloyi), 7.5 km north of Okun, after losing a battle or series of battles to an itinerant warlord and upstart political entrepreneur from the neighboring Ibokun town. Until the late fifteenth century, Ibokun was under the rule of Alare. In the aftermath of the defeat of Alare, Ibokun not only gained its independence from Alare suzerainty but it also vanquished the Alare political formation known as Eka Osun, and the capital of the polity, Ilare I, was deserted. The task facing Otuluuya, the man identified in the oral traditions as the leader of the settlers at Okun (Ilare II), was to reconstitute a second Ilare settlement and Alare institution. He or one of his successors seems to have succeeded in these tasks. By the mid-seventeenth century, Ilare II was a flourishing settlement strategically located on one of the commercial highways in central Yorubaland (for details, see Ogundiran 2001a).

At the time that the political scions and their followers who claimed to be Alare descendants (fictive or real) were setting about building the second Ilare settlement, motivated by different combinations of glory, ambitions for power, and economic interests, among others, "the Atlantic slave system and the slave trade that sustained it" had fully taken off (Eltis 2000, 58). This Atlantic slave system depended on recruiting African captives for enslaved labor in the Americas. Hence factories specializing in trading in enslaved Africans

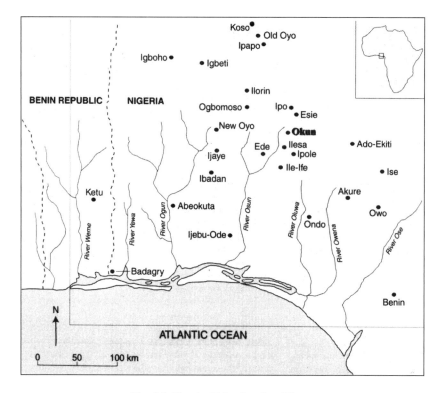

Fig. 3.1. Yoruba-Edo, showing Okun.

developed on the West African coast. These factories were also the conduits through which European imports were funneled into the coastal towns, cities, and villages and from there trickled into the hinterlands. It was in the latter that Okun was located. The substantial period of Okun occupation also took place during the "Atlantic Period" in Yoruba-Edo cultural history (Ogundiran 2003). Between 1600 and 1800, most parts of the Yoruba-Edo region lived in the shadows of Benin and Old Oyo hegemonies and in an expanding regional economic system that was tied to the Atlantic trade. The Benin and Old Oyo hegemonies, among others, and the Atlantic socioeconomic conditions largely shaped the cultural transformations and the trends in production and consumption throughout the region during the seventeenth and eighteenth centuries. This era was marked by proliferation in trade routes and market centers, and old trading networks were either expanded or replaced by new ones.

Okun settlement sprang up, like several scores of others, on one of the commercial highways in the hinterlands of central Yorubaland during the seventeenth century, linking the Benin and southern Yoruba areas with the northern Yoruba towns and villages. It appears that the leaders of Ilare II took advantage

Fig. 3.2. Okun: central artery road during archaeological survey.

of the fact that one of the major roads that crisscrossed Yoruba-Edo region during this period passed through their territory. This road seems to have determined the location of Ilare II settlement (see Figs. 3.2 and 3.3). The intersections of local sociopolitical considerations and regional cultural institutions with the intercontinental Atlantic economic system is the focus in this chapter. The goal is to understand how these intersections impacted the everyday material lives in Okun, a "remote" hinterland town that flourished from the seventeenth century until the mid-eighteenth century. I will examine the material life of the settlement in their local settings and in the contexts of the regional political and transatlantic economic dynamics in which Okun settlement developed and flourished.

Archaeology of Okun Settlement

Like most settlements that historically developed as way stations on major commercial highways, Okun had a linear orientation and was bifurcated by a road that traversed the settlement on an E–W axis. The road, henceforth called "central artery," extended beyond the settlement; archaeological survey traced the remnants of the abandoned road 1 km on the eastern and western outskirts of the settlement. The remains of the central artery vary in width from 4 to 7 m at the center of the settlement to between 1 and 2 m at the periphery of the

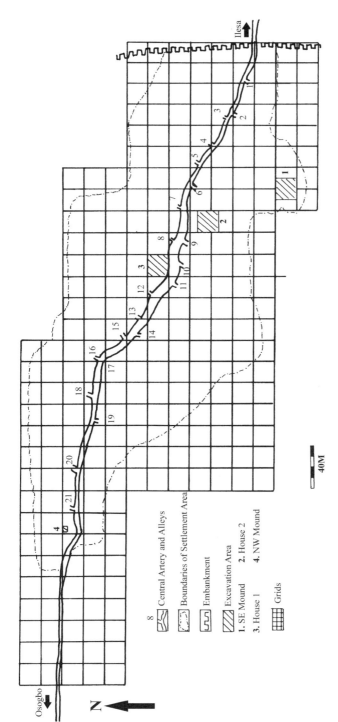

Fig. 3.3. Okun: settlement outline and excavation areas.

settlement. The road must have been much wider during the occupation of the settlement. It appears that the central artery was a significant factor in the settlement layout of Okun. Houses were joined by common walls and arranged in continuous rows and grids on both sides of the road. The frontage walls of these interlinked houses form a continuous linear embankment on each side of the road. Twenty-three alleys branched off from the central artery. The road is described in the oral traditions as part of the network of routes that linked Benin, Ekìtì, and Ijèsà polities in the rainforest region with the Oyó and Igbómìnà polities in the northern savanna region during the heyday of the Atlantic commerce. Informants narrate that Ilare II served as a provisioning rest stop, providing accommodation, food, and refreshment for itinerant traders passing through the area.[2] The increasing activities of itinerant traders in Yoruba-Edo region during the seventeenth and eighteenth centuries as a result of the expansion in the scale of the Atlantic trade would have in turn diversified economic activities in Okun town.

Apart from the road network into which Okun was plugged in the seventeenth century, the other features of the settlement are remnants of house structures that survived as rectilinear and quadrangular mounds. Two main architectural types, the simple module and the courtyard structures, were documented in Okun. The three varieties of the simple module identified are the long-house, the L-shaped structure, and U-shaped structure (Fig. 3.4). The courtyard architecture represents a complex arrangement of the simple-module units into quadrangular clusters around an open atrium (Vlach 1976, 52). The rooms open into the veranda, and the veranda in turn overlooks the courtyard. The daily domestic activities usually take place in both the lobby and the courtyard (Ojo 1968, 15). At the time Okun was abandoned in the mid-eighteenth century, there were 257 courtyard and 115 simple-module structures. Courtyard architecture is found exclusively in the Yoruba township settlements and urban centers, and the simple-module houses, especially the long-house variety, are typical of village settlements and farm homesteads (see Vlach 1976, 51–52). Although the two architectural types often coexist in a township or urban settlement, the presence of any simple-module architecture in the Yoruba township settlements mostly represents a formative stage in the development of courtyard architecture, and it could also represent a devolution in household development resulting from a breakup or disintegration of the courtyard structure. The predominance of courtyard architecture is an indication that Okun was a township by the eighteenth century.

Test archaeological excavations were conducted in a courtyard (House 1), in a simple module (House 2), and at two refuse mounds in order to delineate aspects of the everyday material life in relation to the domestic use of space in a Yoruba hinterland during the seventeenth and eighteenth centuries (see Fig. 3.3). House 1 was about 18 × 16 m in size (Fig. 3.5). The northern section of the structure, opposite the entrance to the building, reveals paved floors with beaten, compact laterite clay, two platforms (A and B), two sitting-podia,

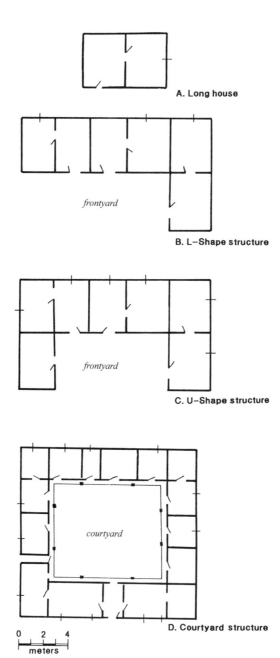

A. Long house

frontyard

B. L–Shape structure

frontyard

C. U–Shape structure

courtyard

D. Courtyard structure

0   2   4
meters

Fig. 3.4. Architectural forms in Yorubaland.

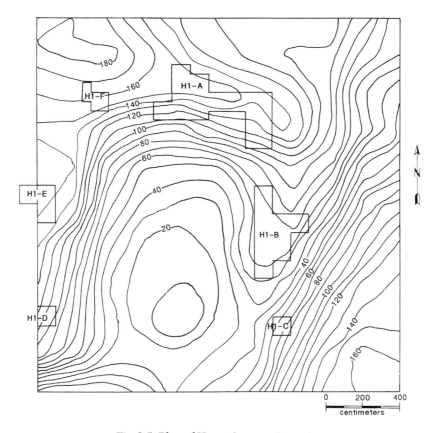

Fig. 3.5. Plan of House 1 excavation units.

and a veranda plane (Fig. 3.6). The artifacts here included pottery, ceramic disks, one bone bead, two cowries (*Cypreae moneta* L), iron pivot and spiral-screw, knives, and pounding stones (Fig. 3.7). The occurrence of ceramic disks in House 1 and the SE refuse deposit reminds us of the 13,500 ceramic disks found at Woye Asiri in Ile-Ife that Peter Garlake (1977, 71–72) recognizes as wall or column tiles "set in the surfaces of mud walls or other vertical features, perhaps columns, as continuous 'mosaic' finish or in decorative patterns." These ceramic disks in Okun would have similarly been used as tiles on the walls, columns, and possibly on the podia. Ceramic disks have also been found in contexts where they were used as top dressing for potsherd pavement floors (Eyo 1974; Willett 1967).

The cooking area for House 1 (unit H1-F), marked by fragments of oxidized red compact clays in a matrix of brittle small pieces of charcoal and ash, was located in the NW corner of the structure where a round-bottomed smoking pipe, with an elbow-shaped base and a flared bowl, was found. Two

Fig. 3.6. Architectural features in House 1-A.

types of guilloche design separated by a band of four excised/oblique lines are etched on the upper and lower parts of the pipe's bowl (see Fig. 3.7e). The upper guilloche design is made of three interwoven excised lines around the bowl. The second, lower, guilloche pattern is a relief that was incised diagonally. The base is about 25 mm wide and it seems to narrow toward the stem. The stem and the bowl are joined at a right angle at the base. The bowl widens gradually upwards toward the lip end. The rim-lip of the bowl is flat, about 5 mm thick, and the orifice of the bowl is 33 mm wide. Much of the stem is damaged, and an accurate measurement of its length cannot be made, but its diameter is approximately 10 mm.

At the western wing of the courtyard house (unit H1-E) is also a reddish, very compact lateritic bench 0.52 m in height and 0.5 m in width with a bulge on one end. An inverted small flask was found "in situ" on the house floor beside the bench. Excavations at the eastern wing of House 1 (H1-B) exposed the cross sections of the veranda and a room. A platform of solid hard lateritic clay was possibly built into the wall of the room into which a small carinated bowl was inserted. At the entrance of the room were three cowry shells of *Cypraea moneta* species stuck into the floor. A smoking pipe and a knife were also found on the floor of the room. The pipe is round-bottomed but single-angled in the sense that its stem and bowl rise directly from the base (Fig. 3.7f). The pipe has an oblong-shaped bowl, 50 mm high and 30 mm wide, decorated with four bands of raised relief. The collared stem rises at an angle of less

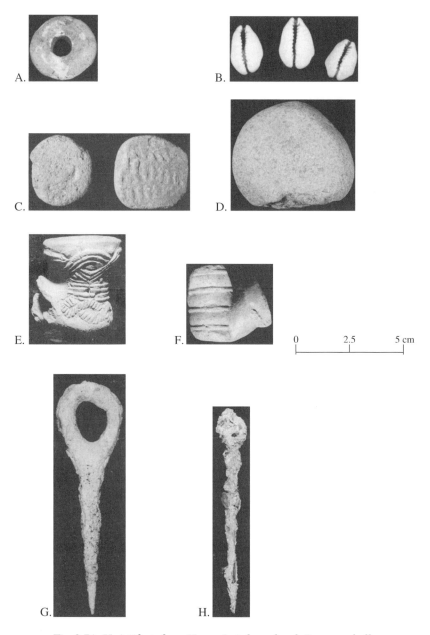

Fig. 3.7A–H. Artifacts from House 1: A. bone bead; B. cowry shells
(*Cypreae moneta* L); C. ceramic disks; D. pounding stone; E, F. tobacco
pipes; G. iron pivot; and H. drilling tool.

than 90 degrees from the base of the bowl, and the stem's socket is 1.9 mm in diameter (Hill 1976, 110; Shinnie and Ozanne 1962, 96).

The three moneta cowries at the entrance of one of the eastern wing rooms deserve further discussion. The use of cowries for making ritual and religious symbols was common in Yoruba-Edo region. The occurrence of cowries as ritual objects, inserted into the platforms and floors of residential structures, temples, and shrines, and associated with burials, has been documented in archaeological contexts in different parts of the region (e.g., Eluyemi 1977, 109). For example, an occurrence similar to the one at Okun was documented in Ondo town by Olupona (1991, 39) at an ancestral temple where "three cowries [were] stuck into the floor." The three cowries in the entrance to one of the House 1 rooms are most likely a ritual signification for protection against ill luck and crisis, and the fact that the cowries are three in number can be sociolinguistically explored by examining the meaning of "three" in Yoruba cosmology. In Yoruba language, the literal translation of three is *eta*. The root word *ta* gives *e-ta* the semantic meaning of "to shoot off," as in "*ta ibon* = shoot a gun" and "*ta ofa* = shoot an arrow." The signifying verb *ta* translates as "to forcefully throw off." Since negative forces are powerful agents that can only be repudiated with a powerful counterforce, three (*eta*) in sociolinguistic terms captures the force of repudiating bad luck, illness, loss, death, and suffering, among others, from one's domain. Hence, the three cowries stuck in the floor in the eastern wing of the house would have formed part of the core of ritual signification used to protect the members of House 1 from hostile forces.[3] The association of this solid earth structure with a flask and the three cowries indicates that the eastern wing of House 1 was a ritual niche and was reserved for religious and sacrificial activities. The flask would have contained liquid libation or medicinal potions.

House 2 is a long house, the most basic form of simple-module architecture. It was approximately 18×6 m in size. The house also faced the central artery. The only architectural feature in House 2 is a clay podium. The cooking area is marked in the western corner of the structure by a concentration of artifacts, mostly pottery, in a matrix of black organic sediments, charcoal specks, fragments of oxidized red clay, ash, and loose fine brown sand. Two stone mullers, a ceramic disk, and a fragment of polished ax blade were present in the deposit.

The excavations of the courtyard of House 1 yielded no archaeological debris, an indication that the courtyard was swept clean in the daily cycle of the house existence. The front yard of House 2 was tested with two excavation units, 1×1 m each. The yard was expected to have served as the central activity arena for the residents of House 2, similar in function to the courtyard of House 1. Few potsherds were found in the yard area. It seems the House 1 courtyard was kept cleaner than the front yard of House 2. Overall, though, the low artifact density in both cases shows that the courtyard of House 1 and the front yard of House 2 were frequently swept and almost free of debris with the exception of a few highly eroded, plain potsherds. These possibly came from the detritus of sherds caught up in the clay used in the construction of the house walls.

The yard was of prime importance in the everyday life of a household; after all, it was the courtyard where "most living is done in full view of family members" (Vlach 1976, 51). In this communal space, according to Vlach (1976, 51):

> elders may discuss family concerns while children dart in between them and chickens scurry under their benches. Not too far away, some women may be pounding yam....Other youngsters may argue loudly...on top of the graves of some ancestors whose remains are buried under the floor.

Similar social activities can be imagined for the front yards of simple-module structures such as House 2. An extension of the courtyard is the veranda; this is the space that connects the courtyard or front yard to the rooms, often with no demarcation. The veranda overlooks the courtyard, while the rooms look onto the veranda. As described by G. J. A. Ojo (1968, 15), the veranda

> is used in the same way as the living-room of modern houses in that all visitors are received there. Mats, stools...and skins of animals are hung on the walls along the veranda from which they are brought down...to seat important guests. In addition, [some]...craft industries take place along the veranda. Such important industries include hair-dressing, ginning, carving, and...weaving...leather working, and wood or calabash carving....Often fowl pens...are placed along the veranda..., and sheep and goats are also tethered there at night. Human beings also share the veranda during the dry season when the rooms may become unbearably hot.

The association of courtyard architecture with township settlement represents a sociopolitical transformation that entails the reorganization of a group of single-family house units of the countryside into an interlocking multifamily (extended family) unit in the township or urban center (Vlach 1976, 53). The limited excavations at House 1 (courtyard structure) and House 2 (a simple-module structure) confirm the ethnographic indices that the simple-module and courtyard architectural types represent different levels of household development and social status. The courtyard structure of House 1 consisted of podia, pavements, and platforms, features that are generally associated with the structures owned by high-status individuals and families in Yoruba-Edo region. In contrast, only one such elaborate architectural feature—a podium—is found in House 2.

Social hierarchy was the overriding basis for the orientation of the structures, internal arrangement of architectural features, and distribution of archaeological objects. The excavations support ethnographic observations that there is a high correlation between the directionality or orientation of a structure and the use of the domestic space in Yoruba architecture (Ogundiran 1991; Ojo 1968; Vlach 1976). Each of the four wings of the courtyard structure reveals different sets of material remains. The ethnography of courtyard architecture in Yoruba-land shows that the quarters of the head of the household is always located at the lobby opposite the house entrance. The results of the excavation of House 1 are consistent with this ethnographic information in the sense that the major architectural features, such as podia and raised platforms, were found in the northern section facing the house entrance. This is the most important section of the house: the platform, podia, and benches would have been used for sitting, although the platform could also be used for sleeping. These architectural features denote permanence, immobility, and potency (Gillespie 2000, 135). The remains of the ancestors could be buried within these platforms, and the fact that the head of the household reserved the right to sleep and sit on this platform demonstrates that he is the bridge between the past and the present. House-hold heads or even institutional heads such as priests and kings, with hereditary duties to keep the ancestral properties and traditions, often "speak of the past in the universal present, making the accomplishment of the past heroes [ancestors] their own and, in a way, seemingly contemporizing past events" (Adjaye 1994, 72). Like the household head, the platforms and podia become the link between the present and the past, structures in which history and memory are lived and of which the men who sat on them are an extension (Fig. 3.8).

The sample size of excavated domestic architectures in Okun settlement is small but they indicate that the occupants of House 1 had better access to the objects of nouveau taste and of long-distance trade than the occupants of House 2. It is even likely that some members of House 1 participated in the long-distance trade networks. The artifact inventories at the courtyard and the simple-module houses demonstrate that there are distinct relationships between the categories/volume of material life/consumption and the house form, and that the organization of domestic space and the range of architectural features could convey information about social hierarchy (e.g., Ashmore and Wilk 1988). House 1 demonstrates more variability than House 2 in the use and specialization of domestic space and in the range of architectural features. The features in House 1, especially the paved floor, the altar, podia, and platforms, demonstrate a greater sense of permanence and continuity than House 2. Moreover, House 1 reveals more artifact variability than House 2, especially artifacts that demonstrate adoption of new tastes and of long-distance origins during the Atlantic period: cowry shells, imported iron tools, and smoking pipes. The cowries and the iron pivots were among the imports via the trans-atlantic contacts, and the transfer of these objects inland about 250 km from the coast demonstrates that Okun was linked to the coastal markets through interregional exchange networks. Local earthenware pipes were also part of the commodities regionally circulating in the seventeenth and eighteenth centuries across western Africa with several production centers springing up at different times in the western Sudan, coastal, and the rainforest belts, and profusely

Fig. 3.8. Podium and platform, Obokun House, Ibokun, 1997.

copying other styles throughout the eighteenth century (Effah-Gyamfi 1981; S. K. McIntosh, Gallagher, and McIntosh 2003; T. Shaw 1960). It is unlikely that they were produced by the potters who made and supplied domestic pottery wares for local consumption in Okun, because the paste, color, and decorations on the smoking pipes are different from those of the ceramic wares. The pipes generally have reddish-brown surface and paste colors, whereas the ceramic ware are predominantly grayish (Ogundiran 2001b, 38). Even if the pipes were manufactured in the vicinity of Okun, they were made by different craftsmen, not the potters, and were likely meant for wider circulation. Thus, like the cowry shells and the iron pivot and drill, the smoking pipes in House 1 were products of the regional exchange networks.

Faunal remains in the form of bones, horns, claws, and shells were also recovered from all the excavated deposits in which the following animals were represented: sheep/goat, domesticated dog (*Canis familiaris*), duiker (*Cephalophus sp.*), giant rat (*Cricetomys gambianus*), squirrel (*Heliescurius gambianus*), grass-cutter (*Tyryonomys swinderianus*), unidentified snake species, and common rat (*Rattus rattus*). Other animals represented in the assemblages include chicken (*Gallus gallus*), land tortoise (*Testudinidae* family), land snail shells (e.g., *Achatina sp.*), and bivalve freshwater mollusk (*Unionidae* family). The faunal remains demonstrate that domesticated and wild animals formed part of the diet of the Okun residents, although the preponderance of wild fauna remains indicates that hunting and trapping wild animals was the major means of everyday meat consumption. It appears that domesticated animals—chicken and sheep/goat—were supplementary sources of animal protein in the diet. The reason for the dependency on wild animals for protein derives from the fact that the long time it would take chicken and sheep/goat to mature made them not readily available for daily exploitation. Rather, these domestic animals would have been killed on mainly ceremonial occasions, as ethnographic sources in the area confirm. Moreover, although ethnographic and ethnohistoric sources show that there were specialized hunters whose primary occupation was the hunting of large game such as elephant, rhinoceros, antelopes, foxes, and members of the big cat family, hunting and setting traps for bush rats and large snakes would have been a leisure activity that many men and boys engaged in, as is practiced today.[4]

A significant portion of domestic life was carried out using pottery. Large storage jars (J1-a and J5) were used for storing water, palm oil, and valuables such as cloth (Fatunsin 1992, 51). They generally outnumber the smaller jars that were used for cooking (J1-c) and transportation of water (J1-b) from the stream to the various vats that would have been located in the yards and verandas of the houses (Fig. 3.9). Other pots were flasks used for serving and storing drinks (J2–J4). The dominant category of pottery in the ceramic assemblage, however, is the serving bowls (Fig. 3.10, 1–9) and to a lesser extent cooking bowls (Fig. 3.10, 10–12). Serving bowls are hemispherical open vessels usually with flat base and shallow depth. With the exception of House 2, serving bowls account for over a third of the vessels in the excavated sites. Cooking bowls, usually with globular-shaped body and round base, with soot stains on the exterior, are represented mainly in House 2 and the SE refuse deposits, 20.7 and 17.6 percent, respectively (Table 3.1). The disparities in the proportions of serving and cooking bowls between the two houses are of interest. The percentage of serving bowls in House 1 is almost double the proportions in House 2, and the percentage of cooking bowls in House 2 almost triples the percentage of cooking bowls in House 1. Whereas one can explain the higher proportions of the serving bowls in House 1 as an indication of the need to feed a larger household, it is not clear why the frequency of cooking bowls in House 2 is three times the number in House 1. This could have resulted from a higher rate of breakage due to commercial cooking activities.

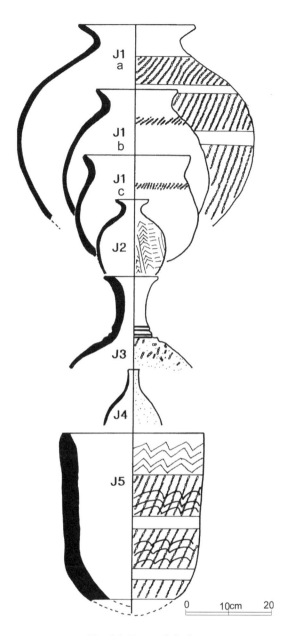

Fig. 3.9. Jars and flasks.

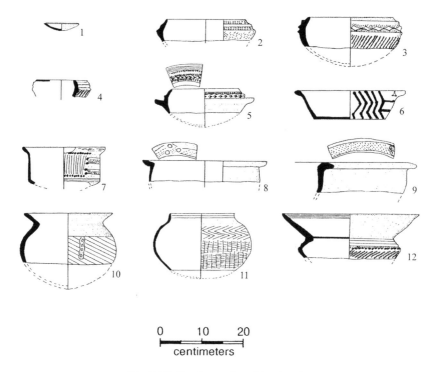

Fig. 3.10. Serving and cooking bowls.

Table 3.1. Distribution of Ceramic Functional Forms

	House 1 %	House 2 %	SE Mound %	NW Mound %
Storage jars	18.1	22.3	12.9	15.2
Cooking/transportation jars	13	14	10	5
Service/storage flasks	1.5	3.3	2.1	1.1
Serving bowls	39.7	23.0	34.2	31.4
Cooking bowls	6.8	17.6	20.7	2.2
Specialized (ritual) bowls	5.5	–	6.4	30.3
Unidentified	15.4	19.8	13.7	14.8
Total number	325	91	140	89

Okun in Regional and Atlantic Africa Perspectives

The artifact inventory at Okun provides evidence for the connection of Okun to the regional exchange networks through which the elements of the transatlantic commerce were transmitted into the interior of Yoruba-Edo region. This evidence is consistent with the oral traditions that describe Okun as a route of interregional exchange between the savanna in the north and the rainforest in the south. By the early seventeenth century when Ilare institution was being revitalized in Okun, the political and economic milieu of Yoruba-Edo region was changing in response to internal politics and external economic forces. Whereas the first Ilare settlement (Ilare I or Iloyi) was aligned with a stable Ife cultural field between the thirteenth and sixteenth centuries (Ogundiran 2002d), the sixteenth century marked the beginning of new dynamics of regional politics and events. The primacy of Ile-Ife as the political-ideological, economic, and religious center in Yorubaland was challenged by the rise of new centers of political power, economic opportunities, and cultural innovations aided in part by the incorporation of the coasts of West Africa into the emerging transatlantic commerce. The Atlantic coast, rather than the trans-Saharan trade termini in the Niger bend area, became the focal point of the long-distance trade networks in most parts of the region starting from the sixteenth century. Hence new interaction spheres, directions of regional interactions, and sociopolitical alignments were created that caused some setback to the political, ideological, and economic influence of Ile-Ife (R. Horton 1992, 136–39). Twenty-four kilometers south of Okun, a new political force — Ilesa city-state — had developed in the late sixteenth century and was the dominant political power in central Yorubaland by the early seventeenth century (Peel 1983). Farther north in the savanna, about 200 km away, was Oyo-Ile, the metropolis of a nascent city-state in the sixteenth century with imperial ambitions. The Oyo polity began a gradual political expansion toward upper reaches of the rainforest belt, including the territories under Ilesa, in the seventeenth century (Law 1977). The two nascent powers clashed, but the result did not deter Old Oyo from establishing a foothold in the uppermost rainforest belt. The expansion of the Oyo political boundaries into the rainforest zone during the seventeenth and eighteenth centuries brought Ilare district within a 30-km range from the western boundary of the Oyo political territory; it also checked the expansionist agenda of Ilesa in the upper reaches of the rainforest belt, but Ilesa maintained its position as a formidable city-state with far-flung hegemonic powers. It must be noted that the attempts by Oyo-Ile and Ilesa to establish links to the increasingly lucrative Atlantic commerce dictated their hegemonic agenda for expansion and was also responsible for their clashes. Likewise, the interest of the harbingers of Ilare dynasty to reestablish a polity with access to the coastal commercial networks dictated the location of the second Ilare settlement at Okun.

The ceramic decoration motifs represented in Okun acutely reflect these flurries of interactions and shifts in the regional political power. The ceramic assemblage in Okun is one of the most diversified in central Yorubaland because it demonstrates the merging of two ceramic spheres in Yoruba-Edo region: Ife and Oyo (Ogundiran 2001b). The stylistic components of Ife ceramic sphere are dominant at Okun in the form of cowry-form bosses, cordon relief, circular stylus impressions, rustication, hyphenated cross-hatching, and red paints. Aspects of Oyo ceramic motifs consist of geometric incisions, dot punctuates, and shell-edge motifs. In fact, the latter account for 7.4 percent of decoration motifs in Okun. The distribution pattern of ceramic motifs in Okun demonstrates that this Atlantic Age settlement occupied a delicate intermediate zone between the expanding Oyo Empire from the savanna north and the influential Ife cultural zone in the rainforest south during the seventeenth and eighteenth centuries. The presence of maize-cob roulette motifs in the corpus of the ceramic decorations at Okun, 3.7 percent of all motifs, also shows that the people of Okun, like most other parts of the hinterland, were already experimenting or actively cultivating maize, a New World crop, by the seventeenth century.

As noted above, Okun developed as a provisioning roadside settlement for itinerant traders and porters carrying goods between the southern rainforest/coastal areas and the northern savanna belts during the early seventeeth century into a maturing settlement of possibly almost 500 house units in the mid-eighteenth century when it was abandoned. As discussed elsewhere (Ogundiran 2001b, 2002a), this highway location meant that Okun was introduced to different ideas and goods associated with the traffic of people along the trading routes. By the time the founders of Okun were laying the foundations for the way station and transforming it into a thriving township in the seventeenth century, the domestic economies in the Bight of Benin and its hinterlands were almost entirely monetized with cowries (Hogendorn and Johnson 1986) brought to the coast by various European nations and factors, mostly from Portugal, the Netherlands, and England. As a contemporary observer, Thomas Phillips (1732: 439), an English trader, noted in Whyday: "When they go to market to buy anything they bargain for so many cowries...and without these shells they can purchase nothing." This process of monetization of cowries in the Bight seems, however, to have begun in Benin Kingdom in the fifteenth century when Portuguese traveler and trader Pacheco Pereira commented that the people of Benin used cowries "to buy everything, and he that has most of them is the richest" (Hogendorn and Johnson 1986, 19). During the two centuries that Okun was occupied, it is estimated that about 16 billion cowries, mostly moneta species, were imported to Atlantic Africa, 3–4 billion in the seventeenth century (Ogundiran 2002c, 441fn), and 12 billion in the eighteenth century (Hogendorn and Johnson 1986, 62, 75–76). The moneta cowries at Okun show that the settlement was integrated into the cowry circuit of the Bight of Benin and its hinterland, although at a smaller scale than the metropolises and major trading towns of the region. The adoption of cowries as currency had far-reaching impacts on the commercial and economic development of Yoruba-Edo region during the seventeenth and eighteenth centuries. Aspects of these impacts on Yoruba culture and society have been discussed elsewhere (Ogundiran 2002c). Suffice to state here that the occupation of Okun coincided with the early period of regionwide adoption of cowry as currency of market transactions in the Bight of Benin and its hinterlands where Okun is located (Lovejoy 1974). Cowries have been dubbed "slave money," since their importation into West Africa after the mid-fifteenth century was achieved largely in exchange for human captives (Hogendorn and Johnson 1986). From the coast and mainly through African slavers and potentates of coastal polities, cowries trickled into the hinterland markets where they were deployed to a large extent in transacting small-scale commercial exchanges. Having cowry as a denominator of value register and exchange at the regional level and across political and ethnolinguistic boundaries made it possible for surplus production to be accumulated individually; standardized the local economic exchange system and made commercial transactions easier; allowed for better management of long distance trade and terms of external trade; provided for more efficient record keeping of the "ever increasing volume and variety of trade goods" (Belasco 1980, 82); and provided the state with an efficient means of tax and levy collection in a medium that could not be counterfeited and whose bulky nature made it difficult to conceal (Law 1978).

The economic valuation of cowries as currency permeated the social and cultural lives of the people so that cowries were also used in religious, ritual, and ornamental aspects of daily life. Apart from the presence of cowries in ritual contexts as attested in House 1 at Okun, cowries were also used for aesthetic purposes, and sometimes the uses of cowries for ritual, aesthetic, and wealth display were interwoven. The supply of cowries to the Bight of Benin peaked in the eighteenth century, and there are references in the European accounts that cowry was a medium by which individuals displayed their wealth, success, and political power. Such individuals particularly incorporated cowries into the aesthetics of architecture for the purpose of displaying wealth and grandeur. Oba Eresoyen of Benin (1735–37), for example, is remembered in the oral traditions of Benin as the king who "built a house of money" because he "decorated the walls and floor of his palace with cowries" (Ben-Amos 1999, 104). This public display did not end in the palace, however, as important and high-ranking chiefs and princes of eighteenth-century Benin also participated in the ostentatious display of wealth by building cowry-decorated floors. In the last quarter of the century, Landolphe described the residential quarters of a powerful Benin chief, Ezomo Ekeneza, as "elegantly encrusted with small Indian shells, called cauris" (Landolphe 1975 [1823], 98; also see Bradbury 1973, 261).

The artifact profiles of Okun demonstrate adoption of imported goods and new taste/consumption patterns (pipe/tobacco smoking) via the Atlantic exchange, but the commercial networks in which Okun was a node carried mainly local products, not imported commodities. In fact, Atlantic imports such as iron tools were used merely as a supplement to the indigenous iron production or were adapted, in the case of smoking pipes, into local forms. For example, although the iron drill and pivot found in House 1 possibly originated from a Western European foundry, the presence of several iron slag and fragments of small iron artifacts such as stems of arrow points, nails, and knives in all contexts attests to the continuity of local iron production in Okun. Moreover, whereas tobacco pipe smoking was a repertoire of Atlantic taste introduced into West Africa, especially via the Senegambia area in the late sixteenth century (T. Shaw 1960), most parts of West Africa did not rely on European imports of tobacco pipes to meet African demands after the sixteenth century. In fact, "there is virtually no evidence to date for pipes of European manufacture moving along trade routes to the interior in the 17th century" (McIntosh, Gallagher, and McIntosh 2003, 192). Rather, distinct West African pipes were adapted from the initial imported prototypes, probably from Florida, and within a few decades metamorphosed into several local varieties to serve both the swelling adoption of smoking pipes as part of social-distinction objects and the addictive taste for tobacco smoking. As the following discussion will show, pipes were indigenized in West Africa as soon as smoking was introduced.

Tobacco and pipe smoking entered West Africa via the Senegambia region, where Native American Florida-type pipes, consisting of stem-socket pipes with round base and flared or hemispherical bowl, were introduced in the late sixteenth century (Shaw 1960). By the first decade of the seventeenth century, however, the region between Senegambia and the Niger Bend not only was producing tobacco pipes based on the Florida prototype but also was supplying pipes to North Africa and the savanna and rainforest belts of West Africa. In addition, local tobacco cultivation was already under way in the early seventeenth century in some parts of West Africa, at least as garden plants. William Finch, for example, observed in 1607 on the Sierra Leone peninsula that "tobacco is planted about everyman's house." He also describes the smoking instrument in a way that reminds us of the Florida prototype and the Senegambian stem-socket forms: "The boll of their tobacco-pipe is very large and stands right upward, made of clay well burnt in the fire. In the lower end thereof they thrust in a small hollow cane a foot and a halfe long, thorow which they sucke it" (cited in Hill 1976, 115).

The region between Senegambia and the Niger Bend dominated the supply of pipes to the West African market throughout the seventeenth century (Shaw 1960; Ozanne 1969). In the second half of the seventeenth century, however, local production of pipes also developed in the coastal area, in the Gold Coast and Bight of Benin (Effah-Gyamfi 1985; Kelly 2001; Ozanne 1969). There is no clear evidence for local manufacture of pipes in the rainforest belt where Okun is located, and the typological sequence of pipe forms is not known in this region either. However, we may be nearer to filling some of these gaps for the rainforest belt when the ongoing neutron activation analyses of some tobacco pipes in Yorubaland, including those at Okun, are completed.[5] The round-bottomed pipes, single-angled and elbow types, seem to belong to the later forms of tobacco pipes manufactured in West Africa, added to the repertoire of the much older forms with pedestal base during the late seventeenth and eighteenth centuries (McIntosh, Gallagher, and McIntosh 2003, 192). Given the prolific adoption of smoking habits across western Africa in the seventeenth and eighteenth centuries and the accompanied prolific production of pipes, it is likely that multiple centers of production mushroomed across regions, with craftsmen incorporating new styles and forms encountered via the travelers and the movement of goods. The tobacco pipes demonstrate that Okun was part of the far-flung networks of the seventeenth and eighteenth centuries, but they also attest to the localization of a taste and habit that originally had external origins.

Conclusion

The existence of Okun had local origins and motives, but the expanding commercial relations on the coast, the networks of trading contacts between the coast and the hinterland, and the dynamics of political transformations of the period shaped the trajectories of the foundation and growth of the settlement. In some marginal ways Okun was incorporated into the Atlantic system, but it was only one of several hundred towns and villages that lived in the shadow of the Atlantic economic system during the seventeenth and eighteenth centuries in western Africa. Although its production and consumption were not fully integrated into the Atlantic economy, the Atlantic exchanges impacted the material life in Okun. In fact, as the current evidence shows, the material aspects of the exchanges—corn, tobacco, cowries, and imported metals—were incorporated into the daily lives of the settlement. With these Atlantic-derived commodities and others that have not been uncovered, such as beads and textiles, new habits and tastes were formed. The technologies of iron production in Okun were possibly altered as new repertoires of iron objects were imitated by local blacksmiths. This technological imitation and adaptation was best illustrated in tobacco smoking, a habit that developed across West Africa in the seventeenth century. In less than a generation from their introduction in the late sixteenth century, pipes of African origins were being manufactured at many centers to cater to the smoking habits of peoples across West and North Africa. The adoption of these new habits and consumption were possibly mediated by age and class/social status differences. The differences in the artifact inventories in House 1 and House 2 indicate the possibilities of how such new consumption patterns were experienced differently across Okun settlement.

The integration of Okun, along with hundreds of other hinterland societies, into the circulation of cowry currency that oiled the engine of domestic
economy contributed to the reasons why the Bight of Benin became one of the
major suppliers of captives into the Atlantic slave economy in the seventeenth
and eighteenth centuries. As elsewhere, the primary European demand on the
coast was human cargo, of which over 40 percent of payment was in cowries
in the Bight of Benin (Eltis 2000, 300). The people of Okun did not have to
participate in kidnapping, raiding, or slave trading in order to have access to
cowries. Servicing the needs of those whose commercial activities were tied
to the coastal trade (slavers, ivory dealers, cotton and dyestuff merchants, porters, etc.) would have given them access to the shell money through complex
chains of social, political, and economic transactions. The extent to which the
people of Okun participated in these export-driven production activities will
only become clearer with further excavations in the future.

The archaeology of Okun serves as a case study of the nature of material life in the hinterland of the Bight of Benin during the era of the Atlantic
trade. In addition to taste making and circulation of new commodities, the
hinterland small-scale societies were important to the Atlantic exchanges
in other ways. With a weak political institution and a poor defense system,
Okun was the typical settlement that could be raided for captives destined
for the Americas. We have no reference in the oral traditions that Okun was
raided and its occupants enslaved, but in the nineteenth century, less than a
hundred years after the site was abandoned, extant traditions state that some
descendants of Okun, now living about a kilometer from the old site, were
captured during the seventy-year Yoruba wars and transported to the coast.[6]
From there they would have formed part of about 500,000 Yoruba who were
forced into the Middle Passage in the nineteenth century, mainly to Cuba and
Brazil, where they identified as Ijesa (Ijexa), Lucumi, and Anago ethnicities
(Eltis 2004).

Notes

1. Alare refers to the title of the potentate of Ilare polity and Eka Osun political
complex in the Ijesa-Yoruba subgroup (central Yorubaland), thirteenth through fifteenth centuries.

2. Informants: Chief J. Aje, Loye of Ilare (October 2 and August 13, 1992); Oba
J. O. Fasoyin, the Alowa of Ilowa (September 10, 1991); Chief Professor Oludare Ola-
jubu, Sokoti of Ilare (October 2 and December 20, 1992); Oba Adejoro Ogidan III, the
Owalare of Ilare (January 23, 1997); the late Prince Adebiyi Adedoyin, Ilare (December 20, 1992).

3. There are other numbers that signify and invoke spiritual actions. For example,
the verb *fa* (pull) in *efa* (six) makes use of six objects that are relevant when one is
engaged in ritual signification connected with seeking friendship, children, money, etc.
Hence, as the Yoruba will say, *"eta ni ta ibi danu"* (it is *three* that throw or shoot away

calamities) and *"efa ni fa ire w'ole"* (it is *six* that draws in good fortunes). I am grateful to the following for this information: Professor Wande Abimbola (Boston, February 1998), Chief Samuel Babayemi (Ilare-Ijesa, May 8, 1997), Pa Iseolu (Ilare-Ijesa, May 8, 1997), and Aworo Olalekan Orisadare (Osogbo, April 5, 2004).

4. Informant: Awogboro Oyedeji, aka Alayo, Ilare, Osun State, Nigeria (July 2, 1997).

5. This procedure is being carried out at the University of Missouri Research Reactor Center, Columbia.

6. Informant: Michael Adebisi, Ilare, Osun State, Nigeria (April 10, 1997).

CHAPTER FOUR

Dahomey and the Atlantic Slave Trade: Archaeology and Political Order on the Bight of Benin

J. Cameron Monroe

West African societies underwent dramatic social and political changes during the era of the Atlantic slave trade. While many polities in the region collapsed as a result of sustained European contact from the seventeenth through nineteenth centuries, some expanded their spheres of influence over hundreds of thousands of subjects. It has long been argued that this transformation was the product of growing interaction with European traders and the new economic and military opportunities resulting from their presence (Austen 1987; Goody 1971; Inikori 1977; Lovejoy 1983; Rodney 1966, 1981; Wallerstein 1974, 1980; Wolf 1982). Only some polities managed to remain stable or expand in coastal West Africa in this period, however, whereas many others succumbed to the debilitating political and economic effects of the slave trade. How such polities managed to survive and expand has been the subject of much historical debate.

Scholars are demonstrating how the archaeological record can contribute to our understanding of West Africa in the era of early contact with Europe. Archaeological projects have examined the nature of European-African interaction at important loci for slave trading in West Africa. Excavations at Fort Ruychaver (Posnansky and Van Dantzig 1976) and Elmina (DeCorse 1992, 1993, 2001a) in Ghana and at Savi in the Republic of Bénin (Kelly 1995, 1997a, 1997b, 2002) have contributed substantially to our understanding of the nature of this interaction, its social effects on local West African populations, and the degree to which European contact affected African worldviews in the long run. Specifically, they have demonstrated powerfully that Africans participated actively in the creation of the Atlantic World System. There is a growing interest in expanding this research beyond the coast, and recent efforts have been directed toward exploring how the slave trade impacted political organization within communities at a distance from the coast (see contributions to DeCorse 2001b for notable examples).

This chapter explores how archaeology is contributing to our understanding of political change in the Kingdom of Dahomey, located in the modern Republic of Bénin. Dahomey has played a prominent role in debates about the nature of West African political order in the era of the slave trade, and archaeology is poised to address this issue. Pioneering studies by local archaeologists have been initiated as either rescue projects (Adande and Adagba 1988; Adande and Bagodo 1991; Adande and Dovie 1990; Bagodo 1993), limited excavation at important sites (Adande 1984, 1987, 1989), or the simple documentation of ancient remains (Iroko 1989). American and European archaeologists are becoming increasingly interested in the archaeology of Bénin as well. Notably, Kenneth Kelly (Kelly 1995, 1997a, 1997b, 2002) and Neil Norman (Norman 2000; Norman and Kelly 2004) have worked at Savi, the capital of the Hueda Kingdom. Recently, a Danish team led by Klavs Randsborg has conducted archaeological research near Abomey (Randsborg et al. 1998). These projects are contributing much to our appreciation of the complex and diverse archaeological record in southern Bénin.

In the summer of 1999, I initiated the Abomey Plateau Archaeological Project in the Republic of Bénin to explore the relationship between the Atlantic slave trade and political order in West Africa (Monroe 2003, 2004, 2005). Drawing on evidence from regional surveys, architectural analysis, and ethnohistorical accounts of Dahomean royal palace sites, this chapter explores the nature of political organization in Dahomey in the Atlantic era. The results presented below suggest that dramatic political change followed the advent of the slave trade in the Bight of Benin, characterized by the extension of state power down to the local level and the rapid bureaucratization of the political sphere. These innovations, I argue, allowed Dahomey to expand and remain stable, despite the destructive tides of Atlantic commerce.

Dahomey and the Slave Trade

The relative impact of the Atlantic slave trade has been a major theme in West African historiography (Austen 1987; Eltis 1987; Eltis and Jennings 1988; Fage 1969; Inikori 1977; Lovejoy 1983; Manning 1982; Rodney 1981; Thornton 1998; Wallerstein 1974, 1980; Wolf 1982). The Aja-Yoruba region of West Africa, spanning Togo, Bénin, and Nigeria, has held a particularly prominent role in this debate. In the seventeenth century, a number of loosely centralized complex societies, locked in intricate tributary relationships with one another, were well documented in this region. Within the western Aja portion of this region, the dominant polities were Allada, Hueda, and Dahomey, all of which were involved in the Atlantic slave trade as suppliers or exporters of human capital (Fig. 4.1).

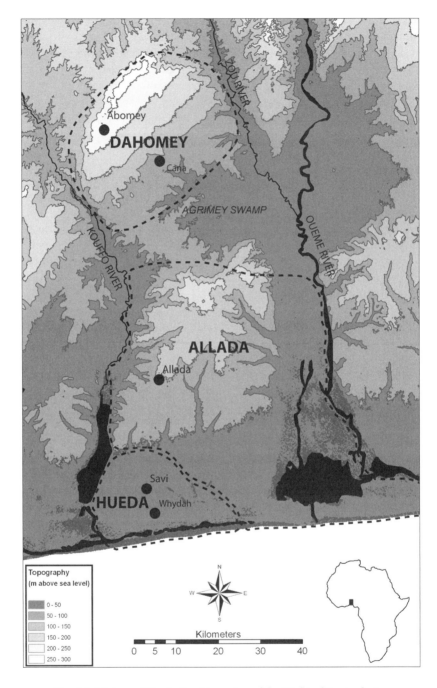

Fig. 4.1. Major polities in the Aja region of the Bight of Benin during the seventeenth and early eighteenth centuries.

Allada was preeminent of the three, exacting regular tribute from Dahomey and Hueda. Although Allada was in a position of political authority in this region, it maintained direct administrative control over neither kingdom. It was precisely this loose control over its suzerain polities that led to Allada's collapse as the slave trade intensified in the late seventeenth and early eighteenth centuries (Akinjogbin 1967). As Hueda grew prosperous from rising levels of trade with Europeans, and Dahomey became strong as provider of slaves for trade, the authority held by Allada dissolved. Hueda revolted from Allada in the 1690s, followed soon after by Dahomey.

Agaja (1718–40), fourth king of Dahomey, seized upon the growing weakness of Allada and began a campaign of conquest, taking Allada in 1724 and Savi, the capital of the Hueda kingdom, in 1727. Agaja thereby conquered a 100-kilometer strip of territory from Abomey to the coast and gained direct access to trade with Europeans. Agaja centralized control over the port of Whydah and all major towns on the road to Abomey. This was the general trend through much of the eighteenth century, as subsequent kings attempted to quell dissent among newly conquered people, thereby solidifying their control over access to coastal ports (Bay 1995, 1998, Law 1987b, 1991). By the nineteenth century, Dahomey achieved expansive control over these and newly conquered territories to the north of the Abomey plateau.

Thus Dahomey rose to power while its contemporaries collapsed under the weight of the Atlantic slave trade. How it accomplished political order in this tumultuous period has been the focus of Dahomean historiography since the eighteenth century (see Law 1991 for a full discussion). This historiography has been dominated by two themes. First, scholars have examined the degree to which Dahomey was economically dependent upon Atlantic commerce for stability. Second, research has focused on whether or not Dahomey represented a radical break from traditional principles of political order on the Bight of Benin.

In the eighteenth century, this debate centered on the writings of pro-slavery and abolitionist authors. Writers like William Snelgrave (1734), Robert Norris (1789), and Archibald Dalzel (1967 [1793]), advocates of the slave trade as a whole, argued that Dahomey was essentially an absolutist and militaristic state. They provided detailed descriptions of human sacrifices and abject servitude among Dahomean subjects to demonstrate the "savagery" and "barbarism" of the kingdom. Thus, for these authors, the slave trade was a positive force for coastal West Africa because it liberated a segment of its population from the horrors of life within Dahomey. Abolitionists in this period, however, presented a contrasting view. John Atkins (1970 [1735]), for example, responded by suggesting that King Agaja was an early abolitionist himself, who sought to wrest control of the region from his coastal rivals in order to end the slave trade. Although Atkins and others, such as Frederick Forbes (1966 [1851]), accepted as true the "barbarous" and autocratic nature of Dahomean society, they argued it was the negative impact of the slave trade itself that encouraged Dahomean militarism in the eighteenth century.

It was with this documentary heritage, heavily flavored with the political agendas of European visitors of the time, that scholars continued to engage this debate. In the early twentieth century, however, ethnographic research in Dahomey began to provide an "insider's" perspective on Dahomean statecraft. In 1911, the French colonial official and anthropologist Le Herissé published a detailed account of Dahomean history and society according to royal oral traditions, shedding much light on political institutions in the precolonial era. In 1958, Melville and Francis Herskovits produced landmark studies of Dahomean political institutions and folklore, adding additional insights into the nature of Dahomean statecraft. These authors largely diverted attention from Dahomey's military qualities, however, highlighting instead the bureaucratic sophistication of the Dahomean state.

Later research by Karl Polanyi and Adeagbo Akinjogbin continued to wrestle with these issues. Polanyi (1966) contended that Dahomean institutions and policies were, in fact, the product of purely local Fon culture and that the slave trade had a relatively minor impact on the essential qualities of Dahomean political organization. He conceded that Dahomean policy was more absolutist than its predecessors, characterized as it was by a state monopoly over trade. Polanyi argued, however, that this strategy was employed to minimize the broader impacts of the European presence on Dahomean society.

Adeagbo Akinjogbin also stressed the destabilizing effects of the European presence on the coast, but suggested Dahomey adapted to this situation by radically altering its political structure. For Akinjogbin, Dahomey in the eighteenth and nineteenth centuries differed dramatically from earlier polities in the Aja-Yoruba region. He argued that, unlike Dahomey, the early Aja-Yoruba kingdoms had limited central authority and were based on what he termed the "Ebi social theory" (Akinjogbin 1967, 16). In this scheme, polities were conceived as a larger version of the family consisting of a federation of autonomous lineages united under hereditary leaders, similar to the chiefdom concept in anthropology (Earle 1991). According to this model, because the kingdoms of this period did not centrally control coastal trade, they found themselves unable to avoid political fragmentation when the slave trade intensified in the seventeenth and early eighteenth centuries. Akinjogbin argued that Dahomey was successful in subsequent centuries because it was able to construct a centralized political apparatus. According to Akinjogbin, then, the rise of Dahomey represented a radical break with the kin-based institutions of the past, characterized as it was by the evolution of centralized bureaucratic institutions.

A great deal of recent scholarship challenged these views (Law 1986, 1987a, 1987b, 1989a, 1989b, 1991, 1997; Pollis 1974; Ronen 1971). Some historians questioned whether or not Dahomey maintained absolute control over the slave trade. These scholars argued that state control over trade was in many ways symbolic, and actual exchanges were carried out by private merchants and officials granted license by the king (Law 1989a; Peukert 1978; Ross 1987). Werner Peukert went so far as to argue that European trade goods were not imported in large numbers at all and thus may have played only a minor role in the political economy of early Dahomey (Peukert 1978). Dov Ronen suggested that the coastal trade in slaves was an economic afterthought for the kings of Dahomey, who were more interested in acquiring captives for sacrifice to their royal ancestors (Ronen 1971). In a sweeping study of West African social and political change in this period, in which Dahomey was included, John Thornton (1998) proposed that although war and trade do appear to have been major concerns for kings in the sixteenth through eighteenth centuries, this may have resulted from internal African political processes unrelated to coastal developments involving Europeans.

Historians also questioned the degree to which Dahomey represented a radical break from previous political forms (Law 1987b, 1991; Ronen 1971). Drawing from admittedly limited seventeenth-century sources referencing the Kingdoms of Allada and Hueda, Robin Law (1987, 1991, 1997) argued that significant continuity existed between Dahomey and its precursors on the Bight of Benin. In particular, Law identified elements of political ideology and organization that Dahomey appears to have drawn directly from Allada. These included the insertion of Dahomey into the dynastic history of Allada's kings, Dahomey's reinvigoration of the Allada kingship in the eighteenth century, and royal ancestor worship in Dahomey. However, the general opinion that Dahomey represented a much more centralized and autocratic form of government, particularly by the nineteenth century, was not countered. Instead, Law argued that although Dahomey appears to have been more dependent on a military ethos than its predecessor, the nature of Dahomean despotism "differed from [its predecessors] more in degree than in the principles of its organization" (Law 1991, 345). Thus the bureaucratic advances highlighted by others were downplayed.

Edna Bay presented an additional perspective that complemented and sometimes contradicted previous reconstructions of Dahomean state formation. Drawing from extensively collected oral traditions, Bay documented the evolution and growth of a state apparatus that, by the nineteenth century, established expansive palatial control over its territory. Like Law, Bay argued that the dynamics of state building in Dahomey were strongly influenced by existing political principles. However, Bay presented compelling evidence that the structure of political relationships within Dahomey was shaped significantly by the need to balance the power of competing political factions within the kingdom, and she highlighted the role of an important class of female officials in this process. Militarism, according to Bay, was merely a by-product of broader attempts at establishing political stability in the era of the slave trade (Bay 1998, 130).

This discussion has illustrated two general themes upon which the historiography of Dahomey has focused since the eighteenth century: the relationship between Dahomey and the Atlantic slave trade, and how this commercial involvement impacted Dahomean political organization. Whereas some have suggested that Dahomey was focused on either ending the slave trade or minimizing its effects, or was relatively disinterested in it altogether, others have argued that coastal trade was, in fact, the primary stimulus for Dahomean political expansion and that its kings depended upon this trade for political power. Scholars generally agree that although an actual monopoly on trade probably did not exist, Dahomey did profit immensely from involvement in the Atlantic slave trade, which became centrally important to its long-term political stability.

Little consensus exists, however, concerning the nature of Dahomey political organization. On the one hand, what may be called the *political transformation hypothesis* posits that Dahomey represented a radical break from its predecessors and was characterized by the development of a centralized state bureaucracy. On the other hand, what may be termed the *political continuity hypothesis* suggests Dahomean political organization continued to depend heavily on the kin-based ideology of its predecessors. According to this hypothesis, Dahomey's expansion was facilitated by a military ethos rather than advances in bureaucratic efficiency. The essential question of whether or not bureaucratic centralization characterized Dahomean state formation can be explored archaeologically.

Archaeologists have sought general patterns that characterize the process of bureaucratization cross-culturally, and commonly cite two evolutionary processes that characterize the emergence of centralized state bureaucracies.[1] These include *segregation*, the amount of internal differentiation within a political system into discrete subsystems, and *centralization*, the degree of linkage between subsystems and highest-order controls (Flannery 1972, 409; Haas 2001). Archaeologically, these bureaucratic processes can be observed in many ways. In general, segregation is suggested by evidence for administrative specialization. The construction of special-purpose state facilities, or the presence of activity areas within such facilities serving specific functions, may suggest the process of administrative segregation (Flannery 1998). Centralization is suggested by the emergence of hierarchical relationships between such specialized units. The presence of administrative central places with satellite communities across the landscape, or the construction of state facilities at the local level are two archaeological indicators of centralization (Schreiber 1987; Stanish 1997).

If involvement in the Atlantic slave trade had little impact on political organization in this region, the degree of centralized administration in Dahomey would have differed little from the seventeenth through nineteenth centuries. Political order would have been characterized by a low level of state intrusion at the local level, with minor changes in administrative structure over time. Contrastingly, if Atlantic commerce did, in fact, shape political trajectories on the Bight of Benin, dramatic change would have characterized the nature of political organization across these centuries. The level of state involvement in local affairs would have risen dramatically over the course of this period, as would the degree of administrative specialization. More specifically, we would expect that regions which played a major role in facilitating Atlantic commerce would have been prime targets for centralization. These competing hypotheses can be examined archaeologically.

The Abomey Plateau Archaeological Project

Anyone who has visited the Republic of Bénin with an interest in its history cannot help but find his or her way to Abomey, the precolonial capital of the Kingdom of Dahomey. Abomey is renowned for its recently restored royal palace, one of many such structures constructed throughout the countryside in the precolonial era and the location of the Musée Historique d'Abomey (Fig. 4.2). In 1999 I initiated the Abomey Plateau Archaeological Project to explore the relationship between palace construction and political order in

Fig. 4.2. Royal and princely palaces at Abomey (after Antongini and Spini 1995). The palace of Prince Agoli-Agbo was constructed in the colonial period and is not included in this discussion.

Dahomey (Monroe 2003, 2004, 2005). This project examined the regional distribution and internal layout of Dahomean royal constructions as an index of bureaucratization over time. Research was limited to the Abomey plateau, the approximate political boundaries of seventeenth-century Dahomey at its greatest extent.

Visitors' descriptions from the eighteenth and nineteenth centuries, as well as local oral traditions, provided an initial window into the presence of royal complexes across the plateau. These structures, made entirely of earth, stand in varying states of decay. In some, wall sections stand nearly to their original heights, whereas others have collapsed so completely as to be nearly invisible under heavy vegetation (Fig. 4.3). Thus aerial photographs were used to identify eighteen royal complexes on the plateau, in addition to the nine precolonial palaces already documented at Abomey and environs (Fig. 4.4). Once identified and confirmed in the field, oral traditions were collected from local informants, and small surface collections were taken to garner information about the age and function of these complexes. Oral and written sources indicated that the royal complexes of Dahomey fall into three general categories: royal palaces, princely palaces, and special-purpose complexes.

The majority of complexes identified were royal palaces. These buildings were the centers of political discourse in Dahomey. They served as residences for the king and his dependents, who may have numbered from two thousand to eight thousand at Abomey alone (Dalzel 1967, xi; Le Herissé 1911, 27–31). They also provided contexts for staging state ceremonies such as the Annual Customs, or *Xwetanu*, in which largesse was distributed to the populace and human sacrifices were performed. Additionally, Dahomean royal palaces served major administrative functions within Abomey and throughout

Fig. 4.3. Earthen walls of the late-nineteenth-century palace of King Glele at Cana-Mignonhi. A southern view of a palace gate on the northern wall *(left)* and the palace wall reaching this gate from the east *(right)*. A 3-m survey rod is provided in both photographs for scale.

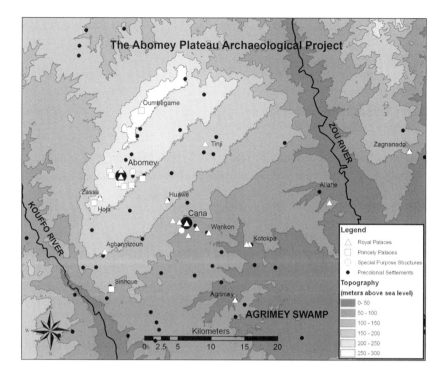

Fig. 4.4. Three types of royal complexes on the Abomey Plateau. White triangles, squares, and circles indicate royal palaces, princely palaces, and special-purpose complexes, respectively. Black circles represent towns and villages known to have existed in the precolonial era.

the countryside. Many of the royal wives were administrators themselves, and the interior courtyards of the palaces at Abomey were stages upon which all the notable dignitaries of the day vied to tip the balance of royal favor in their direction. This fits into a general West African pattern in which the various domestic, ritual, political, and economic roles of the elite were played out behind palace walls (Kelly 1995, 1997a, 1997b; Nast 1996; Ojo 1966).

Oral and written sources indicate that nearly every king of the seventeenth through nineteenth centuries built a royal palace at Abomey (Fig. 4.5). The earliest was built by Wegbaja (1650–80) at the northernmost corner of the royal palace complex at Abomey. His son, King Akaba (1680–1718), lived in an adjacent structure. This structure, referred to as the Dahomey Palace in period sources, stands to the north of the main Agringomey Palace in the Royal Precinct at Abomey. Following Akaba, each king from Agaja (1718–40) to Behanzin (1889–93) built an addition to Wegbaja's palace, thus expanding the total area of the Agringomey Palace to approximately forty-four hectares by the close of the nineteenth century.

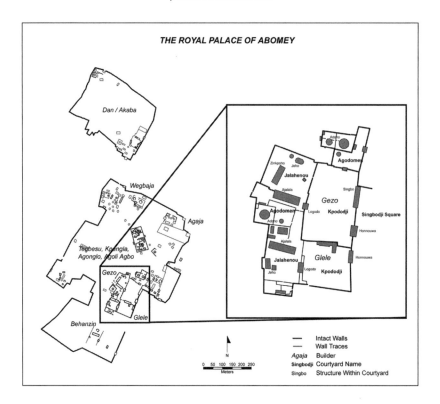

Fig. 4.5. The royal palace of Abomey showing areas constructed by successive kings from the seventeenth through nineteenth centuries (after Antongini and Spini 1995, plan 3). The inset shows courtyards serving specialized functions within the semipublic zone of the palace at Abomey. The northern *kpododji*, *jalalahénou*, and *agodomen* courtyards are attributed to Gezo. Their southern counterparts were added by Glele. This area is the current location of the Musée Historique d'Abomey.

Royal palaces were constructed outside Abomey as well. Oral traditions suggest that the earliest Dahomean palace on the plateau was built at Huawe by King Dakodonu (1625–50) (d'Ans 1997). Until recently, this structure was still inhabited by a descendant of Dakodonu, King Dako Landozin. It is relatively small compared to other palaces identified in this research, and it shares much in common with traditional chiefly compounds on the plateau today (Le Herissé 1911, 359). Much of the construction appears recent, and thus it may have been reconstructed extensively over the centuries. According to J. A. Skertchly, who visited the palace in 1871, this structure was built by Tegbesu (1740–75) to commemorate Dakodonu's conquest of the region (Skertchly 1874, 153). Thus although there is no evidence that a palace did not stand at Huawe during Dakodonu's reign, the structure standing today is probably the remains of Tegbesu's construction.

A royal palace identified at Zassa, west of Abomey, was attributed to King Kpengla (1775–89) by local sources. Oral sources also suggested that King Gezo (1818–58) constructed a palace identified at Tinji, to the northeast of Abomey. These traditions claimed that Gezo built this latter complex to commemorate the memory of his mother, who was a native of Tinji. This story is partially corroborated by Frederick Forbes, who indicated that in 1849 Gezo traveled to Tinji to "make custom" for his mother (Forbes 1851, 1:84). Royal complexes identified at Wankon, Kotokpa, Agbanhizoun, and Allahe were all attributed to King Glele (1858–89) by local traditions. Lastly, six royal complexes were constructed and occupied by seven kings of the eighteenth and nineteenth centuries at Cana, 11 kilometers southeast of Abomey. These latter structures are examined in detail in subsequent pages.

Only one historically attested royal palace was unidentifiable on the ground. In 1844 Thomas Freeman wrote, "We started from Avadi at ten minutes after ten, and in the course of forty minutes afterwards we reached Agremi, where there is another royal residence" (Freeman 1844, 254). Richard Burton also noted this palace (Burton 1864, 1:179). These sources suggest the presence of a palace at Agrimey by the 1840s at the latest or during the reign of King Gezo (1818–58). This structure may have been small, made of perishable materials, or destroyed as a result of modern development, making it difficult to identify on the ground or from the air.

Princely palaces comprise the second category of royal structures identified. Initially these structures were the primary residences of the future king of Dahomey as *vidaho*, or heir apparent. By the nineteenth century, however, princely palaces were also constructed for the brothers and cousins of the *vidaho* to govern Dahomey's territories. Each king from Tegbesu (1740–75) to Behanzin (1889–93) constructed a princely palace at Abomey. Only three such palaces were identified outside Abomey. King Agaja (1718–40) built a princely palace at Hoja to the southeast of Abomey. Additionally King Glele (1858–89) stationed two of his sons in palaces at Sinhoue and Oumbegame, in structures still inhabited by their descendants.

Like the king himself, princes lived inside these buildings with their dependents, held court, and resolved local disputes. Historical sources indicate that princely palaces were initially walled with palm fronds. When a *vidaho* became king, he was allowed to rebuild these structures in earth. Skertchly, for example, indicates that King Glele's princely palace at Jegbe (a suburb of Abomey) was still under reconstruction in 1871, a full fourteen years into his reign (1874, 65).

A number of "special purpose complexes" were identified across the plateau as well. Two structures, a stockade and a hospital for slaves, both of which were attributed to Wegbaja (1650–80), were identified at Abomey. Only a segment of the stockade's outer wall remains. The hospital has been reconstructed continuously over the centuries and is currently used as a private dwelling. Sources also suggested an additional slave stockade at Cana. A number of Abomey and Cana residents indicated this structure was located at Cana in the Mignonhi quarter. This attribution is probably erroneous, however, and it is much more likely that a complex at Cana-Kpohon served this function (Monroe 2003). Additionally, oral sources suggest that Agaja's palace at Hoja was converted by King Gezo (1818–58) into a barracks for female soldiers.

The combined use of archaeological survey methods, oral traditions, and period documents thus provides valuable insight into the presence, function, and age of royal complexes across the Abomey plateau. Surface collections conducted within these structures allowed them to be dated to within a century. To test the utility of using local oral traditions to identify the specific builder of each structure, test excavations were also conducted within the six complexes identified at Cana (Monroe 2003, 2004, 2005). Visible surface features within each palace were excavated which, based on high densities of surface artifacts, appeared to be either trash heaps or backfilled borrow pits. These trenches contained a wealth of materials.

Locally manufactured items dominated all of the assemblages. These included ceramics, tobacco pipes, shell beads in various stages of production, iron implements, and ground stone as well as bone, ivory, and metal finger rings and bracelets. In contexts dating to the late eighteenth and nineteenth centuries, European imports also composed a significant part of the assemblage. European goods included ceramics, tobacco pipes (mostly Dutch), and glass bottle fragments. Numerous beads of unknown origin also characterized all the assemblages and await further analysis. In addition, two flintlock mechanisms were recovered with other gun hardware in one palace excavation (Cana-Mignonhi).

Seriate analysis of carved roulette decorations on local ceramics recovered from these excavations corroborated the sequence of palace construction at Cana suggested by historical sources. Additionally, imported European goods provided *terminus post quem* and *terminus ante quem* dates for three of these structures, again corroborating historical sources. These results generally confirm the value of combining textual, oral, and archaeological data for dating precolonial royal constructions in Dahomey. Broad patterns over time and space can now be identified.

The Regional Distribution of Royal Palaces

Regional archaeological data demonstrate that Dahomey became increasingly centralized over the course of the seventeenth through nineteenth centuries (Fig. 4.6). The regional pattern of palace construction suggests that royal power was relatively indirect in the seventeenth century. Although Dahomey had effectively conquered all corners of the Abomey plateau by the close

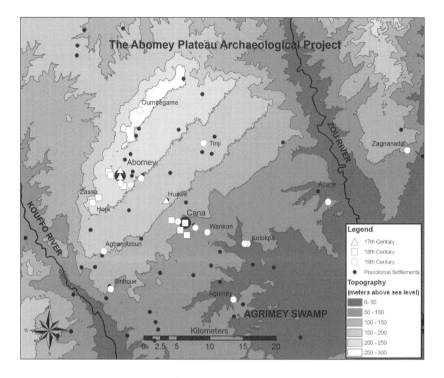

Fig. 4.6. Palaces identified by the Abomey Plateau Archaeological
Project represented by construction date. White triangles, squares, and
circles indicate complexes constructed in the seventeenth, eighteenth,
and nineteenth centuries, respectively. Black circles represent towns
and villages known to have existed in the precolonial era.

of the seventeenth century, the palaces of its kings were constructed within
Abomey and two satellite communities (Huawe and Hoja) alone. Thus direct
royal control was essentially limited to the capital and its immediate environs.
During the eighteenth and nineteenth centuries, however, state complexes
were increasingly constructed throughout the countryside. This may be interpreted as evidence for an expanding political apparatus designed to project
state authority down to the local level.

The direction of political expansion across the plateau over time supports
the argument that Dahomey sought to centralize control over sectors of the
political economy linked to Atlantic commerce. Eighteenth-century palaces
are centered along the road through Cana toward Agrimey, the dominant trade
route through the Agrimey Swamp to the coast (Fakambi 1993). Cana was
also a major waypoint for traders coming from eastern Yoruba kingdoms en
route to southern coastal ports. The presence of a number of state complexes

113

at this town reflects growing state interest in controlling this important node in inland–coastal trade routes. The desire to administer such trade routes to the coast clearly encouraged the southward expansion of Dahomean palace construction in the eighteenth century.

In contrast, multiple palaces were constructed in the nineteenth century in areas to the north, east, and west of this main road, thereby extending direct state control across the plateau. A number of factors may explain this observed shift in the direction of palace construction. This pattern may reflect, in part, a general concern with controlling the roads from Abomey and Cana to Zagnanado. These roads provided access to Ketu and Abeokuta, Yoruba kingdoms that were constant military concerns for Kings Gezo (1818–58) and Glele (1858–89), and palace construction would have facilitated military action in this direction. Le Herissé indicates that soldiers were installed at Zagnanado for five months in the 1860s to guard against invaders from Ketu (Le Herissé 1911, 333). However, royal palace construction along these roads also would have facilitated trade with these eastern Yoruba kingdoms. Oral traditions collected at Allahe, on the road to Zagnanado, suggested the presence of a large market frequented by Yoruba traders in this period.

Palaces constructed in Abomey's countryside may have facilitated the state's growing interest in managing local production as well. The expansion of palace construction into the countryside in the nineteenth century coincides closely with a dramatic decline in royal revenue from the slave trade as a result of abolition, and the rise of "legitimate" trade in palm oil products destined for industrial Europe. Palaces built to the southwest and east of Abomey are located in what are today considered the most agriculturally productive regions of the plateau, and both documentary and oral sources suggest that a number of royal palaces were used to centrally manage palm oil production.

This pattern may indirectly reflect market spacing on the plateau in the nineteenth century, suggesting that internal market forces were driving political expansion. In this part of West Africa, periodic markets (those occurring every two, four, or eight days) tend to be spaced approximately 11.6 kilometers from one another (7.2 miles), servicing an area with a radius of nearly 6 kilometers, or a single day's walk to and from market (Hodder and Ukwu 1969, 62). Towns with royal palaces on the Abomey plateau are spaced an average of 10.75 kilometers from one another, suggesting a possible correspondence between the distribution of royal palaces and local market spacing norms. These complexes would have facilitated Dahomey's ability to profit from a growing domestic economy in this period (Manning 1982). The distribution of local periodic markets thus may also have been a factor in determining palace placement in the nineteenth century.

Based on the observed pattern of palace construction, two conclusions can be made regarding the nature of Dahomean political organization from the seventeenth through nineteenth centuries. First, royal control was relatively indirect in the seventeenth century and increasingly centralized in the eighteenth and nineteenth centuries. Second, Dahomean palace construction in the eighteenth and nineteenth centuries was geared toward capitalizing on economic expansion fueled, to a large degree, by Atlantic commerce. Although these data provide no insights into the question of whether or not Dahomean kings monopolized production and trade, the presence of royal complexes along major trade routes and throughout agriculturally productive zones would certainly have allowed them to profit from the activities of others.

The Organization of Royal Space

Cross-cultural archaeological research suggests that architecture is particularly sensitive to changes in social structure (Ashmore 1989; Canter 1977; Deetz 1996; Fritz 1986; Glassie 1975; Hillier and Hanson 1984; Kent 1984, 1990; Moore 1992; Rapoport 1969). Political order is often reflected in spatial order, and the process of bureaucratization is generally visible in the ground plans of elite facilities. As political organization becomes increasingly centralized and bureaucratic, archaeologists commonly witness an increase in spatial segmentation and hierarchy within such buildings (Flannery 1998; Kent 1990; Moore 1992). Characterizing the nature of spatial organization within the royal palaces of Dahomey illustrates the processes of bureaucratization in Dahomey.

Behind the high walls of the royal palace, space was divided into two zones that can be described as semipublic and private (Monroe 2003). The private zone housed the wives of the king, and access was restricted to the king and a few others. The semipublic zone contained clusters of open courtyards lining the interior palace walls. It was in this semipublic zone that most matters of state and royal interest were discussed and resolved and elements of the state's ritual cycle were conducted. Within this area the king received visitors, held court, resolved disputes, and performed sacrifices before ancestral shrines. The semipublic zone thus may be considered a region for inter-elite discourse, removed from the public gaze.

Traditional descriptions of the names and functions of various courtyards in the semipublic zone of the royal palace at Abomey indicate that each of the courtyards in this zone served specialized political and ritual functions (Antongini and Spini 1995). A tripartite courtyard system containing *kpododji*, *jalalahénou*, and *agodomen* courtyards characterized this area of the palace. In the *kpododji* and *jalalahénou*, visitors to the king were received and issues of state were discussed. It was within *jalalahénou* that temples for royal ancestors were located and judicial hearings were conducted. The *agodomen* housed the actual or symbolic remains of these royal ancestors. Additional areas designated for storage, ritual, and political activities are also suggested by ethnohistorical sources. Because these courtyards appear to have served specialized

115

functions, the relative number and organization of these architectural units over time might reflect the nature of political organization in the kingdom as a whole.

Royal palaces located in the town of Cana were examined in 2001 and 2002 with this goal in mind (Fig. 4.7). Cana was chosen as the research focus for a number of reasons. First, Cana was the nineteenth-century provincial capital of Dahomey and one of the earliest political centers on the plateau. Cana thus presented an ideal setting in which to explore political change in Dahomey. Second, unlike Abomey, Cana declined dramatically following the French conquest of Dahomey in 1893. As a result, its royal palaces have been subject to little restoration in the twentieth century and contain less disturbed archaeological contexts. Third, six complexes were constructed in Cana, built and briefly occupied by successive kings of the eighteenth and nineteenth centuries. Each structure thus represents a relatively thin slice of time and presented an ideal opportunity to examine architectural change based largely on surface remains alone.

These royal complexes, four of which will be discussed here, range in size from approximately twelve to thirty-four hectares.[2] I adopted a method of

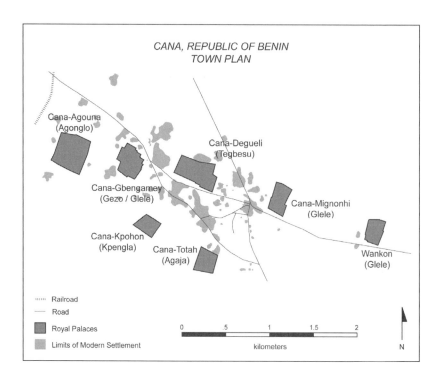

Fig. 4.7. The royal palaces and limits of modern settlement at Cana.

intensive mapping in which 100 percent of obstructing vegetation was cleared from each palace, allowing for the complete documentation of all visible standing walls, mounds and depressions. Architectural analysis suggests a rise in spatial complexity and hierarchy within palaces at Cana over the course of the eighteenth and nineteenth centuries.

The earliest royal palace built at Cana, located at Cana-Totah and attributed to Agaja (1718–40), has a very simple ground plan (Fig. 4.8a). This structure is characterized by a few small courtyards containing the remains of temple complexes and reception halls. Agaja's successor, Tegbesu (1740–75), took only a slightly different approach to palace construction (Fig. 4.8b). The palace of this king, located at Cana-Degueli, is larger than that of Agaja and contains an expansive domestic zone. This area contains abundant grindstones identifiable on the surface and numerous small house-mounds, suggesting a large resident population. Differences in scale aside, spatial planning in Tegbesu's palace consists simply of agglomerations of architectural units similar to those present at Cana-Totah.

The royal complexes at Cana became more internally segmented and hierarchical by the late eighteenth century, as reflected by the presence of major architectural divisions in the palace shared by Kings Kpengla (1775–89) and Agonglo (1789–98) at Cana-Agouna (Fig. 4.8d). This architectural tradition was most fully elaborated in the Gbengamey palace of Kings Gezo (1818–58) and Glele (1858–89) (Fig. 4.8e). Large domestic zones, major dividing walls, and numerous reception courtyards are present in both palaces. Oral traditions from Cana, furthermore, suggested seven functionally specific areas within the palace at Cana-Gbengamey related to domestic, ritual, military, craft, and official activity. These roughly correspond to observed architectural demarcations. It appears, therefore, that the ground plans of Dahomean royal complexes became increasingly complex and spatially segmented over the course of the eighteenth and nineteenth centuries, possibly reflecting growth in the number and types of activities undertaken by officials stationed therein.

These data can be quantified to approximate the degree of spatial segmentation and hierarchy over time. If ethnohistorical evidence that royal courtyards served specialized functions is accepted, then the number of courtyards located within the semipublic zone of Dahomean royal palaces may serve as an index of relative administrative specialization. Furthermore, centralized organization of such activities may be reflected spatially in a number of ways. Courtyards may be clustered into courtyard groups, defined as clusters of courtyards sharing common walls. Additionally such groups may be formally separated from one another through the use of any number of architectural devices.

Table 4.1 summarizes the number of courtyards, courtyard groups, and major divisions within the four royal palaces described above. The number of courtyards per palace increases dramatically after the early eighteenth century and remains relatively high from the mid-eighteenth century onwards,

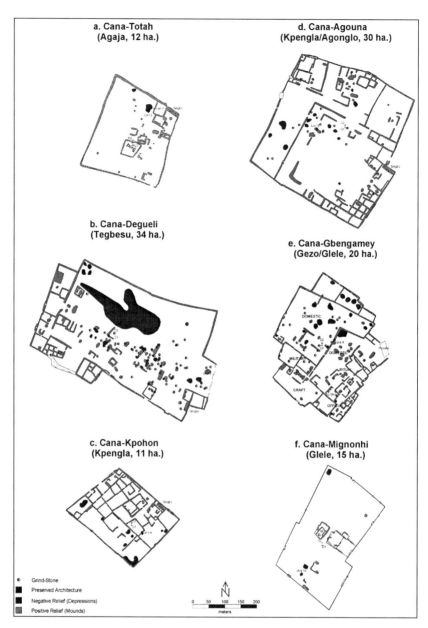

Fig. 4.8. Plans of the royal complexes at Cana. Preserved architectural remains (black), mounded remains (light gray), and depressions (dark gray), as well as the distribution of grinding stones (black and white circles) are represented. The kings credited with the construction of each complex are noted, and each structure's total area in hectares is indicated in parentheses.

Table 4.1. Courtyards, Courtyard Groups, and Divisions for Four
Dahomean Royal Complexes

Architectural unit	Totah (Early 18th century)	Degueli (Mid/late 18th century)	Agouna (Late 18th century)	Gbengamey (19th century)
Courtyards (C)	6	28	42	30
Courtyard groups (CG)	2	9	4	4
Average C per CG	3.0	3.1	10.5	7.5
Divisions	0	0	5	4

suggesting an initial florescence of political, economic, and ritual activities within these complexes. In contrast, courtyard groups also increase significantly in the second palace of the sequence (Cana-Degueli), but then decrease dramatically in subsequent constructions. This pattern appears to have resulted from grouping larger numbers of courtyards into a lower number of courtyard groups over time. The average number of courtyards per courtyard group for Cana-Totah (3) and Cana-Degueli (3.1) is relatively low; higher values are yielded at Cana-Agouna (10.5) and Cana-Gbengamey (7.5).

Assuming these courtyards were used for specialized political and ritual activities, this suggests an initial florescence of such activities at Cana-Degueli, but little change in the manner in which they were organized hierarchically. This provides an example of increasing segmentation of activities with little overall centralization. At Cana-Agouna and Cana-Gbengamey, in contrast, more courtyards are concentrated into fewer discrete courtyard groups. This suggests that palace activities were being reorganized hierarchically by the late eighteenth century. Additionally, courtyard groups at Cana-Agouna and Cana-Gbengamey were separated by high dividing walls. This spatial pattern may also reflect the formal segregation of activities into discrete areas of the palace. The process of bureaucratization is thus suggested by these palatial plans.

Conclusion

This discussion has contributed an archaeological perspective on how the kings of Dahomey responded to the Atlantic slave trade over time. Whereas the destabilizing effects of this trade led to the decimation of many kingdoms in the region from the seventeenth century onwards, Dahomey was able to adapt to the problems presented by European contact. Multiple lines of archaeological evidence corroborate historical arguments that long-term political stability was fostered through political reorganization in Dahomey. This process involved the segregation of administrative tasks and their centralization into a stable political hierarchy or the construction of a centralized bureaucratic apparatus.

In the seventeenth century, Dahomey focused on controlling central nodes within coastal–inland trade routes. Regional power, however, was relatively indirect. In the eighteenth century, the kings of Dahomey centralized control over coastal–inland routes under a state-run administration so as to facilitate the unobstructed traffic in human beings. By the nineteenth century, this control was extended into the countryside to facilitate both war and trade with Yoruba kingdoms, to manage agricultural production, and to profit from local market activity. Architectural evidence from Cana also supports the suggestion that bureaucratic activities increased in number and were integrated into a formal hierarchy over time. Although a rising military ethos probably was a major component of Dahomean political strategies, archaeological evidence suggests that a bureaucratic order emerged over the course of this period that bound the region into a tightly integrated political and economic system.

Archaeological research thus largely supports the political transformation hypothesis for Dahomey. This should not be read to suggest, however, that none of the traditional strategies for expressing political legitimacy persisted into later phases of Dahomey's history. The annual veneration of the royal ancestor cult, for example, appears to have been modeled directly on preceding traditions on the Bight of Benin. It is clear, however, that a great deal of political reorganization did take place in Dahomey, as its kings became more involved in the direct administration of Atlantic commerce as well as local production and exchange. Neither does this evidence support the idea, as some might extrapolate, that Dahomey was anything but the primary agent for political change in its history. It was Dahomean kings who foresaw how a centralized state bureaucracy could successfully stabilize a fragile political system. It was these same kings who succeeded in developing such a system in the face of political and economic turmoil brought on by the slave trade. Adaptability in the face of potentially debilitating forces characterized Dahomean political organization in the eighteenth and nineteenth centuries and contributed to political expansion and stability for nearly two centuries.

Notes

1. This literature is beyond the scope of this chapter. For general discussions see Feinman and Marcus (1998) and Johnson and Earle (2000). I must also note that African cases have been successfully harnessed to dismiss the long-standing argument that the processes of bureaucratization described here are "universal" cultural phenomena. For notable examples see S. McIntosh (1999a).

2. Six royal constructions were identified and mapped at Cana. Two of these have been excluded from this discussion. I have argued elsewhere that the first of these, built at Cana-Kpohon (Fig. 4.8c), was not a palace at all but rather a facility for housing slaves en route to the coast. The second, built at Cana-Mignonhi (fig. 4.8f), was not finished and probably was never occupied to any great extent, limiting its usefulness for this analysis. See Monroe (2003) for descriptions of these structures.

CHAPTER FIVE

Enslavement in the Middle Senegal Valley: Historical and Archaeological Perspectives

Alioune Déme and Ndèye Sokhna Guèye

Historically two slave trade networks were involved in the transfer of Africans outside Africa: the trans-Saharan slave trade and the Atlantic slave trade. Most of the historical research has focused on the Atlantic slave trade, specifically on its relationship with sociohistorical and economic processes in Africa (e.g., DeCorse 1991; Elbl 1991; Gemery and Hogendorn 1978, 1979; M. Johnson 1978b; Law 1980, 1992; Meillassoux 1991; Thomas and Bean 1974; Thornton 1998; Webb 1993). The consequences of the Atlantic trade have raised a debate between the maximalists (Barry 1985, 1988a; Manning 1990; Rodney 1966, 1981) and the minimalists (Curtin 1969, 1975; Eltis 1987; Fage 1969). The maximalists state that the Atlantic trade has had a great and detrimental effect on African societies (warfare as well as demographic and economic downfall). They associate the Atlantic slave trade with the loss of manpower, increased warfare, cultural and religious transformation, and destruction of endogenous technology.

The minimalists, on the other hand, argue that the Atlantic slave trade had a small influence on African societies. Some even go further: that the Atlantic trade was important for the growth of the centralized African states (Fage 1969, 1980). Even though this debate is important in illuminating the demographic, economic, and social consequences of the Atlantic slave trade, it has overshadowed the processes and consequences of the trans-Saharan slave trade. The trade across the Sahara is often analyzed through Arabic documents and archaeological data (Berthier 1997; Cuoq 1975; Devisse 1983; Fisher and Fisher 1971; Garrard 1982; Garren-Marrot 1995; Insoll 1996; Levtzion and Hopkins 2000; Robert-Chaleix 1970, 1991; Vanacker 1983). Such studies have prompted some scholars to argue that the impact of the trans-Saharan slave trade on African societies was equal to or even worse than that of the Atlantic trade (Austen 1979; Hunwick 1992; Hunwick and Trout 2002; Levtzion 1968, 1988; Marmon 1999). This opinion is difficult to verify because of the disparity in the scale of research between the two trade networks. The transatlantic slave trade is far more documented than the trans-Saharan trade. Concomitantly, the former is richer in historiography than the latter. Paraphrasing Hunwick and Trout (2002, ix), for every gallon of ink that has been spilt on the transatlantic trade and its consequences, only one small drop has been spilt on the forced migrations of Africans into the Mediterranean world of Islam. Similarly, the quantitative data used by economic historians to estimate the Atlantic trade is difficult to compare to the trans-Saharan. Ralph Austen summarizes the problems as follows:

> The published literature on the trans-Saharan trade relies almost entirely upon literary records for its quantitative analysis. It is easier to note the shortcomings of such method than to provide any alternative approach. The observations from literary sources are discrete (usually involving only one year or even one caravan) rather than serial in their scope. They report, at best, information at one remove from the actual operation of the trade. Even when slave traders are directly quoted, they cannot be trusted to be making real calculations of annual averages as opposed to what Curtin called capacity estimates of how much the trade should carry under optimal conditions.... Working records would thus be far preferable to literary ones, but unfortunately these are practically nonexistent for the trans-Saharan slave trade. (1979, 27)

Austen's statement is an indication that the quantitative approach developed in illuminating the Atlantic trade (Curtin 1969, 1975; Eltis 1977, 1979; Lovejoy 1982; Richardson 1989; Stein 1978) may not be well suited for the trans-Saharan trade. Hence the debate over the consequences of the Atlantic will remain unsolved as long as the trans-Saharan trade is not well studied.

Fortunately, the comparison of the effects of these two trade systems has started to emerge, thanks to the pioneering work of Patrick Manning. Using a demographic model, Manning concluded that the Atlantic trade was larger than the trans-Saharan trade (1990, 81). However, the fact that the comparison was based mostly on demographic data does not help to illuminate all aspects of these two trade networks. It is difficult to develop a coherent demographic model for the trans-Saharan trade. This is why an alternative approach is needed. We propose an approach that focuses more on the impact of the two trade networks rather than on the number of enslaved. To illuminate the impact of the slave trade, we need to focus on the hinterland or the periphery of the core trade centers. As DeCorse puts it for the Atlantic trade: "Europeans sites can only offer insight into one side of the contact. In order to obtain a more holistic interpretation of West African culture dynamics, the associated African settlements and the vast hinterland from which captive Africans were drawn need to be examined" (2001b, 9).

Our proposed approach is methodologically archaeological. Indeed, archaeology can provide additional information to illuminate issues related to these two trade networks by focusing on their impact on African societies rather than on the number of enslaved. The use of time-space systematic is well suited for that type of analysis. A regional approach aimed at illuminating the settlement organization and evolution as well as the technological and economic changes through time will provide important data, especially in areas that are historically known to have been part of the trans-Saharan and Atlantic trades. The Middle Senegal Valley (hereafter called MSV) is one such area. There are four reasons that explain the suitability of the MSV for the archaeological understanding of the impact of slavery.

First, the Middle Senegal Valley has been an important catchment area for settlement and population expansion (Déme 1991, 2003; Elouard 1962; Lericollais 1975; S. McIntosh 1999a, 1999b; Michel 1973). Its topography comprises several landforms that are suitable for different subsistence activities, trade, and population movement. Throughout history, several groups have occupied the MSV to take advantage of its geography (Adams 1977, 1985; Chavane 1985; Ndiaye 1975; Thilmans and Ravisé 1980). Second, traditional historians agree that a few among the earliest historically known African polities were located in the MSV: Takrur and Silla (Bocoum 1990; Cuoq 1975; Delafosse 1963, 1972; Déme and R. McIntosh 1994; Levtzion and Hopkins 2000; Mauny 1961; Naqar 1969; Soh 1913; Trimingham 1962). According to Arab authors (e.g., al Bakri and al Idrissi), these polities were rivals to the Ghana Empire and were involved in the trans-Saharan slave trade by raiding their non-Islamic neighbors (Cuoq 1975). Third, during the Atlantic trade era, MSV polities took part in the Atlantic trade and witnessed its consequences: slave trade, warfare, and the rise of popular Islam (Barry 1985, 1988a; P. B. Clarke 1982; Curtin 1971, 1975; Kane 1986; Robinson 1975; Robinson, Curtin, and Johnson 1972; Samb 1974; B. Wane 1981; Webb 1985). Fourth, research is being undertaken in the area by S. K. McIntosh, R. J. McIntosh, and H. Bocoum based on large-scale controlled stratigraphic excavations at mounds of various sizes and a survey of a 700-km^2 area (Fig. 5.1). The research is aimed at shedding light on political, social, and political issues in the MSV during the Iron Age. Results from that research provide a picture of a long-term settlement and technological evolution (Bocoum and S. McIntosh 2002; Déme 1991, 2003; Guèye 1991, 1998; S. McIntosh et al. 1992). This chapter takes its roots from that research program in which we participated as investigators. The data from our field research covers both the trans-Saharan and the Atlantic trade networks and their impact on the MSV societies.

Geographical Overview

The MSV is a fertile floodplain located at the core of the Sahel. The MSV is highly advantageous because, contrary to its surrounding areas, it offers the

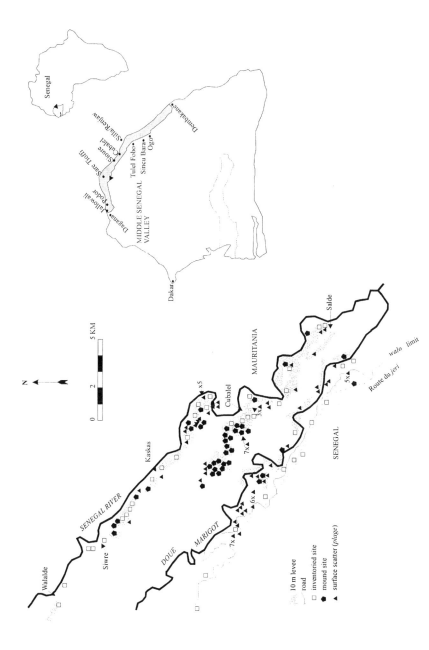

Fig. 5.1. The Middle Senegal Valley and data from the MSV Project study region. (In Déme 2003: 50)

possibility of two cultivation seasons per year: first during the rainy season, and then during the progressive retreat of the flood carried by the Senegal River and its distributaries (Baro et al. 1987; Elouard 1962; Michel 1973; Rochette 1974; Seguis 1990). Overall, four topographic units are found in the MSV: the red dunes, the high levees, the low levees, and the low units. The red dunes are 10–30 m high (Elouard 1962). They were formed during the arid climate phase known as the Ogolien (between 20,000 and 13,000 years ago). The high levees are more than 10 m high and are rarely toppled by the flood. They were formed after 4000 BP. Used for habitation and the cultivation of rain-fed crops, the high levees are the preferred refuge zone during the flood season. The low levees are formed by the undercutting of the high levees. They are mostly found in the convex sides of the Senegal River and its tributaries. The low-slope basins of the floodplain back swamp compose the low units. Fed by the rain and by the flood (through a system of distributaries), they have the highest clay content (40–60 percent) and are mostly used for the cultivation of sorghum and rice. These units are exploited through an integrated land use system. A lateral cross section of the Middle Senegal Valley shows that the land use system recognizes three zones that are defined by the topography of the floodplain (Fig. 5.2): the floodplain (locally called *walo*); the non-inundated areas outside the floodplain (*jeri*); and the transition zone between the two (*jejeengol*).

The walo comprises the river slope, the high levees, and the basins. The jeri is the domain of the high dunes, and it is used for the cultivation of rain-fed millet and for pastoralism. The jejeengol is occupied by agriculturalists and agro-pastoralists (Schmitz 1986). Today the jejeengol contains most of the largest villages. This is due to its strategic position which allows cattle herding and the cultivation of rain-fed millet in the jeri during the rainy season and the *décrue* cultivation of sorghum and rice in the walo (Boutillier 1962, 1989; Elouard 1962; Schmitz 1986, 1994).

The microecological diversity described above is used in a complex subsistence strategy organized along an axis perpendicular to the Senegal River (Schmitz 1986): fishermen, agriculturalists in the floodplain, agro-pastoralists in the transition zone, and pastoralists in the non-inundated zones. The subsistence strategy is not based on strong specialization. During periods of high risk and uncertainty, people shift subsistence activity. They abandon their traditional subsistence activity to adopt a new one that has a better chance of success. Schmitz (1986, 354) provides the cases of some agriculturalists who become agro-pastoralists and those of herders who, having lost their livestock, become fishermen.

Historically, fishermen, pastoralists, and agro-pastoralists have lived in small "agro-halio-pastoral units," called *leydi* (Schmitz 1986). The leydi is a variant of a Senegambian land-based system known as *lamanat* and stressing consensual decision-making among lineage heads (Diagne 1967; Diop 1968; Kane 1986; Ngaido 1993; Niang 1975; Park 1992, 1993; Schmitz 1986, 1994; Y. Wane 1969). In its risk management strategy, the leydi offers the possibility of having

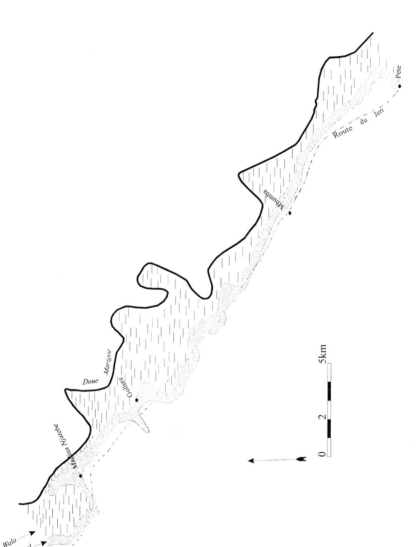

Fig. 5.2. Topography in the jeri and jejeengol. (In Déme 2003: 248)

a portfolio of lands that includes at least parts of each of the three topographic units. The leydi are regularly intersected and overlapped. The different production groups exchange subsistence goods. Little is known about the evolution of the leydi. But it may have a greater time depth. Park hypothesizes that the first form of organization may be related to the organization of the flood recession agriculture. Little is also known about the evolution of that land base system and its relations to other polities that were the first known historically: Takrur and Silla.

Historical Perspectives

First historical evidence came from Arab authors such as al Bakri (ninth century), al Idrissi (twelfth century), and Ibn Said (thirteenth century) (Cuoq 1975). From these authors we learn that Takrur was rival to Ghana. They also inform us that Takrur and Silla were led by Muslim kings who raided their non-Muslim neighbors for booty and human captives.

The MSV during the Trans-Saharan Trade

The trans-Saharan trade established a well-organized trade network between sub-Saharan Africa, the Mediterranean, and Arab worlds. Hasan (1967, 18) states that there were three principal trade routes: (1) by way of the Sinai Desert and Egypt, (2) across the Red Sea, and (3) through northwestern Africa, this third route being the least important. These routes played a major role in the emergence of West African polities such as Takrur, Ghana, and Mali. These polities rose to regional power in part because of their control of the trans-Saharan trade routes. That trade focused mostly on exchange between Mediterranean and Saharan products (salt, copper, beads, cloths, silk, and metalware such as swords) on one hand, and West African products (human cargo, gold, ivory, and kola) on the other (Bovill 1933, 1968; Farias 1974; Levtzion 1994). However, gold is the most important traded commodity. The dominant MSV polity that was involved in the trans-Saharan trade was Takrur. An analysis of Takrur during the trans-Saharan trade will shed light on the effects of the trans-Saharan contact on western Sudanese societies.

The earliest information about Takrur came from al-Bakri in 1068 (Cuoq 1975). He described two polities located along the Niger: Takrur and Silla. Historians generally agree that the section of the Niger being referred to was the Senegal River (Cuoq 1975; Levtzion and Hopkins 2000). Takrur is among the earliest historically known empires to be influenced by Islam (Cuoq 1975; Trimingham 1962, 1980a, 1980b). The Islamization process is linked to the monopolization of the trans-Saharan trade by Muslims, a monopoly so strong that trade and Islam became synonymous (Levtzion 1994, 209). Polities involved in the trans-Saharan trade gained more strength. This was the case for Silla, located along the Senegal River and considered by al Bakri as being as vast as the Ghana Empire (Cuoq 1975).

By the time of Al-Bakri, Islam had started to spread into the MSV. Triming-ham stated that the spread of Islam was mostly caused by Berber merchants rather than the Arabs (1962, 20). The introduction of camels (which provided more mobility) allowed a contact between the MSV and the Mediterranean civilization. This engendered a change in the MSV social and economic fab-ric. Takrur and Silla were converted to Islam by the ruler of Takrur (War Jabi), who in 1040 "embraced Islam, introduced among them Muslim religious law, and compelled them to observe it" (al Bakri in Levtzion and Hopkins 2000, 77). This type of Islamization was one of the two defined by Levtzion as being characteristic of early Islam in West Africa: Militant Islam and Compromising Islam. The first form refers to the conversion of the elite who then used force to convert its own people. It is exemplified by Takrur where "the Muslim king forced his subjects to accept Islam, he introduced the Islamic laws, propagated Islam among neighbors, and waged a war against the infidels" (Levtzion 1994, 208). Compromising Islam was a mixture of Islamic and African traditional beliefs. In the Compromising Islam, elites are converted through contact rather than violence, and in several cases pagan kings ruled over Muslims. This second form, often associated with the Africanization of Islam, is generally considered the most successful. Levtzion (1994, 208) links that success to the simplicity of Islam and its ability to adapt to new contexts.

By the twelfth century, Takrur was larger than Silla and was visited by trad-ers (Levtzion and Hopkins 2000, 107). Takrur was a marketplace for exchange between northern products (wool, copper, and beads) and Sahelian export (gold and slaves). The sultan of Takrur was a powerful ruler who had soldiers. He raided the land of the pagans (known as Lamlam) to enslave them. These raidings in the Lamlam, justified by the difference made by Islam between the Dhar al Islam and the Dar al Harb, engendered probably a change in warfare rules. Trimingham (1962) and R. S. Smith (1989) stated that in most of precolonial Africa, the winning entity superimposed its political authority on the losing polity without impairing it. The leadership of the losing pol-ity had to accept being under the control of the victor. In Senegambia, this political submission had a clause that stipulates the right for the leaders of the losing polity to be part of the advisory council and electoral committee in the winning entity (Barry 1985, 1988a; Boulègue 1987). This involvement of the pagans in the sociopolitical process was impossible during the time of Takrur. Because they were not Muslim, pagans could not be part of the socio-political process. They were not to be recognized. Instead, they were to be destroyed. What were the consequences of the slave raiding? How did it affect the settlement, the subsistence strategy, and the economic production south of the Senegal River? Arab authors are mute on this subject. These crucial questions are addressed below.

There are indications that the regional political domination of Takrur should not be viewed as total. Ibn Said stated that every time the sultan of Takrur became weak, the ruler of Barisa become independent (Levtzion and Hopkins 2002). This suggests that the Takrur was indeed an aggregate of several kingdoms under the domination of the rulers of Takrur. It is also an indication of the important role played by the trans-Saharan trade in shaping the regional political power. According to Ibn Said, towns in Takrur were frequently visited by travelers. Throughout the trans-Saharan trade era, the routes were shifting progressively eastward. That progressive eastward shift of trade route may have played a role in the rise of Barisa. Located east of Takrur (Cuoq 1975, 2), Barisa was among the Takrur towns that were the most visited by Moor/Berber/Arab traders. This importance of Barisa in the trans-Saharan trade may explain the rise in power of its ruler, who became independent every time the political regime of Takrur was weak (Levtzion and Hopkins 2002).

By the mid-thirteenth century, Takrur was a part of the Mali Empire and administrated by a non-Muslim dynasty (the Tondyon), an indication of the loss of political power by the Muslims. In the fifteenth century the Takrur came under the influence of two short-lived Fulani dynasties: the Lam-termes and the Lam-taga. From the fifteenth through the eighteenth centuries, the MSV was under the domination of a Fulani group known as the Denyankee (plural Denyankobe) who, coming from the east, liberated the MSV from the domination of the Jolof Empire (Barry 1988a; Boulègue 1987; Kane 1986; Wane 1969).

The Denyankobe were also known for their non-Muslim practices. The domination of the Muslims by non-Muslim leaders (starting with the Tondyon) suggests that Islam was probably losing its political power in the MSV from the mid-thirteenth century. Why? Is it an indication that the entire society was not Islamized? Or does it stress Levtzion's assertion that when traders become agriculturalists they have a tendency to go back to the traditional belief system? These questions show the complexity of the issues related to the development of Islam in the MSV. There are strong indications that by the fifteenth century, large sections of the population along the Senegal River were not Muslims (Chavane 1985, 83).

The MSV during the Atlantic Trade

The period of the Atlantic has been thoroughly studied by Barry (1985, 1988a), Boulègue (1987), and Kane (1986). Historians have been debating the importance and consequence of slavery in Senegambian societies as well as the number of slaves imported from Senegambia for over thirty years. One school (represented by Barry and Rodney) argues that the Atlantic trade engendered dramatic changes and a high volume of enslavement. Another school, led by Curtin, argues for a smaller number of slaves from Senegambia with less dramatic consequences.

The Atlantic trade started with the construction of European forts along the Atlantic coast. In 1445, the Portuguese arrived. The rivers provided the best opportunity for Portuguese penetration into the interior. In order to penetrate into the hinterland, they built outposts near the major rivers. Between 1445 and 1448, they tried unsuccessfully to build the Fort Arguin (Mauritania). In 1448, another attempt to build a fort at the mouth of the Senegal (Fort Çanaga) was foiled by a flood. W. R. Wood (1967, 43–44) stated that both forts were attempted with the aim of diverting the gold traffic toward the Atlantic coast. Besides gold, the Portuguese were also involved in trading ivory, leather, spices, and slaves (Barry 1988a). They made annual payments to the coastal kings and to those whose territories included the main rivers in exchange for free navigation along the rivers (Barry 1985, 1988a; Bathily 1989; Kane 1986; W. R. Wood 1967).

The Atlantic trade quickly reached the MSV because of the navigability in the Senegal River. Indeed, the Senegal and the Gambia were the main river channels used by coastal traders to reach the hinterland (Barry 1988a). In the MSV, the early decades of the Atlantic trade coincided with the domination of the region by Koli Tenguela, the founder of the Denyanke dynasty (Boulègue 1987; Kane 1986). In the second half of the sixteenth century, Koli defeated the Jolof Empire and contributed to the empire's destruction. The weakening of the empire, combined with the European presence on the coast, led to the independence of the kingdoms of Kajoor, Baol, Walo, Sine, and Salum after a series of wars against the Jolof (Barry 1988a; Boulègue 1987; Diouf 1990). The increased tempo of warfare among these kingdoms profited mostly the Denyanke regime, who, in the seventeenth century, after taking the area of the MSV once under Jolof control, took advantage of the dislocation of the empire by controlling a larger area: from Mali to the mouth of the Senegal River (including the entire MSV). This allowed the Denyanke dynasty to control both the trans-Saharan and the Atlantic trades.

If, until the 1650s, the Atlantic trade was mostly about gold, the nature of the trade changed when the quest for slaves became the dominant activity of the Portuguese along the Senegal. Barry quoted Lavanha, who stated in 1600 that slave trading represented the essential Portuguese activity (1988a, 76). Slaves were traded against North African horses, iron, fabric, alcohol, and firearms (Eltis and Jennings 1988). Contrary to the trans-Saharan trade, when the camel was the most used animal, the horse became the most used animal during the Atlantic trade. Horses allowed for greater mobility in the Sahel and the Savannah. They were also useful in warfare strategy, especially the cavalry.

By the seventeenth century, the Dutch, the French, the British, and other Europeans joined the Portuguese. In 1638, the French built a fort north of Bieurt, on Isle Bocos near the abortive Portuguese Fort Çanaga (Wood 1967, 47). The area was often flooded. Twenty years later, the French built a fort at Saint Louis (Fort Saint Louis). The French commander, Andre Brue, built other forts in the Upper Senegal (specifically in the Galam) in the early eighteenth century (e.g., Fort Saint Joseph, Fort Saint Pierre) (Bathily 1989, Thiaw 1999; Wood 1967). Other small outposts were built at Bakel and Matam a century later (Bathily 1989; Kane 1986; W. R. Wood 1967). There is evidence of construction of other minor outposts at Donguel and Podor, but little is known about these outposts (W. R. Wood 1967, 51).

Because of the presence of the Europeans on the coast, the Atlantic trade increasingly overwhelmed the caravan trade. According to Barker (1978, 3), "by the seventeen century the ocean had been transformed from a barrier into a highway and its coastal states from insignificance to position of power and influence." The major shift in the direction of the trade routes contributed to social, economical, and geopolitical changes in Senegambia: the rise of coastal states and the decline of hinterland polities (such as the Jolof Empire) (Boulègue 1987). Indeed, factors such as the intensification of slave raiding to satisfy the needs of the Europeans, the rivalry between the trans-Saharan trade network and the Atlantic trade network, and climate fluctuations (Becker 1985; Brooks 1993) intensified slave raiding and its corollaries: insecurity, increasing trade with the Europeans, and increasing arrival of prestige goods.

In that context of warfare, a new elite emerged: the crown slaves and the warriors (Barry 1985, 1988a; Boulègue 1987, Diouf 1990). In the MSV, the emergence of a new elite is evidenced by the domination of the political processes by the Sebbe (warriors) who formed the Denyanke regime (Barry 1988a; Bathily 1989; Kane 1986). However, the Denyanke regime was weakened by the intense rivalry between Samba Gelajo Jegi and Bubu Musa. That rivalry coincided with a heavy Berber pressure on the MSV to take a more active part in the Atlantic trade (specifically the trade in gum arabic) and to secure the annual taxes paid by the Fuuta to the Berbers (the *mudo horma*) (Kane 1974). That pressure was evidenced by the presence of armies of Berbers (mostly Krakna) and Moroccans (hormans) in the MSV where they took an active part in the rivalry among members of the Denyanke regime. The presence of these occupation armies was a way for the Berbers and the Moroccans to secure more mudo horma. Barry (1988a, 88) stated that the Berber pressure was caused by the increasing decline of the trans-Saharan trade amid the monopoly of the trade by the French since their construction of Fort Saint Louis in 1659.

The construction of the French fort resulted in the decline of the trans-Saharan trade. Slaves and cereals were now being traded to the French instead of to the Moors and the Berbers. Barry has linked the decline of the trans-Saharan trade to the crisis in the Berber society, which led to the Tubenaan Movement. Nasir Al Din, a Berber cleric, launched a religious war aimed at imposing the Islamic Law (Sharia), reforming the Berber society, and stopping the traffic of cereals and slaves toward Fort Saint Louis. In 1677, his movement succeeded in the MSV because of his populist message: critical of the tyranny of the leader, willing to stop the slave trade (Barry 1988a). He put Muslim clerics in power. However, his success was short-lived. The Tubenaan Movement failed after the death of its founder. France, which helped the old aristocracy to regain power, profited from the reprisals on Muslims by purchasing several enslaved Muslims. The failure of the Tubenaan Movement exacerbated military pressure from the Berber warriors (Trarza and Brakna). That pressure was enhanced by the increasing importance of gum arabic, which became the most important traded product in the MSV during the eighteenth and nineteenth centuries (Barry 1988a) and allowed the Berbers to take an active part in the Atlantic trade.

To lessen the Berber pressure and to eliminate his rival, Bubu Musa, the Denyanke Samba Gelajo Jegi—who came to power with the help of the Berbers—tried unsuccessfully in 1725 to establish a factory at Jowol in exchange for firearms. However, the Denyanke regime had been weakened by internal rivalry and by the slave raiding expeditions mounted by Moors along the Senegal River to satisfy both the trans-Saharan and the Atlantic trades. This Berber pressure was sometimes facilitated and encouraged by the Europeans. For instance, in order to satisfy the increasing demand for slaves in the Caribbean markets, the English governor Charles O'Hara incited the Berber Trarza to invade the MSV to enslave thousands between 1770 and 1775 (Kane 1974, 251).

The climate of insecurity, violence, and warfare rendered the Denyanke regime less and less popular while Islam, using a grassroots strategy, was becoming more and more popular. In 1776, Muslims led by Cernoo Suleyman Baal and Almamy Abdul Kadiri Kane ended up overthrowing the Denyanke regime during the Toroodo revolution. But Kane (1986) states that the Toroodo revolution was largely a reaction to the Berber pressure and influence on the MSV. The Toroodo revolution marks the rebirth of Islam in the MSV. It also marks the beginning of a new type of Islam: an Islam that disconnected itself from the Berbers and that was aimed at stopping the enslavement of the MSV Muslims, an Islam close to the aspirations of the people, and an Islamic theocracy seen as an alternative to the excess of the state. The Toroodo revolution had three main objectives. The first—to get rid of the Denyankobe regime—was easily achieved by the fact that the arrival of Muslims in power was also facilitated by the Islamic conversion of some members of the Denyanke regime who protected Muslims in their territories. The second goal was to stop the Berber pressure. This was achieved by a regional settlement reorganization. Almamy Abdul Kadiri Kane displaced the agro-pastoralists in the south (jejeengol) and put warrior villages on the high levees along the Senegal River (Schmitz 1986; Kane 1986). That regional settlement reorganization has given its form to the actual settlement specialization. Also, the Toroodo regime was involved in the internal Berber rivalry (war between the Brakna and the Trarza). In 1786, Almamy Abdul allied with Brakna to defeat the Trarza and its ally, the Kajoor. The MSV became independent from the Berbers and powerful enough to impose taxes on the Berbers and the Kajoor (Kane 1974, 251).

For the third objective, the Toroodo regime sought to stop the enslavement of Muslims. This opposition to the enslavement of Muslims made them more popular, since MSV habitants had always rejected the enslavement of their own people (Kane 1974, 250). The MSV became the center of the Muslim antislavery movement. Following its anti-Muslim enslavement policy, the Toroodo regime decided to help Muslims in other areas of Senegal fight the aristocracy (Barry 1988a; Diouf 1990). They launched wars against the warrior regime of Kajoor and against the Berbers. This may have played a role in decreasing the number of slaves taken in Senegambia during that period. The Toroodo regime ended during the second half of the nineteenth century with the colonization of the MSV by France.

Archaeological Perspectives

Previous research has focused on two of the three major elements of the topography: the floodplain (walo) (Bocoum 1986; Chavane 1985; Déme 1991; S. McIntosh et al. 1992; Thiam 1991; Thilmans and Ravise 1980) and the upper lands of the jeri (Bocoum 1986; Bocoum and S. McIntosh 2002; Chavane 1985; S. McIntosh and Bocoum 2000; Thilmans and Ravise 1980). Consequently, little is known about the occupation history and process of the third major unit, the jejeengol. This is unfortunate because the biggest villages and the highest number of villages are found today along the jejeengol, due in part to the role played by the strategic location of the jejeengol in the regional subsistence strategy, allowing agro-pastoralists to practice both flood-recession agriculture in the floodplain and rain-fed agriculture as well as pastoralism in the jeri (Boutillier 1962; Kane 1973, 1986; Schmitz 1986, 1994). Moreover, the jejeengol and the jeri are refuge zones during high floods. In some villages located in the jejeengol, there are specific areas (such as temporary settlement zones and cemeteries) reserved for population living in the floodplain. Apart from serving as a refuge for coping with climate crisis, the jejeengol can be used as a refuge zone during political uncertainty, as was the case with the regional reorganization of the settlement undertaken by Almamy Abdul Kadiri Kane to fight the Berber pressure. On the other hand, jeri is a preferred settlement location because it is close to the floodplain and is elevated enough to be above flood level.

Archaeological research in the jejeengol and jeri is therefore important in illuminating the regional settlement patterns and settlement chronology, the buffering mechanisms, the regional organization and interaction, and the regional subsistence strategies in the MSV. Arab-Islamic writers Al-Bakri, Al Idriss, and Ibn Said placed the location of Takrur and Silla along the river in the floodplain (Cuoq 1975; Levtzion and Hopkins 2002). Ibn Said divided the area into two zones: one occupied by sedentary people and the other by nomads. Ibn Said also stated that the south was occupied by non-Muslims. This shows a geographical differentiation based on religious practice between a northern Muslim (the floodplain) and a southern non-Muslim (south of the floodplain). This indicates that the non-Muslim kingdom of Lamlam frequently mentioned in the historical sources was probably located in the jejeengol or in the jeri.

Since northern Muslims raided the south for slaves, archaeological research south of the floodplain would help shed light on the consequences of these raids. An intensive survey of the jejeengol and the jeri was undertaken in 2000 (Déme 2003), consisting mostly of shovel testing of three 1-km² testing zones (located near Madina Njatchbe, Gollere, and Mbumba). These areas are over 15 m high and would have been preferred zones because of their elevation and proximity to the floodplain. In each shovel testing area, small shovel-tested pits were dug along each 100-m transect.

Besides the shovel testing, a pedestrian survey of an area 20 km long and 2.5 km wide was undertaken. The area chosen was located in a 12-m elevation zone. The area was surveyed by walking along transects spaced 50–100 m apart and perpendicular to the road. Sites found were plotted using a GPS, artifacts were collected, and data on the geography of the site were recorded. Also recorded were data on the nature of the surface deposits, house foundations, volume of artifacts, and features (slag, furnaces, house foundations, spindle whorls, prestige goods, etc). In order to illuminate the occupation chronology and dynamic in the jejeengol and in the vicinity of the jeri, an assessment of the preliminary chronology for the surveyed sites was needed. This is done by correlating the surface assemblages of the surveyed sites with the data from other aspects of the MSV Project (S. McIntosh et al. 1992).

The MSV during the Trans-Saharan Trade

This period from AD 990 to 1500 is significant because it marked the expansion of the trans-Saharan trade and the rise of Muslim entities such as Takrur and Silla. Data from the MSV show significant cultural and settlement pattern changes, evidence of trade, and contact with groups bringing copper, spinning technology, glass, and other exotics into the region. The ceramics found in the region between the tenth century and the late fourteenth century indicate that some of these influences flowed from Tegdaoust (S. McIntosh et al. 1992, 57). These ceramics, characterized by cordoned and channeled vessels and by oculi and lozenge motifs (Chavane 1985), appear to copy those at Tegdaoust, a trade entrepôt of Awdaghost in the eleventh century where Berbers are known to have been active as carriers of trade goods across the Sahara (S. McIntosh et al. 1992, 52).

In terms of regional organization, the settlement distribution is characterized by the drastic decrease of the number of sites. Also, all large and medium sites associated with stone circles are abandoned. This was also the case during the MSV Project where the site J1 was abandoned during the trans-Saharan trade period (Déme 1991). This is different from the floodplain where the settlement underwent a significant change from small to large clustered sites

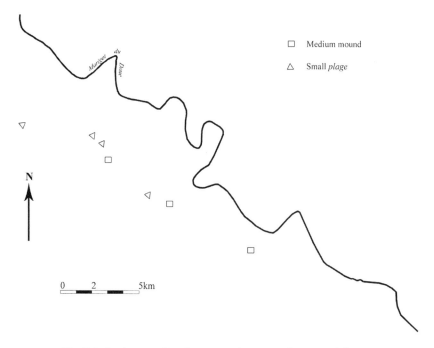

Fig. 5.3. Settlement distribution in the jeri and jejeengol during
the trans-Saharan trade period.

and is associated with evidence of trade and the presence of copper and exotic
goods probably from Tegdaoust (Fig. 5.3). These data, strengthened by historical records from Arab sources (Cuoq 1975; Levtzion and Hopkins 2000), are
indications that the trans-Saharan trade played a major role in the rise of the
floodplain polities.

Why the end of the use of stone circles? Surface material analysis alone
cannot help solve this issue. However, the survey shows that the use of stone
was probably part of the funerary ritual. The dead were buried on ash, accompanied by perforated ceramic vessel and food remains. This is a non-Islamic
burial practice. It shows that before the tenth century the area was occupied by
non-Muslims. Before the end of the tenth century, however, the trans-Saharan
trade stimulated the Islamization process in the valley, pushing leaders to convert to Islam and to raid non-Muslims (Cuoq 1975; Kane 1986; Levtzion and
Hopkins 2000; Trimingham 1962). Hence, the abandonment of the area concomitant to the arrival of Islam was probably due to the expansion of Islam in
the Middle Senegal Valley.

Arab records show the arrival of Islam in the MSV at the end of the first
millennium AD, whereas archaeological data show the abandonment of sites
occupied by non-Muslims. We don't know what happened to the non-Muslims.

However, oral traditions of the Serer (an ethnic group now occupying the center of Senegal and known for its traditional beliefs) claim that the Serer occupied the MSV before migrating south amid the rise of Islam (Bocoum 1986; Gravrand 1983; Kane 1986). Even though data show clearly an abandonment of non-Muslim sites with the arrival of Islam, more research is needed to make any strong relationship between the stone circle sites and the Serer. However, the version of the oral tradition concerning the Serer should be taken very seriously because of the linguistic affinities between the Serer and the Pulaar (the language of the Hal Pulaaren, who are the dominant ethno-linguistic group in the MSV) and because of the use of both food remains and perforated ceramic vessels in Serer funerary rituals (Becker and Martin 1982; A. Faye 1997; L. D. Faye 1983; Gravrand 1990; Touré 1999). According to the Serer, the perforation found in vessels is a passage from this world to that of the dead ancestors (the Jaanuw).

The MSV during the Atlantic Trade

This period is contemporaneous to European influence in the region. Archaeologically, it is characterized throughout the valley by a homogeneous ceramic originally referred to as *toucouleur sub actuelle* by Thilmans and Ravisé (1980). The archaeological research and analyses of the artifacts show that the ceramic complex of the Atlantic period is characterized by simpler forms and decorations than in the trans-Saharan trade period. Three general categories of rims were found: simple open, simple closed, and the everted (Guèye 1991, 1993, 1998). Also there is very little diversity in the decoration, characterized mostly by three types: slip, paint, and twine impressions. But there was a change in temper from grog (which was dominant during previous phases) to organic (dominant during the sub-actual phases) (Bocoum and S. McIntosh 2002; Guèye 1991; S. McIntosh et al. 1992). The texture is dominated by big to medium inclusions. Overall, the ceramic was poor in quality. Also, few other artifacts (metal, small finds, smoking pipes) were found. All these data suggest that the period from the sixteenth through the nineteenth century was associated with a lack of intense production in material culture. There was also a decrease in technology, technological innovation, and exchange. In addition, hamlets and villages proliferated with very shallow occupation debris, an indication of intense mobility due to the insecurity and sociopolitical instability of the period (Fig. 5.4).

Conclusion

We have tried a first comparative analysis of the impact of the trans-Saharan and the Atlantic trades in the Middle Senegal Valley. Data suggest that before

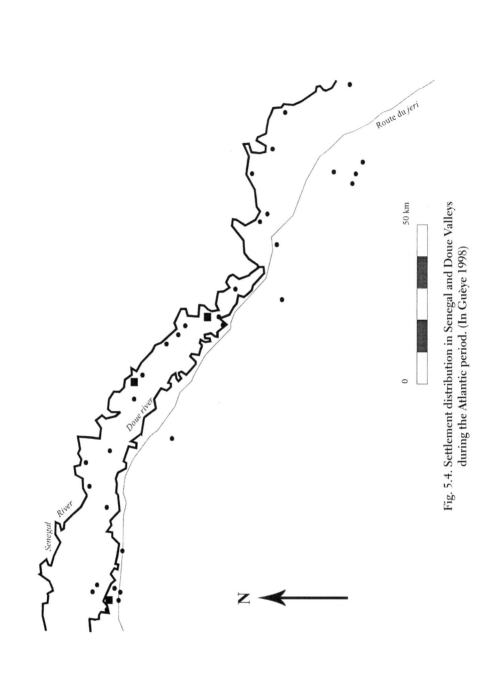

Fig. 5.4. Settlement distribution in Senegal and Doue Valleys during the Atlantic period. (In Guèye 1998)

the trans-Saharan trade, there were different entities in the floodplain, the jejeengol, and the jeri. A major shift occurred during the trans-Saharan trade: entities located in the floodplain took advantage of the trade by becoming more powerful. Arab sources describe that Muslim kingdoms of Takrur and Silla were located along the Senegal River. Also, archaeological evidence suggests contact with the north and a major shift in settlement organization: from small to clustered sites. While the floodplain underwent a major increase in hierarchization and in external contact, the jeri and the jejeengol experienced a decrease in occupation. This decrease in occupation is found in sites previously associated with the use of stone in the funerary rituals. Using oral and historical data, we have suggested that the stone circle users probably moved outside the area because of Islamization processes. This shows the double side of the trans-Saharan trade: improving certain areas and impoverishing others. This shows that the consequence of the trans-Saharan trade is limited to specific areas because it was based on an intersocietal dichotomy between the Muslim entities and non-Muslim entities. Indeed, Arab sources describe Muslim polities raiding non-Islamic entities. However, non-Muslims continued to live as equal and protected citizens within the Muslim-ruled polities of the Middle Senegal Valley.

This situation is very different from that of the trans-Atlantic period. Rather than inter-group hostility and raiding, intrasocietal hostility for enslavement prevailed. Barry (1985) describes how the elites were finding any pretext to sell members and citizens of their own polities (sometimes even their own relatives). Berber pressure, drought, and internal conflict among the elite worsened the situation. This engendered a culture of violence as evidence by the Cebbe song that glamorized blood: they refer to their drums of blood and their songs of blood (Kane 1970, 922). There was also an economy of violence based on the need for firearms and for imported products.

CHAPTER SIX

The Landscape and Society of Northern Yorubaland during the Era of the Atlantic Slave Trade

Aribidesi Usman

Most studies on the Atlantic slave trade have focused on the themes of the European and African traders on the coast and the nearby interior, demography of slaves, profits to the European and African merchants, impact of the slave trade, and African cultural transformations in the New World (Curtin 1969; Fage 1969; Inikori 1982; Lovejoy 2000; Thornton 1998). These studies have provided a regional understanding of the Atlantic slave trade. However, much is still unknown about the slave trade and the effect on the society in the African interior. Unlike societies that traded in slaves, we still know very little about the areas from which the people sold to the Europeans were taken. It is in the area of origins of the victims of the slave trade and slavery, usually located in the distant interior, that one may presume that the effects of the trade were most felt (van Dantzig 1982, 188). This chapter has two major objectives: to examine the early cultural background and condition in northern Yorubaland before the eighteenth century, and to demonstrate the nature and effect of warfare and enslavement in the area, especially after 1750. This chapter relies on a combination of oral, documentary, and archaeological sources.

The northern Yorubaland includes the Yoruba people in the present-day Kogi, Kwara, and Osun states of Nigeria. The area is situated in the woodland savanna belt of west-central Nigeria, characterized by tall grasses, scattered trees, shrubs, plains, and hills. It is a zone of great topographic and ecological diversity, with elevations ranging from 1,000 to 3,000 feet above sea level, with bare rock surfaces and boulder-strewn hills. This area has residual hills bordered by well-developed pediments and includes ridge and exfoliation domes (Buchanan and Pugh 1958). The region includes the Igbomina, Ibolo, and Ilorin, all in present-day Kwara state and part of Osun state. Other groups are the Okun-Yoruba or northeast Yoruba, comprising the Owe or Kabba, Ijumu, Bunu, Iyagba, and Oworo. They are located on the right bank of the Niger above and below the confluence and are presently in Kogi state. Some other Yoruba culture groups, such as the Ekiti, and non-Yoruba groups, such as Bariba, Nupe, Igala, Ebira, and the Kakanda, share borders with the northern Yoruba groups (Fig. 6.1).

There are several sociopolitical and/or kin units among the northern Yoruba groups, each with its own Yoruba dialect. None of the groups ever formed a single large political entity like Oyo, and there are slight variations in the social and political systems of the different groups. They lived mostly in "decentral-ized" societies succinctly referred to as "mini-states" (Obayemi 1976). The oral traditions indicate that the northern Yorubaland was settled at different times

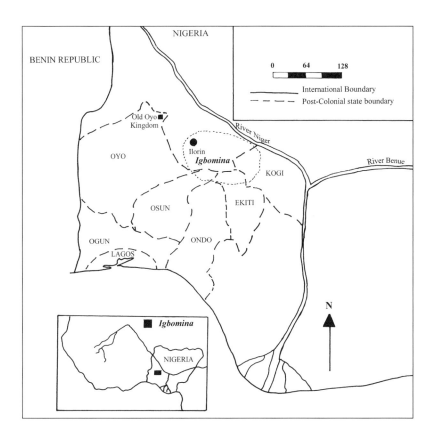

Fig. 6.1. Northern Yorubaland.

and from various places, such as Ile-Ife and Old Oyo. These traditions place the peopling of the area before the emergence of Old Oyo Empire in the sixteenth century. Today it is common to see a lot of cultural affinity between these groups and their Yoruba neighbors in Oyo, Ibadan, Ijebu, and Ijesha, especially with regard to the traditions of age-grades, births, salutations, and marriages (Metiboba 2003).

Early Cultural Background before 1700

The human occupation of northern Yorubaland goes back to at least the fourth century BC with ceramic-using Late Stone Age populations. By the ninth century AD, iron-using and iron-making communities had been established in the region. It was also possibly during this century that permanent settlements, such as Ife-Olukotun, were established in northern Yorubaland (Oyelaran 1998). Large-scale settlements with centralized political formations and occupational specializations (e.g., iron and bead manufacture) were established by at least the twelfth century in different parts of Igbomina (Aleru 1998; Obayemi 1972, 1976; Stevens 1978; Usman 2001).

The fifteenth century was a period of sociopolitical changes throughout Yorubaland. Economic and political pressures forced people to migrate from the central Yoruba area toward northern and eastern Yoruba, establishing new settlements, overrunning older communities, and warring with others in their need and desire for economic stability, political power, and territory (R. Smith 1969). The establishment of settlements in Igbomina, a consequence of this migration process, corresponds to the Intermediate Period of Ile-Ife (c a. 1400–1600). This was characterized by population movement, settlement aggregation, political centralization, factional competition, emergence of hegemonic ambitions, ideological innovations, and diffuse regional interaction networks (Ogundiran 2003, 59). At Ila and Ipo areas of Igbomina, the arrival of new immigrants resulted in considerable political transformation in the form of "centralized" polities with outlying subordinate villages and towns (Akpobasa 1994; Usman 2000, 2001).

The development of the Oyo empire in the sixteenth century brought momentous transformations in the sociopolitical history of Igbominaland. Agbaje-Williams (1983) suggests three major phases for the occupation of Old Oyo. The period from the ninth century to the thirteenth century is considered the earliest phase of the Oyo-Yoruba culture, followed by the intermediate cultural level in the thirteenth through fifteenth centuries, and then the later period from the sixteenth century through the early nineteenth century. The Old Oyo authority extended from the Niger River in the north to the Atlantic Ocean in the south. It covered much of Yorubaland including the Igbomina, Ibolo, parts of Osun, Egba, Egbado, Ketu, Porto Novo, and probably Ijebu (Fig. 6.2). Outside the Yoruba country, the Oyo empire extended

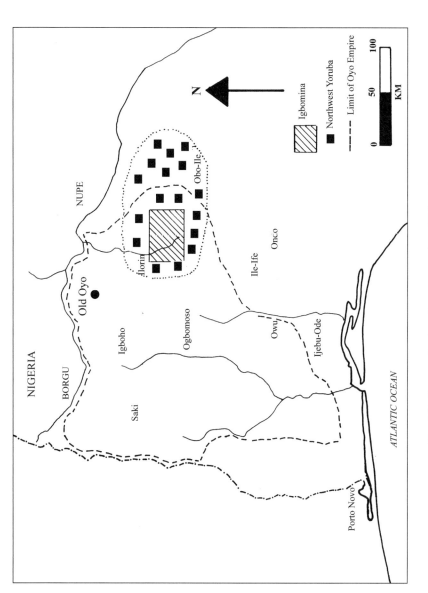

Fig. 6.2. Oyo empire (maximum extent) and Igbomina.

its power to the Ibariba (Borgu) and the Nupe on the Niger River as well as much of the Aja and Fon country of Dahomey, to the borders of the empires of Benin in the southeast and Asante in modern Ghana.

The rise of Oyo as a hegemonic power was not a smooth transition. In fact, the initial attempt by Oyo to expand its political territory during the fifteenth century met with stiff resistance from Borgu (Bariba) and Nupe and even led to the defeat of Oyo during the fifteenth century by Edegi of Nupe. The raiding of Yagba and Bunu was part of a general process of Nupe expansion into Yoruba territory south of the Niger River (Nadel 1942, 74). The Nupe apparently came to settle as well as to raid, for some northern Yoruba towns which later acknowledged the authority of Oyo claim to have been founded or raided by Nupe (Babayemi 1971, 77–79; Obayemi 1980). The sixteenth century was a turning point as Oyo displaced the Nupe and established northern Yoruba frontier communities through expansion and consolidation and the occupation of the conquered land by groups from Oyo-Yoruba-speaking areas. The displacement or partial absorption of the aboriginal inhabitants led to the early frictions between Yoruba and Nupe, which has been described as "frantic efforts by the Nupe to regain the territory" (Adepegba 1982, 105; Aleru 2001, 126). This scenario is likened to "action space" of warfare, a geographic model recently discussed by Ekanade and Aloba (1998, 23). Disputes over space may have occurred after years of peaceful coexistence in Igbomina between the Yoruba group and Nupe in the area.

The location of Oyo's northern frontier next to Nupe and Borgu exposed the fledgling polity to a great deal of political pressure. Such threats may have played a major role in the unification of the Igbomina under Oyo to promote common leadership and defense (Usman 2000). Oyo consequently established Igbaja, a military outpost in Igbomina, to check Nupe raids (Law 1977, 91). Oyo incorporated a number of Igbomina towns east and west of the Osin River, including Ajase-Ipo, Igbaja, Oro, Isanlu-Isin, and Omu-Aran (Elphinstone 1921, 12–15). The success of Oyo in most parts of Igbomina and Ibolo was based on the subjugation of all these kingdoms, but the local chiefs retained a good measure of their autonomy (Law 1974).

Sociopolitical changes occurred in some parts of Igbomina as a result of Oyo expansion into the area from the sixteenth century. In Ipo area, for example, beginning about 1600, there was a trend toward settlement aggregation and the emergence of large centers of unprecedented size such as Gbagede, Okegi, and Iyara that probably dominated satellite communities. The increasing influence of local elite, increasing military tension in the area created by the defeat of Nupe, and the corresponding need for security were important forces behind establishing large centers (Usman 2000). The new migrants, who often included specialized professionals like blacksmiths, iron smelters, woodcarvers, medicine men, and career warriors, could provide labor for public works (e.g., walls, ditches) and craft production, pay taxes, and be organized for defensive purposes.

Oyo Empire and the Atlantic Slave Trade

Social hierarchies and class consciousness were already well established in Yorubaland between the tenth and twelfth centuries. With the development of city-states, empires, chiefdoms, and kingdoms arose differential social status and the institutions that reinforced social hierarchies from the elitism/aristocrats to the servitude. Although interpolity wars yielded captives that were enslaved or reduced to other forms of servitude and made to serve their captors, slave trade did not become a major factor or interest in northern Yorubaland until the rise of Oyo and the involvement of the state in the Atlantic slave trade in the seventeenth and eighteenth centuries. Oyo tradition indicates the establishment of contact with the coast and the Europeans trading during the reign of Alafin Obalokun. A patriarch of Yoruba history, Reverend Samuel Johnson, records that during the reign of Obalokun, the Oyo began importing salt (*iyo*) whereas previously they had had only "rock salt" (*obu*) (Johnson 1921, 168). It is possible that the very name Obalokun, which appears to mean "king at the sea," is an oriki, a panegyric, commemorating this king's establishment of contact with the coast (Law 1977, 218). From his position in the Oyo king-list, Obalokun's reign belongs to the first half of the seventeenth century (Johnson 1921, 58). However, the Portuguese had traded along the coast to the south of the Oyo kingdom before the seventeenth century. They had made contact with Benin in 1486, and in the early sixteenth century they briefly established direct trade with the kingdom of Ijebu (Ryder 1965, 1969). Thus there would have been indirect contacts between Oyo and the Portuguese through the distribution of trade goods. For example, the jasper beads that Benin was selling to European traders in the seventeenth century (Fage 1962, 346) and the horses used for ceremonial purposes by the kings and chiefs of Benin (Egharevba 1987, 8) may have come from Oyo.

In the seventeenth century, Oyo began selling war captives on the coast. The majority of slaves acquired by Old Oyo were Dahomey, Borgu, Nupe, and Hausa, not Yoruba. This was a consequence of Oyo's imperial war of expansion and far-flung trading networks. Morton-Williams (1964, 27–28) has suggested that the eastern Yoruba—the Ijesa, Ekiti, and Yagba—formed the principal reservoir from which the Oyo raided communities for the European slave market. Another argument is that the Oyo invasions of Ijesa and Ekiti were unsuccessful and that the Oyo wars were directed against Oyo's northern and western non-Yoruba neighbors, who were regarded as aliens (Law 1977). Whatever the case, northern Yorubaland before the eighteenth century was not totally safe from raiding conducted by some Yoruba and non-Yoruba groups. The Ijesa were said to be harassing and abducting people in Igbomina in the early seventeenth century. The attacks became so frequent and deadly that the areas where they occurred were named after the event. For example, the name "Ipo" or "Po," an area in western Igbomina, was derived from the expression "*ibi ti Ijesa n po ni si,*" meaning "where the Ijesa harried people" (Afolayan 1998a; Usman

145

2001). The combined forces of the Olomu of Omu and the Olupo of Bagiddi subsequently defeated the Ijesa marauders. Also, Benin's attempts to penetrate Igbomina were resisted as a result of local cooperation by the communities (Afolayan 1998a; Akintoye 1971, 28).

Slaves were exchanged for horses from the Hausa and Nupe traders and for firearms from the Europeans (Lander 1830, 222). The Europeans also probably purchased some Oyo cloth for resale on the Gold Coast or in Brazil (Law 1977; Ojo 1967, 249). The Oyo obtained a variety of goods of European and American origin, such as cloth, earthenware, beads (especially coral), rum, tobacco, iron bars, and cowry shells, which served as currency (J. Adams 1966, 262, 264; Clapperton 1829, 14, 57; Dalzel 1967, 208–209; Lander and Lander 1832, 110, 180). As firearms came into use in Yorubaland in the nineteenth century, slaves became a major article for the purchase of ammunitions (Falola and Oguntomisin 2001, 5–6). Apart from the demand for slaves by Europeans at the coastal markets, many slaves were used locally to supplement free labor in agricultural production (Lander and Lander 1832, 105) and in areas of scarce technical skills such as tending cattle and horses, making rope, and hair barbing (Johnson 1921, 123, 193). Non-Yoruba slaves might be preferred in any of these cases, since there was less danger of successful escape with foreign slaves than with slaves whose homeland was nearby (Law 1977, 206).

By the 1780s, the Oyo empire had been weakened by internal political crisis and was now dominated by her northern neighbors, the Bariba and Nupe. In 1783, Oyo was defeated in a war with the Bariba kingdom of Kaiama (Duff 1920, 28; Hermon-Hodge 1929, 144–45), a revolt of Kaiama against its subordination to Oyo (Law 1977, 149). The Nupe intensified their raids in Igbomina at the beginning of the eighteenth century when the constitutional crisis in Oyo began to preoccupy the aristocracy and thus reduced Oyo's control in the north (Usman 2001). By 1789 Oyo was paying tribute to Nupe, and an Oyo attempt to throw off this subordination was decisively crushed in 1790 (Dalzel 1967, 229).

In the early nineteenth century, Afonja, the Aare-Ona-Kakanfo (military commander) of the Oyo empire who was based in Ilorin, revolted against the Oyo, having failed in his bid for the Alafin throne. In 1817, he recruited the Hausa and other slaves of northern origin living in Oyo and created a formidable force known as Jamma (congregation of the faithful). When Clapperton arrived at Oyo in 1826, the Alaafin told him that the rebel slaves "had joined the fellatahs [Fulani], put to death the old, and sold the young" (Clapperton 1829, 68). The Fulani who turned against Afonja and eliminated him ca. 1823–24 now emerged as the controllers of Ilorin, and Ilorin became an outpost of the Sokoto Caliphate (Ajayi and Akintoye 1980, 283). By 1837 military pressure from the Fulani had caused the Oyo Empire to collapse. Dislocations caused by the collapse of the Oyo empire, the ambition of displaced people led by their more warlike chiefs to find new homes and new opportunities, provoked a series of wars in Yorubaland with devastating consequences (Ajayi and Akintoye 1980). The collapse of the Oyo empire had resulted in a struggle for leadership and control of Yorubaland among the successor states of Ibadan, Ijaye, and Ilorin. The non-Yoruba groups, taking advantage of their own good political fortune and the crisis in Yorubaland, began raiding Yorubaland for captives during the late eighteenth century.

Wars and Slave Raiding in the Eighteenth and Nineteenth Centuries

In the oral traditions of Igbomina, the various wars of the eighteenth and nineteenth centuries have been collectively referred to as *agannigan*. This describes an uncoordinated or poorly organized war with no concrete objective in mind. Surprise attacks, kidnappings, ambushes, theft, and slave raiding characterized these wars. This area, which had been protected by Oyo from the ravages of the Nupe, now became its potential victim. The Nupe raids took place under three notable Nupe kings: Etsu Jubrilu (1744–59), Majiya I (1769–80), and Mu'azu (1780–95) (Elphinstone 1921, 30). Affected by these wars are the Igbomina and Ibolo communities. Most settlements in the areas were destroyed, and some of the inhabitants were carried into slavery. The Oba-Isin, Isanlu, Oke Aba, Oke Ode, Oro Ago, Orangun's town of Yara, Olusin's town of Igbole, the villages of Oniwo, Odo Eku, Ijara, Kanko (Oro), and Iji all suffered this fate (Biscoe 1912). In about 1790, Gbagede, the political center of Olupo, was attacked. Olupo Dalla II, the ruler of the settlement, was killed, and the town was destroyed while a greater percentage of its inhabitants were carried off and enslaved (Dupigny 1921; Elphinstone 1921, 30).

Slaves were an important product of Ilorin's early expansionist wars started by Afonja. Johnson indicated that Afonja captured various towns and "resettled them around Ilorin.... The able-bodied men of these dislocated towns he enrolled among his soldiers, and several women and children he sold into slavery, in order to have wherewith to maintain and supply arms to his war boys" (Johnson 1921, 200). Under the Fulani rule, the expansionist wars against the Igbomina, northern Ekiti, and other groups in northern Yorubaland continued. With their cavalry, the Fulani from 1840 invaded and dominated different parts of the region. In the more open countries of Igbomina and northern Ekiti, the Ilorin cavalry forces inflicted heavy destruction on Ajasepo, Eruku, Omu-Aran, and Ekiti towns of Osi and Obo (O'Hear 1997). Several Igbomina rulers, such as Olupo and Orangun, who were former allies or sympathetic to Oyo, were taken as prisoners to Ilorin, but later allowed to return home (Elphinstone 1921, 16). In many of these campaigns, large numbers of the population were taken away and sold as slaves (Whitely 1916, 10). Daniel May in 1858, while visiting Ejeba, a Yagba town under Nupe control, reported an Ilorin raid on a town nearby in which people were "attacked and carried off.... This is the occupation...of the army from Ilorin here, as of Ibadan and Nupe...on a marauding and slave-hunting expedition" (May 1860, 226; O'Hear 1997, 23).

The Nupe, under Malam Dendo, the Fulani jihadist, sacked the northeastern parts of Yorubaland (e.g., Oworo, Bunu, Iyagba, Owe, and Ijumu) between 1830 and 1850 and took captives who were sold into slavery. Between 1860 and 1870, the Nupe-Fulani under the Emir Masaba invaded communities in the Kabba, Oworo, Akoko, Kurukuru, and Igbiras areas (Dada 1985, 5; Elphinstone 1921, 19; Hermon-Hodge 1929, 37). It was during the reign of Umaru Majigi (1873–82) that most parts of Ijumuland, especially Ekinrin Adde, Iyamoye, Iffe, Egbede-Egga, Ikoyi, and Ayere, were brought under Nupe hegemony (Akinwumi 2003, 26).

The Ibadan, often in competition with the Ilorin for control of the area, emerged as the most powerful state in Yorubaland and by 1875 it was master of most of the communities in this northern part of Yorubaland (Ajayi and Akintoye 1980, 290). In the late 1840s, the Ibadan armies moved northeast through the Ekiti area, conquered most of the Igbomina towns north, south, and west, and stationed their *Ajele* (local warlord and tax collector) (Akintoye 1971, 58–59; Elphinstone 1921, 17–18). All subordinate towns were also mandated to support the Ibadan military expeditions with food, money, and warriors from time to time. A nineteenth-century observer wrote that "all the Efon, Ijesa, and Akoko territories had now become a field for slave hunting for any number of men who could bind themselves together for an expedition" (Johnson 1921, 323).

Throughout the 1850s and 1860s, northern Yoruba towns were laid waste by one army or another. Advancing Ibadan forces destroyed villages and towns, including Offa, Ila, Ora, Ilofa, and Omu-Aran (Pemberton and Afolayan 1996, 14). However, the oppressive actions of some of the Ibadan officials soon led to revolt among the subjugated towns. After killing and expelling the Ibadan officials among them, the Ekiti, Ijesa, Akoko, and Igbomina allied into a confederacy, the Ekitiparapo, to fight for their independence (Ajayi and Akintoye 1980, 291). The Kiriji war started in 1878, and the Igbomina-Ekitiparapo military alliance could not stop the Ibadan forces, even with Ilorin support. Faced with mounting pressures on all sides, Ibadan was compelled to recognize the independence of the members of the Ekitiparapo in a treaty of 1886.

It appears that from the late eighteenth century, slave raiding, both for export and for domestic use, was a major preoccupation of the Nupe, Ibadan, and Fulani (Ilorin) in northern Yorubaland and probably accounted for the frequent raids in the region. The British explorer Hugh Clapperton, on his visit in 1826 to the war camp of a Nupe king, Majiya II, made the following remark: "He has been the ruin of his country through his natural ambition....Through him the greatest part of the industrious population...have either been killed, sold as slaves or fled from their native country" (Clapperton 1829, 128). The fact that these raids were "smash and grab" operations, with little consideration for long-term exploitation, meant that the intention was to take captives.

The Nupe had no intention of permanently controlling the conquered people. The primary goal was to exploit both the human and material resources that were in abundance in the region to prosecute wars. According to Afolayan (1998b, 408), Bishop Tugwell gave an account of the ruler of the Okun-Yoruba town of Ayere in 1894:

> Four years ago, on coming to the throne, the Nupe came and took away three hundred of his people. He told us that oppression has been the rule here for forty years, that first the Nupe only demanded cowries, then farm produce, and that now they will have slaves as well. As all the slaves are gone as tribute, they have to give their own children, and many after giving their children and wives for tribute have left the town and not come back.

The fact that slave acquisition and trading were still prevalent in Yorubaland despite the decline in the Atlantic slave trade in the late nineteenth century meant that slaves captured at this time were not only to satisfy coastal demands. First, as Afolayan put it, "slaves had come to possess for the ambitious and enterprising individual both economic and political values, as they [slaves] had for centuries possessed for Yoruba kings" (Afolayan 1998b, 410). Second, the expansion of legitimate trade in southern Yorubaland created a need for labor which sustained or even increased the demand for slaves. Loyalty, trustworthiness, and martial ability became a more decisive factor in appointment and promotion than ethnic or family background (Afolayan 1998b, 413). Slaves were appointed as resident officials of imperial states of Ibadan and Ilorin, where they were known as Ajele, Ajia, or Ojoo (Afolayan 1998b, 414). Slaves with special training in animal husbandry provided fodder for horses both at home and on the war front (Akintoye 1971). Slaves also served as gatekeepers, toll collectors, potters, escorts to travelers, and armed guards to traders (Johnson 1921, 351). Slaves with special skills were imported to practice their arts. The rulers of Ilorin imported slaves who were experts at bead making from Oyo and Dahomey countries (Pearre 1963, 143–44). The Nupe ruler Etsu Masaba (1859–73) also brought in weavers from the Okun-Yoruba town of Isanlu as slaves to Bida where they were resettled as *Konusi*, king's slaves (Afolayan 1998b, 413).

The chiefs and people of Ilorin acquired many slaves through trade, tribute, and capture in wars. In some cases, slaves were purchased and manumitted. Samuel Johnson gave an account of a man called Esu (or Esubiyi, later the ruler of Aiyede) "who had been a slave at Ilorin...was redeemed by one Laleye for 12 heads of cowries; the latter also redeemed one Oni for 25 heads of cowries and gave her to him to wife" (1921, 308). By 1850 Ilorin under the Fulani had become a major slave trading center in northern Yorubaland. Ann O'Hear has carried out an extensive study of the Ilorin involvement in slave trading. The slaves sold at Ilorin market were provided by war chiefs and other individuals in Ilorin, as well as through northern sources of Kano, Abuja, and Nupe (O'Hear 1997). The buyers were drawn from Ilorin as well as from the south (e.g., Ibadan, Ijebu Ode, and Abeokuta). Egba slave traders appear to have been prominent in the Ilorin market (Awe 1973). Slaves were sold in Ilorin in the Gambari (Hausa) Market and in Emir's Market located outside the palace. As quoted by O'Hear (1997), G. B. Haddon-Smith, political officer attached to Governor Carter's peace mission, in 1893 described the Gambari Market:

> There were a number of slaves in two sheds, about 30 altogether, comprising old men, old women, middle-aged men and women, and children. Their clothes were rather scanty, and they did not appear to suffer from overwashing; otherwise they appear alright. They evidently were well fed and did not seem to mind their position with the exception of one woman who had a very sad expression. Behind the slaves sat the dealers, who appeared to be fairly well-to-do Mohammedans.

Impacts of Wars and Raiding

The wars that the slave trade generated and steadily intensified caused a great deal of misery and bloodshed and altered the landscape of northern Yorubaland. Whole villages and towns were burned down, and as many people were killed as were caught. Populations were displaced or relocated, and traditional economic and cultural activities were impeded. As one travels around the villages and towns in northern Yorubaland today, one finds relics of abandoned habitations, crafts, and defensive works, important reminders of the chaos and devastation of the last two centuries.

Provision of Defense

The oral-ethnohistoric information on military aggressions in Igbomina has been corroborated by surface relics and artifacts from former settlement sites. Military action in the region was more in terms of defensive system. Since offensive activities required more resources and were riskier than defense, people spent more energy providing defense than offense (LeBlanc 1999). The most important response to raiding, warfare, or military threat in Igbomina was the construction of fortifications. A number of settlements were surrounded by earthen ramparts, mud walls, ditches, or stone barriers. Gbagede, Iyara, and Ila-Yara sites in western Igbomina are characterized by massive ramparts and mud walls with deep, continuous ditches, probably dating from the sixteenth or early seventeenth century (Akpobasa 1994; Usman 2001) (Fig. 6.3). Gbagede wall is about 3.4 km in circumference with three main entry gates, probably with sentry, and two or three minor entrances. The Iyara wall is about 2.8 km

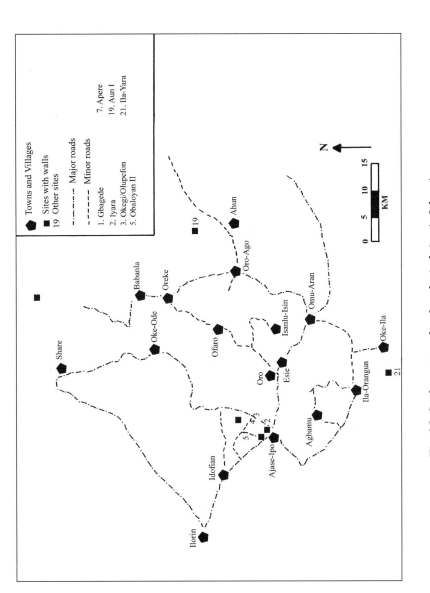

Fig. 6.3. Settlements and archaeological sites in Igbomina.

in circumference with two main entrances and a continuous ditch about 1.3 m deep located outside the wall. Such a deep ditch provided the soil material for the construction of the rampart wall.

These massive walls had at least two purposes: defense mechanism from outside aggression and sociopolitical marker, presenting its valuable resident political elites to outsiders. The walls were erected to ward off or minimize the risk of constant attacks. Rampart walls and ditches in this part of Igbomina indicate a prevailing condition of hostility. Also, the construction of walls following the large-scale immigration of Oyo-Yoruba into Igbominaland may represent internal sociopolitical changes in the society, when warrior leaders were transforming settlements previously organized in terms of a cluster of lineages headed by a council of elders. Both Gbagede and Ila-Iyara settlements were former "capital" or head towns where the royal elites resided (Pemberton and Afolayan 1996; Elphinstone 1921, 5–14; Hermon-Hodge 1929, 37; Temple 1965), and it is not surprising that these centers had the largest and most extensive defensive systems.

In the northeastern Igbomina, rock piles and boulders were important defensive mechanisms. Along edges and entrances to hilltop sites in this area were stone piles and boulders arranged to considerable heights and stretching sometimes up to 1 km or more (Usman 2003). Stones of various sizes were used to form most embankments, but in some cases mud walls were combined with stones as a barrier against intruders (Fig. 6.4). The construction of these walls accompanied the occupation of hilltop sites in this area from the late eighteenth century. The rock piles were meant to slow down an enemy advance, especially cavalry soldiers. In 1854, W. H. Clarke recognized similar stone piles among the Igbeti in northwest Yorubaland and described them as "innumerable small rocks scattered in profusion and confusion.... [This] was the stratagem of mode of warfare resorted to when the Igbeti were attacked by Ilorin" (Clarke 1972, 76).

Settlements Abandonment

In response to war or the threat of war, many people abandoned their settlements and relocated to more fortified sites in the area or retreated from the grassland into the neighboring forest belt to join others at existing settlements. From local traditions, we know that some of the survivors of Nupe raids at Okegi, Apere, and Gbagede either founded or settled at Ago, Eggi-Oyopo, and Ajase-Ipo. The Orangun settlement of Ila emerged out of the remains of Yara, while out of the ruins of Kanko (Oro) emerged the agglomeration of nine villages known as Ekumesan Oro.

Some communities moved to join others at existing settlements. Safety in numbers is undoubtedly a benefit of aggregation, as larger residences are not as open to raiding as are smaller, dispersed settlements. The present Oko town

Fig. 6.4. Remains of a stone embankment.

in Igbomina was an aggregation of seven communities representing Odo-Oko, Iwoye, Idemorun, Inisan, Akowaro, Odo-aba, and Irapa. These communities lived separately before the eighteenth century and decided to come together because of the belief that aggregated settlements provide stronger opposition against external invasion.[1] Also, Oke-Ode, a northeastern Igbomina town located on a hill, became a large refugee center for people who were displaced by the Ibadan army between 1850 and 1860. Babanla in the Ilere area also became an important center for war refugees who were attracted by the military prowess and popularity of its founder, Abogunrin.[2] Typically such amalgamation for defense did not result in any notable increase in political centralization. Instead, it often seems to have resulted in increased factional conflicts that revolved around the concern for ensuring sectional representation in the political affairs of the reconstituted towns and polities (Obayemi 1976, 208).

The northern Igbomina towns of Ofaro, Owa, Aafin, Alaabe, Ikosin, Oke-Oyan, Idera, Obirin, Idoba, Okegbo, Oreke, and Agunjin were abandoned, sometimes on more than one occasion. The people resorted to moving their towns into rugged hills, situated in a naturally fortified position, and building houses on and between rock outcrops. This location facilitated a commanding view of approaching invaders and restricted enemies' advance. Consequently, these areas served as temporary refuge centers for people from Ekan, Omuaran, and Ilofa. Similar situations occurred in the Yagba and Ijumu in northeast Yoruba where the Nupe destroyed settlements and forced the inhabitants to flee their homes and seek refuge on hills and mountains to their total discomfort. Some Yagba people were separated from their family and clans and taken to Lafiagi/Pategi (Nupe capital) (Omoniyi 2003, 17).

Although the hill sites had been chosen for defense, the inhabitants were soon faced with enormous challenges and difficulties. Gleave (1963, 349) identified some of these problems as shortage of farmland, long treks to and from the fields, isolation with its limiting effect on trading and economic development, congestion in the hilltop settlements, and limited physical expansion due to the rocky nature and steep slopes of the available land. Again, some of these hill settlements were taken and destroyed in spite of their natural defenses. For example, Iwawun and Erin in western Yorubaland were situated on high hills surrounded by craggy rocks, while the town wall was built at the foot of the hill (Gleave 1963; Johnson 1921, 347). During the Ijaye war (1860–65), both towns were captured by the Ibadan forces and destroyed in spite of their defensive positions. Several of these communities remained on hilltops until a combination of factors such as those described above, and the increased security in the area following European colonial penetration, provided stimulus for relocation to more accessible areas, a process that continued up to the early twentieth century.

The wars produced enormous demographic changes in Yorubaland. Before the colonial period, the open grassland of northern Yorubaland was the center of the greatest concentration of the Yoruba (Ajayi and Akintoye 1980). In the nineteenth century this was reversed in favor of the forests and the edges of the forest to the south. Johnson indicated that, before the wars of the nineteenth century, most of the Yoruba people lived in the towns of the plain, "the towns in the forest lands being small and unimportant, except for the town of Owu" (Johnson 1921, 93). Clapperton, in his journal, further demonstrated that Kishi, Igboho, Old Oyo, and Ilorin had populations of more than 20,000 people, unlike Badagry and Shaki in the south (Clapperton 1829; Ojo 1967, 106). Archaeological data from Igbomina appear to corroborate this and contrast the widely held views that the societies of northern Yoruba had always been small (Usman 2001).

Economic Impact

It may be correct to say that the economic activities in northern Yoruba were disrupted by wars and the slave trade of the eighteenth and nineteenth centuries. Because of the high insecurity during the period, movements of people were restricted and the warfare created a serious labor shortage that hampered agricultural development and technological production. The concentration of the population within a restricted boundary for agricultural practice could result in rapid deforestation of the immediate vicinities (Ekanade and Aloba 1998, 28). Other economic subsistence activities were also affected by the wars. Until the beginning of the twentieth century, the crafts of the iron smelter, the brass caster, and the smith were familiar in Yorubaland. There were, for example, 143 blacksmiths on the Isero Hill, a reputed manufacturing center of weaponry, before the inhabitants were driven away by the Ibadan army in the early nineteenth century (Johnson 1921, 119–20).

The status of ironworking in northern Yoruba during the wars and slave trade of the eighteenth and nineteenth centuries is not very clear. At most of the hilltop sites in Igbomina (e.g., Owa-Orioke, Aun I, Idoba, Oke-Oyan, and Ofaro I), smelting and smithing debris was located near the hills and mountains, but no strong evidence suggests that these were accumulated during the nineteenth-century wars. However, the combined effect of slave raiding and the concentration of population on hilltops probably resulted in increased ironworking activities. The availability of suitable raw material for ironworking in the area was a plus, but iron was intimately connected to other activities such as farming, hunting, and warfare. With increased production, limited exchange of iron goods between communities located in close proximity may have continued throughout the period.

Iron points are common in archaeological excavations in Igbomina. They have been found at sites from the fourteenth century and later (e.g., Gbagede, Obaloyan, Olupefon, Ila-Yara, Apere, Oke-Oyan) and occasionally with present-day hunters in Yoruba villages. Usually, the arrow (*ofa*) carried an iron point that was attached to a shaft by a long tang (Fig. 6.5). Some oral traditions in Igbomina also described Oro Ago as a major producer of fine bows and

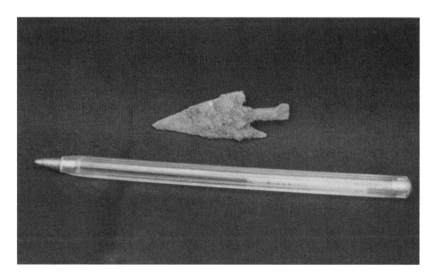

Fig. 6.5. Iron arrowpoint.

arrows that were sought by communities far and wide. Such exchange relations have produced some historical remembrance, as in the naming of settlements after a trade item. For example, the Ofaro village in northern Igbomina derived its name from the *Ofa Oro,* bow and arrow, that its inhabitants procured from Oro Ago.[3] The introduction of firearms into Yorubaland on a scale sufficient to affect the conduct of both war and politics took place between the 1820s and 1840s (R. Smith 1973). However, the availability of firearms to the soldiers and their use in wars during the nineteenth century may be limited. Firearms were probably only regularly possessed by war commanders and a few lieutenants. Most soldiers relied mostly on locally manufactured swords, spears, bows and arrows, clubs, and charms. The continuation of ironworking in Igbomina during the wars was probably aimed at producing defensive, if not offensive, weapons.

The impact of slave raiding and wars on local ceramic exchange in northern Yorubaland is not yet clear, and the imported wares (porcelain) in excavations appears to be too small to have had any significant impact on local ceramic production and consumption. The pre-eighteenth-century middens excavated at Igbomina sites contain dense concentration of pottery (Usman 2000, 2001). The excavated ceramic assemblages from three eighteenth- and nineteenth-century sites (Ofaro II, Oke-Oyan, and Ago) show a large proportion of maize cob roulette decoration, while most of the early decorative types, except twisted string roulette, were absent (Usman 2001) (Table 6.1). Maize cob roulette has the archaeological advantage of being a chronological indicator, since maize was introduced relatively recently from the New World in the sixteenth century (Stanton and Willet 1963; Willet 1962). Among the northern Yoruba, the introduction of maize and its use as decorative motif by potters was much later than the sixteenth century. Unlike pottery made before the eighteenth century, there is a small variety of decorative types in the pottery assemblages from excavations. Since pottery vessels were in the later period infrequently traded over a far distance, it appears that potters probably paid less attention to decoration and produced more vessels that could meet local demand.

Conclusion

Two major historical events occurred and affected northern Yorubaland in the past: the rise of the Oyo empire, and the eighteenth- and nineteenth-century wars and slave trade. These events generated different consequences. The settlement data obtained from Igbomina show large settlement sites with enclosed walls. These settlements (e.g., Gbagede, Iyara, and Ila-Yara) indicate large populations, serving as highly visible indicators of chiefly power. The appearance of large sites may relate to complex demographic, economic, and political developments that accompanied the rise of Oyo. This suggests that at least in part of northern Yorubaland, a well-coordinated and organized

Table 6.1. Comparison of Decorated Pottery Types between Pre-Eighteenth-Century and Later Sites in Igbomina

	Gbagede* (Ipo)	Ila-Yara* (Ila)	Okegi* (Ipo)	Ikorun* (Ilere)	Oke Oyan** (Ilere)	Ago** (Ipo)	Ofaro II** (Ilere)
Decorative types							
Twisted string roulette	421	3132	61	425	168	105	68
Maize cob roulette	?	–	?	–	212	80	198
Groove	25	433	58	14	??	61	??
Incision	–	37	10	16	20	29	8
Circle stylus	–	8	85	–	–	–	–
Painted	–	58	–	–	–	–	4
Wiping (striation)	–	–	–	1524	59	–	34
Snail shell	–	–	619	–	–	1	–
Carved roulette	8	51	70	1	–	–	–
Punctation	15	31	1	2	–	3	–
Scallops	33	9	–	–	–	–	–
Broom/brush	308	–	–	–	7	–	–

* Sites from before the eighteenth century.

** Sites from the eighteenth century or later.

? Counted as twisted string roulette in Usman 2001.

?? Counted as groove in Usman 2001.

sociopolitical structure had developed by the seventeenth century. The internal political growth also meant that there was relative peace in the region at least up to 1750.

One of the major challenges in the examination of Yoruba warfare of the eighteenth and nineteenth centuries in northern Yorubaland is how to distinguish between those wars that were fought for political purposes and those that were solely motivated by the slave trade. While recognizing the political (i.e., expansionist or imperialist) dimension of the nineteenth-century wars in Yorubaland, Falola and Oguntomisin (2001) have provided other possible reasons for the wars: the pursuit of antagonistic policies by states, military assistance given to one state by another, economic or commercial interests (e.g., struggle for markets, trade routes, etc.), and ambitions for war booty and honors. Political war could lead to enslavement and slave trading, since slaves were needed to procure weapons (e.g., horses, firearms). Lovejoy (2000, 147) has suggested that, while the struggle for political supremacy was paramount in the minds of the warlords, the political motive also included enslavement as an effective weapon against rivals and in obtaining human resources that could be exploited domestically or sold on the market. But even if the primary objective of these wars had been political (i.e., to extend and establish authority), no evidence suggests that any of the wars resulted in an effective political establishment over the conquered. Rather, the result was total destruction, plundering, or economic exploitation. The continued importance of the Atlantic slave trade and slavery helped extend the wars and affected both the objectives and direction of the wars. The institution of slavery took new shapes and assumed new dimensions with the advent of agricultural exports in the second half of the nineteenth century. The wars and the economic needs of the states ensured the large-scale diversion of war captives, hitherto meant for export, to internal use (Afolayan 1998b).

The issue raised above also relates to how we should look at the consequences or the devastations of the wars. Should we call relics of an eighteenth- or nineteenth-century abandoned settlement a consequence of wars fought to capture slaves or wars waged for political reason? It is difficult to clearly distinguish the two, since slave trade, both domestic and foreign, persisted during the wars. However, it is important to note that slave raiding associated with Nupe, Fulani, or Ibadan military aggressions did not cause all settlements to be abandoned. There have been cases in Igbomina of settlement abandonment as a result of disputes within or between villages, flooding, or simply a desire to live closer to friendly neighbors.

I have restricted this chapter to a limited area of northern Yorubaland and period because of scarcity of data. More research will be needed to fully understand the situation in northern Yorubaland during the Atlantic slave trade and the effects on the societies. The Ibadan and Nupe military expeditions and slave trade in northern Yorubaland came to an end in 1886 and 1897, respectively, but the bitter memory of the war period remains. Without a doubt, the often-mentioned effects of the slave trade, such as depopulation, disruption of economic and cultural activities, and general insecurity, as well as the strategies devised by the people to contain the problems, abound in northern Yorubaland.

Notes

1. Interview conducted with the ruler of Oko, Joseph Abolarin Jolayemi-Ewedunoye I, at Oko town in Igbomina on April 12, 1991. Others present were Chief Dada Okinbaloye, the Olowa; Chief Ajiboye, the Esa; Chief Oderinde, the Aro; and Chief Adewumi, the Asanlu.

2. An interview with the ruler of Babanla, Aliu Oladimeji Arojojoye II, on December 10, 1988, at Babanla town in Ilere area of Igbomina. Other people present were Chief A. Abolarin, the Esinkin; and Salami Majeobaje, the Odofin regent.

3. An interview with the ruler of Owode Ofaro, Late Oyedunmola, on November 22, 1988, at Owode Ofaro town in Ilere area of Igbomina. Others in attendance were Chief Salami Elegbe, Suberu Ajide (captain of guard), Salau Olore, and Jide Sonibare.

CHAPTER SEVEN

The Collapse of Coastal City-States of East Africa

Chapurukha M. Kusimba

In assessing the collapse of African states and complex societies,
archaeologists and historians have traditionally invoked environmental deterioration, endemic warfare, weak political superstructures, revolts and conquest
by peripheral nonstate societies, harsh and monotonous climates, epidemic
diseases, and foreign conquest to explain the collapse of precolonial African
states (e.g., Connah 2001; S. McIntosh 1999a). Several of these factors contributed to the collapse of many states worldwide (e.g., Tainter 1988; Yoffee
and Cowgill 1988), but how they combined to influence the collapse of complex societies in East Africa between the sixteenth and nineteenth centuries
is not clear. In this chapter, I will address two questions: (1) How and under
what conditions did city-states and polities of coastal East Africa develop and
maintain complex cultural and political systems? (2) How and under what
circumstances did they collapse? It will be demonstrated that, although the
coastal polities developed in the context of the Afrasian economic growth,[1] the
collapse of these polities was a direct result of the Portuguese colonial interests
in the region. Overall, our goal is to understand the impact of the modern
European political and economic expansion on the trajectories of social complexity in coastal East Africa after the fifteenth century. But this is a task that
involves an appreciation of how the coastal societies evolved in the five hundred years before their encounters with modern European expansion.

For a long time, it was held that the rise of city-states, towns, and states in
eastern and southern Africa was the work of Arab and Persian mariners (Bent
1892; Kirkman 1964). Trade and migration were believed to be the prime
movers of social, political, and economic transformations in Africa. However,
recent studies show that early residents of the coastal city-state and urban

polities were mostly indigenous peoples originating from diverse ethnic groups who had settled along the coast from ca. 100 BC (Abungu 1998; J. Allen 1993; Chami 1994, 1998; C. Kusimba 1999a; C. Kusimba and Kusimba 2000). Archaeologists have argued that intra- and interstate conflict and warfare and foreign conquest were the primary factors responsible for the collapse of coastal urban polities. I draw upon ethnohistorical eyewitness accounts and archaeological evidence to show the rise and fall of coastal Swahili states. Both natural and human factors were responsible for the collapse of Swahili states. Prolonged droughts, diseases, and conflicts over resources weakened preexisting intersocietal relationships and pitted neighboring chiefdoms, states, citystates, and nonstate societies against each other. However, the presence of powerful foreign intruders also disrupted the balance of power and prevented constructive ways of dealing with crises and conflicts.

Archaeological Research on the East Coast of Africa

For more than five decades, archaeologists have sifted through the rubble of ancient ruins to explain the rise and fall of the numerous settlements found along the East African coast (Fig. 7.1). To date, more than four hundred archaeological sites have been reported (Freeman-Grenville 1958; M. Horton 1996; Kirkman 1964; Stigand 1913; Wilson 1978, 1980). An equal number of sites are now known in the coastal hinterland (Abungu 1990; Kusimba and Kusimba 2000; Mutoro 1998; Pikirayi 1993; Thorbahn 1979). With a few exceptions (Abungu 1990, 1998; Chami 1988, 1994; C. Kusimba 1993; Mutoro 1987; Wilson 1978, 1980), the most thoroughly investigated sites are large cities with elite residences, royal palaces, courts, and several mosques (Chittick 1974, 1984; M. Horton 1996; Wilson 1982). Some of the large citystates and polities left detailed royally commissioned histories written by court scribes (Stigand 1913; Tolmacheva 1993; Werner 1915). This focus on large urban sites, coupled with the failure to take into consideration the hinterlands upon which these settlements were connected, inevitably introduced significant biases in data collection and interpretation. My own research suggests that 80 percent of the settlements were built of perishable materials—grass on wooden structures and mud on wooden frame structures. Fifteen percent of the structures were built of coral rug stones, and about 5 percent were built of coral blocks and porite coral (a live coral locally mined from the sea and carved, while fresh, into nice blocks and frames for doors, entrances, and tombs). The use of porite coral may well have been reserved for the economic and political elite (Horton 1996).

Like any other complex society, the interpretation of the coast's prehistory has varied from one generation to the next. Each generation of scholars has emphasized some aspects of society and deemphasized others. Late-nineteenth-century and early-twentieth-century scholars proposed that the ruins of the

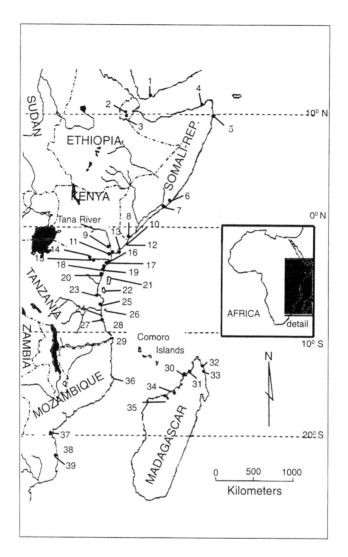

Fig. 7.1. East African coastal settlements: (1) Aden, (2) Zayla, (3) Harar, (4)
Cape Guardafui, (5) Ras Hafun, (6) Warsheikh, (7) Mogadishu, (8) Bur Gao,
(9) Wenje, (10) Bajun Islands, (11) Ungwana, (12) Lamu Archipelago, (13) Ras
Kipini, (14) Tsavo, (15) Gedi, (16) Malindi, (17) Kilepwa, (18) Mombasa, (19)
Mtwapa, (20) Galu, (21) Pemba Island, (22) Zanzibar Island, (23) Mkadini, (24)
Unguja Ukutu, (25) Dar es Salaam, (26) Mafia Island, (27) Kilwa, (28) Songo
Mnara Island, (29) Kerimba Archipelago, (30) Mahilaka, (31) Nosybe, (32)
Irodo, (33) Vohemar, (34) Nosy Manja, (35) Kingany, (36) Mozambique Island,
(37) Sofala, (38) Vilanculos Bay, and (39) Chibuene.

East African coast represented a good evidence for the Asiatic colonization of East Africa. The prime motivator for seeking and acquiring colonies was to control long-distance trade between Africa and Asia, especially Southwest and South Asia (Chittick 1974, 1977, 1984; Donley-Reid 1990; Kirkman 1954, 1964, 19, 1966; Trimingham 1964). The colonization hypothesis was based on a number of reasons. First, East Africa represented the southern-most extension of a Pan-Islamic civilization, having adopted Islam and the teachings of the prophet Mohammad in the ninth century (Horton 1996; Pouwels 1987, 2000; Sperling and Kagabo 2000). Second, both ethnographic and archaeological materials were composed of a variety of artifacts drawn from the Afrasian world (Pearson 1998). Finally, some local origin traditions credited the foundation of some city-states and polities to Persian settlers from Southwest Asia (Gates 1999; Nurse and Spear 1985; Shepherd 1982; Stigand 1913; Tolmacheva 1993). The present generation of scholars agrees with their predecessors that the participation of East Africans in international trade in the Afrasian world was crucial for their development (see Horton 1996; C. Kusimba 1999a; Pearson 1998; Middleton 1992; Mutoro 1998; Sutton 1990). Indeed, interaction with other societies through trade is a necessity for all state societies. However, they have discredited the attribution of state formation and urbanism to Asian colonists. They see the originators of these states as East Africans (Abungu 1998; J. Allen 1993; Chami 1994; C. Kusimba 1999a; Kusimba and Kusimba 2000).

Factors Contributing to the Rise of Social Complexity

The residents of the East African coast played a major role in linking East Africa to Southwest, Southeast, and South Asia from the beginning of the first century AD to the nineteenth century (J. Allen 1993; C. Kusimba 1999a; Middleton 1992; Pearson 1998; Radimilahy 1998; Verin 1986). The wealth accumulated through commercial interactions in the Afrasian world system enabled the coast to develop city-state and urban polities between 1000 and 1500. Several polities had large capitals covering more than fifteen hectares with populations ranging between 10,000 and 25,000 residents. These states were based on both agrarian and maritime economies. The populations of these cities possessed a well-defined social hierarchy including rulers, admin-istrators, the clergy, merchants, craft specialists, and commoners. Coastal city-states were linked to their hinterlands and forelands by elaborate interactive networks that involved barter, gift exchange, and short- and long-distance trade (Beach 1994, 1998; Curtin 1984; C. Kusimba 1999a; Middleton 1992; Pearson 1998). In 1993, I reorganized the chronological record of the coast into four broad periods emphasizing cultural manifestations (C. Kusimba 1993, 1999a, 1999b).

Period I (100 BC–AD 300)

Owing to insufficient research in early periods, few sites are known from Period I. The few Period I sites, several of which have been excavated, are found in close proximity to fresh water and abundant food resources. Called Early Iron Ware (EIW) sites, they possess evidence for craft production and intra/interregional trade. The production of iron at some sites may have exceeded local needs, and this surplus would have been used as export trade goods (Schmidt 1995, 142). The presence of glass and imported ceramics from Greco-Roman Egypt suggests commercial linkages with other regions between the first century BC and the fourth century AD (Chami and Msemwa 1997, 674–75).

Archaeological remains from Period I sites show that the domestic structures were built of grass on wooden frames and mud on wooden frames and that the Period I settlements were probably composed of largely communal tribal organizations (Table 7.1). Evidence of social or class differentiation has not been detected in the archaeological record. The few nonlocal trade artifacts suggest intermittent contact and interaction with maritime transoceanic traders. But the rest of the archaeological record shows no significant hierarchy

Table 7.1. Period I Archaeological Sites

Site	Sample #	Dates	References
KiMa1	24620	1115 ± 126 BC	Schmidt et al. 1992
KiMa1	24619	600 ± 100 BC	Schmidt et al. 1992
Misasa	UA-2593	98 BC–AD 68	Chami 1994, 91
Kivinja	Beta-24626	94 ± 60 BC	Chami and Msemwa 1997, 674
KiNy9	24624	AD 20 ± 105	Schmidt et al. 1992
KiNy9	24626	AD 25 ± 95	Schmidt et al. 1992
KiMa1	24621	AD 35 ± 95	Schmidt et al. 1992
Koma Island	Beta-24623	AD 233 ± 60	Chami and Msemwa 1997, 674
Misasa	UA-2594	AD 239–395	Chami 1994, 91
Limbo	UA-10286	AD 241 ± 60	Chami and Msemwa 1997, 674
Kwale	N-291	AD 270 ± 115	Chami and Msemwa 1997, 674
Kwale	N-292	AD 260 ± 115	Chami and Msemwa 1997, 674
KiNy9	24623	AD 265 ± 95	Schmidt et al. 1992
KiNy9	24625	AD 415 ± 85	Schmidt et al. 1992

or status linked to possession of these exotica. Crucial here is that the potential for differential access to trade goods among different social groups possibly provided a critical first step toward the evolution of individual appreciation and accumulation of preciosities that were later to confer higher social status, privileges, and hierarchy.

Period II (300–1000)

Period II sites contain large quantities of diverse local and nonlocal material culture (Table 7.2). Felix Chami has divided Period II into the Azanian Phase (300–600) and the Zanjian Phase (600–1000). Locally produced material culture predominates at all the sites and makes up over 95 percent of the entire archaeological assemblage (Abungu 1990; Chittick 1974, 1984; Horton 1984, 1996; Mutoro 1979; Wilding 1980). Period II was characterized by a village-level subsistence economy based on local resource exploitation with some participation in local, regional, and international trade. Interactions among coastal and foreign societies on local and regional levels are indicated

Table 7.2. Period II Archaeological Sites

Site	Sample #	Calibrated	References
Kilwa	GX-0398	AD 125	Chittick 1974, 29
Manda	N-339	AD 470	Chittick 1984, 49
Misasa	UA-2597	AD 536–639	Chami 1994, 91
Kiwangwa	UA-2097	AD 556–650	Chami 1994, 91
Masuguru	UA-2096	AD 562–654	Chami 1994, 91
Mpiji	UA-2087	AD 576–658	Chami 1994, 91
Mpiji	UA-2088	AD 582–678	Chami 1994, 91
Ungwana	TO-3891	AD 595–1030	C. M. Kusimba 1993, 180
Kiwangwa	UA-2598	AD 599–662	Chami 1994, 91
Kilwa	SR-77	AD 630	Chittick 1974, 29
Galu	TO-3895	AD 630–890	C. M. Kusimba 1993, 180
Mpiji	UA-2592	AD 642–765	Chami 1994, 91
Misasa	UA-2595	AD 659–775	Chami 1994, 91
Masuguru	UA-2095	AD 660–797	Chami 1994, 91
Kaole	UA-2092	AD 667–801	Chami 1994, 91
Kiwangwa	UA-2599	AD 671–797	Chami 1994, 91
Kiwangwa	UA-2098	AD 676–863	Chami 1994, 91
Manda	N-338	AD 780	Chittick 1967, 49
Kaole	UA-2093	AD 781–984	Chami 1994, 91
Ungwana	TO-3892	AD 785–1785	C. M. Kusimba 1993, 180
Kilwa	SR-78	AD 930	Chittick 1967, 49

by greater diversity in pottery style, especially in the Zanjian Phase, when Southwest and South Asian artifacts became more common (Abungu 1990; Horton 1996). Craft production, especially ironworking, was intensified at many settlements. In addition to gold, ivory, hides and skins, and rhinoceros horns, iron bloom was exported from East Africa (Freeman-Grenville 1962).

Period II witnessed gradual transformation toward social complexity on the coast. Interaction and exchange among East African societies widened in scope. External demand for African products including iron, ivory, rock crystal, and gold created opportunities for wealth accumulation for those East Africans who directly traded with Asian merchants. The bulk of imports included textiles, beads, glass, ceramics, and other processed items. Concomitant with the accumulation of prestige goods is evidence of increasing hierarchy in sociopolitical organization toward the end of the Zanjian Phase. Settlement size increased, and construction became more differentiated by size and building materials. Some settlements were surrounded by perimeter walls and guardhouses, suggesting the increasing need for security, privacy, elitism, and social separation (Horton 1996, 411).

Period III (1000–1500)

Intensification of agricultural and craft production and interregional interaction is most evident in Period III. Village settlements of Period II developed into more diversified towns, city-state capitals, and ports of trade during Period III. Settlement growth was greatest in areas that attracted large volumes of trade, such as the mouths of major rivers or creeks, islands with natural harbors, and coasts of rich hinterlands (C. Kusimba 1999a; Pearson 1998; Radimilahy 1998; Thorbahn 1979). Nearby river mouths and good harbors provided opportunities for direct trade with the hinterland and foreign merchants. Agriculturally rich hinterlands ensured a regular supply of food, raw materials, or finished goods for the urban people which increasingly became more specialized and diversified. Agricultural intensification provided the bulk of the food for towns (C. Kusimba 1999a; Pearson 1998). The urban populations were diverse, including administrative and religious elites, merchants, artisans, artists, and unskilled laborers.

The diversity of archaeological remains that were recovered show that these sites were linked to regional and Afrasian trade networks. Period III local earthenware consisted of diverse motifs, shapes, and vessel types. As coastal towns grew, they attracted both migrants and immigrants. These newcomers may initially have been predominantly men. It is probable that for the first time, neighbors in these towns were not always family members but people linked together by similar interests in craft production and trade. East Africans' growing prosperity increased the market for exotica both from the African interior and from the Indian Ocean. Islamic sgraffito pottery, Chinese

166

Qing bai and Cizhou ware (1200/1250–1400), and chlorite schist from Madagascar and Zimbabwe were imported to the coast. The proportion of imports still remained between 4 and 6 percent despite their increase in volume and distribution. New luxury items, such as bronze mirrors, kohl sticks, and glass beads, also began to be imported regularly in fairly large numbers. Both elite and nonelite women began to wear and display elaborate ornaments including gold, silver, and bronze bracelets and rings. Minting of copper and silver coins began at Kilwa, Manda, and Shanga in the twelfth century (J. Allen 1993, 116). Coinage suggests an attempt to unify the system of exchange in the region and to extend and exert political control beyond the city-state's boundaries.

During the fourteenth century, Chinese celadons, especially Longquan and Tongan (1250–1500) and Sawankhalok or Sisatchanalai jars from Annan or Cambodia (1350–1450/1500), dominated the imported ceramics (Kirkman 1956, 92; 1957, 18). Large quantities of Indian beads, Egyptian and Siraf glass sprinkler bottles, bowls in green, white, smoky, and cobalt glass, and glass beads were imported (Chittick 1974, 485–95; Horton 1996, 329; Kirkman 1956, 94). Weaving and textile production intensified at Kilwa, Pate, and Mogadisho (Freeman-Grenville 1960, 1965, 257).

The coast's prosperity reached its zenith in the fifteenth century. Settlements that had begun as modest fishing and slash-and-burn hamlets in Period I had gradually developed into towns and city-states with close connections to the Afrasian world system (Pearson 1998). East African prosperity increased the demand for exotica among the ruling class elites, Waungwana, and other social groups as well. Despite the cultural diversity in Period III coastal towns, there were few changes in the style, form, and quality of the local bowls, pots, jars, and incense burners. The distribution of local pottery at all the sites investigated revealed no significant difference at elite and commoner residences. Both the elite and commoners continued using the same local utensils. Differences are only manifested in imported and other artifacts where the elite had greater purchasing power.

The main participating city-states and states in interregional trade in eastern Africa included Sofala, Kilwa, Mombasa, Malindi, Pate, Mogadishu, and the Great Zimbabwe state. Interregional trade networks extended over much of modern eastern, southern, central, and parts of western Africa and involved many groups including peripatetic societies, chiefdoms, states, and city-states (Abungu 1998; Mutoro 1998; Pearson 1998). The prominent traders came from the Yao, Nyamwezi, Akamba, Giriama, Shona, and Swahili. Primary trade items destined for inland markets included cloth, glass and shell beads, and dried fish. From a variety of regions in the inland came alluvial and mineral gold, ivory, hides and skins, rock crystal, and grains (Barbosa 1967, 11–12). There were as many production and collecting centers as there were participating societies. The distribution of trade items over inaccessible areas would have required highly sophisticated managers backed by a strong political and military power. It is remarkable that the intensity and scope of long-distance exchange and interactions, reported by Duarte Barbosa and other Portuguese observers, show that there was neither a unified political entity nor a strong military or security force to compel the various chiefdoms and states to enter into commercial relationships with the coast. Chiefs, managers, and inland itinerant traders, peripatetic hunters, gold miners, and panniers would have bought items from the villages and sold them at the nearest trading nodes and market towns (Mutoro 1998; Pearson 1998). The antiquity of trade among various African groups is evident in all periods. Villagers in small settlements would have produced and conveyed their trade goods to merchants of the larger towns, with whom they had both kinship and affinal ties and trading partnerships. These merchants would either have sold the products directly to long-distance coastal traders or organized trading expeditions to the coast in order to trade directly with South Asia and Southwest Asian merchants. Security for long-distance traders was in part a responsibility of the chiefs and rulers of the states that were involved in this commerce. Various groups levied taxes on caravans traversing in their territory. Chiefdoms and states that failed to protect traders risked being excluded in the lucrative trade of the Afrasian world system.

Interregional trade linked many African societies to an increasingly global economy. Trade also helped define regional and interregional sociopolitical hierarchies. Large towns developed along the coast and in the hinterland where trade was most active (Beach 1994; Garlake 1978; Huffman 1996; Pikirayi 1993; Pwiti 1996). In some cases, densely populated villages and towns, some surrounded by perimeter walls, came into being (Fletcher 1998). The numerous nonlocal artifacts including gold, silver, porcelain, glass, and beads recovered at many sites in East Africa attest to this period of prosperity and commercial interaction. Information, ideas, and people were also exchanged (Blanton et al. 1996, 1999). Such exchanges helped shape and transform interacting societies. Interregional trade created opportunities for accumulation of wealth and promoted societal inequalities (Price and Feinman 1995). Expansion in international maritime trade during Period III increased competition among large towns in securing trading monopolies for the international markets. The major coastal city-states had a large fleet of boats that plied along the coast. Entrepreneurship became the cornerstone of cementing political control. According to the *Pate Chronicle*, the king of Pate "owned much wealth (cattle, ships, and gardens are mentioned), acted as an entrepreneur in ship building, trading, and even mining, and relied for emergency on a private army as distinct from the regular troops which he also commanded, and which consisted of gentry, slaves, and mercenaries" (Prins 1961, 93).

Growth in wealth compelled entrepreneurs to invest more of their resources in financing and securing allies among the hinterland chiefdoms that produced trade items required for external markets. Large polities like Pate, Malindi, Mombasa, and Kilwa developed trade partnerships with interior chiefdoms and tribal societies. The rivers linked coastal peoples with their trading partners in the interior. The towns of Zuama and Angoche on the Zambezi Delta, for example, became ports for exchanging gold and ivory from Great Zimbabwe and for textiles and beads from the coast (Barbosa 1967, 15; Pearson 1998; see C. Kusimba 1993, 1999a; C. Kusimba and S. Kusimba 1999). The region's prosperity is illustrated here by Duarte Barbosa's 1917 description of Mombasa at the turn of the sixteenth century:

> a very fair place, with lofty stone and mortar houses, well aligned in streets [after the fashion of Quiloa]. The wood is well-fitted with excellent joiner's work, and it has its own king, himself a Moor. . . . The men are in colour either tawny, black, or white and also . . . their women go very bravely attired with many fine garments of silk and gold in abundance. This is the place of great traffic and has a good harbour, in which are always moored craft of many kinds and also great ships, both of those which come from Çofala and those which go thither, and others which come from the great kingdom of Cambaya and from Melynde; others which sail to the Isles of Zinzibar, and the others of which I shall speak anon. (19–20)

The Portuguese found many local boats and foreign ships docked in towns and ports they visited. Sofala, on the southern coast of Mozambique, was the main artery for trade with the interior Great Zimbabwe, the source of considerable gold, silver, iron, ivory, leather, and slaves. At the time of Portuguese conquest, day-to-day activities and the African end of international commerce were controlled by coastal city-states. Foreign merchants from Southwest Asia and South Asia were present, and some had even settled permanently in East Africa. The main language spoken along the length of the coast and trade routes was Kiswahili. A number of coastal and hinterland peoples, especially those involved in trade, had converted to Islam (Pouwels 2000). The commercial ties with other Afrasian societies were visible in the great diversity of merchants reported by Portuguese observers. Some of the managers and financiers of interregional trade had made huge profits that enabled them to build elegant residences and homes (Garlake 1966). They wore elegant cloths and possessed expensive Chinese porcelain that was proudly displayed in their homes and, after death, on their tombs (Kusimba and Kusimba 2000).

Periods I through III witnessed the creation of socially chartered trading networks and growth attendant upon the exchanges of value between the emergent cities of the coast and the world beyond. By the sixteenth century, a fairly stable and prosperous civilization had been achieved. Fernand Braudel described sixteenth-century coastal city-states in the following terms:

> The towns were busy and prosperous on account of the trade in slaves, ivory, and gold. Gold was found in large quantities upcountry from Sofala, as witnessed by Arab geographers like Masudi (916) and Ibn al Wardi (975). The goldfields and mines seem to have been in Matabeleland, between the Zambesi and

Limpopo. . . . Mainly African, these towns had only a small minority of Arab or
Persian colonists: they also had closer links with India than Arabia. Their apogee
was in the fifteenth century. . . . Far away as it was, it had political structures like
the kingdom of Monomotapa in what is now Zimbabwe. (Braudel 1994, 127)

Coastal entrepreneurs had underwritten the development of a complex,
highly textured society, one which reflected their traditional African origins,
as well as new ideas imported along with the foreign goods that filled their
residences. Little did they realize at the end of the fifteenth century that the
golden age of East African prosperity was about to change.

Period IV (1500–1700)

The collapse of coastal city-states of East Africa has been linked to environmental change, warfare, and foreign conquest (Connah 1998, 11; C. Kusimba
1999a). Below I will examine each of the factors separately with the goal of identifying the primary factor that destroyed the coastal civilization of East Africa.

Climate and Environmental Changes

Climate change affects the balance of culture and nature and makes it difficult to sustain stable and sustainable economic and political systems. These
changes elicit responses in humans that lead to reorganization of their cultural tool kit. Droughts can cause people to migrate or increase or decrease
intercultural dynamics and the flow and exchange of ideas (Harlan 1971;
Harlan, de Wet, and Stemler 1976; Hassan 1996, 2000; Wendorf and Schild
1994; Wendorf, Close, and Schild 1987). Droughts have been responsible
for the decline and collapse of many complex societies.[2] The severe droughts
of the sixteenth century affected all East African societies. Groundwater levels dropped, rivers, wells, and waterholes dried up, crops failed, water- and
wind-borne diseases increased, and in some instances epidemic diseases like
cholera, typhoid, and even plague occurred (Kirkman 1959). Kirkman (1957,
16) proposed that environmental deterioration created a bottleneck effect at
resource-rich areas, forcing former trading partners and neighbors to compete
for decreasing resources.

Assuming that Kirkman's hypothesis is correct, we expect the following to
have occurred: drought and the epidemic diseases would have caused high
mortality among humans, their livestock, and wildlife and severe depopulation. Farmers, foragers, and pastoralists would have migrated to inland freshwater lakes and floodplains. Farmers would have dug canals to divert river
waters for irrigation. Urban residents would have deepened their wells only to
strike saline water. Many urban and hinterland settlements located far from

freshwater sources would have gradually been abandoned. Unfortunately, Kirkman's proposal is yet to be proven archaeologically. There is as yet no evidence of mass deaths or depopulations on the coast. Evidence of decadence and decline occurs at many seventeenth- and eighteenth-century sites, but not earlier. The abandonment of some cities like Gedi is yet to be satisfactorily investigated. Wells appear to have dried up as a result of poor or lack of maintenance rather than drought. It seems that this hypothesis does not adequately explain the collapse of coastal city-states and polities.

Internal Conflict and Warfare

Unlike previous seasonal or temporary shortages of food and grazing land, sixteenth-century droughts lasted longer and affected the entire continent (Hassan 1996, 1997). Competition for securing access to resource-rich areas would have ensued, pitting previously peaceful neighbors against each other. Conflicts over the rights to use hunting grounds, arable farmland, rich pastureland, and water sources were inevitable. The Oromo (Galla) migrated from Ethiopia to escape severe droughts that desiccated their homeland. By the fifteenth century they had began to settle in the hinterland of the coast of Kenya. Tensions over scarce resources developed into full-scale warfare between pastoral peoples, particularly the Somali, the Maasai, the Oromo, and the coastal agricultural and urban societies. Oral traditions of coastal societies, including the Swahili, Mijikenda, Taita, and Oromo, tell of strife and warfare (J. Allen 1993; Cassanelli 1982; Merritt 1975; Spear 1978, 1982). Interethnic warfare may have caused further abandonment of coastal settlements and migration into the countryside and to offshore islands. The Watikuu, a Swahili-speaking people who inhabit the Lamu archipelago, and the Mijikenda assert that they migrated to the coast from their hinterland homeland, Shungwaya, in the sixteenth century following a conflict with the Oromo (J. Allen 1993; C. Kusimba 1999a; Spear 1978, 1982). The Oromo had earlier been displaced by the Somali. Elsewhere in the hinterland of East Africa the pastoral Masai plundered the region as they moved in search of pasture, and after the drought they were to terrorize their neighbors in order to replenish herds lost to the epidemic diseases trypanosomiasis and rinderpest.

Internecine warfare, coups d'état, succession conflicts, interpolity rivalry, and polity expansionism have been reported in Swahili chronicles (Tolmacheva 1993). According to these sources, intercity state conflict arose from competition over access to fertile hinterlands and islands and for trade with hinterland chiefdoms and foreign merchants (Gray 1957; Nicholls 1971). For example, Kilwa and Sofala competed for gold and ivory from Great Zimbabwe. Mahilaka, in Madagascar, often raided the Comorian Island polities for slaves (Ottenheimer 1976). Lamu and Pate battled over access to the fertile Tana Delta and its hinterland. Mombasa and Malindi competed for the fertile island of Pemba, the breadbasket of the coast (Gray 1957). The opulent and consumptive lifestyles of the elites could not be sustained without access to new markets, factories, and marketable commodities. Competition for access to important exchange networks, which had initially made these city-states so successful, also contained the germs for their collapse. Internal conflict weakened their abilities to create lasting alliances and made them vulnerable to external interference, manipulation, and attack.

As prosperous as these city-states were, they still lacked the power, individually, to protect themselves from a determined invader and the political structure to forge the kind of confederacy of cities necessary to provide long-term security in case of attack (Prins 1961). On the other hand, relationships with hinterland groups, on whom the coast depended for trade goods and food, differed from city to city. Not only were those relationships shifting as hinterland groups moved and reconstituted themselves, but they were also increasingly being contested by the various parties (C. Kusimba 2004; Kusimba and Kusimba 2000). Before the Portuguese conquest, the regional and international economy had been based on a traditional person-to-person exchange network in which friendship, brotherhood, alliances, and kinship ties were as important as the trade items themselves. In Kenya, for example, regional and interregional trade was carried out among the Akamba, Oromo, Taita, Waata, Giriama, and Swahili from earlier times (Mutoro 1998; Robertson 1997). The Waata foragers of Tsavo hunted game such as elephant, rhino, zebra, buffalo, and ostrich and sold the skins, dried meat, and ivory to coastal Mijikenda in exchange for *uchi*, palm wine, cloth, grain, and beads. The Oromo pastoralists traded ivory and cattle with Pokomo, Giriama, and Swahili. The Taita agropastoralists visited the coast to sell sun-dried vegetables, meat, ivory, and grains in exchange for uchi, cloth, beads, and hardware. The Taita would travel to Jomvu Market, near Mombasa, to sell ivory and cattle directly to Swahili, Arab, and Indian merchants. The Akamba were trading partners with Giriama, Taita, and Waata. The Akamba would come to Rabai as well, and Jomvu and Giriama traders would travel to Akamba land for ivory and cattle.

These trade relationships were dependent on fictive ties called *undugu wa chale* (blood brotherhoods) in Kiswahili (Herlehy 1984, 293–94). That oath, in which individuals exchanged vows to respect and treat each other as members of the same family, would be honored by the entire chiefdom. The blood brotherhood ceremony involved sacrificing a goat or chicken, then making cuts in their chests and rubbing the meat, usually a liver, into the wounds and exchanging and eating the blood-soaked meat. The participants would then pledge brotherhood, loyalty, and protection of each other and their families. It was believed that misfortune would befall any individual or close members of his family and extended family if that oath was broken (Bakari 1981, 167–68). The oath enabled the participants to become fictive brothers or sisters and for their children to inherit those relationships. It would allow the groups to exploit resources in their neighbor's country while enjoying the protection of the whole community. In this sense, blood brotherhoods and sisterhoods enabled the exchange of ideas and knowledge, eased tensions arising from competition for resources, and provided access to technical and sacred knowledge (Herlehy 1984; Kusimba and Kusimba 2004). For example, the Taita elders interviewed have admitted that their ancestors never would have learned the secret knowledge of elephant hunting which enabled them to benefit from lucrative ivory trade with the coastal Mijikenda and Swahili traders without the compliance and permission of their Waata blood brothers. The nature of these relationships began to shift when the region came under political and economic control of the foreigners, and people became a major article of trade and exchange.

The Portuguese Conquest

The encounter between Africans and Portuguese began in the early fifteenth century and was to change the course of European and African history. The Portuguese established their first African settlement at Ceuta in 1415, the second at Qsar es Seghir in 1458, and the third at Tangiers in 1471. The Portuguese presence in Africa preceded the arrival of Genoan Christopher Columbus in the Americas by seven decades (DeCorse 1998, 221). The year 1488 is significant for African history as it marked the establishment of a permanent European presence in sub-Saharan Africa. During that year, Bartholomew Dias and his crew successfully circumnavigated the Cape of Good Hope in search of a sea route to India around Africa. In 1498, Vasco da Gama ventured on to India, accomplishing the vision of Prince Henry the Navigator (Freeman-Grenville 1973, 81). For the next two centuries, the Portuguese and their rivals, the Dutch and English, would vie for economic and political control in the Indian Ocean and the South Seas. As we have seen, there were several hundred villages, towns, and cities along the length of the East African coast. These settlements were connected through coastal and hinterland trade. They were linked together by a common language, Kiswahili, which was the lingua franca of the region. The residents of the coast were nominally Muslim, having adopted Islam as a regional religion earlier in Period III. Portuguese eyewitness accounts provide testimony about the state of coastal settlement at the beginning of the sixteenth century. For example, Vasco da Gama was favorably impressed by the city of Kilwa and its ruler, Sheikh Wagerage:

> a town of lofty white houses whose king wore a robe of damask trimmed with green satin and a rich turban. He was seated on two cushioned chairs of bronze beneath a round sunshade of crimson satin attached to a pole. . . . There were many players of anafils, and two trumpets of ivory richly carved, and of the size of a man, which were blown from a hole in the side, and made sweet harmony with the anafils. (Freeman-Grenville 1962, 54–56)

173

The Portuguese left many favorable accounts of other coastal towns and cities including Sofala, Kilwa, Mombasa, and Mogadishu. Historical descriptions of luxuriously clad elites, royal regalia, and well-kept towns show a very different picture from that portrayed by Kirkman and compel us to consider another factor that may have caused the collapse of coastal city-states and polities—colonial conquest. The Portuguese mission to Africa and Asia was straightforward: to find the sea route to India, control the spice trade, and, if necessary, to avenge years of domination by the Muslim after they conquered Spain in the twelfth century. The Portuguese *Regimentos*, a handbook of instructions and rules of behavior for captains toward people they encountered, recommended subjugation and, if necessary, extermination. Thus when King Dom Manuel I appointed Dom Francisco de Almeida to serve as India's first viceroy in 1505, he instructed him to use diplomacy and plunder:

> And using this pretense [of peace] you shall leap ashore there from your long-boats and using such dexterity as you may, you shall take all the Moorish merchants who may be there from foreign parts and all the gold and merchandise you find upon them. . . . We do so by reason of their being enemies of our holy Catholic faith. . . . But the natives of the land you shall not hurt either persons or their property, for it is our wish that they be protected. (Mbuia-Joao 1990, 63)

The Portuguese used four methods to subjugate their enemies. First, they offered protection treaties with city-states and polities in exchange for an annual tribute to the king of Portugal. Second, they wedged punitive expeditions against uncooperative city-states and polities, forcing them into becoming tribute-paying subjects of the king of Portugal. Third, they organized punitive expeditions against polities that defaulted on tribute payment. Finally, they often disguised themselves as pirates and plundered merchant ships on the high seas.

The first coastal town to fall to the Portuguese was Kilwa in 1505. The punitive war against Kilwa was organized by Francisco d'Almeida after Kilwa defaulted on a tribute promised to Vasco da Gama in 1502. A conversation between Vasco da Gama and King Ibrahim, recorded by Gaspar Corrêa in *Lendas da India*, illustrates that the Portuguese were determined to conquer and acquire the city-state of Kilwa in order to secure access to and control of trade with Zambezia, the source of much gold and ivory (Beach 1984; Pearson 1998). They reasoned that because of Kilwa's importance in long-distance trade, whoever controlled it would inevitably hold sway over the entire Swahili coast and its trade inland. In the 1502 "diplomatic" exchange, the king of Kilwa had accepted Vasco da Gama's "generous" offer of Portuguese protection and confessed to having been wrong about Portugal's real agenda. But Ibrahim was told that as a pledge of friendship to Portugal he was to pay annual tribute. Gaspar Corrêa (1866, 279) relates the dialogue translated by Tome Mbuia-Joao (1990, 109–10):

> *King Ibrahim:* Good friendship was to friends like brothers are, and that he
>   would shelter the Portuguese in his city and harbor . . . to pay

tribute each year in money or jewelry was not a way to a good friendship, it was tributary subjugation . . . to pay tribute was dishonor . . . it would be like to be a captive. . . . such friendship he did not want with subjugation . . . because even the sons did not want to have that kind of subjugation with their own parents.

Vasco da Gama: Take it for certain that if I so decide your city would be grounded by fire in one single hour, and if your people wanted to extinguish the fire in town, they would all be burned, and when you see all this happen, you will regret all you are telling me now, and you will give much more than what I am asking you now, it will be too late for you. If you are still in doubt, it is up to you to see it.

King Ibrahim: Sir, if I had known that you wanted to enslave me, I would not have come, and I would have fled into the forest, for it is better for me to be a fox but free, than a dog locked up in a golden chain.

Vasco da Gama had told the king to go into the forest if he so wished because he had dogs to go and fetch him (Mbuia-Joao 1990, 82). Knowing well Muslim aversions toward dogs, Vasco da Gama was deliberately provoking the king, whose reaction would have served as an excuse to plunder the city. Wanting to get rid of the intruders, the king had ignored the insult, paid the tribute, and thus saved his city. Three years later, the Portuguese returned led by Francisco d'Almeida, plundered the city, and installed Mohammad Ibn Rakn Al-Din al Dabuli as a puppet (Barbosa 1967; Gray 1954, 26; Mbuia-Joao 1990, 111).

In the same year, 1505, Tristao da Cunha sacked the town of Hoja (now known as Ungwana) at the mouth of the Tana in a punitive expedition on behalf of Malindi. The following year, Lamu, having heard the news of the Portuguese destruction of Hoja, submitted to da Cunha (Barbosa 1967, 29; Ravenstein 1898, 102). After sacking Hoja, da Cunha proceeded to Barawa, where he allegedly demanded the tribute that had been promised to Saldanha in 1503 by certain Barawa inhabitants whom Saldanha had captured off the coast of Malindi. The people of Barawa refused to comply with da Cunha's demand, and in the war that followed the once proud city was reduced to ruins. The city of Barawa was destroyed, its wealth was plundered, and many people were slain or taken into captivity. Some survivors fled into the hinterland (Barbosa 1967, 30). The eyewitness account of Martin Fernandez de Figueroa, Conquista de las Indias, here translated by Mbuia-Joao (1990, 112–13), tells of the brutality that accompanied these conquests:

The Portuguese entered the city by force of arms, killed many Moors, and carried off great riches which their owners had not thought to save, in the belief they could defend the town. They could not even save their own women, very rich and beautiful with seven and eight bracelets on each arm and just as many thick and valuable on their legs. This was an occasion for severe cruelty, for the men, blinded by avarice rather than mercy, in order not to lose time, cut off the arms, the legs, and the ears which bore the jewelry without pity.

The Portuguese adopted a scorched-earth policy. The towns were looted and burned to the ground, making it expensive to rebuild them. Surviving residents were sent into slavery abroad or enslaved locally (Barbosa 1967, 39). According to M. D. D. Newitt, the political instability due to the Portuguese interference in the local politics led to large-scale movements and migrations, frequently violent between the coast and the hinterlands. These instabilities were major factors behind the inability of indigenous industries to capitalize on the increasing trade in the Indian Ocean (Newitt 1987).

The Portuguese dealt a deadly blow to the initiatives of East Africans to participate and take advantage of the global economic boom afforded by high Eurasian demand for African products. The plunder and destruction of the region's economy was often driven by personal greed. Before the Portuguese, all merchant ships complied with the code of trade called Cartaz (Pearson 1987). For example, no foreign merchant ships would navigate the waterways of a region without being licensed by the local commercial communities. All ships that complied with the system were protected from piracy.

After the Portuguese conquered and gained control of the major Red Sea and Indian Ocean ports of trade, they imposed their own tax codes and meted severe punishment to merchant ships that evaded paying taxes. To prevent merchant ships from evading taxes, the Portuguese blocked the Cape of Guardafui, where merchant ships converged to enter the Red Sea (Barbosa 1967, 33). The Portuguese were too few to efficiently police the Indian Ocean. Thus their pledge and determination to maintain law and order were not well enforced. It is probable that some displaced merchants and traders took advantage of loopholes created by the Portuguese Cartaz. The previous code was largely based on an honor system and self-policing, but with the arrival of the Portuguese, cases of piracy and robbery on the high seas increased. Many ships were captured and relieved of their booty. Many investors, particularly those of Egypt, Arabia, and China, reduced their fleet or turned their attention to other investments. Merchants in East Africa were cut off from direct trade with their counterparts, and thus began the rapid decline.

In an attempt to impose a trade monopoly, the Portuguese targeted foreign merchants who visited ports under their control for high tariffs. Smuggling increased as local and foreign merchants colluded to evade paying taxes. During Period III, the regional and international economy had been based on a traditional person-to-person exchange network in which honesty, friendship, brotherhood, alliances, and even kinship ties were as important as the trade items themselves. The rules and regulations imposed by the conquerors weakened those traditional networks of commercial interaction and exchange.

The anti-Islamic policy of the Portuguese affected the organizational structure of the trading groups within the Indian Ocean. According to Jain (1990), Chau (1964), and others, the bulk of the trade in the Indian Ocean between the eleventh and fifteenth centuries was conducted by Arab and Chinese merchants. After the mid-fifteenth century, the Ming dynasty stopped sponsorship of overseas trade and concentrated on control of Chinese ports. The Portuguese, taking advantage of the Ottoman takeover of the Mamluk Empire in Egypt, differentiated between the Arabs and Indians as trading partners. Their definition of "Moors" did not include Indians, either Hindu or Muslim. These traders, mainly Gujarati merchants, were favored by the Portuguese and sought Portuguese protection for trade under the Cartazes (Pearson 1987). Portuguese support, the decline of Arab and Chinese influence, and the emergence of state-sponsored overseas trade by the urban Indian polities (Naqvi 1972) gave Gujarati traders enormous access to the East African ports under Portuguese control. According to Ashin Das Gupta (1987), by the mid-sixteenth century Gujarati capital was dominant in the Indian Ocean trade. Additionally, the scorched-earth technique of destroying and rebuilding soon ran out of targets. The king of Portugal authorized a series of fortresses to be built along the length of the coast to replace destroyed towns and cities. Many of the fortresses had to be abandoned as they became too expensive to maintain after trade in the region declined and indigenous people moved into the interior, some reverting to simpler ways of making a living (C. Kusimba 1999a; Kusimba and Kusimba 2000).

Evidence of Collapse: The Portuguese Conquest and Colonialism

Before the arrival of the Portuguese, the coastal towns and cities were part of a prosperous interregional trading enterprise that Michael Pearson (1998) has called the Afrasian world system. Now their conditions changed. Portuguese interference destroyed local industries. The increase of the Gujarati interest in East Africa, due to Portuguese influence, resulted in two major changes in the production and trade systems of the East African cities and hinterlands. First, the Gujaratis (and other merchants) started flooding the East African markets with very cheap cloth from India. Rahul Oka has estimated that by the end of the sixteenth century, 7,000,000 rupees' worth of Gujarati cloth was being exported by the various merchant groups to East Africa every year (see also Moosvi 1987, 388, 389; Alpers 1975). In 1622, the British East India Company purchased 40,000 pieces of cloth for 53,000 rupees (1.325 rupees per piece) for resale overseas (Krishna 1974). Even if the price appreciated tenfold in value in East Africa, it was still cheaper than locally produced cloth, and this change must severely have affected the indigenous cloth industries

(Pearson 1998). The great weaving industries of Pate, Mogadishu, and Kilwa declined, forcing coastal residents to become consumers of textiles imported from India. The iron-working industries of Malindi, Sofala, and Kilwa stopped production early in the colonial era and were never revived. The farmers and merchant families of Barawa, Sofala, and Kilwa became bankrupt; some became makers of straw mats, baskets, and hats. The trade they once carried out with India and Hormuz was now in the hands of the Portuguese and the Gujarati merchants.

The second major change in the trade activities of the port cities was that they began to respond to increasing pressure to deal in raw materials and not finished products. The Indian markets had a constant demand for East African ivory and gold (Das Gupta 1982; Thorbahn 1979). The Indian merchants used their increasing influence to increase the supply of ivory from the hinterlands. Newitt even suggests that the merchants were unwilling to invest in local industries due to perceived instability, even after Omani takeover of Mombasa in 1698, and concentrated mainly on ivory and gold (1987, 205).

The increasing emphasis on raw material, capital flight to India and Portugal due to trade deficits and emphasis on imports, political instability due to Portuguese interference, and the destruction of the local modes of commercial production—are all intertwined factors that sowed the seeds for the subsequent underdevelopment of East Africa over the next century (see Rodney 1981). Friar Gaspar de Sao Bernardino's description of Mombasa in 1606 captures the inequity that reigned over much of the coast during Portuguese rule. The Portuguese captain lived in luxury in the fortress; the native puppet king lived close by, but under the watchful eye of the fort, the seat of the government; the Portuguese civilian population lived apart, with their slaves; and the natives lived in poverty:

> We afterwards visited the city houses of which are lofty and raised from the ground, but are already very ancient. Their inhabitants are Moors who although formerly rich, now live in utter poverty, their most usual occupation is that of making mats, baskets, and straw hats so perfectly finished that the Portuguese bring them out to wear on feast day. (Freeman-Grenville 1962, 157)

The quality of life under Portuguese rule had deteriorated to such a level that even the puppet king, Muhammad of Malindi, was compelled to intervene on behalf of the people of the coast. He pleaded with the king of Portugal to permit coastal people to carry on trade, freely associate with one another, and participate in the Hajj. Reviewing the letters that the kings of Mombasa, formerly of Malindi, were writing to the Portuguese kings in Lisbon, Mbuia-Joao (1990, 256) writes:

> But in 1597 the king was not asking just for himself, but for all the Moors trading on the coast that they should be given freedom to trade, at a standstill due to the

policies of the captains and the Portuguese merchants of Mombasa who did not allow anybody to compete with them. Included in the idea of free navigation on the coast, the king requested that the Moors be allowed the right of sending at least one ship to Mecca for pilgrimage. In the same letter the king of Mombasa also recommended that all the East African rulers should be relieved of the burden of tribute, imposed on them by Tome de Sousa Coustinho at the time of the Turkish attacks, since they were too poor to keep honoring that obligation.

A request of this kind from a puppet ruler makes clear the difficult conditions East Africans suffered under their colonial masters.

The effects of Portuguese colonialism on the coast are most visible at Malindi, the first true ally of Lisbon. When Vasco da Gama first visited there in 1498, Malindi welcomed the Portuguese and firmly remained an ally. Malindi paid a price for its alliance with Portugal. Trade with the hinterland chiefdoms declined as they began trading with rival Kilifi and Mombasa. Foreign merchants boycotted Malindi for its decision to welcome the Portuguese. Mombasa and its allies Kilifi, Takaungu, Mnarani, and Kitoka repeatedly attacked Malindi (Mbuia Joao 1990, 225). Revenue was lost as the Portuguese ships that docked at the port did not pay taxes or give revenue directly to the town. In 1542, St. Francis Xavier, the first Jesuit missionary to India, stopped in Malindi on his way to take up his see, and found the "city, in a very ruinous condition . . . but what remains standing shows that it must have been very noble in ancient times" (Schurhammer and Wicki 1944–45, 119–28). St. Xavier's observation is a far cry from Vasco da Gama's description given only fifty years earlier.

Although East Africans were defeated, they continued to rebel against Portuguese rule and policies of forced labor, irregular trade practices, and enslavement of their victims. In 1506–1508, the hinterland of Malindi was in anarchy leading to the collapse of agricultural activities. In 1511, King Maulidi of Sofala revolted, and in the conflict that followed he took flight to Inharmoninca and later to Pandene in Zambezia, from whence he waged a campaign to dissuade his interior trading partners from trading with the Portuguese. Maulidi's campaigns were successful as other kings in the interior rose against the Portuguese.

The Portuguese response to rebellions was brutal. In an incident involving the alleged poisoning of Jesuit priests by the local Muslim merchants at Sena, the Portuguese reaction was especially violent and reminds us of the Inquisition that was then ongoing in Europe against Jews and Muslims. The punishment meted on the alleged perpetrators was described in 1570 by Jesuit priest Father Moclaro:

They were condemned and put to death with strange inventions. Some were impaled alive; some were tied to the tops of trees, forcibly brought together, and then set free, by which means they were torn asunder; others were opened up [from] the back with hatchets, some were killed with mortars; and others were delivered to the soldiers, who wreaked their wrath upon them with arquebuses. (Couto 1974, 35; Mbuia-Joao 1990, 188)

The Portuguese colonization wrested political and economic power from coastal communities. Many people responded by emigrating into the interior to escape Portuguese persecution. Others stayed on to be co-opted into the colonial system. Much of the interethnic conflict reported by Kirkman may have been a consequence of, rather than a precursor to, the Portuguese invasion. There was a massive exodus of people from the Portuguese-occupied cities to highland areas of the hinterland, where they set up fortified Kaya settlements (Mutoro 1987). From these fortified settlements, these groups, many of whom survive today as the Mijikenda and Segeju, waged resistance warfare to regain their territories. These hostilities prevented the Portuguese from extending their influence inland. For example, in 1592, the Portuguese surrendered and paid substantial tribute to the Mijikenda after they made an unsuccessful attempt to fortify Makupa on Mombasa Island (Gray 1947, 12).

The Portuguese regularly ambushed and looted villages, chiefdoms, and states in the hinterland. The foreign domination of the coast not only weakened African chiefdoms and states but also prevented them from making long-term development plans. They faced the firepower of the musket with their poisoned arrows. Defeated and severely weakened, many groups retreated to backcountry forests, using their Kaya hill fortresses as protection against slave seekers (Cooper 1981; Maugham 1906; Nurse 1978; Sherif 1987). Some of the walled settlements in southern Kenya and the northern Tanzania coast with guardhouses may also date to this period of refugee movement and insecurity (Bakari 1981; Fosbrooke 1960, 32; Gillman 1944).

Until the late nineteenth century, when Western Europeans partitioned Africa among themselves, the situation in eastern Africa was one of decline and collapse of chiefdoms, states, and kingdoms. Over four centuries, few opportunities existed for indigenous people to make long-term plans. Foreign conquest, colonization, and institutionalization of slavery had devastating and long-term effects. Oral traditions of coastal and inland societies tell of an increase in internecine warfare as various towns and cities fought with one another. The international market for slaves turned neighbor against neighbor who raided each other for prisoners of war to sell to European and Arab slave dealers. The raids were severe and exposed entire communities to risk of enslavement. The anxiety forced abandonment of indefensible settlements. Hilly and forested sites were chosen because they were easy to defend (Kusimba and Kusimba 2000), while other villages were fortified with stone walls or wooden stockades (Fosbrooke 1960, 36).

Differences between the coastal urban and rural groups markedly increased during the colonial period. Trading regulations imposed by the Portuguese created a barrier that in time caused the decline in contact between hinterland and coastal people (C. Kusimba 1999a). Coastal functionaries raided hinterland villages and chiefdoms and conveyed their captives to the slave merchants. The demise of political and economic independence of the coastal city-states diminished the coastal elite's economic and political power. New symbols of power were invented, but these could only be found in collaboration and alliance building with conquerors and colonial masters.

Conclusion

European expansionism, beginning in the fifteenth century, severely affected all aspects of African society. Long-standing economic activities in the Indian Ocean and the East African interior were early casualties. So much of this colonial past was never recorded and may be impossible to recover. The European intrusion into the affairs of East Africans and Asians caused abandonment of many towns. Others declined in importance to become minor trading partners. Yet others continued to flourish under foreign rulers (C. Kusimba 1999a). These are changes that we can detect in the archaeology of these places. What the changes mean is another matter. I have described a region somewhat stressed climatically but which collapsed and lost the basis of its material wealth and power as a result of increasing stress from colonial powers with maritime superiority and a definite agenda for trade control (see also Krishna 1974; Nightingale 1970). I have emphasized that two primary factors, climatic change and foreign conquest, were responsible for the collapse of Swahili urban polities. The drying up of wells and decline in traditional grazing ground increased threats from pastoralists who took advantage of the vulnerability of isolated coastal settlements. The Portuguese were a stronger opponent who wielded a potent maritime weapon and had a more determined governing principle. The Portuguese entrance into East Africa broke down traditional trade networks and set in motion forces that eventually diminished the authority of some long-standing polities as well as the ruling classes' ability to underwrite the civil well-being of their towns and polities.

Although Kirkman (1957, 1964) wrote of violent times preceding the Portuguese conquest, no such archaeological evidence has yet been unearthed on the coast. One might expect that warfare on a systematic, regional scale would be apparent in the archaeological record in the form of burned houses, wrecked villages, trophy heads, and skeletons of individuals burned in rooms or killed with arrows. Archaeologists have yet to find such evidence. One explanation is that people abandoned their settlements willingly as environmental conditions deteriorated.

Another explanation is that the Portuguese conquest, not drought, caused people to abandon the coastal settlements for the safety of the backcountry, which in increasing fashion they fortified against the depredations of slavers and others who might attempt to dominate them. From the sixteenth century on, hinterland settlements were set in defensible locations in heavily forested regions. The atmosphere of terror described by missionaries and early British and German colonial officers offers a valuable explanation of the strict behavioral codes prevailing in the hinterland fortresses (Kraph 1860; Livingston 1874; Steere 1870). Having fortified and established themselves in the hinterland, the coastal peoples waged punitive wars against the Portuguese and their allies to regain their independence and possessions.

Throughout its mercantile history, the commercial enterprises of the coast were an important link in intercontinental commerce. Before the sixteenth century, the coast became prosperous and attracted a variety of immigrant groups, who melded into the indigenous ethnic, cultural, and linguistic societies which so characterize the coast today. Major towns were politically independent entities, enjoying trading privileges with their immediate hinterlands. The coast was then an integral part of the Islamic and African world. Its upper classes were early converts to Islam, establishing themselves firmly in league with their trading partners (Pouwels 2000).

This situation changed when the Portuguese, thwarting Near Eastern merchants, rounded the Cape and conquered bases on the coast to trade in person with the Far East. Portugal was a major world power rivaling the then declining Ottoman Empire. The Islamic world shrank in importance as the Iberians set out to rule the world. The coast remained an important link in the Portuguese seaborne empire, even after some of the cities of the northern coast rebelled with Omani Arab help, only to be subjugated by the Omanis themselves.

In the end, the independence of the merchant city-states was lost to foreigners. The demise of the independent states obviously arose in part from a political culture that emphasized relations between kin-chartered domestic stewards or between trading partners. The coastal cities lacked the wealth to underwrite warfare and the extensive administration of conquered territory and people. Obviously, they achieved their ends through other means. They were unprepared to stave off well-founded cannon-laden warships. Foreign rule brought the independent history of the coastal states to an end.

The armed incursion of the Portuguese in the sixteenth century caused mass exodus of coastal peoples to the hinterland. On the immediate coast, three-quarters of the settlements were abandoned and the remainder severely weakened. Out in the countryside, agricultural communities shifted from open places to secluded hilltops. There was an air of general insecurity and stress following the defeat of local potentates by Portuguese mariners, borne on well-founded cannon-laden sailing vessels. The Portuguese soon dominated the coast, adopting severe restrictions on trade, which ensured their monopoly. They punished dissent and in the process severely weakened long-standing trade networks as well as the other kinds of power relations painstakingly developed by the coastal merchant class. Once-prominent individuals lost control of local crafts, commerce, and political life. Uncooperative sultans were deposed and replaced by puppets. Out of the more than four hundred coastal settlements, only a handful were inhabited by the seventeenth century; the rest vanished (Allen 1977). Even Malindi, the town most faithful to the Portuguese, became a mere shell of its old vital self shortly after Vasco da Gama's visit.

The first casualty of the colonial period was the disruption of traditional African industries. Large-scale production of iron, textiles, and beads declined, finally to be abandoned altogether, as local communities became dependent on cheap mass-produced imports from India and Europe. Local traditions of building construction also declined and were cast aside. The quality of life under colonial rule deteriorated, and with it long-standing modes of exchange that had been important to African traditional culture. The relationships among coastal peoples, which sustained contact between people pursuing very different lifeways and wove a safety net against hard times, came to an end (see Cassey 1998). The trust that bound both trading partners and competitors weakened. The colonial powers used divide-and-rule tactics pitting the ambitions of former partners against one another. The greater interest was the economic well-being of the home countries and their settlers. In the end, the unique qualities of the coastal civilization faded away, replaced by a new set of ideals and attitudes. If the historical evidence about the role of colonialism in the collapse of the coast is so overwhelming, why did archaeologists ignore it for so long?

Acknowledgments

My research was supported by the National Science Foundation (Grant 9615291), the National Geographic (Grant 5816-96), and the Field Museum of Natural History. Permission to conduct surveys and excavations was granted by the Office of the President, Republic of Kenya, through the National Museums of Kenya. I gratefully acknowledge the logistical support of Karega-Munene, George Abungu, Mohamed Mchula, and Salim Mutengo of Kenya. Ahmed Sheikh Nabhany and Sagaff Alawy of Mombasa have taught me the ways of the Swahili in the last fifteen years. More than one hundred American and Kenyan students have participated in my excavations in Kenya and contributed tremendously to my research. Sibel Kusimba, Rahul Chandrashekar Oka, Augustin Holl, and Stephen Nash read the original manuscript and made useful comments.

Notes

1. *Afrasian* bears similar meaning and connotation to the more accepted and commonly used term *Eurasian*. The noted Indianist historian Michael Pearson is among the first authorities to use the term in his book *Port Cities and Intruders: The Swahili Coast,*

India, and Portugal in the Early Modern Era (1998). The word simply means African and Asian interaction spheres across and around the rims of the Indian Ocean.

2. The large-scale decline of the urban centers after AD 500 in India (Dhavalikar 1996; Sharma 1987), the collapse of the Ethiopian kingdom of Aksum (Butzer 1981), and the devastation reported in the thirteenth-century American Southwest (Haas and Creamer 1993) have been blamed on prolonged drought and resultant stress.

CHAPTER EIGHT

Ghana's "Slave Castles," Tourism, and the Social Memory of the Atlantic Slave Trade

Brempong Osei-Tutu

This chapter focuses on the different perspectives that Ghanaians and African Americans bring to the recent restoration of Ghana's "slave castles." The project raises several layers of complexity, including questions about ownership, commodification, and representations of the monuments with African Americans and Ghanaians as stakeholders on a transnational landscape. This chapter highlights the contradictions between the Ghanaian authorities' quest for increased national revenue through the restoration and commodification of Cape Coast and Elmina castles and African Americans' preference for preserving these monuments as sacred sites not to be desecrated.

The transatlantic slave trade, which led to the forceful removal of Africans to the Americas, has not only left its mark on the very tropes of African American collective memory. It has also led to African Americans' search for their roots in Africa as they remap the exit routes from the continent centuries ago. Cape Coast and Elmina castles, which were used as entrepôts in the infamous enterprise, are two such powerful exit routes where history meets memory. In addition, Ghana may hold a special place in the hearts of many African Americans. Their attachment to Ghana can largely be attributed to President Nkrumah's philosophical projection of the "African personality" during his tenure as Ghana's head of state in the 1950s and 1960s (see, e.g., Birmingham 1998; Pellow and Chazan 1986; Petchenkine 1993). Deborah Pellow and Naomi Chazan (1986, 185) describe Nkrumah "as the embodiment of African nationalism and the personification of the quest for continental unity."

Ghana's historic link with prominent African Americans such as W. E. B. Du Bois and his wife and Maya Angelou may be another consideration. All three lived in Ghana, and Dr. and Mrs. Du Bois, who were also pioneers of

Pan-African affairs, have been entombed in Ghana. It is not surprising, then, that Ghana continues to be a place of pilgrimage for many members of African Diaspora communities, especially African Americans (Gaines 1999, 65; Lewis 1999, 41). Ghanaian policy makers assumed that these considerations and the memorialization of the castles and the transatlantic slave trade would motivate African Americans to travel to Ghana. Such assumptions, which seem to be premised on Pan-African images that essentialize brotherhood, cooperation, and togetherness, downplay the differing historical experiences of Ghanaians and African Americans. On the contrary, this chapter highlights the complexity of such a transatlantic enterprise.

Restoration and Preservation Efforts for Ghana's "Slave Castles"

Between the late fifteenth and the early nineteenth centuries, Europeans constructed several structures along West Africa's coastline. Ranging from castles to smaller forts and lodges, these well-fortified bastions became centers of colonial administrative, economic, and political power as well as staging posts for the transatlantic slave trade (Figs. 8.1 and 8.2). The initial function of these structures was to safeguard the merchandise of the various European interests between visits by trading ships as well as to accommodate their resident citizens and their associates (Lawrence 1963, 17; Walker 1998, 17–18). The monuments have a long history of structural changes, having been rebuilt and expanded by the various European factions that controlled them over the centuries, as well as by the postcolonial governments (Anquandah 1982, 133; Bech and Hyland 1978; Hyland 1995, 46; Kankpeyeng and DeCorse 2004, 107–17; Lawrence 1963, 18, 25; Schildkrout 1996, 36; van Dantzig 1980, 82).

The Foundation for the Preservation of Castles and Forts in Ghana was established in 1985 to assist with the restoration of some of the monuments (DeCorse 1987, 28). In the 1970s, the African Descendants Association Foundation of Ghana attempted to mobilize funds to restore Fort Amsterdam at Abandze in the Central Region as a shrine for Africans in the Diaspora. This mainly African Diaspora initiative also provoked controversies, but at that time the opposition came from white and local people. While a group of white people perceived the project as the foundation of a black power movement for antiwhite propaganda, local residents protested that anticipated changes would anger the spirits that protected them (*Ebony*, January 1972, 89–91). The initiative fell through for lack of funding.

Further, as recently as 1992, a newly formed African American Society to Preserve Cape Coast Castle, represented by Isaac Hayes and Dionne Warwick, pledged to raise US$30 million to support the restoration. The pledge, however, did not progress beyond the signing of a memorandum of understanding with

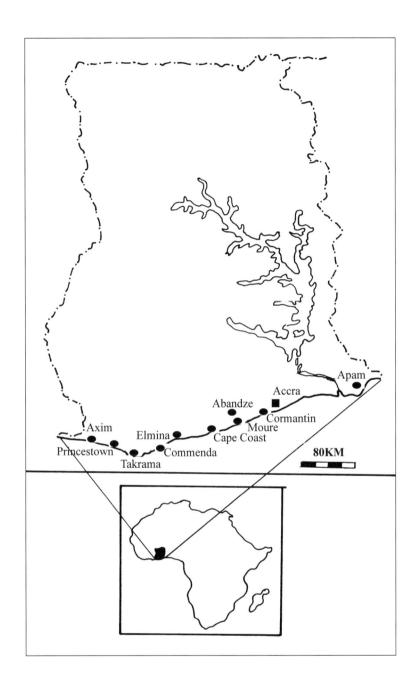

Fig. 8.1. Ghana.

Fig. 8.2. Castle with tourists.

Ghanaian authorities. These initiatives and intentions, as well as my interviews with some African Americans, demonstrate that they do not object to the restoration of the country's "slave castles" per se. This evidence calls for a consideration of the issue of who has the power to represent the monuments, for as some authors have emphasized, not only are the representations of the past contested but they are also imbued with power (e.g., Meskell 1998, 3; Nash 2000, 27).

The Central Region Development Commission initiated the restoration and commodification of Cape Coast and Elmina castles in the 1990s as part of a broader integrated development program to stimulate socioeconomic development in the region (Hyatt 1997, 5; Hyland 1995; Kreamer 2002; MUCIA 1991). This program also involved the creation of a tropical rainforest, wildlife, and nature parks. The Kakum Nature Park, located about thirty kilometers north of Cape Coast, is an example of this initiative. Another aspect of the project involved the development of hotels and auxiliary service industries in the region (MUCIA 1991; West Africa, April 22–28, 1991, no. 3842, 610–11). To accomplish these objectives, the Ghanaian authorities collaborated with USAID and UNDP to fund the restoration of three World Heritage monuments (Fort St. Jago makes the third) between 1991 and 1996 (Hyatt 1997, 6, 31). The project initially sought to stabilize the monuments to make them watertight and put them to adaptive uses. These included refurbishing rooms and installing restaurants and gift shops (Hyatt 1997, 6). In addition, the project sought to transform the castles into a museum complex with facilities for new exhibits, storage, conservation, and training (Singleton 1999b, 156).

Controversies and Compromises

African American Reactions

While restoration is crucial to the preservation of monuments, it can also produce unintended consequences. The restoration of Cape Coast and Elmina castles has evoked several reactions from concerned Diaspora Africans who felt deliberately excluded from a project that significantly impacts their emotional experiences. These include painting the monuments, providing a better lighting system, and opening modern visitor facilities. Some critics see these changes as "Disneyfication" and desecration of what they have regarded as sacred sites, as well as acts of falsification and "whitewashing" designed to mask the evils of slavery. Imahkus Vienna Robinson (now Imahkus Nzingah Okofu), an expatriate in Ghana, characterized the restoration work as "renovation and destruction of an important monument of the African Holocaust." She also questioned why black history was being "whitewashed" by the descendants of those who enslaved Africans. Afrikadzata Deku described the restoration of the monuments as a "tele-guided falsification" in the name of preservation for the promotion of tourism (Deku 1993; I. V. Robinson 1994a, 1994b; Tyehimba 1998, 28).

Critics also challenge the designation of the monuments as castles because they did not house nobility. Disaffection has also been expressed toward all aspects of the commodification of the castles, including the requirement of admission fees from visitors. Some feel that the commercial transaction compromises the solemnity of the buildings (Tyehimba 1998, 30). In spite of the protestations, African Americans continue to be classified as international tourists and are required to pay the same admission fee as other international tourists. African Americans have suggested a more friendly strategy of contributing toward the preservation of the monuments through pledges and donations rather than having to pay mandated entrance fees. Some of them have alleged the underrepresentation of the horrors of the slave trade in the castles' exhibition while others have criticized the exhibition's overemphasis on the experience of enslaved Africans in North America (e.g., Schildkrout 1996, 38; Singleton 1999b, 156). My interview with African Americans showed that some want the Ghanaian authorities to restore the various rooms in the castles to their previous functions to emphasize the disparity in living conditions between the European slavers and the enslaved Africans.

Reactions from the Ghanaian Authorities

While the Ghanaian authorities have shown an appreciation for some of the concerns by African Americans and have taken steps to address them, they have expressed problems with others. A few examples of these reactions will suffice. In 1994, the Ghanaian authorities organized a seminar to discuss some of the problems (National Commission on Culture 1994). One of the outcomes was the closure of a restaurant-bar in Cape Coast Castle out of respect for African American feelings. Further, Ghana's museum officials placed plaques in Cape Coast and Elmina castles with the following inscriptions:

> In everlasting memory
> Of the anguish of our ancestors
> May those who died rest in peace
> May those who return find their roots
> May humanity never again perpetrate such injustice against humanity
> We, the living, vow to uphold this.

Cape Coast Castle's "Door of No Return," the final exit of slaves who were forcefully taken out of the country, was also reopened. This initiative was intended to symbolize the reversal of the original dispersal that had created the African Diaspora.

It is also significant to note that in contrast to the omission of an atonement ritual in neighboring Benin's attempts to commodify that country's slavery heritage (see Sutherland 1999), Ghanaian chiefs have performed rituals, both in Ghana and in the United States, to atone for the ancestral role in the slave trade to appease African Americans (*Washington Post*, August 3, 1995, B1). In addition, exhibits in both Cape Coast and Elmina castles devote a considerable space to the Black Diaspora. Guided tours of the castles/dungeons represent another arena where the Ghanaian authorities and some African American expatriates negotiate productions that ensure that the latter's perspectives are represented. This is achieved through narratives and stage performances that involve reenactments of the horrors of the slave trade. For example, expatriates Nana Okofo Iture Kwaku I and his wife, Imahkus Nzingah Okofu (formerly Benjamin and Imahkus Robinson), own One Africa Productions Tours and Specialty Services Limited, which conducts tours in Cape Coast Castle. This company reenacts a three-part narrative of slavery depicting an initial horror, Diaspora resistance, and a joyous return.

A standard narrative describes how greedy white slavers seized defense-less Africans from their homes and drove them into crowded dungeons with little ventilation and no toilet facilities for months before they were shipped to the Americas (Schildkrout 1996, 36; Tyehimba 1998). A recurrent theme in these narratives draws attention to how the European captors sexually assaulted female captives. Cape Coast and Elmina castles provide space for African Americans to highlight some of the horrors of the transatlantic slave trade. Scholarship on the politics of memory shows how memory can be appropriated and related to what a group considers important (e.g., Early 1999; Nora 1989).

On the other hand, the Ghanaian officials have been critical about other matters of concern to African Americans. For example, even though partici-pants at the 1994 conference recommended that the castles be designated as "castles and dungeons" (Bruner 1996, 294), Ghanaians still anachronisti-cally refer to them as "slave castles" (Osei-Tutu 2003, 16). Only some Ameri-cans consistently use "castles and dungeons." The Ghanaian authorities have also argued that the castles needed to be restored to ensure their preservation (Hyatt 1997, 6; Singleton 1999b, 157). While Ghanaian museum profession-als have devoted considerable attention to the slave trade in the castles' exhibi-tions, they also wish to emphasize the monuments' multifunctional histories as trading posts, slave dungeons, military fortifications, colonial administra-tive centers, prisons, schools, offices, and heritage sites (*U.S. News and World Report*, September 18, 1995, 33). Cape Coast and Elmina castles have served different functions since they were built (Bruner 1996, 293; Hyatt 1997, 29; Schildkrout 1996, 36). Martha Norkunas (1993, 6) reminds us that monu-ments represent complex historical events. The Ghanaian authorities further urge African Americans not only to criticize the restoration project but also to provide funds for the preservation of the monuments.

Commodification, Power, and Identity

African Americans' objection to the commodification of Ghana's "slave castles" recalls the long history of scholarship regarding the perception that commodification contaminates the sacred (e.g., Greenwood 1977; Marx 1967; D. Miller 1995; Parry and Bloch 1989; Upton 2001). The issue is embedded in many mainstream formulations of religious piety and personal identity and the common assumption that commodified identities are less authentic. Most advocates of the search for African Americans' African roots disassociate that quest from commodification (e.g., Asante 1988; Karenga 1982). Paulla Ebron (2000, 912) argues that, for many blacks, the return to their African roots is to escape from the grip of Western materiality and commercial greed.

The problem with this conceptualization of commodification is the dichotomous distinction it makes between spirituality and commodification without reflecting on their mutual constitution (Askegaard and Firat 1997, 115–16; Ebron 2000, 912). Yet the representation of slavery and commodification need not be mutually exclusive. For example, African American tourist companies profit from the new tourist environment created by the commodification of Ghana's "slave castles" through the commercial tours that they organize for blacks in search of their roots. Harold Cook, a director at Henderson Travel Service in Silver Spring, Maryland, notes that commercial tours to Africa have been a major part of their business (*Washington Post*, October 2, 2000, B1–2). Further, Ebron shows how corporate sponsorship enabled some African Americans to fulfill their dreams of undertaking a pilgrimage to Africa in 1994. In the summer of that year, Alex Haley's son, William, facilitated a "homeland" tour to Senegal and Gambia financed by the McDonald's Corporation (Ebron 2000, 915). The involvement of African American tourist companies in the commodification of Africa's heritage complicates the Diaspora's criticism of Ghana's "slave castles." However, American involvement in the commodification of Cape Coast Castle/Dungeon ensures that the African American interest is represented. Above all, the controversies surrounding the restoration project have helped to draw global attention to the lessons of the slave trade (Osei-Tutu 2002, 124).

Situating the Tensions within the Disparate Historical Experiences of Ghanaians and African Americans

The tensions over the restoration project can partly be attributed to the perception among some African Americans that Ghanaians do not have the requisite experience to represent the monuments to their satisfaction. They feel that Ghanaians do not fully understand slavery and its implications, for which reason some of them have attempted to "educate" Ghanaians about life in the Diaspora. Significantly, one of the objectives of the African American Association of Ghana is to "educate" Ghanaians about the African American experience instead of striving for a mutual education of both Ghanaians and African Americans about their respective experiences. In addition, some African Americans have not only spearheaded the commemoration of Juneteenth in

Ghana but have also stormed classrooms in Ghana to "educate" Ghanaians on slavery (Bruner 1996, 295).

I suggest that black Americans' perception of local knowledge of slavery contradicts the Ghanaian reality. For example, it neglects the fact that slavery used to be an important component of Ghanaian school curricula at all levels of education. I recall how my schoolmates and I were upset when confronted with pictures of the tightly packed Africans in slave ships that appeared as illustrations in our history books. Akosua Perbi (pers. comm.), a historian at the University of Ghana, Legon, and Ella Keren (pers. comm.) of the History Department of Tel Aviv University in Israel, however, note that there is very little coverage on the slave trade in the country's schools before college. I also recall Ghanaians' positive reception of Alex Haley's epic docudrama series *Roots* when it made its debut in Ghana.

African American critique of Ghanaian sensibility of slavery also fails to take into consideration what Elmina Castle may mean to the Asante people of Ghana, whose king, Prempeh I, was imprisoned in the fortress for nearly a year before his exile in the Seychelles (Boahen 1972, 7; Moore 1972, 169). Further, it does not take into account the impact that the prolific writings of the expatriate African American community in Ghana on slavery may have had on Ghanaians during the late 1950s and 1960s. For example, some authors note the extent to which these expatriate writers informed Ghanaians about the civil rights demonstrations in the United States through extensive reportage in the local Ghanaian media (Gaines 1999, 65–69; Lewis 1999, 45). Ultimately, one will have to examine the disparate historical trajectories of Ghanaians and African Americans to appreciate their different perspectives on slavery as well as the restoration and commodification of the monuments.

Scholars such as Kwame Appiah (1992, 6–7) and Edward Bruner (1996, 293) locate the complexity of these tensions within the disparate and unequal historical experiences of Ghanaians and African Americans. Even though slavery is an important issue for both Ghanaians and African Americans, they react to it differently. While black Americans long to remember this tragic episode, Ghanaians tend to suppress it, and whereas many black Americans project issues of racism into the controversies, Ghanaians do not. Kwame Arhin argues that most Ghanaians did not even see the British colonial masters and have not endured centuries of slavery and legal segregation, as such racial problems have been less salient in Ghana (*Washington Post*, April 17, 1995, A10). Even under colonization, Africans lived in a society with an overwhelmingly black majority where black people were largely in charge of their own sociocultural and political institutions. For African Americans, on the other hand, daily life was and has been a painful struggle by a minority group against racism and economic marginalization within a dominant white society (O. Davis 1997, 158). Further, racism was the driving force behind the slave trade and colonialism and was also responsible for the deeply rooted racial stereotyping of blacks (Ackah 1999, 12; Dei 1998, 144; Minter 2000).

African American Interior Perspectives

African American criticism of the restoration and commodification of Cape Coast and Elmina castles recalls a long historical tradition. Examples include the 1969 exhibition *Harlem on My Mind* in the Metropolitan Museum of Art in New York City, the accidental discovery of the African Burial Ground in New York City, and the planned excavation of the Foster property in Charlottesville, Virginia. In all of these examples, African Americans protested against the handling of their heritage by outsiders. They also raised the issues of paternalism, self-determination, and the symbolic ownership of their history and identity. They felt that outsiders did not have the requisite insight and spiritual sensitivities to investigate black heritage (Crew 1996, 80, 86; Harrington 1996; *Washington Post*, January 18, 1994, D4). The African American photographer Roy DeCarava better articulated the perspective when he noted, "The fundamental thing is that Blacks want to say their own things about themselves. White people, no matter how sympathetic, can't do it" (Dubin 1999, 38). The fundamental issue being raised in all these instances regards the lack of African American interior perspectives (Ruffins 1992, 512). This problem has also surfaced on Ghana's landscape. Not satisfied with the representation of the castles and the transatlantic slave trade, some African Americans hope to purchase one of the monuments to turn it into a shrine where African American interior perspectives can be presented (Phillips 2000, 206–207). While this position may be problematic, it also cautions that commodification of heritage can provoke intense conflicts when the process results in the trivialization of what some interest groups consider important or when the process is controlled by outsiders with little insight or understanding of the meanings and historicity of the group's past. What is significant about the situation in Ghana is the fact that the controversies have unfolded not in America but in the "ancestral" homeland (Osei-Tutu 2004, 198).

African American Reactions to the Monuments' Restoration

African American reactions to the restoration and commodification of Cape Coast and Elmina castles can partly be linked with their search for history and memory as well as their increasing sense of ownership over their heritage in Africa and elsewhere (Ebron 2000, 911). Further, the conflicts cannot be isolated from the dilemmas that confront African Americans as a Diaspora people returning to the ancestral homeland (Akyeampong 2000, 185–186; Angelou 1986; Clifford 1994, 311; J. Harris 1993, 3–8, 6; Kaur and Hutnyk 1999, 1–13; Safran 1991, 83–84; Shepperson 1993, 44; Skinner 1993, 11). Several African Americans, including Maya Angelou (1986) and Richard Wright (1975), have documented their complex experiences in Ghana. Bruner (1996) and Ebron (2000) have shown specifically that the terrain becomes even more complicated for those whose return to Africa coincides with the unexpected representations of slavery.

Summary and Conclusion

This chapter has highlighted some of the problems surrounding the restoration and commodification of Cape Coast and Elmina castles. Tensions have been noted over attempts to present the monuments and the transatlantic slave trade to African Americans and the way in which power is transmitted through the process. Most of the problems can be attributed to the disparate historical experiences of Ghanaians and African Americans. Whereas African Americans project issues of slavery and racism, Ghanaians tend to be mute about them. In general, issues relating to slavery have always been problematic (e.g., Devenish 1997, 49). While some compromises have been reached on Ghana's landscape, there are still some lingering issues, including ownership of the monuments. Having been declared World Heritage sites by UNESCO, these structures have assumed global significance and ownership. Besides, as Arjun Appadurai has shown in his discussion of the social life of things, ownership over things may come about through avenues such as kinship ties and spiritual connection. I suggest that this is the sense within which the ownership over Ghana's "slave castles" must be approached. From this perspective, Ghana's Museums and Monuments Board remains the statutory national institution that holds these World Heritage sites in trust for humanity. Future attempts at restoring and presenting any of these monuments will require consultation with all stakeholders, including Ghanaians, African Americans, and Europeans. They will also require dialogue, sensitivity, and tolerance.

III
African Diaspora

CHAPTER NINE

BaKongo Identity and Symbolic Expression in the Americas

Christopher C. Fennell

Archaeologists have recovered a variety of objects that appear to have been used for religious purposes by African American occupants of sites in the late seventeenth through nineteenth centuries in North America. Examples include pottery bowls with crosses incised on their bases; white clay marbles, coins, and pewter spoons with X marks scratched into them; and caches of quartz crystals, polished stones, pieces of chalk, ash, iron nails, and bladelike fragments, bird skulls, crab claws, coins, and bone disks secreted under the brick and wood floors of dwellings (see, e.g., Brown 1994; Ferguson 1992, 1999; Franklin 1997c; Galke 2000; Leone and Fry 1999; McKee 1995; Patten 1992; Samford 1996; Wilkie 1995, 1997; Young 1996, 1997). These objects typically appear in contexts that indicate they were used in private, often covert, settings. The symbolic composition of these items also appears to be significantly abbreviated in comparison to key symbols of African religions from the relevant periods. These characteristics raise intriguing issues concerning the processes of symbolic expression and the blending of cultural beliefs and practices over time.

This study explores the ways in which such artifacts likely served their creators and users as significant components of private religious rituals, as potential communicators of group identities, and as expressions of individual creativity in the forging of new social relationships (for further details, see Fennell 2003a, 2003b). Moving beyond a simple assumption that African Americans retained static and conservative cultural traditions with which they shaped such material culture, this study examines the creative uses of facets of African cultural beliefs over time and in new social settings (see Posnansky 1999, 22; Raboteau 1980, 4–8; Singleton 1999a, 8; Singleton and Bograd 1995, 25). In particular, I examine an array of artifacts that appear to have been created as expressions of certain beliefs within the BaKongo culture of West Central Africa, and the changes over time and space in the modes of symbolic expressions derived from that belief system. This analysis is also designed to avoid the tendency of assuming that there existed forms of "pan-African" cultural beliefs and significant degrees of homogeneity among African religions that were diverse and rich in their beliefs and practices (Morgan 1998, 610–11; Posnansky 1999, 22; Thomas 1995, 149, 153).

This chapter sets forth an interpretative framework in which these artifacts can be viewed as possessing meaning and significance derived from a core symbol utilized as a material expression within the BaKongo culture. This interpretative exercise illustrates the dynamics of three interrelated processes. First, core cultural symbols are used in a broad spectrum of expressive modes. I will refer to the use of a core symbol to express a social group's collective identity as an "emblematic" expression of that symbol. At the other end of the spectrum, private expressions of components of a core symbol for personal purposes can be referred to as "instrumental" symbols. Thus, for any particular core symbol of a social group, there will typically exist both emblematic expressions of that core symbol and instrumental versions. Second, such a core symbol is typically expressed in its most fully complex and embellished form in the emblematic expressions of public and group rituals. When a core symbol of a religious belief system is used for more private and personal ends, it is typically expressed as an instrumental symbol that uses only selected and abbreviated components of the full array of the core symbol's composition. Third, such an individual and private use of abbreviated forms of core symbols can lead to stylistic innovation and the creation of new symbolic repertoires to express membership in social networks formed in new settings.

These three processes unfolded when persons who subscribed to the BaKongo culture in Africa were abducted into slavery and were able to continue their religious practices only in covert, individualized settings in the slave quarters of plantations and "big houses" located in North America. In such social settings, those persons could not easily continue the group rituals and public expressions of their religious beliefs and associated core symbols. They focused instead on individualized and private uses of those core symbols to invoke spiritual powers for self-protection.

This study is organized into three parts. First, I set out a theoretical framework concerning core symbols and their varied expressions within religious belief systems. This framework includes interpretative schemes for examining group and emblematic expressions of core symbols, more individual and instrumental expressions, and the varying deployment of such symbols by dominant and subordinated social groups. I then employ these theoretical insights to formulate a methodology for assessing the significance of religious artifacts uncovered at African American domestic sites in North America that date within the late seventeenth through nineteenth centuries. I construct a form of ethnographic analogy, using ethnohistorical data concerning the past beliefs and practices of the BaKongo religion in West Central Africa. I then outline the patterns of symbolic expressions one might expect to see in new settings. Then I examine an apparent divergence in the way this creative process played out at sites in North America, the Caribbean, and South America. The use of private, instrumental symbolism is prevalent in the religious artifacts uncovered at African American sites in North America. With rare exception, there is little evidence of newly elaborated core symbols of blended African religions emerging in the material culture of African Americans. This contrasts significantly with the material culture and symbolism of African descendant groups in Caribbean and South American locations, such as Haiti and Brazil. In those locations outside the United States, new forms of embellished symbolism were developed out of the blending of elements of diverse African religions, including the BaKongo, Yoruba, and Dahomean belief systems. These embellished symbols were often displayed publicly and in ways likely intended to signal new social networks and group identities.

Individual and Group Manifestations of Core Symbols

In individual and private exercises of spiritual power, the creator of a particular material symbolic expression will often design it to embody an array of metaphors, making the symbolic expression polysemous by design (Douglas 1975, 150; 1996, 10; Firth 1973, 207; Wagner 1975, 90, 98, 122). Other persons within the same social networks who view and react to that symbolic representation will often see in it one or more of the metaphors intended by the designer, but may also read from it metaphoric meanings not intentionally communicated by the author (Bruner 1993, 332; Fabian 1985, 145–47). The symbolic expression can thus be created and used in a way that has a separate polyvalent impact (the array of metaphoric meanings read into the expression by viewers of the symbol) that overlaps to some degree with the polysemous design of the author (Tilley 1999, 28–33; Turner 1967, 20–31).

However, these dynamics do not leave us at a loss to say anything useful in attempting to analyze the creation and use of particular symbolic expressions in different cultural settings and periods. When particular forms of symbolic expression appear and reappear with some degree of consistency in related cultural circumstances, that persistent pattern and its changes provide a subject for analysis (Rosaldo, Lavie, and Narayan 1993, 5–6). While the spoken words of past rituals may be lost to us, the archaeological record often shows patterns of persistent material forms of symbolic expressions that can be interpreted in the context of one or more past cultural traditions and associated meaning systems (Tilley 1999, 31; Turner 1973, 1101). Thus analysts can detect patterns of expressions and attempt to interpret the cultural traditions that inspired past actors in their creation and use of varied symbols and associated metaphors.

The analyst's interpretative construction of the primary array of metaphors and meanings expressed in particular material symbols over time will not fully capture the array of metaphors intended by specific creators of those symbols. Nor will it fully capture the array of metaphors and meanings that other readers within a past cultural tradition would have taken away from the symbol. Yet the analyst's interpretative construction, if assembled with rigor and constrained by a closeness of fit to the available evidence, will overlap at least in part with the primary and repeated metaphors intended by past authors and read by past viewers of the material symbols (Firth 1973, 208; Hegmon 1992, 527; Janzen 1985, 243; Thompson and Cornet 1981, 45; Tilley 1999, 260–66).

A number of anthropologists have addressed ways of analyzing "core" cultural symbols, which have also been referred to as "dominant" or "key" symbols (e.g., Geertz 1973, 126–41; Ortner 1973, 1338–39; Schneider 1980, 8, 113–14; Turner 1967, 20–31; 1973, 1101–1104; Wagner 1986, 11–12). For example, Sherry Ortner analyzed key symbols within individual cultures as being characterized along a continuum of expressions. At one end of this spectrum are expressions of a key symbol that I will refer to as "emblematic" expressions, which are meaningful and significant as expressions of group identity and solidarity. At the other end are expressions that have a more limited, instrumental purpose.

According to Ortner, emblematic symbols typically have the effect of "summing up, expressing, [and] representing for the participants in an emotionally powerful way, what the system means to them." These emblematic expressions usually invoke "a conglomerate of ideas and feelings" and an array of metaphoric meanings communicated by the different elements composing the emblem. This type of expression is emblematic in that it stands for all those ideas, feelings, and metaphors "all at once" and "does not encourage reflection on the logical relations among these ideas, nor on the logical consequences of them as they are played out in social actuality." Ortner sees examples of such emblematic symbols in the American flag, the crucifix of Christianity, and the churinga of Australian Aborigine groups. Thus emblematic symbols can be expressive of a variety of identity types, such as subscription to a particular cosmology, or membership in a particular social network, or membership in a specific nationality (Ortner 1973, 1339–40).

In contrast, an "instrumental" symbol has a more practical and immediate purpose and is "valued primarily because it implies clear-cut modes of action appropriate to correct and successful living" (Ortner 1973, 1341). These instrumental symbols are thus "culturally valued in that they formulate the culture's basic means-ends relationships in actable forms" (Ortner 1973, 1341). Over time, actors may take components of an emblematic symbol and create a derivative, but more limited, instrumental symbol. In turn, that derived instrumental symbol may become further developed and embellished so that it comes to function as a summarizing symbol for a different identity and worldview in a later social setting (Firth 1973, 236–37; Ortner 1973, 1344; Wolf 1972, 150).

This spectrum of emblematic versus instrumental, abbreviated expressions of a core symbol can be illustrated with the BaKongo cosmogram. The BaKongo people consisted of a cluster of ethnic groups who spoke the KiKongo language, who shared a cultural system called the BaKongo, and who inhabited the area referred to historically as Kongo. That geographic area consisted of territories now located in the nations of the Democratic Republic of Congo, Gabon, the Republic of Congo, and Angola, in a region that historians often refer to as West Central Africa (MacGaffey 2000c, 35–36; Janzen 1977, 112).

A core symbol of the BaKongo culture was an ideographic religious symbol, or cosmogram, which can be referred to as *tendwa kia nza-n' Kongo* or *dikenga dia Kongo* in the KiKongo language and which I will refer to as the *dikenga*. Ethnohistorical sources and material culture evidence demonstrate that the dikenga existed as a long-standing symbolic tradition within the BaKongo culture before European contact in 1482 and that it continued in use in West Central Africa through the early twentieth century (Janzen 1977, 81; Janzen and MacGaffey 1974, 34; MacGaffey 2000b, 8–11; Thompson and Cornet 1981, 27–30, 43–45; Thornton 1998, 251). In its fullest embellishment, this symbol served as an emblematic expression of the BaKongo people and summarized a broad array of ideas and metaphoric messages that represented their sense of identity within the cosmos (see, e.g., Gundaker 1998, 8–10; MacGaffey 1986, 136, 169–71; R. F. Thompson 1997, 29–30).

Figure 9.1 depicts a rendering of the full dikenga, with a composition consisting of multiple components that summarize and represent a remarkable array of key ideas and metaphoric meanings. The dikenga consists of intersecting vertical and horizontal axes, set within a circle or ellipse, with smaller circles or disks at the four ends of those crossed lines (Jacobson-Widding 1991, 182–83; MacGaffey 1986, 43–46; Thompson 1997, 29–30). The small disks represent the "four moments" of the sun and cosmos, with the top symbolizing the direction of north, the sun at noon, a masculine element, the land of the living, the apex of a person's earthly life and power in that life, and the upper realm of the Godhead. The bottom disk represents the direction of south, the sun at midnight, a female element, the land of the dead and the spirits, and the apex of a person's spiritual power. The right-hand disk represents the direction of east, the sun at dawn, the power of potentiality and transition, and nascence of the spirit, soul, and earthly life in a cosmic cycle. The left-hand disk represents west, the sun at dusk, the power and transition of death, and movement from the living to the spirit world. Movement in this depicted symbolic cycle is conceptualized as proceeding counterclockwise (Gomez 1998, 148–49; Janzen and MacGaffey 1974, 34; R. F. Thompson 1983, 108–109).

The surrounding circle or ellipse conveys the cyclical nature of earthly life and the natural world, the spiritual journey of the soul, and the evolution of

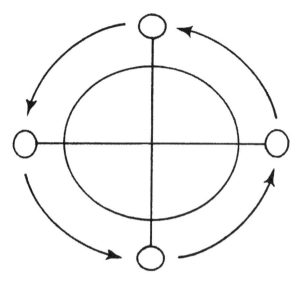

Fig. 9.1. Dikenga dia Kongo, the BaKongo cosmogram.

spirits. The crossed lines communicate an array of meanings concerning both the oppositional ordering of the cosmos and the invocation of spiritual powers into the land of the living. The vertical "power line" connects the Godhead above with the lower realm of lesser spirits, ancestor spirits, and the dead. It also communicates the invocation of spiritual power from below into the land of the living above. The horizontal line is the "line of Kalunga," which is the boundary line between the supreme God and the lesser spirits and also the boundary between the land of the living and the realm of the spirits and the dead (Thompson and Cornet 1981, 28, 44; Thornton 1983, 9). Both living persons and the souls of the dead are conceptualized as cycling through incarnations, the living becoming the dead, the dead forming souls and ancestors, and ancestors evolving into more powerful spirits, as depicted by the wheeling element of the surrounding circle and the progression of the four moments of the cosmos (Balandier 1968, 155; Thompson 1997, 29–30).

The opposing realms of upper and lower unfold in even more metaphoric oppositions expressed in this emblematic version. The upper land of the living is inhabited by people with dark complexions, opposed and mirrored by the lower realm of the land of the dead and spirits, inhabited by souls colored white. The east and west points are powerful points of transition from birth to death and rebirth, and they are associated with red as the color of birth and death. The upper land of the living is conceptualized as a mountain range, mirrored at the Kalunga boundary by a comparable mountain range in the land of the dead. The Kalunga line is a boundary for which the surface of water

204

is a metaphoric image, and the mirroring flash of water and other reflective surfaces invokes this immediate interrelation of the land of the living and the spirits. The crossed lines represent the BaKongo belief that spirits pervasively imbue the land of the living and can be summoned to cross the boundary and come to the aid of an individual, family, or community to provide aid in subsistence and protection against disease, misfortune, and other harmful spirits (Janzen and MacGaffey 1974, 34; Thompson and Cornet 1981, 27–30).

A more abbreviated and instrumental form of the dikenga, consisting solely of the crossed axes, omits the surrounding cycle of lives and souls and the four moments of the cosmos with their multiple, metaphoric oppositions (Jacobson-Widding 1991, 183; MacGaffey 1988b, 516; Thompson and Cornet 1981, 43–44). The crossed lines provide a more focused and selective invocation of the intersection of the spirit world and the land of the living for immediate social action. Among the BaKongo people, this was the "simplest form" of dikenga rendering, and it was used when individuals took oaths of truthfulness or undertook private rituals to seek spiritual aid (MacGaffey 1986, 118). These crossed lines were typically drawn upon the ground, and a person would stand at the intersection of the lines when swearing an oath, or a ritual specialist would draw the lines upon the ground to demarcate a private ritual space in which a spirit would be summoned for the aid of an individual supplicant. The crossed lines could also be drawn or etched onto objects in combination with vocalized prayers to create protective objects and amulets. Thus an abbreviated version of the emblematic form of the dikenga usually served more private and instrumental purposes (Jacobson-Widding 1991, 201; MacGaffey 1991, 4; Thompson and Cornet 1981, 43–44).

Ethnohistorical Analogy and the Interpretation of a BaKongo Diaspora

Can one credibly interpret the crossed lines scratched into bowl bases, marbles, spoons, and coins or the crossed lines demarcated by the position of buried caches of objects at African American sites in North America as the solemn expressions of the BaKongo cosmology? Such a proposition would be greatly strengthened if there existed specific evidence that persons enculturated in BaKongo beliefs and practices had lived at each of those sites. This observation raises the initial issue of whether individuals abducted into slavery and subjected to the horrors of the "middle passage" across the Atlantic could have retained any of their cultural beliefs and practices.

Some historians have contended that the traumatic experiences of enslavement effectively destroyed Africans' memories and knowledge of the cultural traditions that existed in the homelands from which they were abducted (e.g., Frazier 1966a, 1966b; Whitten 1962). In addition, some scholars of African cultures and religions have argued that many of those belief systems lacked a concept of individuality similar to that found among Western cultures, so that an "individual" could not "exist alone except corporately" (Mbiti 1990, 106; Mogobe 1988, 10; cf. R. Handler 1994, 31–34).

Other studies have demonstrated that enslaved Africans succeeded in retaining detailed memories of the belief systems of their original cultures and that they passed these traditions on to later generations throughout the Americas (e.g., Herskovits 1958; Perdue, Barden, and Phillips 1976). Similarly, other analysts find extensive historical evidence of concepts of individualism among a variety of African cultures, which should have facilitated a person's ability to adapt to new group settings (e.g., Morris 1994, 139–40, 145–46). While enslaved Africans were unable to transport their social structures to America, individuals could bring their learning and cultural knowledge with them. Torn from their previous social relationships and thrown into new settings on American plantations and in big houses, Africans needed to apply their cultural knowledge creatively in forging new relationships. In addition to the average members of each cultural group abducted into slavery, healers, diviners, priests, priestesses, and political leaders were frequently abducted as well, and they brought with them even more specialized beliefs and practices (Mintz and Price 1976, 10; Raboteau 1980, 50; Sobel 1987, 6).

Sidney Mintz and Richard Price argued persuasively that enslaved African Americans most likely forged new social relationships with one another by focusing on their common cultural and cosmological assumptions, creating innovative forms of expression in their new settings. Such subjugated persons would have focused less on trying to retain the "formal elements" of their different African cultural traditions, such as specific kinship or political modes of organization (Mintz and Price 1976, 6–7, 21). One avenue for these creative efforts would have involved individuals' greater use of instrumental symbols to invoke spiritual aid and protection for themselves and their new cohort and a lesser focus on using emblematic symbols expressive of their past group identities.

To explore these processes, consider an array of artifacts uncovered at sites occupied by African Americans in the late seventeenth through nineteenth centuries in North America. For example, archaeologists excavating the basement level of the Charles Carroll house in Annapolis, Maryland, occupied between 1721 and 1821, uncovered deposits of objects, including quartz crystals, a smooth black stone, a glass bead, pottery pieces decorated with cross and asterisk marks, and pierced discs and coins. These objects had been deposited in caches under the floorboards of adjacent work rooms (E. Adams 1994, 1–2; Galke 2000, 23–25; L. H. Jones 2000, 2; Leone and Fry 1999, 372–73; Logan 1995; Russell 1997, 64–65). Similar finds were uncovered at the nearby Brice and Slayton houses, dating from the mid- to late nineteenth century (Neuwirth and Cochran 2000).

At plantation sites in South Carolina and Virginia, archaeologists recovered pieces of "colonoware" pottery associated with use by African Americans. A number of these pieces of pots and bowls had crosses scratched into their round bases and were recovered from rivers near the sites of past rice plantations in South Carolina (Ferguson 1992, 110–16; 1999, 121–27; Orser 1994a, 38–39). At the Locust Grove Plantation in Kentucky, archaeologists uncovered a white clay marble and a silver teaspoon with X marks incised into them and glass prisms from a chandelier dating from the 1790s through 1860 (Young 1996, 1997).

The Levi Jordan Plantation site in Brazoria, Texas, yielded particularly intriguing artifacts. This site was occupied from 1848 through 1888, when it was rapidly abandoned due to eviction proceedings. African Americans lived in slave quarters and later lived and worked at the site as tenant farmers. They were forced off the land in 1888 by the plantation owner's heirs in a manner that resulted in sudden abandonment of their dwellings (Brown 1994, 96–98, 102–103). Artifacts uncovered at several of those house sites presented distinct assemblages indicating that a number of the dwellings had been occupied by persons who possessed well-defined social and economic roles. For example, the archaeologists referred to one house site as the residence of a seamstress and others as past residences of a carver, a carpenter, a political leader, and a curer (also referred to as a healer, magician, or conjurer) (Brown 1994, 101, 106–107; Brown and Brown 1998; Brown and Cooper 1990, 15).

The curer's cabin contained four caches of objects in the floor space of one room. These caches were not located at the corners of the room but rather along the perimeter at each of the cardinal directions. They contained round iron kettle bases and white chalk, a concentrated deposit of iron wedges or knife-blade fragments, a series of silver coins, two iron kettles with heavy chain fragments, white ash and clay, and burned iron nails, shell, and ash (Brown 1994, 108–10; Brown and Brown 1998, 2). Another African American dwelling nearby, which the archaeologists referred to as the "political leader's cabin," contained a concealed brick embossed with crossed lines surrounded by an ellipse (Brown 1994, 112, 115).

Archaeologists investigating these sites in Maryland, Virginia, South Carolina, Kentucky, and Texas have each interpreted these artifacts as representing objects of religious significance derived from the beliefs of the BaKongo religion. Based on material similarities and contextual evidence, the artifacts are viewed as expressing symbolic compositions consistent with the BaKongo dikenga or with related objects of spiritual invocation called *minkisi* in the KiKongo language (Brown 1994; Brown and Cooper 1990; Ferguson 1992, 1999; Franklin 1997c; Galke 2000; Leone and Fry 1999; Neuwirth and Cochran 2000; Patten 1992; Samford 1996; Young 1996, 1997). These interpretations have been viewed skeptically by some commentators, who caution that archaeologists should be careful and explicit in the logical steps taken in arriving at such inferences (e.g., Deetz 1995, 1996; Fennell 2000; Howson 1990; Thomas 1995).

For example, it is often unclear whether these interpretations are based on an approach that invokes a direct and specific historical link between the occupation site and persons known to have come from the BaKongo culture (cf. Steward 1942). Some analysts, such as Leland Ferguson (1992, 1999), have attempted to show that persons abducted into slavery from the Kongo area were brought to the general region in which the archaeological finds were located. However, if more direct and specific types of evidence exist, they have not been identified in the archaeologists' studies. Similarly, it remains unclear whether these interpretations are based on an approach that employs some form of ethnographic analogy (see Ascher 1961; Stahl 1993; Thomas 1995; Trigger 1995; Wylie 1985). If such a method has been applied, these analysts have yet to set forth their specific methodologies.

Interpreting Particular Cultural Expressions through Analogy

There typically existed corroborative and contextual evidence to support the proposition that the artifacts in question, at each of the sites described above, were located in the living quarters of enslaved or free African Americans (see, e.g., Brown and Cooper 1990, 18; Wilkie 1997, 102). However, there is no direct documentary or archaeological evidence at any of those sites to demonstrate that one or more of the past inhabitants was abducted from the area of West Central Africa or was in some way closely associated with a member of the BaKongo culture. Such specific evidence would be required if one were to apply a direct historical approach and interpret these artifacts as particular expressions of core symbols of the BaKongo culture.

Other potential sources of direct evidence typically fall short of such proof as well. For example, the records of individual slave shipments arriving in North American ports are often unhelpful, because those records usually fail to identify individuals or the locations within West or West Central Africa from which each person was abducted (DeCorse 1999, 135; Lovejoy 1989, 378). Identifying the ports on the African coast from which slave ships departed also fails to provide specific evidence for particular persons. Slave ships embarking from African ports often carried persons abducted from various locations in the interior and transported long distances to those ports (DeCorse 1999, 136–37; Posnansky 1999, 25; Walsh 2001, 141).

In the absence of direct evidence linking an occupant of these sites with someone known to have been enculturated in the BaKongo belief system, an analyst should instead formulate an explicit interpretative framework based on a form of ethnographic analogy. One can then compare and contrast in a more systematic manner the ethnohistorical information concerning a specific African cultural system with the material culture evidence found at the relevant sites in North America. "Ethnohistorical" data in this context means evidence based on the oral histories, writings, and material culture of a particular African society, and also evidence carefully compiled from critical readings of Europeans' (often biased) descriptions of that society in the past. Such an approach using an ethnohistorical analogy requires one to compile a detailed account of the beliefs and practices of an identifiable culture in one place and time (often referred to as the "source" of the analogy), and then to compare and contrast the attributes of that belief system with the material culture of another time and place (Ascher 1961; Stahl 1993; Wylie 1985).

A first step in constructing an ethnohistorical analogy is to demonstrate that the selected cultural system that will provide the source information for the analogy is relevant to the subject of material culture to which it will be applied (Stahl 1993, 248–50; Thomas 1995, 153; Trigger 1995, 450–52; Wylie 1985, 101). The BaKongo religion was practiced by a large percentage of the population in West Central Africa throughout the period of slavery. However, people abducted into slavery and brought to the North American colonies came from a variety of regions in Africa. Nonetheless, the general relevance of West Central African culture to the potential cultural beliefs and practices of occupants of slave quarters in North American sites is readily demonstrated.

Continuing studies of the Atlantic slave trade, building on the work of Philip Curtin (1969), David Richardson (1989), and others, have estimated that approximately 26 percent of enslaved Africans brought to North America came from West Central Africa, 24 percent from the Bight of Biafra, 15 percent from Sierra Leone, 14 percent from Senegambia, 13 percent from the Gold Coast, and 4 percent from the Bight of Benin (Gomez 1998, 29; also see Lovejoy 1989). Other studies similarly estimate that over one-third came from West Central Africa (Eltis 2001, 44, table II; Morgan 1998, 62–68; Thompson and Cornet 1981, 32).

The dynamics of the slave trade could present further obstacles to the ability of individuals to retain and practice their BaKongo (West Central African) beliefs over time. It is possible that persons abducted from West Central Africa could have lost their original cultural beliefs and practices before arriving in North America if they were first forced to adapt to the settings of plantations in the Caribbean for a number of years. However, recent studies show that most Africans abducted into slavery and brought to British North America were transported there directly from Africa and not from the Caribbean or South America (Eltis 2001, 36–37). For example, Lorena Walsh has recently calculated that 93 percent of persons abducted into slavery and brought to the Chesapeake region came directly from Africa "or were transshipped from the West Indies after only a brief period of recuperation from their transatlantic ordeal." Examining newly expanded databases of slave shipment records, she found that "almost all of the 18,000 slaves estimated to have been imported into Maryland in the eighteenth century came, as in Virginia, directly from Africa" (Walsh 2001, 144–45, 148).

A significant percentage of those slaves brought to Maryland came from West Central Africa as well, ranging from 13 to 48 percent in the period of

1731–73 (Walsh 2001, 167, table I). Between 1710 and 1769, 3,860 slaves were imported into Virginia from the Angola region within West Central Africa, out of a total of 52,504 slaves imported into that colony from all African locations (Holloway 1990, 11). Other census calculations show that enslaved persons imported from the Angola region of West Central Africa into South Carolina comprised 59 percent of all slaves imported into that colony in the period of 1733–44, 14 percent in 1749–87, and 52 percent in 1804–1807 (Holloway 1990, 7).

Significant numbers were abducted from the Kongo, Angola, and adjacent regions in West Central Africa and taken directly to the areas in which the North American archaeological sites in question were later uncovered. While this fact is not sufficient to provide a direct historical link for each site, it demonstrates the relevance of using the attributes of the BaKongo beliefs and practices in formulating an ethnohistorical analogy for use in interpreting the potential meaning and significance of the material culture uncovered at slave quarters in North America. After compiling a detailed description of this source for our analogy, we need to apply it to the artifacts and context of the North American sites to determine the degree to which the attributes of the source provide a closeness of fit for interpreting the meaning and significance of those objects. In addition, the context in which the artifacts are found at each site is of critical importance when formulating inferences of their meaning, use, and significance in those settings (Brown and Cooper 1990, 16–19; Posnansky 1972, 34; Stine, Cabak, and Groover 1996, 64–65).

The particular character of the interpretation proposed here raises another relevance criterion for the source of the analogy. My research question proposes that persons learned in BaKongo cultural beliefs and practices were abducted into slavery in the sixteenth through nineteenth centuries and brought to North America, where they continued their practices and taught these traditions to others. Therefore, the ethnohistorical evidence should provide details of a BaKongo culture that existed in Africa in periods predating the related artifacts uncovered in North America. The level of specificity involved in this type of analysis makes a requirement of chronological relevance appropriate. I am not proposing the use of an ethnographic analogy to yield only a general interpretation that these artifacts at North American sites were simply of a general spiritual or ideological character, rather than purely utilitarian in nature. Nor do I seek to assess an interpretation that such artifacts simply exhibit some form of homogeneous "pan-African" spiritual character (Lovejoy 1997, 10; Thomas 1995, 153). The ethnohistorical analogy proposed here is designed for the purpose of credibly assessing an interpretation that these artifacts show the attributes of spiritual expressions consistent with the BaKongo religion in a West Central cultural context. The use of such a specific analogy also provides a means to assess the extent to which there may have been changes and innovations in those expressive motifs over time and in the new settings in which African Americans lived.

There have been two main difficulties related to this requirement of chronological relevance. A much greater body of ethnographic data concerning many African cultures was compiled in the late nineteenth and early twentieth centuries than in earlier periods. One should not rely solely on ethnographic data of a particular African society compiled in the late nineteenth or early twentieth century to construct an analogy for application to artifacts in North America that date from earlier periods (Handler and Lange 1978, 210; Howson 1990, 78–81; Jamieson 1995, 43; Palmer 1995, 224; Thomas 1995, 152–53). To do so, one would have to assume that the characteristics of the African society under analysis had remained static for centuries preceding the time of ethnographic description (Posnansky 1999, 22; Singleton 1999a, 8). While some facets of a culture may have remained consistent for decades or centuries, this fact should not be assumed but established by ethnohistorical and material culture evidence from the earlier periods relevant to the study.

Finally, when employing ethnohistorical analogies, analysts should refrain from "mapping" a "wide range of social traits" from the source-side of the analogy onto the subject of interpretation based only on limited similarities in some forms of belief systems and associated material expressions. For example, one may find evidence of symbolic objects in North American sites that are consistent with the attributes of an instrumental and abbreviated expression of the BaKongo dikenga in private settings. However, one should not assume, based on that finding alone, that occupants of those sites in North America also displayed symbolic renderings consistent with an emblematic expression of the dikenga to assert group identity in public settings. Similarly, one should not assume that an individual who performed a role as a ritual specialist and healer within the slave quarters of a North American plantation would have possessed all the social status and attributes of a comparable specialist within the BaKongo culture in West Central Africa (Schmidt 1995, 125; Stahl 1993, 252–53; Thomas 1995, 154).

Formulating a more explicit and detailed ethnohistorical analogy, which compares primary facets of the BaKongo culture in Africa with the characteristics of the African American artifacts under consideration here, yields two main benefits. First, a more systematic study provides a greater body of evidence with which to judge the accuracy of these interpretations of artifacts. Second, a more thorough consideration of the BaKongo religion as practiced historically in West Central Africa reveals dynamics of the emblematic and instrumental symbolism utilized within that belief system. A comparative use of an ethnohistorical analogy points out not only elements of correspondence, but instances of divergence (Stahl 1983, 252–53; Wylie 1985, 107) between the repertoire of material expressions utilized within the BaKongo culture in Africa, those expressed in African American domestic sites in North America, and those expressed in newly embellished forms by African Americans in settings in the Caribbean and South America. This, in turn, permits a richer analysis of the social significance of the artifacts uncovered at these sites.

BaKongo Beliefs and Practices in West Central Africa

Extensive historical information about the BaKongo people's culture and religion is available from Europeans' ethnohistorical accounts dating back at least to the time of Portuguese colonists' arrival in Kongo in 1482 (see, e.g., Janzen 1977, 77; MacGaffey 1986, 21–24; 2000b, 7–8; Vansina 1966, 6–7). Numerous accounts of Christian missionaries and European officials in the sixteenth and seventeenth centuries must be read critically to extract useful ethnographic information while avoiding reliance on biased characterizations (Balandier 1968, 22; Vansina 1966, 8–9). Anthropologists and historians working with these ethnohistorical accounts and later ethnographic observations find notable continuity in the principal facets of the BaKongo religion from the sixteenth century through the late nineteenth century (e.g., Balandier 1968; Hilton 1985; Jacobson-Widding 1979, 1991; Janzen and MacGaffey 1974; MacGaffey 1986, 2000b; R. Thompson 1993; Thornton 1983, 1998). Their observations are not based on mere assumptions of constancy or the "conservative" character of religions, but rather on the critical reading of numerous ethnohistorical accounts that span that period (cf. DeCorse 1999, 134). This continuity resulted largely from the particular historical dynamics of political strategies of BaKongo ruling factions over time and the related effects of indirect European colonial rule and Christian missionary strategies (see, e.g., MacGaffey 1986, 179).

Extensive documentary, material culture, and oral history evidence indicates that the core elements of BaKongo religion survived the period of the slave trade (Janzen 1977, 81; MacGaffey 2000b, 8–11; Thornton 1998, 251). Through much of the eighteenth and nineteenth centuries, the BaKongo people were able to retain and speak the KiKongo language and to practice many of the central facets of the BaKongo religion, particularly in more private settings. Although members of the BaKongo culture adopted Christianity, they did so in a very selective manner, translating most of the Christian concepts and icons into the BaKongo worldview (Balandier 1968, 65, 80; Berlin 1996, 259–60; 1998, 73; Thornton 1983, 63; 2002, 83–90).

In addition to the BaKongo beliefs discussed earlier, primary elements of the BaKongo religion included a concept of a supreme Godhead, called Nzambi Mpungu in KiKongo, who was the creator of all things (Laman 1962, 53; Raboteau 1980, 9). The crossed lines of the dikenga were viewed as "Nzambi's writing" and should not be drawn by any person without solemnity (Laman 1962, 56). However, Nzambi was viewed as a remote creator, uninvolved in the daily affairs of the living (Vansina 1966, 30). Nzambi created a variety of intermediary spirits, known as *basimbi* (also spelled *bisimbi* for the plural and *simbi* in the singular) to whom the living may make supplication for aid in subsistence and for protection from disease, misfortune, and the attacks of adversaries (Janzen and MacGaffey 1974, 34–35; MacGaffey 1991, 6; Raboteau 1980, 9). This BaKongo concept of intermediary simbi spirits was notably distinct from

212

the Yoruba and Fon concepts in West Africa of a pantheon of subdeities, each with specific personalities (see, e.g., Raboteau 1980, 9–12).

BaKongo people made supplications and requested the aid of particular simbi spirits, ancestor spirits, or the souls of the dead by creating physical containers, such as bowls, gourds, or cloth bags, into which a manifestation of one of those spirits could be summoned and focused (Laman 1962, 34, 44–45, 67; MacGaffey 1991, 1–6; 2000b, 82–83). These physical objects were called *minkisi* in KiKongo (*nkisi* in the singular). Minkisi were created by ritual specialists called *banganga* (*nganga* in the singular). The compositions of various types of minkisi were replete with metonymic and metaphoric meanings that were summarized and represented in the components of the dikenga (MacGaffey 1991, 4–6; Thompson and Cornet 1981, 37). The minkisi were typically created and used in association with a ritual space demarcated by crossed lines drawn upon the ground, and the crossed-line motif was often incorporated into the decorative design of individual nkisi objects themselves (Laman 1962, 149, 152, 156; 1968, 37; MacGaffey 2000b, 107–108; Van Wing 1941, 86). These rituals included both divination, to determine the causes of misfortune or illness, and enactment of supplications to obtain protection, cures, or retribution (Thornton 1983, 59–62). A variety of minkisi were created over time, some designed to contain more powerful spirits capable of lethal actions and others to contain more benign spirits for the purposes of healing or protecting an individual or household (Janzen and MacGaffey 1974, 37; MacGaffey 1991, 5–6, 33–34; Van Wing 1941, 86–87).

A nkisi was thus viewed as the container for a manifestation of an invoked spirit, and the object itself was not worshiped as an idol (Jacobson-Widding 1979, 132; Janzen 1977, 71; Van Wing 1941, 86). The nkisi was animated by the powers represented metaphorically and metonymically by the *bilongo* substances placed within it and upon it. White clay, soil, or ash provided metaphors of the purity of God, the spirits, and the dead. Reflective surfaces of seashells, quartz crystals, and mica or mirror fragments were metaphoric for the water boundary of the living and the world of spirits, and thus communicated the invocation of spiritual forces into the world of the living. Seashells, nutshells, and some types of roots also provided metaphors for wombs and containers of lives, souls, and spirits. Bird skulls or feathers supplied metaphors for spirits through the connotation of flight and the realm of the sky. Animal claws and teeth provided metaphors of the power and forcefulness of particular spirits. Fragments of clinging vines and roots were used as symbols of the ability of a summoned spiritual force to locate malevolent spirits and to bind and subdue them (MacGaffey 1986, 132, 137–48; 1993, 32–42; Van Wing 1941, 86).

Other items used as bilongo invoked metaphors through the punning association of the item's name and a word for a desired attribute of a summoned spirit or a word descriptive of the affliction that the spirit would be able to cure (Jacobson-Widding 1979, 140; Janzen and MacGaffey 1974, 6; MacGaffey

1991, 5). For example, the bilongo might include a nut named *nkiduku* to invoke *kidukwa*, the KiKongo word for protection (MacGaffey 2000b, 44). The nganga who created a nkisi likely recited these names of the bilongo in a solemn, ritualized manner while composing the object (Jacobson-Widding 1979, 140; MacGaffey 2000b, 38). These bilongo expressed the invocation of the spirit world into the land of the living and the relevant attributes of the summoned spirit (Janzen and MacGaffey 1974, 35–36; MacGaffey 1988a, 190–191; Laman 1962, 68).

The banganga ritual specialists were often viewed as possessing and exercising a sacred form of power that could be contrasted with the political power of the ruling class. However, they were not viewed as a caste of priests. Any member of the BaKongo people could become a nganga if they experienced a simbi's calling and dedicated themselves to the proper use of minkisi. The banganga were feared for their powers, but they were also viewed with respect and appreciation for their abilities to cure and bring blessings on communities and individuals seeking aid. A nganga who created, possessed, and worked with a greater number and variety of minkisi would be able to provide a greater array of specific divination, healing, and protective measures to those who sought her aid. She would in turn obtain higher status and earnings if her efforts were believed to be effective (Jacobson-Widding 1979, 68; Janzen and MacGaffey 1974, 37; Laman 1957, 132; Van Wing 1941, 86–91).

Minkisi were often employed for private purposes as well as for more public displays and applications. When a nkisi was employed for the use and protection of a village, "nkisi-houses" were often built with "low walls, so that anyone could see the nkisi and call upon him" for aid. Some nkisi houses were carefully concealed, so they could not be desecrated by outsiders, and would be accessible only to members of the community. A nganga might take up residence within such a nkisi house at times, necessitating an expansion of the structure. Banganga also frequently kept many of their minkisi in their own dwelling houses and conducted related rituals in their homes or transported the minkisi to the houses of persons who sought their services (Laman 1953, 83; MacGaffey 1986, 136, 169–71; 2000b, 82; Thompson 1993, 48–54; Van Wing 1941, 88–89).

Some forms of minkisi were created and used in prominent public rituals (Janzen and MacGaffey 1974, 37). For example, the powerful *nkisi Nkondi* was often used in oath-taking, consecration of political and social agreements, and enactment of laws or treaties among multiple chiefdoms (Laman 1957, 113, 117, 159–60; MacGaffey 2000b, 109–10). In efforts to protect an entire village from disease or misfortune, two banganga might convene at a crossroad leading into the village, draw a cross upon the ground, pour water onto the crossed lines, and undertake other ritual measures to protect the village (Laman 1962, 156). Similarly, households or villages could be protected by burying selected minkisi in their vicinity and avenues of approach (Janzen and MacGaffey 1974, 45).

Forms of the nkisi Nkondi were often viewed as "hunter" minkisi, which contained manifestations of a powerful simbi spirit that could track down, bind, and vanquish malevolent spirits and other forces that were assailing the persons who made supplication to Nkondi for aid (MacGaffey 1988a, 199). The container was usually designed as an anthropomorphic or zoomorphic figure in a pose conveying power and lethal capabilities. These containers ranged in size from a few inches to a few feet in height, with larger forms typically used for more public rituals. The bilongo of such a nkisi often included fragments of binding vines, animal teeth, and claws as metaphors for its lethal powers. Other metaphoric bilongo, such as fragments of reflective crystals and white clay, were often included, as well as decorations of crossed lines on the exterior of the wooden body of the nkisi. The bilongo were typically placed inside a cavity created in the body of the sculpture and enclosed with a reflective piece of seashell, mica or mirror (MacGaffey 1993, 32–42, 75–79).

Personal supplications for aid from nkisi Nkondi were often undertaken in a private ritual attended by the nganga who possessed and interacted with the nkisi and the person seeking help. The nganga would typically draw crossed lines on the ground, oriented along the cardinal directions, to demarcate the ritual space in which this supplication would be made. The intersection of these lines represented the desired intersection and communication between the spirit world and the land of the living. The nganga and supplicant would first swear their righteous and truthful purposes by taking oaths while standing upon the crossed lines and addressing the Nkondi (Jacobson-Widding 1991, 201; Thompson 1990, 153; Thompson and Cornet 1981, 44).

If the supplicant as ill, the nganga would often have him lie on the crossed lines with feet pointing west, perhaps adding a circle to surround the person and crossed lines. The nganga would then symbolically drive the illness out of the person and westward into obliteration (Jacobson-Widding 1991, 201; Laman 1962, 144, 149; MacGaffey 1986, 118). In the course of the ritual the nganga would often place the nkisi at the intersection of the crossed lines as well. The nganga and supplicant would then recite prayers to request specific aid from Nkondi and to incite it into action. In addition, they would drive a small iron wedge or iron nail into the body of the wooden Nkondi to record this act of supplication and oath-taking and to further animate the nkisi to exercise its powers (Laman 1957, 113, 117, 159–60; MacGaffey 2000b, 98–99, 106–107; Thompson 1990, 153; Thompson and Cornet 1981, 38, 151).

European colonization and Christian missionary activities from the late fifteenth century through the late nineteenth century failed to destroy this rich belief system expressed in the BaKongo dikenga and minkisi (Balandier 1968, 50–51; Thornton 1983, 67–68). Catholic missionaries were most active in the region from the time of initial European contact onward, with the assistance of Portuguese colonial interests. Protestant missionaries sponsored by the English and Dutch also became active in the region in the eighteenth and nineteenth centuries (MacGaffey 2000b, 38). The BaKongo people converted to Christianity and adopted its beliefs only in a highly selective manner throughout this period. This process of selective adoption was aided by the fact that European missionaries often used KiKongo terms for key Christian concepts, thus translating Christian beliefs into the BaKongo counterparts (Thornton 1977, 512–13; 1983, 63; 2002, 83–90).

The BaKongo easily understood and assimilated the Catholic concepts of saints, seraphim, and the holy spirit as entities translatable into the BaKongo belief in basimbi and other intermediate spirits (Thornton 1998, 259). In contrast, the BaKongo largely rejected Catholic concepts of heaven and hell, which were highly inconsistent with their traditional cosmology (Hilton 1985, 94; Thornton 2002, 84–85). Priests were viewed as performing the same roles as banganga, and the crucifix, statues of saints, eucharist, and church buildings were viewed the same as minkisi and related ritual buildings (Balandier 1968, 54; Hilton 1985, 94; Thornton 1977, 512–13; 1983, 63). By the mid-seventeenth century, the BaKongo people had come to view the crucifix as the principal nkisi of the Christian banganga (the priests), and they erected wooden crosses throughout the region (Balandier 1968, 102, 242, 254; Hilton 1985, 102). Thus, the symbol and object of a Christian cross was not adopted as a cosmological symbol that displaced the BaKongo dikenga, but rather as a new form of nkisi container. The missionary priests also found that baptism was the primary Christian sacrament of interest to the BaKongo people, due to the BaKongo belief in the transformative character of the water boundary, and the priests frequently used baptisms as a favored way to attract potential converts (Thornton 1977, 514). The blending of the dikenga with the Christian cross and other sacraments thus occurred in many forms, typically in a way that served to reinforce the BaKongo cosmology, rather than displace it.

Predicting Patterns of Symbolic Representations in New Settings

This extensive and detailed body of ethnohistorical information of the BaKongo culture and religion in West Central Africa provides the elements for constructing an ethnohistorical analogy for use in analyzing and interpreting the potential meaning, significance, and use of artifacts of spirituality created by members of a BaKongo Diaspora. The principal elements of material culture delineated and characterized in this analogy consist of the BaKongo dikenga and related forms of minkisi. More specifically, the BaKongo dikenga was manifested in different forms depending upon the specific context and use to which it was placed. When used for public rituals to express group identity and solidarity, the dikenga would typically appear in its fully embellished and emblematic form of expression, with crossed lines, surrounding cyclical ellipse or circle, and four moments of the cosmos. When used in community or private rituals for the purpose of invoking spiritual aid to protect or heal a village, household, or individual, the dikenga would often be expressed in an abbreviated form of crossed lines and associated with forms of minkisi positioned along the axes or intersection of that cross.

Within the Kongo Kingdom, the more emblematic uses of the dikenga were often associated with public rituals conducted by political and religious specialists. However, it is unlikely that the political and religious organizational structures of the BaKongo cultures would be replicated by those abducted into slavery and transported to New World settings (see Mintz and Price 1976, 6–7, 21). In such circumstances of subjugation, members of the BaKongo Diaspora would likely exercise their beliefs and expressions of cosmology and self-identity in private and covert settings (Orser 1994a, 39, 42; Raboteau 1980, 215). The BaKongo people had practiced a broad array of such private rituals within West Central Africa, typically by demarcating the appropriate spaces with the crossed lines of the dikenga, and using nkisi objects in association with that space. While minkisi were at times maintained within public "nkisi-houses," they were frequently utilized within the dwellings of the banganga or their clients, or positioned to protect individual households and villages.

Banganga within the Kongo Kingdom held positions of heightened status and played vital roles in a broad array of political rituals, public religious rituals, and invocations of spiritual aid for individuals seeking healing, protection, or retribution. While many banganga were no doubt abducted into slavery, it is less likely that they were able to enjoy comparable status within plantation settings in the New World (Mintz and Price 1976, 10; Raboteau 1980, 50; Sobel 1987, 6; Thomas 1995, 154). In time, they could adjust to their new circumstances and begin performing the services of a healer, diviner, and specialist in invocations of spiritual aid within their immediate communities (Genovese 1976, 221; Orser 1994a, 37). In turn, they could teach their evolving sets of beliefs and practices to other members of their communities, with some facets of the BaKongo traditions continuing, some changing, and others falling away.

The degree to which such beliefs and practices were exercised, both in frequency and intensity, was dependent in part on the degree to which plantation owners and overseers precluded slaves from engaging in such conduct (Levine 1977, 60; Raboteau 1980, 53, 66). The rate of change in those beliefs and practices depended, in turn, upon the degree to which particular slave communities consisted of a significant number of persons enculturated in the BaKongo culture, or instead consisted of persons enculturated in a number of varied cultures of West and West Central Africa. In many New World settings, Africans and African Americans enculturated in the traditions of diverse cultures interacted within local slave communities. The religions of the Yoruba, Fon, Bambara, and BaKongo, to mention just a few, are notable in their richness and diversity of beliefs, practices, and modes of ritual and symbolic expression (see, e.g., Gomez 1998; Morgan 1998, 610–11; Thomas 1995, 153). The broad array of minkisi designs created by the BaKongo people present particular challenges to the effort of predicting discernible patterns in related material culture in New World settings. Due to the compositional emphasis on metaphoric meanings, both the containers and contents of minkisi are often made of naturally occurring and fairly prosaic materials. Containers made of wood or natural fibers will typically decompose in the archaeological record. Bilongo consisting of pieces of vines or other organic materials will similarly perish. Bilongo which invoke the reflective flash of the water boundary, such as quartz crystals, shells, or polished stones, are naturally occurring objects which may have been collected and deposited in New World house sites without any relationship to such religious beliefs and practices. White clay and white chalk have similar characteristics. Such objects as crystals, shells, and polished stones also could have been collected and deposited by persons who subscribed to European American religious beliefs and practices entirely separate and independent from the BaKongo (Fennell 2000, 286–87; Perry and Paynter 1999, 303). Similarly, other African religions treated white objects or grave dirt as religiously symbolic as well (Mbiti 1970, 155; Raboteau 1980, 34; Thompson 1983, 134–38).

The particular context in which artifacts are found is critically important to the strength of an interpretation that those objects were created pursuant to beliefs and practices derived from the BaKongo culture. Such an interpretation will be stronger if a variety of bilongo-like objects are located in a concentrated collection, rather than being dispersed throughout the space of a dwelling. Such an interpretation will be stronger still if there exist multiple concentrations of bilongo-like objects, located in a spatial pattern that indicates the demarcation of the crossed lines of a dikenga along the cardinal directions within a private space. However, these elements of contextual evidence alone should not suffice. Archaeologists should look for multiple lines of supporting evidence to establish that the site was inhabited by persons likely to have been enculturated in BaKongo beliefs. They should also assess the degree to which the site may have been inhabited or used by persons likely to have been enculturated in other European American or African American belief systems that could have generated similar artifacts (Fennell 2000, 286–87).

Archaeologists should proceed with similar care when interpreting crossed lines inscribed upon artifacts as representing expressions of the BaKongo dikenga. A significant number of such artifacts have been found at historic-period sites in the United States. These are often small, everyday items with crossed lines scratched into them, such as ceramic bowls and pots, white marbles, pewter or silver spoons, and coins. Some of these objects include white material, such as the bright color of pewter and silver metals when scratched, or objects made of kaolin (Ferguson 1992, 1999; M. Franklin 1997c; Young 1996, 1997). This bolsters the interpretation of these objects as expressions of BaKongo beliefs, because it presents two known metaphoric features that were often used in combination by the BaKongo in West Central Africa.

However, the presence alone of crossed lines on small amulet-like objects could as easily be interpreted as the product of other European American or African American beliefs. Anglo-American and German American religious traditions included the use of a cross mark or "saltire" as an invocation sign on objects designed to create protective charms or curses (Fennell 2000, 299–302; Smith, Stewart, and Kyger 1964, 156). Other African religions also utilized the symbol of crossed lines and the crossing of paths as representations of an invocation of the spirit world (Gundaker 1998, 65; Stuckey 1987, 92). The interpretation of crossed lines on particular artifacts or in the spatial configuration of features upon the ground as a primarily BaKongo expression will be stronger if evidence exists of other metaphoric references that are also consistent with BaKongo beliefs and practices. The surrounding circular motif of the shape of an inscribed marble, coin, or bowl base provides reinforcing evidence of related metaphors. Additional supporting evidence should be sought, however, because the symbol of a circle as representative of cosmic cycles was not unique to the BaKongo.

Instrumental Symbolism and the Generation of New Emblematic Expressions

In his extensive study of "slave religions" in the Americas, Albert Raboteau stated that "in the United States the gods of Africa died" and that various forms of "African theology and African ritual did not endure" in the slave communities of North America "to the extent that they did in Cuba, Haiti, and Brazil" (1980, 86). More recently, Laura Galke (2000), one of the archaeologists who worked on the Carroll House site in Annapolis, Maryland, declared that Raboteau was mistaken. Surely, she argued, the numerous findings of nkisi-like objects at slave sites in the United States show that the BaKongo religion was alive and well in America in the seventeenth, eighteenth, and nineteenth centuries. In essence, they are both correct.

Spiritual Invocations in Private Rituals in North America

Documentary, oral history, and archaeological evidence shows no evidence that the BaKongo religion was observed in public displays of group-oriented rituals using emblematic forms of the core symbol of the BaKongo in North America. Instead, only private and covert forms of ritual were undertaken, each employing instrumental and abbreviated forms of the religion's core symbol to obtain protection and well-being for the individuals involved. The institution of slavery and the dominant religion of Christianity had pushed the BaKongo beliefs off the stage of publicly displayed group rituals. However, adherents to the BaKongo religion were able to continue practicing forms of the private, instrumental rituals that the BaKongo people had observed regularly in West Central Africa.

The artifacts uncovered at the Carroll House in Annapolis provide a persuasive example of such a continuation of private nkisi rituals in North America. Documentary evidence showed that Charles Carroll of Carrollton maintained this house as one of his family's principal residences from the mid-1700s through 1821. He maintained up to nineteen enslaved African Americans at this location in the early 1780s and a lesser number in the early 1800s (Galke 2000, 22–23; Jones 2000, 2). Many enslaved Africans imported into the Maryland and Chesapeake areas came from the region of West Central Africa (Walsh 2001, 148). Thus there was a considerable probability that Carroll obtained enslaved laborers from the Kongo area, although direct evidence is lacking.

A diverse array of objects was located in concentrated collections under the floorboards of one room in the basement level of the Carroll House. Supporting evidence indicated that this room was likely used as the living and work space of house servants. The objects could have been viewed as reflecting multiple metaphors of significance within the BaKongo tradition. Quartz crystals, polished stones, and glass fragments invoked the flash of the water boundary. Disks of white bone invoked the color of the spirit world and the dead and the circular form of the cosmic cycle. A fragment of a pearlware bowl, with an asterisk mark as a decoration, could have been viewed as both a symbolic container of other bilongo-like objects and as providing an invocation of the crossed lines of the dikenga (Galke 2000, 23–24; Jones 2000, 2; Logan 1995).

Crossed lines appear as well on the round bases of colonoware pottery uncovered in the Carolinas and Virginia. This form of earthenware pottery was produced as a result of a blending of African and Native American ceramic forms and production techniques. Many of these incised pottery fragments were located in rivers in the Carolinas. These locations are in areas occupied in the past by enslaved Africans and African Americans who worked on nearby plantations. A large percentage of these enslaved persons were imported into South Carolina from West Central Africa (Ferguson 1992, 111–16; 1999, 121–23; Holloway 1990, 7; Mouer et al. 1999; Orser 1994a, 38–39).

Four attributes of these colonoware artifacts thus correlate with the potential composition of a nkisi-like object produced pursuant to inspirations from BaKongo beliefs. Ceramic pots and bowls were used as containers for some forms of minkisi by the BaKongo people. The crossed lines scratched within the circumference of a surrounding circular bowl base could invoke elements of the dikenga. The use of such objects at sites along the edges of bodies of water also could have been consistent with private rituals invoking the boundary with the spirit world or invocations of simbi spirits associated with bodies of water (Ferguson 1999, 124–26; see Denbow 1999, 420). Ferguson (1998, 4–6) believes one can infer that the small jars and bowls were likely used in the preparation of medicines in ritual undertakings, and the vessels were later

cast into the water. However, the use of cross and circle motifs and the association of water with religious rituals were beliefs and practices common to
a number of Native American, African American, and European American
religions (Ferguson 1999, 118, 124, 127; Stuckey 1987, 34–35, 92). Ferguson
(1999, 127) suggests that the multivocal character of these core symbols facilitated cultural interactions and the sharing of ideas among African Americans
and Native Americans who worked and lived together under the burdens of
enslavement.

Such a blending of multivocal, instrumental symbolism appears at the Levi
Jordan Plantation site in Brazoria, Texas. No direct evidence established that
persons enculturated in the BaKongo religion lived at that site (Brown 1994,
96–98; Thomas 1995, 153). However, general information on the history of the
Atlantic slave trade shows that members of the BaKongo culture were likely
imported into the region, either directly or through points in the Caribbean
(Brown 1994, 97; Brown and Cooper 1990, 12). The artifacts uncovered in
four caches in the curer's cabin present a number of poignant attributes. The
four caches were deposited at the four cardinal directions along the perimeter
of the room. This is notable, since the room itself was not oriented along the
cardinal directions (Brown 1994, 108–14). Thus the deposits could have been
intended to demarcate the crossed lines of a dikenga within the space of this
cabin. The objects could have been components of minkisi that were placed
along the axes and intersection of this dikenga when ritual invocations were
undertaken.

One deposit consisted of a concentration of small iron wedges, which
could be described as contrived fragments of a knife blade (in area 1 in Fig. 9.2).
Kristine and Kenneth Brown, the archaeologists working on this site, propose
that these are the remains of a form of nkisi Nkondi–a hunter nkisi into which
one would drive an iron wedge to record the taking of an oath and a request for
aid. If such a nkisi had been created in this space, the body would most likely
have been made of wood, which would perish in the archaeological record. A
cavity within the wooden figure would have held a cache of bilongo objects,
some of which may have been inorganic and some organic and perishable
over time. Close to the iron wedges the archaeologists found water-worn peb-
bles, fragments of mirrors, several seashells, and a part of a small white porcelain doll (Brown 1994, 108–109, 111–13; Brown and Brown 1998, 2–3).

The Browns refer to this cabin as a curer's cabin in part because of the variety of nkisi-like deposits within it. This variety suggested that an experienced
curer or healer had lived there and performed his or her services for others in
private rituals undertaken in the space of the cabin. This view supports the
likelihood that a nkisi of the Nkondi style may have been created and used
there, because such a nkisi was viewed by the BaKongo people as very powerful and as manageable only in the hands of an experienced ritual specialist.
Such hunter minkisi, if misused, were believed to inflict harm on those persons who mishandled them (Janzen and MacGaffey 1974, 37).

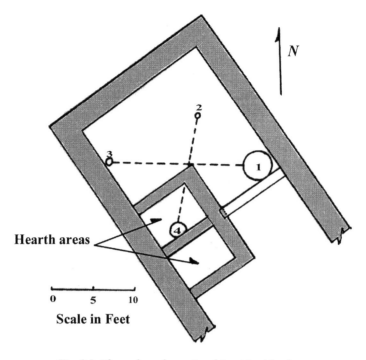

Fig. 9.2. Floor plan of curer's cabin at Levi Jordan.

Adjacent to the concentration of iron wedges were two round bases of cast-iron kettles with a piece of white chalk, fragments of medicine bottles and a glass thermometer, and two bullet casings sealed into a tube form (area 1 of Fig. 9.2). Objects uncovered in the other deposits included silver coins stacked along a line running north–south at the northern point in the room (area 2 of Fig. 9.2). On the south side of the room, a cavity created and covered by bricks inside the hearth contained a concentrated deposit of burned shells, burned iron nails and spikes, and white ash (area 4 of Fig. 9.2). These could be interpreted as objects consistent with other minkisi deposits and items used in divination, with the iron kettles used as trays on which crossed lines would be drawn with white chalk when commencing a divination ritual. The series of coins, fragments of glass, burned shell, iron nails, and ash could invoke the flash of the spirit world, land of the dead and ancestors, and cycles of the cosmos, while being placed to demarcate the axes of a dikenga (Brown 1994, 108–15; Brown and Brown 1998, 2–4).

The west end of this configuration presented artifacts that did not directly fit the predictable attributes of BaKongo-inspired religious items (area 3 of Fig. 9.2). At this location, the archaeologists uncovered two iron kettles deposited upright, with one inside the other and ash placed in between their bases.

The upper kettle contained soil, small bone fragments, seashells, and metal objects. Fragments of a smaller kettle rested on top of the two larger kettles, and heavy iron chain was wrapped around the circumference of the larger kettle. Other objects were located in the space immediately surrounding these kettles, including seashells, metal buttons, bone fragments, a bolt, several spikes, a bayonet, a hinge, and a piece of a plow. It was not clear whether all of these objects were placed in this area purposefully (Brown 1994, 113–14; Brown and Brown 1998, 2–3).

This configuration of nested iron kettles wrapped in heavy chain does not correlate directly with the known forms of minkisi design typically utilized by the BaKongo people. While BaKongo beliefs included the use of iron materials as a form of bilongo object, such a concentrated use of iron containers was seldom employed. It is a design far more consistent with the *amula* compositions of the Yoruba religion, which were typically dedicated to the deity named *Ogun*. Although the archaeologists made this interpretation by examining forms of amula known in New World settings, such as examples from Cuba (Brown and Brown 1998, 3; Thomas 1995, 153; Thompson 1983, 54–56), their interpretation is supported by historical information concerning the Yoruba religion as practiced in earlier periods in West Africa as well.

The Yoruba religion possessed a large pantheon of deities, called *Orisa*, to which believers could make supplication and prayers for the Orisa's protection or intervention into the affairs of the living (Cuthrell-Curry 2000, 460–61; Thorpe 1991, 90–91). Members of the Yoruba religion prayed to individual Orisa in the privacy of their homes, in public shrines within their villages, and at regular, larger-scale ceremonies (Mbiti 1970, 240, 268; Thorpe 1991, 92, 99). Ogun was the god of war and iron, and supplicants would make offerings of iron to Ogun at shrines within their homes when seeking this deity's aid and protection (Thorpe 1991, 94). Amula were objects composed primarily with elements of iron to make supplication to Ogun and focus the protective powers of that deity into the space in which an amula was placed (see, e.g., Thompson 1983, 54–56).

The artifacts of this cabin thus appear to present evidence of the interaction of distinct traditions and practices derived from separate African religions. It is in such a setting that the powerful utility of instrumental and abbreviated symbolism becomes apparent. The fully embellished and emblematic dikenga of the BaKongo would have little direct import as a summarizing symbol to someone who was instead educated in the Yoruba religion and culture. Yet a configuration of four altars at each of the cardinal points within a private space would be consistent with the Yoruba practice of individual ritual supplications to the Orisa (Mbiti 1970, 240; Thompson 1997, 30–31). Thus the spatial layout of the four ritual caches in the curer's cabin would make sense to a member of the Yoruba culture as well, but through the application of different religious metaphors that could be read off the similar symbolic configurations.

Focusing on such dynamics will increase our appreciation of the cultural flexibility of such past actors and their innovativeness in creating new social networks and shared symbolic expressions under difficult circumstances (see Gundaker 2000, 128; Howson 1990, 90–91; C. H. Long 1997, 27; Mintz and Price 1976, 23–24; Sacks 1979, 144). In individual uses, we see evidence of the symbolism being selected in the form of simpler instrumental compositions. Consider the possible choices of an African American who was educated in the traditions of the BaKongo religion, lived in slave quarters, and interacted with persons more familiar with other African religious traditions. By reducing the extensive array of design components from the fully embellished BaKongo dikenga (cross, circle, and four disks) down to a simpler form of cross symbol, this person would increase her ability to communicate in a spiritually mean-ingful way with those African Americans with whom she interacted (see Firth 1973, 211, 215–16, 222, 238–40; Sacks 1979, 6–7).

Over time, their interactions could solidify into new social networks for which they could develop emblematic symbols to express their new group identity. Those emblematic symbols could be composed of the components of their previously varied instrumental symbolism. Yet, in the African American communities of North America, we do not see evidence of such a develop-ment which blends the instrumental symbolism of different African religions to form new emblems of group identity. Instead, the vast majority of religious artifacts recovered reflect private, instrumental symbolism. Why?

Two primary dynamics inhibited the development of new, emblematic symbolism from the components of instrumental symbols of multiple African religions. First, in the early generations of slaves in North America, from the seventeenth through the early eighteenth century, heightened levels of sur-veillance and control of slaves' lives largely precluded their ability to develop and deploy such emblematic symbols. Plantation owners and overseers in the North American colonies typically implemented a much greater level of con-trol over the daily lives of their labor force than did many plantation operators in the Caribbean and South America (Genovese 1976, 179, 211; Raboteau 1980, 53). Second, from the early eighteenth century onward, many enslaved persons in North America adopted evangelical Christianity as a new set of beliefs and practices which they could employ to promote group solidarity and to undertake associated conduct and symbolic expression in open, public display (Blassingame 1972; Harding 1997).

Historians often emphasize a third factor as well: the United States formally outlawed the importation of slaves after 1808 (see, e.g., Genovese 1976, 211). As Raboteau (1980, 92) stated, in "North America, a relatively small number of Africans found themselves enslaved amid a rapidly increasing native-born popu-lation whose memories of the African past grew fainter with each passing gen-eration." However, this factor is of questionable significance. Scofflaws no doubt continued a considerable amount of illegal importation of enslaved persons into the United States throughout the antebellum period. Moreover, the question remains of the degree to which persons enculturated in particular African traditions succeeded in passing those beliefs and practices on to others within their community in America, regardless of where those other persons were born.

The earlier generations of Africans and African Americans could only practice rituals derived from their African religions when outside the scope of surveillance. The twentieth-century narratives of former slaves report that such meetings, when held, were typically convened in hollows, hush arbors, and other secret locations in the vicinity of the plantations (C. H. Long 1997, 26; Perdue, Barden, and Phillips 1976, 53, 94, 124; Raboteau 1980, 215; Rawick 1978, 23). These limitations greatly inhibited the formation of new styles of group ritual and group expression that could have been developed out of a blending of different African religious traditions. However, such a blending of African traditions occurred more frequently in those parts of the Caribbean and South America in which European American colonial institutions were less fixed and surveillance was less strict (Barrett 1977, 193; Mulira 1990, 35).

In that same period, up through the early eighteenth century, plantation owners in North America typically preferred that their slaves exercise no religious observances. Plantation owners, overseers, and their associates typically disapproved of the exercise of African religious beliefs, fearing such conduct would lead to group solidarity and resistance. They comparably disfavored the conversion of enslaved persons to Christianity. Many feared that conversion would lead to arguments that Christianized African Americans should not be subjected to enslavement. Some feared they would lose significant amounts of labor time if their slaves began attending services regularly. Plantation owners primarily feared, however, that enslaved persons would become increasingly restive after conversion, due to Christianity's concepts of religious equality and self-determination (Berlin 1998, 60–61; Genovese 1976, 211; Levine 1977, 60; Raboteau 1980, 66, 98–99, 103).

By the early eighteenth century, two trends made it easier for African Americans to adopt Christianity as a dominant religion for public observance. An increasing number of colonies passed laws declaring that conversion to Christianity would have no effect on a person's status as a slave. In addition, successive waves of evangelical movements within the Christian faith spread across the colonies, promoting conversion of as many persons as possible (Berlin 1998, 138; Gomez 1998, 21; Levine 1977, 60–61; Raboteau 1980, 98–99). Many African Americans were attracted to this religious movement, with its emphasis on the value of every soul, no matter their station in life, and the comparable struggle of every individual against sin and corruption. The evangelists frequently expressed religious grounds for condemning material opulence, pretension, and unequal wealth. An emphasis on the sacrifices and pains of the Savior during mortal life, and comparable salvation after death, presented sympathetic and familiar themes. Old Testament promises of God's liberation of the chosen and downtrodden provided comparably attractive beliefs (Berlin 1998, 138–39; Levine 1977, 60–61).

The evangelical movements were particularly strong in the Virginia Tidewater area and Maryland, moving northward from there from the 1740s onward. Such evangelical "awakenings" occurred in waves of revivals (Berlin 1998, 138, 272; Levine 1977, 61; Raboteau 1980, 66). This process accelerated in northern states in the late 1790s as new evangelical churches were formed with the aid of local African American leaders (Berlin 1998, 252). Elsewhere during the eighteenth century, such as the low country of the Carolinas, many African Americans continued to resist and reject the evangelists' efforts to convert them to Christianity, and instead endeavored to retain various forms of their African religious heritage (Berlin 1998, 172; Genovese 1976, 211; Raboteau 1980, 149).

The core symbols of Christianity contained motifs that resonated with the symbolism of a number of African religions. Sterling Stuckey argues persuasively that persons learned in the BaKongo religion would have viewed the Christian cross, as it was used in group worship in the colonial and antebellum periods in the United States, as a symbol consistent with the dikenga. Moreover, as those persons converted to Christianity and participated in its group rituals of worship, they shaped their liturgical practices to reflect the ring shouts and call-and-answer techniques of traditional BaKongo ceremonies (Gomez 1998, 4; Raboteau 1980, 64; Stuckey 1987, 34–35, 92–95). "By operating under cover of Christianity, vital aspects of Africanity, which some considered eccentric in movement, sound, and symbolism, could more easily be practiced openly" (Stuckey 1987, 35).

Crossed lines would have been read in varying ways by members of different African religions, such as the Fon, Yoruba, Asante, or BaKongo. However, that symbol was still meaningful in a spiritual sense to members of each of those religions, even if interpreted differently in the details (Raboteau 1980, 34, 85; Stuckey 1987, 92; Thompson 1997, 21–27). Through the dynamics of these interactions and constraining social influences, many African Americans continued to practice African religious beliefs in private, instrumental uses, while shaping evangelical Christianity into a new form for public observance and the promotion of their group interests and solidarity (Genovese 1976, 211).

Innovation and Blending of Instrumental Symbols in Haiti and Brazil

The blending of instrumental symbols of African religions into new emblematic symbols occurred more fully in those regions in which the European colonial institutions were less rigid and surveillance and control were frequently lax. Plantations and slave communities within western Saint Domingue (later called Haiti) and Brazil provided such opportunities (Mulira 1990, 35). In each region, the abbreviated forms of core symbols from multiple African religions were combined to create new, ideographic symbols which served as "virtual national expressions" of group identity (Thompson 1990, 155). Such a blending of varying religious beliefs and practices in the formation and consolidation of new social networks can thus be viewed as examples of "ethnogenesis" (Yinger 1994, 263).

In both Haiti and Brazil, a number of factors contributed to this rich blending of African traditions. The population of enslaved Africans and African Americans was far greater than the number of European plantation operators and their associates. Control and surveillance were less strict, and plantation operators tended to seclude themselves from the daily affairs of the workforce. Social interaction and communications between enslaved persons were undertaken with greater ease and regularity. Religious and political leaders were able to assert themselves within local slave communities, organizing the residents socially while employing beliefs, practices, and expressive motifs derived directly from African traditions (see, e.g., Barrett 1977, 193).

Europeans first brought enslaved Africans to Saint Domingue in the sixteenth century. The majority of those persons were abducted from the areas of the Gulf of Benin, Kongo, and Angola, with most coming from the region in which the BaKongo people resided. The religion of Vodun developed as a blending of African belief systems in Saint Domingue from the early 1700s onward, a period in which increasing numbers of enslaved persons were imported from varied locations. Elements of the Catholicism of the French colonialists were incorporated as well. With strong instigation from the ritual specialists of Vodun, the enslaved population rebelled and won their independence by 1804, creating the nation of Haiti (Barrett 1977, 199; Eltis 2001, 46, table V; Genovese 1976, 174–75; Metraux 1972, 25–26; Rigaud 1985, 11, 13).

The word *Vodun* (or *Vodou*) was derived from the Ewe language and referred to lesser deities within the religious beliefs of the Fon people of the Dahomey region in West Africa. However, Vodun represents a rich blending of numerous African religions, including the Fon, Yoruba, and BaKongo. As Leonard Barrett stated, Vodun represented "a divine confederation honed on African pragmatism" and an example of the "flexibility" that enabled Africans traditions to survive and evolve in Saint Domingue. Vodun beliefs include a broad array of lesser deities, called *loas* (or *lwas*), each with variant names from the principal contributing religions. The loas called *Legbe, Guede,* and *Dambella* are typically treated as the most prominent in Vodun rituals. Legbe represents the guardian of gates and boundaries between worlds and is a direct variant of the Yoruba deities named *Eshu* and *Elegba*. Supplication is typically made to Legbe at the start of any ceremony to request permission to seek spiritual intercession into the land of the living. Thereafter, other spirits or loas might be requested to provide specific forms of aid (Barrett 1977, 199–200; MacGaffey 2000a, 234; Metraux 1972, 28–29; Rigaud 1985, 9, 92; Thompson 1997, 31).

Each of the principal Vodun loas is represented by an ideographic symbol, typically drawn upon the grounds of ritual spaces displayed to the public.

These are called *vèvè* ground blazons (or the *vever*) and typically cover two to three square feet (Barrett 1977, 200; K. M. Brown 1976, x–xi; Metraux 1972, 163). *Vèvè* was originally a word from the Fongbe language of the southern Dahomey region and was used in that area of West Africa to refer to ceremonial circles drawn on the ground to demarcate a protective space (Brown 1976, ix; Thompson 1997, 23). Like the crossed lines of the BaKongo, the Vodun vèvè denote the center of the ritual space on which supplications can be made for spiritual assistance. Each rendering of a blazon is believed to summon the associated loa to become manifest in that space, and other ritual objects are typically placed at the center of intersecting lines within the blazon's pattern (K. M. Brown 1976, xi, 46; Laguerre 1980, 30, 166; Metraux 1972, 165; Rigaud 1985, 92; Thompson 1997, 21). Ethnohistorical sources record the appearance of early forms of ground blazons in a slave community in Saint Domingue in the late eighteenth century (Thompson 1997, 26–27). Haitian vèvè are typically rendered on the floors of Vodun temples, at the exterior entrance to those temples, at the base of trees deemed sacred to particular loas, and in cemeteries (Brown 1976, 46; Rigaud 1985, 79–80). Some may be rendered as adornments on the walls of temples. These detailed drawings are rendered with a variety of media, including kaolin, wheat flour, cornmeal, wood ashes, red brick powder, rice powder, gunpowder, or powdered leaves, bark, roots, or charcoal (Gundaker 1998, 165; Rigaud 1985, 92).

Figure 9.3 shows an example of a Vodun blazon associated with the loa called simbi. Simbi is a loa of many variant forms, derived in part from the BaKongo concept of simbi spirits (Gundaker 1998, 165; MacGaffey 2002, 223–26; Rigaud 1985, 93). In this vèvè the crossed lines of the BaKongo

Fig. 9.3. Vèvè of simbi from Vodun of Haiti.

dikenga have been combined with numerous symbolic motifs along the axes that represent blended concepts from the Yoruba and Dahomean cosmologies (Brown 1976, 412). As Grey Gundaker observed, such "designs sum up the attributes of the lwa . . . and are composites spreading out from central cross marks—the cross mark itself being the intersection of worlds mediated by the lwa Legba, the master of thresholds, uncertainty, and writing." These ideographic renderings, combining an array of instrumental core symbols into new emblems, were not used in solely private rituals, but were instead deployed as part of a public expression of group identity (Gundaker 1998, 165; Thompson 1990, 155).

A similar but separate process unfolded among the enslaved Africans and Native Americans on Brazilian plantations. Portuguese colonial efforts promoted the establishment and operation of large-scale plantations in this region, focused primarily on sugar production, from the early sixteenth century onward. The first slaves imported into Brazil were abducted primarily from the areas of Senegal and Sierra Leone. However, from the late sixteenth century onward, the Portuguese obtained most enslaved people for import into Brazil from the areas of Angola, Kongo, and the hinterlands of West Central Africa (Eltis 2000, 189; Orser 1996, 42, 51–52; Sturm 1977, 218). Plantation owners in this region typically ran large-scale operations with less consistent control and surveillance of their workforce than occurred at locations in North America. As a result, greater opportunities were available to enslaved persons to engage in social interactions within their communities over time. Moreover, many rebelled and won their freedom from the plantations, creating "maroon" communities of escaped slaves (Orser and Funari 2001, 66). Nonetheless, slavery persisted in Brazil until the late nineteenth century, and nearly 2 million new slaves were imported into the region between 1811 and 1870 (Wolf 1982, 316, 373).

Such communities within Brazil developed a new set of beliefs and practices, later to be called *Macumba*, through a blending of African religions, Catholicism, and Native American religions. The concepts of BaKongo minkisi, Dahomean Vodun, Yoruba Orisa, and the intercessionary saints of Catholicism were carefully combined using the correspondences and complementary characteristics of those religions. Similarly, the indigenous Tupi-Guarani people of Brazil, called Tupinambá by the Europeans, possessed religious beliefs concerning ancestor spirits that blended easily with ancestor beliefs of the BaKongo and the Yoruba concepts of Orisa (Genovese 1976, 179–80; Orser 1996, 48–49; Sturm 1977, 219; Thompson 1983, 113; 1990, 156).

This blending of religious concepts included a careful combination of abbreviated symbols from the contributing religions. Ground blazons, called *pontos riscados* (for "marked points" of invocation), developed independently in this Brazilian tradition as well. These pontos were typically rendered in chalk or sand on the floors of shrines or other public ritual spaces. Each intercessionary spirit, often characterized with the combined names and attributes

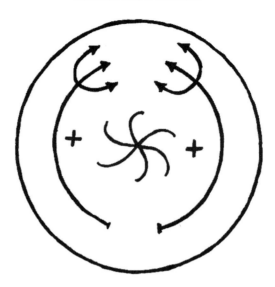

Fig. 9.4. Ponto of Eshu Elegba from Macumba of Brazil.

of different saints, ancestors, Orisa, or basimbi, possessed a ponto which would summon a manifestation of that spirit to render aid. These pontos were rendered both in transient forms at particular rituals and as permanent expressions in publicly visible locations (Thompson 1983, 113–16; 1990, 155–56).

For example, the crossed lines of the BaKongo dikenga were combined with the concept of Eshu Elegba as the mediator of the crossroads between the spirit world and the land of the living. Elegba was viewed as being unpredictable and inclined to punish those who trifled with the spirit world. In turn, Elegba's attributes were merged selectively with symbols for the Satan of Catholicism, with Elegba challenging and testing the righteousness of individuals but not representing an opponent to the Godhead. Figure 9.4 shows an example of a ponto for Eshu Elegba within the Macumba tradition, which blends the intersecting lines of the dikenga with the pitchfork motifs of Elegba, and a spinning pinwheel motif suggestive of the dynamism and unpredictability of that guardian of the crossroads (Thompson 1983, 114; 1990, 156).

This blending of elements from African religions, as well as facets of European and Native American beliefs, developed in Haiti a nd Brazil with "a depth and visibility virtually unknown in the United States" (Genovese 1976, 179). The resultant religious systems and associated material expressions of key symbols were deployed as part of larger-scale processes of social organization and the consolidation of new group identities. Central elements of a variety of African religions were combined and developed for continuing observance, not just in the private rituals of households and covert meetings, but in public displays which signaled an evolving group cohesion to anyone within view.

Conclusion

By focusing on the spectrum of emblematic and instrumental expressions of core symbols, this study makes two contributions to studies of African Diasporas. First, the artifacts of African American religious practices found in North American sites did not represent the shreds and tatters of past African religions. Rather, those artifacts represented the continuing use and development of a typical spectrum of private ritual undertakings that was a vital component of those religions even when they were practiced as dominant belief systems in West and West Central Africa. Such points of correspondence are highlighted by analyzing those artifacts through the application of a detailed ethnohistorical analogy. Second, the diachronic interplay of disparate instrumental symbols in the creation of new emblematic expressions is highlighted by the points of contrast between developments in North America with those at locations in the Caribbean and South America.

These examples illustrate larger processes of symbolic communication and social ordering. The interpretative approach outlined here provides a vehicle for examining the ways in which social group memberships shift over time and space, as individual members decrease their expression of a previous group identity in their material culture, increase their expression of individually assertive and creative styles, and in turn create and adopt new group identities. Individual exercises of creativity and instrumental symbolic expression provide the drawing boards for the formulation of new emblematic symbols that will facilitate communications and enhance the cohesiveness of new social networks in which those individuals participate.

I have refrained in this study from referring to this blending of communicative forms as a process of "creolization." A symposium of the Society for Historical Archaeology addressed the issue of whether concepts of creolization represented an "emerging paradigm" for the analysis of material culture. No consensus emerged even as to a definition for this term as applied in archaeological studies (Dawdy 2000, 1; Gundaker 2000, 124–25). Some studies of creolization in material culture tend to focus on a limited mixing of new "lexicons" with old "grammars," without analyzing the internal logic of such grammars and how they might change as well (Singleton 1995, 133). Others emphasize the importance of the dominant status of one group over another in past social settings (Gundaker 2000, 125–26).

Archaeologists borrowed the creolization concept from linguistic analysis. As used in linguistics, creolization and pidginization are processes that usually involve different cultural groups in contact and a purposeful simplification of communicative forms in a process of accommodation within a context of asymmetrical power relations between the groups (Bickerton 1999; Hymes 1971; Kapchan and Strong 1999; McWhorter 1997; Polomé 1980). Concepts of "syncretism" or "acculturation" also typically view one cultural system as dominant and imposing itself upon lesser systems (Shaw and Stewart 1994, 6–7).

The simplification and abbreviation of instrumental expressions of core symbols, however, occurs in an internal process that is initially independent of intercultural contact. It is a communicative process that occurs within the expressive range of core symbols within any coherent, shared meaning system. Yet that abbreviation and increasing multivalency yield an instrumental expression that will be useful beyond its initial employment in private rituals for individual interests. Such abbreviation also produces multivalent expressions which can aid those social actors in their later attempts to build new relationships with persons from other cultures in contact settings. For persons abducted from different regions of Africa and brought together on American soil, that interaction process involved individuals from groups in comparably subjugated positions, rather than an asymmetry of power relations between them.

This was not a matter of conservative grammars seeking new lexicons, or of the subjugated making accommodations to their oppressors. Instead, those African and African American social actors creatively blended the more multivalent features of their disparate cultural systems to generate new symbolic repertoires to aid the formation and consolidation of their new social networks. If an ethnicity is viewed as a socially constructed concept of group identity, this process is more aptly viewed as a form of combinatory and instrumental ethnogenesis.

Acknowledgments

This study presents an analysis of the interrelationships of group and individual identities and the symbolic analysis of material culture in African Diasporas, for which I have received very helpful comments, critiques, and encouragement from Anna Agbe-Davies, Kenneth Brown, Fred Damon, Michael Dietler, Leland Ferguson, Garrett Fesler, Maria Franklin, Grey Gundaker, Jeffrey Hantman, Michael Klein, Adria LaViolette, Mark Leone, Wyatt MacGaffey, Jessica Neuwirth, Charles Perdue Jr., Warren Perry, Paul Shackel, Brian Thomas, Robert Farris Thompson, Mark Warner, and Anne Yentsch. My sincere thanks to Lee Anne Fennell for her invaluable support. Any shortcomings remain the author's responsibility.

CHAPTER TEN

"In This Here Place": Interpreting Enslaved Homeplaces

Whitney L. Battle-Baptiste

It is true that domestic life took on an exaggerated importance in the social lives
of slaves, for it did indeed provide them with the only space where they could
truly experience themselves as human beings.

—*Angela Davis*

During a casual conversation with my grandmother about her childhood
on a farm, I learned that her family considered the yard an extension of the
living room. They ate, played, and socialized outdoors. As a second-generation
apartment dweller, I was amazed. I quickly realized that the enslaved household also would have extended beyond the four walls of a 20 × 20–foot dwelling (see also Gundaker 1993; Heath and Bennett 2000).

To understand the lives of enslaved communities, archaeologists often look at
the meanings of environment and space. In my analysis, however, the enslaved
community occupied a bounded and culturally significant space that was not just
the background but the epicenter of black cultural production. The slave quarters were what a number of scholars have referred to as spaces of autonomy and
independence (Berlin 1998; Blassingame 1972; Davis 1981; M. Franklin 1997c;
White 1999; Heath and Bennett 2000; Joyner 1984; Wilkie 2000). The major
protected social spaces in which the culture of the enslaved could be developed were largely within the quarters and adjacent yard areas. These were
zones of domestic production dominated by women, and it was there that food

preparation, child care, clothing repair and adornment, recreational storytelling, and music making served as the focal point of enslaved domestic life and provided avenues for strengthening social relationships. It is more than the place that holds the answers that connect the study of slavery and archaeological theory; it is the beginning of a journey to understanding how landscapes and people come together to tell a story of community and survival.

Gendered Perspectives on the Black Family

Black feminist scholars like Angela Davis, Toni Morrison, and bell hooks bring a different perspective to understanding the structure of the black family under slavery. The family structure of the mid-nineteenth century, as in the previous century, was a strategic response to the rigors and terror of slavery. Significantly, the role of women was magnified as they labored in the Big House and the fields at the behest of masters but also spent much of their time and energy ensuring the survival of the slave community. While African Americans had alternative family structures, I argue that these were not the result of a pathological black culture (see, e.g., Moynihan 1965) but a consequence of the constraints of enslavement. For example, the practice of abroad marriages, where spouses lived on different plantations, affected domestic arrangements, as did the sale of family members (Berlin 1998; Malone 1992; Walsh 1997).

Consequently, slave families differed from those of their African homelands and also from the Euro-American families who held them in bondage. At the same time, there were some aspects of African cultural and family practices that were reinforced by the conditions of slavery. These included fictive kin networks, premarital or bridal pregnancies, diffuse responsibility for parenting, and women-centered domestic production (Robertson 1996, 18). Yet the typical view of enslaved family formation does not take into account its African roots and the dire consequences that slavery had on family structure. Rather, as Claire Robertson argues, it is the sexist and racist assumptions of the matrifocal/matriarchal arguments that underlie these stereotypical representations of black family structure.

Carol Stack demonstrated how participants in domestic exchanges were defined by one another, not by people from outside of the community. She was able to observe what performances and behavior members of the community expected from one another, who was eligible to become a part of existing cooperative networks, how they were recruited, and which participants were actively involved in multiple series of exchanges. Although Stack's study was based on a contemporary urban community, there are definite connections that may add weight to the arguments about the black family that hark back to enslavement. For this study, the family is defined as the smallest organized, durable network of kin and others who interact daily, providing domestic needs of children and ensuring their survival. The family network was diffused over several kin-based households. That is, each household was composed of more than one family. Further, fluctuations in household composition do not significantly affect cooperative familial arrangements (Stack 1974, 28, 31).

Exploring the Enslaved Homeplace

I propose here that a study of the household as a social unit should be given much more attention than has previously been the case. While domestic sites abound in the study of plantation life, there are few works that theorize about the household. Household-level analysis can allow archaeologists to develop a better sense of the everyday actions of a slave quarter community. The concept of the complex household and how that directly influenced the use of exterior areas is crucial to understanding domestic life and social formation among black families. In order to understand the social networks established by the enslaved living in separate families, it is important to focus research on activity areas. I will be focusing on specific activities that occurred around the Kitchen Quarter of President Andrew Jackson's Tennessee plantation, the Hermitage. Here I will use material evidence to demonstrate functions such as yard sweeping, communal cooking, music, and leisure activities.

The development of meaningful extended kin networks and collective labor and knowledge were integral parts of the enslaved experience. I will also demonstrate how the concept of a nuclear-based household structure differed from the composition of the enslaved household. Using the First Hermitage site as a microcosm of the larger Hermitage community, I argue that archaeological features, material culture associated with specific tasks, and oral and written history support the idea that enslaved peoples lived in a shared and multifamily household.

The domestic sphere was the only place where enslaved Africans could enjoy the comfort and support of family and friends. In this chapter, I bring together theories of "homespace" and "yardspace" in African Diaspora archaeology. These two concepts have been interpreted separately. My research at the Hermitage demonstrates that yardspace and homespace are one and the same. Indeed, the study of enslaved landscapes must include people, and in order to do this, we must take into account the various ways in which members of quarter communities used exterior spaces.

The lives of enslaved Africans were structured by racism, sexism, and oppression. As such, the solace of a place called home takes on an added dimension for the daughters and sons of slavery. It provided a place to regroup, to find the strength to resist. I discovered the concept of homeplace when reading bell hooks's *Yearning*. For hooks, homeplace is the foundation in the making of the black subject: "Despite the brutal reality of racial apartheid and domination, one's homeplace was the site where one could freely confront the issue of humanization, where one could resist" (hooks 1990, 42). Similarly, in *Incidents in the Life of a Slave Girl*, Linda Brent described her grandmother's home with feelings of comfort and nurturing, a place somewhat removed from the reality of slavery (Yellin 1987). When Brent escaped from slavery, she concealed herself for many years in a small crawl space in her grandmother's attic. It was here that she painstakingly regained her humanity.

When I began the archaeological project at the First Hermitage, I was obsessed with learning about yards and how the enslaved population used these spaces to reflect their own social and cultural needs. The fascination with how yards were swept, maintained, and cultivated was a part of my attempt to use archaeological material to study life under slavery. I initially felt that the yard would provide all of the information needed. Yet it was my approach that hindered my original concepts of how significant the enslaved landscape was in the development of African American culture. Although many archaeological studies highlight the significance of Africanisms and African cultural practice (K. L. Brown 1994; Y. D. Edwards 1998; Epperson 1999a; Ferguson 1992; Franklin 1997c; Leone and Fry 1999; McKee 1994; Russell 1997; Thomas 1995b; Wilkie 2000; Yentsch 1994), the role of landscapes in the daily constitution of African American identity formation has not been as thoroughly addressed. Beyond identifying sites and structures, archaeologists must also uncover material on the enslaved landscape to help address how and why people created spaces to reflect their culture and spiritual worldviews.

A part of the problem rests in how archaeologists understand the enslaved family and the relation between the landscape and the domestic realm. My research interprets the landscape as the domestic sphere. It symbolizes the space in which enslaved families shaped the built environment into sites of comfort and support and therefore their homeplaces. A broader understanding of landscape as the cultural and social place shaped by enslaved women and men is reflected in the spatial distribution of material culture. Landscape is more than a visual arrangement; it becomes the backdrop for human action. The relationship between people and landscape is an element in the articulation of everyday actions. It is this connection which allows the researcher to see the landscape as a text, a source of study that enhances the dialogue of people and their lives. Writes Norrece T. Jones, "When time and opportunity presented themselves, sacred symbols and signs became part of who Africans were in the New World. For the most part, their meanings are now faded from traditional history. African American homes and yards abound with African characteristics of expression which still speak to the power and the protection of the ancestors" (1990, 107).

The manipulation of the natural and built (i.e., cultural) landscape became a part of how slaves communicated social meaning (Edwards 1998, 248). They were able to shape specific spaces into a concept known as "homeplace." For bell hooks, the concept of houses is more universal than just thinking of home or simply the place she grew up; it shaped her very being and association with the larger world. It was a safe space that was defined by what took place there.

I would argue that this concept of home can also be interpreted in a plantation context like the First Hermitage. It was this space which defined generations; it was this place where activities shaped the various members of the enslaved community.

The Hermitage Plantation

The Hermitage is presently a parklike setting dedicated to telling the story of Andrew Jackson and the many complexities of plantation life. Jackson's Greek Revival mansion sits on more than 600 acres of farmland (see Fig. 10.1).

The First Hermitage was established between 1804 and 1821, and it was a large farm rather than a working plantation. The Jacksons and their ten or twelve slaves lived in cabins less than forty feet apart, and their primary goal was to clear the land and plant crops (R. Jones 2002; Remini 1977). During the "Middle Quarter" (1821–50), Jackson expanded his landholdings, slave-holdings, and financial capabilities. He moved his family into a new mansion and left the cabins to his slaves. These cabins lay midway between the Mansion Backyard Quarters and the Field Quarters (approximately 250 yards north of the First Hermitage site).

Jackson's death in June 1845 marked the end of financial success and growth at the Hermitage plantation. His adopted son, Andrew, had neither the good fortune nor the business sense to maintain the plantation through lean times. The impact this had on the enslaved community is still unclear, and this period (1850–88) has been neglected by archaeological and historical research at the museum.

In 1889, the Ladies Hermitage Association was founded to protect the mansion and surrounding areas. The LHA used the First Hermitage land-scape to demonstrate Jackson's humble beginnings before his rise to national prominence.

Excavations

Excavations were conducted at the First Hermitage site for three years. During this period, researchers investigated several areas around the standing cabins. These areas were later divided into archaeological zones. The excavated areas of the First Hermitage site included structural remains of the Southeast and South Cabins (Fig. 10.2), the interiors of the standing structures (the Kitchen Quarter and the Farm House), and areas surrounding the buildings referred to here as "yard areas." The First Hermitage site was separated into six excavation zones or yard areas. This study will focus on Zone I (the Kitchen Courtyard), Zone II (the Kitchen Quarter backyard), Zone III (the outdoor hearth and cooking area), and Zone IV (the Central Courtyard).

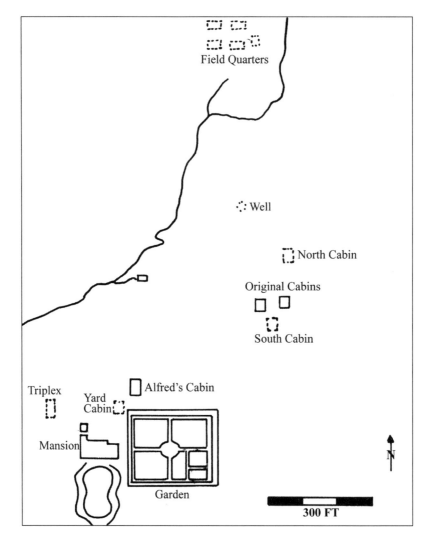

Fig. 10.1. The Hermitage plantation as it appeared in 1834 based on archaeological excavations and surveys. The First Hermitage is referred to as the Original Cabins.

Material Culture Analysis

Artifacts are often overlooked, yet without them it is impossible to find the subtle aspects of people's lives. James Deetz (1993) contends that archaeology has produced a rich body of evidence that, if used correctly, can offer insights into aspects of culture that are often ignored by documentary sources.

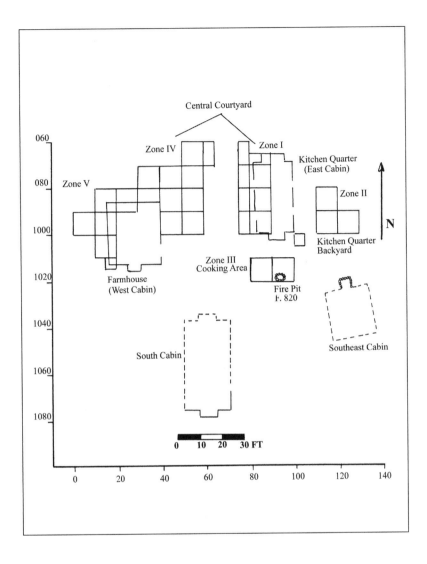

Fig. 10.2. The First Hermitage site with structures, zones,
and excavation units.

Material culture, therefore, can enhance archaeological interpretations
of the pedestrian features of life under the system of slavery. Although archaeologists use material culture as the main source of interpretation, the artifacts
are not the only sources. At historic sites, artifacts are enhanced by the support
of aboveground information, such as architecture and activity areas (Deetz

1996). At the Hermitage plantation, archaeologists already knew where a number of structures were located. Still, they uncovered additional structures from the earliest Jackson years. After an extensive shovel-test survey in 1996, the main questions shifted from the location of additional structures to the nature of a frontier farm that later served a unique type of enslaved community. The original excavation units dug in 1997 were based on the 1996 survey artifacts.

African Diaspora archaeologists in the United States have moved well beyond the search for artifact patterns or African cultural continuities reflected in African American material culture. More recent research has focused on the analysis of material culture and its relationship to social relations. Shifting from the overused concept of hand-me-downs, I argue that slaves used various methods to obtain materials, whether it be a bowl or glass, than simply waiting to receive discarded objects from their masters. In the case of the Hermitage, the diversity of material assemblages throughout the property supports this notion.

"Home" Is Where the Hearth Is: An Archaeological Example

The idea of a communal cooking area seems logical based on the fact that Jackson never assumed responsibility for feeding the enslaved population. Many nineteenth-century plantation owners complained about how their workers were not knowledgeable about proper nutrition and how to eat a meal properly. "It cannot be expected that the slave who is all day at hard work can pay a proper attention to preparing his food after the day's labor. He generally comes home tired, and before he has half cooked his meal, hunger induces him to devour it" (Breeden 1980, 92).

Certain plantations would have found it impossible to feed large numbers of people, even just concentrating on field-workers. And although some planters were wary of how and what workers were preparing to eat, it was the planter's decision whether to employ a cook to prepare two or three meals per day or to leave that chore to the workers themselves. Even when the planter chose to stay independent of the daily food preparations, there was always concern about the time that enslaved workers gave to eating and their attention to maintaining proper health.

"The great object is to give them out enough, have it well cooked, and *give them time to eat*. Negroes cannot, or will not—they do not—eat in as short a time as whites; I can and do eat my meals in from ten to fifteen minutes; they will eat thirty by watch, and ofttimes forty-five; but I have timed them and know it to be a fact" (Breeden 1980, 95). Eating was a social activity for slaves. So much of their time was spent working, yet it was after the work was done when interactions between community members became a reality. "At night, especially in the summertime, after everybody had eaten supper, it was a common thing for us to sit outside. The old folks would get together and talk until bedtime. Sometimes somebody would start humming an old hymn, and then the next-door neighbor would pick it up" (Raboteau 1980, 220).

Faunal Remains

A brief overview of the faunal remains from the Communal Cooking area indicates the presence of a massive amount of material, spread thick and heavy over the area, through several layers. The species present were pig, turkey, chicken, sheep, cow, fish (catfish, gar, most likely from the Stones and Cumberland Rivers), horse, cat, squirrel, groundhog, and rabbit. The most abundant was pig. Pig bones from all parts of the body were present. This represents carcass-processing activity in the vicinity (six skulls, two split down the middle for brain extraction) or the gathering of elements left over from carcass processing to trim remaining meat scraps. There were a lot more heads, spines, ribs, and feet than limbs.

Cow bones were "randomly" present with no set pattern. There were a few ribs, some broken limb bones, a few teeth, and no skull fragments. Most likely this indicates that no one on the plantation was eating large amounts of beef and may represent opportunistically gathered or acquired cuts of meat from the occasional slaughter of surplus animals (typically a young male) from the dairy herd, eaten on a special occasion or to give a little variety to the pork-heavy mansion diet. A more detailed analysis is being conducted on the material from several archaeological zones.

The social nature of the cooking area is reflected in some of the material remains. For example, three mouth harps and part of a harmonica were recovered from the area (Fig. 10.3). The fact that there were no instruments found in other regions may support my contention that this space not only was used for cooking but was also important in the social lives of Middle Quarter occupants.

Archaeologically, it is the outdoor cooking hearth that I believe is the center and social heart of the First Hermitage extended household. Barbara Heath and Amber Bennett (2000, 53) have noted that "together, house and yard form a nucleus within which the culture expresses itself, is perpetuated, changed, and reintegrated." Similarly, the yard served as an extension of the house at the Hermitage (Y. D. Edwards 1998; Gundaker 1998) and household activities were carried out in these yard areas. This area was a space where multiple families would meet and engage in various activities beside the warmth of the fire. It was the type of space that masters would either restrict or ignore. In other words, the enslaved community often used space around their homes in a way that was not understood or even appreciated by slave owners.

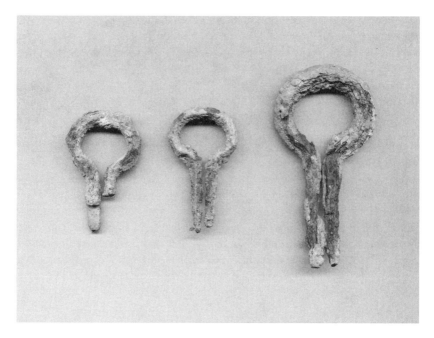

Fig. 10.3. Mouth harps found in the communal cooking area.

The Cooking Pit

Feature 820 was a food-related pit. In addition to all of the bones found, this area addresses the probability of in-ground cooking and adds to the evidence of this area as an active social space. It was because of this feature that Zone III is described as the BBQ area, for lack of a better expression. Within these cultural layers are several significant finds. This area is described as a social space not only because of the evidence of cooking but also because of the presence of leisure artifacts such as clay and ceramic marbles, straight pins and buttons, mouth harps, and fish hooks.

When exclusively enslaved families occupied the First Hermitage site, the central yardscape (area between the Kitchen Quarter and Farm House, see Fig. 10.2) served as what I would term the "visible" center of the community. Yet within the confines of the four standing structures was an area surrounded by multiple ash deposits and evidence of a variety of activities. Feature 820 was surrounded by dwellings, which obscured its view from the Jacksons and possibly the direct view of the overseer. It was well within the boundaries of the complex Quarter Household and could serve as the space that tied the various dwellings together, providing a gathering space where multiple families participated in daily functions of the extended household. The importance of looking at the enslaved landscape has several dimensions. At the forefront of the elite plantation during the Middle Quarter was a demonstration of prestige, power, and mastery in general. In this case, a large brick mansion complete with white columns and a guitar-shaped driveway was the means of conveying the message of dominance. Beyond that initial realm was the private mansion backyard, where entry was not given to all. There had to be a reason to be in this space. Associated with the brick mansion were the garden, main kitchen, smokehouse, and orchard. As the plantation system took off, the workspaces became the sphere of influence of enslaved peoples, yet the disconnecting of the plantation landscape and plantation power was constantly reinforced. Separating Jackson's private backyard from the working plantation was a white picket fence. This fence provided a physical and social boundary between the protected space of the Big House and the workspaces of the larger plantation. This also ensured that there would not be a mistake about where one ended and the other began.

However, the enslaved community at the First Hermitage created similar forms of boundaries. These boundaries may not have been in the form of a white picket fence of the later Middle Quarter, but they were shaped in a way that was meaningful to the inhabitants of the quarter. The visually and culturally hidden aspects of life under slavery were a daily negotiation of all enslaved populations. The ability to construct an outdoor hearth was very real for the members of the First Hermitage who sat outside on warm nights and shared music, gossip, stories, and good food cooked in ways distinct to the families sharing the space and in ways appreciated exclusively by its community members.

Jackson or any overseer might not have found any of these activities threatening or dangerous. They most likely appeared as one less obligation to provide for or worry about for effective plantation management. For the First Hermitage community, however, these actions were the very foundation of their complex household. Therefore, slaves were active participants in their own cultural production.

Before enslavement, African people had family and kinship structures that were altered once they arrived in the Americas. Jackson's belief in simple family units was practiced on a surface level among the enslaved community. In order to accomplish daily goals and tasks, enslaved workers pooled their resources in order to maintain a communal way of living. For the inhabitants of the First Hermitage site, communal living was not simply a choice but a necessity.

The Enslaved Family

Different people define landscapes differently. John Michael Vlach (1993) sees a landscape not only as a visual scene or an environmental setting but as a cultural construction. The enslaved inhabitants of plantations may not have had a say in the design, construction, and location of their individual dwelling structures; however, they did shape the way landscape functioned. By the nineteenth century, southern agricultural journals suggested various reforms to maintaining quarters. There was a call to "promote orderly family life within the slave community" (McKee 1992). Health and housing were among the top priorities of a slave owner, yet overcrowding was mentioned often as a main concern in several planter documents and letters. For reasons of health and happiness, masters believed that only one "family" per structure was the proper formula for success (Breeden 1980).

Several leading scholars of black family life have argued against viewing the black family structure as "pathological" in comparison with the Eurocentric concept of the nuclear family (Davis 1981; Stack 1974). However, black feminist scholars have long understood how domestic production was directly linked to black cultural production and the formation of African American identity (Carby 1987; M. Franklin 2001; Gray White 1999; Hill Collins 2000; hooks 1990; Steady 1993). As Angela Davis explains, the significance of the quarters for enslaved women and men was that they became the single space on the plantation that could possibly facilitate any sense of autonomy or semblance of safety. The homeplace, or quarter, served as a setting where activities of resistance occurred with greater frequency, and therefore it represents a useful line of evidence with which to use a gendered perspective of the enslaved landscape.

To unravel these landscapes, it is important to see how spaces were transformed into sites of comfort and safety. According to Edwards-Ingram, "The slave landscape incorporated both the apparent and the hidden" (1998, 270). The quarter, therefore, was formed into the "homeplace," where there is relief from the stresses of everyday hardships experienced by enslaved people. My reading of homeplace in the case of the First Hermitage is an example of how one enslaved community transformed the landscape into a location of reprieve from the daily rigors of enslavement. Although physically there was no "real" place away from the master's gaze, there were spaces constructed and understood by those who lived there as protected.

Several circumstances led me to concentrate on the exterior spaces at the First Hermitage site. The confining dimensions of each cabin forced a great deal of activity to shift outdoors. I believed that the yard was not empty space between the two structures but a bridge connecting several families. The yard can therefore be understood as an extension of the house, a "living room," so to speak (H. Lawrence Jones, Chesapeake, pers. comm., 1997). Edwards-Ingram further explains how "African American houses and yards also embodied complex and simple rhythms of time, space, energy, and change during slavery, as they do today" (1998, 249). The courtyard was not only socially significant to inhabitants of the Middle Quarters but also served as a connection across a culturally defined landscape.

To move toward an analysis of the centrality of landscapes and homeplace, the role of material culture used in activities associated with these symbolic spaces will enhance the study of enslaved domestic organization and the related social relationships. Further, it is pertinent to emphasize the connection between the enslaved household as a complex social unit and the yardscapes. As enslaved individuals were inextricably tied to all plantation affairs through forced labor, they were members of multiple "households" simultaneously. They were members of their own simple family units, the larger plantation household, and, in my research, the complex household of the First Hermitage quarter. Thus the enslaved household of the Hermitage plantation (Franklin 1997c, 53–54) "was a domestic network which served to mediate the social relations that revolved around production, distribution, and reproduction," whereby members "variously contributed their efforts and resources to the subhousehold as circumstances and needs varied."

At the First Hermitage site, daily activities connected the household by linking multiple families living within the quarter, not necessarily under the same roof. Thus there existed a system of cooperative individual families working together, forming a single complex household. As follows, the "yardscape" (or transformed exterior spaces) functioned as the nucleus of this household structure. The yardscape was central to the quarter, a significant component to all the members of the complex household. The analysis of the natural and built environment has proven to be central in the comprehension of how people actively shape and are shaped by the places they occupy. The First Hermitage provided the material and archaeological evidence to address methods employed by slaves to form semiautonomous, secure spaces, where various forms of black cultural production were taking place.

My interpretation of the enslaved household seeks to add a new dimension to how daily life differed from Jackson's emphasis on a "simple" family structure. As they performed household-related tasks throughout the plantation, individual families constantly shifted social divisions to meet their varying needs. In doing so, the typical divisions of "field, skilled, and house" were not meaningful to workers when it came to household performance. All were involved in Middle Quarter domestic-related activities such as gathering wood, cultivating herbs and vegetables, sweeping yards, or watching small children and the sick. These individuals were not listed on inventories as domestic occupations, but they were central to the well-being of the quarter subcommunity. The owner's records do not take into account the layers of domestic responsibilities performed by slaves.

When the First Hermitage shifted from the center of a small plantation to one of three large quarter areas, there was a gradual and visible transformation of how the landscape looked. Among the Middle Quarter community, there was a need to reshape the natural environment to support the physical, spiritual, and functional needs of the increasing populace. For example, the growing numbers of enslaved children and long lives of elders meant that there probably were networks of support and exchange only available to a cooperative community structure.

245

Spiritual Dimensions of Landscapes

Courtyards also served the needs of the living and the dead (Heath and Bennett 2000, 39). By this I am referring to the spiritual aspect of landscape. There has been a strong connection among peoples of African descent to the ancestors. Family members provided stories and lessons to shape the needs of successive generations. For example, the importance of connection to nature was a real aspect of how people from western Africa, the Caribbean, and ultimately the plantation South organized daily actions. It was this spiritual connection which remained beneath the radars of Eurocentric modes of behavior and understanding. Heath and Bennett contextualize this spiritual connection with the earth: "Among the Bakongo of Central Africa, 'sweeping is an ordinary ritual gesture for ridding a place of undesirable spirits' in a landscape populated by day with ghosts of witches and others who have not been accepted into the villages of the dead, and by night with the ancestors" (2000, 43). African American spirituality is often couched with religion, specifically black Christianity, yet I would argue that much of what enslaved Africans experienced and practiced was beyond what their masters or white counterparts would have considered spiritual.

There are several discussions in historical archaeology about ritual and items that demonstrate the presence of alternative forms of worship among enslaved peoples. The connections to African worldviews have long been discussed and debated, yet it is obvious that African spirituality has continued to influence black cultural production throughout the Diaspora (R. F. Thompson 1983). Music, folklore, and conjuring demonstrated the direct connection to the African continent (Paris 1995). Black literature, however, adds another dimension to this interpretation of the spiritual diversity of enslaved Africans. In Toni Morrison's *Beloved* (1987), the spiritual realm is a very real aspect of everyday life for Sethe and her daughter, who live in a world filled with ghosts of the past.

The yardscape is an excellent place to conceptualize how enslaved communities maintained a complex balance between work, spiritual, and communal efforts. When former slaves remembered their lives in bondage, a common point of discussion for interviewers was how their cabins looked. This emphasis on domestic sites seems logical when researchers think about where African American culture was in constant motion. The yard was for socializing, playing, performing household chores, raising animals, gardening, and "spiritual and cultural expression" (Heath and Bennett 2000, 43).

I have argued that enslaved landscapes are imbued with meaning. As homeplaces, they are sites of human action, the location of culturally prescribed and understood action, yet the power of these spaces must not be overlooked. In contemporary African America, the yard can be the site of conformity or resistance. For many, the yard and soil around the home is private, protected, and in many ways sacred. Included in the function and meaning of household are the spiritual and cultural needs that the collective household fulfilled for enslaved peoples. The connection is more substantial than simply recognizing how enslaved men and women used exterior spaces to reflect and meet their cultural and social needs. It is an argument to demonstrate how archaeology can be a tool in the understanding of the dynamics of enslaved homeplaces or alternative notions of how home functioned in the everyday lives of slaves.

Communication of ideas and meaning is also directly connected to the notion of identity formation. For Africans, slavery became the "root of an emergent collective identity" and therefore an emergent collective memory. Although the individual experiences differ, the overall impact on African American identity has to be linked to the collective nature of the system of slavery, for it was slavery that "distinguished a race, a people, or a community" depending on the level of abstraction (Eyerman 2001, 1). It was also slavery that informed generation after generation of the details and rules needed for survival. Without the ability and social space to communicate these details and rules, the social reproduction of African American identity would have been impossible. The collective memory of the older generations nurtured the succeeding generations, but the social spaces of yardscapes made the articulation and the "passing on" of these memories possible. Although I posit that communication between enslaved peoples often went unnoticed by slaveholders, landscape was a meaningful aspect of plantation construction in general. Slaveholders were very specific in how they ordered their properties. The placement of the main house, outbuildings, crops, workspaces, and quarter areas was a concept prescribed to maintain order and the display of power.

Conclusion

Ultimately, my research supports the understanding of how central the domestic realm was to the foundation of African American cultural production. Therefore, this analysis contributes to the fields of African Diaspora studies and African Diaspora archaeology in a number of ways. First, I seek to emphasize the connection between the enslaved household and the landscape. I argue that archaeologists typically take on two methodological approaches. One is the exploration of the enslaved community or family, and the other is a focused interpretation of the enslaved landscape. However, I seek to combine these interpretive methods to emphasize the daily importance of the enslaved household within the context of, and with regard to their relationship to, the landscapes.

The reason that the social group and the landscape must be considered together is because landscapes only have meaning when used and given meaning by people. Further, my research reveals that in order to interpret enslaved social groups from a more comprehensive and meaningful viewpoint, one should take into account what these groups practiced and within what specific spaces. At the Hermitage, the center of the complex household was the courtyard. The exterior areas were the sites where domestic production took place. The outdoor cooking hearth came to symbolize the social center of the compound. It was where meals were prepared, stories were told, music was performed, and games were played. Therefore, there is no way to separate the landscape from the household, since they were parts of a whole.

Second, my research supports understood notions of the protected social spaces of a quarter. For the enslaved, the domestic realm was the site of comfort, love, and support. Yet by the Eurocentric standards, it was also supposed to be the domain of women based on patriarchal concepts of gender-specific spheres and racist notions of a black pathological culture. The centrality of enslaved women, however, was not the result of pathological culture. Black women played an important role in black social life, partly as a response to African-influenced cultural practices and family organization and partly in response to the rigors of slavery, which deeply influenced enslaved family formation. Third, although historical archaeology has traditionally been an interdisciplinary field, I employ oral histories and African American literature in order to interpret enslaved life. These significant sources have yet to be used to any large extent within this field. Further, I conceptualize the black family and black women's roles using black feminist theory. This body of scholarship has not had much influence within historical archaeology, although research on African Americans has grown tremendously over the past thirty years (for exceptions, see M. Franklin 2001; Wilkie 2000, 2003).

The social memory of people of African descent is linked to the experience of slavery from the way a community shaped its built environment, to the material remains of social and cultural activity, and how the distant past acts as the foundation of contemporary notions of black identity. This being said, the potentials of African Diaspora archaeology are yet to be fully tapped in the fields of African American and African Diaspora studies. The material and expressive elements of enslavement should not be used simply to enhance the written word or oral testimony. By combining these elements, the potential for a wider reading of life under slavery should contribute to the ever-expanding notion of black cultural identity.

Bringing the Out Kitchen In? The Experiential Landscapes of Black and White New England

Isaac Royall Sr. (1677–1739) was born of modest means to a carpenter and his wife in the wilds of North Yarmouth, Maine, but he made a fortune as a young man through his participation in all three of the principal elements of the Triangular Trade. For thirty-three years, he had a sugar plantation and rum distillery in Antigua and one foot in the slave trade. Years of hardship on the island, however, involving drought, failed crops, epidemic disease, and slave insurrections in which two of the Royalls' own were implicated, brought the Royalls and a number of their slaves back to New England in 1737. The Massachusetts tax valuation of 1771 (Massachusetts Historical Commission [MHC]) shows that the New England estate, known as Ten Hills Farm, was a very different operation from the sugar plantation in Antigua, being engaged in wool and cider production, the raising of livestock, and the growing of English and Upland hay (Fig. 11.1). The Royalls seem also to have rented at least two slaves in town, perhaps more, and transported others between their farms in Medford and Stoughton, Massachusetts, wherever work was needed (Royall account book, June 25, 1737, Royall House Slave Quarters; Hoover 1974, 83).

Twombly and Moore (1982, 154) have called the dispersed task system of New England slavery a "lack of repression." And indeed, while no serious scholar today would claim that northern slaves were happy, substantial differences in population structure and economy, as well as in religion and law, have led some scholars to conclude that slavery in the North was somehow gentler than in plantation settings (Berlin 1998, 57; Greene 1942, 219). Some have also argued that the close working and living conditions of New England masters and their slaves made relations in the region more incorporative or "familial" in nature than elsewhere (Piersen 1988, 26). And it has

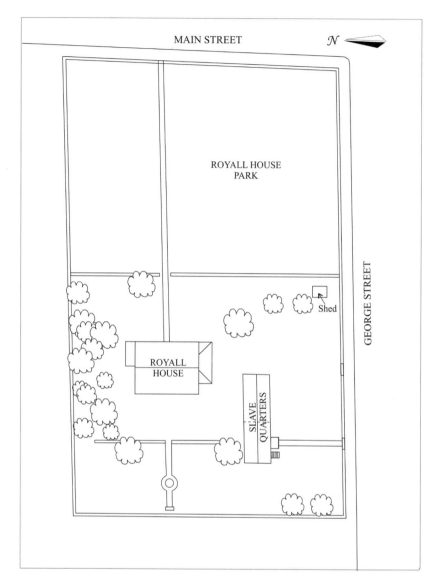

Fig. 11.1. Site plan for Ten Hills Farm, Medford, Massachusetts.

been implied that northern blacks, vastly outnumbered in a region that was at least 95 percent white throughout the colonial era, may have been more quickly and completely assimilated into European cultural forms than in the predominantly black regions of the South and Caribbean.

Recently such statements have begun to receive criticism from archaeologists (e.g., Chan 2003; Fitts 1996; Garman 1998) who have sought to provide, through a multiplicity of evidence, a view of master-slave relationships that recognizes and explores the diversity of the American slave experience but that does not downplay the oppressive social and economic impositions of slavery within which such relationships were negotiated. This chapter focuses particularly on documents and archaeological evidence of the use of space at the Isaac Royall House in Medford, Massachusetts, with regard to this problem.

Studying Landscape in Historical Archaeology

Rodman (1992, 643) has criticized anthropologists for being slow to problematize the concept of place, stating that place "is more than locale." Archaeologists, however, have long realized that people have always lived in cultural and natural landscapes that varied widely and have been experienced in multiple ways—what Rodman calls "multilocality," the "dynamic, socially constructed qualities of place" (651). Broadly defined, landscape constitutes all the natural and cultural features within and without human settlement—not just forests, creeks, and mountains but also houses, roads, fields, and walkways (Orser 1996, 368). Landscapes have reflected and shaped human relations, controlled social interaction, and given meaning and context to everyday life. Leone (1984) uses the notion of landscape as ideology, for example, to argue that the William Paca garden in Annapolis was not just a passive collection of trees, plants, and flowers but also a material symbol of Paca's rank and status in Maryland society. Yet if landscape studies have been able to do anything, it has been to demonstrate that "intention" and "reality" rarely coincide (Hudgins 1990; McKee 1992; Mrozowski and Beaudry 1990; Orser 1988b; Upton 1988). At best we may treat the Georgian gentleman's preoccupation with the manipulation of material symbols, such as landscape or artifacts, as but one side of an ongoing discourse that might be more telling about his own fears and desires than about any universal eighteenth-century "social reality."

What has come to be known as the "dominant ideology thesis," for example, has come, directly or indirectly, under considerable analysis. Most scholars no longer accept the notion that an elite or dominant class can create and perpetuate a societal ideal that then trickles down to the masses intact, making them internalize and accept their low status and thus contribute to their own oppression. On the contrary, many scholars have been able to demonstrate quite compellingly, through landscape, some of the ways that "the masses" have been able to respond to, reject, or ignore dominant ideologies and create ideologies of their own within and in spite of the external limitations placed on their lives (Beaudry, Cook, and Mrozowski 1991; DeCunzo 1998; Fitts 1996; Hall 1992, 2000; Hudgins 1990; Isaac 1982). Landscape studies do not just physically reconstruct landscapes but also try to interpret what they meant to the people who manipulated them and "experienced" them. In so doing they all attempt to understand a broader interaction sphere, including individuals, residential units, communities, regions, etc.

Scholars of landscape also now recognize that there are many kinds of landscapes and that they can have multiple meanings that change through time. Some of the best studies focus on human agency, the multiple levels of involvement in a landscape, and the idea of processional or experiential landscape (e.g., Barrett 1994; Beaudry and Mrozowski 2001; Isaac 1982; Mrozowski and Beaudry 1990; Rodman 1992; Upton 1988). Hence such questions as who designed and ordered a particular landscape, who built and maintained it, who displayed it, who visited it, and who altered his or her unobserved patch of it have become relevant in landscape studies. What the answers to these questions imply about the way we should be interpreting a landscape's social meanings is at the heart of the present discussion.

There are inadvertent landscapes as well. They can reveal the nuances of social life and relationships because they are often shaped by unconscious attitudes and values. Unlike purposeful landscapes, the inadvertent landscape is not anyone's attempt to make a statement about anything, and yet it might come closest to the truth about many things as a result. Ten Hills Farm was a patchwork of advertent and inadvertent landscapes that melded seamlessly. The Royalls and their slaves may have crossed the boundaries between them unknowingly, but they would always have been aware at some level of what the landscape was telling them about who they were, where they belonged, and where they were headed.

The Medford Landscape

In 1736, the year before the Royalls took up residence there, Medford was what one might almost call a hamlet, with only 665 inhabitants (Seaburg and Seaburg 1980, 100). It was located on the tidal Mystic River, whose steep banks and deep waters made it navigable by ships bound for Boston markets and whose great undulating curves ran through vast open marshes and wetlands that became saturated with Atlantic seawater twice daily. Here one could find geese, quails, partridges, and a variety of ducks in the spring. The river itself was home to bass, shad, frost-fish, and oyster beds (Brooks and Usher 1886). Annual runs of alewives and smelts choked the river and the many small freshwater streams and creeks that snaked their way into the salt marsh. The fish weirs that were set up there caught fish that would eventually find their way into the southern colonies and British West Indian markets, where cash crops were king.

Beyond the lowland salt marshes that immediately surrounded the river, there are wooded uplands that had been smoothed into rolling hills by glaciers thousands of years earlier. "The Rocks" were a range of such wooded granite hills that defined the north-northwest boundaries of the town. By the time the Royalls arrived, most of the town had been cleared of forest and transformed into an agrarian landscape with signs of exclusive landownership clearly demarcated through field boundaries, fences, bridges, and roads. The woods continued to hover at the outskirts, however, and not so far from human settlement. There the wolf, bear, wildcat, boar, and deer roamed at will. The woods were also a resource for food to supplement the meat of farm animals. Throughout the eighteenth century, there were annually elected town offic- ers called Deer Reeves and Hog Reeves, whose job it was to preserve the wild populations of deer and boar in the forests (Medford Town Records through 1830, MHC).

Apart from the physical landscape, however, is the landscape that is per- ceived, interpreted, and experienced by its inhabitants. The fields, fences, bridges, roads, and boundary markers can be read as a map of relations between people and their environment as well as a map of the "distribution and control of access" to resources (Isaac 1982, 19). As Medford carved its tiny niche of civilization out of the supposed "wilds" of Massachusetts, it was pur- posefully shaped in accordance with European social values about what was appropriate, desirable, or necessary. One of the great social values in the new colonies was that of private ownership of land. It was one of the primary attrac- tions for colonists to come to the New World in the first place. By the early eighteenth century, Medford town had been intensively divided and demar- cated into private landed property. The conditions of these properties would reflect the individual owner's standing and respectability, the size of his labor force, and his ability to keep them in order (Isaac 1982). Highways, roads, and lanes further divided the town. These grew in number in the eighteenth century as Medford became an important stopover for travelers going between Portsmouth and Boston or Salem, but they were still relatively few. By the mid-eighteenth century there were three principal streets extending from Medford Town Square like spokes on a wheel: the Road to Woburn, the Road to Malden, and Mystic Street (present-day Main Street), where the Royalls lived (Fig. 11.2). In addition there were cart paths leading to places of business such as the Distill House or taverns, the brickyards, and the wharves (Seaburg and Seaburg 1980). There were likely other ways of moving about the land- scape, however, that were not recorded in maps, for they were informal: foot- paths that led from field to barn, highway to tenement, house to house, and field to forest. These would probably have been the domain of the lesser folk: common farmers, tenants, artisans, and slaves.

Material Culture and Power in the Landscape

One's family, friends, and mode of dressing, walking, and talking informed a person's perception of the landscape on a more intimate, detailed level (Isaac 1982). A wig, for example, or lace cuffs, silver buttons, and brass or gold

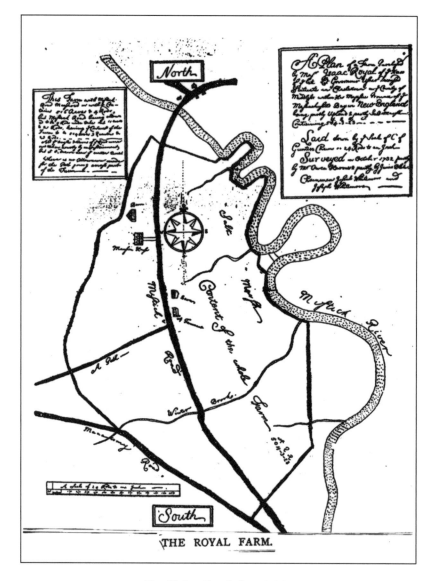

Fig. 11.2. a. Deed plan, 1732.

shoe buckles were unmistakable marks of a gentleman. They showed a gentleman's freedom from material necessity and toil. Reverend Devereux Jarratt, a
carpenter's son, writing of his boyhood in the 1730s and 1740s, observed:

> We were accustomed to look upon, what were called *gentle folks,* as beings of
> a superior order. For my part I was quite shy of *them,* and kept off at a humble
> distance. A *periwig,* in those days, was a distinguishing badge of *gentle folk*—and

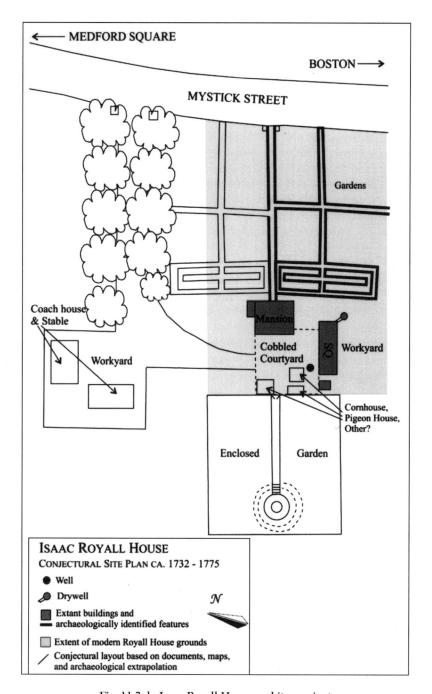

Fig. 11.2. b. Isaac Royall House and its precincts.

when I saw a man riding the road, near our house, with a wig on, it would so alarm my fears, and give me such a disagreeable feeling, that, I dare say, I would run off, as for my life. (1806, 14; emphasis in the original)

The quotation is suggestive of some of the awe with which the Royalls would have been beheld after they moved to Medford. It is also interesting to note, however, that Reverend Jarratt was the son of a carpenter, just as Isaac Royall Sr. had been. It is possible that Isaac himself had once harbored similar feelings as a boy, but rather than run in fear, he determined that one day it would be *he* who would ride down the street on horseback wearing a powdered wig, a bootspur, and shoe buckles (Fig. 11.3).

The gentry cloaked themselves with an authority that seemed to draw from time immemorial. The "appropriate demeanor, dress, manners, and conversational style . . . accompanied by a familiarity with the sources of sacred, Classical, or legal learning" led to a "presumption of gentility" (Isaac 1982, 131). The Royalls met all of these requirements with apparent effortless ease. Their estate ledger shows the degree to which both father and son concerned themselves with keeping au courant with the latest fashions. Silk hose, wigs, hats, yards of lace, "puffs" (soft gathers of fabric, ribbon, or small feathers for accenting dress), gowns, great coats, breeches, gloves, pumps, gold buckles, silver buttons, and watch crystals were frequent entries in the ledger. Isaac Sr.'s letters reveal that in addition to being well dressed, he was an educated, articulate, and genteel man. His erstwhile neighbor in Antigua, Samuel Martin, wrote in his *Essay upon Plantership*: "A liberal education is undoubtedly the principal ingredient necessary to form a good planter; who ought at least to know the rudiments of all the sciences" (Martin 1745 [1765], viii). Both father and son studied law, and Isaac Jr. became a Suffolk County judge during his tenure in Medford. They had numerous legal, scientific, and classical works on the shelves of their library and almost certainly considered themselves to be among the heirs apparent of the ancient world's cultural legacy (Middlesex County Probate Court File Papers, 1st ser. 1648–1871, case 19545, 1739). Martin, once again expounding upon the genteel planter, drew comparisons between the modern and ancient worlds when he noted the similarities between the modern, genteel planter and the Roman husbandman in his *Essay upon Plantership*: "The best plowmen were the bravest generals, and the wisest politicians of the Roman commonwealth; as if the same qualifications were equally requisite to form those very different characters. This I confess seems a paradox at first view; but upon closer examination will appear not less true of a good planter" (viii).

Within the white world there were many shades of respectability. A person of the times would have been able to read the clues to other people's station in life effortlessly from their manner of speech and their clothing fabric and style. Gentlemen of the caliber of Isaac Sr. and Jr. would have been a small but highly conspicuous minority in the Medford landscape. Both Royalls are said

Fig. 11.3. Artifacts: A. bootspur; B. shoe buckle; C. arrowhead amulet; D. stone
bead; E. gaming pieces; F. sewing kit.

to have paraded their illustrious guests out regularly on pleasure drives in their four-horse carriage driven by a fine-liveried black coachman (Hoover 1974). A common farmer, deeply tanned and gritty from the relentless demands of planting and harvesting crops, his simple unbleached linen sleeves rolled to the elbows and his hair a natural brown, might have paused to look up as the Royalls swept through the public landscape of Medford like elusive and exotic birds, in their colorful velvets and flowing silks. Such conspicuous, and at some level ritualized, performances served at once to underscore their authority by appropriating public spaces for personal pleasure, but also, in so doing, re-created the Royalls as an elite anew every time.

The world of the less fortunate is much more fragmentary and elusive. Not much is known about the lives of common farmers, tradesmen, widows, migrants, the poor, the elderly, or servants and unskilled laborers. Court records are the primary source of information about their lives and often the only evidence of their existence at all. The fact that court records usually represent extraordinary circumstances rather than ordinary ones must be taken into consideration when trying to reconstruct the townspeople of the eighteenth-century Boston area. Nevertheless, such records do indicate that the Royalls' lifestyle was not representative of the general colonial experience (Chan 2003, 370–74). It would have been highly visible, however, for its vast difference. Perhaps the second-most conspicuous or visible portion of the population at that time would have been the numerous African and Creole (American-born) slaves that seemed to exist in a separate but parallel universe to the white world.

Medford would have been about 4 percent black at the time of the 1754 slave census, when twenty-seven black males and seven black females over the age of sixteen were reported for the town, twelve of whom belonged to the Royalls (MHC; Brooks and Usher 1886, 355). Thirty-four people, with some number of children and elderly, were certainly not many, but they would have been a visible and exotic minority, lending a distinctly foreign flavor to the town, and they probably knew each other well. Implicit evidence also suggests that white New Englanders did not perceive African and Creole slaves to be an assimilated or organic component of their own society (as suggested by Twombly and Moore 1982; Berlin 1998; or Piersen 1988, 22) but rather as an alien presence that could be alternately amusing, irritating, or menacing.

Isaac Sr.'s son-in-law, Robert Oliver, who settled in Dorchester with his wife, Anne, and their slaves, is said to have looked with "scornful pity" on his slaves who refused to see the merits of the "proper use of a Yankee wheelbarrow" and persisted, despite his efforts, in carrying all of their burdens on their heads (Jackson 1907, 4). The fact that many of the Royall slave children, who would have been island- or Massachusetts-born, also had Akan-derived names, such as Abba, Quaco, Coba, Jemmy, and Nuba, further suggests that the slaves belonging to the Royalls and their immediate family were still actively cultivating their African heritage in New England (Table 11.1).

Table 11.1. Enslaved Population Belonging to the Royalls in 1738–39,
Derived from the 1739 and 1752 Probate Inventories of Isaac Royall
Sr.'s Estate (Middlesex County Probate 1739)

Men	Women	Children/adolescents
Fortune	Trace	Girl, 6[a, b]
Barron	Ruth	Quacoe
Ned	Sue	Diana
Peter	Jonto	John
House Peter	Black Betty	Nancy
Cuffe	Abba	Betty
Smith	Abba	George
Phillip	Old Cook[a, b]	Sarah
Quamino		Jacob
Robin		Jemmy
Captain[a, b]		Robin
George, about 45[a, c]		Coba
Santo, Lame, 50[a, b]		Walker
Old Negro Man, about 70[a, c]		Nuba
		Trace
		Tobey
		Present

[a]Individuals added in a retroactive inventory of 1752.
[b]Individuals held at Stoughton, Massachusetts, farm (now Walpole).
[c]Individuals held at Mount Hope Farm (Freetown, Massachusetts, now Fall River).

One place to find documentary accounts of these people's physical appearance is in contemporary newspapers, particularly in advertisements for runaway slaves. Greene (1944, 127) surveyed sixty-two of these advertisements from eleven newspapers in various New England colonies between 1704 and 1784, in search of what he called the "slave personality" in New England—admittedly a rather suspect agenda and of limited use to us here. Some of the data he presents, however, are revealing if interpreted for the purpose of looking at blacks as figures in the New England landscape. For instance, forty of the sixty-two fugitives (65 percent) had African names, probably reflecting the relatively high proportion of African-born individuals in the region, and mastery of the English language was by no means a given in the eighteenth century. Many were said to speak "good English," "pretty good English," or "tolerable good English" (quoted in Greene 1944, 138), while two Boston runaways I encountered in newspapers were said to speak only "broken English" (*Boston Weekly Post-Boy*, September 25, October 16, 1749).

Fugitive slaves were most often described in traditional European attire, but that was true of most slaves in the Americas, and there is oblique documentary evidence that some enslaved individuals in New England continued to cultivate an African aesthetic in their modes of self-adornment and self-presentation. A young runaway in 1767, for instance, was described as having a shaved forehead, which was probably an African or African-derived hairstyle, possibly "Coromantee" or Mandingo (*Boston Gazette and Country Journal*, November 23, 1767). White and White conclude that the styling of hair was one area in which blacks in the eighteenth century were able to flaunt their distinctiveness, coming up with syncretistic styles influenced by traditional African forms, Native American forms, and even European wig fashions of the day. They further argue that while these "striking arrangements" were both jarring and confusing to white observers, they could have served as an outlet for individual self-expression and even resistance for slaves (White and White 1998, 47–48, 54–55).

Other styles of self-adornment that American colonials may have encountered are suggested by archaeological finds. A stone flake with two chipped side notches that give the object the distinct shape of an arrowhead, for instance, was recovered from excavations in the Royall House slave quarters' west yard (Fig. 11.3c). Although it is certainly not a functional arrowhead, a groove scratched between the side-notches likely facilitated suspension (for example, from around the neck) by a length of twine or leather thong, and the object has been preliminarily interpreted as a charm or protective amulet. Given the apparent ethnic makeup of the Royall slave population, as evidenced by their names, we may also speculate that it belonged more specifically to a belief system of Akan derivation in which prehistoric stone projectile points were believed to have magical powers. *Nyame akuma*, or God's axes—thunderbolts that resulted when lightning struck the earth—were excellent vessels for powerful indwelling spirits (Ward 1958, 32). What is more, it is a belief demonstrably carried over to parts of the Americas as well. Both Orser (1985) and Wilkie (1995, 2000) document the curation of Native American lithics both in the archaeological and ethnohistorical record of slave sites in the South, and Wilkie (1995, 143) adds that "arrowheads" continue to be sold in New Orleans today as good luck charms. The object at the Royall House was not a "found" artifact but made by hand by someone who was no doubt familiar with the Native American lithics that would turn up periodically in fields and streambeds. It was not just the accidental find, however, that could be imbued with power. Chireau (1997, 228) says that "created objects" were used throughout West and Central Africa as vessels of the supernatural. Incantations or libations could invoke the ancestors over the vessels and turn any object into a charm (Puckett 1926, 171; Wilkie 2000, 188). The "amulet" suggests a private spiritual agency on the part of slaves, perhaps as an attempt to exert a measure of control over the largely uncontrollable circumstances of life under slavery. It is not clear, however, whether the worst threats were seen to come from a generally malign spirit world, the whimsies of white society or the Royalls themselves, or from other slaves on the estate. It is likely that all were perceived as threatening at different times and under different circumstances.

A hand-drilled stone bead was also recovered from the Slave Quarters excavations (Fig. 11.3d), and beads have long been found at, and associated with, slave sites. This bead, however, is unusual in that, while it reflects a distinctly non-European aesthetic, it has none of the gay, vibrant colors typically associated with beads recovered from other slave quarter sites as part of an African-American woman's "garments of gladness" (John Davis 1803, quoted in Yentsch 1995, 52). It is plain, handmade, and crude, but the task of drilling it by hand does reveal something of its symbolic importance to the person who made and used it. It may have been worn in the hair, in a necklace, or in a string around the waist.

Anne Yentsch has situated the role of beads within an African-American cultural framework of maintaining ideas of African womanhood: that African-American girls wore beads because their mothers and grandmothers had. It was a tradition never broken because whites dismissed beads as decorative baubles of the weaker sex, and they were therefore able to inadvertently become a means of expressing oneself, forging transgenerational kinship ties among black women in America (Yentsch 1995, 48–49). It is an interesting possibility that may well have been true at the Royalls' own estate, where naming practices that show several instances of young girls sharing names with older female kin suggest the importance of those transgenerational ties in the structuring of family and the socialization and rearing of children. The bead, as an item of handcraftsmanship and personal adornment, may have served to strengthen symbolic ties of kinship through their embodiment in something tangible.

On the other hand, it should not be overlooked that men in many parts of West Africa also wore beads for various cultural, political, and aesthetic reasons at this time. Beads, as prestige objects, had played a role in establishing and maintaining social hierarchies and relationships in West Africa since the eleventh century, and they could be mobilized in public arenas as a kind of social and/or political capital—to reaffirm status or to consolidate and legitimate power (Ogundiran 2002c, 433). In this sense, beads were very much more than mere personal adornment and were often restricted to persons of authority. Of course, the very act of transporting millions of Africans to the New World would tear the cultural fabric within which such symbols had originally been used and had significance. Nevertheless, while the Middle Passage and the new cultural context of enslavement would have altered the precise meanings and social valuations of beads, the idea of "beads-as-social-objects" may well have continued to signify for Africans and their descendants in the New World. Within an American context, beads might have had slightly different meanings among the enslaved, but could still have generally been understood to distinguish among persons of different status, authority, respectability, or desirability—for both women and men.

Finds such as the ones discussed here, while elusive in revealing their true significance, provide evocative evidence of a non-European aesthetic and belief system being cultivated at Ten Hills Farm that is inconsistent with assumptions of greater assimilation (Chan 2003). It could perhaps be argued, however, that the scarcity of New England slaves' numbers may have reduced the cultural expression of their "otherness" to these more private and individual actions.

The Royalls' Experience of Landscape

Upton (1988, 363) claims that the white world of the eighteenth century, contrary to the black, was designed to be experienced "dynamically." It is an interesting way of looking at landscape because it implies that social life, shaped by and played out in these very landscapes, is a kind of performance in motion, or *praxis* (Bourdieu 1977). The public landscape of roads, drives, and public architecture, and the private landscape of a landed estate with mansion house, fields, and outbuildings are but a spatial context or a collection of visual referents to guide the intricate dance among participants in a discourse negotiating their positions and roles in reference to each other. Such performances create a kind of "cultural geography" from which people get their bearings and learn "how to act" (Barrett 1994, 56, 19). In other words, it is only through the practice or performance of social life that the rules of social discourse are created, its meanings determined. The importance of place derives not just from what takes place there in the present but also from what took place and what is expected to take place there in the future. Robert St. George (1998, 2) calls this phenomenon cultural "implication," the poetic art of conveying thoughts, ideas, or things without specifically referencing them; bringing associations and evocations to mind as things, places, ideas, or words from another time and place and cultural milieu are appropriated into a new context. Place is a metaphor that gives what happens there meaning and power because it recalls other places, other events, other interactions.

The Royalls' Georgian mansion was situated on slightly raised ground that commanded a view of the hills and marshes that led down to the Mystic River itself. There the bustling ship traffic served as a visual reminder of the Royalls' personal "connectedness" to international markets, as their own "boat" brought tons of hay, cider, and wool down that artery to Boston markets and from thence to the world. The house was set back from Mystic Street, where most traffic coming in or going out of Medford would pass by and see its grandeur. In fact, a long stretch of Mystic Street cut right through Ten Hills Farm, so travelers would be surrounded for some time on all sides by the Royalls' grounds. Drake (1906, 123) quotes one such traveler as saying, "On our journey past through Mistick, which is a small Town of ab'a hundred

Houses, Pleasantly Situated, near to which is a Fine Country Seat belonging to Mr. Isaac Royall being one of the Grandest in North America."

The links between the public landscape of roads, rivers, and wharves, however, and the private landscape of Ten Hills Farm itself, though seemingly part of a single articulated landscape, were carefully orchestrated with an eye to outside visuals and processional effect, and to the establishment of a series of barriers to restrict access. From the public space of Mystic Street, one could see and admire the Royalls' house, grounds, and sprawling vistas, but one was also meant to be awed by the symbols of power that inhabited the landscape and be intimidated by their inaccessibility. The house itself could be approached on foot or horseback through a gate on Mystic Street flanked by wooden posts and opening onto a "grand avenue . . . bordered with box" that led you to the door. Farther to the north were massive stone gateposts that marked the entrance to the carriage drive that also turned off of Mystic Street and led, "under the shade of magnificent old elms," to the cobbled courtyard in back of the house (Drake 1906, 120–21). Here, too, was the separate entrance for the barn, stables, and coach house complex. St. George (1998, 273) claims that the Royall "plantation represents the first documented impact of a new generation of English agricultural reform," which sought to keep animal yards "at a polite distance" from the house and to "segregate farm labor . . . from the fictive allegorical scene [Royall] was contriving." The house was in a neoclassical architectural style that recalled the villas of ancient Rome. It was extremely fashionable, the more so for its relative rarity so long before the Revolution, and processing along the carriage drive allowed the privileged social visitor to admire the house from three sides before reaching the ornate front door. There they might enter the house and take tea in the Best Room, which overlooked the pleasure gardens and drew the eye to the distant and tantalizing focal point of the summer gazebo on a hill in the orchards. After tea one might be invited to take a turn in the gardens and catch the late afternoon breezes in the summerhouse, which, according to St. George (1998, 273, 276), was located perfectly according to John Mortimer's *Whole Art of Husbandry*, a book that Isaac Sr. had in his library. The path to the summerhouse was aligned with the mansion's central axis and led to the top of a hill that afforded fine prospects of the orchards, gardens, and lands. In fact, although the mansion house was of neoclassical design, the Royalls' estate might have more immediately implicated the English landed gentry and their country houses. Girouard (1980, 3) states that the country house was the "image-maker" of the emerging English gentry in the eighteenth century and that the building of a country seat was the critical culmination of a man's rise to affluence and influence. Thus, while the classical references in the architecture of the house and summer gazebo would certainly have been recognized, the Royalls, who continued to be active and influential members of the Boston political and social scenes, might also, in retiring "to the country" in Medford, have been symbolically aligning themselves with the English ruling class.

The procession was truncated for people there to conduct business. The Royalls' office where they collected outstanding debts and loans was a single room annexed to the northern elevation of the house and had its own entrance. Debtors came and went without ever gaining access to the inside of the house or any of the hospitality and gentility that it seemed to promise. The placement of the office would have defined its visitors' relationship to the Royalls in no uncertain terms. Then there were the people who had no business at the Royalls' estate at all—common farmers, tradesmen, servants, etc.—who passed the house day in and day out, driving their goods to market in open carts or running errands on foot. They could but imagine what lay beyond the massive stone gates that barred them from the Royalls' world.

In the immediate vicinity of the house were, of course, the slave quarters, which—visible from the street—were one obvious, tangible symbol of their lordly stature in the landscape. There were other symbols, though, in the built environment that seemed to justify the Royalls' authority and rightful domination. The Royall House estate is laid out much like an urban townhouse compound of the American South, such as one finds in Charleston, Savannah, or Richmond. In those cities, large slaveholders kept some of their slaves in a building behind the main house, usually a two-story structure housing a kitchen, laundry, and other workrooms on the first floor, and slave bedrooms on the second. These buildings, as part of the social display of the whole estate because of their proximity to the main house, matched the main house in architectural design, detail, and integrity, and together they formed an L-shaped enclosure on a common courtyard. The whole design mirrored the social relationships of the people who inhabited the structures: the master's spatial control of the land, and viewscapes that centered on the main house—the master and his place (Herman 1999; Tate 1965; Vlach 1991). The Royalls' mansion house, with its neoclassical quoined corners and pedimented windows and doors would, according to Epperson (1990, 31), have worked to "appropriate the ahistorical aura and authority of classical culture, making specific relations of domination appear timeless" (Fig. 11.4). By extending the same style to the Slave Quarters, the Royalls may have attempted to incorporate the quarters into the formal landscape of the estate and hence into the ideology of domination and control on which it rested (Fig. 11.5).

But Isaac Sr. was not just a master of black men. In addition to one white servant named William Beven whose indentures Isaac Sr. held briefly in the 1720s, Isaac's account book shows that he collected rent from or held mortgages on the Skinners, Farrows, Fosters, and Clevelands of Medford and Charlestown. Isaac Jr. held the same on the Tufts, Wises, Greys, Crofts, and Olivers. Some of these were tenants on the Royalls' property, paying rent to use houses, barns, and fields on Ten Hills Farm. Others were forced to relinquish partial ownership of their own farms by taking out a mortgage with the Royalls for defaulting on payments for slaves or monetary loans that the Royalls put out at 6 percent. Part of this money-lending scheme was Isaac Sr.'s

Fig. 11.4. Mansion's western façade.

Fig. 11.5. Slave quarters.

strategy to stabilize his fortune in a time of great inflation and uncertain colonial currency. As he informed Edmund Quincy in a letter dated August 15, 1736, investing in land and putting money "out to interest" was the only way to make sure his fortune did not lose value over time, for he shrewdly guessed that land values in and around Boston would "never" fall. Another part, however, was surely a means of establishing a kind of hegemony in the township. Girouard (1980, 2) states that power in the eighteenth century was based on ownership of land, not for farming but for the tenants who lived on it and the rental income it produced. Isaac Sr.'s account book shows that literally dozens of families were perpetually indebted to the Royalls, either for tenements, mortgages, monetary loans, or slaves. Tenant farms that dotted the landscape, then, were another visual symbol of the Royalls' dominance in the town.

The Black Experience of Landscape

It may be that only white landscapes were designed with processional effect in mind—what we might call purposeful landscapes—but I do not agree with Upton (1988) that only white landscapes were dynamic. All landscapes are really processional or experiential, and all people moving through them are processing, intentionally or not. Who one is will affect how one moves through a particular landscape and thus how one experiences that landscape. Indeed, Rhys Isaac (1982) has said that one's experience of a landscape is not just affected by, but actually contingent upon, rank. So it is not that blacks and common whites failed to process or that they were denied the opportunity to process; they processed differently, often through what may be thought of as inadvertent landscapes, those that do not make a blatant social statement but rather are shaped by and help to perpetuate unconscious values and attitudes. By processing through the landscape in alternative ways, the Royalls' slaves would have made their own implicated places. The "social 'art' of living" for a slave would have been very different from that of his master (Bourdieu 1977, 19). His understanding of "reality" would have been shaped by personal experiences and interactions with the physical world and other actors in it who were themselves vastly different.

Most scholars of landscape agree that landscape, as artifact, works to reflect as well as shape social and class relations (Beaudry and Mrozowski 2001; Hudgins 1990; Luccketti 1990; McKee 1992; Mrozowski and Beaudry 1990; Orser 1988b). Planters in particular designed their estates to be part of their "strategy of social control," meant to facilitate control over the lives and labor of their slaves and to maximize production and profits, while convincing social inferiors to internalize their own inferiority (Delle 1999, 151). Such statements of power were mitigated by the degree to which their intended audience saw or paid attention to them (e.g., Hudgins, 1990; cf. also McKee, 1992), but Garman (1998, 133) claims that "conflict-driven models" of dominance and resistance are inadequate for understanding the complexities of master-slave relations in southern New England anyway. Piersen (1988, 143) suggests a model of "resistant accommodation," which is more rigorously developed by Garman, as more suitable to understanding the nature of the encounters between colonial New England masters and their slaves. Master-slave relations, under such a model, consisted of a series of mutually uneasy compromises and grudging concessions.

Blacks and whites in New England lived under a system in which white surveillance and monitoring of blacks (both formal and informal) were an inescapable part of daily life. Close living arrangements were coupled with curfews to curtail slaves' movements and legal acts to control their behavior, ability to engage in trade, their right to assemble, and their right to attend houses of entertainment. At the same time, however, while segregation in everything from meals, work, and living spaces to processional access, church seating, or burial grounds cast slaves as inferior and outsiders, it also ensured that they would have space and time to themselves (Garman 1998; Jones 1990).

The slave quarters at Ten Hills Farm were at the interface of two landscapes—the white and the black—and they would have belonged in some ways to both (Upton 1988). There can be no question that they belonged to the white landscape the Royalls had explicitly created, centered on the mansion house, as part of the workscape and visual statement of the Royalls' dominance. On the other hand, they also belonged to the black landscape that included the quarters and surrounding yards, but may in fact not have been centered on them, for the black domain could be far-reaching. These were "shared but contested" spaces (Garman 1998, 134).

Three seasons of excavations have helped to shed light on the way the Ten Hills Farm landscape may have been perceived by those who lived there, black and white. Although I have argued that the estate was laid out in a way that seemed to proclaim the natural inferiority and dependency of blacks on whites (Chan 2003) and to physically draw the slave quarters into the center of the estate, excavations of the grounds suggest ways in which this centripetal force might have been counteracted. Most notably, there seems to have been a pronounced difference in the social and functional use of space surrounding the mansion and the slave quarters that relegated work, construction, and waste-disposal activities to the relatively out-of-sight side and back yards of the slave quarters, while the north yard where the slave quarters fronted onto the courtyard that is shared with the main house seems to have been swept relatively clean. There was a certain amount of sheet refuse recovered from immediately atop the cobbled surface of the courtyard and in the matrix of the stones, but fully two-thirds of the artifacts in the courtyard came from a midden layer found beneath the cobbled surface and dating to the late seventeenth and early eighteenth centuries. The cobbles, believed to have been laid as part of the Royalls' beautification efforts of the estate when they first bought the property in 1732, mark a shift in the use of that space, from a work yard to a formal receiving area. No trash pits were located in the courtyard after the laying of the cobbles. The attention to cleanliness is not particularly peculiar. The Royalls entertained guests of the highest order, including the governor himself. To lead their visitors down the long avenue of elms only to greet them in a courtyard filled with stinking piles of rubbish would hardly have been appropriate. Table 11.2 compares the artifact assemblages from the slave quarters' west, east, and south yards with those of the courtyard and indicates that the west and south yards of the slave quarters contained nearly 79 percent of the total artifact assemblage in these four areas. Table 11.3 was created to help correct for sampling error. Because the yards were not equally sampled, the average number of finds per unit was determined in order to partially balance out the raw frequency distribution numbers, which do not take into consideration issues of sampling.

Among the work yards, the west yard was more heavily used for these purposes than the south yard, and both were more heavily used than the east yard, probably because the latter two would have been visible from the street to passersby, and the east yard would actually have been part of the house's main frontage on Main Street. In the west yard, small trash pits were dug to contain some of the larger deposits, while buckets of ash and the remains of the latest meal were thrown carelessly on the ground. Rats and other small rodents rummaged for scraps, and pungent smells must have wafted across the grounds on hot days. Broken cooking and storage pots, discarded utensils, and rubble from old building activities were strewn across the ground, with little care given to appearances. It was in both of the side yards, too, that most of our artifacts suggestive of family life, leisure time activities, and craftsmanship of slaves were found, suggesting that when the work day was done, these were the areas in which the slaves gathered to unwind, largely beyond the watchful eye of the master (Figs. 11.3e and 11.3f).

The functional division in the use of space would have had various social implications. For one, it would have made the slaves' domain an unpleasant one and reinforced slaves' inferior and altogether separate social position. It also would have kept the most blatant and unpleasant evidence of human bondage out of sight and perhaps out of mind while the Royalls got down to the serious business of entertaining and living lavishly. Another possibility, although documents particular to the Royalls do not survive to support or contradict it, is that these areas were dirty in spite of the Royalls. McKee (1992) argues, for instance, that slave house yards were often untidy and unclean in spite of owners' best efforts to the contrary; that dirty house yards were in point of fact a form of workplace aggression on the part of slaves, in retaliation against the various controls placed on their lives. He also argues that since few slaves were likely to feel any real emotional attachment to their quarters as "home," and the "slave domain" extended far beyond the walls of the quarters in any case, there was even less reason to keep the yards neat.

Table 11.2. Artifact Assemblages of the Slave Quarters' West, East, and South Yards Compared with Those of the Cobbled Courtyard, Showing Differential Use of Space for Waste Disposal on the Royall Estate

Material	SQWY No.	% Total from These Areas	SQEY No.	% Total from These Areas	SQSY No.	% Total from These Areas	CY No.	% Total from These Areas
Ceramic (n = 22,837)	13,492	59.08	2,090	9.15	4,662	20.41	2,593	11.35
Glass (n = 10,052)	7,173	71.36	729	7.25	1,373	13.66	777	7.73
Organic (n = 8,893)	4,411	49.60	546	6.14	2,539	28.55	1,397	15.71
Metal (n = 6,534)	3,232	49.46	382	5.85	1,457	22.30	1,463	22.39
Other mineral (n = 244)	111	45.49	40	16.39	93	38.11	–	–
Stone (n = 59)	32	54.24	6	10.17	18	30.51	3	5.08
Synthetic (n = 5)	–	–	2	40.00	1	20.00	2	40.00
Other (n = 628)	148	23.57	44	7.01	404	64.33	32	5.10
Unidentified (n = 1)	–	–	–	–	–	–	1	100.00
Total (n = 49,253)	28,599	58.07	3,839	7.79	10,547	21.41	6,268	12.73

Table 11.3. Average Number of Artifacts/Ecofacts Recovered per Unit in the
Four Yards Surrounding the Slave Quarters

Location	No.	No. of Units Sampled	Average Artifacts/Unit
SQ West Yard	28,591	13	2,199
SQ East Yard	4,390	4	1,097
SQ South Yard	10,457	10	1,046
Courtyard	6,274	15	418

In light of the claim that northern bondage was more familial and incorporative in nature than plantation slavery, the interpretations of the finds at the Royall House in this respect take on added significance. Although one can certainly argue that there is a difference between retaining and enforcing social distance, the observed spatial segregation between master and slave is, in either case, inconsistent with family relationships. The Royalls and their slaves were clearly not living together as a single social and economic unit. They were not using the land collectively as one might expect in a familial form of bondage. Thus the architectural layout of the farm seems to convey but an ideal of incorporating slaves and their place into the center of the white-dominated landscape and its ideology. Archaeology seems to betray, however, the inherent contradiction involved in giving such importance to physical segregation to make these attempts at social domination effective. Epperson (1999a) points out, for example, that slaveholders were never able to fully reconcile the need to incorporate slaves, through landscape, into the ideology of their own inferiority, when their inferiority was defined in large part through their systematic exclusion from the white spatial domain. The Royalls' slaves did not see or experience the formal landscape in the same way as the Royalls themselves, their honored guests, or tenant debtors did, because they traveled through it differently. What is more, taking footpaths and shortcuts and inhabiting marginal areas of the "formal" landscape—such as the side and back yards of the quarters—was not only likely a forced condition of their existence but also one way for these people to make the formal landscape informal and familiar.

At the Royall House, in addition to the functional division in the use of space, there is evidence of alternative processional ways that would have allowed for multiple experiences of the landscape, depending on one's background, one's business there, and one's routes of access to various parts of the estate. A slave's "procession" began not at the stone gates but at the kitchen door at the back of the house. Excavations revealed a historical walkway that once connected the out kitchen to the main house kitchen door. From there, a narrow servant stair made all three floors of the house accessible from the kitchen and this backdoor entry. It hid the inner workings of servicing the house from the Royalls and their guests. However, it also gave slaves a backdoor view of all that happened there. They would probably have kept themselves abreast of the financial state of the family and the various events and happenings of the Royalls and their acquaintances; they would have listened for news from the outside world, rumors of imminent sale, or other threats to slave family stability. They would have been invisible to the house and its occupants in a way that the house and its occupants were *not* invisible to them. This idea has been illustrated in dramatic fashion by Bernard Herman (1999, 88), who used court records from the defense of a slave named Billy Robinson in the 1822 Denmark Vessey insurrection trial to reveal the "cultural blindness in masters" in their perceptions of space. He argues that blacks were able to gain an invisibility "engendered by white custom, habit, and arrogance" that stemmed from the misguided belief that the spaces in an urban townhouse compound made slaves "perpetually visible" (Herman 1999, 100). Robinson was able to take advantage of this false sense of security to help plan the insurrection under his master's very nose and then to use the same presumptions of perpetual visibility to get himself acquitted of any wrongdoing.

Urban townhouse compounds were tightly knit, incorporative landscapes that made the mansion, kitchen, washhouses, quarters, privies, workyards, gardens, sheds, and warehouses appear to be part of a unitary whole. The master family, situated at the center, felt they could survey all, while the architectural layout of the estate seemed to confirm blacks' inferiority to and dependency on whites. The idea of perpetual visibility would have been especially seductive in New England where most slaveholders housed many if not all of their bondsmen in their own homes—ferreted away in kitchens, garrets, closets, or hallways. Isaac Sr.'s 1739 probate inventory lists eight "Negro beds and beding" in the main house kitchen, garrets, and chambers, although there may have been as many as twelve. The constraints and pressures of living in the main house in close proximity to the Royall family must have been formidable. N. T. Jones Jr. states that house servants paid a high price for the material improvements in living conditions they may or may not have had, for a house slave's work was never done, and close surveillance made slipping out for "nocturnal and illicit travels," crucial for forging and maintaining family ties, friendships, and community, more difficult to do (Jones 1990, 116). There can be little doubt that the proximity of the Royalls' slave quarters to the main house, and the housing of several individuals within the mansion itself, would have made absences or transgressions more immediately apparent. One can also see quite readily how masters might have been seduced into thinking in such a situation that they had a good idea of what their slaves were doing at all times.

Of course, the idea of perpetual visibility would not have been taken literally. There were several places in the immediate vicinity of the mansion house that would have been more or less out of sight from the Royalls' central post. Indeed, this fact partially explains the differences in the use of space around the mansion and slave quarters outlined above. And if Mistress Royall went to the kitchen daily to dictate the day's meals, she would have had little occasion to go to the kitchen chamber or the third-floor garrets. Thus these segregated areas and whatever was done or said in them, though easily monitored if desired, would have been mostly unsupervised. Likewise, in their servicing of the house and its inhabitants and visitors, perhaps standing discreetly by the wall, or coming and going silently to serve and clear tea, lace up stays, or deliver wax-sealed letters, slaves became "backdrops" or "props" who found in their "transparency" a measure of autonomy (Herman 1999, 97).

Not all of the Royalls' slaves lived in the Great House, however, and even those, in their varied and sundry tasks, may have been able to circumvent the formal landscape in unsuspected ways. Historical documents obliquely suggest that the Royalls, in addition to having a bevy of house slaves, also had in-house specialists for performing tasks from baking to boating to cider pressing. In 1737, for example, a "Negro man" likely on the hire-out system was "taken again of Henry Neal," a baker in Boston, "and sent up to Stoughton, he not being able to pay for him" (Royall account book, June 25, 1737). In June 1768, Plato drowned (New England Historic Genealogical Society 1907). Could he have been the boatman responsible for taking hay, cider, and wool produced at Ten Hills Farm down the Mystic River to Boston markets? Garman (1998, 148) has also linked cider production, which was engaged in at Ten Hills Farm, to specialized and seasonal slave labor in New England. These occupations likely afforded considerable unsupervised mobility. Fortune, whose occupation is unspecified, was sometimes entrusted with large amounts of cash and a degree of autonomous movement to buy things for the farm, as seen in account book entries such as "To Cash sent P Fortune . . . £25" and "To Cash to Fortain [sic] to buy beef 27/ 1 pr Wool Cards 10/ . . . £1.17" (account book, November 21, 1737; May 10, 1738). He must have been a trusted slave and able to go where he pleased on such errands. The baker's apprentice may also have been sent here and there regularly, and working in town would have allowed him access to the shadow lands and alternative landscapes of "alley society"—tavern, workyard, and waterfront life—among the city's 1,000 black slaves and vast numbers of poor whites, free blacks, and Indians (Twombly 1973, 26). He may have seen or even participated in the "gross immoralities" of "tumultuous companies of men, children, and Negroes" that plagued the streets and lanes of Boston at the time (*Massachusetts Acts and Resolves*, vol. 3, Province Laws 1756–57, 4th session, ch.14, 997). He may have heard news from abroad about slave conspiracies and revolts, smelled the ghastly odor in the air that signaled the recent arrival of a slave ship in Boston harbor, or seen the latest imports from Africa or the West Indies stumble ashore in all of their filthy misery, perhaps by now exotic and strange even to him. Perhaps he also attended festivals such as Black Election Day or met in private homes with Boston's free blacks. We will never know. But we can probably say with certainty that he brought news of what he had done and seen in town back to Ten Hills Farm. In so doing he would have been able to give his fellow slaves a feeling of belonging to a larger community of their brethren in suffering that went beyond the bounds of their immediate surroundings and existed in spite of the landscapes of inequality that seemed to deny their independence. Those slaves who, because of the nature of their work, had mobility and relative freedom of movement, became a ray of hope and the umbilical cord between those left at home and the wider black community. Indeed, the fact that the Royalls' slaves may have felt community ties to the black population of Boston is evidenced by Fortune's having been one of the cofounders of the Prince Hall African Lodge after emancipation and Prince Hall's having drafted the aged Belinda's 1783 petition to the General Court for a pension because she could not read or write herself (Royall House Association Files). These ties were no doubt first forged under servitude, when the nature of several slaves' work for the Royalls took them far afield. In being hired out, the baker's apprentice escaped the confines of the Royalls' incorporative landscape and was exposed to alternative landscapes and ideologies where the Royalls, if only temporarily, had no mastery over him. Through his stories, the quarter community back home may have felt a vicarious thrill.

Back home, however, even the consummate generalists who were responsible for the daily ins and outs of running the estate were probably able to appropriate various landscapes of Ten Hills Farm as their own. These general farmhands and jacks-of-all-trades probably used the main Medford highways only to transport goods on their carts. They likely got their bearings from the backs and sides of houses and traveled along field boundaries, following the river, creeks, fence lines, or the edge of the forest rather than roads. There were orchards to be planted and maintained, herds of pastured livestock to feed and protect from predators, friends to visit at the next estate, and clandestine meetings to attend deep in the forest. Garman (1998, 151) states that the necessary spatial dispersion of many New England slaves in the construction of "workscapes" undercut the "spatial proximity and surveillance" experienced by domestics, and probably constituted a source of "constant interaction" and "dialogue" between master and slave.

The Royalls' slaves inhabited a patchwork of natural and cultural landscapes that they would have seen with two different sets of eyes, for they led a dual existence. On the one hand, they were members of a discounted and despised class of people who were bound for life to labor for another. From this perspective, all the natural world seemed to be cut up and divided among the ruling class; the fields, the forests, the land, and the waterways belonged to Master Royall or his neighbors and were physical manifestations of the system and ideology that allowed his ownership and power over themselves (e.g., Isaac 1982, 53). Everywhere around them was evidence of their role as unfree laborers: the fields they planted and harvested, the orchards they tended, the pastures their livestock grazed, the fences and boundary walls they maintained and that seemed to enclose them, too, in their statement of all-encompassing power. Where Isaac Royall Jr. may have looked at the land around his house and been reassured by its beauty and symmetry of the legitimacy of his position, his slaves must have looked at the same landscape and seen only the rigidity of their imprisonment.

On the other hand, slaves led an alternative existence as individuals. In 1735, Sampson, a black slave of the town, was "sorely frightened" by a bear and her cub in the woods near Governor Cradock's house, which lay directly across the river from Ten Hills Farm (Brooks and Usher 1886, 495). At first glance little more than an anecdote, the story of Sampson suggests that slaves may have had a more intimate, organic relationship with their environment, and certainly that they had access to and perhaps sought solace in the forests. While the Royalls tried to structure movement through the landscape, those they enslaved roamed freely along paths and across boundaries. Slaves were surrounded, too, by their own implicated places. Perhaps for Sampson, the distant line of trees at the edge of the forest called to mind the smell of damp earth and the cool silence where confusion, frustrations, and fears could fall away. Cato Pearce, a slave in Rhode Island who eventually served as a minister to his black community there, said he "used to go into the woods every night," seeking meditation, mental escape, and personal space to practice his sermons (Pearce 1842, 18). Sampson may have visited the woods in a more utilitarian capacity as well, though. Piersen (1988, 98) states that Africans from the "forest regions" of West Africa (such as the Gold Coast) were "especially artful in the use of snares and traps for capturing small game . . . [and] certain Yankee blacks won local renown for their hunting skills, like Black Nim the deer-hunter or Roswell Quash the 'scourge of foxes.' "

An opening in the brush, invisible to the uninitiated, may have led to a clearing that welcomed weary minds, there for a few minutes or hours to think or pray, gather informally with friends, or simply "quit the master for awhile" (Upton 1988, 367; see also Fitts 1996; Isaac 1982). Perhaps that creek led to a good fishing hole. Down by the marshes, when the tide receded, one could be sure of finding a good oyster bed or a nest of quail eggs. The paths along the fence lines, worn to hard-packed dirt tracks by the long passage of feet, recalled the connectedness of the black community across white boundaries.

I imagine Plato, or whoever the boatman actually was, would have had the most freedom of movement. He would have been one of the more important slaves to the success of the estate and implicitly trusted by the Royalls. He may also have achieved particular status in the slave community because of his ability to carry news up and down the river from Medford to Boston and all the ports in between. Frederick Douglass (2000 [1845], 286) said that the boatmen on his master's plantation outside Baltimore were "esteemed very highly by the other slaves, and looked upon as the privileged ones of the plantation; for it was no small affair, in the eyes of the slaves, to be allowed to see Baltimore."

The Royall boatman's trips to town may have kept him away from the farm for as many as two or three days. What is more, unlike the baker's apprentice, the boatman was not passing from one master to another. There was no one at the other end of his journey to take him in hand and put him to work for their own purposes. He was there to deliver the goods and return to Ten Hills Farm, where eager slaves would gather round to hear the latest tales. Who could tell how long such a trip would take? Who would know if he stopped off along the way to visit with friends, a new wife, or a lover? Garman (1998, 151) has argued that throughout New England, just what a master could expect from a day's work must have been at least partly negotiable:

> For example, how many apple trees could be pruned in a day's work? Or how long would it take to transport a wagonload of salt pork to Newport? There were no established answers to these questions. Time expectations were likely set, contested, negotiated, and renegotiated. . . .

Plato, whose classical name suggests he was an African by birth, may have found especial pleasure in these temporary escapes. He would have felt the loss of his freedom in a way that little Joseph, son of Diana, or Prine, daughter of Belinda—both born in Medford—could not.

Conclusion

Landscape can be read as a physical map of social relations and realities of the past. Planned landscapes often reflect conscious attempts by those who commission them to state an ideal, to force behavior from surroundings. The landscapes of inequality found in various American slave regimes, for example, betray the hope that white spatial and visual dominance in architecture and the landscape will translate into an internalized acceptance of social and political dominance, both by their social inferiors as well as their own peers. Fields, boundary lines, fences, formal drives, and grand avenues seemed to divide the eighteenth-century white landscapes of Boston and surrounding areas into discretely owned and controlled spaces. Their architecture, layout, and processional ways sought to appropriate the ahistorical aura and authority of the ancient world to make the inequalities of the modern era appear to be grounded in antiquity. Archaeologists have for some years now, however, been able to demonstrate convincingly the existence of alternative landscapes, as well as multiple levels of involvement and experience of the same landscapes, that challenged the power presented in such implicated places.

Landscape is also experiential and the social interactions played out upon its stage a kind of performance in motion (e.g., Barrett 1994; M. Hall 2000). The same landscape may be experienced differently, depending on one's status, life history, and personal relationships with other actors (e.g., Rodman 1992). The Royalls succeeded in creating a landscape that seemed to reflect, and legitimate at least to themselves, their hegemony in the town, but their many slaves experienced these spaces in alternative ways. On the one hand, they must surely have felt the restrictiveness of close living and working conditions with the Royalls that characterized New England slavery. On the other hand, because landscapes become implicated only insofar as they recall how one has experienced them on an individual level, the same landscapes that legitimated the Royalls' power to the Royalls and their peers would have held different implications for the slaves, whose experience of the landscape was structured by their servitude and ways of adapting to it. The differential use of the work yards surrounding the slave quarters from the courtyard it shares with the main house illustrates how these were "shared but contested" spaces (Garman 1998, 134). The land immediately surrounding the mansion house, from the Royalls' perspective, might have served as a daily reminder of their legitimate mastery over land and men. The neoclassical architectural elements of house, quarters, and gardens implicated the rightful hierarchy of men that stemmed from time immemorial. The trash-strewn work yards emphasized the separation between master and slave, work and leisure, clean and unclean. To the slaves these same work yards might have represented a welcome retreat from constant surveillance, despite their appearance or smell. To them, they might have implicated family ties and time away from Master: long smokes on the stoop out back, an impromptu game of checkers or marbles, quiet time to sew, make beads, or tell stories about Africa and freedom to the children who had never known it.

Primary Documents

Account books of Isaac Royall Sr. and Jr. (1724–49). Photocopied manuscript at the Royall House slave quarters.
Isaac Royall Sr. to Edmund Quincy, 15 August 15, 1736. Typed transcript at Royall House Association.
Massachusetts Acts and Resolves, vol. 3, Province Laws 1756–57. Massachusetts Historical Commission.
Massachusetts Historical Commission (MHC). Archives.
Massachusetts slave census, 1754. Microfilm. Massachusetts Historical Commission.
Massachusetts tax valuation, 1771. Massachusetts Historical Commission.
Medford town records through 1830. Microfilm. Massachusetts Historical Commission.
Middlesex County Probate Court File Papers, 1st ser., 1648–1871. Will, probate inventories, accounts of administration of Isaac Royall, Sr. of Charlestown, 1739. Case #19545.
Vital Records of Medford, Massachusetts, to the Year 1850. New England Historic Genealogical Society, Boston, 1907.

CHAPTER TWELVE

African Metallurgy in the Atlantic World

Candice L. Goucher

This chapter considers the history of African metallurgy in the wake of the Atlantic era. The transfer and cultural continuity of African metallurgical technologies to the Caribbean reveals the vital dependence of the plantation and colonial economies on African technical expertise. The extent to which the African contribution to this technological history exceeded a mere labor component is suggested by a closer examination of African-European interactions. A focus on the Atlantic world offers insights for the investigation of African-derived ideology and culture in the Caribbean and seeks to assist archaeologists and historians studying similar situations of multicultural interaction in the African past.

The development of an Atlantic economy forged lasting links between Europe, Africa, and the Caribbean and between slavery and the rise of merchant capitalism. These links were partially constructed of African metals. Ferrous and nonferrous metals, whether imported or locally produced, were traded and exchanged as currencies. When manufactured, they were essential to the acquisition of slaves and the maintenance of the Atlantic commercial system. The period between 1500 and 1850 witnessed major technological changes within the participating metallurgical industries, including those identified with the British industrial revolution, those linked with the decline of some African industries and the transformation and intensification of others, and those connected with the introduction of new metal technologies across the Western Hemisphere. The interaction between competing technological systems also appears to have been an important feature of the emerging Atlantic economy.

The ways in which Africanists and Caribbeanists have studied the technologies of this era have varied. The intersection of this scholarship owes much to

277

the encouragement of Merrick Posnansky. African archaeology has played a major role in shaping the historical questions and knowledge about metals. Previous scholarship has discussed how designations like the Early Iron Age (EIA) and Late Iron Age (LIA) have been as problematic as they have been useful (see Fagan and Kirkman 1967; Connah 1998). The technological history of the transition between periods is not marked by uniform technological change, nor are the categories themselves satisfactorily described by reference to coherent material cultural contexts: African LIA societies systematically employed stone tools even in the large-scale production of iron and steel. Another historical distinction hinges on the presence or absence of Europeans rather than on any particular configuration of material complexes or even technological domination. Archaeologists on both sides of the Atlantic have only recently begun to explore the cultural complexity implicit in these distinctions. The basic historiographical assumption has been that African technology faltered in the shadow of a European presence (Goucher 1981; Pole 1982; D. Williams 1974, 73–75). The specific technical parameters remain largely unexamined, yet iron has been viewed as a symbol of the vulnerability of African technologies and economies to the European presence. Europe's impact on local African technology has been neglected or imperfectly understood.

West Central African Forges and Foundries

On the African side of the Atlantic, archaeological and documentary evidence is limited for such questions as might be of interest to the historical reconstruction of transatlantic technology. Few inventories of metal products exist, and when they occur, they pay scant attention to production processes. The best understood African technologies are generally far from the coastal scene of African-European interactions. The range of variation in those few technological systems studied suggests that Caribbeanists will face great difficulties in attempts to identify continuity or change. African contexts do provide windows on the processes of technological change (Childs 1991; David et al. 1989; Herbert and Goucher 1987; van der Merwe 1980; van der Merwe and Avery 1982), but opportunities to investigate preindustrial technological systems will soon vanish together with their living contexts. Smelters, blacksmiths, casters, and other metallurgists are nearly extinct in other parts of the world, but in sub-Saharan Africa the smaller local industries have persisted in rural areas and even in large towns. In rapidly dwindling numbers, they are potential repositories for the history of technology. The ethnoarchaeological potential may be limited, but in too many instances it will soon be irretrievably lost (Childs 1991; David et al. 1989; Herbert and Goucher 1987; MacEachern 1996).

The coastal regions of West Central Africa provided the earliest and most sustained arenas for African-European economic as well as technological interactions (DeCorse 2001b). Early European permanent settlements, forts, and castles generally employed a number of African and European blacksmiths (De Gregori 1969, 149; Lawrence 1963, 91). These establishments were, of course, also centers for the introduction and distribution of European manufactures (Sundstrom 1974). Their archaeological potential has been noted by Posnansky and van Dantzig (1976) and pursued by DeCorse (1987, 1993) at Elmina and elsewhere, although not with the specific focus of technology transfer. African towns were only in some instances repositories for the transfer of skills acquired at forts and castles. They constitute another source of interaction and change (Hull 1976), as they also attracted smiths and products from their hinterland. As European manufactured goods reached inland markets, they necessarily wrought changes in local industry: for example, the cheaper (and inferior, according to many local smiths) European hoes required new techniques of repair. The introduction of European firearms also presented opportunities for the growth of ancillary metalworking industries. Villages and towns in the interior developed as specialized centers in the repair and limited manufacture of guns. The village of Brawhani in Brong Ahafo, Ghana, is such an example. In 1979, the raised forge was proudly pointed out as being "European" in style; that it supported a furnace sculpted in the shape of a woman suggests the ideological, cultural, and stylistic continuities attendant on, and probably necessary for, the successful transfer of non-African technologies.

Marion Johnson, rare among historians, considered the relationship between African technological change and competition; she tested the assumption of inevitable replacement of African industry by European technology. Although she concentrated on textiles, Johnson (1978b, 268) suggested that iron working might have responded similarly to patterns of demand, organization of production, and European imports. Because smelting industries were capital-free, their decline was attributed to qualitative differences in product. African smiths adjusted their forging technology to the drastically different products, thus flourishing or declining in response to the European market. But did such competition necessarily produce a pernicious consequence? Brian Fagan (1961, 209) suggested that the invigorated mid-eighteenth-century trade in iron hoes from the Luba resulted in the standardization of form and techniques in Zambia. In parts of Ghana and Togo, the impact seems also to have been more varied. Although European manufactures, including farming implements and cutlasses, reportedly appeared in markets connecting the hinterland and coastal towns, some technology was observed to be unaffected by European imports as late as the 1880s (Klose 1899, 175). J. C. Miller (1988, 19) even reports that south of the Zaire River, Africans were exporting their own metalware.

Elsewhere, the supply of imported metals, new forms, and borrowed techniques were not necessarily coeval. The Central African reports on locally preferred weapons and tools indicate that styles might change, while the source of the metal remained constant. Alternatively, new sources of metal could be utilized in traditional ways and with little change in meaning or significance. The eighteenth-century Kasanje king's army fought with locally manufactured weapons, while in Lunda imported European muskets were forged into blade weapons (Miller 1988, 88). Factors inhibiting the transfer of European metallurgical technology appear to have depended upon more than cost-related, capital-intensive features.

The relative availability of fuel and labor figured heavily in the equations of technology transfer. Temporal change within African metallurgy is obviously complex and not well understood. For example, several researchers have noted the transformation of West African iron-smelting furnace function and form, including an increase in furnace height and the utilization of induced draught rather than forced draught techniques. The correlation of these features (constituting "blast furnaces") would have produced fluid products, even cast iron (David et al. 1989; Wertime 1962, 45–47), such as occurred in medieval Europe and in China. The innovation also appears in LIA contexts at Bassar, Togo, by the eighteenth century (Fig. 12.1; Goucher 1984). This West African technical change may be related to the demographic change, especially population loss, attributed to slaving activities in the hinterland. Since induced draught furnaces no longer required bellows, a significant labor-saving advance would have reduced further the costs of production, making those African industries more competitive with imported European metals. While the increase in West Central African slave-raiding activities contributed to the vulnerability of much African production (Rodney 1981), slave labor was increasingly available to state systems and their elites for industrial and other applications (Inikori 1982; Lovejoy 2000; Meillassoux 1991). Industries that persisted in the Atlantic era's climate of heightened insecurity and violence seem to have been located on major slave-trading routes, such as the one connecting the Bassar region to Asante, Hausa, Kabre, and Dahomey. Although contemporary informants deny that slave labor was used, Klose (1899) and others record this slave labor market in the 1880s and relate the prices of slaves to iron hoes.

The nature of the fuel supply represented a considerable factor distinguishing European from African-based metallurgy. Industries in both parts of the world suffered the consequences of deforestation as a result of the overuse of forest resources (Goucher 1981; Wertime 1962). In Britain, critical developments after the mid-eighteenth century made possible the widespread use of coal and coke by the iron industry. Even then, British forgers outside Exeter welded steel-reinforced agricultural implements from imported Swedish iron, as noted by Angerstein around 1753 (Hildebrand 1958, 22). In Africa and the Caribbean, suitable coal was not available locally and had to be imported at high prices, or substitutes had to be found elsewhere. The continued availability of charcoal, despite rising costs, meant that its use easily remained cost-effective and was preferred to coal in the African-European interactions of the Atlantic world. In parts of Africa where large iron ore deposits attracted the entrepreneurial attention of European colonizers, the issue of fuel prevented the wholesale transfer of European technology and thus exploitation of local resources (for example, in German Togo at the turn of the century). The case of

Fig. 12.1. Bassari furnace, Togo.

fuel supplies in the Caribbean and in the Americas is discussed below. Suffice it to say that despite an inordinate English pride in the "sooty mineral" and its technological significance, the global outlook suggests that this innovation had little to do with the first three centuries of African-European interactions.

The Caribbean Crucible

Studies of African cultural continuities in the Caribbean have suggested some of the potential for technology transfer in the Atlantic world (Agorsah 1992a, 1994a; Alleyne 1988; Braithwaite 1971; Price 1979; R. F. Thompson 1983). The concepts of situational ethnicity and fluid boundary conditions have recently been discussed by Africanist archaeologists (MacEachern 2001). Discrete packages of neatly bounded cultural attributes have given way to interdependent "mosaics" (see Denbow 1990 for an EIA application). Knowing the vectors of transformation and change in Caribbean contexts of African technology constitutes a valuable contribution to understanding processes of cultural negotiation that are implicit in so much of the discussion about links between technology, style, and ethnicity. Well-documented cases of ethnic identification in the decidedly multicultural African-Caribbean cultural contexts are relatively few (DeCorse 1987; Posnansky 1984; Postma 1990), but strong African retentions in the ritual and symbolic fields of Caribbean technology have been documented (Goucher 1990, 1991, 1999; Rickford 1987; Schuler 1980). This observation has implications for the study of African technological systems and styles carried across the Atlantic. Like his contemporary African counterpart, the Jamaican blacksmith repairs automobile axles on an anvil he calls the "mother" of his forge (Fig. 12.2).[1] Technology was an important component of cultural systems,

Fig. 12.2. Blacksmith, Ginger Ridge, Jamaica.

influencing the expression of gender and other power relationships (Childs 1991). Yet it has not been studied in historic perspective as an equally inevitable consequence of the newly constructed Atlantic world. Where ideological transfers have been noted, as in the case of the transatlantic journey of Ogun (the Yoruba deity associated with iron) to Haiti, Cuba, Brazil, and Trinidad, the technological implications of these transfers have been completely ignored (Barnes 1989; Lawuyi 1988).

In the technological continuum of the Caribbean, the eighteenth century holds a particularly pivotal position. Communities of African refugees escaped repeatedly from slave masters and were known as maroons (see Agorsah, this volume). In Jamaica and elsewhere, maroons initiated a series of wars that plagued European domination throughout the eighteenth century. They also encouraged the persistence of metallurgical skills presumed to be African-based (Goucher 1990). Jamaican Maroons were reportedly armed with guns; each and every man, woman, and child carried an iron hoe. The political basis of power and resistance often depended upon the support of armies of blacksmiths on both sides of the Atlantic, as demonstrated by the likes of the West African Samory or the rulers at Palmares in Brazil. Where African metallurgists congregated in the Caribbean, they wrested considerable independence from the more typical constraints of plantation slavery. For example, at Winkle Village, Guyana, the 1796 uprising of slave blacksmiths and leather workers led to increased wages and early emancipation. Even as individual craftsmen, the transplanted African blacksmiths negotiated positions of leadership in the plantation hierarchy and were presumably instrumental in the exercise of ritual continuities (Curtin 1970, 34–35; Schuler 1980).

Metals and metal products constituted a significant part of the cargo of transatlantic ships. Iron was considered a particularly useful export commodity, both heavy and stable. Throughout much of the eighteenth century, the British West Indies was the largest market for wrought iron. This was due no doubt to the reliance on imported agricultural implements used on plantations. However, the tool shapes of Europe gave way to West African styles: the short-handled hoe and cutlass. Shipping records, underwater archaeology, and the cobblestone streets of Caribbean ports like San Juan testify to the inclusion of cast-iron blocks and iron slag as ballast (Samuels 1980). Swedish bar-iron imports to Great Britain nearly doubled between 1740 and 1770, and their prices rose dramatically toward the end of the century (Hyde 1977, 80–81). Export figures for iron bars, iron nails, ordnance, and wrought iron from England to Jamaica (1748–73) similarly reflect tremendous increases after 1769.[2] American industries, many of which were still dependent upon wood charcoal for fuel, constituted yet another source of metal for the Caribbean markets; this source proved to be extremely unpredictable, especially around 1776 following the U.S. declaration of independence.

By the eighteenth century, smithies dotted the Caribbean. Every significant town and harbor and nearly every plantation employed a blacksmith.

Documented smiths were African, European, and Creole. Michael Craton (1978) alludes to a color bar in apprenticeship systems operating on the Worthy Park Estate in Jamaica; this is hardly visible among surviving Caribbean blacksmiths and not likely to have been routinely enforced (Goucher 1990, 40). In some respects, the documented, large-scale involvement of African metallurgists in Caribbean technology is uniquely limited to the Reeder site described below. No other evidence of cuprous metalwork or casting by transplanted Africans has yet emerged; the transfer of West African gold-working techniques and styles in the circum-Caribbean seems probable but unstudied. That blacksmiths achieved mobility and traveled widely across the Atlantic world is not surprising. One African blacksmith who accompanied Mungo Park in West Africa reportedly made the transatlantic journey to British Guyana (Rickford 1987). When European planters moved from island to island, as they frequently did in response to the vagaries of the imperial chess game, they carried with them skilled slaves. Among them were "blacksmith jobbers," who were in high demand (Higman 1976). The Jamaican planter John Stewart (1808) suggested the late-eighteenth-century value of metallurgical skills when he boasted that the fortunes to be made in the Caribbean by the clergy and lawyers were nearly surpassed by those of the coppersmiths. In Brazil, the development of steelmaking was attributed to "the technical skills of a few African slaves" (Furtado 1965). The case of Reeder's foundry in eighteenth-century Jamaica suggests that the African skills are critical to the understanding of the history of Caribbean technology.

African-Caribbean Metallurgy: The Case of Reeder's Pen

Reeder's Pen is located in the parish of St. Thomas-in-the-East, Jamaica, where it occupied a considerable portion of the area west of the late-eighteenth-century coastal town of Morant Bay and east of the Morant River (170 53′ N. 760 25′ W). The site's approximate location was identified by the use of oral and archival sources, including an uncataloged sketch map by Thomas Harrison in the collections of the Institute of Jamaica, Kingston. Archaeological investigation (1989–93) began as part of an ongoing project on African-Caribbean technology. The study has incorporated survey and surface collections, local interviews with Jamaican blacksmiths, archival research, the excavation of two main portions of the site, and comparative technical studies of metals.

The Reeder site appears to be unique in the history of Caribbean technology, at least with respect to the extent of documentation (Buisseret 1980). Established in 1772, the foundry at Reeder's Pen produced iron and brass two years later. John Reeder was a Devon coppersmith by trade, but he planned to engage in iron-working activities as well. By 1781, the industry was immensely profitable, valued by the island's plantations and the Royal Navy.

Reeder relied heavily on African metallurgical expertise. The slaves, maroons, and "free coloreds" who operated the foundry were "perfect in every branch of the iron manufacture, so far as it relates to casting and turning . . . and in wrought Iron."[3] On the basis of this, Reeder applied for and received permission from the island assembly to erect iron-smelting furnaces and cut wood for charcoal. The prosperity of the foundry operations was short-lived. In 1782, Governor General Campbell, fearing a combined invasion of the island by French and Spanish forces, ordered the dismantling of the Morant Bay foundry.[4]

The main purpose of the research thus far has been to assess the nature of the operation of the iron and brass foundry established at the site during the last quarter of the eighteenth century; to locate and study the various technical facilities of the industry and to describe the nature of their operation and function; and to assess the cultural identity and technological contribution of the different components of the labor force operating and maintaining the foundry during its brief existence. The study has closely investigated areas of African technological continuity within the metallurgical activity represented at Reeder's Pen.

Description of Sites and Features

The earliest existing map of Reeder's Pen, providing the foundry's location and bearing (SE 860) is an undated sketch map by Thomas Harrison, a cartographer active in the nineteenth century. Incorporating Edgar's notes of 1777, the map identifies several features partially standing today. One such feature is the area referred to today as Church Corner, which, in addition to the eighteenth-century church building now in ruins and its adjacent gravesites, shares location with what is indicated on later maps as a "House of Corrections," a convalescent residence for the aged and mentally impaired. The National Heritage Trust investigated the Church site some years ago; thus we collected only a few items (green glass bottles and three pieces of imported ceramics) from the surface of the slopes facing the main Morant Bay road that today passes by the ruins on their south side.

Another main feature is an old bridge located to the south of milestone 31 approaching from the Kingston direction. This feature appears to have been part of a water-control system in the western part of Morant Bay. However, it is unclear whether or how it might have functioned in the operations of Reeder's Pen or exactly how the river course might have changed over the past two centuries. The possible site-related eighteenth-century canal and waterway construction is discussed below. East of the bridge is a road, referred to by residents as the "Old Road," which connects the pen to the wharf at Morant Bay. Only minimal investigation was possible because the area is now a dense residential extension of the town. However, local informants mentioned structural features and identified footpaths of "slavery days" (i.e., pre-1830s).

The area between 48 and 52 Church Street, Morant Bay, appears to have been a central part of the foundry. The widespread distribution of iron slag across this and adjacent lots and concentrations of slag and other metalworking by-products at selected spots indicate metallurgical activity. At one such concentration (48 Church Street), also containing large (10-kg) chunks of slag, samples were taken for analysis. Surface collections made in this area of the site also revealed concentrations of nail fragments, imported ceramics, and green glass bottles. Other significant features of the area include building foundations visible between, and incorporated into, the foundations of several house structures along the southern side of the modern Morant Bay main road. Their extension into the empty front lot at 52 Church Street became the focus of excavations described below.

One of the two pillars that marked the main gate of Reeder's Pen still stands on the north side of the modern main road. This eastern pillar contains a legible engraving: *PEN*. According to local residents, the western pillar (presumably containing the word *REEDERS*) was broken down only recently in the course of construction at the site. These pillars probably supported a cast-iron gate. Some of the forged-iron fencing is still attached to the eastern pillar, but some has collapsed and been abandoned nearby. A sample post was collected for analysis.

Leading from the gate in a northeasterly direction is the approach to what has been tentatively identified as the site of John Reeder's residence, or Great House. Early foundations appear to have been built over by later structures now in ruins. The approach has been partially covered by a road built by the current owner in preparation for a housing development on the site. The main finds from the area consist of a few seashells, green glass bottles, and several pieces of imported ceramics. Along the slope facing northwest are several apparently modern metal artifacts.

A feature of much local interest is a large stone believed to be at a site marked "store" on the Harrison sketch map. The foundry bearing according to this map is SE 860, while John Reeder's residence is NE 810. The stone is situated on the hillside property of Mr. Dudley Fyffe (23 Church Street), across the contemporary main road from what are believed to be the remains of the foundry buildings. The stone, a variety of milky quartz, is huge, measuring 1.25 m at its widest part (north–south) and 2.15 m on its long axis (east–west). Local residents frequently identify such prominent stones as markers for buried treasure, especially rumored caches of Spanish gold. To prevent destruction of the Fyffe property and to protect the stone site, it was deemed necessary to investigate these claims and satisfy public interest.

Curiously, the upper surface of the stone has two large iron pegs, 65 cm apart, driven into the upper surface at its wider part. Information from Mr. Fyffe confirmed the opinion of other residents. Fyffe, together with others who had previously heard of or seen the stone years earlier, maintained that there had originally been four pegs, two having rusted away or been otherwise removed. Upon closer examination, the stone's surface revealed several worn indentations but no obvious peg holes. The two surviving metal pegs are 3–4 cm in diameter.

What was the function and importance of the stone, and what was the meaning or purpose of the two (or possibly four) pegs driven into its surface? As mentioned above, some local informants claimed that the Spaniards may have buried some treasures under the stone; others mentioned that the stone seems to disappear and reappear, and therefore it was thought that it had some mythical connections.

In summary, the pre-excavation studies clearly identified many features of Reeder's Pen known from documentary sources, although the definite boundaries could not be established because much of the area has now been built over. Also, the historical records indicate that the foundry itself was dismantled and partially destroyed, first intentionally, then by an island hurricane in the 1780s. Parts of the foundry were even purported to have been buried during dismantling in 1782, when foundry operations were halted abruptly. Such a deliberate attempt to conceal important structural features that otherwise might have remained in the archaeological record is significant for identifying the subsequent use to which the buildings and site may have been put and also for any interpretations of the archaeological remains.

Excavation

The excavation of 52 Church Street sought to expose and identify the nature and configuration of building foundations and their associated structures as a means of explaining activities that may have been related to them. The southern section of this feature is referred to as the "ramp area" or Area 1-A, while the northern section, which is the section nearer the main road, is Area 1-B. It consists of foundations or platforms of what appears to be part of the factory built by John Reeder. It is bounded on the property's eastern side by the remains of a canal system.

A 2×2-m square was opened along the wall, adjacent to the ramps referred to above, in order to expose the wall, locate floors, and eventually extend the excavation to expose the ramp area itself. The first level (0–35 cm) was a fairly compact and dark reddish brown soil (Munsell 5YR 3/3) and contained material very like the surface collection, consisting of several pieces of iron slag, green glass bottle, wire nails, and a few fragments of ceramic tile. The ramp area was particularly productive, yielding much green glass and iron slag. Level 2 (35–75 cm) yielded a number of almost complete ceramic artifacts within the area between the two ramps. The ramp interior sides are lined with red brick down to its base level at 75 cm, which is characterized by a wide scatter of pieces of limestone and fragments of brick. Between the first excavation square and the ramp area, the distribution of brick is suggestive of a collapsed structure.

Also identified in the ramp area was a semicircular iron ring or hoop. This hoop seems to mark the mouth of a structure that spans an opening 45 cm in diameter, passes under the wall at the ramp entrance from its southern to its northern side, and then extends to the building's center. The soil around this feature (75–90 cm in depth) was heavily laden with ash. Within the same area was recovered the largest collection of artifacts. The foundations were clearly exposed and the outline of the rooms in that part of the excavation was noted. It was also clear that building foundations continue under the three houses immediately to the west of Mr. Ray's house, indicating that the factory was much larger than the portion under excavation. This would seem to be in keeping with the sketch map that locates a line of several structures, and also consistent with known British foundries contemporary with the Reeder site.

Finds

The main items consist of the structures around the ramp area, the cast-iron hoop, several imported ceramics of various manufacture and derivation, tiles, iron slag, glass, and metal artifacts. The ceramics include creamware, earthenware, pearlware, porcelain, stoneware, whiteware, and yelloware. The ceramics and other evidence should be treated with caution as the archaeological investigation has only just begun and so far extends over only a small portion of the site. However, several tentative and general observations are possible. The earthenware consists mainly of rim and body sherds, some with blue or mottled blue glaze. One piece appears to be of a polygonal-shaped vessel and another of the lateral terminal of a handle with stamped geometric patterns on both handle and body. Most earthenware comes from level 2, the level that seems most likely to date to the period of foundry operation. However, almost half of the earthenware could be classified as local pottery, referred to as *yabba* in Jamaica.

Of the remaining pottery types, the creamware consists mainly of body sherds and would date from between 1775 and 1820. One piece seems to be a chamber pot rim; three others appear to be footings. The whiteware pieces are mainly undecorated fragments of cups, bowls, and footings of plates or saucers. They are all from level 2 and date from between 1830 and 1860. Annular ware is the most popular of the pearlware ceramics. An almost complete bowl of this type was recovered from the ramp area at 72 cm. The porcelain recovered includes sherds of export ware: a few have red, green, and blue floral pattern overglaze, and a few have gilded wavy edges with incised lines in red, green, and blue floral transfer print. Most are derived from level 2 and may be dated from between 1790 and 1825. A stoneware bottle, probably used for ginger beer and possibly of nineteenth-century American origin, was recovered complete from level 2.

Also found in the level is a body/rim jar with salt glaze suspected to be of nineteenth-century English manufacture.

The metal finds consisted of large quantities of iron and copper-alloy objects, including a horseshoe, file, wire, nails (including some with flat heads), buckle, bolt, spike, rim and body of a large cast-iron pot, square shanks, barrel hoop, and sheets of iron scrap. Slag and droplets of various metallic compositions confirm that a variety of metallurgical activities were undertaken at the site. Samples of some metal finds have been selected for laboratory identification and characterization. This aspect of the research should provide data for determining the sources of the raw materials as well as for characterizing the smelting and other refining technologies employed.

Almost all glasses recovered consisted of fragments of green cylindrical wine bottles with conical kick-up bases. The distribution of glass is even across the levels, and it appears that most are from the twentieth century. Of the remaining glass, all the thin clear pieces in the deposits are probably medicinal bottles, and these were derived from level 1. Other finds include fragments of clay pan tile, glazed ceramic wall tiles with traces of adhesive and probably dating to the twentieth century, and several fragments of stone, which were recovered mainly from level 1 and surface areas. Only four pieces of white clay smoking pipe were recovered. The bore of the stems measured 1.6 mm, which, with the embossed floral bowl decorations, dates the pipes to between 1820 and 1840.

The "mystery stone" was only partially excavated in the limited time available. Initially we believed the stone to be peripheral to the foundry site, perhaps serving as an early boundary marker. A 2×2-m square was opened over the stone's exposed upper surface and overlapping it on the eastern side, the main objective being to determine its shape and size and to investigate any associated structures or objects. One restriction was that the stone is situated extremely close to the property owner's current building, and it was thought that the excavation could easily damage the foundation and the pipelines.

No finds were recovered above 1.0 m depth, with the exception of a few pieces of iron slag and broken bottle. An auger test was conducted in order to determine the presence of any structural features; nothing was detected. At 1.92 m depth, large pieces of molded clay pan tile approximately 2.5–3.5 cm thick were reached. All of the 15 pieces collected appear to belong to the same tile, identified as similar to seventeenth-century molded examples from the site of Port Royal, Jamaica. The association of this tile with a large chunk of iron slag is interesting, especially as no object was encountered in the levels above them. Although the complete size and nature of the stone is unclear, its association with the slag and iron pegs, as well as its location within the territory of the foundry map, suggests that it may indeed be linked in some way to the operations of the Reeder foundry. Further work may help to answer fully the questions regarding its function and meaning.

Discussion

Limited portions of the Reeder site have been investigated, but much remains to be learned. Archaeological excavation and survey work has confirmed that we are indeed dealing with the structural features that were once part of John Reeder's eighteenth-century foundry complex. The range of metallurgical finds and their distribution are consistent with late-eighteenth-century descriptions of the foundry as a site of manufacture and repair of ferrous and nonferrous items. Tentative identification of hearth and forge areas inside the foundry building should he confirmed by further investigation of the limited area open to excavation.

The ramp area of the foundry needs to he understood better in its relationship to the location of the forge and the possible source of waterpower. According to the original foundry plans put forward by John Reeder during his attempts to secure a Jamaican Assembly loan, the plant operations were intended to rely on a water-powered mill and a series of support canals from the Morant River. The river appears much nearer to the foundry buildings in the eighteenth-century sketch map, and this discrepancy may reflect the changing course of the river itself and/or the subsequent rechanneling of waterways through the area of the site. The early sketch map indicates several separate buildings, but only one set of foundations has thus far been identified. It is hoped that the complete configuration or plan of the buildings will be established during subsequent excavation.

At this point, identified ceramic types confirm that the excavation covers the late eighteenth and early nineteenth centuries, dates that agree with the historical documentation of the Reeder site. The ratio of yabba to other types of vessels compares favorably with the suggestion that the foundry workers were predominantly of African origin. According to archival sources, the industry employed as many as 276 "Negroes." On the basis of this documentation, the Africans and their descendants can be identified as slaves, maroons, and free coloreds. Only occasionally were European craftsmen employed; frequently their tenure was cut short by illness and death.[5] No comparable industrial context is known in the entire Caribbean region. Metal finds and various casting, forging, and possibly smelting by-products, including varieties of slag, have been identified. Clearly, a range of metallurgical activities involving both ferrous and nonferrous metals existed at the site. The full extent and nature of production at the foundry remain to be determined through analytical studies of the metal remain already under way and through further archaeological research.

Conclusion

Many more questions have been raised than answered by research in the Atlantic world; they are expected to direct attention to new field strategies. The unanticipated importance of the stone and its relationship to the Reeder house and foundry remains to be explored, as do the locations of worker accommodations. The actual size and plan of the factory are of particular interest in answering questions regarding the degree of continuity between European (contemporary British industries at Ironbridge, for example) and African (contemporary West and Central Africans, and the maroons). Comparative research on British- and African-derived technologies and contexts like the Reeder foundry site will be essential for characterizing the technological styles of African-Caribbean metallurgists. Finally, greater areal coverage will be needed to comprehend the nature and significance of the Reeder industry. Identifying the location of smelting sites in the Bath region and residences at Morant Bay will be critical to the recovery of cultural identity. As we begin to inventory and map the material traces of Atlantic technologies, cultural and ideological aspects may be opened to comparative study. Until then, the early industrial site of Reeder's Pen is a tantalizing Jamaican monument to the complexity of African-European technology transfer during the Atlantic era.

Acknowledgments

Research was partially funded by grants from the National Endowment for the Humanities, the Oregon Council for the Humanities, and a Faculty Development Grant from Portland State University. My thanks go to David Schoenbrun for editorial comments, to Roderick Ebanks for his encouragement, to my research assistant Katherine Sadler, and to Charlene Fair and Doreen Frankson for clerical and logistical assistance. I am particularly grateful to Dr. Kofi Agorsah, who made equipment and facilities available in Jamaica, and to his students who participated in the 1990 excavations at Reeder's Pen. I can think of no more gracious or cooperative a colleague. This collaboration is made possible by the foundations laid by Merrick Posnansky, to whom I owe an enormous debt of gratitude. Finally, I thank the editorial staff of Springer Netherlands, publisher of *African Archaeological Review*, for the permission to reprint a version of this essay.

Notes

1. Lindsay Rickettes, Ginger Ridge, pers. comm., August 17, 1988.
2. Great Britain, Public Record Office, Treasury T.64 273. I am grateful to Dale Simon for her assistance in retrieving these records.
3. Devon Record Office, Exeter, John Reeder Papers, J16.
4. Institute of Jamaica, Memorial of Stephen Fuller, Esq., Agent for Jamaica… 1789, ms. 1718.
5. Letter from Fuller to Lord Sydney, June 28, 1788, John Reeder Papers, J7, Devon Record Office; Church of England Parish Records, St. Thomas-in-the-East, Spanish Town Archives, Jamaica.

CHAPTER THIRTEEN

Between Urban and Rural: Organization and Distribution of Local Pottery in Eighteenth-Century Jamaica

Mark W. Hauser

There has been a general assumption that local pottery associated with the African diaspora was made on a small-scale basis, feeding local demands (Beuze 1990; Crane 1993; Ferguson 1980, 1992; Handler 1964; Wheaton and Garrow 1985). This article questions the strength of that argument through an analysis of archaeological ceramics recovered from contexts associated with eighteenth-century Jamaica. Through ethnographic, documentary, and archaeological evidence I establish that the scale of production of pottery in Jamaica was large and focused around the Liguanea plain. The study shows that the nature of economic interaction among enslaved and free African Jamaicans was not restricted by the arbitrary divisions of rural and urban contexts. The nature of economic behavior was more fluid and far-reaching than anticipated by the planter class or the archaeologists who study them.

Analysis of urban and rural contexts in the archaeology of the African Diaspora, with very few exceptions (Crane 1993; Hauser 2006), has often been separate endeavors. In light of the important work on landscape and capitalism (Delle 1998; M. Johnson 1996; R. Williams 1972), this phenomenon can be explained as a result of the ways in which agro-industrial production impacted the cultural landscapes of the colonial world. This disconnect is also, in part, an artifact of arbitrary analytical models of scholars studying the African Diaspora and in the end reproducing the dichotomous social constructs of the social sciences (Wurst 1991). Most archaeological studies of the Caribbean during the slavery period have focused on the plantation life (e.g., Armstrong 1990b; Delle 1998; Handler and Lange 1978; Higman 1998; see Farnsworth 2001; Haviser 1999) or the commercial nature of urban centers (Hamilton 1992; Hamilton and Woodward 1984). Few studies have tried to draw the connection between these two spheres.

Rather than taking the dichotomies of urban and rural slavery for granted, more attention should be paid to unraveling the nature of social relations both within and between rural and urban contexts. One of the loci of these social relations was the Sunday street market, a meeting place of the enslaved and what in the end became a space of their own. They were places of tension, where the enslaved introduced disorder to the slave regime. This disorder existed on an abstract level providing a level of economic agency from the plantation economy (Olwell 1996), but it also provided a real and material means for resistance (Higman 1996). While there has been much written about the transgressive potential of the Sunday markets, the evidence for the development of social networks has come largely from anecdotal evidence and extrapolations from entire populations. To see the interrelatedness of the rural and the urban, archaeology offers a method for establishing the real material links between communities in Jamaica. To determine whether social relations operated on a localized level and were restricted to either urban or rural milieus, I examined the production and distribution of ceramics found in archaeological contexts associated with the eighteenth century. For many reasons, pottery proves to be an incredible material through which to understand the political economy and social networks of a particular society. Yabbas, as a local ceramic and commodity, sold on the Sunday markets (Hauser 2006), can be used to determine the scale and extent of social relations forged through the internal market economy.

Many items were sold on the internal markets, and most were of local manufacture (Edwards 1793; Hauser 2001; E. Long 1774; Mintz and Hall 1991; Reeves 1997). Of the items sold in the Jamaican street markets (including vegetables and fruits grown on the provision grounds of enslaved laborers and locally produced goods such as ropes, mats, and calabash), the only archaeologically visible products were earthen jars (Edwards 1793). This pottery, called yabbas, are poorly fired and coarse; they may be glazed, slipped, or untreated. Like all pottery, yabbas are a plastic form of material culture in that they betray their provenance through aplastic inclusions found within the clay matrix and through the methods of their manufacture. Hence we can discern the level of organization required in manufacturing the pottery and the degree to which it was distributed across the island. The ethnographic, documentary, and archaeological record I examined challenges the assumption that pottery production and distribution were localized in nature. Analysis of this pottery not only addresses the level to which pottery production was organized among the enslaved but challenges in a broader sense the need to examine interrelatedness of social relations of the enslaved in urban and rural contexts.

Pottery Production

There is relatively little information on ceramic production or distribution in the ethnographic or documentary record of Jamaica. This evidence is largely anecdotal from the accounts of planters and visitors to the island. All told, I have been able to glean only five accounts mentioning pottery manufacture and two more mentioning its sale (*"Characteristic Traits"* 1797; Edwards 1793; Sloane 1707; E. Long 1774; Phillippo 1843). What does exist, however, points to a complex system of production reliant on kinship ties and a method of distribution that included sale at Sunday markets. Below, I detail ethnographic evidence recorded by Roderick Ebanks in the 1970s and documentary evidence from the eighteenth and nineteenth centuries.

Many scholars argue that pottery manufacture, as part of a larger sociotechnical system in which relations of pottery manufacture exist, bespeaks broader social relations. This system can be accessed through an understanding of the pottery's production and distribution (Pfaffenberger 1992; Sinopoli 1986, 1988, 1991). Craft production can also be seen as a way to access and challenge normative constructions of identity in the past (see Costin, Wright, and Brumfiel 1998). Local craft production, however, is also impacted by the indeterminacies of colonial structures (Stahl 2002) and therefore can be seen both as a result and a reaction to larger economic domains. Through an analysis of the aplastic inclusions found in ceramics, one can gain a sense of the systems of exchange used to distribute them. However, because of their inherent plasticity, the analysis of ceramics can reveal contexts of production and organization in which they were manufactured.

The debates that have centered on local ceramics of the African Diaspora by archaeologists have generally focused on cosmological meaning or the identification of ethnicities of potters who made them (Ferguson 1999, 1992, 1985; Heath 1988). This debate has been somewhat flawed in its concentration on a shallow interpretation of identity and its meaning (Armstrong and Hauser 2004), and on ceramics of the African Diaspora and what they indicate about the fluidity of African identities in the Americas (Hauser and DeCorse 2003). That is not to say that the ceramics do not offer great potential in understanding the formation of African social networks and concomitant identities in the Americas. However, ceramics also bespeak the contacts made through the commercial networks developed by Africans forced into slavery in the Americas.

Archaeologists working with ceramics of the African Diaspora have generally assumed that the production of these materials occurred at the level of a household craft industry within enslaved residences for use on a given plantation (Beuze 1990, 40; England 1994; Handler 1963, 1964; Wheaton and Garrow 1985, 183) and that the pottery that made its way into urban settings was a result of indirect links created by the planter (Crane 1993). There is indeed little evidence to challenge the model that local, low-fired, coarse earthenware was the product of part-time potters who had access to only intermittent distribution networks. To the contrary, well-fired glazed ceramics, like those discussed by Handler and England, are said to be the result of more intensive production and distribution systems. In initiating my analysis of ceramics in Jamaica, I framed, rather uncritically, my models around these rather dichotomous production strategies, mirroring the two predominant types of local pottery in Jamaica: slipped and glazed yabbas.

Yabba actually refers to the form rather than the specific method of manufacture or decoration. The term itself is believed to be derived from the Twi word *ayawa* meaning "earthenware dish" or a local Taino word for "big mouth" (Mathewson 1972b, 55). The strongest evidence of production comes from ethnographic evidence. In his analysis of a modern analogous Spanishtown potter, Roderick Ebanks (1984) described the method of manufacture for slipped yabbas. Ma Lou made coiled pots that were smoothed with a piece of wood and evened with a scraper (Ebanks 1984, 33) (Fig. 13.1). The pots were dried, burnished, and fired with green wood (Ebanks 1984, 35). Similar coiled pots were recovered from seventeenth-century contexts in Port Royal. Also represented in the archaeological record are glazed pots of a similar shape,

Fig. 13.1. Waster sherd from Ma Lou's house yard.

which Ebanks identifies as "Syncretic." The glazing presupposes a kiln firing for this particular type of pottery. There is absolutely no ethnographic evidence of production of this type of ceramic with the exception of oral history citing a large number of kilns along the Río Cobre.

It appears that the industry responsible for production of this pottery was concentrated in family compounds and organized around female members of the family.

> Fanny Johnson [Ma Lou] was a potter, as was her mother before her. The yard in which Mother Lou was born contained a large external family of maternal aunts and their children. All of these aunts made pots, and almost every yard in the district was occupied by a family of potters. By the time Ma Lou was nine, she and her female cousins had begun to learn pottery from her mother, three aunts, and uncle's wife. (Ebanks 1984, 3)

This account implies that a potting industry organized by matrilineal bond and based in the natal home was concentrated in Spanishtown. The industry was neither isolated nor changeless. What is of considerable interest was the susceptibility of this industry to increasing global economic pressures. The local industry was disrupted by the introduction of imported metal equivalents. Ebanks recounts, "Ma Lou continued to perfect her skills until the end of the 1940s, when the introduction of the aluminum pot all but destroyed the potting industry, which appears to have relied heavily on cooking pot sales to sustain it" (1984, 31).

Impossible though it is to disentangle this industry from the broader colonial economy, this change decimated the local industry of which there are but a few remaining potters mostly meeting the demands of a burgeoning tourist trade. While the ethnographic record provides some details on organization and methods of production in recent years, there is even less documentary evidence on the production of local coarse earthenware. In the eighteenth and nineteenth centuries, most references are sporadic allusions to the existence of local pottery or the presence of potential resources. James Phillippo asserts, "Particles of golden mica have been found in districts near the source of the Rio Cobre, and sometimes, near Spanishtown, it has been incorporated with the potter's clay" (1843, 72). An anonymous writer in 1797 describes the domestic utensils of enslaved Jamaicans in *Columbia Magazine*: "Some negroes are expert in manufacturing pots and other common vessels on which they bestow a coarse glazing. Their pans (called yabbas) are convex at the bottom without a ring as ours" ("Characteristics Traits," 293). These pots were used primarily for cooking in the following manner: "The trivet for supporting the vessel in which he prepares his food, consists of three large stones" (292). In 1774, Edward Long described these pots as "a better sort of earthenware, manufactured by the Negroes" (3:851). They can be defined as coarse, internally glazed, restricted, direct rimmed vessels. They are ubiquitous in the archaeological record and can be found as early as the seventeenth century.

While the evidence is partial, it does point to two alternatives of ceramic manufacture. An understanding of ceramic manufacture must include the organization of its production and of its distribution. Two alternative models will be assessed: (1) If ceramic production was an outgrowth of the domestic economy, a craft industry taken on independently on each plantation to meet specific needs, one would expect a system of internal production that was limited to local distribution. This parochial model of manufacture would bespeak a limited range in economic systems and resultant social networks. (2) If pottery was more intensively produced, we would expect a more centralized production scheme, and distribution would be regional in scope. This islandwide model of production would indicate a robust economic system and concomitant social network of the enslaved.

Archaeological Analysis

In my analysis I focused on two distinct issues: the change in the ceramic inventory over time and the relative provenance of ceramics in the eighteenth century. I examined 10,049 sherds of coarse earthenware of which 7,695 sherds were germane to the analysis presented below. While most sherds in this sample (n=4,836) were analyzed as part of a larger project looking at marketing in eighteenth-century Jamaica (Hauser 2001), access to the collection gave me an opportunity to study a collection from one locus, Port Royal, in the seventeenth, eighteenth, and nineteenth centuries (n=2,859). I examined ceramics recovered by Marx from the underwater component of the Port Royal site[1] (n=118), recovered by Tony Aarons from Fort Charles (n=179) and Old Naval Hospital (n=73), recovered by Anthony Priddy from St. Peter's Church (n=1,640), and recovered by Philip Mayes from the Old Naval Dockyard (n=849).

Coarse earthenware excavated from historic contexts includes both imported as well as locally produced ceramics. Coarse earthenware identified as locally produced (yabbas) was primarily utilitarian in function, had little decorative inventory, was handmade, and came in three varieties: glazed, slipped, and untreated. These ceramics, while varying in frequency, have been recovered as early as the seventeenth century (Fig. 13.2). Many of these ceramics recovered archaeologically have analogs in the documentary record. Due to the heterogeneity of local coarse earthenware, much of my analysis of production and provenance is dependent on the degree of variation. This analysis shows there is little difference in the manufacture of the pottery within each type of pottery from different sites.

Following Costin (1991, 1999) and Mills (1999), as a measure of variation I looked at the diameters of rim openings within specific forms of slipped coarse earthenware, including cooking vessels and water pots. In contexts from the seventeenth to nineteenth centuries in Port Royal, I recorded the rim diameters of 183 slipped yabbas. During the seventeenth-century occupation of Port

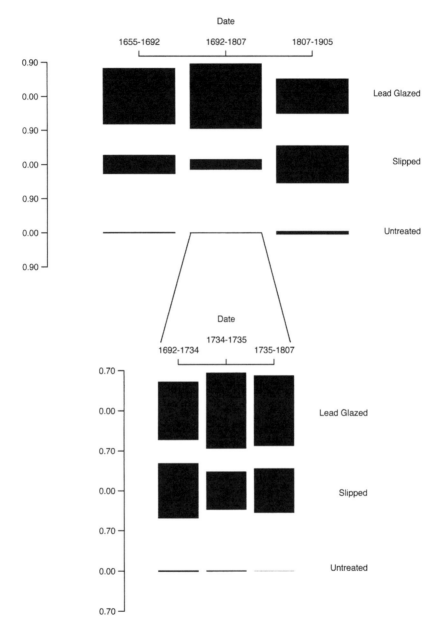

Fig. 13.2. Seriation of yabba: temporal changes.

Royal, there was a considerable degree of variation in the diameter of the rims of slipped yabbas. During the eighteenth century, this variation decreased considerably. Beginning in contexts associated with occupations after 1807, the variation in rim diameter increased again (Fig. 13.3). While not necessarily an indication of standardization, the data do indicate that significant transformation took place in the potting industry during the eighteenth century.

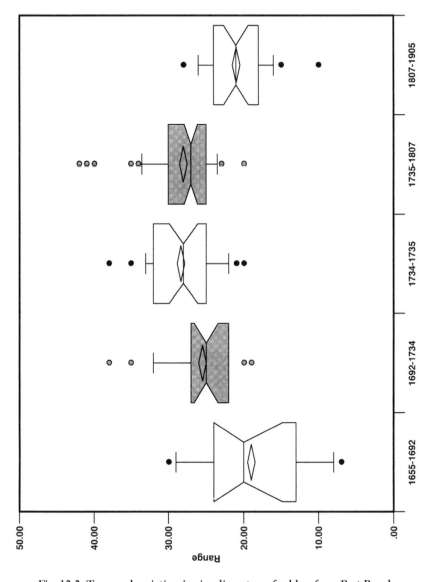

Fig. 13.3. Temporal variation in rim diameters of yabbas from Port Royal.

299

Evidence of this transformation is further buttressed by changes in the decorative inventory of the ceramic assemblage during the eighteenth century (Fig. 13.4). Seventeenth-century potters used seven distinct techniques in decorating the slipped yabbas. These decorations included punctation using the end of a reed, impressions with rice grains, fiber rouletting, grooved incisions, fluted rims, geometric incisions, and maker marks. In all, 10 percent of the sherds were decorated. By the eighteenth century there were only three decorations: fluted rims, groove incisions, and maker's marks. The decorated sherds at this point were only 1.2 percent of the overall assemblage. In the nineteenth century there was an explosion of decorative techniques including appliqué, perforations, fiber impressions, fluted rims, perforations, and maker's marks (6.7 percent of the ceramic assemblage). These results suggest a growth and transformation of the pottery industry in Jamaica during the seventeenth century. While many of the slipped yabbas were not decorated in the three contexts, there was a distinct reduction and then florescence in the decorative inventory. This coincides with a decrease in the variability in rim diameters followed by a sharp increase. It is my belief that in the eighteenth century we see the development of these yabbas as a trade item produced in a somewhat larger scale than suggested by domestic manufacture.

Analysis of similar measures of variability of ceramics recovered from eighteenth-century contexts across Jamaica tends to support this argument. Sites examined included St. Peter's Church and Old Naval Dock Yard from Port Royal, Old King's House in Spanishtown, which was excavated by Duncan Mathewson (1972a) (n=984), Seville (n=775), Drax Hall (n=27) near St. Anne's Bay, which was excavated by Douglas Armstrong and Juan Debollas (n=178), and Thetford (n=135) in central Jamaica, which was excavated by Mathew Reeves. Taken as a whole, the eighteenth-century Jamaican ceramic assemblage is highly varied in apparent manufacture, form, and size. Glazed, slipped, and untreated yabbas all seemed to have been exposed to varying firing environments indicated in the multiple types of cores and abundant clouding I recorded on the vessels. While this variation might be an artifact of the different skills that potters adopted in attempting to incorporate technologies like glaze, it does not seem to be the result of regional variation in pottery production.

In this analysis I wanted to establish that intrasite variation among the ceramics was less than intersite variation. In other words, there would be greater difference between ceramics from different sites than among ceramics within a site. Box and whisker plots of glazed and slipped yabbas recovered from the seven sites mentioned above show that island assemblage is quite varied. This heterogeneity, however, does not seem to be correlated with sites or regions. Rather, the variation within site-specific assemblages is greater than variation between sites (Fig. 13.5). In addition, the relative dearth of decorative inventory in the eighteenth century in Port Royal seems to be mirrored across the island as a whole. The trends I observed in the Port Royal assemblage, such as the disappearance of a decorative inventory and the relative increase in homogeneity,

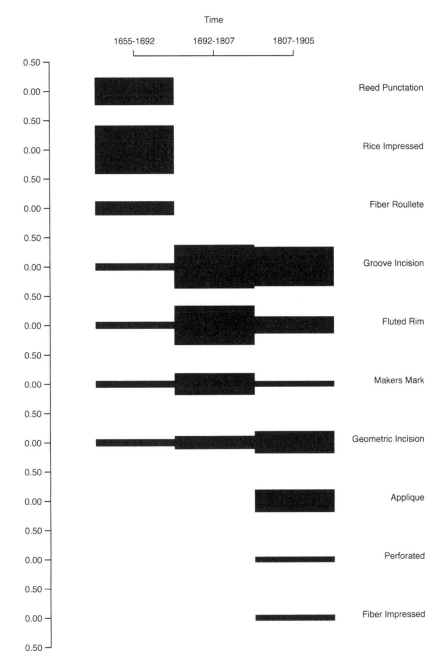

Fig. 13.4. Temporal change in decorative inventory.

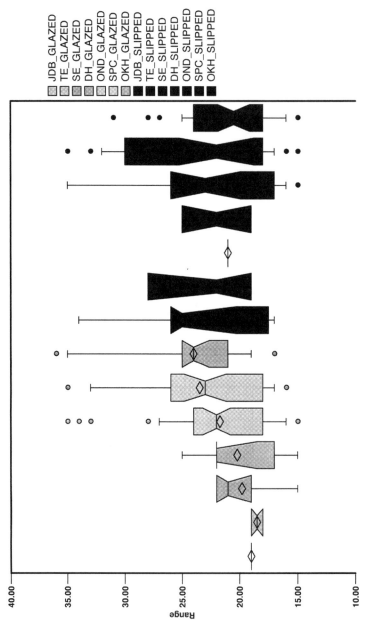

Fig. 13.5. Variation of rim diameters, sorted by glazed and slipped varieties of yabbas.

seem to bear out across the island and are the result of a bourgeoning ceramic industry.

As a means to test whether the decreased variability in ceramic assemblages was a result of islandwide trends among disparate potters or the consolidation of a ceramic industry, I examined the relative provenance of the slipped, glazed, and untreated yabbas. Ceramic petrography identifies aplastic mineral inclusions within the body of the ceramic and seeks to determine the relationship between these inclusions to identify potential source materials (C. Allen 1997). This analysis also includes more quantitative analysis attempting to identify the kinds of sediments from which the clay was mined (Fieller and Nicholson 1997; Gibson and Woods 1990; Stoltman 1989, 1999). Following Stoltman (1999), I employed point counting as a strategy to acquire qualitative information about aplastic mineral inclusion but also to quantify these results. Many of the results of petrographic analysis were published elsewhere (Hauser 2005), but I shall attempt to summarize the results and illustrate the significance to this study.

I examined a random selection of 149 rim sherds from eighteenth-century contexts across Jamaica and 15 sherds from prehistoric contexts representing the three regions within the study area. What emerged were five major compositional groups that were concordant with specific archaeological types. All of the glazed yabbas represented one fairly homogeneous composition group with the exception of four examples. There were two compositional groups identified from the slipped yabbas and two compositional groups identified from the untreated yabbas.

Four of the compositional groups interpreted from petrographic analysis contain inclusions which are consistent with the alluvial sediments from the Río Cobre in the region of Spanishtown. This includes abundant potassium feldspar, quartz, plagioclase feldspar, laterite fragments, and minor amounts of biotite. Of note was the recrystalization of quartz indicating a metamorphic source material for the clays used to construct the pottery. One of the compositional groups contained inclusions that were consistent with sediments from the Liguanea Plain around Kingston. These soils had considerable feldspar and quartz but also contained high quantities of arkose fragments. One group contained smaller inclusions of quartz, potassium feldspar, and plagioclase feldspar. This compositional group is significantly different from sediment in both the Liguanea and the Río Cobre. There was significant variation in the clays used to produce the slipped, glazed, and untreated yabbas.

This variation, however, did not correlate to the sites from which the sherds were excavated (Fig. 13.6). Groups 2, 3, and 4 are the most interesting for the purpose of this analysis. All of the communities were getting their ceramics from the same place. There does seem to be some difference in preference for where the ceramics originated. For the most part, the communities decided to acquire their slipped yabbas from potters working in the Río Cobre area (group 3). The communities at Juan de Bollas and Tethford seemed to prefer

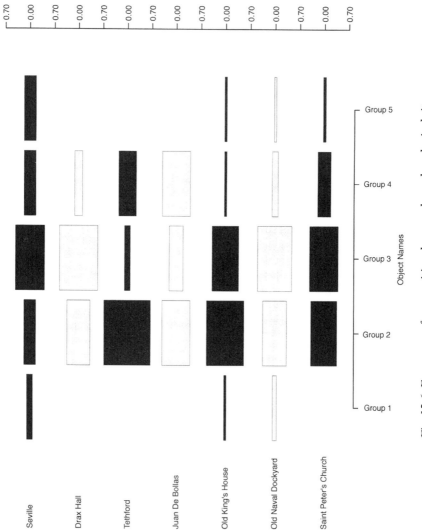

Fig. 13.6. Frequency of compositional groups by archaeological site.

slipped yabbas from an unknown source (group 4). A personal communication with Matthew Reeves indicates that in the nineteenth and twentieth centuries these communities would purchase their yabbas from Old Harbor.

What the archaeological data suggest is an organization of manufacture which creates large amounts of highly variably ceramics from a limited number of loci. Indeed, the volume and distribution of ceramics seem to indicate an intensive strategy of pottery production. The variability, however, in rim diameter, decorative inventory, and firing would seem to suggest that there was no standardization of pottery. While this does not conform to normative definitions of industrial or artisanal modes of ceramic production, it also does not conform to assumptions of ceramic manufacture implicit in the literature of pottery manufacture in the African Diaspora. If we were to extrapolate from Wheaton and Garrow's 1985 study, we would see hundreds of ceramic workshops throughout Jamaica, associated with plantations and pens, meeting only direct and local demand. But what we see is a rather restricted number of production sites producing highly variable pottery, but with similar mineralogical characteristics.

The Markets

Since yabbas were recovered on multiple sites including rural plantations, urban tenements, and elite households, it is important to understand the linkages between these contexts. In the case of Jamaica, it was the street markets and peddlers who sold wares, between urban and rural, to enslaved laborers who required the pottery for their own consumption and to urban servants who used them for their own meals and for the meals of the elite. Rather than being a single economic relationship, the internal market system was really a vast array of economic exchanges that developed on the island of Jamaica since the seventeenth century. The internal economy of Jamaica provided a flexible set of trade relationships. This mechanism served several communities in Jamaica, including slaves, both urban and rural, the free African Jamaican population, the merchants, the planters, the administrators, and the lawyers. Interactions ranged in the degree of formality from legal agreements between planters facilitated by lawyers in order to obtain commodities or livestock to a highly informal form of gift exchange between enslaved laborers on the same plantation (Fig. 13.7). Informal interaction could also be both internal and external. In short, the internal market system encompassed a range of activities that cannot be reduced to any single institution or group.

As Higman has noted, the internal economy went beyond the realm of the enslaved. Planters also engaged in more informal aspects of the internal economy. Thomas Thistlewood was a skilled horticulturalist who grew European vegetables. He made ketchup to sell to the taverns in Savanna La Mar (Hall 1999, 121), and he sold produce to other plantations. "A girl from Mr. Meyler's came to buy garden stuff. Wrote to Mr. Meyler, and sent two

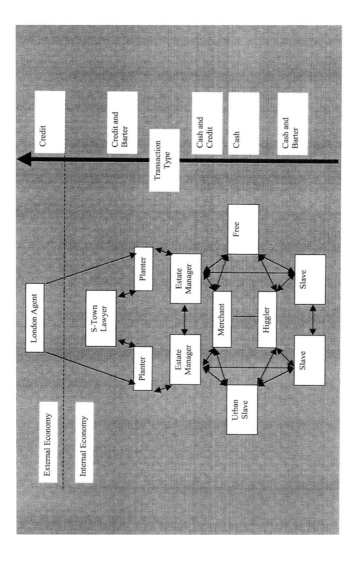

Schematic of transaction types and actors | Using Thistlewood 1778-1804

Fig. 13.7. Schematic of internal exchange in eighteenth-century Jamaica.

watermelons, some tomatoes, green peas, dry peas, and dry kidney beans to plant as a present" (Thistlewood in Hall 1999, 164).

Higglers were itinerant traders who were either enslaved or were free independent operators (Katzin 1971, 340). The enslaved higglers, who were often women, were the selling agents for planters and merchants alike. Thomas Thistlewood's higgler sold items for him on other plantations or at the market in Savanna La Mar, Negril, or Hatfield Gate (Thistlewood in Hall 1999, 69). For example, in 1767 Thistlewood's chief higgler "Sold at Savanna La Mar for me, 14 eggs, 2 bitts; Indian kale, 2 bitts; Cabbage & savoys, 3 bitts" (Thistlewood in Hall 1999, 156). Higglers represent the lower end of the middle range of formality. These higglers were vital in transactions linking the rural with the urban and the planter with the slave. They traveled between the plantation village and the market, or between plantation villages, exchanging goods either through cash or barter.

Higglers were not viewed much better than the merchants of the town. They were common in remote areas with poor access to markets and were often blamed for price inflation (Katzin 1971, 341). In the eighteenth and nineteenth centuries, these country sellers, mostly townswomen, traveled between plantation and market, selling and bartering goods. An editorial in a newspaper complained about "the prevailing practice of vending all kinds of merchandise and stores upon Sugar Estates.... This practice if permitted, must soon destroy the establishment of the Regular Trader, and consequently ruin in the Towns" (Simmond 1987). Another writer describes higglers as follows:

> They are sent abroad by their owners, to work out as it is called, for which liberty they are obliged to pay a certain rate per week or month.... Turned loose on the community, they are guilty of every kind of fraud and forestalling, to make up their respective allotments. They are the receivers and vendors of stolen goods and occasionally thieves themselves; the most honest part of their employment being to monopolize roots, greens, fruit and other edibles, which they produce from the country Negroes, and retail at exorbitant prices. ("Characteristic Traits" 1797, 702)

There was much concern about the higglers, but they were also vital in maintaining Jamaica's economic health. They were necessary in economically linking the urban with the rural. Most important, they proved a crucial means through which enslaved laborers provisioned themselves by linking different plantation villages and the towns.

On the less formal end of the economy were the transactions between slaves. These transactions employed barter or cash.[2] Slaves would engage in this economy themselves by attending a market or would rely on higglers as intermediaries. Although these types of transactions are seldom mentioned as much as higgling or market transactions in the documentary record have been, some authors claim these exchanges were crucial to the creation and consolidation of enslaved communities (Olwig 1977, 1985). In 1826, Alexander Barclay stated that "upon many of the estates a sort of business is made by some of the slaves of baking bread and selling it to others" (1826, 70). He goes on to note that slaves "brought in Irish salt pork, butter, mackerel, cod-fish, linens, printed cottons, muslins, handkerchiefs and crockery-ware," which they would sell to other slaves in the plantation village (Barclay 1826, 273).

The Sunday street markets were a mechanism through which enslaved and free peoples negotiated the conditions of the plantation system. On the one hand, the markets provided a degree of economic independence from the plantation, giving enslaved and free African Jamaicans a venue to sell surplus produce and obtain cash or other goods through barter (Hauser 2001; Higman 1998; Mintz and Hall 1991; Reeves 1997). On the other hand, according to Mintz and Hall, "the market diversified the social interaction of its participants, allowing for a temporary respite from the planter and plantation" (329).

The social interaction involved in the market relationships goes deeper than simple commodity exchange. Margaret Katzin highlighted this in her ethnographic description of higglers in the late 1950s:

> Higglers and country people make the trip to market every week, not out of economic necessity, but because they enjoy it. As the story goes, if one meets a country higgler on the way to market with a big load while she is still near her home, and offers to buy the whole load and pay more than she can expect to get for it in the market, she will refuse to sell. The reason for the refusal, according to those who tell the story, is that she wants to go to Kingston for some high life, to be able to do things that would not be approved by her rural neighbors. (Katzin 1959, 316)

Markets continue to be of enormous social import in Jamaica. Victoria Durant-Gonzalez describes the social nature between the wholesaler, retailer, and consumer:

> A higgler buys from a number of wholesalers so that she is assured of a constant supply of available produce. I was told by higglers that if this practice is not maintained and a higgler limits her buying to one wholesaler, she runs the risk of being boycotted by the other wholesaler.... This practice seems to be related to a general rule which governs the buying and selling of commodities at the marketplace: "you buy from me and I sell to you," or the converse: "You don't buy from me before, now I won't sell to you." This governing rule applies to wholesaler and retailer as well as to retailer and customer, suggesting there is an emphasis on reciprocity at each level of the market system. (Durant-Gonzalez 1983, 5)

While this is a very recent account, there is little reason to doubt that the nature of exchange and the relationship between retailer and consumer has changed much over time. Indeed, the very fluid nature of the exchange required these social networks. While operating in the realm of hard currency, it also employed barter as a mechanism of exchange (Mintz 1955, 95). The material scale and social nature of these markets provided mechanisms for subtle and not-so-subtle transgressions against the slave regime. In his article on the internal economies of Jamaica, Higman (1996) suggests that through these systems of markets the enslaved organized the 1831 rebellion.

I have described the variety of economic interactions that took place in Jamaica during the eighteenth century. The internal economy is markedly diverse in its range, its mechanisms, and its actors. The locus of these interactions was the Sunday street markets. They were a fulcrum of tension within the slave regime because they were an institution where rural and urban slaves came together and created a space of their own.

The market provided a subtle and not-so-subtle space for resistance. In describing his illustrations "French Set Girls" and the "Red Set Girls," Isaac Mendez Belisario (1837) reveals the tensions implicit in the slave society:

> The degree of jealousy heretofore existing between the Rival Sets can scarcely be conceived. The writer has been credibly informed, their animosity some twenty years back, was of so inveterate a nature, that their meetings in public, seldom passed without violent affrays: proving fatal in most instances, to their articles of dress, if not also to their persons, the struggle for pre-eminence.

Such spaces also provided the space through which acts of resistance could be organized. Higman (1996) suggests that it was through markets like Falmouth that the rebellion in 1831, known as the Baptist War, was organized by the enslaved.

To integrate the archaeology into this discussion, pots made by the same people were found in Drax Hall, Seville, Juan de Bollas, Thetford, Old King's House, Old Naval Dockyard, and St. Peter's Church. The people who lived on these sites in the eighteenth century were of various economic and social backgrounds. The one commonality that all of the residents shared was their access to the street markets and higglers of eighteenth-century Jamaica. While some of the residents, like the governor of Jamaica, bemoaned the necessity to rely on these markets, this economy proved to be a vital system for maintaining and transforming the social landscape of Jamaica.

Conclusion

The partial nature of the documentary record in Jamaica leaves much room for the interpretation of internal market exchange and pottery production. More so, the ethnographic evidence of contemporary potters in the Caribbean producing analogous ceramics point to small-scale production but an unstable market and an early-twentieth-century crash in the demand for pottery. While suggestive, hints about the scale of pottery production and distribution can be gleaned from their oral histories. Archaeological evidence indicates that ceramic production of yabbas, though highly variable, was focused in one location for three centuries. This in turn requires that we reconfigure our constructions of ceramic production associated with people of African descent in the Americas.

To extrapolate from the archaeological data, our understanding of commodity flow has an enormous impact on our understanding of Jamaica's economy as a whole. The local street market system employed by the enslaved population of Jamaica had formal and informal components that fed both internal and external markets. The enslaved population participated in this system, as did planters, administrators, and merchants. Although we can see this complexity from the documentary record, the system's extent can only be understood through material remains. More important, archaeological evidence establishes material links of the social relations between laborers on the plantations and laborers in the cities. It also leaves room for future examination of the interconnection of maroon communities traditionally isolated from the mainstream Jamaican black population by choice and geography. We must therefore reconfigure our understanding of the social relations of the enslaved as not only being informed by the context of labor but also being transformed by the social networks established among themselves.

Notes

1. Ceramics recovered by Marx were used only as a diagnostic tool and type collection due to the poorly recorded provenance of each artifact.

2. Some have also interpreted this exchange to involve reciprocity/gifting (see Olwig 1985).

CHAPTER FOURTEEN

Allies, Adversaries, and Kin in the African Seminole Communities of Florida: Archaeology at Pilaklikaha

Terrance Weik

The archaeology of Africans in the Americas needs to be redefined so that it can accommodate issues beyond the popular recognition of African roots and the agonizing memories of slavery. Even the "creolized" perspective has not widened our view enough to capture the full complexity of life for people of African descent in the Western Hemisphere. A group that shared both African and Native American cultural beliefs, biology, and traditions also emerged out of the conflicts and encounters that marked the African expansion into the Americas. Carter G. Woodson, pioneer of African American studies, labeled African–Native American contact the "longest unwritten chapter" in black history (in Katz 1986). In this chapter, I discuss my efforts at filling this void, using archaeology to answer fundamental questions about identity and social relations that historians and anthropologists have been grappling with for a few decades. I argue that African Seminole Maroons at a nineteenth-century site called Pilaklikaha (central Florida) produced a unique society that left behind a material culture both comparable and unlike what has been found at other sites across the Southeast.

Early chroniclers identified people of this dual heritage by many names, including black Indians, half-breeds, or *zambos*. The meanings behind these racial identities varied from continent to continent hundreds of years ago, as they do today (J. Forbes 1993). In some places, people of both African and Native American descent were called mulattos, a name that is usually reserved for those who have African and European parentage. "People of color" faced brutal re-definition and cultural erasure, as Europeans attempted to fit them into cat-egories that were used to justify warfare, colonization, and enslavement (Forbes

1993). Rights and resources continue to be manipulated or denied based on how governments choose to define "tribal" or racial status.

In the past two centuries, scholars, artists, journalists, politicians, and others have contributed to a growing discourse on Africa-Amerindian contacts (Katz 1986; Willis 1963). Descendants of both African and Native American ances- tors have also articulated their origins, celebrating their diverse family trees and remembering histories of defiance to racism and slavery (Jones 1990). In a number of places, fears over being associated with "blackness" or over being ridiculed for favoring one's Indian ancestry over one's African ancestry have prevented people from claiming all parts of their heritage. Other descen- dants have been selective in the way they represent their past, emphasizing the strengths of their "Africanness" or "Indianness" (Brooks 2002).

African Seminole archaeological sites provide us with a relatively new lens through which to view African–Native American contacts, identities, and sociocultural formations. African Seminole archaeological sites have been studied in only four locations (Fig. 14.1). Three of the four locations have been explored in Florida (Carr and Steele 1993; Griffin 1950; Herron 1994;

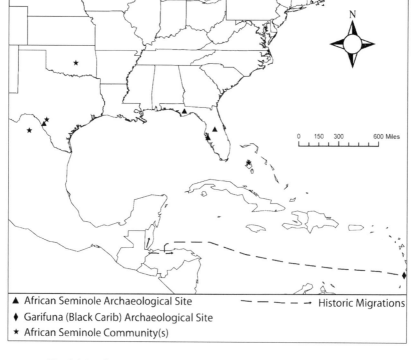

▲ African Seminole Archaeological Site   − − − − → Historic Migrations
♦ Garifuna (Black Carib) Archaeological Site
★ African Seminole Community(s)

Fig. 14.1. African Seminole archaeological sites and communities
in the United States.

Poe 1963; Weisman 1989). Pilaklikaha, or Abraham's Old Town, was one of the largest and best-known African Seminole Maroon sites in Florida—if not North America—during the nineteenth century (Herron 1994; Weik 2002). The historical and anthropological questions that have guided research at this Florida site inform my archaeological approach. First, we must ask the most fundamental type of anthropological question: who were the African Seminole? Were they a unique group with a sociocultural identity that was significantly different from that of the Seminole Indians and slave societies of the South? What was the relationship between Africans who escaped from slavery and Native Americans? What can material culture add to the stories that have already been told from archives, oral histories, and ethnographies? What are the social implications of archaeology for the modern-day African Seminole?

The historical archaeology of Pilaklikaha addresses a gap in our knowledge of the earliest periods of cultural genesis among the African Seminole. African Seminole societies have been studied in various parts of the circum-Caribbean and western United States (Boteler-Mock and Davis 1997; Foster 1935; Gallaher 1951; Littlefield 1977; Mulroy 1993, 2004; Porter 1943, 1996; Twyman 1999; Weik 2004). Archaeologists can offer material data concerning African Seminole history and help us expand our view beyond the limited but interesting observations of chroniclers.

One gathers mixed messages from the documentary record concerning the Florida African Seminole. They were viewed by European or Euro-American writers as Maroons or "runaway slaves." Many assumed they were slaves of the Seminole Indians. Colonial chroniclers were biased by their proslavery, white supremacist political views, which prevented them from questioning the possibility that some African Seminole were free before they left slave societies or were never subjected to forced labor. These Africans or Afro–Native American societies were said to have paid tribute in a few cases to the chiefs of Seminole Indian settlements (McCall 1974 [1868]; Porter 1996). Some of the few chroniclers to observe their towns noted that the African Seminole lived in a state of almost complete equality with Seminole Indians. Others noted that Africans were forced to labor under certain Seminole chiefs, in one case at gunpoint (Weik 2002). Many early African Seminole lived in remote enclaves, which limited the Euro-American commentators from making lengthy observations. Moreover, many chroniclers were not trained or critical cultural observers. Thus we should eschew blanket statements about African Seminole status, identities, and social relations. Some of our knowledge of the African Seminoles' past comes from oral histories and traditions. National policies of genocide and economic pressures are threatening the survival of Maroon societies throughout the Americas (Price 1998). African Seminole descendants in Texas proudly explained to me their ancestors' accomplishments, but they were also aware of how intermarriage and absorption into African American or U.S. society have threatened their group existence.

African Seminole descendants elsewhere face displacement from their historic lands, absorption into wider society through intermarriage, and alienation from claims to their Seminole heritage (see Price's 1998 commentary on similar problems in other Maroon descendant communities). Archaeologists are in a position to contribute time, funding, ideas, and data that can help African Seminole identify and protect their cultural resources (compare with Weisman's 1999 collaboration with Seminole Indians in Florida; see also Carr and Steele 1993 on archaeological service to the state of Florida and the Seminole Nation of Florida). Archaeologists could also help descendants gain access to material culture and historic places that tell their history by negotiating with landowners and museum staff. We may also assist descendant communities in educating the future generations through programs that promote a greater consciousness of the places, artifacts, traditions, and people who created their heritage. The aforementioned activities are the first steps in promoting an applied archaeology, one that avoids older anthropological practices of "salvaging forgotten cultures" from the destructive forces of "development" for interment in reports or museums (compare with Rubertone 2000).

In addition, a better dialogue between insiders (indigenous or descendant people) and outsiders (non-native or not connected by birth, social membership, or personal identification) should be cultivated so that outsiders proceed by respectful rules of engagement. Experience has suggested to me that there are descendants who are capable spokespersons for their history. Some are uninterested in the interpretations of academics who make authoritative claims about their past. Our best intentions have to be weighed against the legacy of intellectual and economic exploitation that many anthropological "subjects" have faced over the discipline's history. Moreover, we must be conscious of the wider public arena of cultural representation within which the insights of those who are not viewed as "authorities" are sometimes downplayed or ignored. More collaboration is necessary to give descendants a greater voice in publications and media. There are also venues where descendants should be allowed to tell their own story, free from interference.

What's in *Their* Name?

"African Seminole" is an ethnonymy or cultural label formed from the confluence of two words charged with multiple meanings. Africans were transformed into "blacks" (Negroes, etc.) by the racialized ethnonymy of chroniclers over the past few centuries, one of the many forms of oppression they faced in the Americas. By the twentieth century "black" took on a number of meanings that also reference skin color, political consciousness, and cultural expression. I prefer to use African here, as it invokes important old-world biocultural heritages. Africans came from a wide variety of societies, spoke many languages, and had a constellation of experiences, which have to be factored into conceptualizations of their transformations in and contributions to the Americas. "Seminole" may have come from the Creek word *Ishti semoli*, "wild Indian." Europeans attached the label "Creek Indian" to a range of indigenous cultural groups from Alabama, the Carolinas, and Georgia (Covington 1993; Weisman 1989). Seminole Indians are descended from the Creeks and other southeastern peoples who had moved into Florida by the eighteenth century.

Some have also proposed that the name "Seminole" derived from the Spanish word for Maroon, *cimarron* (Fairbanks 1978; Sturtevant 1971; Weisman 1989, 1999). As Europeans began their colonial ventures in the western hemisphere, they reduced people of various nations into "Indians." Even the label "Native American" is problematic because it does not contain any indigenous views on self-definition, recognizing instead a European. As the earliest enslaved peoples in this hemisphere were indigenous, those captives who escaped forced labor were called *cimarrones* by Spanish colonial chroniclers through the seventeenth century, in the circum-Caribbean (Arrom and García Arévalo 1986).

As resistance to slavery progressed, people of African descent became "Maroons" or "runaways" (Price 1979; Weik 2004). From the 1600s onward, Africans fled slavery in the southeastern part of North America, where they came into contact with Native Americans. After they reached Florida, enslaved Africans, freed blacks, and Maroons became what I will refer to as "African Seminole" because of their associations with the Seminole Indians. Over time, people of combined African and Native American parentage also became African Seminole.

By the nineteenth century, a plethora of terms were used to refer to African and Seminole Indian ancestry. Besides Maroons, nineteenth-century Euro-American accounts concerning African Seminole refer to them as "fugitive Negroes." "Indian Negroes" and "slaves" are listed along with individuals' names, sex, age, owner's name, and family on a military report that describes people who went to Fort Jupiter under a truce in 1838 (25th Cong., doc. 225, 1839, 83). After they were sent west, some fled to Mexico where they acquired the title "black Muscogulges" or "Indios Mascogos" (Porter 1996). Upon returning to the United States, they became "scouts" for the army, which needed their skills to battle groups such as the Apache. A gateway that marks a cemetery in Fort Clarke, Texas, bears the name "scouts cemetery," and it has been used by African Seminole from the late 1800s until now. Officials in the Bureau of Indian Affairs referred to them as "Freedmen."

Twentieth-century African Seminole ethnonyms are equally as variable as those in the preceding century. By the 1940s, Kenneth Porter referred to his informants as "Seminole Negros," although some explained to him that they were "colored not Indians." Arthur Gallaher (1951, 6) interviewed descendants who used a variety of self-identities, including "colored," "negro," "Indian Negro," and "Seminole Negro." Some of the labels that Gallaher observed clearly overlapped with wider African American group identifiers. A female descendant in

Texas explained to me that they used to be called Indians, not African Seminole. Subsequent historians and anthropologists have used the terms "Afro-Seminoles," "Negro Indians," "black Indians," and "Seminole Maroons" (Hancock 1980; Mulroy 1993, 1). One elder in Texas handed me a bright red bumper sticker with the words "Black Seminole" on it. In comparing the African Seminole narratives with documents, ethnographies, and histories, it is apparent that the terms that mark their identities have changed over a long period.

Similarly, the central Florida African Seminole town that I will discuss below has been referred to by different names. A surveyor's map constructed by government surveyors in the 1840s bears the name "Abraham's Old Town." This is the name that was given to the site by archaeologists who reported it to the State of Florida's Division of Historic Resources. Abraham was a African Seminole leader who advised the Seminole Indian chief Micanopy in his negotiations with the United States during the 1800s (Porter 1996). U.S. military records and travelers' accounts, which provide the majority of the documentary record on the African Seminole, refer to the town as Pilak-likaha (Cohen 1964 [1886]; McCall 1974 [1868]). The origin and meaning of Pilaklikaha is a matter of debate. Historian Kevin Mulroy (1993) has proposed that Pilaklikaha derives from *pakalala*, a challenge stance in the Kongo. Many of the earliest enslaved Africans who escaped from South Carolina plantations and joined the Seminole in Florida were from the Kongo and Angola areas of Africa (Landers 1990). An alternative origin for the site's name comes from the Micosukee and Muskogee languages of Seminole and Creek communities. Historians and linguists claim it is of Creek derivation, from *opilwa* (swamp), *lako* (big), and *laiki* (site). One nineteenth-century soldier translated Pilaklikaha as "Land of Many Lakes." Although there are plentiful swampy areas in the region, especially near the Withlacoochee River, the countryside definitely had its share of hardwood and pine forests. A similar word, "Palatklakaha Creek," is located several miles east of the archaeological site on modern USGS topographic maps. Armed Occupation Act land claims from the 1800s reflect the transition from communal African and Indian Seminole occupation to Euro-American private property. This transition was made possible by legal and violent means, as the United States enforced the Indian Removal Act of the 1830s through their pursuit of the "Seminole Wars" (Boyd 1958). The Florida Armed Occupation Act land claims and modern topographic maps refer to the area as Palatklakaha Prairie. A government surveyor referred to the area around the African Seminole site as "Abraham's Old Town." It is not clear whether Abraham's Old Town or Pilaklikaha was used by Africans and Native Americans during the nineteenth century, or whether both were used interchangeably.

I use the term "African Seminole" with the assumption that the selection of ethnonyms will remain a contentious issue. Some authors have proposed alternatives such as "self-emancipated Africans" in place of Maroon, because the original Spanish word, *Cimarron*, is a denigrating referent that first was applied to cattle and hogs who escaped from colonial ranches (Arrom and García Arévalo 1986; Ogunleye 1996). Today the word remains in popular use, as in the case of *pollo Cimarron*, served in some Latin American restaurants. I retain the word Maroon as one identifier for African Seminole because it retains a positive connotation for descendants in some parts of the African Diaspora such as Jamaica.

Naming is a potentially empowering or confining act, often contested by those to whom the names are directed. I hope to encourage readers to engage the dissonance surrounding labeling discourses such as anthropology, in order to understand the complexities of ascribing identity. I advocate no one identity term here where people or places are concerned, but would definitely place greater emphasis on the self-identifications ascribed by the ancestors and descendants of those I call African Seminole. Likewise, selecting only one name—Pilaklikaha or Abraham's Old Town—to refer to the town inhabited by African Seminole society may be a point of contention for some. I will use the terms "African Seminole" and "Pilaklikaha" because they are already familiar to many academics and descendant communities. I also do this out of convenience and the need for an economy of language.

Archaeologies of Africans and Indians

Like other disciplines, archaeology has been slow to transcend compartmentalizing approaches to culture contact and identity. Archaeologists usually discuss contact in the Americas by elaborating on trade, conquest, intermarriage, or "Creole" cultures (examples include Deagan 1985; Lightfoot 1995). African and Native American interactions generally get subsumed under archaeologists' concerns with world systems of inequality. "People of color" are generally discussed as part of a multicultural society where each population is dominated by Europeans or whites and has unique interactions with these colonists. However, African and Native American interactions outside of labor or marriage relations are rarely discussed.

The debate over colonoware is a good example of the problems that can occur for archaeologists who compartmentalize the roles played by Africans or Amerindians in colonial archaeological sites. Colonoware is a low-fired, undecorated earthenware made in mostly European forms and produced in the colonial Americas. Ivor Noel Hume first identified "colono-Indian" wares at Virginia sites, and his designation was used for similar pottery discovered in the southeast. It was first attributed to Native American potters in the south. Later, studies from the Chesapeake to South Carolina plantations helped to show that Africans also made colonoware in the south (see summaries in Ferguson 1992). Noel Hume and his proponents have answered this challenge to their original attribution of Native Americans as the potters in certain areas, emphasizing the continued Native American presence. In northwestern Hispaniola, at the town of Puerto Real (1503–78), archaeological and historical evidence suggests that enslaved Africans and Tainos exchanged pottery traditions, responding to European demand with one of the earliest colonoware traditions in the Americas (C. G. Smith 1995). Research that refines our knowledge of production, distribution, and circulation will flourish to the extent that it does not become too absorbed in trying to prove either African or Native American—or European for that matter—origins of production. Moreover, there need to be more efforts that seek the meanings, uses, and traditions that shaped and derived from colonoware (Ferguson 1992; Singleton and Bograd 2000).

African American and Native American archaeological sites have been interpreted through the framework of culture history or ethnicity. In their attempts at portraying the depth and content of each group's identity, archaeologists have hindered their ability to understand the complex interconnections of groups within wider populations. Hence the presence, the sociocultural impact, and the activities of one group are ignored or downplayed in sites interpreted as solely the domain of another group.

African American and African Diaspora archaeology has traditionally focused on ethnic or racial identity, creolization, or African influences (Ferguson, 1992; Singleton 1999a; C. G. Smith 1995). Deagan and Landers, Ferguson, and C. G. Smith have all discussed the Native American and African interchanges using pottery making, pipe production, enslavement, and military service as contexts of such interactions. Beyond these political, economic, or materialistic realms, studies of cultural interactions, shared interests, and worldviews are few.

Historical archaeologies of Native Americans have taken longer to develop than those of the African Diaspora. Native American historical archaeologies have explored a range of issues: identity, missions, settlement patterns, landscape, migrations, symbolism, and colonial contact (Lightfoot 1995; Rubertone 2000; Weisman 1989). Scholars have begun to question interpretations of Native American sites that do not fully account for the role of Africans where history suggests they existed. Southeastern sites (e.g., Creek, Cherokee) are a growing area of research (Rubertone 2000; Waselkov and Smith 2001), but unfortunately archaeologists have been silent about the role of Africans in these societies. Historians provide us with incentives for asking more pointed questions about Africans who were enslaved or married to people in these societies during the eighteenth and nineteenth centuries (Littlefield 1977; Saunt 1998; Wright 1986, 73–99). Brent Weisman (1989) has investigated Seminole Indian sites for a number of years, and in the process he has located African Seminole sites that have been studied with his support (Herron 1994; Weik 2002).

Likewise, plantation archaeology in southern and eastern North America will have to be reconceived to account for the role of enslaved Native Americans who have been ignored or blackened by chroniclers (see historical contacts in various chapters of Brooks 2002). Charles Fairbanks was a pioneer in

African American and Seminole Indian archaeology (see Singleton and Bograd 1995 and Weisman 1989 for bibliographic summaries). Ascher and Fairbanks's writings concerning Kingsley Plantation made mention of Maroons in the slave society that they studied, an acknowledgment that was ahead of its time in archaeology. However, they failed to explore the impacts of sizeable Seminole and Creek Indian societies near the plantation (Ascher and Fairbanks 1971; Fairbanks 1971). For instance, African and Indian Seminole forces raided Kingsley Plantations, kidnapping (or liberating?) forty slaves (Porter 1943; Rivers 2000; Schafer 2000). Moreover, the WPA slave narratives suggest that "kidnappings," intermarriage, conflicts, and friendships occurred between enslaved Africans and Seminole Indians in Florida (Rawick 1976, 27–29, 81). Fairbanks briefly mentioned the African Seminole in a 1978 essay on Seminole Indian history, explaining that they were slaves, cultural brokers, and forces of European acculturation.

Archaeological studies that focus on people of both African and Native American descent are few (Boteler-Mock and Davis 1997; Weik 2002). Black Creek, Black Choctaw, African Seminole, Black Garifuna, and other Afro–Native American settlements may provide fruitful sites that can be explored archaeologically, with the opportunity to build on the groundwork laid by historians and anthropologists in these areas (Gonzalez 1988, 24–37; Katz 1986; Willis 1963). Particular African and Native American interactions must be assessed in their own terms, in order to examine how each group may have experienced things differently from Euro-American colonists and how their worldviews affected their use of space, built environment, and material culture. People of African and Native American descent should not be expected to have operated the same way within their own communities, as they did when impinged upon by colonial or slavery societies.

Some of the criticisms above apply to other subfields of anthropology. Physical anthropology has traditionally been mired in studies of racial typology and pathology when it comes to studies of African Americans. African Diaspora physical anthropology has been slowly moving toward more sophisticated approaches that account for African American studies, health, and biocultural approaches (Blakey 2001). Part of the reason that African American populations have become attractive to physical anthropologists is because Native American activism and NAGPRA have regulated academic access to Native American remains since the 1980s (Blakey 2001, 402). Blakey's biocultural study of the Nanticoke-Moors in Delaware is one of the few examples that illustrate how to approach communities that have African, Native American, and European ancestry without submerging particular relations of "people of color" under their individual reactions to Euro-American political and economic hegemony. Blakey conducted demographic analyses of data gleaned from gravestones, government documents, and interviews in order to illustrate how each of the three Nanticoke-Moor populations dealt with racism and twentieth-century industrialization.

Histories and Anthropologies of the African Seminole

There are a number of reasons why scholarship concerning African and Native American contact has grown slowly, compared with other areas of study. Colonial Eurocentric chroniclers only focused on intergroup antagonisms, perhaps supporting this view out of fear for potential black and Indian military alliances against the colonists (Landers 1990; Willis 1963). Twentieth-century "areas studies" and ethnicity paradigms have discouraged scholars from venturing into murky intellectual waters where they would have to contend with cultures or offspring of African/Native American interaction. Some writers have assumed that Native Americans were not enslaved or present in the eastern United States during its slavery period (see criticisms by various authors in Brooks 2002). Jack Forbes has argued that Native Americans have been undercounted or erased from documents over the centuries by government officials who redefined them in racial terms, thereby weakening Native American land claims. Finally, the *zambo*, someone who has both African and Native American ancestry, has not fit into the North American bipolar racial model of society (Forbes 1993; Katz 1986).

One of the most prolific historians of the African Seminole was Kenneth Porter. He viewed Maroons as living in an unequal, but relatively free, feudal relationship with the Seminole Indians. Porter's feudal perspective focused on cases where Maroons gave Seminole Indians tribute and military assistance in exchange for allowing them to live in Seminole Indian territory. The feudalistic view has shaped most subsequent scholarship on African Seminoles (Littlefield 1977; Mulroy 1993). Porter and later writers such as Mulroy used military events and biographical case studies in their analyses of African Seminole social history. African Seminole leaders such as Abraham and John Horse have been the focus of these studies (Mulroy 1993; Porter 1996). Daniel Littlefield (1977) also focused on African and Native American contacts as well as political and economic history.

Laurence Foster (1935) analyzed "Negro-Indian" relations in a long-term regional perspective. Like Porter and many later researchers, he conducted months of fieldwork among African Seminoles in Mexico, Texas, and Oklahoma (see also Mulroy 1993). Foster noted that both alliances and antagonisms existed between Seminole Indians and Maroons in the past and ethnographic present (compare with Price 1979 and 1998 on other Maroon societies).

William Willis's anthropological perspective focused on how missionaries and Euro-American politicians feared the alliance of blacks and Indians. Willis argued that Europeans and whites actively sought to "divide and rule" Africans and Native Americans. Euro-Americans in colonial South Carolina paid Native Americans to reenslave African Maroons. At the same time, the colonists restricted Native American access to enslaved populations (Willis 1963). Conversely, Africans were employed in colonial expeditions against

Native Americans. The same thing happened in Florida a century later, involving Seminoles, Creeks, and people of African descent (Porter 1996). Willis argued that the American Revolution was the critical event that led to an influx of African people into Florida (cf. Landers 1999, Littlefield 1977; Rivers 2000; Wright 1986). As a result of the overt and clandestine slave trade and regional instability of the late eighteenth and early nineteenth centuries, separate African Seminole towns were established by some first-generation Africans. Willis concluded that "self-interest frequently prevails over the brotherhood of color." That is, for many Native Americans in the southeast—the Seminole were an exception—Eurocentric racial and eco-nomic ideas, indigenous beliefs about status, and political interests all pre-vented Native Americans from establishing major alliances with Africans and other Native Americans (cf. Foster 1935; Saunt 1998).

My research builds on previous colonial history, African Diaspora archaeol-ogy, and African Seminole studies. I seek to challenge Kenneth Porter's (1996) view that all African Seminole lived in a feudalistic relationship with the Semi-nole Indians. I believe that African Seminole interests and skills gave some of them great influence over the Seminole or the ability to engage Seminole Indians on more equal terms. This is not to say that all Africans exercised the same level of power in Seminole Indian territory. Some Africans were enslaved, and some did give gifts or tribute to Seminoles to gain their favor or protection (Cohen 1964 [1836]; McCall 1974 [1868]; Simmons 1973 [1822]). But we lack data from most African Seminole towns. Seminole Indians certainly relied on the Maroons during wars and negotiations with whites. These wartime con-flicts and contacts, illustrated in many military and government records, are a primary source of information on the African Seminole Maroons. However, Euro-American documentary sources usually viewed Africans as a subservi-ent "race." This slant should be critically analyzed with the awareness that (1) African Seminoles incorporated African, European, and Native American cultural beliefs into their societies (for examples, see Mulroy 1993; Porter 1996; Willis 1963) and (2) African and Native American influences probably dif-fered in their strength and importance in each African Seminole settlement.

Similarly, I suspect that the African Seminoles' sense of group identity both intersected and diverged from neighboring Seminole Indians and enslaved or free African populations. People of African descent probably had a variety of interactions with Seminoles. Africans and Seminoles formed alliances during wars, and they shared kin. Other Africans lived with Seminole. A number of people of African descent came and went from Seminole or African Seminole towns periodically. African Seminole such as John Horse had both African and Seminole Indian parents. The majority of African Seminole may have selected from a continuum of affiliations, beliefs, and practices from Semi-nole Indian, African, African American, and European cultural systems.

It seems unreasonable to assume that all African Seminole would have self-identified or claimed a common identity and community to the same extent.

We should consider which symbols, traditions, and interests affected African Seminole identities. The culture concept is rooted in a historical lineage of ideas that tend to reduce the complexities of human relations and beliefs into entities ("cultures") that are assumed to operate with solidarity. Ethnicity theorists have laid out a vast universe of ideas (conceptual frameworks) that should be addressed when assessing cultural identity and social formation. These ideas include "primordialist," "instrumentalist," and "constructivist" perspectives. The primordial view defines groups by seemingly inherent, locally defined features such as language. The instrumentalist approach assesses factors, interests, and loyalties that are manipulated by leaders in the maintenance of social and cultural life. The "constructivist" view explores how groups are created or dismantled by institutions and individual actions. Some African Seminole may have perceived the benefits of forming separate villages, perhaps in pursuit of a well-defined, cohesive community that could be mobilized in defense of territory and resources, as well as in opposition to the hostile neighboring groups. In a setting where slavers and military forces sought to reenslave them and where different Seminole Indians related to them in unpredictable or periodically changing ways, it would have been advantageous for African Seminole to mobilize around a common identity and devise collective strategies for ensuring their safety and subsistence. If ethnicity studies of Maroons, the Balkans, and colonial Africa are any indication, we should be wary of any assumptions that African Seminole only took up arms to defend their freedom, for group members could have also manipulated crises to oppress (or eliminate) their peers. Maroon histories suggest that the very people who obtained their freedom from slavery sometimes made deals with their oppressors, gaining freedom in return for their help with preventing others from escaping slavery. In light of the ways some popular and traditional ethnicity studies have downplayed race or simplistically assumed Africans followed European patterns of immigrant adaptation to life in the Americas, ethnicity should be applied to African Seminole societies with caution.

Ethnicity has been viewed in more processual ways by a growing number of scholars. Ethnogenesis theory, as articulated by pioneers such as William Sturtevant (1971), refers to the creation, change, and fissioning of distinct sociocultural groups from culture contact situations (Bilby 1994; Mulroy 1993; Sattler 1996). Each of these three ethnogenetic processes had profound impacts on Seminole Maroons, and all three created circumstances that cannot be fully understood by focusing on the creative moments and structuring forces of cultural trajectories alone. Dissolution, voluntary fissioning, and ethnocide also occurred. Kevin Mulroy (1993) emphasized that African Seminole ethnogenesis involved a number of factors, including African heritage, plantation creolization, and the emergence of the Seminole Indians. Mulroy observed that the African Seminole survived by international diplomacy and migration. Echoing earlier views of Maroons (see Price 1979), Mulroy writes, "As with other neoteric societies, they incorporated adaptations of the most useful elements of their past and present experiences into a complex cultural whole" (23). Asa Hilliard (1995, 10) eloquently illustrates this point, noting that colonizers are often able to enact oppression because of their victims' loss or lack of a cultural basis for solidarity in resistance.

The adaptations and cultural wholeness of African Seminole should not be overemphasized or explored without also considering countervailing forces. Not all decisions that African Seminoles made or cultural developments allowed them to continue to survive. People chose to leave African Seminole or Maroon towns. When early African Seminole towns were destroyed, new ones were built in other locations, and African Seminole societies were forced to change or disappear. Behaviors and ideology probably changed as people started new towns, joined Native American towns, or returned to slavery (Porter 1996). Some towns may have shifted over time as the residents varied in their commitment to African, Native American, and syncretic worldviews. Thus our framework for understanding African Seminole must balance attention to the forces of communal cooperation and the sense of wholeness that people may have gained from forming social identities with the divergent interests and individual aspirations that impeded social and cultural unity.

An Archaeology of African Seminole Ethnogenesis

The African Seminole had roots that were grounded in various parts of Africa. Planters such as Zephaniah Kingsley ran a lively slave trade from East, West, and Central Africa to the Americas that became covert after the abolition of the slave trade in 1808. Planters like Kingsley who operated in Florida, Georgia, and Alabama faced devastating losses as Seminole Indian and Maroon forces attacked and "stole" (in the words of the authorities) Africans workers during the "Indian Wars" (Mahon 1967; Porter 1943; Rivers 2000).

Landers (1990) outlined the racial, geographic, and cultural identities of Maroons and freed Africans at colonial St. Augustine and Fort Mose, an outpost inhabited by ex-Maroons. Congo, Mandingo, Fara, Mulatto, Black, Caravali, Minas, Gangas, Lecumis, Sambas, Gangas, Araras, and Guineans were among the terms used to describe the people present at these locations (Landers 1999, 49). Her comparison of mid-1700s slave registers from South Carolina and St. Augustine church records suggests that nearly 70 percent of the black population that inhabited Fort Mose may have originated in the Congo. Research on names has provided the most lucid evidence of African connections with the African Seminole up to this point, particularly regions around Ghana and the Congo (Bateman 2002; Hancock 1980; Mulroy 1993). The other groups that Landers (1999) outlined may have also helped to found African Seminole societies.

Africans had been escaping from Spanish slavery in the southeast for over a hundred years by the time Seminole ethnogenesis reached its peak in

Florida (Weik 2002). Africans fled British plantations in the Carolinas during the seventeenth century, and the Spanish crown exacerbated the situation by proclaiming religious sanctuary to runaway converts who fled to Florida after 1693. Without the Maroon and free black recruits who built Fort Mose, the Spanish colonists in St. Augustine would not have withheld the British and American military incursions of the eighteenth and nineteenth centuries (Deagan and Landers 1999; Landers 1999). Hence the African Seminole emerged from an older stream of resistance that preceded the Revolutionary War.

African Seminole Maroon towns first emerged in northern Florida in the same place as Seminole Indians towns. Population counts are hard to establish, for Seminole Indians were reluctant to divulge their numbers. Historians estimate that 1,400 African Seminole lived in the oak hammocks and swamps of Florida, where they joined forces with thousands of Seminole Indians in the eighteenth and nineteenth centuries (Mulroy 1993; Porter 1996). However, we should use population estimates with much caution. By 1830, one U.S. census agent complained that the Seminole Indians denied his request for a count of Africans living in their midst. Africans who escaped from slavery either established their own communities or lived with Seminoles and Creek Indians as slaves or adopted members of society. As the Seminole and Creeks controlled their territories, Africans would have had to negotiate their existence in many cases. The Maroon and Indian Seminole alliance was powerful enough to threaten U.S. expansion. As a result of the "Seminole Wars" (1816–55) in Florida, the United States lost millions of dollars and thousands of lives (Covington 1993; Mahon 1967; Porter 1996). People of African descent were kin, adversaries, or military allies to the Seminole Indians during this last great challenge to U.S. hegemony on the East Coast.

More than ten early African Seminole settlements have been documented on government records and military maps (Fig. 14.2). From documents, it appears that men such as Abraham and John Horse shared leadership positions in Pilaklikaha. In one settlement, the biracial leader's authority depended on "the affection of his peers" (McCall 1974 [1868]; Young 1953 [1818]). Buckra Woman's and Mulatto Girl's towns may signify the role of women leaders in African Seminole society as well as a complex African-Indian-European ancestry for some leaders (Mulroy 1993). The historical contribution of African Seminole women has yet to be told with detail in Florida. Researchers in Texas are using oral histories to balance older male-centric African Seminole histories (Boteler-Mock and Davis 1997).

Africans lived with Seminole Indians in various towns, such as Sim-e-no-le-tal-lau-has-see and Thlonto-sassa (Carr and Steele 1993; Dexter 1823 [in Boyd 1958]; Landers 1999; Rivers 2000, 195). In a northeastern Florida settlement called Topkoliky, the Seminole leader named Phillip owned Africans who were forced to grow crops at gunpoint, according to a U.S. soldier (Cohen 1964 [1836]). The Seminole slaveholders did not base their slavery on race initially, for the indigenous people called Yamasee were also enslaved (Saunt 1998).

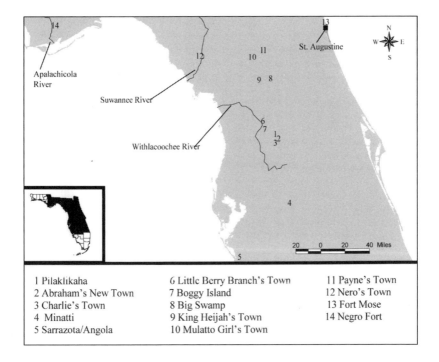

1 Pilaklikaha
2 Abraham's New Town
3 Charlie's Town
4 Minatti
5 Sarrazota/Angola

6 Little Berry Branch's Town
7 Boggy Island
8 Big Swamp
9 King Heijah's Town
10 Mulatto Girl's Town

11 Payne's Town
12 Nero's Town
13 Fort Mose
14 Negro Fort

Fig. 14.2. African Seminole towns in Florida.

Pilaklikaha's main period of occupation was between 1813, when Seminoles were forced to flee north Florida settlements that were invaded by U.S. armies, and 1836, when General Abraham Eustis's troops burnt down the town (Mahon 1967; Weisman 1989). A mean ceramic date of 1811 was derived from over 800 pottery sherds at the site (Weik 2002). Clay pipe and dark-green bottle glass fragments also suggest a late-eighteenth- or nineteenth-century occupation. A visitor in 1826 stated that over one hundred "runaways" from Georgia were living at Pilaklikaha. He identified three leaders: "Abram, July, and August" (McCall 1974 [1868], 160). Abram, the best known of the three, was a skilled interpreter, religious leader, and war strategist (Porter 1996). Besides Africans, Seminole Indians such as chief Micanopy and his wives built homes in the African Seminole town of Pilaklikaha. Some inhabitants were of "mixed" African, Native American, or European descent, as was Micanopy's "half breed" wife (Cohen 1964 [1836]; McCall 1974 [1868]; Simmons 1836).

During the nineteenth century, the African Seminole were successfully farming near Pilaklikaha (Cohen 1964 [1836]; McCall 1974 [1868]; Simmons 1836). They cultivated a variety of crops that were common in the south. Their fields may also have been close by the town, as "indian old fields" appear within a mile or two of the present-day archaeological site (see reference for Whitner's 1849 surveyor's map of central Florida in Weik 2002). In addition, they had livestock such as horses, cattle, and fowl. Some of the cattle in their large herds may be the same ones depicted in the painting *The Burning of Pilak-li-kaha by Gen. Eustis*, found in the Library of Congress.

Wooden structures probably predominated in Pilaklikaha (Cohen 1964 [1836]; H. Young 1953 [1818], 100). Building materials such as wrought and cut nails and brick fragments have been recovered from excavations at Pilaklikaha (Weik 2002). Like at Seminole sites in Florida, brick and nail fragments seem to be a rare occurrence at Pilaklikaha (see site summaries in Weisman 1989). Log cabins were also constructed by a number of Seminole and Creek Indians (Downs 1995; Weisman 1989, 1999). Traditional Seminole Indian homes known as "chickees" were constructed of four large corner posts, overlaid with a roof of crossbeams and palm thatch. These structures were often open on all sides, with a raised platform in the middle (Downs 1995; Weisman 1989). Young (1953[1818]) explained that some houses at other African Seminole towns had fenced gardens. According to General Abraham Eustis, who destroyed the town in 1836, Pilaklikaha had walls. It is unclear whether these were walls containing each household or surrounding the town.

Fig. 14.3. Fragments of an incised pottery rim, a clay pipestem,
a beverage bottle, and a porcelain button.

326

From the depiction found in the image entitled *The Burning of Pilak-li-kaha by Gen. Eustis*, it appears there may have been a small fence around the base of the hill upon which the town was built.

The artifact assemblage from Pilaklikaha is similar to other regional colonial period settlements because Maroons took part in the wider global economic and social systems of the Americas (Fig. 14.1; Parris 1983). The mechanisms for artifact acquisition and distribution included trade, raids, barter, gift giving, and local production (Porter 1943; Simmons 1973 [1822], 137; Weisman 1989).

Metal and glass fragments were found in great quantities, which is not surprising for such durable materials. Some of the unidentified metal fragments found at Pilaklikaha may have been part of kettles and hand tools. Lead shot and bullet fragments were the only weaponry found on site. Glass items such as clear and rose-colored patent medicine bottles and dark-green spirits bottle shards were found at the site (Weik 2002; compare with Ferguson 1992, Singleton 1990; Weisman 1989). Glass items may have been recycled for carrying liquids, and the shards may have been used as cutting implements (Neill 1977; Weisman 1989, 73).

Adornments recovered in excavations at Pilaklikaha need to be further explored so that we can determine what aesthetic, spiritual, or other beliefs may have been attributed to them. For example, clear and blue faceted beads and green and black wound beads have been recovered from Pilaklikaha (Herron 1994; Weik 2002, 122). Blue beads found on North American plantations and African American burials have been interpreted as items used to ward off evil, as status markers, or as clothing accessories (H. B. Foster 1998; Singleton 1990, 75; Stine, Cabak, and Groover 1996, 55). In contexts of African belief, beads were imbued with various functions and meanings: as forms of wealth, as aspects of color symbolism in ritual paraphernalia, or as manifestations of aesthetic values in clothes and crafts (H. B. Foster 1998; Ogundiran 2002c; Stahl 1999, 55–57). Seminole Indians used beads to decorate their clothing, sashes, and pouches (Downs 1995, 166–67; Goggin 1951; Weisman 1989). Early-twentieth-century photos illustrate that some native Seminole women wore beads in great quantities, and this practice has continued. Little has been written about Seminole beliefs concerning beads. Portraits of Seminole Indians, such as the leader called Osceola, show them wearing elaborately beaded necklaces and silverwork (see Johnson [in Weik 2002, 125, 191] regarding Native Floridian silverwork). Teardrop-shaped silver artifacts have been found at Pilaklikaha as well as Seminole Indian burials in Florida and Creek Indian sites in Alabama (Weik 2002, 125; Weisman 1989, 67).

We recovered sherds of American- or European-made pottery at Pilaklikaha that hint at the use of cups, bowls, storage vessels, and plates (Weik 2002, 116). British ceramic production was so prolific that it dominated European ceramics found at eighteenth-century Fort Mose and Jamaican Maroon towns, just as it did for North American Maroons at Pilaklikaha and the Dismal Swamp in North Carolina a half-century later (Agorsah 1994a; Deagan and Landers 1999;

327

Nichols 1988). Pilaklikaha's pottery assemblage includes cream, ironstone, pearl, stone, slip, white, and annular wares. The same predominance of British ceramics marks southeastern plantations and colonial sites after the mid-eighteenth century. We should interpret the white and ironstone wares items with caution, as there was a nineteenth-century homestead occupation in the same location as Pilaklikaha within a decade of its abandonment by African Seminoles.

Pilaklikaha differs from late-eighteenth-and nineteenth-century slavery or colonial sites because of its close proximity to Native American populations. It is not surprising that Native American artifacts dominate Pilaklikaha's assemblage. Ceramic fragments from the "Withlacoochee Brushed" category constitute over a third of all the pottery remains at Pilaklikaha, making it the most numerous artifact category at the site (Weik 2002). Goggin (1951) and Weisman (1989) have described the Creek and Seminole Indian origins of this "brushed" pottery tradition. The ceramics have a rough, scratched surface, probably made with reeds or grass. Vessel forms include small bowls, lozenge-shaped jars, and large globular pots. Carinated, wide-mouthed bowls occasionally are found at Seminole sites. The Seminoles used the brushed pots to prepare soffkee, a dish resembling pudding that was made from the coontie root (McCall 1974 [1868], 222). Native American pottery was used at other Maroon sites, such as Fort Mose (Florida), Palmares (Brazil), and Jose Leta (Dominican Republic) (Arrom and García Arévalo 1986; Deagan and Landers 1999; Orser 1994b; Weik 2004).

Rim decorations are one of the most interesting characteristics of the hand-made pottery at Pilaklikaha. The majority of the brushed pottery lip forms at Pilaklikaha were plain and rounded. Notched and notched-fillet rim sherds, when considered as a combined category, formed the majority of Pilaklikaha's five rim decoration styles. Pilaklikaha exhibited a wider diversity of brushed rim decoration styles than those found at twenty of the most accessible Seminole Indian site assemblages that date to the eighteenth and nineteenth centuries. More of the Florida sites that were home to over five thousand Seminoles in the nineteenth century need to be sampled to strengthen this conclusion.

Brushed pottery rim styles may have been clan or cultural group signifiers or may have had symbolic significance within the Seminole Indian societies (Weisman 1989). Archaeologists have argued that the brushed pottery at nineteenth-century Seminole Indian sites features one or few rim styles because the resident potters at each site decorated the wares in ways that expressed the local cultural or matrilineal clan affiliation. Many nineteenth-century Seminole Indian sites were "clan camps," small groups of people who lived in family homesteads (Weisman 1989). Clans may have been the main mechanism by which individuals from other clans and cultures were incorporated into Seminole and Maroon settlements. Kinship and conversion have been a historical means by which some Native American and African societies have integrated slaves, prisoners, or others with ambiguous statuses (Miers and Kopytoff 1977; Saunt 1998).

Triangular punctuate rim sherd styles observed at Pilaklikaha are one aspect that distinguishes the site from Seminole Indian sites sampled to date (Fig. 14.1; cf. Goggin 1951, Weisman 1989). It is easy enough to find mention of both brushing and triangular punctates on West African sites from Ghana to Nigeria that existed during the time of the transatlantic slave trade (DeCorse 2001b; Ogundiran 2002a). However, triangular punctation may have been created for one or many reasons. Classic archaeological studies of plantations and other sites have searched for "ethnic-identifiers," but this is too simplistic an approach (see critiques by Posnansky 1999; Singleton 1999a). Contexts of use and meaning have to be constructed from cultural beliefs and practices that African Seminoles derived from African, European, and Native American societies. The African Seminole also may have created their own meanings and uses for their material culture. An alternative interpretation is that the triangular punctates on Pilaklikaha's sherds may have been a personalized potter's mark. Future research on pottery characteristics at African Seminole and Seminole Indian sites may clarify whether older traditions or independent invention were responsible for the styles found at Pilaklikaha. Perhaps all these forces or a combination of some were at work.

African Maroon potters have produced ceramics at various archaeological sites, which raises the possibility that Pilaklikaha's brushed pottery was made by residents of African descent. A descendant from South America explained that Matawai women created pots, but few other observers have described Maroon pottery production in the Americas (see King in Price 1979, 299). S. J. Allen's (1995) work at Palmares suggests that Maroons were making their own pottery in the seventeenth century. Jamaican Maroons employed an Afro-Jamaican style similar to colonowares (Agorsah 1994a). Some of the people who became African Seminole came from South Carolina, where a number of Africans were working in pottery factories by the nineteenth century. Ferguson (1992) and others have explored the transmission of African potting through colonoware traditions. Preliminary analysis of clays near Pilaklikaha indicates that they could have been used to make pottery (Ann Cordell, personal communication, 2002). A neighboring property owner showed me a fired pot that he said was made out of clays found in his backyard. More detailed analysis of the pottery at Pilaklikaha is necessary to see whether clay choices, manufacturing techniques, tempering materials, or other factors can provide clues to the origins of pottery at this African Seminole site.

In addition to the pottery rim styles, the spatial distribution, measured in surface area, indicates another difference between Pilaklikaha and Seminole Indian sites. Pilaklikaha's surface area is over 10,000 m^2 greater than the average surface area of seven of the better-known Seminole Indian sites. Few features—postholes and thin amorphous stains—have been discovered in twenty test excavation units of various sizes and over one hundred shovel tests (30 cm^2) done at Pilaklikaha. It seems that this African Seminole site is like nineteenth-century Seminole Indian sites in regard to the paucity of features it left behind.

However, a very small percentage of the nearly 15,000 m² area of Pilaklikaha has been excavated. More of Pilaklikaha needs to be sampled so that my observations can be strengthened or revised. Also, the site, as defined by artifacts discovered to date, is just a small portion of the area that was used by past inhabitants at Pilaklikaha. Finally, a stripping technique that exposes larger subsurface areas may allow us to connect disparate and ambiguous features.

If maps, land grant records, and historical descriptions did not so strongly suggest Pilaklikaha was home to African Seminoles, we might have mistaken it for a Seminole Indian town, based on the large amount of brushed pottery. The mutually reinforcing evidence from documentary descriptions, maps, and European-made artifacts that date to the period are usually offered as proof that Maroons inhabited certain archaeological sites (Agorsah 1994a; Arrom and García Arévalo 1986; Nichols 1988; Orser 1994b). "Abraham's Old Town" (Pilaklikaha) is written on a trail that was sketched on a 1840s surveyor's map. This location correlates with Pilaklikaha's mapped position on modern USGS maps, which can be linked using section, township, and range information. The proximity of Pilaklikaha to the Dade Battlefield State Historic Site also supports my argument that the site I excavated is the famed African Seminole site. The battlefield was the location of the "Dade Massacre," an event where a whole company of U.S. troops was wiped out in an ambush by Seminole forces. Military maps of the 1830s identify both Pilaklikaha and the battlefield.

In light of what history and archaeology are uncovering in places like Pilaklikaha, other eighteenth- and nineteenth-century sites in Florida may have to be reinterpreted to account for the impact of various African, Native American, and syncretic cultural practices and social relations. Both Seminole Indian and African Seminole towns had occupants of Indian, African, and dual lines of descent. There may have also been opportunities for people to share political power and cultural beliefs, making it hard to assign a single sociocultural identity to some sites.

Conclusion

Archaeological research shows that the society at Pilaklikaha was an amalgam of Africans and African Americans who incorporated Seminole and Creek Indians. African Seminole societies like the one at Pilaklikaha survived for a number of reasons. They maintained their autonomy through self-sufficient subsistence and artisanry. They were mobile when necessary, fighting or fleeing attackers. Their multilingualism and diplomacy skills allowed them to form alliances and incorporate a wide range of backgrounds into one society. They relied on African skills in activities such as cultivation and guerrilla warfare. Many learned European languages, crops, and religion from plantation socialization. African Seminoles took advantage of Euro-American manufactures when they were accessible. The Maroons also shared or borrowed practices and material culture such as ceremonial names, pottery, and foods from their Native American peers.

Documents suggest that Seminole Indians' relationships with those who became African Seminole varied over time and space, but a primary relationship of alliance and cooperation characterized their interactions before the end of the Seminole Wars. Even after they went out west to Oklahoma, Texas, and Mexico, a portion maintained the previous ties of kinship, alliance, and friendship (Mulroy 1993; Porter 1996). In the past few years, Seminole Indian and African descendants have met in friendly and more adversarial contexts. The federal lawsuit *Sylvia Davis vs. the United States* is named for a African Seminole woman who was denied benefits from the Seminole Nation of Oklahoma (U.S. Court of Appeals for the 10th Circuit 1999). She was a member of the "Tribal Council" at the time her request for aid was rejected by the Oklahoma Seminole Nation (Staples 2002). Conversely, the Seminole Nation of Florida sent a representative to the community of African Seminole descendants who live on Andros Island in the Bahamas. Howard's (2002) ethnographic research has helped bring about an awareness of the African–Native American–Bahamian links that began during the African Seminoles' flight from the troubles created by General Andrew Jackson's invasion of north Florida in 1816. African Americans in Florida and African Seminole descendants in Oklahoma have organized annual ceremonies at the Loxahatchee Battlefield (southeast Florida) over the past few years. I visited the celebration in 2001 and listened to an Oklahoma African Seminole descendant describe the part his ancestors played in the Seminole Wars. Thus the modern African Seminole have reconnected with the land of their ancestors.

CHAPTER FIFTEEN

Scars of Brutality: Archaeology of the Maroons in the Caribbean

E. Kofi Agorsah

The portrait of freedom fighters that emerges in black history is often complex and contradictory. History is replete with scenarios in which exclusive groupings were created on the basis of ethnicity, race, social status, warfare/conquest, and occupation, and their rights and privileges were denied so that the group could be exploited for social, political, and economic purposes. Rarely would an individual volunteer to be enslaved. The people drawn into the vortex of the Atlantic trade and funneled into the sugar fields, the swampy rice lands, or the cotton, coffee, or tobacco plantations of the New World during the seventeenth and eighteenth centuries saw no future in their survival and had no alternative but to risk their lives for freedom. The plantations were filled with exhausting work, frequent punishments, and personal injustice of every kind. The process was unbelievably painful and bewildering. Unfortunately, however, their struggles to free themselves from bondage have not received the proportionate attention and analysis as other aspects of their history. Those who sought freedom by all means necessary are often referred to in the literature as runaways, Maroons, or Bush Negroes.

Lust for power and precious metals attracted Columbus and the Spaniards into the New World, where they encountered the Lucayanos living in the Bahamas (Keegan, Stokes, and Nelson 1990; the Borequinos in Puerto Rico (Alegria 1980), the Tainos in Cuba, the Dominican Republic, and Haiti (Arrom and García Arévalo 1986; Barroso 1984), and much of the eastern Caribbean inhabited by the Caribs, whose ferocity prevented European colonization of islands such as Grenada and St. Lucia. Parry and Sherlock (1956) record that there were "Negroes" on board the vessels that brought the Spanish adventurers to the New World. Some of them reportedly escaped to join the

332

local groups in the inaccessible regions. As the Spaniards forced the Indians and their slaves onto their vessels, they escaped. For example, it is reported (Price 1973) that as early as 1502 an African slave escaped from his enslaver into the interior hills of Hispaniola and that during the early sixteenth century, strongholds established by escaped African slaves already existed on one of the islands referred to as Samana, off the coast of Hispaniola. These groups eventually developed into Maroon communities who fought to retain their freedom. Maroons were certainly not the only resistance group in the Caribbean, but they were the only one whose activities have recurred throughout and, in many cases, shaped the history of the colonial period in the New World.

Maroon societies or "runaways," wherever they were, formed colonies of core communities that preserved their freedom and identity as the pioneers in freedom fighting, after escaping from bondage in the New World and becoming the symbol of a special type of nationalism. Relentlessly pursued by the colonial forces in a new, harsh, and mostly hostile environment, these people faced a protracted struggle against slavery. In fact, they were the first in the Americas, in the wake of 1492, to resist colonial domination. Recent studies demonstrate that the Maroons, against the odds of colonialism and imperialism, with all its manifestations of exploitation and oppression, forged independent communities, new cultures, and identities and, out of diversity, developed solidarity against slavery, through processes which only later took place on a larger scale in many parts of the world.

Evidence from recent archaeological studies suggests a redefinition of the heritage of runaway slave communities. As societies in their own right and now fully recognized and identified as one of the existing cultural groups or societies in the New World, they are now generally referred to as *Maroons* with an uppercase *M* similar to *Britons* with the capital *B*. Some scholars, particularly those who do not want to accept the fact that they are viable and real and who use various linguistic arguments, continue to use the lowercased *maroons*, but this must change. Second, contrary to the previous views and descriptions, which suggest that these communities derived only from African slave escapees, archaeological evidence from the Caribbean and other parts of the Americas is now revealing that the heritage of Maroon communities stemmed initially from the union forged between native American communities and Africans. The partnership-in-arms for freedom is documented among the Maroons of Jamaica, Suriname, and Brazil, the U.S. South, and Mexico. Corroborative evidence from various parts of the entire New World supports the call for the redefinition of the status and role of these "small-scale" societies in the making of New World heritage. Aspects of Maroon heritage requiring revision include the currently known picture of the distribution and composition of Maroon societies and sites, the archaeological potential of the settlements, material culture, and their implications for the historiographic concepts about Maroons and other small-scale societies in the past of the New World. It is concluded that, through the archaeological study of the material culture of the Maroons at their past settlements, it should be possible to redefine the nature, context, and mechanism of the functional adaptation of their communities and the implications of these for our understanding of New World history and heritage.

Recent archaeological, ethnographic, and historical studies have ignited interest in the reappraisal of the contributions of these "runaway" societies to the material culture of freedom-fighting societies in the New World (e.g., Agorsah 1993a; Hoogbergen 1990, Weik 1997; Weisman 1989). From their past one could find the best examples of the contributions of small-scale societies to freedom fighting and the achievement of respect for human dignity in the New World. Although the Maroons were fighting while on the move, because they lived a purely guerrilla lifestyle, yet with good knowledge, ingenuity, and hardiness to live off the rough environments in which they found themselves, some of them fought the colonial forces relentlessly to a military stalemate forcing treaties that ensured their freedom, territorial control, and coexistence. Unfortunately, some of the societies such as those in Brazil did not benefit from treaties that would have defined them territorially on a permanent basis. Nevertheless, the Maroons forged new behavior patterns and identities and developed new alliances out of the great diversity as well as carried forward cultural heritage such as the social, political, and artistic expressions characteristic of their original roots, thereby culturally defining themselves (Carter, Govinden, and Peerthum 2003; Carvalho, Doria, and Oliveira 1996; Deive 1989).

Distribution of Maroon Societies

As shown in figure 15.1, Maroon communities were widespread in New World, but particularly in eastern and western Jamaica, Suriname, and French Guiana (Price 1976). Others include the Palenqueros of Colombia, the Palmares in Brazil (Orser 1992, Orser and Funari, 1992), the Garifuna of the Atlantic coast of Central America (Belize), the Maroons of the Costa Chica region of Mexico (Price 1973), and the Cimarrones of Cuba (Barroso 1984; Pereira 1990), of Haiti and the Dominican Republic (Arrom and García Arévalo 1986), and of the Blue Hills of the central province of the Bahamas. There were also the Maroons of St. Vincent, St. Lucia, and St. Thomas, the Black Warriors of the Seminole of Texas and Florida and of Mexico in Costa Chica de Guerrero, the Moskitos of the Honduras, and the Maroons of Mount Misery of St. Kitts, Guadeloupe, Martinique, Grenada, Shekerly Mountains of Antigua, St. John, and St. Christophe. Evidence is becoming available that there were many more rebellious communities in the New World than has been known. For example, in the geographical region of British North America (that is, much of modern United States), more than fifty Maroon settlements, many of them probably very small, were known to have been established

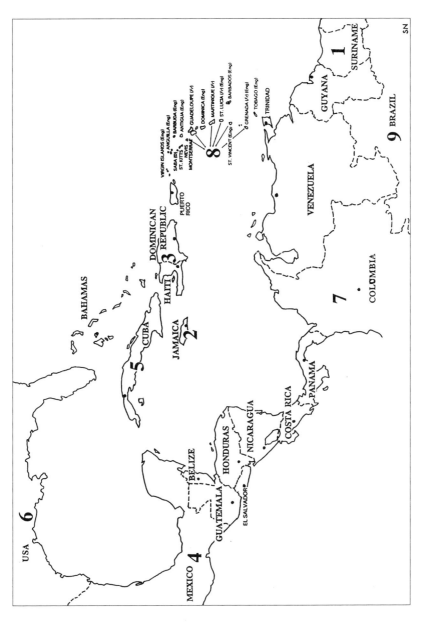

Fig. 15.1. Major Maroon societies in the New World.

between 1672 and 1864 (Aptheker 1943). Maroon societies can also be found in Canada (Halifax and Nova Scotia) and in Sierra Leone (West Africa). The very life of all these groups revolved around fighting for freedom and against oppression.

The widespread distribution of Maroon sites is directly related to the composition of Maroon communities. Archaeological and historical data on the Seminole Maroons and Maroons of Jamaica, Mexico, Suriname, and Columbia support the view that the earliest freedom fighters in the New World consisted of combined forces of Amerindian groups and Africans and not only Africans as previously has been suggested. Recent historical analysis of the survival of the Seminole Maroons (Thybony 1991; Mulroy 1993), recent archaeological evidence from northern Florida (Weisman 1989; Porter 1996; also see chap. 14, this volume), the historical sources on early Jamaican Maroons (Bryan 1971; Dallas 1803), archaeological evidence from the Blue Mountains of Jamaica (Agorsah 1993b, 1994a), and the historical and archaeological data on the formation of the *mocambos* or *quilombos* in Brazil (Bastide 1967, 1971; Carvalho, Doria, and Oliveira 1996) provide strong support to the proposition regarding the importance of the partnership between Amerindians and Africans right from the very beginning of the formation of Maroon societies. Owing to guerrilla strategies of the Maroon defense and the constant need to fight back against imperialism and slavery, the Maroons were always on the move, and many of the Maroon settlements would obviously have been short-term, leaving very little archaeological evidence. The size of Maroon sites appears to lie anywhere between 0.5 and 3.5 acres (Agorsah 1994a). This is not only because the Maroons were "marooned" in rough, inaccessible, and concealed areas but also because it was impossible for them, in a guerrilla lifestyle, to congregate in large numbers.

How much reliability one can place on the historical records on Maroon populations is a question that needs to be more seriously addressed. Who went to the Blue Mountains of Jamaica, for example, to take a census of Maroons? What were the mechanics for counting warriors who were constantly on the move? Linked to the demographic speculations about the Maroons is the erroneous notion very popular in every history book in the Caribbean about the extermination of the Amerindians before enslaved Africans were brought in. Archaeological evidence from Jamaica indicates that the Maroon stronghold of Nanny Town, perhaps established during the Spanish period, still had a few Amerindian residents as late as 1668 (Agorsah 1994a). There is no doubt that the colonial people made deliberate attempts to exterminate the native Americans and, as has been documented, worked them to death or enslaved them (Blassingame 1979). In the 1700s, the Brazilian *mocambos* and *quilombos* were clearly defined to include Africans, Indians, and "free people," and this confirms the partnership between them in the face of a common enemy—slavery, colonialism, oppression, and deprivation by European colonists.

Archaeology of Maroon Sites

Maroon sites in Suriname, Florida, and Jamaica, among others, have yet to be examined. We still have no knowledge about the formation and transformation of the material culture of these societies, although oral traditions and history have been recorded among some of the groups (for example, by Richard and Sally Price among the Saramaka of Suriname) and a lot of translations, paraphrasing, and publication of Dutch colonial records and descriptions have been made. These previous works continue to be useful sources for the archaeologist collecting data. It is erroneous to assume that there is not much more that we need to know about the Maroons.

Florida

The Seminole Maroons escaped from South Carolina and Georgia and settled in Spanish Florida. They established good relationships with the Seminole Indians. Together with their Indian allies, they were deported to Oklahoma after the Seminole wars, and some later moved to Mexico where they are referred to as *Negroes Mascogos*. A century later, some of them moved to Texas, where they were engaged to serve as a special military unit called Seminole Negro Indian scouts.

The heritage of the black warriors of the Seminole may be linked with many sites known in the Florida peninsular, particularly Boggy or Wahoo (now considered to be Kettle Island and the site of Pilaklikaha). Many other sites such as Paynes Town, Cuscowilla, Lattchaway, Talahasochte, and Oven Hill in the Gainesville area; Fort King near Ocala, Roles Town, and Spauldings Store near St. Augustine; and Powells Town, Newman's Garden, Wicki Wachee, Nicholson Grove, Fort Brooke, and Opauney's Town in the south could reveal archaeological material on African continuities among the Maroons of that area. Brent Weisman, who has conducted archaeological research in the area, concedes that available evidence is far from demonstrating the ethnicity and related features of the Maroon communities. The allotment of land made to the black warriors of the Seminole at various times around the mid-nineteenth century marked a turning point in their struggle for freedom. It was an attempt to prevent them from taking up arms against enslavement and to disorganize their alliance with the natives. Although much of the territory given out to them was barren and unsuitable for food and other productive activities, the allotments formed a basis for them to define themselves territorially, strengthen their alliances, and regroup (Porter 1996). In the end they won recognition and freedom. Studies carried out by Weisman (1989), Weik (1997), and Deagan and Landers (1999) continue to provide evidence regarding the process of the formation and material culture of these societies.

Haiti and Dominican Republic

Early Maroon sites have been identified in the Bahoruco Mountains in the parish of Vallieres on the Mulatto bluff near the river of that name. Sites with names such as Peak of Blacks, Peak of Darkness, and Crest of Congos and sites on the Tarare Mountains in the parish of Saint-Louis de Nord relate to the African elements at those Maroon sites (Laguerre 1989). In 1977, the attacks of the Maroon chiefs Canga and Gillot in the parish of Trou are referred to as devastating. Also on record are the sites of Morne Mantegre near the village of Tannerie between the Grand Reviere and Lamonde in the parish of that name, sites in the hillock of the parish of Mirebalis, in the mountains of the parish of Grande Anse, and in the district of Plymouth, this last having been named after a Jamaican escapee to Haiti in the late 1700s. Descriptions of these sites by Laguerre need to be backed up by further archaeological investigations.

Suriname

The Saramaka escaped from plantations in the seventeenth century, fought against the Dutch for more than a century, and finally signed a treaty in 1762 giving them the right to control the rainforest region of the basin of the Suriname River, while the Okanisi (Aukaners), popularly known as the Ndjuka, who signed their peace treaty in 1760, controlled the Tapanahoni and the Cottica basins. The Aluku or Boni, having come over from Suriname into French Guiana and struggled to maintain their freedom sealed by a treaty in 1860, lived across the Marowijne and Lawa rivers in French Guiana. Although volumes of literature exist on Suriname Maroons, practically nothing exists on the archaeology of their settlements simply because archaeological research has concentrated solely on Amerindian sites. Historical records have led to the identification of many sites, some of which could date to the very first Maroon settlements (Hoogbergen 1990). Oral traditions abound among the Maroons about many of these sites, some of which are sacred. These sites include Claes, Pedro, and Papa, identified as the earliest settlements of the Saramaka Maroons, who inhabit the basins of the Suriname and Saramaka rivers (Fig. 15.2). The location and identification of these sites continue to elude archaeologists, although some of the early sites such as Kumako and Tuido mentioned in the oral traditions have been located and are being excavated. The sites of Bakakum and Sentea, located farther south and in the upper reaches of the Suriname River, are also remembered in their traditions even more vividly, as they are more recent and need to be archaeologically examined.

Sites located in northeastern Suriname (Hoogbergen 1990) inhabited by the other Maroons include Kosay, Nomerimi, Kromotibo, Buku, Kofi-hay, Gado-Sabi, New Tesisi, Kwamigron, Kormantin-Kadjogron, and Makamaka,

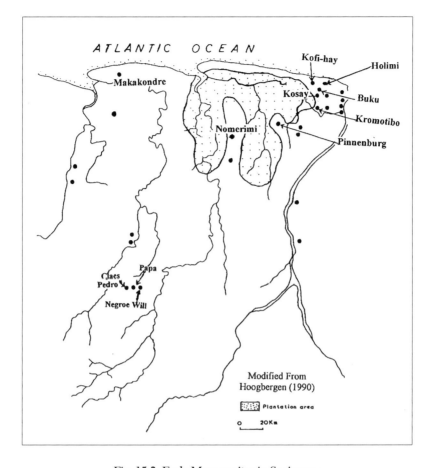

Fig. 15.2. Early Maroon sites in Suriname.

all located in the basin between the Marowijne and the Commewijne rivers. South of that area and in Ndjuka area are the sites of Animbaau, Kiyoo-Kondre, and Mama-Ndjuka. Animbaau is located on the Tapanahoni River; it was a paramount village but is now a sacred burial ground of the Ndjuka. Kiyoo-Kondre, also on the Tapanahoni River, is said to have been the place from which modern Ndjuka dispersed to found other places. Mama-Ndjuka appears to be the earliest settlement where the initial Ndjuka Maroon settlement was founded and is located on a creek of that name. Until this day, the Ndjuka go to the site to offer prayers and libations to their ancestors. Archaeological sites in Suriname could help answer many of the questions regarding settlement or spatial patterns and the functional adaptation of the Maroons to their new and mostly harsh environments, particularly at the time of their struggle against slavers. With archaeology at almost a zero point in the country, a lot of work lies ahead. The most tangible evidence that will reinforce the fight of the Maroons for the right to their lands will eventually consist of the material evidence that is being archaeologically recovered and that is already beginning to indicate the very strong ties that the Maroons have had with their lands for the past several hundred years.

Colombia

During the seventeenth century, slaves who escaped from Spanish planta-tions in Colombia established their community at Palenque de san Brasilio near the port of Cartagena. They gained recognition and permanent control of the area after several failed attempts by colonial authorities to exterminate them. The result was a peace treaty signed with the colonial government in 1717. Sites in Colombia need to be identified, surveyed, and excavated.

Mexico

Many of the slaves who went into flight in the Costa Chica area of Guer-rero and Oaxaca in Mexico had escaped from the Spanish cattle ranches and estates on the Pacific coast. Their retreat into mostly inaccessible areas made it impossible for the colonial government to subdue them. The conflict ended with the abolition of slavery in Mexico in 1829. Mexico provides a very good example of the mixed nature of earliest Maroons in the New World. For example, evidence indicates that within three years of the decline of the Aztec Empire, reference was made to African slaves who had fled to live among the Zapotee Indians (Pereira 1994). By 1576, blacks and mulattoes were well established in a place called "Canada de Negros" and were "terrorizing" the Spaniards' newly established settlements in Mexico.

Jamaica

Since 1990, the Maroon Heritage Research Project of the University of the West Indies has conducted expeditions to Maroon sites or settlements in Jamaica (Fig. 15.3). Sites excavated include Nanny Town in the Blue Moun-tains (1990–93), Accomong Old Town in St. Elizabeth (1992), and the Sea-man's Valley (1994, 1995). Maroons of Jamaica are well known because of their long struggle with the British colonial authorities. One of the areas settled by the earliest Maroons was the Guanaboa Vale in the Juan de Bolas hilly areas located in the modern parish of St. Catherine between the towns of Linstead and Chapelton and including the Ginger Ridge, Pindars, and Marlie Hill areas,

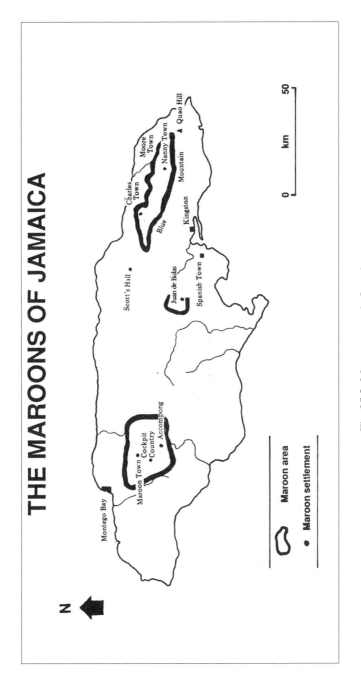

Fig. 15.3. Maroon areas in Jamaica.

which are dominated by the Rock River drainage system. Another settlement referred to as Los Vermmajales in the Juan de Bolas mountain area has also been described (Campbell 1997).

Located south of Cave Valley near the border of Clarendon and St. Ann in a grassland area lying between the Macho Mountains and the modern town of Porus was another early Maroon settlement. Its exact location is not known, but it is conjectured that there may have been several temporary settlements in the area. Maroon settlements belonging to the Spanish period are less known probably because they may not have been well established by the time the English took over the island. Another group resettled in the Cockpit country in the vicinity of modern Accompong in St. Elizabeth at Maroon Town in Trelawny. Accompong and its surroundings controlled the groups living in adjoining modern St. Elizabeth, St. James, and Clarendon parishes. The maps of Jamaica are useful in identifying territories occupied by the various Maroon groups in the seventeenth, eighteenth, and nineteenth centuries, as well as their dwelling sites, guerrilla war camps, hideouts, cemeteries, battlegrounds, military tracts, and fortifications. Many maps indicate the changing nature of the settlements over time. By 1700, several Maroon settlements of varying sizes and composition had been established. Some were fishing and hunting villages, and there was a particular one near Quoa's Town that had seventy-four huts. Another fairly large settlement, Men's Town, was described as being located on the way "toward Nanny Town with a dancing place." It is not clear what exactly was the function of the dancing place mentioned in the record, but it suggests a place for some kind of community activity. English reports observe that the main town (Nanny Town?) was located on the ridge of the Blue Mountains with two smaller towns in the same area but fairly far apart. Also reported is a "large cave with two great troughs to hold water" that was an important Maroon hideout. Guy's Town is mentioned as a refuge for Nanny Town Maroons after the British forces had taken control of the Nanny Town site in 1734. In a confession to the English authorities, one Seyrus is reported to have mentioned "Hubby's," a "Negro town," and settlements in the Carrion Crow Hill. The locations of these sites are yet to be confirmed.

As one of the conditions of the peace treaties signed between the British and the Maroons, grants of land as well as the survey of land occupied by Maroon groups were made. Consequently, Maroon settlements became more and more clearly defined spatially. A grant in 1741 of a square parcel of land situated on the Negro River, an eastern arm of the Rio Grande in eastern Jamaica, was awarded to Nanny, described as "a great Negro woman," and her followers in the parish of Portland. This land grant refers to the location of New Nanny Town, which is modern Moore Town in the parish of Portland. Other Maroon settlements that resulted from land grants include Bath, a splinter town to the south of Nanny Town surveyed and documented in the 1760s; Scott's Hall, with the Wag Water River serving as the main boundary in that area; Crawford Town, relocated and documented in 1754; and Charles Town, which was a new settlement of Crawford Town several kilometers from the latter located on the Buff Bay River close to the south shore. In western Jamaica, the Maroon lands, like those of the east, became more clearly defined. Accompong was granted some 1,500 acres of land, 1,000 of which was for Accompong itself. Trelawny Town (Dallas 1803) was another settlement in the west. The examples noted above indicate that only vague information exists about early Maroon sites. It appears as if the British did not know about several sites, especially in the mountainous areas where accessibility was problematic for their forces. Names such as Parade, Gun Hill, Watch Hill, Lookout Point, Kindah, Bathing Place, Pette River Bottom, Gun Barrel, and Killdead are mentioned in Maroon oral traditions (Agorsah 1990, 1991; Bilby 1994; Harris 1994), and some of these sites have been located. In Scott's Hall area of Jamaica is a site referred to as Konkonsa Ceitful—*Ceitful* being an acronym for "deceitful" and *Konkonsa* being an Akan word for "liar." According to oral traditions, Maroons accused of various crimes, especially for circulating false information, were tried at that spot in Scott's Hall.

West of the island is the Cockpit country (see Fig. 15.3) with a tropical karst terrain and unique vegetation. This is one of the main Maroon areas in Jamaica. Archaeological sites in the neighborhood of Accompong include Kindah, interpreted to mean "We are a family." Kindah is northeast of modern Accompong and the venue for the annual celebrations of the 1739 treaty involving several Maroon rituals. Also present at Old Accompong Town are the burial sites of Kojo, the Maroon leader at the time, and other leaders of the Maroon community. Another archaeological site is the Peace Cave site located almost on the eastern border of the Accompong Maroon lands. Strategically located closest to the opponent is a military camp situated in the then Aberdeen Plantation to the east. The Peace Cave is also often referred to as "Ambush" and was used as a hideout. The last battleground of the British-Maroon wars, before the treaty of 1739, took place in the valley referred to as Pette River Bottom. Within this area is located what is called Guthrie's Defile, an important point of access to Maroon lands. The location of the present elementary school at Accompong marks the location of the site currently known as Parade but which traditions refer to as an important "lookout point" of the Maroons. Other sites to the north and west of Accompong include Gun Hill, Trelawny Town, Flagstaff, and Vaughsfield, where structural features such as burials and house foundations can be observed.

Archaeological Excavations at Maroon Sites in Jamaica

It is apt at this point to examine three Maroon sites excavated in Jamaica and the nature of the archaeological finds from the sites.

Old Accompong Town

Accompong has been known as one of the main areas of the encounter between the Maroons and the British forces (Cawley and Agorsah 1995; Eyre 1980), and it remained a powerful Maroon stronghold until they signed treaties. The Accompong settlement was surveyed and mapped in 1991, and the boundaries of the Old Town were determined. The excavation zone near the burial ground of Kojo was selected in cooperation with the colonel at the time, as we were to be careful not to interfere with the actual burial ground.

Finds recovered from Accompong include local earthenware, a bead (probably imported), a copper bracelet, fragments of green glass bottles, a few musket balls, and a cowry shell. Although not an extensive excavation, the finds were of great significance. No specific period has been assigned to the excavated material, but many of the artifacts point to the late seventeenth/early eighteenth century, although occupation of the area could have been much earlier.

Nanny Town and Other Blue Mountain Sites

Maroon sites identified in eastern Jamaica include Nanny Town, Pumpkin Hill, Mammee Hill, Watch Hill, Dinner Time, Marshall's Hall, Gun Barrel, and Brownsfield. These sites are located in and around Windsor, Seaman's Valley, Ginger House, and Comfort Castle in and around the Blue Mountains. The environment is generally fragmented because of its mountainous nature and the deep gullies of the Rio Grande, Negro, and Dry rivers, which cut through the region. The Blue Mountain region has been particularly suitable as settlements for the Maroons. Documentary sources indicate that in 1601 the Spanish government sent troops to flush out some "Arawak" escapees who had taken to the Blue Mountains (Bryan 1971). This confirms the speculation that some of the Indian groups who escaped from the Spaniards' slavery had built settlements in the Blue Mountains before the African Maroons. This also supports the view that Maroons were not all of African origin.

The Nanny Town site is strategically located within the loop of the Stony River, and the main features of the site include stone structures considered to be military fortifications. These structures are rectangular piles of dry stones, large and small. A large block of stone located near one of these fortifications has an engraving with a message that the settlement was taken and briefly controlled by the British forces in 1734 (Agorsah 1992a, 1992b; Bonner 1974; Teulon 1967).

The excavations covered approximately 40 percent of the total site. The stratigraphy, particularly the texture and humus content of the soils, vary from area to area, depicting differential site utilization, which could be related to different periods or to the same period but for different activities. Local ceramics (earthenware) became more common as the excavation moved away from the west toward the east and southeastward of the site. At the entrance of one of the fortifications was what appears to have been the location of a flag post, perhaps erected by the British. Much of the local earthenware was obtained from this fortification at levels that indicate the fortification was built over a previous living floor that would have been the Maroon level. This level was dated by a coin to approximately 1668.

Artifacts recovered from this site (First Fortification) of Nanny Town (see Agorsah 2001) include local earthenware and terracotta figurines, imported ceramics such as a Belarmine jar, tin glaze, and delftware, fragments of wine, alcoholic, and medicine bottles, metal implements and fragments of gun barrels, musket balls of various sizes and weights, nails, lead, knives, spearheads, door hinges, crockery, red clay and kaolin (white clay) smoking pipe stems and bowls, grinding stones and other stone implements, fragments of worked and unworked flint, glass and stone beads, and buttons. Spanish coins, popularly known as "pieces of eight," one of which dates to 1668, define the upper limits of the earliest occupation phase at the Nanny Town site. That date was only thirteen years after the British occupation of the site and indicates that some slaves who had escaped from Spanish domination had already set up settlements in the heart of the Blue Mountains a few years after the British left the area. At the second stone structure, excavated in 1993, two occupation levels were observed. The upper occupation level appears to have a combination of two cultural features—the Maroon material culture (characterized by poorly fired ceramics) and the European materials (mainly British military equipment). The lower level consisted of the terracotta figurines and the associated thin local and highly fired earthenware, which, from all indications and comparisons, appear to be typical Amerindian occupation level (Fig. 15.4).

The presence of smoking pipes at the site is significant because of their potential importance for establishing a chronological framework for the site. Although making up a small percentage of the total artifact assemblage, the pipes provide an insight into the historic occupations at the site. A total of 363 pipe fragments were recovered, with most coming from the surface and uppermost levels of the excavation. All but two of the pipes are European imports made from white clay. The majority (224 fragments) are represented by pieces of pipe stems. None of these fragments have maker's marks or any traces of decoration. Pipe stems may, however, be dated through measurement of the stem bore diameters. Studies pioneered by I. C. Harrington have demonstrated that the bore diameters of British pipes decreased in a regular way between 1620 and 1800 (Binford 1978; Harrington 1978; Noel Hume 1964). By calculating the relative proportions of the bore diameters found within a particular site, feature, or level, the approximate age of the deposits can be inferred. The stem bores measured were in increments of 4/64 to 9/64 of an inch using standard drill bits. Notably, all of the median dates are after the 1734 fall of the Maroon stronghold. This perhaps suggests an association with the British military force rather than the Maroons. Stem bores do not, however, provide

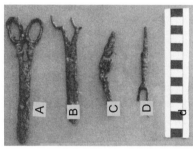

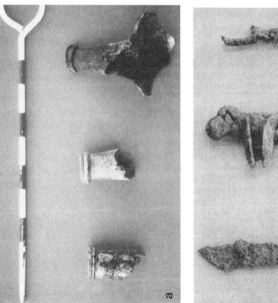

Fig. 15.4. Finds from Nanny Town, Jamaica.

absolute chronologies, especially when the number of specimens is relatively small. Harrington (1978) indicates that 5/64-in. bores (217 stems, or 88.9 percent of the Nanny Town sample) were most common between 1710 and 1750, dates that include much of the Maroon occupation of the site. Depending on the archaeological context, the pipes could be consistent with either the Maroon or British Military occupations. One might expect the median dates to be rather earlier if, in fact, Maroon occupation began in the seventeenth century or much before 1720, but an association with the Maroons cannot be ruled out.

One hundred nineteen pipe bowl fragments were also recovered. The most common form is a simple bowl without a foot or spur at the base. These are comparable to the British pipes produced throughout most of the eighteenth century. But the majority of the bowls are really too fragmentary for one to be certain of their exact shape. Some appear to suggest nineteenth-century forms in which the bowls are more perpendicular to the stem. The clearest example of the latter is from the general surface collection area designated as Area 4 of the site. There is also the single pipe, which seems to have traces of an impressed decoration, though these are so faint and fragmentary that no pattern can be identified.

Some of the bowl fragments possess feet, and their form is consistent with an early-eighteenth-century occupation. In the absence of manufacturer's marks, however, they cannot be definitely associated with either the Maroon or British occupation. A single bowl recovered from Level I in unit R-5-6 at the site would seem to predate the British occupation. This is of interest as it was found within the stone structure (structure B) considered to be a military fortification. The broad foot of this pipe is more characteristic of the seventeenth-century than the eighteenth-century British pipes. The pipe is, unfortunately, too fragmentary for us to really get an idea of the entire form. It could be said, however, that it was certainly "old-fashioned" by 1734. Two pipe fragments are of particular interest because they are clearly non-European. Distinctive in form, decoration, and paste, these two pieces appear to represent products of two manufacturers. The source of these pipes was likely to have been in Jamaica, perhaps Kingston, but the origins and output of Jamaican pipe manufactures are poorly known. As is the case with the "old-fashioned" pipe, both of these fragments were recovered from Level I of unit R-5-6, within the stone structure B. This is significant, as it would seem to confirm a clearly pre-British component at the site.

Although the pipes from Nanny Town can help to make some speculations about the period of occupation, one cannot rely solely on one group of artifacts. The Nanny Town site has been recognized as having seen three phases of occupation (Agorsah 1992b, 1993b, 1994a), the first of which appears to predate the Maroon presence in the area, with its mixture of local ceramics, stone artifacts, and shell material. In some areas, this phase is represented by artifacts that have been referred to as pre-Maroon or Amerindian. I have suggested that the makers of the artifacts of this phase, particularly the clay figurines and vessels, might be the "Arawak" group of Native Americans (Agorsah 1994a). No date can be assigned to the Amerindian phase at this time, although age between 1,500 and 2,000 BP years is not unlikely.

The second phase at the Nanny Town site is the Maroon occupation. It is represented by ceramics (mostly local), grinding stones, and a considerable amount of charcoal which, if dated, should facilitate our understanding relationships among the three phases. Much of the charcoal came from levels that contain plenty of ash layers on surfaces that appear to have been trampled upon or beaten, though not very hard. The red clay pipe bowls, gunflint, fragments of gun barrel, musket balls, iron nails, and green and clear glass bottles are finds from the Maroon phase. Many of the artifacts from the Maroon phase are difficult to separate from the third phase. More refined dates will be needed to determine if there was any overlap between the first and second and the second and third phases. Assessment of possible Maroon-Amerindian connections should consider documentary evidence of "maroonage" in the Blue Mountains as far back as the early sixteenth century (Bryan 1971), meaning that a range of dates between 1500 and 1734 for the second phase will not be an exaggeration.

The archaeological evidence seems to suggest that Nanny Town had been occupied for a fairly long time and that its occupation could date to periods before colonial contact (Agorsah 1993b, 1995). The dates obtained from analysis of the pipes cover a very short range, centered on the 1740s. But one piece of evidence that appears to link the first two occupation phases at the site are coins (Spanish pieces of eight), one of which dates the lower levels of the Maroon phase to 1668, indicating, at least, that some kind of contact existed between that location and the Spanish presence in the island.

The third phase represents the period of Maroon encounter with British forces at the site. It includes stone fortification as well as a stone with inscriptions (Agorsah 1994a). The main finds of this phase include fragments of imported smoking pipes (described above), fragments of gun barrel, musket balls, buttons, pharmaceutical bottles, nails, imported ceramic bowls, plates, and cups, buckles, and a large quantity of green glass bottle fragments. A few postholes are associated with this phase at the site. One of them appears to represent the location of a flag post, possibly erected by the British forces. This hole, approximately 1.5 meters deep from the surface, was lined with stones and located against the back wall of the stone structure. As indicated earlier, many of the smoking pipes were associated with the stone structures, suggesting its relationship to the British forces, but the British may have come to use a structure that already existed at the time of their capture of the site. The early pipes associated with the stone structures at Nanny Town also suggest that structures could have been built by the Maroons as claimed in the Maroon oral traditions. Many of the pipes apparently were associated with this structure in level I and on the surface. The stone structures may also have been used by the Maroons after the British left Nanny

Town in 1735. As has been remarked above, these data appear to be consistent with either the Maroon phase or the phase of the British military occupations of the site, both of which appear to have had access to European imported material.

Seaman's Valley Site

Seaman's Valley (Fig. 15.5), located about 3 km north of Moore Town (New Nanny Town), is a battleground where the Maroons defeated the colonial forces. The archaeological site spans both sides of the modern main road, but much more the east side of it, approximately 3 km north of Moore Town. The entire length of a stone-lined aqueduct—approximately 124.5 m and the main feature of Area 5 of the site—was excavated (for details, see Agorsah 1994b; Agorsah and Bandara 1995). The thickness of the stone walls at both sides of the aqueduct was approximately 52 cm. The duct itself is only 41 cm wide. It appears that the course of the aqueduct was changed from a higher to a lower ground, probably indicating a change in the level of the river or the source of the water supply. Waterwheel housing was also excavated, but no parts of the waterwheel, the drive mechanism, the gears, the drive shaft, bucket paddles, or other major structural features were found. Although the waterwheel housing appeared to be of a sturdy construction, it does not appear to contain any metal rods or metal enforcement. Other features and finds include building foundations, a circular feature (possibly a fireplace), locally made and imported ceramics, roofing slates, fragments of bricks, glasses, bottles, metal scraps and implements, fragments of a gun barrel, musket balls of various sizes and weights, nails, and fragments of metal objects such as knife and cast-iron pot (three-legged), kaolin (white clay) smoking pipe bowls and stem, glass and stone beads, and metal buttons. Several graves were identified but were left untouched.

The cache of arms, ammunition, and pharmaceutical and possibly some of the weapons abandoned or buried in the wake of the panic and flight of the colonial forces from the Maroons in the encounter, remain hidden somewhere in the Seaman's Valley area. Burial grounds, possibly of the defeated colonial soldiers, locally (i.e., Maroon) manufactured arms and other fighting equipment, as well as the main combat point in the encounter, have not yet been uncovered. But it was the impact of the Maroon successes at Seaman's Valley in 1733 on the morale and aspirations of the colonial forces that accounted for the colonial army's two-pronged attack on the main Maroon stronghold, Nanny Town, in 1734. This demonstrates why the events related to the site must be more fully investigated. Several questions about Seaman's Valley remain unanswered. Rather, new questions are being raised. Although the trend of the research appears promising, subsequent field seasons in the area would have to contend not only with the elusive data being sought but

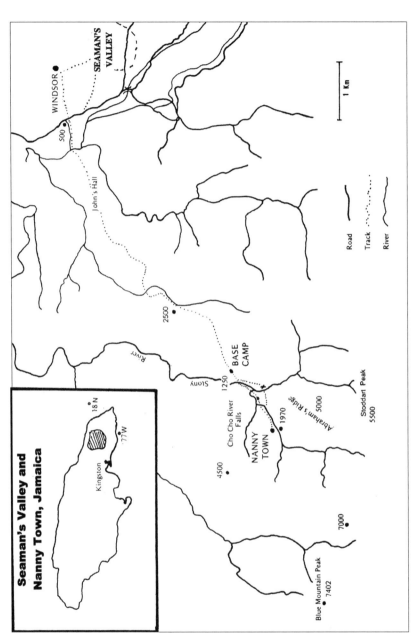

Fig. 15.5. Seaman's Valley and Nanny Town, Jamaica.

also with other challenging but surmountable situations. Although the misfortune met by the colonial forces at the hand of the Maroons in the early 1730s is documented (Hart 1985, 66–68), it was the archaeological excavation at this site that uncovered some of the details of this incident and provided the necessary data for a reenactment of the memorable events at Seaman's Valley.

Maroon Heritage Studies

Maroon historical and archaeological studies (e.g., Agorsah 1994a; Handler 1982; Hoogbergen 1990; Weik 1997; Weisman 1989) are beginning to open up new avenues that should provide the material context for explaining the whole process of cultural formation and adaptation of the groups who came from several parts of the world and divided by great differences in language and cultures. Whereas considerable analyses have been conducted on historical and ethnographic evidence (Campbell 1997; Craton 1982; Price 1976), the archaeological evidence has received little or no attention. The distribution of Maroon sites in Jamaica provide us with evidence supporting the view that the Maroons were both African and Amerindian; that many of the early Maroon sites such as Nanny Town may have been sites strategically located in inaccessible areas by the natives of the island, meaning that the Maroon sites have greater antiquity than had been known; and that the successes of the Maroons depended considerably on the maintenance of a network of footpaths and trails that enabled them to live as guerrillas and maintain security. However, several questions such as the formation and transformation processes that created Maroon settlements, their size as well as spatial and decay patterns, family networks, and many other aspects of cultural traditions remain unknown. As the archaeological study extends to the study of Maroon sites elsewhere, it will be possible to fill in some of these gaps. Results from Maroon archaeological sites in Jamaica clearly indicate the potential that sites in other parts of the New World hold for a better understanding of the response of these early freedom fighters to all the various transformations and processes occurring during the period of struggle against slavery and colonialism.

Maroonage and the Demise of Colonies

Between 1783 and 1843, parts of the British and Spanish North American empire collapsed one by one, many of them principally as a result of the pressure from freedom-fighting groups as well as the internal and external stirs caused by those pressures. Hispaniola became independent from France and Spain between 1791 and 1804. Central and South America were separated from metropolitan Spain as a result of wars of independence between 1819 and 1830. The military expedition undertaken by the Portuguese against the *mocambo* of Buraco de Tutu near Itapoa northeast of the city of Salvador in Brazil in 1763 generated greater cooperation among the free population, the slaves, and the Maroons. Successfully fought by the leaders of Maroons, creole, and blacks in the New World, these wars paved the way for the rise of a string of republics from Mexico to Argentina and ended over three hundred years of Spanish rule on the mainland of the Americas. In the Caribbean by 1830, for example, only the West Indian islands, Honduras (Belize) and the Guianas were still in the hands of their European colonizers. Meanwhile, the Portuguese, Dutch, and English were losing their hold on territories in South America, particularly in Suriname, Brazil, and Colombia as maroonage intensified in those areas, often also playing the colonial powers against each other as happened in Suriname. Names of known leaders of these freedom fighters such as Bayano of Panama, Yanga of Mexico, Ganga-Zumba of Brazil, Benkos Bioho of Colombia, Nanny, Kojo, and Paul Boggle of Jamaica and also Boni of Suriname, John Horse also known as Caballo or Gopher John of the southern United States and Mexico stirred terror in the hearts of the imperialists. These were the pioneer freedom fighters in the Americas.

The last straw took place in the 1930s. Owing to the long years of colonial neglect, the Depression, and political restrictions on the colonial governments, there were serious outbursts of strikes and rioting in Mexico in 1934 led by Antonias Soberanis; strikes riots in Jamaica in 1935 led by Alexander Bustamante; a strike in St. Kitts in 1935; rioting in St. Vincent in the same year; a strike and demonstrations in Trinidad in 1937 under the leadership of Uriah Butler, strikes in British Guiana in 1935–39, riots in Barbados in 1937, and strikes in St. Lucia. That era coincides with Marcus Garvey and the emergence of Rastafari as a social and religious movement. All the accompanying violence constituted a manifestation of rising nationalist feeling and active descendant of the black and other dispossessed people who continued to be oppressed. Many later West Indian leaders, from Franz Fanon to the Rastafarian, strongly drew on the legacy of Garvey and the United Negro Improvement Associations (UNIA), which reportedly commanded twenty million people worldwide. Clearly, the main goals of resistance in black history were achievement of freedom. Maroonage pioneered and dictated the course of colonial policies and resistance against slavery. Maroonage was a reaction that demonstrated the complexities and inversions inherent in the dialectic of the powerful and the dispossessed. Such diagnostics can inform how the politically and socially disadvantaged defined power, justice, and the cultural system in which they lived.

Peace treaties, abolition of slavery, and many other measures appeared to have spelled the end of the suffering of Maroons and other disadvantaged communities. Political oppression, torture, and its attendant undignified treatment had ceased, but many Maroons and their descendants remained dispossessed, some on their own land and many in new, harsh environments and without any resources for rehabilitating themselves (Beckles 1986; Beckles and Shepherd 1992). The Maroons of Jamaica, Mexico, Suriname, and the Black Warriors of the Seminole signed treaties with colonists and managed to cling to the territories defined in those treaties. The most important issue after the freedom fighters had won their freedom through various means, especially by peace treaties, was getting settled. Palmares by all standards, reports, and observations was a large conglomeration of runaway settlements. Not only was it powerful, but it maintained a considerable amount of authority and influence in Brazilian history since the seventeenth century or possibly earlier (see chap. 16). Although its general area of occupation is historically documented, its demise left their inhabitants landless and almost absolutely dispossessed. Unlike Jamaica, Suriname, and other runaway groups who enforced designated territories in the treaties that they signed with the colonists, Palmares and other *quilombos* of Brazil, despite their greatness, had no such lands and property to hold on to, nor were there any plans put in place for a future consideration. However, the people of *quilombos*, hereafter referred to as Maroons, managed to maintain their identity and history through new cultural forms that they developed during and after their long struggle and brought into the history and culture of Brazil, a record of a most respectable achievement as a highly revered group of pioneer freedom fighters of the Americas.

Conclusion: Searching for Africa in the Caribbean Diaspora

The complexity and expanding geographical coverage of the archaeological record that is emerging in the Caribbean (Singleton 1985; Singleton and Bograd 1995; Weik 1997) calls for improved interpretations and comparative analyses that go beyond the immediate borders of the cultural region, for as will be observed in this chapter, the archaeological and historical patterns of cultural transformation in the Caribbean appear to have been mosaic in character. The fact that the Caribbean accommodates one of the most racially mixed groupings in the world has been addressed in some detail (Parry and Sherlock 1956). Archaeological evidence from the Caribbean and the neighboring areas (Kozlowski 1974; Rouse and Allaire 1978) support the view that the Caribbean has featured as a dominant factor in the development of the diversity and intercultural relationships that we observe in much of the New World, particularly in the general Central American archaeological region since prehistoric times (Agorsah 1993b).

Some of the more recent attempts to reaffirm Africa's vital enduring cultural contributions to the New World and the global community have included reconstruction of possible pre-Colombian African–New World contacts (Sertima 1976), identification of African continuities in the diaspora through artifact pattern analyses (Armstrong 1990a), demographic evidence and racial types or ethnicity and bio-archaeological studies (Blakey 1995), African technological transfer (Goucher, this volume), spatial and settlement pattern studies (Higman 1986), migrations (Kozlowski 1974; Rouse and Allaire 1978), and archaeology of Maroon heritage (Agorsah 1993a, 1994a; Cawley and Agorsah 1995).

The emphasis on the Maroons in this chapter is only an illustration of the significance of one of the many areas that can be explored in the African Diaspora to widen our understanding of the extended arms of African culture in the Americas. Emerging themes arising from all these include ethnic identity; settlement patterns and spatial behavior; cultural formation, retention, continuities, and transformations; and functional adaptation of Africans in the Caribbean. Crucial questions to be considered include how archaeological research on both sides of the Atlantic can enhance our understanding of the African heritage in the Caribbean. Consideration of some of these issues should possibly raise several other issues and generate discussions that should help place archaeological study of the African heritage in the Caribbean Diaspora and indeed the entire Diaspora in its rightful place.

Research in the diaspora, particularly the Caribbean, is pointing to the need to identify historiographic themes in the cultural history of the Diaspora with African continuities (Posnansky 1984). This goal will help bring under the lens of archaeological research the search for roots or origins of African institutions and practices in the diaspora, cultural identity and continuity, as well as the heroic roles played by small-scale societies such as the Maroons whose history constitutes a major thread that weaves through the entire historical period of the New World (Agorsah 1994a).

Acknowledgments

Support for the Maroon Heritage Research Project came from the University of the West Indies, particularly the Department of History, Mona, Jamaica National Heritage Trust, Center for Field Research and Earthwatch, USA, the Wenner-Gren Foundation for Anthropological Research, National Geographic Society, USA, the Department of Black Studies and the Office of Research and Sponsored Projects, Portland State University, the chiefs and people of the Maroon communities of Jamaica and Suriname, the Suriname National Museum, Archaeological Society of Jamaica, and the Jamaica Defense Force. I wish to thank them and all Maroon Heritage Research Project volunteers as well.

CHAPTER SIXTEEN

The Archaeological Study of the African Diaspora in Brazil

Pedro P. Funari

The Greek origins of the term *diaspora* refer to the "dispersion" of people, not necessarily forced to disperse, but usually scattered against their will. This is precisely the meaning associated with the transfer of millions of Africans to the New World. Brazil has the largest number of people of African descent outside Africa, and archaeology has a special role in the recovery of the African heritage in the Diaspora through the study of material culture, the only direct evidence we can count on to search for African mores. In the period between the sixteenth and nineteenth centuries, most Brazilians were Africans. Today some 40 million Brazilians are of Indian descent, another 40 million are of African descent, and 80 million are descended from other nationalities (Portuguese, Arab, Jewish, Italian, Japanese, and Korean, among others).

In this chapter, I address some issues relating to African ethnicity in Brazil and the role of archaeology through a case study, Palmares, the seventeenth-century rebel polity. I first deal with the mixed features of Brazilian society, then show how archaeological theory and praxis are linked to politics. Next, I turn my attention to Palmares and other African Diaspora archaeological studies in order to highlight the development of aspects of African identity in Brazil. The chapter ends with an assessment of the tools for the archaeology of African Brazilians.

Mixed Features of Brazilian Society

The two main features of Brazilian society are the huge social inequalities and the seclusion of the so-called non-Europeans from the institutional

355

public spheres. These conditions have existed since the inception of colonization and have resulted from the racial hierarchies of the colonial social system
(Da Matta, 1991, 399) and, as a consequence, of the dominance of patronage.
Considering the cultural diversity within the country, at least in the first four
centuries, the historian Luís Carlos Soares (1991, 101) went so far as to deny
the existence of a single structure within the area now known as the "Brazilian
territory." He proposed instead that "there existed not one but many precapi-
talist economic and social formations within the area that is today Brazil."
Accepting the main contention that there were huge differences of social
organization within the Portuguese colony, it is also clear that patronage was
ubiquitous and pervasive.

Brazil has one of the most uneven income distributions in the world, and as a
result only some 20 million inhabitants can be considered ordinary consumers,
whereas 130 million survive by consuming very basic products, like staple food
and cheap clothing. As Brazil has developed a strong industry, producing almost
everything from cars to aircrafts, it is clear that in the past centuries, when only
raw materials were produced (Brazil wood, sugar, gold, coffee), social imbal-
ances were at least as important as today. The culture of the elite has always
been integrally Western (Hale 1989, 225), and unfortunately there is no irony in
the popular saying that "Brazilian intellectuals like to discuss Brazilian affairs on
the banks of the Thames, Hudson or Seine rivers."

Most of the ordinary excluded majority is considered by the elite as
"non-European" (cf. Skidmore, 1994, 13). There should be no need to stress
that the term *subordinate races*, notably when referring to blacks, mulattoes,
Indians, and their mixed results, does not refer to *actual* biological differences
but does constitute an ideological concept (Wade, 1993, 32). The elite is white
and European by definition, and there is thus no need to prove ethnic purity.
David Babson (1990, 22) links racism in the modern society in general and the
masking of economic and social gain. There has been, however, a false theory, as warned by M. Harris (1972, 218–19), that in Brazil there was a lack of
prejudice against dark-skinned people. It is true that there is no racial segregation as such, but ordinary people are labeled as dark-skinned and the elite as
white, and although it is not impossible to overcome the subtle line dividing the
two groups, it is difficult. The subtlety is only skin deep, however, as Fernando
Henrique Cardoso reminds us: "The fact that blacks were emancipated did not
of course change their slave mind and habits, which were incompatible with free
wage labor in industry" (Cardoso, 1969, 196–97). As summed up by Thomas
E. Skidmore (1993, 375), "Brazil's 'racial democracy' does not exist," and in a
recent review of major studies in Brazilian history, Skidmore (2000, 572) notes
that such studies "reach the kitchens or the servant's quarters."

Cláudio Bojunga (1978, 177) emphasized that even though more than
80 percent of the population at Bahia State was nonwhite, the university there
continued to be "a white institution." Although there is no legal injunction
against people of African descent, the exclusion of this large majority from the

mainstream society at Bahia, as elsewhere in the country, is institutional and systemic: poor people are uneducated and usually do not succeed in going to universities. Different authors refer to this appalling situation as a direct result of slavery (Morner 1992, 20) and as a consequence of its disenfranchising character (Graham 1979, 40), its subordination of ordinary people, and the acculturation and "whitening" of non-elite cultures (Fernandes 1969, 282). The black scholar Eduardo de Oliveira e Oliveira (1984, 70) accepted the validity of the famous dictum by Fernando de Azevedo that "culture in Brazil is the elite and we, the blacks, in terms of both race and class, we do not belong to the elite." All other things being equal, skin color matters. While black cultural identity has become widely accepted and even celebrated in the form of music, dance, food, and sometimes religion, there is no equality (Lovell, 1999, 414). The idea that Brazil is a color-blind society masks everyday racism and has helped to internalize racism in Brazil (Goldstein 1999, 573).

Archaeological Theory and Politics

It is in the context of a divided society that we must consider the role of archaeological theory in Brazil. Recently Robert Paynter (1990, 59–60) reminds us that "history is written by the winners [but] in studying Afro-American sites, archaeologists should seek a better understanding of the realm of racism and resistance to it." Archaeology, however, does not necessarily challenge current prejudices, and there is still a strong tradition in Brazil to consider archaeology as a handmaiden to history, with no interpretive role whatsoever: "far from being a pursuit in itself" (Meneses 1965, 22). Archaeological theory is thus particularly important if we aim at empowering subordinate groups, as proposed by Ian Hodder (1991, 10), and archaeologists must work closer with related humanities disciplines, such as history, anthropology, and semiotics to develop a more international perspective placing interpretation in a wider context (D'Agostino 1995, 104).

We face two problems that can be addressed with theory: ethnicity in the material culture and the political implications of our interpretive efforts. Ethnicity in the material record is a complex issue in itself, and noting the politics involved in the recovery and interpretation of material record, Michael Blakey (1990, 39) suggested that "American archaeologists exhibit an ethnic bias that 'whitens' national heritage and identity." In this way, it is impossible to dissociate ethnicity and archaeological interpretations from present social and political contexts (Wood & Powell, 1993, 407). Archaeology is not a neutral source–discipline, as dreamed by Leo Klein (1993, 729). Since theory mediates data and vice versa (Shanks & Tilley, 1987, 1), we must study the connection between the present and the past as a source of power within society (Wilk 1985, 319).

Personal views and class interests, as well as the elite social milieu, are at the root of interpretation (Trigger 1989, 777–78), which is inevitably subjective

(Ucko 1989, xii). Traditionally, "archaeological work and interpretation has always reflected and contributed to the class relations of power and domination" (Handsman and Leone 1989, 134). However, I do agree with Brian Durrans (1989, 67) when he proposes that "the most useful way in which archaeologists can contribute to a wider political movement is by exploring the ideological bias of archaeology, thereby encouraging people to recognize and therefore transcend ideology in their own lives." It is thus symptomatic that Martin Bernal (1990, 128) was able to link Renfrew's *archaeological interpretation* and his activities for the British Conservative Party, and we must acknowledge that usually 'objective' interpretations of the archaeological record are in reality ideologically charged (Nassaney 1989, 76). Hence, given the fact that a positivistic outlook is related to the political aspirations of the U.S. establishment (Rowlands 1982, 159), it is not surprising that positivist archaeologists in Brazil were in close contact with military and intelligence authorities during the dictatorship era (1964–85) in the heyday of the cold war.

It is in this context of politics of power and hegemony that the study of black (African) material culture—or rather ordinary, mixed-race, nonlearned expressions—must be considered. This consideration must be cognizant of two parallel situations: that "all survivals in colonial Brazil of African traditions in dance, song, music, religion, or social mores were persecuted" (Russel-Wood 1974, 573) and that "Africans did not abandon or lose their cultures during enslavement…[yet] the cultures they forged in the New World were not exact duplications of those in Africa" (Orser 1994a, 34).

Since the inception of the European colonization in the sixteenth century, Brazil has been characterized by the mixture of nationalities. A plethora of indigenous peoples mixed early on with the Portuguese, whose ethnic background was varied, comprising Iberians, Celts, Germans, Phoenicians, Jews, and Moors, originally from North Africa. Africans were brought as chattel slaves and in the following centuries mixed furthermore with people from all over the world who immigrated to Brazil. In this context, it is no surprise to discover that, after a recent genetic study of groups of self-defined blacks, 40 percent had African genes, 27 percent European and/or Asiatic, and 33 percent both African and non-African, while self-defined whites had 7 percent African, 55 percent European and/or Asiatic, and 38 percent both African and non-African genes (Table 16.1). Self-defined mixed people had 29 percent African, 35 percent European and/or Asiatic, and 36 percent both African and non-African genes (*Veja* 20 December 2000, 106–109). It is thus clear that African genes are not restricted to people who consider themselves to be of African descent or are classified as blacks by official statistics. Official data offer the ethnic portrait of the country and its regions, as detailed in Table 16.1.

Because of racism, self-definition masks ethnic affiliation, for the percentages of whites and mixed people are probably higher than expected, as a way of escaping discrimination by "whitening" self-definition. In other words, people define themselves as white or mixed in order to escape from discrimination

Table 16.1. Regional Population Distribution in Brazil by Race

	Brazil	North	Northeast	Southeast	South	Midwest
White %	55.2	28.4	30.6	65.4	85.9	48.3
Black %	6.0	3.7	6.1	7.4	3.2	3.9
Mixed %	38.2	67.2	62.9	26.7	10.5	46.6
Others %	0.6	0.7	0.3	0.5	0.4	1.2

Source: Adapted from Lopez 1999, 14.

against black people, so that the figures must be considered with a pinch of salt. In a recent survey in the state of Rio de Janeiro, 93 percent of people thought there was racial prejudice against blacks in the country (62 percent said there is a lot of prejudice, while 31 percent stated that mild prejudice prevailed) (Jansen 2000). There is clear evidence that people classified as blacks or mixed race face more difficulties than self-styled whites. Whites study 6.3 years, blacks and mixed people 4.3. The average salary of whites is 4.9 minimum wages, while blacks earn 2.4 and mixed people 2.2. Whites with a monthly wage lower than the minimum wage (that is US$ 40) are 33.6 percent, blacks 58.1 percent, and mixed people 61.5 percent. Illiteracy is 9 percent among whites and 22.2 percent among blacks and mixed people (Vieira 2000, 72). Still according to official statistics, 30.7 percent of whites, 70.7 percent of mixed people, and 61.2 percent of blacks are considered poor. Salvador, the capital of Bahia State, where a large majority are of African descent, blacks earn no more than half of an average white income (_Folha de São Paulo_, 20 November 2001, B4). On the average, whites are 2.5 times richer than blacks (Farid 2001). In Brazilian colleges and universities, blacks are only 2.2 percent and mixed people 13.5 percent, and in some prestigious careers like medicine, blacks are 1 percent and mixed people 12.3 percent (Gois 2001). Blacks have not fared well in the private business world either. A recent survey showed that 94 percent of top executives at the biggest Brazilian corporations are white. Nonwhites make up 45.3 percent of the population, but only 17.8 percent of all registered entrepreneurs. Nearly half of all black proprietors left school by the eighth grade, and only 15.8 percent completed twelve years of schooling, while 35.8 percent of white entrepreneurs have a minimum of twelve years of schooling (Figueiredo 2002).

Archaeology as an academic endeavor must be framed in relation to this overall context. Although the interest for African Brazilian culture has been felt for decades in such fields as anthropology, sociology, and history, the archaeology of African-Brazilian topics has been marginal. Archaeology, however, was particularly affected by military rule (1964–85), and an overall conservative outlook prevailed even after the dictatorship ended. Historical archaeology has paid attention to upper-class material culture; the material remains linked to exploitation, and the oppressed were not at the heart of the discipline

(Funari 2002). In the early 1990s, the archaeological study of Palmares, the seventeenth-century maroon, opened new avenues for the study of African Brazilian material culture.

Palmares, Ethnic Identity, and Archaeology

Resistance against oppression has been studied as a way of avoiding the traditional disenfranchising role played by the scholarship. The slave system was not benign (Conrad 1973, 50); racial slavery and oppression were not abnormalities (Higgins 1991, 25). Yet there has been a continuous struggle against slavery and oppression (Schwartz 1977, 75). Runaway communities are the clearest evidence of this resistance (Reis 1992, 17). The archaeology of these communities has the potential of denying the once accepted view of Negro docility (Davidson 1979, 82) and of challenging the delightfulness of the slave system (Aptheker 1979, 165). According to Glassman (1991, 278), "The construction of distinctly African-American cultures and communities is eloquent testimony of the frequent success of the New World slaves' struggle to build autonomous institutions of local social reproduction." Maroons were the strongest expression of nonconformity (Bakos 1990, 51), and the fact they were unable, up to the mid-nineteenth century, to change the social structure of slave society, as Ciro Flamarion S. Cardoso (1988, 82) reminds us, does not diminish their importance in comparison with short-term violent confrontations like revolts, uprisings, and insurrections (Orser 1991, 40).

Palmares was a runaway settlement established in the beginning of the seventeenth century in northeastern Brazil and able to grow for almost a century (Fig. 16.1). In its heyday, it comprised several villages, and the largest site, at the Serra da Barriga, or Belly Hill, was a town with hundreds of houses. After many attacks, the *bandeirantes* or pioneers from São Paulo in the south were able to destroy that polity in 1694 and to kill the last black ruler, Zumbi, on November 20, 1695 (Carneiro 1988). In the 1970s, Palmares would return to the forefront of public interest thanks to Afro Brazilian institutions. The Hill was declared a national heritage monuments in the 1980s, and Palmares and Zumbi were considered strong symbols against oppression:

> At Palmares, there was an organized slave uprising, and the result was a multiethnic society strongly anticolonial in outlook. This was the first liberation movement in the Americas.... There is now the opportunity to reenact the pluralistic experience carried out at Palmares. If you look at this most glorious page of Brazilian history, you will remember that at Palmares there were not only blacks but also Indians, Jews, and all other people subjected to discrimination. (Serra 1984, 107–108)

Aquiles Escalante (1979, 74) described maroons as "communities where they could keep their original cultures alive." At Palmares, however, different

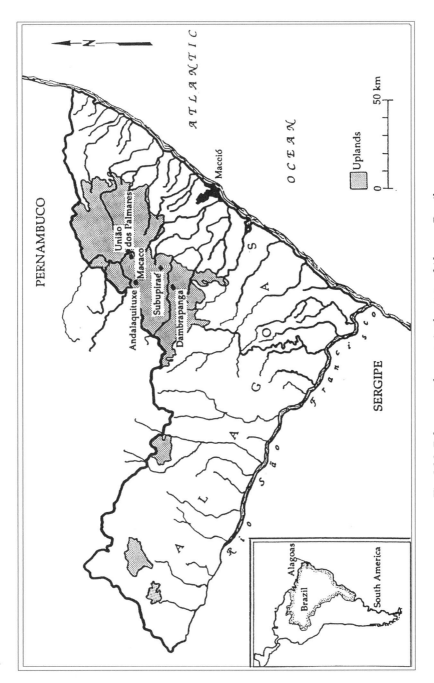

Fig. 16.1. Palmares settlements in the state of Alagoas, Brazil.

authors refer to the *mix* of African, Native American, and European elements (e.g., Saraiva 1993, 46). This is the result of references in the written documents about different ethnic groups in this polity, but it is also an ideological assumption. Serra's citation is clear on that matter: it was the first multiethnic state, and we should re-create it. Other social activists, like Abdias do Nascimento (1980, 1995), would take a completely different stance, interpreting Palmares as overwhelmingly African and rejecting any racial interaction, in the past and in the present. In any case, the archaeologist is faced with strong symbolism when studying Palmares.

In the early 1990s, Charles E. Orser Jr. and I decided to set up an archaeological project on Palmares. We have been acting in close contact with the Afro-Brazilian Studies Centre at the Federal University of Alagoas and its director, Zezito de Araújo, and through him also with the black community at large. Archaeological theory has been at the heart of our concern as we must deal with ethnicity on two levels: archaeological artifacts related to ethnic groups and modern perceptions, by social agents, of the pristine ethnicity and its contemporary consequences. Since 1990, several books and papers have been published on the archaeological study of Palmares by Charles Orser, Pedro Paulo Funari, Michael Rowlands, and Scott Allen (for overviews, see Funari 1999; Orser and Funari 1992). Allen (2001, 214) has recently summed up a decade of archaeological research at Palmares emphasizing that "combined archaeological research has unequivocally determined that there are multiple narratives to the Palmarino past...Palmares is a site that requires a reflexive approach as only then can we reach a true multivocality." The fact that we found mostly Native American–related pottery is meaningful in itself (Orser 1994b, 12–13). We should also not forget that European and African society were much more similar than is usually thought (Thornton 1981, 186), and it is thus not surprising to find evidences of a mix of cultural traits at Palmares. Scott Allen has proposed that the archaeology of Palmares can use a model of ethnogenesis that places neither Africans nor Native Americans at center stage in archaeological analysis, but rather the Palmarino themselves, as a specific, freedom fighting polity. Perhaps the main message of the archaeology of this so important free polity is to show that Africans fought not only for their own freedom as individuals or as Africans. Africans contributed to the struggle for the freedom of all those oppressed, be they black, Indian, Jew, Moor, "witch," sodomite, or whatever. Africa in the Americas means fighting for freedom and justice, and archaeology has a special role in showing this to society at large.

An Archaeology of the African Diaspora: Palmares

Palmares provides a good example of the importance of archaeology to the study of the African diaspora in Brazil (Orser and Funari 2001). Limited archaeological research at Palmares has yielded evidence that runaway people did not live in isolation, that historical accounts of the rebel state were biased, that maroons often resemble indigenous settlements, and that there are multiple ways of venerating them by descendant communities and by other ways.

The Portuguese developed sugar plantations in Brazil early in their colonial history, and by 1570 there were already several estates combining African and Native South American slave workforces (cf. Costa e Silva 2002 on the African background). These Portuguese plantations were in the northeast of the colony, while sugar processing and financing were in the hands of the Dutch, who managed to occupy Pernambuco in 1629 and to stay at Recife until 1654. Runaway slaves settled in the hilly forest areas, some fifty miles from the coast, at the beginning of the seventeenth century. During its initial years, Palmares ("palm groves" in Portuguese) derived its name from the many palmetto trees and referred to their scattered hideouts. Several villages grew up in the foothills from 45 to 75 miles inland from the coastal plantations stretching out over almost 100 miles running roughly parallel to the coast (Allen 1999, 144).

The first expedition against Palmares in 1612 attested to the importance of the polity already in the first years of the century. The polity continued to grow up and the Dutch considered Palmares a serious danger, attacking it several times. In the mid-1640s, Palmares already comprised nine villages. After the Dutch left Brazil, the Portuguese carried out several expeditions against Palmares, with a systematic campaign to destroy it beginning in the 1670s (Funari 1999). Between 1670 and 1687, under the rule of Ganga Zumba, or Great Lord, there seems to have been an active trade between Palmares and the coastal settlers (Rowlands 1999, 333). The decline in prices for sugar and competition from the Caribbean led to the increase in social tension among the planter-elites, and force was used to maintain order in the slave-holding society, including an increase in the attacks against Palmares. From the late 1670s, a new ruler of the polity, King Zumbi, was in charge of the defense of the maroon. Pioneers from the south of Brazil, known as Paulistas or bandeirantes, destroyed Macaco, the capitol of Palmares, in 1694, and the following year they executed its leaders, including Zumbi.

Much has been written about Palmares from historical evidence, but there was no archaeological study before the 1990s (cf. Funari and Carvalho 2005). Pedestrian surveys to locate archaeological materials began in the early 1990s and were followed by archaeological testing. Fieldwork continued to be carried out in Palmares in the late 1990s (Allen 1999). Most of the material evidence consists of coarse pottery and ceramics. Three specific wares have been identified in the collection: native unglazed pottery, European glazed ceramics, and locally made glazed ceramics.

The archaeological study of Palmares substantiated the notion that maroon people struggled for freedom and resisted oppression (Funari 1995a). Documents often assume that slaves internalized their master's *Weltanschauung* and mores, thereby producing a biased description of the subaltern groups.

In 1613, the people of Palmares were described as the "lazy and insulting inhabitants who run away from work" (Carneiro 1988, 50), and in the 1670s, they were said to be "barbarians who had all but forgotten their subjugation" (Allen 1999, 147). The pottery produced or used in the capital tells a different story, as it reveals the cultural autonomy of the community (cf. Glassman 1991, 278). This autonomy, however, did not imply a lack of outside contacts, for the ceramics provide clear evidence of interaction with both native South Americans and transplanted Europeans. Interaction with the Europeans is evident in the use of European ceramics, with four varieties of lead-glazed, coarse earthenware in use. These wares were not greatly dissimilar from contemporary Portuguese and Dutch wares, suggesting relations with different colonists. The wares were utilitarian in nature, suggesting that they were intended for non-elites living on the coast. If this interpretation is correct, then the coarse earthenwares indicate contacts between maroon residents and non-elite European colonists (Figs. 16.2 and 16.3).

Pottery fragments comprised more than 95 percent of the overall artifact assemblage. Regional pottery typologies and classifications are rare in Alagoas State, complicating classification. However, Scott Allen has proposed several possible pottery types for the region, as shown in Table 16.2.

The distribution analyses took into account the fact that the site has been seriously impacted by cultural activities. Much of the pottery excavated is well known, and a large proportion of it can be attributed to what several archaeologists call Aratu, as defined in the late 1960s. These vessels have a geographical distribution from the Bahia State to Ceará and west to Goiás. Red slipped ware similar to known Tupinambá manufactures of the late woodland period is also present, as well as a brown burnished type with a perforated handle, known as Papeba elsewhere in northeastern Brazil.

Contact with native Brazilians is thus clear in the pottery of native style. These Tupinambá vessels are similar to Ovimbundu African pottery, probably indicating a convergence of African and native traditions. Locally made wares were wheel-thrown, and so far they have not been identified elsewhere. The pottery used at Palmares thus attests both to the integration of the runaway polity into a much wider world of exchanges—from the Brazilian coast to Africa and to Europe—and to the polity's unique character. The material world of the maroon people was not native, European, or African; it was specific, forged in their fight for freedom. The same conclusion was reached by Claudi R. Cròs (1997, 81): "Palmares was at the heart of a large area of 27,000 square km, occupied by a federation of 11 maroons and several hamlets where lived, free, ... 20 to 30 thousand Africans, mixed people, and even Native South Americans." But freedom had a price: war.

Palmares was a community at war, fighting for its very existence, and the state of continuous warfare strongly influenced every aspect of life in the villages. Archaeologically, it was possible to note that all the sites at the Serra da

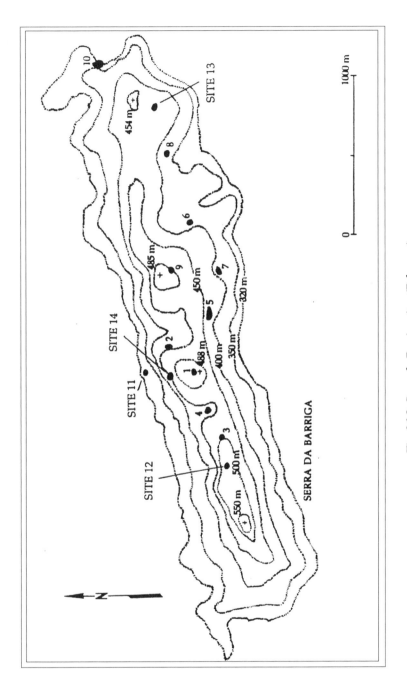

Fig. 16.2. Serra da Barriga sites (Palmares).

Table 16.2. Pottery typologies in Alagoas

Type	Temper treatment	Surface treatment	Thickness	Forms	Level
Yellow red	Stone, moderate	None	>10 mm	Restricted	II
Brown	Stone, abundant	None	>10 mm	n/a	II
Red	Sand, sparse	Slipped	<10 mm	n/a	II
Black	Sand to stone	Burnished	<10 mm	Large bowls Aratu	III
Brown	Sand, sparse	Burnished	<10 mm	Large bowls Aratu	III
Light brown	Stone, abundant	None	>10 mm	Urns Aratu	III
Red	Sand, sparse	None	<10 mm	n/a	II
Strong brown	Stone, moderate	None	>10 mm	n/a	–
Tan	Stone, abundant	None	>10 mm	n/a	III
Palmares ware	None visible	None	<10 mm	Bowls, Whell Turnê	II

Source: Data from Allen 2001, 112–24.

Barriga are located facing the south, in a strategic position in relation to the River Mundaú, used by colonial troops to attack the capital (Fig. 16.2). This landscape is both natural and a cultural artifact. Its significance and the uses to which it was put were understood by Palmarino people and were culturally prescribed (cf. Palmer 1998b, 183). Resistance is thus written in the settlement pattern itself.

Historical accounts are biased against resistance fighters almost by definition. It is not possible to take at face value a contemporary document in which the author attempts to explain the growth of the maroon as a result of slaves being "taken out of plantations against their own will" (Carneiro 1988, 66). In other words, that Palmarinos menaced the enslaved with knives to impel them to join the maroon. The biased view continued to be accepted by later authors, most notably by German historian Heinrich Handelmann (1987, 446) who, in 1860, reproduced the same argument: "The inhabitants of Palmares kept people of their own race in slavery, blacks and colored; if they fell in the hands of the runaways in expedition, they were split by the victors and used, they and their descent, as bonded maids. Only when they were recruited to the maroon of their own free will were they accepted as citizens." Handelmann thus makes the assumption that slaves would rather remain as chattel on the plantations than become servants at Palmares. The available archaeological evidence, however, does not support the idea that life at Palmares would be any harsher than in the plantations—even for servants—considering that there is no evidence of inhuman installations such as sugar mills at the maroon. Despite the bias of the German historian, it is symptomatic that he uses the word *Bürger* to refer to the Palmarinos, for it means both citizen and freeman.

With its 20,000 inhabitants, Palmares sheltered probably one in three slaves in the colony, and the archaeological evidence from the capital of Palmares, despite the destruction of the site, is enough to substantiate the claim that it was a huge settlement, comparable only to the largest cities in the colony. The remains of this polity have been gaining attention only recently, but folklore and tradition kept alive several rituals commemorating the saga of these rebels. The residents of several towns in the northeast of Brazil hold festivals to celebrate their churches' patron saints. Many of these celebrations incorporate a mock fight that remembers Palmares. Called "Quilombo," the fight pits runaway slaves against native Brazilians and occurs around a fortress. Inside the protected area are two thrones, one for the black king and one for the queen, a non-African girl. At one point during the reenactment, the natives appear armed with bows and arrows, led by a king clad in a red tunic and carrying a sword. This oral exchange then occurs between the two groups:

Natives: Come on, come on, knives are not capable of killing even women…
Africans: Don't worry, black man, the white man cannot come here. If he comes, the devil will take him. (Carneiro 1988, 80–81)

The fight terminates with the victory of the natives, who capture the king and the queen. Church bells then ring, the fortress is destroyed, the Palmarinos are sold, and the queen is given to a local potentate.

This story reinterprets Palmares in a rather conservative way, but it also betrays some historical facts: the multicultural character of Palmares, the Indian troops used to assail the polity, and the mixed Indian/Portuguese heritage of the bandeirante Domingos Jorge Velho, who commanded the final assault (Funari 1995b). Black and social activists in general have been reinterpreting Palmares for several decades, constituting the symbolic descendant community of the rebels (cf. McGuire 1992, 828). Since the 1970s, the Serra da Barriga has been used as a meeting place for all those concerned with raising the black consciousness in Brazil, and with the restoration of national civilian rule in the 1980s, it was declared a national heritage monument (Santos 1995). The archaeological study of the Serra da Barriga has focused the discussion on the importance of the site for a more democratic, less partial, and racist interpretation of the Brazilian society at large. Given this high profile, the national media have paid special attention to the site and have helped to contribute to a wider debate about the history and culture of Palmares.

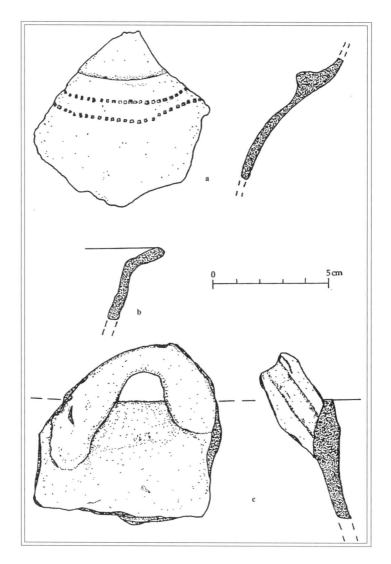

Fig. 16.3. Pottery (Palmares).

Conclusion: Beyond Palmares

Other maroons were studied by archaeologists, most notably in Minas Gerais and Goiás. In the eighteenth century, the back lands to the west of the coast were exploited by the colonial power, Portugal, in order to get access to precious gold sources. Even more than in the earlier sugar cane plantations,

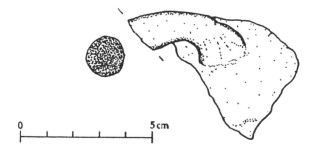

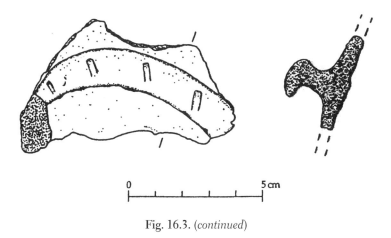

Fig. 16.3. (*continued*)

African slaves were the backbone of colonization in the back lands. Three-quarters came from Bantu areas in Africa, and two-thirds were male (Cròs 1997, 77). Mining is usually an urban activity, and slaves were kept in slave quarters in urban houses. These slave quarters are still to be studied by archaeologists. An ever-present feature of mining life was the existence of camps of runaway slaves. These settlements were usually not far from the colonial towns, as maroons were reasonably safe in the surrounding hills, where the fugitives could interact with the colonial society, at least with ordinary people. Carlos

Magno Guimarães has studied the largest maroon, Quilombo d'Ambrósio, and produced evidence of slave resistance (1992).

Quilombo d'Ambrósio was a settlement in a swamp in the Serra da Canastra. The village itself was on a hill (Morro do Espia, "spies' hill") enabling the settlers to control the main road linking the two most important mining areas, Minas Gerais and Goiás. The study area is 1.5 ha and surrounded by a ditch. The destruction of the maroon in 1746 by 400 colonial troops left most of the site destroyed but uninhabited afterwards, so that the preservation of the evidence is quite good. Dwellings were built using traditional wattle techniques. Walls were 8.5–13 cm thick with no apparent decoration. The floor, on the other hand, was carefully kept by the dwellers and the dwellings were covered by grass/thatched roofs. Pottery was used, as well as pipes, attesting to the consumption of tobacco. Through the study of material remains, it was possible to know that the fugitives consumed cultivated plants, wild animals, and fruits. There is also clear evidence of the importation of artifacts from outside the settlement, indicating a continuous exchange between maroon settlers and the colonial society.

Nineteenth-century slave quarters and maroons are not well known, but archaeologists are beginning to pay attention to such archaeological evidence (Agostini 2002), and the interaction between Africans and other ethnic groups, particularly natives, has been receiving growing attention (Morales 2002, 65–69), as well as on black architecture (Maestri 2001). Another important archaeological research avenue is the study of iconography. Maria Lígia Quartim de Moraes (1999) has studied iconographic documents from seventeenth and nineteenth centuries. This is a most promising avenue, for there is a plethora of paintings and drawings full of material culture details, some of them difficult to find archaeologically. So it is possible to study the clothes used by slaves, the way slaves were controlled, how they transported people and cargoes, and the way they used water (Lago 2001, 73, 89, 105). Most interesting are those paintings depicting everyday life of blacks (Lago 2001, 113, 177), working situations (Lago 2001, 164; 178; 180; 193), and slave punishments (Lago 2001, 182) (Figs. 6–15). Another promising avenue is the archaeological study of popular strata, where the presence of African Brazilian culture is always relevant (see Domínguez 1999, on a similar situation in the Cuban archaeology of the African diaspora). Paulo Eduardo Zanettini (1996; 2002) and associates are studying the remains of Canudos, a rebel state in northeastern Brazil, destroyed in the early twentieth century. At the rebel settlement lived people of different ethnic backgrounds, but most were of African descent, and the material culture reflects the mix of people so common in ordinary Brazilian material culture.

All in all, the outlook for the archaeological study of African Brazilian material culture is bright. Archaeologists can learn from the rich experience of historians and social scientists who have been studying the African diaspora in Brazil for decades. Archaeology can contribute to a deeper knowledge of the African contribution to Brazilian society, particularly to the understanding of the original ways Africans contributed to shaping diversity as a main feature of Brazilian cultural life.

Acknowledgments

I am grateful to Scott Joseph Allen, Zezito de Araújo, Margarete Bakos, Martin Bernal, Alberto da Costa e Silva, Lourdes Domínguez, Donna Goldstein, Brian Durrans, Jonathan Glassman, Peggy A. Lovell, Mário Maestri, Randall McGuire, Charles E. Orser Jr., Michael Rowlands, Thomas Skidmore, John Thornton, Bruce G. Trigger, and Peter Ucko for their collegial support. The responsibility for the ideas rests fully with me. I must also acknowledge the support from the National Science Foundation, the National Geographic Society, the Brazilian National Science Foundation (CNPq), the São Paulo State Science Foundation (FAPESP), Illinois State University, and Campinas State University (NEE/UNICAMP).

CHAPTER SEVENTEEN

The Vanishing People: Archaeology of the African Population in Buenos Aires

Daniel Schávelzon

Theresa Singleton writes, "The archaeological study of African-American life has become a well established research interest within American historical archaeology" (1999a, 1). This position, well accepted across the United States, takes on a different meaning when it is considered from other places on the continent. For example, in Argentina, not more than two or three archaeologists have demonstrated interest in the subject in spite of the importance that this topic should have. This fact has a negative repercussion in the national archaeological community. Is this a simple delay in the national research lines? I believe not. I believe it is due to racist attitudes within academia and due to the views and understanding of the role of archaeology in society. Let us take another example: the bibliographical compilation *The Archaeology of the African Diaspora in the Americas* (Singleton and Bograd 1995), which does not have a single reference on Argentina. Is this the authors' mistake? No, there was not a single reference on this subject in Argentina back in 1995.

The archaeology of African Argentina is at its very beginning stage. Not a single book has ever been published on this subject, and only some papers have dealt with the topic. On the other hand, the history of the African population in Argentina has experienced some growth and, from the 1980s, there has been an increase of publications and studies, including some recent books (Coria 1997; Morrone 1995; Picotti 1998) and an extensive list of researchers such as Ricardo Rodríguez Molas (1955, 1958, 1959, 1961, 1962, 1969, 1993), Marta Goldberg (1976, 1994, 1997, 2000), Silvia Mallo (1991, 1997), and Miguel Angel Rosal (1978, 1982, 1988, 1996), who followed the first academic studies by Diego Luis Molinari (1944), N. Ortiz Oderigo (1974), and

Elena Studer (1958). From the public outreach point of view, the first publications on this topic were by Vicente Rossi (1925) and José Luis Lanuza (1946). The immediate challenge facing the archaeologist of African Diaspora in Argentina is to find the earliest indications of the African presence in the country. Yet the denial of the existence of African Argentinean population in the past or in the present is so strong that in August 23, 2002, a woman was stopped at the Buenos Aires airport because "she couldn't be Argentinean and black." The indirect accusation here was either the passport was false or her skin color was fake (Clarín, 24-8-02, cover). This incident, with all the evidence of discrimination and racism it projects, shows the prevailing image of Buenos Aires as a white-only city whose seven million inhabitants are "white," no matter what definition of "white" is used or what the reality shows.

The contemporary racial makeup of Argentina was profoundly shaped by the large white immigration in the 1900s, and since then the African presence in the city has been denied. If we take the already exaggerated statistical figures, blacks do not even reach 0.2 percent of the total population. Nevertheless, when looking at the historical sources, we know that in the early nineteenth century there were towns and cities where the African population surpassed 50 percent, and at that time Buenos Aires was 30 percent black (Ravignani 1919). The rejection of this past visibility ties in well with the position taken by the traditional archaeology where the presence of the African population and their contribution to the making of Buenos Aires is rarely acknowledged. Yet it is through archaeological remains that we can assess the extent of African presence in the city. Granted, it is difficult to determine the ownership of an object or a group of objects to a specific ethnicity or social group. Many of the diagnostic artifacts that we assign to the African community can be ascribed to any poor population: Caucasian, Mestizo, or Native American.

This subject of material culture and racial/ethnic identity arose in Buenos Aires when we were digging a garbage pit that belonged to the house of an important woman in Buenos Aires society during the mid-nineteenth century, Mrs. Josefa Ezcurra, located at 455 Alsina Street. She had many servants living in her basement at the end of the eighteenth century, and they were mostly Africans (Seró Mantero 2000). The objects found at this house were ascribed to an African origin. This discovery came along with the uncovering of the first handmade ceramic pot, of about 12 cm in height, so common within the Diaspora context and so different from all the other Creole or Indigenous material culture. These findings opened the door to understanding the material culture of the African population in Argentina and how objects were deployed in daily lives to ensure individual and group survival. Unlike the plantation systems, it is impossible to dig slave quarters in Buenos Aires because slaves were part of the urban population and they lived in their masters' homes. Therefore, there was only one other possibility: to be able to identify objects of African cultural provenance within the garbage produced by the residents of a large house, we also need to have a wide range of collection of artifacts from public and private settings, but with no archaeological context, for comparative purposes.

The African Culture in Buenos Aires

Today, the Buenos Aires population shares mainly white European physical and cultural features, from both Western and Eastern Europe, and also Asia Minor features, due to the large immigration between 1880 and 1920. Today, the African presence is almost nonexistent, or at least it is not clearly visible. Buenos Aires was founded in 1580 after an initial failed attempt in 1536. It started as a poor village but soon became a major port city. The population from South America wanted to have an easy access to the sea so they could communicate with Spain, but the great city of Lima and its trading monopoly made it impossible. Thus the role of Buenos Aires as a city was left in a second place until almost the end of the eighteenth century (Schávelzon 2000a). African slaves had to travel by the Magallanes Strait on the southern tip of the continent, and then sail up to the port of El Callao, later travel to Lima, where they would take a road trip of several months to reach the different exchange points, specially the silver mines of Potosí, which were the main buyers of slaves. This system took a slave or any product almost a year to travel from Spain to Buenos Aires, and it increased incredibly the merchandise prices. In response to this problem, an illegal exchange system rapidly developed that brought produce, including silver from the Potosí mines, and slaves directly to Argentina thereby circumventing the official authorities (Crespi 2000; Moutoukias 1989). Thanks to these illegal market activities, the city of Buenos Aires was able to survive, and within two centuries it was able to overcome Lima in terms of regional power.

The fact that most slaves entered Argentina illegally makes it difficult to know how many Africans were forcefully brought to Argentina. Many details from this period have been impossible to reconstruct: there are few written registries, and those that exist are inaccurate. However, the entry of 250,000 to 300,000 Africans is accepted among researchers (Curtin 1969; Studer 1958; Torre Revello 1979). For example, between 1606 and 1625, when Buenos Aires was only a remote village, 12,778 slaves were registered as entering the city, of which 11,262 had entered illegally but were detected by the authorities.

The rapid depletion of Africans during the late nineteenth century is another problem that we face when conducting research. Slavery in Buenos Aires and its surrounding region was not devoted to working on plantations like in Brazil or in the Caribbean, nor was it for working in the mines like in Peru or Bolivia. Slaves raised cattle in the rural areas and made handicrafts and worked in homes in urban centers. This made the living conditions different from those of plantation slaves. In Buenos Aires, there were no "Large Houses" where slaves were locked up at night, as was typical in Brazil. The Buenos Aires slaves enjoyed the benefits that the anonymous urban life offered, and the fact that they lived in the same houses as their masters would have enabled a large segment of the enslaved population to receive better treatment (Fig. 17.1). This fact possibly gave some of them access to better food and material goods, although with attached paternalistic attitudes from the masters of the house. Artisans from the city were sometimes able to have their own workshops and were even able to have some slaves under their command in exchange for paying their master a daily salary. During the nineteenth century, some employers allowed adult slaves to manufacture simple products, sell them, and pay back to the masters their daily salary (Andrews 1980). It is also a fact that there are few references to runaways and slave rebellions.

The data from 1806 and 1807 show that there were 6650 "blacks and mulattos," 347 natives, and 15,708 whites in Buenos Aires. These figures put the percentage of the African population at 26.20 percent. However, 13 percent of the population did not participate in the census, a high percentage of whom were probably of African descent. In 1810 there were 9,615 "blacks and mulattos," 150 natives, and 22,793 whites, which means that the percentage had increased to

Fig. 17.1. A store in Buenos Aires where Africans, whites, and mestizos interacted, dressed similarly, and had access to the same goods in 1830. Painting by César Hipólito Bacle.
Archivo Centro de Arqueología Urbana.

29.53 percent. However, the image that the travelers had of the city at that time was slightly different, since they calculated that the African population reached up to 50 percent of the residents, a situation similar to a place like Tucumán, which was 64 percent African during the same time period. Obviously, the census figures did not take into account the slaves in the "Companies" waiting to be sold or transferred, since they were merely objects.

The urban houses could be large or small, but normally they sat on large lots. Depending on the owner's social status, these houses range from a living room and a bedroom all the way to a dozen rooms. However, the place for the slaves was what has been called the "the patio at the bottom," a place physically separated from the main house but without an absolute racial barrier. It is common to state in the nineteenth-century chronicles that white people had been raised by an African slave—or free servant—and played with the African children, but when the white kid reached puberty this situation abruptly came to an end. In 1813, the first law was passed where they gave conditional freedom to the slaves' children, although in Buenos Aires slavery did not completely end until 1861.

The Process of "Disappearance" of the African Population

The 1813 law that conditionally freed the slaves' children, the British abolitionist activities in West Africa against the slave trade, and the changes taking place in Argentina between 1810 and 1816 as a result of the independence movement made the arrival of slave shipments less frequent and more expensive in the early nineteenth century. Most of the soldiers in the Argentinean independence movement were slaves who offered their service in exchange for potential freedom or who were simply taken away from their masters. The disruptions inflicted on the economic life by the wars of independence rapidly decreased the imports of human cargo into the country. Moreover, the death rates among the slaves was already high and the fact that a large percentage of the slaves who enrolled in the army never came back from the independence wars that took place in Chile, Peru, Bolivia, and Paraguay drastically decreased the number of slaves in Buenos Aires. Afterwards, Africans who lived close to the port area, who were without doubt the poorest population in the city, suffered several serious epidemics such as cholera and yellow fever, and these poor Africans descendants recorded a higher death rate among the population. Earlier in the 1860s, the war against Paraguay killed hundreds of thousands of Africans who were almost exclusively the only members of the army troops—a true human genocide. All these facts reduced the number of Africans in Buenos Aires. Moreover, there was also a decrease in the life expectancy among these populations where there were no newcomers and the old residents were dying faster (Schávelzon 2003).

However, other countries that suffered this same situation did not have their African population erased: something different had happened in Argentina. It was difficult to find an explanation for this abrupt reduction of the African population that took place in less than half a century. This situation turned out to be the sum of two phenomena: (1) Africans had a birth rate of only 1 percent (Goldberg 1997, 2000) and almost half of all infants died, and (2) the large group of non-African immigrants accounted for the "whitening" of the Argentinean population. At the turn of the twentieth century, more than one million Europeans and Asians entered Argentina.

Artifacts of African Traditions

The international bibliography has identified a group of artifacts as characteristic to the African culture in the Diaspora. These artifacts have been documented several times in excavations, and although it has been impossible to identify who used them, the fact that they appeared in excavations is a first step for the studies on this topic. Some of the most important artifacts are ceramic pipes (Fig. 17.2). There are many shapes, but all are small, made of a dark ceramic paste, without a tube, and with an enlargement in the mouthpiece. They have star-shaped decorations, triangles, crosses, or areas decorated with dots and lines, which were well-known decorative motifs from West and West Central Africa (Schávelzon 2003).

Round colored stones were found, together with glass pieces or some other objects that were slightly altered or polished and that apparently were used in divination ceremonies. There are also ceramic pots or containers less than 15 cm tall, handmade, irregular, with fingerprints on their surface (Fig. 17.3). There is nothing similar to these artifacts in the European or local indigenous collections. In other regions, like Santa Fe la Vieja (1560–1650), human heads with African features made of coarse clay have been identified. In nearby areas, such as Arroyo de Leyes, some human figures or containers depicting deformed human and animal heads were found at a cemetery (Aparicio 1937; Bousquet 1936). These figures were similar in style to what was found at sites dating to the nineteenth century in the southeastern United States (Burrison 1978; Vlach 1990). On at least one occasion at Buenos Aires, a handmade wooden figure was found buried in the shore of a small artificial lake, with a noose around its neck and a thorn made out of bone in its heart (Schávelzon 2003, 148).

There are a wide variety of objects that, thanks to the written sources, have been identified as belonging to the African population. For example, the wooden swords (*sables de palo*) were worn with ceremonial outfits. The so-called king of each nation (congregation) was expected to own one, since they were forbidden to carry real weapons. Pieces of these swords have been found at least twice in domestic trash pits in the southern area of the city where the African

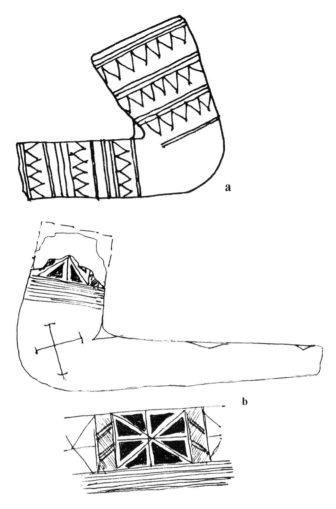

Fig. 17.2. Ceramic pipes with African decorations, San Telmo.
Private collection, Buenos Aires.

community used to live in the nineteenth century, especially associated with the *libertos* (those slaves who were able to run their own businesses).

Several types of archaeological contexts are associated with the African population, but the most common are trash pits and the living quarters. A combination of the two contexts has been found at 455 Alsina Street, the house that belonged to Mrs. Josefa Ezcurra. According to the written sources, the trash pit dates from 1801. We found a ceramic pipe decorated with white dots inside triangle motifs, a knife made from a cow rib, polished stones, exquisite carved glass from Spain, magnificent creamware pottery, and an almost complete Talavera plate set. It is

Fig. 17.3. African ceramics from Buenos Aires: a cooking pot,
a pipe, and a candlestick, eighteenth and nineteenth centuries
(excavation by the Center for Urban Archaeology).

possible that all the trash, from the masters and the slaves, ended up in the same trash pit. When excavating under the floors of the servants quarter, we found irregular ceramic disks of different sizes (Fig. 17.4), a modeled dark ceramic pipe without decoration, and blue glass beads (Schávelzon 2003, 145–50).

A completely different situation was found in the trash pit of the Santo Domingo church, dated to 1780–1820, where a group of six fragments of bone objects were found, including a fan handle (Fig. 17.5), thrown together into the trash pit, probably wrapped up in a leather bag. However, the rough conditions inside the pit have made this hypothesis hard to prove. The priests from this church and from the other Catholic Orders from this city had a large number of slaves living in specific buildings in the south area of the convent (Schávelzon and Silveira 1998). Could we identify this as a group of objects used for divination ceremonies? We find a similar case while excavating under the house on Alsina Street where, in the last patio, a group of objects was found, each less than a centimeter in height, some made from a well-cut piece of a kaolin pipe, some from two blue necklace beads, and some from two copper pieces, one of them possibly a button (Fig. 17.6). We think that some African slaves used such objects for ceremonial or divination activities (MacGaffey 1987).

The third category is that of the nonarchaeological discoveries which nonetheless have partly preserved their context and for which we have at least one source, whether oral or written, that identifies their owners. There is a house in the southern end of the city that still had an oral tradition preserved by its owners about how some objects that belonged to a king from the African Nation had been thrown into its well. This king (a direct ancestor of the house owners)

Fig. 17.4. Pieces of ceramic disks from African-descendant servant quarters at the house of Josefa Ezcurra, ca. 1800 (excavation by the Center for Urban Archaeology).

played an important role until 1852, during the government of Juan Manuel de Rosas. He became important because he politically supported the African community, and when he was murdered his family threw all his belongings into the well. When the house was torn down, the owners cleaned the remains from the well and the objects that were found dated to the 1850s, clearly related to the Rosas political power: an army shield, flags, banners with inscriptions, and a snake-shaped wooden scepter. We know from the chronicles that this was the type of scepter used during the dances to determine the rhythm of the group, and it could only be used by the ceremony's leader.

The well-known symbol of the Diaspora called BaKongo is a cross with small dots at the end of each arm. Numerous objects carry this symbol on their surface (interior or exterior) in the Americas, and it is impossible for us to reference them all (Ferguson 1992). In Argentina, this symbol has been documented, too, but rarely in controlled archaeological excavations. In the 1940s, a ceramic pipe was found in the Riachuelo, a small river that runs through the southern part of the city and has been modified several times. The pipe was located

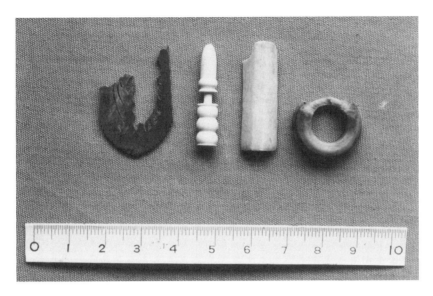

Fig. 17.5. Artifacts made of animal bone found in the trash pit of the Santo Domingo convent, 1780–1820 (excavation by the Center for Urban Archaeology).

Fig. 17.6. Group of small objects found together in a trash pit from the servant quarters at the house of Josefa Ezcurra, ca. 1800: two blue beads, a mother-of-pearl button, fragment of an English kaolin pipe, and two unidentified copper objects (excavation by the Center for Urban Archaeology).

during one of the river modifications. This is a ceramic pipe with a very mestizo shape, and hundreds of such pipes have been found in the city of Santa Fe La Vieja (Teresa Carrara and Nelly de Grandis, pers. comm. 2000). This is the only pipe that has been located outside the Santa Fe's context with the engraving of the classic BaKongo symbol. At least one other dark gray ceramic pipe that comes from a nineteenth-century landfill shows a similar though more abstract symbol. This symbol was applied to the exterior of the pipe and was excavated at Defensa #751 street, the landfill area of the city.

In 1996 and 1999, several excavations took place at the city square where we knew that a cemetery for poor people supported by the nearby Catholic church had existed during the eighteenth century. This was where abandoned slaves, suicide victims, unidentified bodies, or paupers were buried. Anyone who could not afford a funeral was buried there, no matter the skin color (Quatrín 2000). There was also a women's hospital and a girls' asylum at this location. The construction of these later buildings during the nineteenth century destroyed many of the graves. However, seventeen graves were archaeologically excavated (Techenski 2003). The materials that were found corresponded to different time periods and to different activities. These materials appeared mixed, but there were significant elements such as pipes and containers from the African culture. At least one burial did not belong to the Catholic tradition.

Skeleton #17 was found in a flexed position, with the back slightly in a higher location and with a long necklace inside the mouth. We know from local chronicles and comparative archaeology of the African Diaspora that necklaces were a symbol of power among the dignitaries of the African Nations in the Americas (Stine, Cabak, and Groover 1996). A description dating to this period says that the king of one of the communities "preserves as valuable relics two necklaces that may measure approximately three meters" (Gallardo n.d.). Although the skeletons from this cemetery are still being studied, they have already been identified as African (Zunilda Quatrín and Xavier Perussich, pers. comm. 2003).

Conclusion

Although the archaeology of the African population in Buenos Aires is just starting to take its first steps, a few discoveries deserve being mentioned in this chapter. First, we have already accepted the existence of a past population that until now had not been taken into consideration. Whether this group is a social group, a social class, or a culture is a discussion that should be our concern in the future. Second, we accept that this group of people interacted in different ways with the other groups, maintained its cultural traditions from its original place in Africa, and created new ones. Third, archaeology is revealing aspects of African cultural life unknown in the written history until now, such as divination practices and religious ceremonies, and the existence of non-Catholic burials. The fact that we are finding African or African-inspired ceramic forms and styles possibly indicates that this African population maintained the African ways of cooking, eating, and planting vegetables (Schávelzon 2000b). The preservation of these traditions by this population implies some sort of resistance that we are only beginning to identify and understand. The lack of evidence for slave rebellions in the city hid the other ways the Africans used to challenge their masters' hegemonic control and culture. This field of studies is finally open for inquiry with exciting possibilities of unexpected results.

Acknowledgments

I appreciate the personal communications from Zunilda Quatrín and Xavier Perussich about their excavations in the Square Roberto Arlt and from Teresa Carrara and Nélida de Grandis about Santa Fe la Vieja. We also want to thank Theresa Singleton, David Webster, Verónica Aldazábal, and Editorial Emecé for allowing us to reference my book *Buenos Aires Negra*, and the CONICET, which has supported the research project on the African presence in Buenos Aires. Appreciations to Dr. Chantal Esquivias, research fellow in the Department of Archaeology, Boston University, for translating the original manuscript from Spanish into English.

CHAPTER EIGHTEEN

Maritime Archaeology and the African Diaspora

Fred L. McGhee

The study of the seafaring component of the African Diaspora, particularly for African Americans, has an almost intuitive appeal. So much of African and Diaspora life in one way or another revolves around maritime themes and metaphors. Examples include Kongo cosmologies, wherein the water was seen as the conduit into the spirit world, in the Candomble goddess of the sea, Yemanja, who protects the men and women making their living in the seas off the Bahian coast, or in many of the traditions and practices observed by Garifuna seafarers along the central Belizean coast and elsewhere in Central America. Certainly the poetry of Langston Hughes ("The Negro Speaks of Rivers") is another classic example of how important the role of water has been in black culture. It is also certainly not by accident, as Bolster (1997) points out, that the first six autobiographies written by black men in the English language were written by mariners.

Although it could be approached from many directions, the major aim of anthropological African American maritime archaeology is to figure out the role of the sea and seafaring in the development and ongoing cultural practice of black identity. As many writers such as Paul Gilroy (1993) have noted over the years, the unique geographies of ships afford us singular and powerful vantage points from which to investigate the advent of modernity and the development of blackness within it. By identity, I essentially mean what Eric Wolf (2001, 354) noted in 1984 when he argued that "processes of identity-making and -unmaking refer to the creation and abrogation of the cultural markers and culturally informed activities by which populations define themselves and are defined by others in the process of incorporation." Identity is a historical phenomenon that emanates "primarily from the dynamics of labor mobilization, as well as from the closely connected consolidation of competitive political power" (Wolf 2001, 368). Seafaring is in many ways the ultimate "everyday" practice; it is therefore a fertile place to study these questions.

Methodologically, the African American study of the sea owes much to the modern development of maritime archaeology as an accepted archaeological subfield. Regrettably, however, maritime archaeology has very little to offer theoretically to those interested in studying black identity and the social and economic transformations that its development engendered. Although the scene is slowly beginning to change, the field is marked by pervasive Eurocentricity and a somewhat clumsy scientism that frequently have limited the scope of maritime archaeological investigations to mostly pale, male, and stale caricatures. The stereotype of the "macho" archaeologist/diver has also not helped things; it has distanced this field from seriously engaging the larger African American studies community and the realities of contemporary black life with which it is at least partly engaged. The amount of scientific information available about the transatlantic slave trade, for instance, is far more scarce than it should be, given the fact that the trade was perhaps the single most defining characteristic in the development of the modern world.

Conversely, although the plantation was an obvious early geographic choice for African American archaeologists, it has now become apparent that the plantation was only one of many places where African and African American culture and identity were exercised and negotiated. The maritime environment serves as a particularly powerful metaphor for the black experience, in that the dynamic and intense circumstances in which so many Africans and African Americans found themselves acted as a marker for the commonly acknowledged things that make contemporary black culture unique: improvisation, displacement, strength, spirituality, music, and so forth. Archaeological research is the primary method by which the ethnogenesis of varying "shipmate" identities (Blackburn 1997; Mintz and Price 1992) can be investigated.

Work in this arena is inherently political. It is also often polemical, but this is not necessarily a bad thing. Slave trade studies have been political since the publication of W.E.B. Du Bois's landmark 1895 doctoral dissertation on the subject, and they were episodically considered blasphemous. Ultimately, albeit somewhat indirectly, this is policy-oriented—and thus applied—work. The archaeological study of the transatlantic slave trade, one of the most wretched chapters in world history, cuts to the heart of ongoing debates about the origins and development of modernity and stands to furnish further insight that can be used by pro-reparations activists, for instance. The famous U.S. walkout of the 2001 World Conference Against Racism in Durban, South Africa, illustrates that this subject remains significant. Moreover, the study of *internal* slave trading within New World countries is also important. In the American case it raises all sorts of questions about the true meaning of American democracy and what "freedom" has historically meant. It also sheds greater light on the business history of the United States and the importance of "free market" dynamics in the socioeconomics of "negro speculation" (a euphemism for slave trading). Lastly, the stories of black sailors constitute a novel literary and cultural genre that can be investigated archaeologically. The often ignored detail that a disproportionate number of blacks worked on ships (whaling ships, for instance) up until the mid-nineteenth century and were eventually almost completely Jim Crowed out of work is another emblematic story about the history of race in American labor relations. It also explains a great deal about how the legal manipulation of work, life, and love can almost completely erase multigenerational traditions of "shipping out" and full participation in a maritime life. But the traditions remain embedded beneath the surface awaiting excavation.

Maritime Archaeology

Casual observers may have some difficulty distinguishing between the different forms of archaeology conducted under or near water. Delgado and Staniforth (2002, 5) have produced generally accepted definitions that shed light on the different emphases archaeologists have placed on submerged cultural material. Generally speaking, the term *underwater archaeology* refers to "the systematic study of past human life, behaviors, activities, and cultures using the physical (or material) remains (including sites, structures, and artifacts) as well as other evidence found in the underwater (or submerged) environment. Such evidence may exist beneath fresh (or inland) waters or beneath salt (or marine) waters. It may be visible on the bed of the water body (i.e., seabed) or buried beneath sediment. The term *underwater archaeology* simply refers to the environment in which the practice of archaeology is undertaken."

The term according to Delgado and Staniforth (2002) overlaps with the following definitions, which can be taken to mean that these are subspecializations within underwater archaeology:

> *Maritime archaeology*—the archaeological study of humans and their interactions with the sea, including sites that are not underwater but that are related to maritime activities such as lighthouses, port constructions, or shore-based whaling stations.
> *Marine archaeology*—the archaeological study of material remains created by humans that are submerged in the marine (or saltwater) environment such as submerged aircraft.
> *Nautical archaeology*—the archaeological study of ships and shipbuilding. Like maritime archaeology, it can include sites that are not underwater but that are related to ships and shipbuilding, including ship burials, shipwreck remains in the terrestrial environment, or shipbuilding yards.

Of the three, a maritime archaeology approach is best for studying the African Diaspora, although in practice there is considerable overlap between the categories. It should be noted that for most maritime archaeologists it is *humans* and their interaction with the maritime environment where emphasis is mostly and ultimately directed, whereas most nautical archaeologists are trained to focus first on the *ship* and its construction. Both approaches provide mutually reinforcing information and have proved fruitful in investigating the diverse methods humans have used to adapt to the marine environment.

The Maritime Archaeology of the Transatlantic Slave Trade

Extensive information is available on the slave trade, much of it produced by eighteenth- and nineteenth-century abolitionists, and the various slave narratives generated over the years are important starting points. Research designs in this area are generally targeted toward establishing the living conditions onboard a typical slaver, for both cargo and crew, investigating the maritime design innovations brought about by the need to carry and safely transport human cargo numbering in the hundreds (and later the thousands), and gathering information about the types of material culture that were involved in the trade, such as the dreaded "speculum oris," a cruel device used to force open the mouths of newly enslaved blacks who refused or were incapable of eating (for some photographs of this device and discussion of its role in the development of dentistry and gynecology, visit the French Museum of Medicine Web site at http://www.bium.univ-paris5.fr/aspad/expo09.htm). In seeking answers to such questions, we are also able to understand how material culture usage and the individual ability to "express" one's "culture" are constrained and enabled by the exercise of various forms of power. Thus the study of the transatlantic slave trade is also an important research site in the archaeological investigation of power (for some brief discussion of Foucault and Weber, see Blackburn 1997, 588).

The shipwreck of the British merchant/slaver *Henrietta Marie* is probably the most famous example of a vessel engaged in the transatlantic slave trade to have been studied by archaeologists. The wrecksite, which is still being investigated by the Mel Fisher Maritime Historical Society, has also produced the most extant middle passage artifact assemblage yet available. Since the late 1990s, the society has coordinated a national tour of the shipwreck artifacts under the banner *A Slave Ship Speaks*, as well as a permanent display of some of the objects in its Key West headquarters. An accompanying book, *Spirits of the Passage*, provides a comprehensive discussion of the ship and its history and a general discussion of the slave trade utilizing the noted narrative of the enslaved West African Olaudah Equiano. The society has placed much of the information available on the Henrietta Marie shipwreck on its excellent Web site at http://www.melfisher.org.

Transatlantic slave trading was big business. According to Roger Anstey (1975, 47), whose calculations on the British slave trade have stood the test of time, between 1761 and 1807 approximately 6,000 voyages resulted in the landing of 1.4 million enslaved persons, at a profit of about £4.4 million. The Caribbean island of Barbados "in 1699–1701 was the richest of the English plantation colonies. Although it had little more than half the total population of Virginia . . . its exports were worth nearly 50 percent more" (Blackburn 1997, 267). Jamaica's sugar crop tripled in size in the second half of the eighteenth century, and the French island of Martinique produced 6.5 million pounds of coffee in 1740, which began displacing the customary Arabian and Moroccan product in Europe (Blackburn 1997, 432).

The Henrietta Marie wrecked on New Ground Reef, approximately thirty-six miles west of Key West, Florida, in 1700. With the exception of the ship's bell containing the inscription "Henrietta Marie 1699" (used to positively identify the ship), the most famous and emotionally resonant artifacts from the shipwreck are the eighty sets of shackles or "bilboes" found between the early 1970s and the 1990s. Of varying sizes, made of iron, and forged in various weights, they were used to bind the ankles and/or wrists of the enslaved cargo. These, along with the presence of a sizeable copper cooking pot or cauldron found on the site are now signature markers being used by maritime archaeologists to identify slave ship sites.

A fairly impressive pewterware collection dating to the reign of William III of Great Britain (1689–1702) was also recovered and includes basins, flagons, plates, spoons, and tankards. Pewter eating and serving utensils are also used as diagnostic markers for British slave ship sites. For instance, the wreck of the *Queen Anne's Revenge* off the North Carolina coast, the flagship of the notorious brigand Blackbeard, contained pewter plates and chargers bearing inscription marks similar to those found on the *Henrietta Marie*. Eight ivory elephant tusks and thousands of beads were also recovered from the site (for a fuller discussion and photographs of the artifacts, see Burnside and Robotham 1997 and Steinberg 2002). These artifacts are of particular interest because they provide tangible evidence for the sorts of transactions that would take place on the African coast and demonstrate how quickly the British could act in their usurpation of previously existing Portuguese, Spanish, and Dutch human commerce. Great Britain's concerted efforts in the late seventeenth and early eighteenth centuries to establish Caribbean and North American colonies entailed the chartering of various slave trading concerns such as the Royal African Company. By 1700, European merchants had developed a sophisticated understanding of the trading patterns of West Africans with whom their ships and supercargoes came into contact.

It is clear that both ivory tusks and beads were valued highly in pre-Atlantic slave trade Africa. Ivory bracelets and carvings dating from the eleventh century onwards were found, for instance, at Begho in Ghana (Anquandah 1995, 649), and glass trade beads of Mediterranean and Asian origin have been found in many places in the continent's interior, including at Kgaswe B55 in Botswana by James Denbow (Kiyaga-Mulindwa 1993, 388) and in southern Malawi at the Matope Court site (Juwayeyi 1993, 394).

The Venetian beads from the *Henrietta Marie* shipwreck can likewise provide meaningful information not only about the value of the objects to both Africans and Europeans but also about the contexts in which they functioned as media of exchange. Beads found in terrestrial sites (the Jordan plantation, for instance; see Brown and Cooper 1990) are often interpreted to be "example[s] of the slaves' reinterpretation of manufactured objects to meet their own cultural uses" (Singleton 1991, 148). The *Henrietta Marie* assemblage, however, opens up another interpretation that has already been well established historically: slave trading Europeans made beads to fit African tastes and attempted to produce tradeworthy material that would entice the Africans. On one occasion, for instance, slave trader James Barbot noted that a local African king "objected much against our basins, tankards, yellow beads, and some other merchandise, as of little or no demand at the time.... The blacks objected much against our wrought pewter and tankards, green beads and other goods, which they would not accept of" (cited in Burnside and Robotham 1997, 116).

European slave traders' responses to diverse African tastes, therefore, played a significant role in the evolution of the trade and, of course, on the sorts of materials recovered from slave shipwrecks. What matters most in interpreting these sorts of situations is attention to context (especially geography) and especially power. In the late seventeenth century, African polities still possessed a considerable range of options with which to influence the manner and style of slave trading transactions, and European supercargoes had to respect that. An enslaved African *American*, on the other hand, was probably operating under a rather different set of power constraints, although plantation archaeology has, of course, revealed the remarkable degree of agency that disempowered and enslaved African populations in the New World were still able to exercise under relatively horrific conditions.

Displaced Geographies

For Paul Gilroy (1993, 16–17), ships "need to be thought of as cultural and political units rather than abstract embodiments of the triangular trade." They were something more—a means to conduct political dissent and possibly a distinct mode of cultural production. Gilroy's ambitious efforts to reposition the cultural geography of race beyond the borders of the modern nation-state were an important theoretical development. His formulations, such as his focus on a "new topography of loyalty and identity" (1993, 16), creatively dynamized identity formation processes. The idea of a black Atlantic and of the ship in its creation constitutes powerful metaphors for Gilroy because they reinforce the simultaneous resilience and flexibility of black identity formation under complicated geographies in motion. Gilroy pointed out that a focus on nation-states was inadequately encapsulating of the fluidity of what he termed the "black Atlantic" experience. The logic of his argument can and should be extended to include the rest of the planet, because the European conquest and colonization of the Pacific and Indian oceans took place at about the same time as the "development" of the Atlantic world and played a very important role in the development of modernity. Both the extension of the "roots" and the various "routes" Gilroy discusses were more than simply an Atlantic phenomenon. African American scholars have long recognized this. When W.E.B. Du Bois, about a century ago, posited that the color line was going to be the problem of the twentieth century, he did not limit his discussion to North and/or South America or even to the western hemisphere. He was making a global argument about the relationship between the "darker and lighter races" in, among other places, "the islands of the sea."

Hawai'i is a good example. The postcontact history of this fascinating archipelago is bursting with cross-pollinations of varying diasporas, including the African Diaspora. Not only were black seamen part of the eighteenth-century English and French expeditions to the Pacific (something which the traditional Eurocentric and the "newer" Pacific Islander histories of the region have been rather slow to acknowledge), but many black mariners took the opportunity to escape potential enslavement in North or South America to fashion new lives for themselves in the islands. One noteworthy example is Anthony D. Allen, a New York native and sailor who came to Hawai'i from Boston in 1810 and stayed until his death in 1835. Allen acted as a confidant of Kamehameha the Great, received a land grant near present-day Punahou School, and operated a business on O'ahu provisioning the increasing numbers of ships making port calls in Hawai'i. Allen married a Hawaiian woman, and their descendants eventually blended into the "local" culture.

The influx of Portuguese-descended blacks from southeastern New England who came to the Pacific aboard whaling ships starting in 1820 has also left distinctive traces in both places. In Hawai'i, the men who stayed behind to make new lives for themselves were initially identified as "African" or "Portuguese" in nineteenth-century census records, but over time they came to be identified as "Part-Hawaiian" as their descendants assimilated. In New England, the stories these men brought back were part of the extensive "informal" (informal only in the sense that it took place "under the radar screen" as it were) communication networks that kept blacks well informed on the condition and status of the "darker races" around the world, especially in relationship to themselves and their always tenuous freedom. The discovery of a whiskey bottle near a nineteenth-century settlement now occupied by Hickam Air Force Base (McGhee and Curtis 2002) reinforces similar points made by James Deetz (1996) in his historical archaeology classic *In Small Things Forgotten* (artifact similarities between Virginia and South Africa) and by Charles Orser in a *Historical Archaeology of the Modern World* (similar artifact relationships between Palmares, Brazil, and Ireland). The glass bottle found near the Fort Kamehameha portion of Hickam Air Force Base bears a striking resemblance to similar bottles found during African American archaeology excavations in the five points section of New York City. Traveling artifacts that are reused in novel ways are a hallmark of what make historical archaeology truly "global" and interesting.

The "displaced geographies" include other anthropological and biological linkages between the Atlantic and Pacific, including the famous British attempt to transplant breadfruit from the Pacific for use by enslaved Caribbean plantation workers (immortalized by the famous *Mutiny on the Bounty*) and the noteworthy Indian and Chinese labor migration to the Caribbean, which have left their mark on islands such as Trinidad, Cuba, and Jamaica—not to mention Mississippi on the American continent (see Loewen 1988). Certainly the "global" nature of the African Diaspora has not gone unacknowledged (J. Harris 1993); however, the generation of more specific evidence establishing the worldwide character of the dispersal and its linkages is another challenge that lies before maritime archaeologists and historians. How can one fully acknowledge the geographic variety and vibrancy of the black diasporic experience while appreciating the utility and necessity of regional approaches? Investigations of "internal" slave trades may be one answer, because their investigation furnishes examples of specific political, social, and economic situations where identities were forged.

The Nineteenth-Century Internal Slave Trade in the United States

The nineteenth-century United States saw the movement of over one million enslaved African Americans from the states of the Upper South such as Virginia and Maryland to Lower South states such as Mississippi, Louisiana, and Texas. The trade grew in size and sophistication over the course of the century and shifted the maritime center of this commerce from ports such as Richmond and Charleston to ports such as New Orleans, Mobile, and Galveston. Although much of this trade was conducted inland via the movement of slave coffles or the settlement of migrants on newly acquired lands in the west, a significant portion of this trade was conducted—as one might expect—via the sea. Perhaps the most famous illustration of the turns this trade could take involved the famous slave insurrection aboard the *Creole*, an American vessel that was transporting an enslaved cargo from Richmond to New Orleans. On November 7, 1841, 135 *African Americans* (as opposed to Africans in the famous *Amistad* case) under the leadership of Madison Washington revolted and forced the ship to sail to the Bahamas, where they were eventually freed by the British government.

In many ways what happened on board the *Creole* mirrored events on the *Amistad*: a group of enslaved people of African heritage rose up against a slave-holding crew of European heritage, took control of the vessel, and demanded to be taken somewhere where they would be free....The case of the *Creole* differed from that of the *Amistad* in one crucial aspect: the *Creole* rebels were from the United States and had been legally held as slaves by the state from which they escaped. Because of this, the ways in which the rebels were represented and their rebellious acts were interpreted differed dramatically from reactions to the Mendians in the *Amistad* affair. Their differing status according to U.S. and international law made them into completely different kinds of subjects. (Sale 1997, 121)

The *Creole* case is notable for many reasons, including the conflicts it engendered between the United States—which regarded the rebels as lost and compensable property—and Great Britain, which had abolished slavery in 1833 and regarded the insurrectionists as persons. Sale (1997, 144–45) goes on to note that the claims commission, which eventually awarded the former slave-holders $110,330 in compensation, based their decision on the premise that the revolt was really a conflict between white persons and their recognized nations, not as a conflict between enslavers and a group of persons seeking their freedom. The ruling "erased the agency of the rebels—and Nassau's black population—by figuring the conflict as a struggle between armed national entities. It thereby drew upon, displayed, and supported the logic of nation-states, which not only authorized but also acknowledged the existence of the [white] citizens of recognized nations" (Sale 1997, 145). The significance of "internal" slave ship revolts such as the *Creole* affair lies in their affirmation that much of the black experience has been about the fight for freedom, the fight for full acknowledgment of black humanity, and by extension recognition of black folks' rights as human beings, something which nineteenth-century America was not prepared to do. By thus keeping a sharp focus on this central contradiction within the black experience, the maritime archaeologist/historian is able to shed further light on the processes involved in the struggle for human rights and later on full citizenship.

The Texas example is also illustrative of the wide influence of "negro speculation" in American westward "migration." As Michael Tadman (1996) has so eloquently shown, the westward movement of Africans and African Americans across North America should not be considered an "immigrant" experience. The truth is that slaves who accompanied their masters westward mostly did so involuntarily. In fact, a large percentage of the movement of enslaved persons to new nineteenth-century American colonies such as Louisiana, Missouri, and Texas is directly attributable to the internal slave trade. When Stephen F. Austin began settlement of a Texas empresario land grant his father had been able to obtain from Spanish authorities in 1820, the Negro population of the area was small. Forty years later, the enslaved population of Texas stood at nearly 200,000. Both internal and external slave trading contributed to this fairly remarkable increase, which dramatically influenced Texas economics, politics, and culture.

The dynamics of slave trading in Texas were complex and consisted of both illicit smuggling of enslaved people from Latin America or the Caribbean to slave markets in New Orleans via Texas, or "legal" importation of *African American* slaves from the Upper South or older Lower South states. Between 1820 and 1836 the political status of slavery in Texas was uncertain; Mexico's position on the matter was somewhat inconsistent—understandable given the revolutionary climate of the time and the difficulties inherent in the establishment of a new nation—but the abolitionist sentiments of Mexican officials were a matter of record, particularly the attitude of Afro-Mestizo president Vicente Guerrero, who outlawed slavery in Mexico in 1829. Not surprisingly, the cauldron eventually boiled over. When it became obvious that the Mexican government took the abolition of slavery seriously, the insurrectionists in Texas took matters into their own hands in order to safeguard their investments in "life, liberty, and property." The colonists understood that their future economic prosperity depended on the Texas property right to possess, acquire, and control slaves. In fact, proceeds from slave trading were utilized to finance the Texas Revolution. It is a well-known fact that James W. Fannin, later martyred in the "Goliad Massacre," was an active slave trader who purchased a cargo of 152 souls in a Havana slave market shortly after arriving in Texas from Alabama in 1834 (McGhee 2000, 159).

Whereas Cuba served as an important purchase point in the 1820s and 1830s, Nicaragua figured prominently in Texas history in the 1850s as various "filibustering" schemes sought to extend American-style slavery south of the border. The entire Gulf of Mexico teetered with vessels carrying enslaved cargoes, and smugglers seeking to avoid capture sought refuge in the navigationally difficult barrier islands near the Texas gulf coast, in addition to Honduran "Bay Islands" such as Roatàn, Utilia, and Guanaja. Following the navigational routes of these ships produces unexpected and swift lines of connection that clearly demonstrate how disparate yet interconnected trade routes *within* regions could be. These back and forths open up conceptual space to keep scholarly focuses "regional" while acknowledging the hybridity, pace, and depth of commercial maritime linkages.

Conclusion

Racial formation entails simultaneously global and localized processes that dynamically interpenetrate and produce a rich diversity of experiences and identities (Omi and Winant 1986). Maritime archaeology can contribute much to this discussion. Its insights are inherently cross-disciplinary, and its primary strength lies in its ability to traverse geographic boundaries; indeed, ships are geographies unto themselves. Maritime archaeological insights can expand understandings of how racial formation works and can also stretch the theoretical paradigm in newer directions by demonstrating how *even more* complicated racial meanings can be when investigated at a more global level. Eric Wolf, one of the earliest proponents of an "interconnected" and process-oriented approach to the study of humankind, famously noted that "only by understanding these names [such as "nation," "society," and "culture"] as bundles of relationships, and by placing them back into the field from which they were abstracted, can we hope to avoid misleading inferences and increase our share of understanding" (1982, 1) The Hawai'i examples I furnished in this chapter demonstrate that "blackness" is not immutable and perhaps never has been. Recent attention in interracial relationships and the increasing hybridity of twenty-first-century youth culture may seem like hot topics today, but the phenomenon is in fact nothing new whatsoever. Maritime archaeology's insights into the development of modernity can historicize these sorts of discussions into practically innumerable new directions.

CHAPTER NINETEEN

Archaeology of the African Meeting House on Nantucket

Mary C. Beaudry and Ellen P. Berkland

Through archaeological and historical research and architectural restoration, the African Baptist Meeting House, long a forgotten landmark, has been returned to its rightful place as a center for commemorating and celebrating the African American contributions to history and daily life on the island of Nantucket. The Meeting House, although surviving in plain sight, was long lost to memory as the island became a summer resort, tourist destination, and playground for the rich and as its black population steadily declined (Hayden and Hayden 1999, 231; Karttunen 2003a, 2003b; see also Beaudry and Berkland 2001; Berkland 1999, 2003).

Archaeological investigations in 1993 and 1996 provided evidence about the structure and the activities that took place there, about its landscaping, and about the people who used the site for worship, education, socializing, and forging community identity. The archaeological evidence, considered in the light of the recent interpretive turn of scholarship on African diasporic peoples (see, e.g., Franklin and McKee 2004), contributes to our understanding of how African Nantucketers took action to establish autonomy and to create a communal experience of dignity, place, and belonging.

Nantucket lies in the Atlantic approximately 25 miles south of Cape Cod (Fig. 19.1). Before the Europeans arrived in the seventeenth century, some 2,500 Indians affiliated with the Wampanoag tribes of southeastern Massachusetts and eastern Rhode Island lived on the island (Byers 1987, 18–19), but even though they continued to live there as it became increasingly the domain of English settlers, their control of the island, such as it was, was effectively ended with European contact. Their abiding presence is well recorded, however, and their ongoing participation in island affairs was considerable

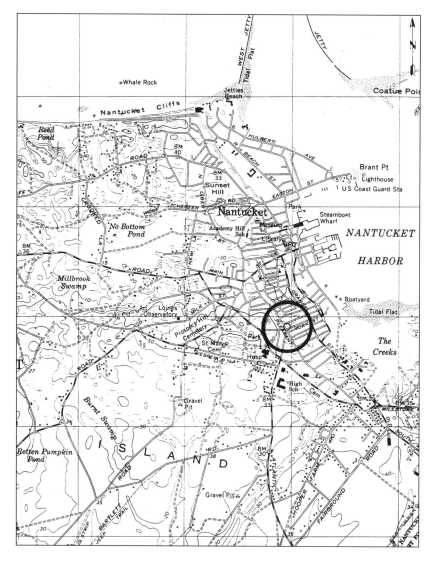

Fig. 19.1. Nantucket, showing the location of the
African Baptist Meeting House.

(see, e.g., Karttunen 2003a, 2003b; Little 1980, 1981a, 1981b, 1983, 1990, 1996; Vickers 1983, 1985).

In 1659, missionary Thomas Mayhew Sr. sold Nantucket to nine men from the Merrimack Valley area of New England for £30 and two beaver hats (Byers 1987, 28). These men became known as the proprietors; they took on additional partners and other investors, then divided the island into twenty-seven shares or divisions, one for each of the original proprietors. The divisions included large parcels of common land that were used for pasturing sheep and cows (Worth 1906, 59–60).

Africans on Nantucket

Enslaved Africans were brought to the island by the first white settlers in 1659, and although by the early eighteenth century some blacks were manumitted upon the deaths of their owners, wills reveal that many were passed down from one generation of owner to another as transferable property (Hayden and Hayden 1999, 219; Karttunen 2003b). The black population was not formally enumerated until 1764 when 44 persons were counted. By 1820 the number of blacks on Nantucket had grown to 274, and in 1840, 571 "free people of color" were reported (Byers 1987, 255, 298).

As the black community grew, its members established institutions that paralleled the white organizations to which they were denied access, including stores, churches, and an abolitionist society. By the second quarter of the nineteenth century, two black churches existed: the Baptist Society, formed in 1831, and the African Methodist Episcopal Church, established in 1835. By 1825 an "African School" was serving the black community (Linebaugh 1978, 4). Land for a cemetery was granted "to the Black people to fence in for a burying place by the proprietors as by a vote" (Nantucket Town Clerk's Records, June 3, 1805).

As the number of free blacks increased, this group, in conjunction with Nantucket's Quakers, initiated an antislavery movement that culminated in 1770 with the abolition of slavery on the island. This made Nantucket a haven for refugee slaves and for free blacks from both the North and the South (Hayden and Hayden 1999, 219). Nantucket was the center of the east coast whaling industry during the 1800s and a base for black mariners. Indeed, Farr and Burne have noted that "between the Revolutionary War and the Civil War, the New England maritime world was operated by more freed and fugitive blacks than any other industry and in greater proportion than in the general population" (1991, ii).

Before whaling and maritime trades began to dominate Nantucket's economy, blacks were employed in various trades and as laborers and others raised sheep and other livestock. In an account of the early days on Nantucket, Henry Barnard Worth describes "the years before 1821 when thousands of sheep roamed from one end of the Island to the other" as justification for extensive fencing near town (1906, 271). The documentary record abounds with mention of sheep herding, underscoring how important wool was to the island's early economy. An 1803 journal entry of a Nantucket farmer (journal 1, PT096, Peter Foulger Museum) is noteworthy for the clear link it provides to the African origins of a Nantucket practice that, it would seem, reveals the extent of African American participation in an ancillary aspect of sheep raising, treatment of wool with indigo dyes.

Method of Dying Blue in Africa

Take the leaves of Indigo Weed when fresh gathered & pound them in a Wooden mortar, & mix it in an Earthen Jar with a strong lye of Wood Ashes; Char lye is sometimes added. The Cloth is steeped in this mixture, & allowed to remain until it has acquired the proper shade. Or collect the leaves & dry them in the Sun, & when used powder them & mix it with the lye as above. Either way, colour is very beautiful, with a fine purple gloss equal to the best European blue.

This passage is copied directly from *Travels in the Interior Districts of Africa*, a book published in 1799 by the Scottish explorer Mungo Park after his return from a journey from Gambia through the present states of Senegal and Mali and along the course of the river Niger (Marsters 2000; see also Gwynn 1935; Lupton 1979). It would seem, therefore, that a copy of Park's popular account of early African exploration must have found its way to Nantucket. It is not known whether the journal writer was a person of African descent, but Parks's description of the process of indigo dyeing must have struck the journalist as remarkably close to what he observed on Nantucket. This suggests that black Nantucketers continued a process that was unmistakably African in its details, particularly in its use of specific items of material culture: a wooden mortar and an earthen jar. Holloway (1990, 12) notes that Europeans who imported Africans to the Americas often took special care to purchase captives from the Windward or Grain Coast for their intimate knowledge of the cultivation and uses of crops such as rice, indigo, and tobacco, accounting for the survival of identifiable African practices in various locales of the Atlantic African Diaspora. For many Africans, resumption of familiar skills, especially with herbs and plants, helped keep alive a memory of Africa that "served these exiles well, especially when conditions became simply intolerable" (Okpewho 2001, xv). The small island of Nantucket was not an exception to this cultural phenomenon.

Yet another document highlighting the significance of sheep raising on Nantucket describes the participation of the black community in an important celebration. On June 24, 1826, the *Nantucket Inquirer* carried an article on the annual June shearing festival that provides a glimpse into the lives of black sheepherders.

As these are the only important holidays which the inhabitants of Nantucket have ever been accustomed to observe it is not to be marveled at, that all other business should on occasions be suspended; and that the labours attendant thereon, should be mingled with a due share of recreation. With the mind's ear they distinguish the spirit-stirring screak of the fiddle, the gruff jangling of the drum and the somniferous *smorzando* of the jews-harp, and the enlivening

scuffle of little feet in a helter-skelter jig upon the deal platform.... For the accommodation of those merry urchins and youngsters, who choose to "trip it on the
light fantastic toe," a floor is laid at one corner; over which presides some African
genius of melody, brandishing a cracked violin, and drawing most moving notes
from its agonized intestines, by dint of griping fingers and right-angled elbows.

This description is an example of a celebration involving all Nantucketers and
focuses on the importance of music and dance at the festival. The importance
of music to black community life is emphasized by Portia Maultsby, who notes
that the "fundamental concept that governs music performance in African
and African-derived cultures is that music-making is a participatory group
activity that serves to unite black people into a cohesive group for a common
purpose" (1990, 187).

New Guinea/Newtown

A distinct black community began to coalesce by the second quarter of the
eighteenth century, and like similar neighborhoods in other towns (e.g., Boston
and New Bedford), it was variously called Newtown, New Guinea, or sometimes simply Guinea (Hayden and Hayden 1999, 220; Karttunen 2003a, 2003b,
69, 78–80). A plat map produced in 1821 and stored in the Nantucket Town
Clerk's Office shows Newtown, Newtown Gate, Burnt Swamp Gate, ropewalks,
four windmills, and the black burying ground, with a structure labeled "Negro
Hall" in the center of the community. The Newtown Gate, a barrier located
near the first milestone, demarcated the bounds of the African American community. In use as late as 1840, the gate as a landmark of the late-eighteenth-
and early-nineteenth-century landscape served as a clear indication that the
African community was "beyond the pale" or outside of what was then considered the town proper, separated as it was by the same gate intended to keep
sheep from roaming freely in the town (Worth 1906, 271). Newtown was further
separated from Nantucket Town by a large sheep pasture. Native Americans,
it seems, were also forced to lived outside town proper, in or near the Newtown community. For example, the proprietors' records for November 29, 1794,
show that "James Dier an Indian Man" obtained "A Piece of Land Near Newtown at a Place where the Black People Live" (book 1, Nantucket Town Clerk's
Records, 180).

The neighborhood as depicted on an 1834 map included the "Five Corners"
intersection formed by York Street, West York Lane, Pleasant Street, Atlantic
Avenue, and Prospect Street as well as a network of lanes and alleyways (Hayden
and Hayden 1999, 220). The original street names often reflected the African
origins of their inhabitants: Angola Street was one of the original alleyways; New
Guinea Street was the original name for Atlantic Avenue. One writer (quoted
in Burns 1981, 31) noted that "a century ago, this part of town was so dark that

coming through at night" gave a traveler the sensation of "being in a place as dark as 'Job's Pocket.'"

Absalom Boston was Nantucket's only black whaling captain, a trustee of the African School, and the son of one of the earliest settlers of Newtown. "Between 1770 and 1790 Tobias (Absalom's uncle) a whalefisherman, Seneca (Absalom's father) a weaver, and Essex (another uncle) a shoemaker, for example, all bought land in the West Monomoy shares...and during the next half-century would buy part or most of the land in the third, fourth, fifth, sixth, and seventh lots of the West Monomoy shares" (Cary and Cary 1977, 16–17). Most of Newtown is located in the original West Monomoy shares, as is the Meeting House.

The African Meeting House

The African Baptist Society Meeting House, located at York and Pleasant Streets, Nantucket, was constructed in the 1820s. The exact year is not certain, but Karttunen (2003b, 102) infers from documentary evidence that construction had begun before the land for the school was legally obtained on March 26, 1825, from Jeffrey Summons, a successful black laborer who sold the parcel and a *standing structure* to the African School trustees for $10.50, "so long as they shall keep a school house standing on the said land which is kept in good repair and a school to be kept in it forever...and the said house is by these presents conveyed & confirmed to the Society occupying the same under the name of a Baptist Society" (Nantucket Town Clerk's Records, book 20, 208; see also discussion in Karttunen 2003b, 94–95). A structure referred to as the "Negro Hall," certainly a community center, was in existence at least by 1821 (Elizabeth Oldham, Nantucket, pers. comm., 1999). The African Baptist Meeting House thrived as a church and community center until the last decade of the nineteenth century, but it was not until 1911 that its doors were shut and locked. A Nantucket city directory, dated 1897, stated that services were no longer held there. The building served as a garage at the end of the first quarter of the twentieth century. Since its acquisition by the Museum of Afro-American History in 1989, the Friends of the Meeting House have restored it and maintained its grounds. The building was rededicated in August 1992, and since being reopened to the public in 1999, it has been the location for concerts, lectures, and other events.

A photograph taken from the southeast ca. 1912 shows a centrally placed door in the front of the building with a window on either side (Fig. 19.2). Two fairly large trees are located in front in the southwest and southeast corners. The photo shows a wood post, pale, and rail fence surrounding the parcel on the southern and western bounds and lining the walkway up to the front door. The photo also shows that the area to the north of the Meeting House property was

Fig. 19.2. African Meeting House, facing north, ca. 1912.
Courtesy Nantucket Historical Association.

not developed. The emblem over the door is a Greek key: a labyrinthine, maze-like, rectilinear relief. The reason for the use of this symbol is not known, but the Baptist Church (ca. 1848) on Summer Street, Nantucket, bears it as well; it could have been a decorative detail added by an architect who worked on both structures (Helen Seager, Nantucket, pers. comm., 1999). The photograph also shows the fence that bounds the Pleasant Street side of the property in a lower position than it occupies today as well as what may be a gate along the northwest run of that same fence. Another pictorial source illustrating the Meeting House, albeit from the rear, is J. J. Stoner's 1881 *Bird's-Eye View of Nantucket* (Fig. 19.3). This map shows two windows on the north face of the structure, three windows and a door (located in the southeast corner) on the east face, and possibly a chimney in the northeast corner of the building. There is no privy visible on the property.

The Meeting House as Church and Community Center

As noted above, the earliest evidence of a meeting house for the black community is the 1821 plat showing the "Negro Hall." Although the name of the structure does not identify its function, one can deduce that it was a meeting place for various activities. W. E. B. Du Bois describes African American meeting houses as serving multiple purposes—school, church, workplace,

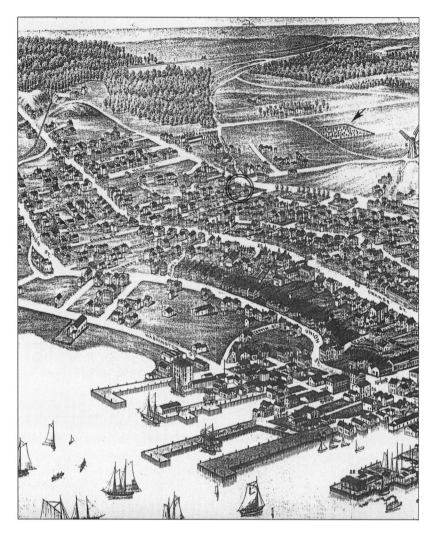

Fig. 19.3. Detail of J. J. Stoner's *Bird's-Eye View of Nantucket* (1881),
showing the Meeting House (#15); the African cemetery is in
the upper right.

theater, and center for community activity. The African Baptist Meeting House
built at the corner of Pleasant and York served multiple purposes as well. Documents indicate that the church and school were contemporary and that both
were established between 1823 and 1825; they also record that smallpox vac-
cinations were administered at the Meeting House in 1834 and that the abolitionist meetings were held there (Linebaugh 1978, 7).

The African School

The establishment of the African School, its role in the institution of public and desegregated schools on Nantucket and in Massachusetts, its instructors, and even the students have been researched and discussed in detail in the literature. Founding of the African School has been attributed to many individuals, including Frederick Baylies, Deacon William Rawson, Absalom Boston, and Edward J. Pompey. Linebaugh (1978, 7) notes that Baylies and Rawson, both white, are usually credited with founding the school, although Boston and Pompey, who were both leaders in the black community, also played a significant role in its establishment. Most of the records pertaining to the African School are school committee reports or items that appeared in the *Nantucket Inquirer*. The 1827 school committee report (stored in the Town Clerk's Office) revealed that "a School for coloured children has also been maintained, under the superintendence of the Town Committee which has embraced about 40 scholars." On April 18, 1829, the *Inquirer* reported that "the present number of scholars in the African School in this town, is forty-seven; of whom 34 write, 30 read in the Testament, 12 in Spelling books and 5 in the alphabet—their writing would do credit to scholars whose opportunities would have been much greater than those children have had, and their reading, spelling, exercises in arithmetic &c, &c were very creditable both to their instructor and themselves."

During the 1840s the school was well documented, although not in a favorable light. The 1840s were a time of turmoil for Nantucketers as well as the rest of the nation. Integration became a topic much written about in the local papers. In June 1840, a move was made to enter black children into the public schools; it was not until 1843, however, that the schools were desegregated (Linebaugh 1978, 12–13). During the spring of 1844 the schools of Nantucket were segregated again; the African School therefore reopened and operated until 1847, closing down after the reintegration of Nantucket schools made it possible for black children to attend public school (Linebaugh 1978, 37, 49). The history of the black community of Nantucket is extensive and rich. The Meeting House was an important center not just for the African Baptist congregation but also for the larger community of black Nantucketers; it is a place where much of its identity and history were created and maintained. Archaeological investigations have contributed in many ways to our understanding of the significance of the Meeting House.

Archaeology at the Meeting House Site

Excavations at the lot on which the Meeting House stands included testing both inside and outside of the existing structure (Fig. 19.4). Investigations were aimed at learning about the former appearance of the Meeting House and its grounds, the sorts of activities that took place in and around it, and whether

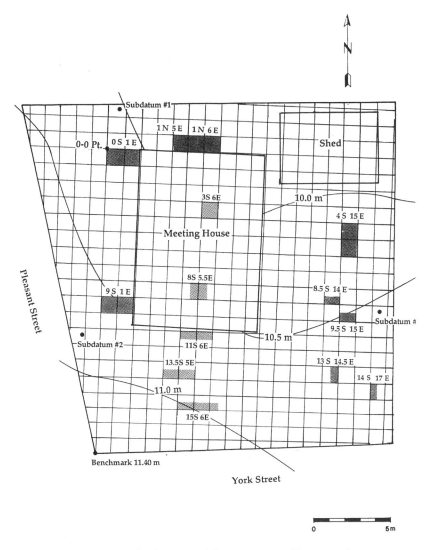

**Fig. 19.4. The footprint of the structure and location of
test trenches at the Meeting House site.**
Drawing by Gerald MacComber.

there was evidence of any activities on the site before the Meeting House was
built. The results of the excavation contributed to our understanding of the
site in three areas: landscaping; architecture and furnishings of the Meeting
House; and artifacts lost or left behind by people who came to the Meeting
House to worship, attend school, listen to lectures or concerts, or enjoy social
gatherings.

404

Landscaping

Archaeology was limited to exploratory trenches, but these were placed strategically in order to examine deposits both inside and around the Meeting House. The most striking result of excavations was the evidence of formation processes at the site—especially about alterations to the topography of the land before the Meeting House was constructed.

Several of trenches were excavated to considerable depth to reach the original land surface and the underlying sterile glacial deposits. This proved that the land purchased by the African Baptist congregation for its Meeting House had originally been bisected by a deep ravine. There was evidence that the ravine began to fill in through natural erosion some time in the late eighteenth century, probably just after the American Revolution. The deepest of the slope-wash deposits produced pottery dating to the third quarter of the eighteenth century. The British occupied the island and cut down all the trees for fuel during the conflict, and lack of ground cover led to considerable erosion here. But this did not fill up this declivity entirely; a great deal of fill was brought in to level the land before the Meeting House was erected. Several of the stone piers upon which the Meeting House rests extended deeply into the fill in order to stabilize the structure. The building never had a continuous foundation, but it survived the decades without visible subsidence, so the footings or piers functioned well.

All around the structure there was evidence of a hard-packed sandy surface that served as the yard during the time the Meeting House was in use, much different both in appearance and in cultural significance from the green lawn that is such a prominent feature of the site today. The archaeological record revealed that throughout the nineteenth century, the yard had been meticulously maintained and swept clear of refuse as well as of vegetation. This practice is a culturally distinctive way of organizing and maintaining communal space that results in a compact "living floor" affording open space for a variety of activities: in this instance, children's play, picnics or church socials, and perhaps crafts or production of some type. There is a strong tradition of "swept yards" in Africa and in the rural American South (e.g., Gundaker 1993; Westmacott 1992), and archaeologists regularly find evidence of swept yards at slave quarters and freed slave sites in the southeast and in the Caribbean (for recent discussions of the significance of swept yards in the Atlantic African Diaspora, see Battle 2004; Franklin 2004), but other examples of swept yards have not been encountered in New England. Documents provide clear evidence that black Nantucketers considered themselves to be African (see Karttunen 2003b); what is more, both black and white residents of Nantucket, a major whaling port, were in constant contact with the world beyond the island's shores via the masters, crews, and passengers of sailing vessels that put in at its harbor. It is therefore not surprising to find evidence of a traditional African manner of yard treatment even in this far-flung outpost of the Atlantic African Diaspora.

Another feature of the landscape that proved somewhat unusual was the original walkway leading from York Street to the door through which people entered the Meeting House. This was a carefully mounded ramp of tamped sand and earth (Fig. 19.5), elevated well above the surface of the Meeting House yard, which lies considerably lower than Pleasant Street to the west. It was flanked by a drainage trench on either side. The walk and sides of the ditches were revetted with planks studded with copper nails. The planks were recycled from the hull of a ship. The copper nails were hammered into the planks in an effort to protect the ship from ship's worm. So the walkway employed a construction technique, tamped earth, with African connections, and at the same time exhibited the African American adaptation of imaginative reuse of available materials. The result was a raised, well-drained ramp-style walk that allowed people to enter the Meeting House without having to negotiate puddles or standing water during inclement weather.

The Building

The Meeting House has survived to the present, far from intact but nevertheless retaining much of its original fabric. Architectural historians and the project's architect have therefore relied almost solely upon the building itself to tell its story and to guide them in its restoration. Although no ecclesiastical artifacts (or none recognized as such) were found, some of the finds contributed small details about lighting and heating the building.

Various means of artificial illumination were used within the Meeting House over time, and this was reflected by the fragments of glass lamp chimneys and globes found in every trench excavated, indicating that lamps, using whale oil and then kerosene, were used throughout the nineteenth century. Parts of gaslight fixtures, along with several graphite arc-lamp cathodes, speak to the adoption of technological advances in indoor lighting. The cathodes date to the last quarter of the nineteenth century and may reflect a partial transition from gas to an early form of electric lighting. A Sanborn Fire insurance map from 1904 indicates that the Meeting House had kerosene lights, with stoves as sources of heat, and the 1909 Sanborn map reveals that the lighting and heating sources were the same but adds that "no chimney, stove pipe passes through north side of building."

Small Things Lost or Left Behind

As expected, many artifacts relating to the use of the structure as a school, including writing slate and stylus fragments, were found. Artifacts that could have been used by students included marbles (with the caveat that adults also used marbles), a porcelain doll face, a doll eye and arm, a jackknife, a possible

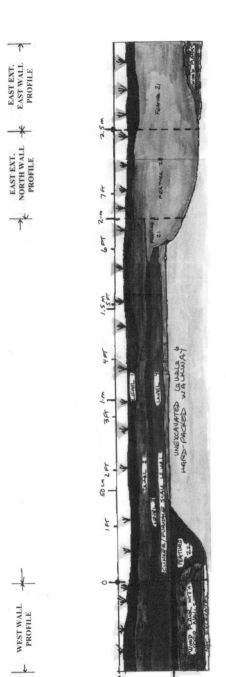

WEST WALL
PROFILE

EAST EXT.
NORTH WALL
PROFILE

EAST EXT.
EAST WALL
PROFILE

SOIL KEY:

Level 1: 10YR 2/2 Very dark brown fine sandy silt
Level 2: 10YR 2/2 Very dark brown compact sandy loam with gravel
Level 3: 10YR 3/2 Very dark grayish brown compact silty fine and medium sand
Level 4: 10YR 6/1, 10YR 4/1, and 10YR 3/1 silty sand and clinkers and furnace scales
Level 5: 10YR 4/4 Dark yellowish brown medium sand mottled with small pockets of
         10YR 5/4 Yellowish brown medium sand with gravel. Loose matrix.
Level 6: 10YR 5/4 Yellowish brown fine to coarse sand mottled with
         10YR 5/6 Yellowish brown fine to coarse sand. Unexcavated.

SCALE

50 cm   1 FT

Fig. 19.5. Profile of the tamped-earth walkway.
Drawing by Ellen P. Berkland.

gaming piece, two rubber balls, two harmonica parts, a red wax crayon, a copper alloy tip from a writing pen, and the top ferrule or finial from a small flag pole. These artifacts bear close similarities to the assemblage of "student artifacts" excavated at the site of the Abiel Smith School in Boston (Mead 1995). There was ample evidence of smoking in the form of pipe stem fragments, some made of coarse red earthenware and most made of undecorated white ball clay and dated 1750–1800, prior to construction of the Meeting House. This is perhaps evidence that people came together to socialize in this out-of-the-way spot before it became a formal site for congregational worship.

The Meeting House served not just as a place of worship and as a school; it also was a gathering place for the congregation and the community as a whole. It seems logical, therefore, to infer that the pristine surface of the Meeting House's swept yard served as a staging point for many a church supper. The Meeting House lacked cooking facilities, so such events for the most part would have been covered-dish or potluck meals. The site produced plenty of evidence, mainly in the form of utilitarian crockery, some large serving platters, sauce bottles, Mason jars and lid liners, seeds, eggshells, bones with knife marks, and eating utensils.

The ceramic assemblage was diverse, but fragments of decorated white improved earthenware plates were most numerous. Second-most abundant were fragments of decorated pearlware vessels for brewing and drinking tea. Fragments of plain creamware plates and many pieces of utilitarian lead-glazed redwares—crocks and bowls—round out the assemblage.

Most of the glass fragments found were from mold-blown and machine-made bottles, some of which once contained patent medicines. A perfume bottle was something of a curious find. The assemblage contains fragments of only two beverage alcohol containers, so it is possible that members of the congregation adhered to temperance codes common among black activists during the 1830s (Hodges 1997, xxxiii), but it is also quite likely that other types of containers were used for transporting and drinking alcoholic beverages (Robert Hall, Boston, pers. comm., 1999).

One item stands out among the glass: a fragment of a clear circular molded bottle. The glass bears the embossed image of a periwigged male face with a factory vignette in the background. But this is no mere piece of broken glass: along one edge a series of small flakes have been deliberately removed through a process similar to flint-knapping (Fig. 19.6). Berkland's research has linked this find to a distinctive class of artifacts recovered by Wilkie at the slave quarter of the Oakley Plantation in Louisiana and at the Lucretia Perryman site in Mobile, Alabama (Wilkie 1996; 2000, 153–55; 2003, 127). Wilkie identified these as handmade glass scrapers, knapped from bottles. Using oral histories, she concluded that these were tools made on the spot by women for tasks such as sewing and minor cutting, but she sees them primarily as elements of women's healing kits, used in preparing herbal remedies. Knowledge of traditional healing and of glass-knapping would have been handed down from

Fig. 19.6. Flint glass tool, obverse and reverse sides.
Drawing by Bice Perruzi and Ellen P. Berkland.

mother to daughter. Wilkie sees these as distinctive African American cultural products that are also gendered artifacts. Our find does not fit into the category of a knapped tool per se, but has the characteristics of what one expert has referred to as "opportunistic implements" (Curtis Runnels, Boston, pers. comm., 2004). The recovery of a possible glass implement at the site of the African Meeting House on Nantucket is provocative and intriguing, but there is no larger context in which to interpret the artifact. Further investigation into the material culture of the African community on Nantucket might shed light not just on this object but on many as yet unexplored facets of the experiences of African Nantucketers.

The site produced little in the way of material related to dress or personal adornment, which is not unusual given that this was an institutional site without any domestic component. The personal items tended to be small things like beads or clothing fasteners that could have been lost easily by the wearer. Fasteners included a clothing snap, grommets, and many buttons. Among the items of personal adornment were three beads: a cobalt blue hand-worked faceted glass bead, a clear glass bead, and a tan glass bead. Given the popularity of beadwork in the nineteenth century, it is difficult to state with certainty whether these beads came from garments to which they had been sewn, from jewelry, or from other items such as bags, parasols, hats, and so on. Much has been made of the significance of beads as tangible symbols of gender identity and social signaling among African, Afro-Caribbean, and African American cultural groups (e.g., Franklin 2004, 127–28, 222; Stine, Cabak, and Groover 1996; Yentsch 1995), but it is very difficult to use the minimal evidence from the Nantucket Meeting House to offer nuanced interpretations. The beads were more likely to have been worn by women or girls than by men, but it would be a mistake to assume that only female members of Nantucket's African community adorned themselves with beads and jewelry. Jeffrey Bolster notes that Captain Absalom Boston (Fig. 19.7), master of the Nantucket whaler *Industry*, posed in 1822 for his portrait in gold hoop earrings and a white shirt and tie, "revealing a man comfortable with several identities and conscious of his status" (1997; see also Cary and Cary 1977). As if to remind us that men as well as women may have adorned themselves in meaningful ways that expressed gender, age, status, and pride in appearance and accomplishment, the assemblage includes a fragment of a pressed copper alloy pendant or medal bearing the image of a man with

Fig. 19.7. Portrait of Absalom Boston, probably painted
during the mid-1820s.
Courtesy Nantucket Historical Association.

a rifle. This may have been awarded for marksmanship or skill in hunting or served as a badge of membership in a men's shooting or hunt club. Three additional artifacts of personal adornment are likely evidence of male display in dress: a metal and celluloid pin bearing the image of a naval flag; a copper alloy pin with a clip for securing something, perhaps a badge, in place; and a small white metal bar with links attached to it, possibly a watch fob.

There were a few sewing implements in deposits dating to the period when the Meeting House was in use as a school and church, and these can be interpreted as additional clues to the ubiquitous presence of women, who were important and active members of the congregation as well as of the community (Karttunen 2003b, 94–95), who brought their "work"—their sewing—along with them to meetings and other gatherings. Items possibly lost from women's workbaskets or workbags included a tiny turned bone cap with screw threads, possibly the lid for a pin poppet or needle case, and a deep-drawn machine-made copper alloy thimble of a form typical of the first half of the nineteenth century (Deagan 2002, 203). The thimble had been pressed flat into the walkway; indeed, it was so embedded into its upper surface that it seems to have been tamped down as part of the matrix when the walk was created. But it could also have been dropped and accidentally trodden into the walkway's surface. A single copper alloy straight pin was found just above the walkway, and three others were found in the upper level of a trench excavated inside the meetinghouse. It seems likely these fell through the meetinghouse's leaky floor of loosely fitted wide pine boards.

Conclusion

Archaeological investigations at the African Baptist Society Meeting House on Nantucket provided evidence of an African-informed aesthetic of landscape treatment in the form of a swept yard maintained as a space for communal assembly and socializing. The tamped earth walkway revealed ingenuity both in its construction and in its reuse of materials drawn from the close links that many African Nantucketers had to the sea and to maritime activities. The material culture reflected the emergence of blended identities; members of the community considered themselves Africans, but they were African Americans or, at the very least, African Nantucketers, and as such they used the Meeting House as a stage upon which to form a collective identity and from which to express their solidarity in seeking the rights of full citizenship as members of the larger community.

The Meeting House has now been restored and again serves as a focal point for the community and as a tangible link with Nantucket's past as a multiracial, multiethnic society. It was not feasible for the restoration to make use of what archaeologists have brought to light: neither the swept yard nor the walkway conform to contemporary aesthetics or regulations about safety and accessibility. In the nineteenth century this site was as pleasing to the eyes of many beholders as it is today, but for very different reasons. It was well used and scrupulously maintained; it was a place where all members of the black community—men, women, and children—came together to worship and to learn, to socialize and to strengthen the bonds of mutual support and obligation.

In the early nineteenth century, churches and meeting houses were crucial centers in the black community. Often forced to live in unwelcoming situations and to experience daily the effects of informal as well as legalized racial discrimination, African Americans sought to establish a sense of autonomy, a sense of African community, and a sense of dignity, place, and belonging. The African Baptist Society Meeting House, the center for the black community of Nantucket, became a place of centering for an otherwise diverse group in an isolated and little-known outpost of the Atlantic African Diaspora.

Acknowledgments

Archaeology at the African Meeting House on Nantucket was sponsored by the Museum of Afro-American History, Boston, with the support of the Tupancy-Harris Foundation. John James, the architect for the restoration and liaison between the archaeologists and the museum, provided valuable assistance. Helen Seager, the convener for the Friends of the Meeting House, coordinated the volunteer and public outreach component of the project and secured equipment from local shops. Wesley Tiffney Jr., director of the University of Massachusetts Field Station on Nantucket, provided accommodations for the field crew. We also thank Doug Beattie, overseer at Gouin Village, and Eleanor Jones for assistance and logistical support.

Additional businesses and individuals supporting the project included Marine Home Center, Island Pharmacy, Nantucket One-Hour Photo, Friends of the African Meeting House on Nantucket, Nantucket Historical Association, Nantucket Bike Shop, Educational Management Network, Unitarian Church, Nantucket Bake Shop, Carl Crossman, Christine Vining, Mara Cary, Belinda Phillips, Russell A. Sibley, Robert Lindvall, Tamsen Merrill, and Mrs. Sara David. On Nantucket, the staff at the Town Clerk's Office and the Athenaeum were exceedingly helpful with archival research. Special thanks to Jacqueline K. Haring, Elizabeth Oldham, and Betsy Tyler at the Foulger Museum for their attentiveness and thoroughness in helping to locate documents. Professor Robert Hall of Northeastern University offered many helpful insights that strengthened our interpretations, and Professor Curtis Runnels of Boston University aided us in interpreting our glass "tool."

Archaeologists Zachary J. Davis, Ann-Eliza Lewis, Timothy Scarlett, and Carolyn White served as field crew members, and Gerald MacComber donated his time to produce a topographical map of the site.

CHAPTER TWENTY

Practicing African American Archaeology in the Atlantic World

Anna S. Agbe-Davies

When Adelaide K. Bullen and Ripley P. Bullen excavated "Black Lucy's Garden," they were far ahead of the curve; in fact, there was no curve. In 1943, there was little precedent for excavating post-contact North American sites, let alone those associated with ordinary people and everyday life. Certainly there were few attempts to use archaeology to investigate the lives of people outside the "mainstream"—racial minorities, women, the working classes—all labels that could be applied to Lucy Foster. The excavation report describes the site and its contents admirably. The authors treated Foster's story with dignity and furthermore noted that "the history of the specimens dug up cannot be properly separated from the history of those who used them" (Bullen and Bullen 1945, 26). Yet no attempt was made to examine the finds in light of Lucy Foster's place in society as a single black woman and former slave. There was no existing intellectual or disciplinary framework within which to understand this domestic assemblage from nineteenth-century rural New England.

Fast-forward to the present day: historical archaeology has emerged as a full-fledged specialization, taking as its subject the emergence and transformation of the modern world (Schuyler 1999), including the global interchange of people, products, and ideas since 1492. Among the specific themes that historical archaeology has confronted is the massive forced migration of Africans across the Atlantic and its worldwide consequences. Thus African American archaeology (Singleton 1995, 121) has proved a subject of great interest to historical archaeologists (Agbe-Davies 2002a). Here I discuss the social significance of this work as practiced today. I have taken "practice" as an organizing concept to evoke the idea of a process of continual improvement, a habitual act, and finally an occupation or vocation. These meanings are also implied

413

in the concept of "practice theory," which furthermore posits a reciprocal relationship between social action and social structure (Ortner 1984).

After a brief summary of the early trajectory of research in African American archaeology, I review major aspects of its practice and discuss the relationships among selected theoretical and thematic trends, namely, ideas about cultural distinctiveness, consumption, and power. Next, I describe the settings within which African American archaeology has flourished and contrast its popularity as a research topic with the slow integration of practitioners of African descent into the profession. Finally, I examine the intersection of African American archaeology with the public sphere. How does this work reach and impact a nonarchaeological audience? Is African American archaeology empowering for people of African descent in the Americas today? I conclude with comments on the contexts within which these points matter, for archaeological practice and for us as inheritors of a world shaped by Atlantic Africa and its diasporas.

Ideas of African American Archaeology

In the United States, African American archaeology emerged in earnest in the late 1960s and early 1970s. Excavations of free black communities like Weeksville (1968), Sandy Ground (1971), the African Meeting House in Boston (1975), and Parting Ways (1975), as well as the plantation quarters at Kingsley (1968), Cumberland Island (1969), Kingsmill (1972), and Cannon's Point (1973), were spurred by a heady mix of civil rights activism, new historic preservation laws, and the twin influences of the new social history and Black Power on the academy (see especially Schuyler 1980). Soon, even at sites previously concerned with the glorification of the elite and powerful, attention turned toward the previously ignored black presence, for example, at Monticello (1981),[1] Colonial Williamsburg (1986), and Annapolis (1989). Important early research elsewhere in the Americas included the plantations at Newton (1971), New Montpelier (1973), Drax Hall (1980), and Gallways (1980).

The theoretical lines along which African American archaeology is practiced today were set early on and to a certain extent they paralleled those in other disciplines. Archaeologists found themselves facing the same conundrums that confronted historians, sociologists, and sociocultural anthropologists, particularly, how to think about evidence of Atlantic Africa in the Americas (Herskovits 1958; Mintz and Price 1976). For a time, the search for "Africanisms" was paramount. Anticipating that few artifacts would accompany Africans through the Middle Passage in any literal sense, archaeologists set their sights on objects with stylistic similarities to African precedents as well as site and assemblage patterns that reflected African sensibilities.

Africanisms come in many and varied forms. Archaeologists have made compelling, if not uncontested, arguments for the African antecedents of certain ceramic- and pipe-making traditions in North America and the Caribbean (see, e.g., Haviser 1999, *contra* Mouer et al. 1999). Beads, crystals, coins, and other small finds are often interpreted in light of magical/religious practices rooted in Africa (e.g., Leone and Fry 2001; Russell 1997), particularly when excavated from provocative contexts such as isolated caches or portals to the spirit world (Yentsch 1991). Attempts to isolate the "African" in African American extended to the tabulation of artifact types to identify a "slave pattern" (see multiple contributions to Singleton 1985).

However, the emphasis on Africanisms and uniquely African-derived traits led to unintended consequences. Archaeologists interpreted a lack of obvious distinctions between the material world of African Americans and that of their Euro-American contemporaries as evidence of acculturation, concluding that the force of European hegemony had overwhelmed the African heritage of African American culture. As Jean Howson (1990, 82) has noted, this interpretation confuses behavior with culture, and such simplistic approaches to the archaeological record provoked a number of essays, like Howson's, that explicitly discussed the implications of this research and the theoretical underpinnings of African American archaeology.

Archaeologists whose work is informed by critical theory were quick to point out that efforts to identify the characteristics of African American cultures usually avoided discussion of the structuring influence of the institution that placed them in the Americas. Before the emancipation edicts of the nineteenth century, slavery was a key paradigm structuring the lives of Africans in the Americas. The same may be said of racism, for the enslaved as well as their free contemporaries and descendants. This critique urged archaeologists to address the power differentials that have long characterized American societies, identifying the material correlates of racial ideologies that simultaneously reinforced and fed off of a general hegemony of white over black. This perspective, it is argued, would shift archaeologists' attention away from attempts to define the material distinctiveness of African Americans. By adopting the (mostly mass-produced) objects they found in American contexts, Africans and their descendants had not necessarily internalized the meanings accepted among those who controlled the design, production, and distribution of those objects (Urban 2001, 45–66). There is no one-to-one relationship between artifacts and their meanings. In fact, archaeologists should be able to identify alternate meanings for familiar artifacts based on a knowledge of African and African American history and practices, closer attention to the attributes of artifacts and their contexts, or an awareness of the processes by which material culture becomes a tool in ongoing social relationships, particularly relationships characterized by inequality (Williams 1992). For example, the discussion of root cellars turned from their possible African antecedents to their role in concealing contraband and avoiding the surveillance of watchful slave owners (McKee 1992), as well as to their importance for preserving privacy and property for people forced to live among strangers (Neiman 1997). When "power" replaces "tradition" as the guiding principle behind research, it provides a theoretical framework that bypasses dead-end debates about acculturation and "cultural" survival. It encourages us to focus on the relational aspects of human behavior rather than essentialist identities of human groups.

Yet a focus on power does not preclude investigation of the nature of African American identities. Although the predominant paradigm for such research continues to be "ethnicity," some historical archaeologists have embraced "race" as a useful concept. Indeed, I have argued elsewhere (Agbe-Davies 1999) that the modern anthropological concept of race as a socially constructed category (Mukhopadhyay and Moses 1997) shares a great deal with the more widely applied idea of ethnicity, provided we take ethnicity to be the practice-based concept described by Frederick Barth (1969), rather than the essentialist category found in popular discourse. A recent edited volume demonstrates the utility of a race concept for archaeology, placing race at the center of investigations of identity, with a majority of contributions discussing the African Diaspora (Orser 2001). Archaeologists have begun to appreciate the body of literature, labeled "critical race theory," that aims to expose the foundations of contemporary racism, explaining its structure and thereby robbing it of its "naturalness" and power (Delgado 1995). Not only does this school of thought force archaeologists to envision the applications of their work (Epperson 2001), but archaeology brings new data sets to the project, examining the material infrastructure of American racism over time.

Such research responds to the most pointed critiques of African American archaeology that focus on the contemporary implications of its practice. Parker Potter Jr. took archaeologists to task for failing to appreciate the political uses of archaeological interpretations. He argued against the prevailing practice among U.S. archaeologists of evaluating slave quarter sites in the United States and the Caribbean in terms of the original price of the ceramics excavated, observing that such work plays into the hands of apologists who would divert questions about quality of life to the cost or quality of material goods instead of the right to one's own person and labor. Potter further asserted that plantation archaeology was seldom of any use to contemporary African Americans, but that it should be. By "useful," he meant that archaeology should provide information or arguments that black people could use to participate in heritage production and challenge contemporary domination (Potter 1991, 100–101). Contributions to Carol McDavid and David Babson's *In the Realm of Politics: Prospects for Public Participation in African American and Plantation Archaeology* (1997) indicate that a number of archaeologists have taken such exhortations to heart and practice their craft accordingly. However, we should note that the critical stance is the subject of a countercritique. This position maintains that archaeologists should avoid political agendas and that research is ultimately *more* effective in contemporary settings when it can claim ideological neutrality (McKee 1994). While the debate is by no means settled, the fact that archaeologists are

416

addressing these questions at all suggests we have begun to recognize that our work has ramifications beyond the discipline.

Trends and Emerging Perspectives

The abrupt introduction of "plantation archaeology" as a synonym for "African American archaeology" at the end of the previous section should signal the way in which theory is inextricably bound up with research themes. Surely, debates about African heritage and power have completely different implications depending on whether one is talking about plantation archaeology or African American archaeology more generally. One can argue that they are not identical, but they are indeed difficult to distinguish. At first glance, it appears that studies of slavery, particularly plantation slavery, are the most common form of African American archaeology. An examination of the first thirty-five years of *Historical Archaeology* (1967–2001) confirms the impression. Of the sixty-six contributions describing research about members of the African Diaspora, forty-eight (72 percent) are wholly or predominantly concerned with pre-emancipation topics. For mainland North America, the rate is 69 percent; for the Caribbean, 100 percent; for South America, 100 percent; and for articles discussing or comparing multiple regions, 63 percent.[2] Of course, pre-emancipation topics are not restricted to the lives of African Americans as slaves. Articles emphasizing maroonage, or otherwise living outside of slavery in opposition to an existing slave regime, constituted 6 percent of the pre-emancipation grand total (see also Weik, Funari, this volume). Overall, nearly 60 percent of the articles dealt in whole or in part with plantation life before and after the American emancipations.

As noted, studies of slavery and of the plantation run the gamut of African American archaeology. Some work addresses "quality of life" questions, emphasizing hardship or revelations of unexpected "flexibility" within the strictures of slavery: evidence of limited autonomy, access to material wealth, or bending the rules. Other studies focus specifically on the struggle for power, the continual tension between domination and resistance. And yet, as perceptive archaeologists have noted, the focus on slavery is by no means universally attractive to people of African descent today, regardless of the theoretical orientation of the archaeologists concerned (Derry 1997).

Another significant, sometimes overlapping, body of work discusses African Americans as consumers. Consumerism, taste, and fashion are themes that underlie a great deal of historical archaeology's output, ranging from assertions that the working classes consume above their station to emulate their betters, to the idea that elites compete among themselves using luxury goods and that they deploy the trappings of material wealth in their power struggles with their subordinates. In archaeological research, African Americans appear as consumers in a variety of ways. As mentioned, some studies operate under the assumption that buying the products of the dominant sectors of society is tantamount to buying into the dominant ideology. However, alternative stances abound.

Archaeology allows an inquiry into the degree of African American partici-pation in local and, indirectly, transatlantic markets. Through careful analysis, archaeologists have determined that not all luxury goods found on slave quar-ter sites are hand-me-downs from the Big House, though certainly some were (Edwards 1990). Archaeology reveals the extent to which slaves had access to the full range of consumer goods circulating in the Americas (e.g., Heath 1999c) and how their choices among mass-produced consumer goods may have differed subtly from their Euro-American contemporaries (e.g., Wilkie 1999). Archaeology has shown how, post-emancipation, consumer choice was one of many means by which African Americans asserted their dignity in socie-ties that continually denied it (e.g., Mullins 1999) and oriented their consump-tion habits to avoid and subvert the racism of certain markets (e.g., Warner 1995). Clearly, studies of African American consumer behavior have gone beyond arguments about acculturation and authenticity.

And yet what does it mean to position consumption as a form of power? Have we as archaeological practitioners "bought into" the dominant ideology, just as we once suspected past African American populations of doing? I remember when the U.S. public sphere was rich with stories about people, particularly black people, perpetrating or suffering violence over the value or symbolism of their clothing. Conspicuous consumption is the hallmark of celebrities of all backgrounds, and yet it seems to carry extra symbolic weight when those celeb-rities are of African descent (see the rise of "bling bling"). Furthermore, U.S. citizens are being told that spending money is our patriotic duty, that citizen-shoppers are the only force propping up a weakened economy. In the early twenty-first century, many of us are used to thinking about people in terms of what they own and buy. To what extent is this idea our inheritance from previ-ous centuries, and to what extent is it a recent development? When archaeolo-gists study the consumer behavior of African Americans in the past, we might consider the influence of the contemporary consumer ideology that prepares us to think of ourselves and others as shoppers in a global marketplace and to see purchases of mass-marketed goods as a form of agency.

I have limited my discussion to only a few of the many research avenues in an African American archaeology that grows more complex and diverse with each passing year. And yet I wish to close by recalling the mid-1990s assess-ments of the field that claimed that analysis has yet to catch up with our rapidly expanding data set (Samford 1996, 113; Singleton and Bograd 1995, 29). Since the partial turn away from pattern analysis, there have been few new ideas about how to synthesize the available material. Studies of individual sites and site clusters have become increasingly sophisticated, but there has been less effort toward advancing comparative studies. One attempt to revitalize comparative research is under way among archaeologists who began by studying the lives of enslaved Virginians. The Digital Archaeological Archive of Comparative Slavery mission is to standardize and computerize the information recovered from the excavation of slave quarter sites and to make that data available for comparative study (www.daacs.org). While many practitioners have embraced the archaeological study of the African Diaspora as a viable and exciting endeavor, we have now reached a point where we need tools like the Digital Archive, in addition to theoretical advances, for larger-scale understandings.

What If You Practiced African American Archaeology, and No Black People Came?

That African American archaeology holds a growing interest for archaeologists can be readily demonstrated by looking at milestones in publishing. The first article in *Historical Archaeology* that focused on African American archaeology appeared in 1971. Similar contributions were sporadic through the mid-1980s but have exhibited a steadily upward trend since then (Schuyler 1980; Singleton 1985), and the newsletter *African-American Archaeology* debuted in 1990.

Any number of factors might explain the growing prevalence of African American archaeology. It may be as simple as the attraction of a novel topic—a new intellectual territory—or even the fact that preservation laws prescribe the excavation and study of many sites, regardless of the individual or collective research interests of archaeologists (but see Barile 2004). Yet in many instances, interest in African American archaeology seems to arise out of contemporary social conditions. It allows archaeologists to bring their expertise to bear on what W. E. B. Du Bois optimistically called "the problem of the Twentieth Century...the problem of the color-line" (1996 [1903], 1). A more complicated cause could lie in the culture of archaeology itself, a discipline that evolved from antiquarianism and treasure hunting and that perpetuates a romantic notion of fieldwork in strange and exotic locations, however those might be defined. In this scenario, past African Americans serve as one of several local versions of the foreign. In countries where archaeologists are traditionally trained as anthropologists, there are additional reasons for the fetishism for the foreign, the Other (see also the discussion in Blakey 2001, 402; Singleton 1995, 121).

For while it is a generalization, one can say that today African American archaeology is largely the study of an Other. Unlike the field of history, in which many early scholars of the African American past were themselves of African descent, few of the professionals practicing African American archaeology—at any point in its brief existence—identify themselves as African Americans (Agbe-Davies 2002a; Franklin 1997b). This should come as no surprise when we consider that archaeology as a whole includes few Americans of African descent.[3] One way to measure this participation is to consult surveys conducted by professional archaeological organizations. The Society for Historical Archaeology reports that barely 0.1 percent of its respondents characterized themselves as African Americans (DeCorse and DiSanto 1999). While the perception within the field is that more African Americans are becoming archaeologists and that some of these men and women are pursuing African American archaeology (Franklin 1997b), there are few benchmarks by which to measure the shift (Agbe-Davies 2002a).

If the archaeologists are seldom African Americans, what about the audiences? Because archaeologists of African America practice in different kinds of settings including university, museum, and cultural resource management archaeology, there are several routes by which the research reaches a non-archaeologist audience. There are few prescribed vehicles for disseminating university-based research other than university classrooms and academic texts. While university archaeologists often create their own opportunities for public access—lectures, lay publications, documentaries, etc.—there are few professional inducements to encourage the practice. Furthermore, the information, styles, and formats appropriate to an academic setting are not always suitable or useful for a lay audience (Gibb 1997; Potter 1991). Museums are another important setting for making research public. For example, the reconstructed slave quarter at Carter's Grove[4] provided a venue for discussing eighteenth-century plantation slavery in a museum initially dedicated to the role of elite Virginians in the Revolutionary War. When archaeology is performed as a commercial undertaking to preserve or rescue endangered sites (as with cultural resource management), the work is usually done in the public's name. However, as with academic archaeology, members of the general public might not have the tools or the inclination to seek out and decipher the final product. Yet regardless of setting—university, museum, or rescue excavation—experience shows that it is not always easy to get an African American audience to turn out for African American archaeology (see also Derry 1997; Haviser 2001; Singleton 1995).

Then Again, What If They Did?

Perhaps noting the worldwide trend of indigenous challenges to archaeological authority, archaeologists of African America have become conscious of the need to be responsive to the African American public(s). This awareness does not preclude controversy, of course, which can be prompted equally by worries about either exclusion or unequal treatment. At a recent excavation in Barbados, my colleagues and I tried mightily to emphasize information about the lives of black Barbadians when we felt that their story was in danger of being eclipsed by the site's brief association with an elite Euro-American visitor from the colony of Virginia (Agbe-Davies, Ladd, and Brown 2001; Agbe-Davies in press). In part, we hoped to reorient the focus of the associated heritage tourism project, one that a local editorial writer had criticized for glorifying "a foreign slave-owner" (Hughes 1999). Well-publicized controversies at the New York African Burial Ground illustrate the determination of African Americans to see their bioarchaeological patrimony treated with dignity and to obtain results that are meaningful for the descendant community (LaRoche and Blakey 1997).

The case of the New York African Burial Ground begs the question, though, of what we mean by "descendant community." Often African American archaeology touches the lives of direct descendants of a site's inhabitants. In some cases that means unearthing distressing information that resonates within the family and the larger community (McDavid 2002). In other cases, it offers the archaeologist insight into important research questions or provides a setting for renewing family ties (Reeves 2004). Sometimes, "descent" is based on institutions other than the biological family (neighborhoods, schools, or churches, for example) or even something as difficult to define as shared identity. All such groups have a claim on the archaeologist's attention, and for the most part, archaeologists of African America recognize that claim and current practice reflects this (Agbe-Davies 2002b; Edwards-Ingram 1997; Franklin 1997b).

However, descendants—whether direct or indirect—are not the only important audience for African American archaeology. Clearly, Americans of all backgrounds and nations would benefit from a more complete understanding of our shared past. American societies would be better off if those who benefit from racism were confronted with its material correlates and structural embeddedness (Farnsworth 1993). Yet how useful is African American archaeology to these or any constituencies? How can we assess its effectiveness? In the fifteen years that the Carter's Grove slave quarter was open to the public, it educated thousands of visitors and had a significant impact on the museum world (Chappell 1999). The Office of Public Education and Interpretation of the African Burial Ground reached over 40,000 people with its publications and many thousands more through on-site programs and the media (LaRoche and Blakey 1997). Yet apart from the numbers of people who are directly informed by these and similar projects, how can we conceptualize and assess the impact of African American archaeology. To what extent is knowledge power?

The Power of African American Archaeology

I suggest that we think of African American archaeology as a potential force for empowerment in two overlapping arenas. First, it can serve as a source of information for deployment in struggles for equality. Second, it is a practice that by its very enactment can undermine the status quo, in part by questioning its "naturalness."

A vindicationist thread runs through much of historical archaeology. Researchers aim to draw attention to neglected facets of the American story or to valorize people and groups whose importance was denied in their own lifetimes (B. J. Little 1994). Indeed, this is a large portion of what our public expects of African American archaeology: to fill in the gaps left in the documentary record and round out a partial and/or biased understanding of the past (LaRoche and Blakey 1997). The search for Africanisms was and still is an important component of this project. Despite the problems associated with essentialist or simplistic applications, archaeologists did not set out to demonstrate cultural capitulation—quite the opposite. On one level, the search for African cultural continuities in the Americas was an attempt to highlight the resilience of men, women, and children who, far from being brainwashed by their captors, persistently maintained their own ways of being human. Such findings are often particularly appealing to contemporary African Americans for whom the idea of African practices in the New World fits well with popular notions of identity and authenticity.[5] Sometimes this information is also available from texts, yet it is rendered more immediate by the very physicality of material culture.

To the idea of archaeology-as-corrective, we can add the dimension of time. Like other historical disciplines, archaeology allows us to observe the trajectory of American societies through time and the changing strategies and counterstrategies for living in a multiracial world in which race played a significant role in social hierarchies. Whether enslaved or free, African Americans used such varied devices as respectability (Singleton 2001c), separatism (Weik 1997), religion and magic (Brown and Cooper 1990; Leone and Fry 2001), and education (Reeves 2004; Wilkie and Shorter 2001) to make their way in the Atlantic world. While information about these strategies does provide tools for contemporary audiences to do the same, it also provides a context for understanding present social conditions, the roots of these conditions, and therefore their mutability.

The ways in which African American archaeology, by its very practice, changes the world are less tangible but no less important. First, the importance of African Americans "get[ting] a piece of the ink" (Dick Gregory, quoted in Deetz 1996, 213) lies not only in the more complete picture provided but also in an awareness that the picture is incomplete—indeed, that pictures *can* be incomplete—to begin with. When I discuss my work with nonarchaeologists, they are often surprised (and delighted) to learn that our understanding of the past is a work in progress, that current research does far more than just fine-tune established facts. When this awareness is achieved, one possible outcome is a dialogue—whether in the public sphere or among archaeologists—about the role that knowledge about the past can play in changing the present. These dialogues prompt action in the specific communities in which archaeology is practiced (e.g., LaRoche and Blakey 1997; Wilkie 2001) and within the professional community as a whole (e.g., Edwards-Ingram 1997; Franklin 2001). African American archaeology, perhaps even more than other topics, prompts archaeologists to use their unique skills to challenge contemporary ideologies (Leone 2005). But if archaeologists fail to recognize the importance of mounting these challenges from within, they do find expression elsewhere. Reactions to archaeological orthodoxy (e.g., those described in Haslip-Viera, Montellano, and Barbour 1997; Trigger 1992) find easy purchase outside the profession. These surrogate archaeologies thrive, in part, because African American archaeology has only partially penetrated the public sphere and perhaps still is insufficiently oriented toward the needs and political objectives of contemporary African Americans.

Conclusion: African American Archaeology in the World

The points made here—about whether African American archaeology is empowering to African Americans; about whether archaeology as a profession reflects the diverse backgrounds of American societies; about the interplay between research topics and theory; about the contexts within which we practice African American archaeology—are relevant for global efforts toward social justice and the advancement of human knowledge.

The modern world, like the worlds that preceded it, is a vastly unequal place. Racism is not the only ideology of oppression. And, contrary to the tropes that dominate U.S. discourse, racism is not a problem exclusively for people of African descent. One of the ways that the dominant powers (whether extragovernmental bodies, governments, corporations, or individuals) maintain their hegemony is by perpetuating the idea that there are no connections between structural racism, the troubles of the poor, problems of gender equity, or equal protection under the law. While it is commonplace for archaeological anthologies to organize studies of the disenfranchised in terms of race, *or* gender, *or* class (Delle, Mrozowski, and Paynter 2000; Scott 1994), the grouping makes it clear that these were strands in a single cable. This awareness can also be applied to the present.

A second motive for examining the themes discussed in this essay is their implications for archaeology as a discipline. Clearly, African American perspectives are lacking in African American archaeology in the United States, and I suspect the same could be true elsewhere in the Americas. We might make an argument for greater participation by people of African descent based on principles of fairness and equality (*pace* Leone and Preucel 1992). Or we might resort to essentialist ideas about cultural knowledge, privileging a presumed emic perspective on the archaeological record. Although archaeology, like other knowledge-producing enterprises, does not exist apart from its practitioners, I have argued that African American practitioners have a special stake in African American archaeology because its findings reflect on us in a way that they do not on other archaeologists (Agbe-Davies 1999). I would further argue, drawing on the idea of "situated knowledge" (Haraway 1988), that every view, because it comes from some particular perspective, is partial. Therefore, we may expect that when a discipline like archaeology is more thoroughly integrated, its findings will more closely approximate a complete truth. The more perspectives we have on the African American past (including those of black practitioners), the more complete the picture becomes.

Archaeologists point out the need for African and Africanist (perhaps even Afrocentric)[6] perspectives on African American archaeology (Agorsah 1996; DeCorse 1999; Posnansky 1999). One of the factors that constrains such perspectives and diminishes their impact on the field is the global distribution of power in contemporary archaeology. Immanuel Wallerstein noted that

> the whole archaeological enterprise from its inception—the social investment in this branch of scientific activity, the research orientation, the conceptual tools, the modes of resuming and communicating the results—are functions of the social present. To think otherwise is self-deceptive at best. Objectivity is honesty in this framework....Objectivity is the vector of a distribution of social investment in such activity such that it is performed by persons rooted in all the major groups of the world-system in a balanced fashion. Given this definition, we do not have an objective social science today. On the other hand, it is not an unfeasible objective within the foreseeable future. (Wallerstein 1974, 9–10)

Let us end by examining the present essay in light of this statement. Clearly I have written from a U.S. perspective and one centered in a particular region at that. Although I have tried to include examples from elsewhere in the Americas and to express general concepts in pan-American terms, I am painfully aware of the narrowness of my perspective, a narrowness that anthologies like this one—which spans the Atlantic and runs the length of the Americas—will no doubt help to alleviate.

I will say in my own defense that the structures of the discipline reinforce such parochial tendencies. For example, English remains the dominant language for international publication, even in a hemisphere in which English speakers are a minority. Likewise, archaeological societies and journals that are nominally international or pan-American in scope (such as the Society for American Archaeology and the Society for Historical Archaeology) are dominated by U.S. practitioners and, to a lesser extent, sites in the United States. In cases where sites are located outside the United States, research may still conform to the patterns identified by Bjørnar J. Olsen (1991) with "metropolises" and "satellites," in a relationship of scientific colonialism. Research topics within African American archaeology that are popular stateside, namely, plantations and forts, are not necessarily congruent with the interests or needs of host countries (see the commentary in contributions to Farnsworth 2001). While we can point out these facts and argue about their legitimacy, we should not forget how they shape our views of the field and, indeed, the field itself.

Practicing African American archaeology in the Atlantic world demands attention to power differentials in the past and in the present, in the public sphere as well as within the profession, along racial lines and national lines. We are steadily building a body of work that has the theoretical, self-reflexive, and methodological tools to take advantage of a complex and rich archaeological record and, I hope, leave the world a better place for having done so.

Acknowledgments

I am grateful to the editors for their invitation to participate in this volume and their sharp editorial eyes, which greatly enhanced this essay. Many thanks also to Marley R. Brown, J. Eric Deetz, Ywone Edwards-Ingram, Maria Franklin, Robert Preucel, Matthew Reeves, and Amy Speckart. Their comments helped me improve an earlier draft of this chapter and provoked several fascinating discussions.

Notes

1. An earlier excavation of the structures on Monticello's Mulberry Row—including dwellings and work areas for Thomas Jefferson's enslaved labor force—took place in 1957.

2. I reviewed volumes 1–35 of *Historical Archaeology* and recorded the presence or absence of several general themes in each article that I judged to constitute "African American archaeology." An article was included if it emphasized at least one of the following: plantation economies in the Americas, racial slavery in the Americas, African American culture(s), people of African descent in the Americas, or commentary on the archaeological study of Americans of African descent. The total number of articles reviewed was 69, slightly more than 10 percent of the total number of contributions published in those volumes.

3. This assumes, of course, that we ignore the contribution of untold thousands of men and women who despite their excavation work—from Thomas Jefferson's mound study to the Civilian Conservation Corps—are classed as "laborers" rather than "archaeologists."

4. At the time of writing, Carter's Grove—including the reconstructed slave quarter—is closed to the public pending a review by its parent organization, the Colonial Williamsburg Foundation.

5. Of course, in some more conservative communities, evidence of Africanisms can be a source of embarrassment, perhaps out of a desire to fit non-African norms—or at least to appear to do so (Derry 1997, 20; Wilkie and Shorter 2001, 5).

6. "Afrocentric," meaning inclined to emphasize the place of Africa in world events, committed to understanding people of African descent in terms of concepts and theories derived from Africa, or designed to establish intellectual, political, or cultural distinctiveness for people of African descent.

References

Abungu, G. H. O. 1990. "Communities on the River Tana, Kenya: An Archaeological Study of Relations between the Delta and the River Basin, 700–1890 AD." PhD diss., Cambridge University.

———. 1998. "City States of the East African Coast and Their Maritime Contacts." In G. Connah, ed., *Transformations in Africa: Essays on Africa's Later Past,* 204–18. Leicester: Leicester University Press.

Achebe, C. 1978. "An Image of Africa." *Research in African Literatures* 9: 1–15.

Ackah, W. 1999. *Pan-Africanism: Exploring the Contradictions: Politics, Identity, and Development in Africa and the African Diaspora.* Aldershot: Ashgate.

Adams, A. 1977. *Le long voyage des gens du fleuve.* Paris: Maspero.

———. 1985. *La terre et les gens du fleuve.* Paris: Harmattan.

Adams, E. 1994. "Religion and Freedom: Artifacts Indicate That African Culture Persisted Even in Slavery." *African American Archaeology* 11: 1–2.

Adams, J. 1966. *Remarks on the Country Extending from Cape Palmas to the River Congo.* London: Cass.

Adande, A. B. A. 1984. "Togodu-Awute, capitale de l'ancien royaume d'Allada, etude d'une cite precoloniale d'apres les sources orales, ecrites et les donnees de l'archeologie." Thèse 3ᵉ cycle, Université de Paris I Panthéon-Sorbonne.

———. 1987. "Recherches a Togudu-Awute: le Grand Ardres retrouvé." *Cahiers des Archives du Sol* 1: 13–56.

———. 1989. "Recherche sur la capitale de l'ancien royaume d'allada." In A. Kuevi and D. Aguigah, eds., *Actes de la Quinzaine de l'Archéologie Togolaise 10 Janvier– 4 Fevrier,* 103–16. Lome: l'Association Togolaise de la Recherche Scientifique.

Adande, A. B. A., and C. Adagba. 1988. "Dix années de recherches archéologiques au Benin (1978–1988)." *Nyame Akuma* 30: 3–8.

Adande, A. B. A., and O. B. Bagodo 1991. "Urgence d'une archéologie de sauvetage dans le Golfe du Bénin: Cas des Vallées du Mono et de L'oueme." *West African Journal of Archaeology* 21: 49–72.

Adande, A. B. A., and A. K. Dovie. 1990. *Archéologie de Suavetage dans la Vallee du Mono.* Cotonou/Lome: Equipe de recherche archéologique Beninoise/Programme Archéologique Togolaise.

Adepegba, C. O. 1982. "Ife Art: An Enquiry into the Surface Patterns and the Continuity of Art Tradition among the Northern Yoruba." *West African Journal of Archaeology* 12: 95–109.

Adjaye, J. 1994. "Time, Identity, and Historical Consciousness in Akan." In J. Adjaye, ed., *Time in the Black Experience,* 55–78. Westport, Conn.: Greenwood Press.

Afolayan, F. 1998a. "War and Change in Nineteenth-Century Igbomina." In A. Akinjogbin, ed., *War and Peace in Yorubaland, 1793–1893,* 77–90. Ibadan: Heinemann.

——. 1998b. "Warfare and Slavery in Nineteenth-Century Yorubaland." In A. Akinjogbin, ed., *War and Peace in Yorubaland, 1793–1893,* 407–19. Ibadan: Heinemann.

Agbaje-Williams, B. 1983. "A Contribution to the Archaeology of Old Oyo." PhD diss., University of Ibadan, Nigeria.

Agbe-Davies, Anna. 1999. "The Legacy of 'Race' in African American Archaeology: A Silk Purse from the Wolf's Ears?" http://www.wac.uct.ac.za/wac4/symposia/papers/S074gbd1.pdf.

——. 2002a. "Black Scholars, Black Pasts." *SAA Archaeological Record* 2 (4): 24–28.

——. 2002b. "Archaeology of the Old Elliot School." *Bermuda Journal of Archaeology and Maritime History* 13: 129–54.

——. In review. "Scales of Analysis and Scales of Value at Bush Hill House, Barbados." *International Journal of Historical Archaeology.*

Agbe-Davies, Anna, K. Ladd, and M. Brown III. 2001. "An Interim Report on the Archaeological Study of Bush Hill House." *Journal of the Barbados Museum and Historical Society* 47: 35–51.

Agorsah, E. K. 1990. "Archaeology of Maroon Heritage in Jamaica." *Archaeology Jamaica* (Newsletter of the Archaeology Society of Jamaica), n.s., 2: 14–19.

——. 1992a. "Archaeology and Maroon Heritage in Jamaica." *Jamaica Journal* 23 (2): 2–9.

——. 1992b. "Jamaica and Caribbean Archaeology." *Archaeology Jamaica* 6: 2–14.

——. 1993a. "Archaeology and Resistance History in the Caribbean." *African Archaeological Review* 11: 175–95.

——. 1993b. "An Objective Chronological Scheme for Caribbean History and Archaeology." *Journal of Economic and Social Studies* 42 (1): 119–48.

——, ed. 1994a. *Maroon Heritage: Archaeological, Ethnographic, and Historical Perspectives.* Kingston: Canoe Press.

——. 1994b. "A Brief Report on the Excavations at Seaman's Valley, Portland, Jamaica." *Archaeology Jamaica,* n.s., 8: 15–19.

——. 1995. "Vibrations of Maroons and Maroonage in Caribbean History and Archaeology." *Proceedings of the XV International Congress for Caribbean Archaeology,* 401–14.

——. 1996. "The Archaeology of the African Diaspora." *African Archaeological Review* 13 (4): 221–24.

——. 1999. "Ethnoarchaeological Consideration of Social Relationship and Settlement Patterning among Africans in the Caribbean Diaspora." In J. Haviser, ed., *African Sites: Archaeology in the Caribbean,* 38–64. Princeton, N.J.: Markus Weiner; Kingston: Ian Randle.

———. 2001. "The Secrets of Maroon Heroism, as Pioneer Freedom Fighters of the African Diaspora." In E. K. Agorsah, ed., *Freedom in Black History and Culture*, 1–25. Middletown, Calif.: Arrow Point Press.

Agorsah, E. K., and S. Bandara. 1995. "Seaman's Valley 1995 Excavations: A Preliminary Report." *Archaeology Jamaica* 9/10: 33–43.

Agostini, C. 2002. "Entre Senzalas e Quilombos: 'Comunidades do Mato' em Vassouras do Oitocentos." In A. Zarakin and M. X. Senatore, eds., *Arqueologia da Sociedade Moderna na América do Sul*, 19–30. Buenos Aires: Tridente.

Ajayi, J. F. A., and S. A. Akintoye. 1980. "Yorubaland in the Nineteenth Century." In O. Ikime, ed., *Groundwork of Nigerian History*, 280–302. Ibadan: Heinemann.

Akinjogbin, I. A. 1967. *Dahomey and Its Neighbours, 1708–1818*. Cambridge: Cambridge University Press.

Akintoye, S. A. 1971. *Revolution and Power Politics in Yorubaland, 1840–1893*. New York: Humanities Press.

Akinwumi, O. 2003. "The Imposition of Colonial Rule and Its Impact on Owe/Ijumu Relations, 1900–1937." In A. Olukoju, Z. O. Apata, and O. Akinwumi, eds., *Northeast Yorubaland: Studies in the History and Culture of a Frontier Zone*, 25–33. Ibadan: Rex Charles.

Akpohasa, J. 1994. "Settlement Studies of Ila-Yara, Osun State: An Ecological Approach." Master's thesis, University of Ibadan.

Akurang-Parry, K. O. 2004. "'We Shall Rejoice to See the Day When Slavery Shall Cease to Exist': The Gold Coast Times, the African Intelligentsia, and Abolition in the Gold Coast." *History in Africa* 31: 19–42.

Akyeampong, E. 2000. "Africans in the Diaspora: The Diaspora and Africa." *African Affairs* 99: 183–215.

Alegria, R. E. 1980. "El Rey Miguel: Héroe Puertorriqueño en la Lucha por la Libertad de Los Esclavos." *Revista de Historia de América* 85: 9–26.

Aleru, J. O. 1998. "An Investigation into the Aspect of Historical Archaeology of North Central Yorubaland." PhD diss., University of Ibadan.

———. 2001. "Igbomina/Nupe Relations: A Historical and Archaeological Reconstruction." *Nigerian Heritage* 10: 126–34.

Allen, C. S. M. 1997. "Thin Sections of Bronze Age Pottery from the East Midlands of England." In A. Middleton and I. Freestone, eds., *Recent Developments in Ceramic Petrology*, 1–16. British Museum Occasional Papers no. 81, London.

Allen, James de Vere. 1977. *Swahili History Revisited*. Nairobi: Institute of African Studies, University of Nairobi.

———. 1993. *Swahili Origins: Swahili Culture and the Shungwaya Phenomenon*. London: James Currey.

Allen, S. J. 1995. "Africanisms, Mosaics, and Creativity: The Historical Archaeology of Palmares." M.A. thesis, Brown University.

———. 1999. "A Cultural Mosaic at Palmares? Grappling with the Historical Archaeology of a Seventeenth-Century Brazilian Quilombo." In P. P. A. Funari, ed., *Cultura Material e Arqueologia Histórica*, 141–78. Campinas: Instituto de Filosofia e Ciêcias Humanas da UNICAMP.

———. 2001. "'Zumbi nunca vai morrer': History, Race Politics, and the Practice of Archaeology in Brazil." PhD diss., Brown University.

Alleyne, M. 1988. *Roots of Jamaican Culture*. Kingston: Pluto Press.

Alpern, S. 1995. "What Africans Got for Their Slaves: A Master List of European Trade Goods." *History in Africa* 22: 5–43.

Alpers, E. A. 1975. *Ivory and Slaves: Changing Pattern of International Trade in East Central Africa to the Late Nineteenth Century.* Berkeley: University of California Press.

——. 2005. "'Moçanbiques' in Brazil: Another Dimension of the African Diaspora in the Atlantic World." In J. C. Curto and R. Soulodre-La France, eds., *Africa and the Americas: Interconnections during the Slave Trade,* 43–64. Trenton, N.J.: Africa World Press.

Amselle, J. 1993. "Anthropology and Historicity." In V. Y. Mudimbe and B. Jewsiewicki, eds., *History Making in Africa,* special issue of *History and Theory: Studies in the Philosophy of History,* 12–31.

——. 1998. *Mestizo Logics: Anthropology of Identity in Africa and Elsewhere.* Trans. Claudia Royal. Stanford: Stanford University Press.

Andah, Bassey. 1995. "Studying African Societies in Cultural Context." In P. Schmidt and T. Patterson, eds., *Making Alternative Histories: The Practice of Archaeology and History in Non-western Settings,* 149–82. Santa Fe, N.M.: School of American Research Press.

Andrews, G. R. 1980. *The African Argentines of Buenos Aires, 1800–1900.* Madison: University of Wisconsin Press.

Angelou, M. 1986. *All God's Children Need Traveling Shoes.* New York: Vintage Books.

Anozie, Frank. 1998. "An Archaeological Study of Ironworking at Umundu, Nigeria: The Decline and Continuity of an Indigenous Tradition." In K. Wesler, ed., *Historical Archaeology in Nigeria,* 259–72. Trenton, N.J.: Africa World Press.

Anquandah, J. 1982. *Rediscovering Ghana's Past.* Harlow, Essex: Longman.

——. 1995. "Urbanization and State Formation in Ghana during the Iron Age." In T. Shaw, P. Sinclair, B. Andah, and A. Okpoko, eds., *The Archaeology of Africa,* 642–51. New York: Routledge.

Anstey, R. 1975. *The Atlantic Slave Trade and British Abolition.* London: Brill Academic.

Antongini, G., and T. G. Spini. 1995. *Les palais royaux d'Abomey: Espace, Architecture, Dynamique Socio-Anthropologique.* Paris: UNESCO.

Aparicio, F. de. 1937. "Excavaciones en los paraderos del Arroyo de Leyes." *Relaciones de la Sociedad Argentina de Antropología* 1: 7–19.

Appadurai, Arjun, ed. 1986. Introduction. *The Social Life of Things: Commodities in Cultural Perspective.* Cambridge: Cambridge University Press.

Appiah, Kwame. 1992. *In My Father's House: Africa in the Philosophy of Culture.* New York: Oxford University Press.

Apter, A. 2002. "On African Origins: Creolization and *Connaissance* in Haitian Vodou." *American Ethnologist* 29 (2): 233–60.

Aptheker, H. 1943. *American Negro Slave Revolts.* New York: Columbia University Press.

——. 1979. "Maroons within the Present Limits of the United States." In Richard Price, ed., *Maroon Societies,* 151–67. Baltimore: Johns Hopkins University Press.

Arhin, K. 1970. "Aspects of the Ashanti Northern Trade in the Nineteenth Century." *Africa* 40: 363–73.

——. 1987. "Savanna Contributions to the Asante Political Economy." In E. Schildkrout, "The Golden Stool: Studies of the Asante Center and Periphery." *Anthropological Papers of the American Museum of Natural History* 65 (1): 51–59.

———. 1989. "West African Trading Settlements in the Asante Hinterland in the Nineteenth Century." *Research Review*, n.s., 5 (1): 1–20. Legon: Institute of African Studies, University of Ghana.

Armstrong, D. V. 1990a. "The Afro-Jamaican House-yard: An Archaeological and Ethnohistorical Perspective." *Florida Journal of Anthropology*, Special Publication 5: 51–63.

———. 1990b. *The Old Village and the Great House: An Archaeological and Historical Examination of Drax Hall Plantation, St. Ann's Bay, Jamaica.* Urbana: University of Illinois Press.

———. 1998. "Cultural Transformation within Caribbean Slave Communities." In J. G. Cusick, ed., *Studies in Culture Contact: Interaction, Culture Change, and Archaeology*, 378–401. Carbondale: Center for Archaeological Investigations, Southern Illinois University.

———. 1999. "Archaeology and Ethnohistory of the Caribbean Plantation." In T. A. Singleton, ed., *"I, Too, Am America": Archaeological Studies of African American Life*, 173–92. Charlottesville: University Press of Virginia.

Armstrong, D. V., and K. Kelly. 2000. "Settlement Patterns and the Origins of African Jamaican Society: Seville Plantation, St. Ann's Bay, Jamaica." *Ethnohistory* 47 (2): 369–97.

Arrom, J. J., and M. A. García Arévalo. 1986. *Cimarrón.* Santo Domingo: Ediciones Fundación García-Areévalo.

Asante, M. K. 1988. *Afrocentricity.* Trenton, N.J.: Africa World Press.

Ascher, R. 1961. "Analogy in Archaeological Interpretation." *Southwestern Journal of Anthropology* 17: 317–25.

Ascher, R., and C. H. Fairbanks. 1971. "Excavation of a Slave Cabin: Georgia, U.S.A." *Historical Archaeology* 5: 3–17.

Ashmore, W. 1989. "Construction and Cosmology: Politics and Ideology in Lowland Maya Settlement Patterns." In W. F. Hanks and D. S. Rice, eds., *Word and Image in Maya Culture: Explorations in Language, Writing, and Representation*, 272–86. Salt Lake City: University of Utah Press.

Ashmore, W., and R. Wilk. 1988. "Household and Community in the Mesoamerican Past." In R. Wilk and W. Ashmore, eds., *Household and Community in the Mesoamerican Past*, 1–28. Albuquerque: University of New Mexico Press.

Askegaard, Soren, and A. Fuat Firat. 1997. "Towards a Critique of Material Culture, Consumption, and Markets." In S. Pearce, ed., *Experiencing Material Culture in the Western World*, 114–39. Leicester: Leicester University Press.

Atkins, J. 1970 (1735). *A Voyage to Guinea, Brasil, and the West Indies in HMS* Swallow *and* Weymouth. London: Frank Cass.

Austen, Ralph A. 1979. "The Trans-Saharan Slave Trade: A Tentative Census." In H. A. Gemery and S. J. Hogerndorn, eds., *The Uncommon Market: Essays in the Economic History of the Atlantic Slave Trade*, 23–76. New York: Academic Press.

———. 1987. *African Economic History.* London: James Currey.

———. 2001. "The Slave Trade as History and Memory: Confrontations of Slaving Voyage Documents and Communal Traditions." *William and Mary Quarterly* 58 (1): 229–44.

Awe, B. 1973. "Militarism and Economic Development in Nineteenth-Century Yoruba Country: The Ibadan Example." *Journal of African History* 14: 72–73.

Azevedo, E. S. 1983. "Sobrenomes no Nordeste e suas Relaçoes com a Heterogeneidade étnica." *Estudos Econômicos* 13: 103–16.

Babayemi, S. O. 1971. "Upper Ogun: An Historical Sketch." *African Notes* 6 (2): 72–84.

Babson, D. W. 1990. "The Archaeology of Racism and Ethnicity on Southern Plantation." *Historical Archaeology* 24 (4): 20–28.

Bachmann, H.-G. 1982. "The Identification of Slags from Archaeological Sites." *Occasional Publication* no. 6. London: Institute of Archaeology.

Bagodo, O. 1993. "Archaeological Reconnaissance of the Lower Mono Valley: A Preliminary Report." *West African Journal of Archaeology* 23: 24–36.

Bakari, M. 1981. *Customs of the Swahili People: The Desturi za Waswahili of Mtoro bin Mwinyi Bakari and Other Swahili Persons.* Ed. and trans. J. W. T. Allen. Berkeley: University of California Press.

Bakos, M. 1990. "Sobre a mulher escrava no Rio Grande do Sul." *Estudos Ibero-Americanos* 16: 47–56.

Balandier, G. 1968. *Daily Life in the Kingdom of the Kongo: From the Sixteenth to the Eighteenth Century.* Trans. H. Weaver. London: George Allen and Unwin.

Barbosa, D. 1967 (1917). *The Book of Duarte Barbosa: An Account of the Countries Bordering on the Indian Ocean and Their Inhabitants, 1518 AD.* Vol. 1. Milwood: Kraus Reprint.

Barclay, A. 1826. *A Practical View of the Present State of Slavery in the West Indies.* London: Beufort Books.

Barile, K. 2004. "Race, the National Register, and Cultural Resource Management: Creating an Historic Context for Postbellum Sites." *Historical Archaeology* 38 (1): 90–100.

Barker, A. J. 1978. *The African Link: British Attitudes to the Negro in the Era of the Atlantic Slave Trade, 1550–1807.* London: Frank Cass.

Barnes, S. T., ed. 1989. *Africa's Ogun: Old World and New.* Bloomington: Indiana University Press.

Baro, M. A., A. T. Dia, D. Ba, and A. Gacko. 1987. *Recherche sur les Systèmes de Production Rurale dans la Vallée du Fleuve Sénégal: Une mission de prospection des cultures de Décrue (walo) dans les regions de Guidimaka, Gorgol, Brakna et Trarza.* Tucson: University of Arizona, College of Agriculture.

Barrett, J. 1994. *Fragments from Antiquity: An Archaeology of Social Life in Britain, 2900–1200 BC.* Oxford: Basil Blackwell.

Barrett, L. 1977. "African Religion in the Americas: The 'Islands in Between.'" In N. S. Booth Jr., ed., *African Religions: A Symposium,* 183–215. New York: NOK.

Barroso, E. 1984. *Yan el Cimarron.* Havana: Ed Gente Nueva.

Barry, B. 1985. *Le royaume du Waalo: Le Sénégal avant la conquête.* Paris: Karthala.

———. 1988a. *La Sénégambie du XVè au XIXè Siècle: Traite Négrière, Islam et Conquêtes.* Paris: Harmattan.

———. 1988b. *Senegambia and the Atlantic Slave Trade.* Trans. A. K. Armah. Cambridge: Cambridge University Press.

Barth, F. 1969. Introduction to F. Barth, ed., *Ethnic Groups and Boundaries: The Social Organization of Cultural Differences,* 9–38. London: Allen and Unwin.

Bastide, R. 1967. *Les Amériques noir.* Paris: Payot.

———. 1971. *African Civilizations in the New World.* New York: Harper and Row.

Bateman, Rebecca. 2002. "Naming Patterns in Black Seminole Ethnogenesis." *Ethnohistory* 49 (2): 227–57.

Bathily, A. 1989. *Les portes de l'or: Le royaume du Ngalam (Sénégal, de l'ère Musulmane aux Temps des Négriers, VIIè–XVIIIè Siècle).* Paris: Harmattan.

Battle, W. 2004. "A Space of Our Own: Redefining the Enslaved Household at Andrew Jackson's Hermitage Plantation." In K. S. Barile and J. C. Brandon, eds., *Household Chores and Household Choices: Theorizing the Domestic Sphere in Historical Archaeology*, 33–50. Tuscaloosa: University of Alabama Press.

Bay, E. 1995. "Belief, Legitimacy, and the Kpojito: An Institutional History of the 'Queen Mother' in Precolonial Dahomey." *Journal of African History* 36 (1): 1–27.

———. 1998. *Wives of the Leopard: Gender, Politics, and Culture in the Kingdom of Dahomey*. Charlotteville: University of Virginia Press.

Beach, D. 1984. *Zimbabwe before 1900*. Gweru (Zimbabwe): Mambo Press.

———. 1994. *The Shona and Their Neighbours*. Oxford: Blackwell.

———. 1998. "Cognitive Archaeology and Imaginary History at Great Zimbabwe." *Current Anthropology* 39 (1): 47–71.

Beaudry, M. C., and E. P. Berkland. 2001. "Constructing/Reconstructing Community: The African Meeting House on Nantucket." World Archaeology Congress Intercongress on the African Diaspora, Willemstad, Curaçao.

Beaudry, M. C., L. Cook, and S. Mrozowski. 1991. "Artifacts and Active Voices: Material Culture as Social Discourse." In R. McGuire and R. Paynter, eds., *The Archaeology of Inequality*, 150–91. Cambridge: Basil Blackwell.

Beaudry, M. C., and S. A. Mrozowksi. 2001. "Cultural Space and Worker Identity in the Company City: Nineteenth-Century Lowell, Massachusetts." In A. Mayne and T. Murray, eds., *The Archaeology of Urban Landscapes: Explorations in Slumland*, 118–31. Cambridge: Cambridge University Press.

Bech, A., and A. Hyland. 1978. *Elmina: A Conservation Study*. Kumasi: University of Science and Technology.

Becker, C. 1985. "Notes sur les Conditions Écologiques en Sénégambie aux 17ᵉᵐᵉ–18ᵉᵐᵉ Siècles." *African Economic History* 14: 167–216.

Becker, C, and V. Martin. 1982. "Rites de sépultures Pré-Islamiques au Sénégal et Vestiges Protohistoriques." *Archives Suisses d'Anthropologie Générale* 46 (2): 261–93.

Beckford, W. 1790. *A Descriptive Account of the Island of Jamaica*. Vol. 2. London: T. and J. Egerton.

Beckles, H. 1986. "From Land to Sea: Runaway Slaves and White Indentured Servants in Seventeenth-Century Barbados." In G. Heuman, ed., *Out of the House of Bondage: Runaways, Resistance, and Maroonage in Africa and the New World*, 79–94. Totowa, N.J.: Cass.

———. 1990. "Caribbean Anti-Slavery: The Self-Liberation Ethos of Enslaved Blacks." *Journal of Caribbean History* 22 (1/2): 1–19.

Beckles, H., and V. Shepherd. 1992. *Caribbean Freedom: Society and Economy from Emancipation to the Present. A Student Reader*. London: James Currey.

Behrens, Joanna. 1999. "Navigating the Liminal: An Archaeological Perspective on South African Industrialization." In A. Reid and P. Lane, eds., *African Historical Archaeologies*, 347–73. New York: Kluwer Academic/Plenum.

Belasco, Bernard. 1980. *The Entrepreneur as Culture Hero: Preadaptations in Nigerian Economic Development*. New York: Praeger.

Belisario, I. 1837–38. *Sketches of Character, in Illustration of the Habits, Occupation, and Costume of the Negro Population in the Island of Jamaica*. Kingston: Privately published.

Ben-Amos, Paula. 1999. *Art, Innovation, and Politics in Eighteenth-Century Benin*. Bloomington: Indiana University Press.

Bent, J. T. 1892. *The Ruined Cities of Mashonaland: Being a Record of Excavation and Exploration in 1891.* London: Longmans, Green.

Berkland, E. P. 1999. "The Centering of an African American Community: An Archaeological Study of the African Baptist Society Meeting House, Nantucket, Massachusetts." M.A. thesis, Boston University.

———. 2003. "An Island Perspective: The African American Community on Nantucket." Presented at the 36th annual conference of the Society for Historical Archaeology, Providence, R.I.

Berlin, I. 1996. "From Creole to African: Atlantic Creoles and the Origins of African American Society in Mainland North America." *William and Mary Quarterly* 53 (2): 251–88.

———. 1998. *Many Thousands Gone: The First Two Centuries of Slavery in North America.* Cambridge: Harvard University Press.

Bernal, M. 1990. "Responses." *Journal of Mediterranean Archaeology* 3: 111–37.

Berthier, S. 1997. *Recherches archéologiques sur la capitale de l'Empire de Ghana. Etude d'un secteur d'habitat à Koumbi Saleh, Mauritanie. Campagnes II-III-IV-V (1975–1976)–(1980–1981).* London: BAR International Series 680.

Beuze, L. 1990. "La Poterie en Martinique." *Les Cahiers du Patrimoine: Artisanat et Petit Métiers*, 7: 39–46. Conseil Regional de la Martinique, Fort-de-France.

Bickerton, D. 1999. "Pidgins and Language Mixture." In R. Rickford and S. Romaine, eds., *Creole Genesis, Attitudes, and Discourse*, 31–44. Amsterdam: John Benjamins.

Bilby, K. 1994. "Maroon Culture as a Distinct Variant of Jamaican Culture." In K. Agorsah, ed., *Maroon Heritage*, 72–85. Kingston: Canoe Press.

Binford, L. R. 1978. "A New Method of Calculating Dates from Kaolin Pipe Stem Samples." In R. L. Schuyler, ed., *Historical Archaeology: A Guide to Substantive Contributions*, 66–67. Farmingdale, N.Y.: Baywood.

Birmingham, David. 1998. *Kwame Nkrumah: The Father of African Nationalism.* Athens: Ohio University Press.

Blackburn, R. 1997. *The Making of New World Slavery: From the Baroque to the Modern, 1492–1800.* London: Verso.

Blake, Lady. 1898. "The Maroons of Jamaica." *North American Review* 167 (November): 558–68.

Blakey, M. 1990. "American Nationality and Ethnicity in the Depicted Past." In P. G. Gathercole and D. Lowenthal, eds., *The Politics of the Past*, 38–48. London: Unwin Hyman.

———. 1995. "Preliminary Results from the Skeletal Remains of the African Burial Ground, New York." American Anthropological Association Conference, Washington, D.C., November 1995.

———. 2001. "Bioarchaeology of the African Diaspora in the Americas: Its Origins and Scope." *Annual Review of Anthropology* 30: 387–422.

Blanton, R. E., G. M. Feinman, S. A. Kowalewski, and L. Nicholas. 1999. *Ancient Oaxaca: The Monte Albán State.* Cambridge: Cambridge University Press.

Blanton, R. E., G. M. Feinman, S. A. Kowalewski, and P. N. Peregrine. 1996. "A Dual-Processual Theory for the Evolution of Mesoamerican Civilization." *Current Anthropology* 37 (1): 1–14.

Blassingame, J. W. 1972. *The Slave Community: Plantation Life in the Antebellum South.* New York: Oxford University Press.

——. 1979. *The Slave Community: Plantation Life in the Antebellum South*. 2nd ed. New York: Oxford University Press.

Boachie-Ansah, J. 1986. *An Archaeological Contribution to the History of Wenchi*. African Occasional Papers, no. 3. Calgary: University of Calgary Press.

Boahen, A. A. 1972. "Prempeh I in Exile." *Research Review* 8 (3): 3–20. University of Ghana, Institute of African Studies, Legon.

Bocoum, H. 1986. "La métallurgie du fer au Sénégal: Approche archéologique, technologique et historique." Thèse 3ème cycle, University Paris I.

——. 1990. "Contributions à la connaissance des origines du Tékrur." *Annales de la Faculté des Lettres et Sciences Humaines* 20: 159–78.

Bocoum, H., and S. K. McIntosh. 2002. *Fouilles à Sincu Bara, Moyenne Vallée du Sénégal*. Nouackchott: CRIAA.

Bojunga, C. 1978. "O Negro Brasileiro, 90 anos depois." *Encontros da Civilização Brasileira* 1: 175–204.

Bolster, W. J. 1997. *Black Jacks: African American Seamen in the Age of Sail*. Cambridge: Harvard University Press.

Bonner, T. 1974. "The Blue Mountain Expedition." *Jamaica Journal* 8 (2/3): 46–50.

Boteler-Mock, S., and M. Davis. 1997. "Seminole Black Culture on the Texas Frontier." *CRM* 20 (2): 8–10.

Boulègue, J. 1987. *Le Grand Jolof (XIIIè–XVIè siècle)*. Paris: Façades-Blois.

Bourdieu, P. 1977. *Outline of a Theory of Practice*. Translated by R. Nice. Cambridge: Cambridge University Press.

——. 1984. *Distinction: A Social Critique of the Judgement of Taste*. Trans. R. Nice. Cambridge: Cambridge University Press.

Bousquet, M. A. 1936. "Investigaciones Arqueológicas en el Arroyo de Leyes." *Revista Geográfica Americana* 8: 161–74.

Boutillier, J. L. 1962. *La Moyenne Vallée du Sénégal: Étude Socio-Économique*. Ministère de la Coopération (République Française), INSEE, Service de Coopération.

——. 1989. "Irrigations et problématique foncière dans la Vallée du Sénégal." *Cahiers des Sciences Humaines* 25 (4): 469–88.

Bovill, E. W. 1933. *Caravans of the Old Sahara: An Introduction to the History of Western Sudan*. London. Oxford University Press.

——. 1968. *The Golden Trade of the Moors*. London: Oxford University Press.

Boyd, M. F. 1958. "Horatio Dexter and Events Leading to the Treaty of Moultrie Creek with the Seminole Indians." *Florida Anthropologist* 11 (3): 65–95.

Bradbury, R. E. 1973. *Benin Studies*. Ed. P. Morton-Williams. London: Oxford University Press.

Braithwaite, E. 1971. *The Development of Creole Society in Jamaica, 1770–1820*. Oxford: Clarendon Press.

Braudel, F. 1994. *A History of Civilizations*. Trans. R. Mayne. New York: Allen Lane.

Bravmann, R. 1972. "The Diffusion of Ashanti Political Art." In D. Fraser and H. M. Cole, eds., *African Art and Leadership*, 153–71. Madison: University of Wisconsin Press.

Bravmann, R., and R. D. Mathewson. 1970. "A Note on the History and Archaeology of 'Old Bima.'" *African Historical Studies* 3: 133–50.

Bredwa-Mensah, Y. 2004. "Global Encounters: Slavery and Slave Lifeways on Nineteenth-Century Danish Plantations on the Gold Coast, Ghana." *Journal of African Archaeology* 2 (2): 203–27.

Breeden, J., ed. 1980. *Advice among Masters: The Ideal in Slave Management in the Old South*. Westport, Conn.: Greenwood Press.

Bronk-Ramsey, C. 1995. "Radiocarbon Calibration and Analysis of Stratigraphy: The OxCal Program." *Radiocarbon* 37: 425–30.

Brooks, C., Rev., and J. M. Usher. 1886. *History of the Town of Medford, Middlesex County, Massachusetts, from Its First Settlement in 1630 to 1855*. Boston: Rand, Avery.

Brooks, G. 1993. *Landlords and Strangers: Ecology, Society, and Trade in Western Africa, 1000–1630*. Boulder, Colo.: Westview Press.

———. 2003. *Eurafricans in Western Africa: Commerce, Social Status, Gender, and Religious Observance from the Sixteenth to the Eighteenth Century*. Athens: Ohio University Press.

Brooks, J. F., ed. 2002. *Confounding the Color Line: The Indian-Black Experience in North America*. Lincoln: University of Nebraska Press.

Brown, Canter, Jr. 1990. "The 'Sarrazota, or Runaway Negro Plantations': Tampa Bay's First Black Community, 1812–1821." *Tampa Bay History* 12 (2): 5–19.

Brown, K. M. 1976. "The Vèvè of Haitian Vodou: A Structural Analysis of Visual Imagery." PhD diss., Temple University. Ann Arbor, Mich.: UMI.

Brown, K. L. 1994. "Material Culture and Community Structure: The Slave and Tenant Community at Levi Jordan's Plantation, 1848–1892." In L. E. Hudson Jr., ed., *Working toward Freedom: Slave Society and Domestic Economy in the American South*, 95–118. New York: University of Rochester Press.

Brown, K. L., and D. C. Cooper. 1990. "Structural Continuity in an African American Slave and Tenant Community." *Historical Archaeology* 24 (4): 7–19.

Brown, K. N., and K. L. Brown. 1998. "Archaeology and Spirituality: The Conjurer/Midwife and the Praise House/Church at the Levi Jordan Plantation." Society for Historical Archaeology Annual Conference, Atlanta, January 9, 1998.

Bruner, E. M. 1993. "Epilogue: Creative Persona and the Problem of Authenticity." In S. Lavie, K. Narayan, and R. Rosaldo, eds., *Creativity/Anthropology*, 321–34. Ithaca: Cornell University Press.

———. 1996. "Tourism in Ghana: The Representation of Slavery and the Return of the Black Diaspora." *American Anthropologist* 98 (2): 290–304.

Bryan, P. 1971. "African Affinities: The Blacks of Latin America." *Caribbean Quarterly* 17 (3/4): 45–52.

Buchanan, K. M., and J. C. Pugh. 1958. *Land and People in Nigeria: The Human Geography of Nigeria and Its Environmental Background*. London: University of London Press.

Buisseret, D. 1980. *Historic Architecture of the Caribbean*. London: Heinemann.

Bullen, A. K., and R. P. Bullen. 1945. "Black Lucy's Garden." *Bulletin of the Massachusetts Archaeological Society* 6 (2): 17–28.

Burns, S. 1981. *Selected Papers*, vol. 2, *Nineteenth-Century Black Life on Nantucket*. Boston: University of Massachusetts Humanities Program.

Burnside, M., and R. Robotham. 1997. *Spirits of the Passage: The Transatlantic Slave Trade in the Seventeenth Century*. New York: Simon and Schuster.

Burrison, J. A. 1978. "African American Folk Pottery in the South." *Southern Folklore Quarterly* 42: 175–99.

Burton, R. F. 1864. *A Mission to Gelele, King of Dahome*. London: Tinsley Brothers.

Butzer, K. W. 1981. "Rise and Fall of Axum, Ethiopia: A Geo-archaeological Interpretation." *American Antiquity* 46: 471–95.

Byers, E. 1987. *The Nation of Nantucket: Society and Politics in an Early American Commercial Center, 1660–1820.* Boston: Northeastern University Press.

Calvocoressi, D. 1968. "European Traders on the Gold Coast." *West African Archaeological Newsletter* 10: 16–19.

——. 1977. "Excavations at Bantama, near Elmina, Ghana." *West African Journal of Archaeology* 7: 117–41.

Campbell, M. C. 1997. *The Maroons of Jamaica, 1655–1796.* Trenton, N.J.: Africa World Press.

Canter, D. 1977. *The Psychology of Space.* New York: St. Martin's Press.

Carby, H. 1987. *Reconstructing Womanhood: The Emergence of the Afro-American Woman Novelist.* New York: Oxford University Press.

Cardoso, C. F. S. 1988. "A Abolição Como Problema Histórico e Historiografico." In C. F. S. Cardoso, ed., *Escravidão e Abolição no Brasil: Novas perspectivas,* 73–110. Rio de Janeiro: Zahar.

Cardoso, F. H. 1969. "Condições sociais da industrialização: o caso de São Paulo." In F. H. Cardoso, *Mudanças sociais na América Latina,* 186–98. São Paulo: Difel.

Carneiro, E. 1988. *O quilombo de Palmares.* São Paulo: Cia. Editora Nacional.

Carney, J. 1996. "Landscapes of Technology Transfer: Rice Cultivation and African Continuities." *Technology and Culture* 37 (1): 5–35.

——. 2001. *Black Rice: The African Origins of Rice Cultivation in the Americas.* Cambridge: Harvard University Press.

Carr, R., and W. Steele. 1993. *Seminole Heritage Survey: Seminole Sites of Florida.* Miami: Archaeological and Historical Conservancy.

Carter, M., V. Govinden, and S. Peerthum. 2003. *The Last Slave.* Port Louis: Center for Research on Indian and Oceania Societies.

Carvalho, J. J. de, S. Z. Doria, and A. N. de Oliveira Jr. 1996. *O Quilombo do Rio Das Ras: Historias, Tradicoes, Lutas, Salvador.* Editoria Da Universidade Federal Da Bahia.

Cary, L. L., and F. C. Cary. 1977. "Absalom F. Boston, His Family, and Nantucket's Black Community." *Historic Nantucket* 25: 15–23.

Casey, J. 2005. "Holocene Occupations of the Forest and Savanna." In A. Stahl, ed., *African Archaeology: A Critical Introduction,* 225–48. Oxford: Blackwell.

Cassanelli, L. 1982. *The Shaping of Somali Society: Reconstructing the History of a Pastoral People, 1600–1900.* Philadelphia: University of Pennsylvania Press.

Cassey, J. 1998. "The Ecology of Food Production in West Africa." In G. Connah, ed., *Transformations in Africa: Essays on Africa's Later Past,* 204–18. Leicester: Leicester University Press.

Cawley, H., and K. Agorsah. 1995. *The Heroic Hearts of Jamaica.* Montego Bay: Speedy Prints.

Chambers, D. 1992. "Afro-Virginian Root Cellars and African Roots? A Comment on the Need for a Moderate Afrocentric Approach." *African American Archaeology* 6: 7–10.

Chami, F. A. 1988. "The Coastal Iron Age Site in Kisarawe, Tanzania." M.A. thesis, Brown University.

——. 1994. *The Tanzanian Coast in the First Millennium* AD. Studies in African Archaeology 7. Uppsala: Societas Archaeologica Upsaliensis.

——. 1998. "A Review of Swahili Archaeology." *African Archaeological Review* 15: 199–218.

Chami, F. A., and P. Msemwa. 1997. "A New Look at Culture and Trade on the Azanian Coast." *Current Anthropology* 38: 673–77.

Chan, A. A. 2003. "The Slaves of Colonial New England: Discourses of Colonialism and Identity at the Isaac Royall Estate, Medford, Massachusetts, 1732–1775." PhD diss., Boston University.

Chappell, E. A. 1999. "Museums and American Slavery." In T. A. Singleton, ed., "I, Too, Am America": Studies in African American Archaeology, 240–58. Charlottesville: University Press of Virginia.

Chau, Ju Kua. 1964. On the Chinese and Arab Trade in the Twelfth and Thirteenth Centuries. Trans. R. Hirth and W. W. Rockhill. Taipei: Literature House.

Chavane, B. A. 1985. Villages de l'ancien Tékrur. Paris: Karthala.

Childs, S. T. 1991. "Styles, Technology, and Iron Smelting Furnaces in Bantu-Speaking Africa." Journal of Anthropological Archaeology 10: 332–59.

Childs, S. T., and E. W. Herbert. 2005. "Metallurgy and Its Consequences." In A. Stahl, ed., African Archaeology: A Critical Introduction, 276–300. Oxford: Blackwell.

Chireau, Y. 1997. "Conjure and Christianity in the Nineteenth Century: Religious Elements of African American Magic." Religion and American Culture 7 (2): 225–46.

Chittick, N. H. 1967. "Kilwa: A Preliminary Report." Azania 2: 1–36.

———. 1974. Kilwa: An Islamic Trading City on the East African Coast. British Institute in Eastern Africa Memoir no. 5.

———. 1977. "Pre-Islamic Trade and Ports of the Horn." Proceedings of the VII Pan African Congress of Prehistory and the Quaternary, Nairobi.

———. 1984. Manda: Excavations at an Island Port on the Kenya Coast. British Institute in Eastern Africa Memoir no. 9.

Clapperton, H. 1829. Journal of a Second Expedition into the Interior of Africa, from the Bight of Benin to Soccatoo. London: Frank Cass.

Clark, J. D. 1990. "A Personal Memoir." In P. Robertshaw, ed., A History of African Archaeology, 189–204. London: James Currey.

Clarke, P. B. 1982. West Africa and Islam: A Study of Religious Development from the Eighth to the Twentieth Century. London: Edward Arnold.

Clarke, W. H. 1972. Travels and Explorations in Yorubaland (1854–1858). Ed. J. Atanda. Ibadan: Ibadan University Press.

Clifford, James 1994. "Diasporas." Cultural Anthropology 9: 302–38.

Cohen, M. 1964 (1836). Notices of Florida and the Campaign. Facsimile of the 1836 ed. Gainesville: University Press of Florida.

Collins, P. H. 2000. Black Feminist Thought: Knowledge, Consciousness, and the Politics of Empowerment. New York: Routledge.

Connah, G. 1975. The Archaeology of Benin: Excavations and Other Researches in and around Benin. Oxford: Clarendon Press.

———. 1998. "Static Image: Dynamic Reality." In G. Connah, ed., Transformations in Africa: Essays on Africa's Later Past, 1–13. Leicester: Leicester University Press.

———. 2001. African Civilizations. 2nd ed. Cambridge: Cambridge University Press.

Conrad, R. 1973. "Neither Slave nor Free: The Emancipados of Brazil, 1818–1868." Hispanic American Historical Review 53: 50–70.

Cooper F. 1981. "Islam and Cultural: The Ideology of Slave Owners on the East African Coast." In P. Lovejoy, ed., The Ideology of Slavery in Africa, 247–77. Beverly Hills: Sage.

Corrêa, Gaspar. 1866. Lendas da India. Vol. 4. Lisbon: Typ. da Academia real das sciencias.

Costa e Silva, A. da. 2002. *A manilha e o limbambo. A África e a escravidão de 1500 a 1700.* Rio de Janeiro: Nova Fronteira/Biblioteca Nacional.

Costin, C. L. 1991. "Craft Specialization: Issues in Defining, Documenting, and Explaining the Organization of Production." In M. B. Schiffer, ed., *Archaeological Method and Theory*, 1–56. Tucson: University of Arizona Press.

———. 1999. "Formal and Technological Variability and the Social Relations of Production: *Crisoles* from San Jose de Moro, Peru." In E. Chilton, ed., *Material Meanings: Critical Approaches to the Interpretation of Material Culture*, 85–102. Salt Lake City: University of Utah Press.

Costin, C. L., R. Wright, and E. Brumfiel, eds. 1998. *Craft and Social Identity.* Arlington, Va.: American Anthropological Association.

Couto, D. D. 1974. *Da Asia de Diogo do Coiuto.* 12 vols. Lisoboa: Livraria Sao Carlos.

Covington, J. 1993. *The Seminoles of Florida.* Gainesville: University of Florida Press.

Cox, G., J. Sealy, C. Schrire, and A. Morris. 2001. "Stable Carbon and Nitrogen Isotopic Analyses of the Underclass at the Colonial Cape of Good Hope in the Eighteenth and Nineteenth Centuries." *World Archaeology* 33 (1): 73–97.

Craddock, P., J. Ambers, D. Hook, R. Farquhar, V. E. Chikwendu, A. Umeji, and T. Shaw. 1989. "Metal Sources and the Bronzes from Igbo-Ukwu, Nigeria." *Journal of Field Archaeology* 24: 405–29.

Crane, B. 1993. "Colono Ware and Criollo Ware Pottery from Charleston, South Carolina, and San Juan, Puerto Rico, in Comparative Perspective." PhD diss., University of Pennsylvania.

Craton, M. 1978. *Searching for the Invisible Man: Slaves and Plantation Life in Jamaica.* Cambridge: Harvard University Press.

———. 1982. *Testing the Chains: Resistance to Slavery in the British West Indies.* Ithaca: Cornell University Press.

Crespi, L. 2000. "Contrabando de esclavos en el puerto de Buenos Aires durante el siglo XVII: complicidad de los funcionarios reales." *Desmemoria* 26: 115–33.

Crew, Spencer. 1996. "African Americans, History, and Museums: Preserving African American History in the Public Arena." In G. Kavanagh, ed., *Making History in Museums*, 80–91. London: Duckworth.

Cròs, C. R. 1997. *La Civilisation Afro-Brésilienne.* Paris: PUF.

Crossland, L. B. 1976. "Excavations at Nyarko and Dwinfuor Sites of Begho—1975." *Sankofa* 2: 86–87.

———. 1989. *Pottery from the Begho B-2 Site, Ghana.* African Occasional Papers no. 4. Calgary: University of Calgary Press.

Crumley, L. C., and W. H. Marquardt. 1990. "Landscape: A Unifying Concept in Regional Analysis." In K. Allen, S. W. Green, and E. B. W. Zubrow, eds., *Interpreting Space: GIS and Archaeology*, 73–79. London: Taylor and Francis.

Cruz, M. D. 1996. "Ceramic Production in the Banda Area (West-Central Ghana): An Ethnoarchaeological Approach." *Nyame Akuma* 45: 30–37.

———. 2003. "Shaping Quotidian Worlds: Ceramic Production and Consumption in Banda, Ghana c. 1780–1994." PhD diss., SUNY Binghamton.

Cuoq, J. M. 1975. *Recueil des Sources Arabes Concernant l'Afrique Occidentale du VIIIè au XIVè Siècle.* Paris: CNRS.

Curtin, P. 1969. *The Atlantic Slave Trade: A Census.* Madison: University of Wisconsin Press.

——. 1970. *Two Jamaicas: The Role of Ideas in a Tropical Colony, 1830–1865.* Cambridge: Harvard University Press.

——. 1971. "Jihad in West Africa: Early West Africa: Early Phases and Inter-relations in Mauritania and Senegal." *Journal of African History* 12 (1): 11–24.

——. 1975. *Economic Change in Precolonial Africa: Senegambia in the Era of the Slave Trade.* Madison: University of Wisconsin Press.

——. 1984. *Cross-Cultural Trade in World History.* Cambridge: Cambridge University Press.

Cusick, J. G., ed. 1998. *Studies in Culture Contact: Interaction, Culture Change, and Archaeology.* Occasional Paper no. 25. Carbondale: Southern Illinois University, Center for Archaeological Investigations.

——. 2000. "Creolization and the Borderlands." *Historical Archaeology* 34 (3): 46–55.

Cuthrell-Curry, M. 2000. "African-Derived Religion in the African American Community in the United States." In J. K. Olupona, ed., *African Spirituality: Forms, Meanings, and Expressions,* 450–66. New York: Crossroad.

Daaku, K. Y. 1966. "Pre-Ashanti States." *Ghana Notes and Queries* 9: 10–13.

——. 1970. *Trade and Politics on the Gold Coast, 1600–1720: A Study of the African Reaction to European Trade.* Oxford: Clarendon Press.

Dada, P. O. 1985. *A Brief History of Igbomina (Igboona).* Ilorin: Matanmi.

D'Agostino, M. E. 1995. Review of *Flowerdew Hundred: The Archaeology of a Virginia Plantation* by James Deetz. *Historical Archaeology* 29 (1): 103–104.

Dallas, R. C. 1803. *The History of the Maroons.* London: T. N. Longman and O. Rees.

Dalzel, A. 1967 (1793). *The History of Dahomy: An Inland Kingdom of Africa.* London: Cass.

Da Matta, R. 1991. "Religion and Modernity: Three Studies of Brazilian Religiosity." *Journal of Social History* 25: 389–406.

d'Ans, A. M. 1997. "Culte Royal et Patrimoine: Le Palais du roi Dako Donou à Houawé Zounzonsa." *Ethnographie* 121: 129–39.

Das Gupta, Ashin. 1987. "Introduction II: The Story." In A. Das Gupta and M. N. Pearson, eds., *India and the Indian Ocean, 1500–1800,* 25–45. Oxford: Oxford University Press.

David, N., R. Heimann, D. Killick, and M. Wayman. 1989. "Between Bloomery and Blast Furnace: Mafa Iron-Smelting Technology in North Cameroon." *African Archaeological Review* 7: 183–208.

Davidson, D. 1979. "Negro Slave Control and Resistance in Colonial Mexico, 1519–1650." In Richard Price, ed., *Maroon Societies,* 82–106. Baltimore: Johns Hopkins University Press.

Davies, O. 1964. "Gonja Painted Pottery." *Transactions of the Historical Society of Ghana* 7: 4–11.

Davis, A. 1981. *Women, Race, and Class.* New York: Random House.

Davis, O. 1997. "The Door of No Return: Reclaiming the Past through the Rhetoric of Pilgrimage." *Western Journal of Black Studies* 21 (3): 156–61.

Dawdy, S. L. 2000. "Preface to Symposium on Creolization." *Historical Archaeology* 34 (3): 1–4.

Deagan, K. 1985. "Spanish-Indian Interaction in Sixteenth-Century Florida and Hispaniola." In W. Fitzhugh, ed., *Cultures in Contact,* 281–317. Washington, D.C.: Smithsonian Institution Press.

———. 2002. *Artifacts of the Spanish Colonies of Florida and the Caribbean, 1500–1800*, vol. 2, *Portable Personal Possessions*. Washington, D.C.: Smithsonian Institution Press.

Deagan, K., and J. Landers. 1999. *Fort Mosé: Earliest Free African American Town in the United States*. In T. A. Singleton, ed., *"I, Too, Am America": Studies in African American Archaeology*, 261–82. Charlottesville: University Press of Virginia.

Deagan, K., and D. McMahon. 1995. *Fort Mose: Colonial America's Black Fortress of Freedom*. Gainesville: University Press of Florida/Florida Museum of Natural History.

DeCorse, C. R. 1987. "Historical Archaeological Research in Ghana, 1986–1987." *Nyame Akuma* 29: 27–31.

———. 1989. "Beads as Chronological Indicators in West African Archaeology: A Reexamination." *Beads: Journal of the Society of Bead Researchers* 1: 41–53.

———. 1991. "West African Archaeology and the Atlantic Slave Trade." *Slavery and Abolition* 12 (2): 92–96.

———. 1992. "Culture Contact, Continuity, and Change on the Gold Coast, AD 1400–1900." *African Archaeological Review* 10: 163–96.

———. 1993. "The Danes on the Gold Coast: Culture Change and the European Presence." *African Archaeological Review* 11: 149–73.

———. 1998. "The Europeans in West Africa: Culture Contact, Continuity, and Change." In G. Connah, ed., *Transformations in Africa: Essays on Africa's Later Past*, 219–44. Leicester: Leicester University Press.

———. 1999. "Oceans Apart: Africanist Perspectives of Diaspora Archaeology." In T. A. Singleton, ed., *"I, Too, Am America": Archaeological Studies of African American Life*, 132–55. Charlottesville: University Press of Virginia.

———. 2001a. *An Archaeology of Elmina: Africans and Europeans on the Gold Coast, 1400–1900*. Washington, D.C.: Smithsonian Institution Press.

———, ed. 2001b. *West Africa during the Atlantic Slave Trade*. Leicester: Leicester University Press.

DeCorse, C. R., F. G. Richard, and I. Thiaw. 2003. "Toward a Systematic Analysis of Archaeological Beads? A View from the Lower Falemme, Senegal." *Journal of African Archaeology* 1: 77–109.

DeCorse, C. R., and B. E. DiSanto. 1999. The Society for Historical Archaeology Membership Survey: Preliminary Draft. Manuscript Report to the Society for Historical Archaeology Board. Maxwell School of Citizenship and Public Affairs.

DeCunzo, L. 1998. "A Future after Freedom." *Historical Archaeology* 32 (1): 42–54.

Deetz, J. 1993. *Flowerdew Hundred: The Archaeology of a Virginia Plantation, 1619–1864*. Charlottesville: University Press of Virginia.

———. 1995. "Cultural Dimensions of Ethnicity in the Archaeological Record." Presented at the 28th annual meeting of the Society for Historical Archaeology, Washington, D.C., January 1995.

———. 1996. *In Small Things Forgotten: An Archaeology of Early American Life*. New York: Knopf.

De Gregori, T. R. 1969. *Technology and the Economic Development of the Tropical African Frontier*. Cleveland: Press of the Case Western Reserve University.

Dei, G. 1998. "Interrogating 'African Development' and the Diasporan Reality." *Journal of Black Studies* 29 (2): 141–53.

Deive, C. E. 1989. *Los Guerrilleros Negros*. Santo Domingo: Fundación Cultural Dominicana.

Deku, Afrikadzata. 1993. "The Truth about Castles in Ghana and Africa." *Ghanaian Weekly Spectator,* May 8 and 15.

Delafosse, M. 1963. *Chroniques du Fouta Sénégalais, Traduction de Deux Manuscripts Arabes Inédits de Siré Abbas Soh.* Paris: Ernest Leroux.

——. 1972. *Le Haut-Senegal-Niger.* Paris: Larose.

Delgado, R., ed. 1995. *Critical Race Theory: The Cutting Edge.* Philadelphia: Temple University Press.

Delgado, J., and M. Staniforth. 2002. "Underwater Archaeology." In *The Encyclopedia of Life Support Systems.* Paris: UNESCO. Online at http://www.eolss.co.uk.

Delle, J. A. 1998. *An Archaeology of Social Space: Analyzing Coffee Plantations in Jamaica's Blue Mountains.* New York: Plenum.

——. 1999. "The Landscapes of Class Negotiation on Coffee Plantations in the Blue Mountains of Jamaica, 1790–1850." *Historical Archaeology* 33 (1): 136–58.

——. 2000. "Gender, Power and Space: Negotiating Social Relations under Slavery on Coffee Plantations in Jamaica, 1790–1834." In J. A. Delle, S. A. Mrozowski, and R. Paynter, eds., *Lines That Divide: Historical Archaeologies of Race, Class, and Gender,* 168–203. Knoxville: University of Tennessee Press.

Delle, J. A., S. A. Mrozowski, and R. Paynter, eds. 2000. *Lines That Divide: Historical Archaeologies of Race, Class, and Gender.* Knoxville: University of Tennessee Press.

Déme, A. 1991. *Evolution Climatique et Processus de Mise en Place du Peuplement dans l'Ile A Morphil.* Mémoire de Maitrise, Université Cheikh Anta Diop.

——. 2003. "Archaeological Investigations of Settlement and Long-Term Complexity in the Middle Senegal Valley (Senegal)." PhD diss., Rice University.

Déme, A., and R. J. McIntosh. 1994. "Antecedent Settlement Dynamics of the Takrur Heartland." Presented at the 12th biennial conference of the Society for Africanist Archaeologists, April 28–May 1, Indiana University, Bloomington.

Denbow, J. 1990. "Congo to Kalahari: Data and Hypotheses about the Political Economy of the Western Stream of the Early Iron Age." *African Archaeology Review* 8: 139–75.

——. 1999. "Heart and Soul: Glimpses of Ideology and Cosmology in the Iconography of Tombstones from the Loango Coast of Central America." *Journal of American Folklore* 112 (445): 404–23.

Derry, L. 1997. "Pre-Emancipation Archaeology: Does It Play in Selma, Alabama?" *Historical Archaeology* 31 (3): 18–26.

Devenish, D. 1997. "Exhibiting the Slave Trade." *Museum International* 49 (3): 49–52.

Devisse, J. 1983. *Tegdaooust III: Recherches sur Aoudaghost.* Editions Recherches sur les Civilisations. Mémoire no. 25.

Dhavalikar, M. K. 1996. "Environment: Its Influence on History and Culture in Western India." *Indica* 33 (2): 81–118.

Diagne, P. 1967. *Pouvoir Politique Traditionnel en Afrique Occidentale.* Paris: Presence Africaine.

Diop, A. B. 1968. "La Tenure Foncière en Mileu Rural Wolof (Sénégal)." *Notes Africaines* 118: 48–52.

Diouf, M. 1990. *Le Kajoor au XIXè siècle: Pouvoir Ceddo et Conquête Coloniale.* Paris: Khatala.

Diouf, S., ed. 2003. *Fighting the Slave Trade: West African Strategies.* Athens: Ohio University Press.

Domínguez, L. 1999. *Los Collares en la Santería Cubana.* Havana: Editorial José Marti.

Donley-Reid, L. 1990. "A Structuring Structure: The Swahili House." In S. Kent, ed., *Domestic Architecture and the Use of Space: An Interdisciplinary Cross-Cultural Study*, 114–26. Cambridge: Cambridge University Press.

Douglas, M. 1975. *Implicit Meanings: Essays in Anthropology*. London: Routledge and Kegan Paul.

———. 1996. *Natural Symbols: Explorations in Cosmology*. London: Routledge.

Douglass, F. 2000 (1845). "Narrative of the Life of Frederick Douglass, an American Slave." In W. L. Andrews and H. L. Gates Jr., eds., *Slave Narratives*, 267–368. New York: American Library.

Downs, D. 1995. *Art of the Florida Seminole and Miccosukee Indians*. Gainesville: University of Florida Press.

Drake, S. A. 1906. *Historic Mansions and Highways around Boston*. Boston: Little, Brown.

Dubin, S. C. 1999. *Displays of Power: Memory and Amnesia in the American Museum*. New York: New York University Press.

Du Bois, W. E. B. 1939. *Black Folk, Then and Now: An Essay on the History and Sociology of the Negro Race*. New York: Henry Holt.

———. 1996 (1903). *The Souls of Black Folk*. New York: Penguin.

Duff, E. C. 1920. *Gazetteer of Kontagora Province*. London: Frank Cass.

Dupigny, E. G. M. 1921. *Gazetteer of Nupe Province*. London: Frank Cass.

Dupuis, J. 1966 (1824). *Journal of a Residence in Ashantee*. 2nd ed. London: Frank Cass.

Durant-Gonzales, V. 1983. "The Occupation of Higglering." *Jamaica Journal* 16: 2–12.

Durrans, B. 1989. "Theory, Profession, and the Political Role of Archaeology." In S. J. Shennan, ed., *Archaeological Approaches to Cultural Identity*, 66–75. London: Unwin.

Earle, T. K., ed. 1991. *Chiefdoms: Power, Economy, and Ideology*. New York: Cambridge University Press.

Early, G. 1999. "Adventures in Colored Museum: Afrocentrism, Memory, and the Construction of Race." *American Anthropologist* 100 (3): 703–11.

Ebanks, R. 1984. "Ma Lou, an Afro Jamaican Pottery Tradition." *Jamaica Journal* 17: 31–37.

Ebron, Paulla. 2000. "Tourists as Pilgrims: Commercial Fashioning of Transatlantic Politics." *American Ethnologist* 26 (4): 910–32.

———. 2002. *Performing Africa*. Princeton: Princeton University Press.

Edwards, B. 1793. *The History, Civil and Commercial, of the British Colonies in the West Indies*. 3 vols. London: Printed for J. Stockdale.

Edwards, Y. D. 1990. "Master-Slave Relations: A Williamsburg Perspective." M.A. thesis, William and Mary.

———. 1998. "'Trash' Revisited: A Comparative Approach to Historical Descriptions and Archaeological Analysis of Slave Houses and Yards." In Grey Gundaker, ed., *Keep Your Head to the Sky: Interpreting African American Home Ground*, 245–329. Charlottesville: University of Virginia Press.

Edwards-Ingram, Y. 1997. "Toward 'True Acts of Inclusion': The 'Here' and the 'Out There' Concepts in Public Archaeology." *Historical Archaeology* 31 (3): 27–35.

Effah-Gyamfi, K. 1981. "Clay Smoking Pipes and the Dating of Archaeological Sites in Ghana: A Reassessment." *West African Journal of Archaeology* 11: 75–92.

———. 1985. *Bono-Manso: An Archaeological Investigation into Early Akan Urbanism.* Occasional Papers no. 2. Calgary: University of Calgary Press.

Egharevba, J. 1987. *Short History of Benin.* 4th ed. Ibadan: Ibadan University Press.

Ekanade, O., and O. Aloba. 1998. "Nineteenth-Century Yoruba Warfare: The Geographer's Viewpoint." In A. Akinjogbin, ed., *War and Peace in Yorubaland, 1793–1893,* 21–31. Ibadan: Heinemann.

Elbl, I. 1991. "The Horse in Fifteenth-Century Senegambia." *International Journal of African Historical Studies* 24 (1): 85–110.

Elouard, P. 1962. "Etude Géomorphologique et hydrogéologique des formations sédimentaires du Guelba mauritanien et de la Vallée du Sénégal." Mémoires B.R.G.M. no. 7.

Elphinstone, K. V. 1921. *Gazetteer of Ilorin Province.* London: Frank Cass.

Eltis, D. 1977. "The Export of Slaves from Africa, 1821–1843." *Journal of Economic History* 37: 410–15.

———. 1979. "The Direction and Fluctuation of the Transatlantic Slave Trade, 1821–1843: A Revision of the 1845 Parliamentary Paper." In H. A. Gemery and J. S. Hogerndorn, eds., *The Uncommon Market: Essays in the Economic History of the Atlantic Slave Trade,* 271–30. New York: Academic Press.

———. 1987. *Economic Growth and the Ending of the Transatlantic Slave Trade.* New York: Oxford University Press.

———. 2000. *The Rise of African Slavery in the Americas.* Cambridge: Cambridge University Press.

———. 2001. "The Volume and Structure of the Transatlantic Slave Trade: A Reassessment." *William and Mary Quarterly* 58 (1): 17–46.

———. 2004. "The Diaspora of Yoruba Speakers, 1650–1865: Dimensions and Implications." In T. Falola and M. Childs, eds., *The Yoruba Diaspora in the Atlantic World,* 17–39. Bloomington: Indiana University Press.

Eltis, D., S. Behrendt, D. Richardson, and H. Klein. 1999. *The Trans-Atlantic Slave Trade: A Database on CD-ROM.* Cambridge: Cambridge University Press.

Eltis, D., and L. Jennings. 1988. "Trade between Western Africa and the Atlantic World in the Pre-Colonial Era." *American Historical Review* 93: 936–59.

Eluyemi, O. 1977. "Excavations at Isoya." *West African Journal of Archaeology* 7: 97–115.

England, S. 1994. "Acculturation in the Creole Context: A Case Study of La Poterie, Martinique." PhD diss., Cambridge University.

Epperson, T. 1990. "Race and the Disciplines of the Plantation." *Historical Archaeology* 24 (4): 29–36.

———. 1999a. "Constructing Difference: The Social and Spatial Order of the Chesapeake Plantation." In T. A. Singleton, ed., *"I, Too, Am America": Archaeological Studies of African American Life,* 159–72. Charlottesville: University Press of Virginia.

———. 1999b. "The Global Importance of African Diaspora Archaeology in the Analysis and Abolition of Whiteness." World Archaeological Congress 4, University of Cape Town, January 10–14.

———. 2001. "'A Separate House for the Christian Slaves, One for the Negro Slaves': The Archaeology of Race and Identity in Late-Seventeenth-Century Virginia." In C. E. Orser Jr., ed., *Race and the Archaeology of Identity,* 54–70. Salt Lake City: University of Utah Press.

Escalante, A. 1979. "Palenques in Colombia." In R. Price, ed., *Maroon Societies*, 74–81. London: Johns Hopkins University Press.

Eyerman, R. 2001. *Cultural Trauma: Slavery and the Formation of African American Identity*. Cambridge: Cambridge University Press.

Eyo, E. 1974. "Excavations at Odo Ogbe Street and Lafogido, Ife, Nigeria." *West African Journal of Archaeology* 4: 99–109.

Eyre, L. A. 1980. "The Maroon Wars in Jamaica: A Geographical Appraisal." *Jamaican Historical Review* 12: 5–18.

Fabian, J. 1985. "Religious Pluralism: An Ethnographic Approach." In W. van Binsbergen and M. Schoffeleers, eds., *Theoretical Explorations in African Religion*, 138–63. London: KPI Limited.

Fagan, B. 1961. "Pre-European Ironworking in Central Africa with Special Reference to Northern Rhodesia." *Journal of African History* 2: 199–210.

Fagan, B., and J. S. Kirkman. 1967. "An Ivory Trumpet from Sofala, Mozambique." *Ethnomusicology* 11: 368–74.

Fage, J. D. 1962. "Some Remarks on Beads and Trade in Lower Guinea in the Sixteenth and Seventeenth Centuries." *Journal of African History* 3: 343–47.

———. 1969. "Slavery and the Slave Trade in the Context of West African History." *Journal of African History* 10 (3): 393–404.

———. 1980. "Slaves and Society in Western Africa, c. 1445–c. 1700." *Journal of African History* 21: 289–310.

Fairbanks, Charles. 1971. "The Kingsley Slave Cabins in Duval County, Florida, 1968." *Conference on Historic Site Archaeology* 7: 62–93.

———. 1978. "The Ethno-Archaeology of the Florida Seminole." In J. Milanich and S. Proctor, eds., *Tacachale: Essays on the Indians of Florida and Southeast Georgia*, 120–49. Gainesville: University Presses of Florida.

Fakambi, J. 1993. *Routes des Esclaves au Bénin (ex-Dahomey) dans une Approche Régionale*. Ouidah: République du Bénin.

Falola, T., and M. Childs, eds. 2004. *The Yoruba Diaspora in the Atlantic World*. Bloomington: Indiana University Press.

Falola, T., and G. O. Oguntomisin. 2001. *Yoruba Warlords of the Nineteenth Century*. Trenton, N.J.: Africa World Press.

Farias, P. F. 1974. "Silent Trade: Myth and Historical Evidence." *History in Africa* 1: 9–24.

Farid, J. 2001. "Brancos são 2.5 vezes mais ricos que negros." *O Estado de São Paulo*, July 8, 2001: A15.

Farnsworth, P. 1993. "What Is the Use of Plantation Archaeology? No Use at All, If No One Else Is Listening!" *Historical Archaeology* 27 (1): 114–16.

———, ed. 2001. *Island Lives: Historical Archaeologies of the Caribbean*. Tuscaloosa: University of Alabama Press.

Farr, F., and L. R. Burne, eds. 1991. *A Diary of the Visits of Frederick Douglass to Nantucket Island*. Boston: Museum of Afro American History.

Fatunsin, Anthonia K. 1992. *Yoruba Pottery*. Lagos: National Commission for Museums and Monuments.

Faye, A. 1997. *Le Thème de la mort dans la Litterature Sereer: Essai*. Dakar: NEA.

Faye, L. D. 1983. *Mort et naissance: Le Monde Sereer*. Dakar: NEA.

Feinberg, H. M., and M. Johnson. 1982. "The West African Ivory Trade during the Eighteenth Century." *International Journal of African Historical Studies* 15: 435–53.

Feinman, G., and J. Marcus, eds. 1998. *Archaic States*. Santa Fe, N.M.: School of American Research Press.

Fennell, C. C. 2000. "Conjuring Boundaries: Inferring Past Identities from Religious Artifacts." *International Journal of Historical Archaeology* 4 (4): 281–313.

——. 2003a. "Group Identity, Individual Creativity, and Symbolic Generation in a BaKongo Diaspora." *International Journal of Historical Archaeology* 7 (1): 1–31.

——. 2003b. "Consuming Mosaics: Mass-Produced Goods and Contours of Choice in the Upper Potomac Region." PhD diss., University of Virginia. Ann Arbor: UMI.

Ferguson, L. G. 1980. "Looking for the 'Afro' in Colono Indian Pottery." In R. Schuyler, ed., *Archaeological Perspectives on Ethnicity in America*, 14–28. Farmingdale, N.Y.: Baywood.

——. 1992. *Uncommon Ground: Archaeology and Early African America, 1650–1800*. Washington, D.C.: Smithsonian Institution Press.

——. 1998. "Early African American Pottery in South Carolina: A Complicated Plainware." 63rd annual meeting of the Society for American Archaeology, Seattle, March 25.

——. 1999. "'The Cross Is a Magic Sign': Marks on Eighteenth-Century Bowls from South Carolina." In T. A. Singleton, ed., *"I, Too, Am America": Archaeological Studies of African American Life*, 116–31. Charlottesville: University Press of Virginia.

Fernandes, F. 1969. *A integração do negro na sociedade de classes: No limiar de uma nova era*. São Paulo: Dominus.

Fieller, N. R. J., and P. T. Nicholson. 1997. "Grain-Size Analysis of Archaeological Pottery: The Use of Statistical Models." In A. Middleton and I. Freestone, eds., *Recent Developments in Ceramic Petrology*, 71–112. British Museum Occasional Papers no. 81, London.

Figueiredo, A. 2002. "The End of 'Social Whitening.'" *Newsweek*, February 18, 33.

Firth, R. 1973. *Symbols: Public and Private*. Ithaca: Cornell University Press.

Fisher, A. G. B., and H. J. Fisher. 1971. *Slavery and Muslim Society in Africa: The Institution in Saharan and Sudanic Africa and the Trans-Saharan Trade*. New York: Doubleday.

Fitts, R. 1996. "Landscapes of Northern Bondage." *Historical Archaeology* 30 (2): 54–73.

Flannery, K. 1972. "The Cultural Evolution of Civilizations." *Annual Review of Ecology and Systematics* 3: 399–426.

——. 1998. "The Ground Plans of Archaic States." In G. Feinman and J. Marcus, eds., *Archaic States*, 15–58. Santa Fe, N.M.: School of American Research Press.

Fleisher, J. 2004. "Behind the Sultan of Kilwa's 'Rebellious Conduct': Local Perspectives on an International East African Town." In A. B. Stahl, ed., *African Archaeology: A Critical Introduction*, 91–123. Malden, Mass.: Blackwell.

Fletcher, R. 1998. "African Urbanisms: Scale Mobility and Transformations." In G. Connah, ed., *Transformations in Africa: Essays on Africa's Later Past*, 104–38. Leicester: Leicester University Press.

Forbes, F. E. 1966 (1851). *Dahomey and the Dahomans; Being the Journals of Two Missions to the King of Dahomey and Residence at His Capital in the Years 1849 and 1850*. 2 vols. London: Frank Cass.

Forbes, Jack. 1993. *Africans and Native Americans: The Language of Race and the Evolution of Red-Black Peoples*. Urbana: University of Illinois Press.

446

Fosbrooke, H. A. 1960. "The 'Masai Walls' of Moa: Walled Towns of the Segeju." *Tanganyika Notes and Records* 41: 30–37.

Foster, H. B. 1998. "African American Jewelry before the Civil War." In L. Sciama and J. Eicher, eds., *Beads and Bead Makers*, 177–92. New York: Berg.

Foster, L. 1935. "Negro-Indian Relations in the Southeast." PhD diss., University of Pennsylvania.

Franklin, M. 1997a. "'Power to the People': Sociopolitics and the Archaeology of Black Americans." *Historical Archaeology* 31 (3): 36–50.

——. 1997b. "Why Are There So Few Black American Archaeologists?" *Antiquity* 71: 799–801.

——. 1997c. "Out of Site, Out of Mind: The Archaeology of an Enslaved Virginian Household, ca. 1740–1778." PhD diss., University of California, Berkeley. Ann Arbor: UMI.

——. 2001. "A Black Feminist-Inspired Archaeology?" *Journal of Social Archaeology* 1 (1): 108–25.

——. 2004. *An Archaeological Study of the Rich Neck Slave Quarter and Enslaved Domestic Life.* Colonial Williamsburg Archaeological Reports. Williamsburg: Department of Archaeological Research, Colonial Williamsburg Foundation.

Franklin, M., and L. McKee. 2004. "African Diaspora Archaeologies: Present Insights and Expanding Discourses." *Historical Archaeology* 38 (1): 1–9.

Frazier, E. F. 1966a. *The Negro Church: The Negro in America.* New York: Academic Press.

——. 1966b. *The Negro Family in the United States.* Chicago: Academic Press.

Freeman, T. B. 1844. *Journals of Various Visits to the Kingdoms of Ashanti, Aku, and Dahomi in Western Africa.* London: J. Mason.

Freeman-Grenville, G. S. P. 1958. "Some Recent Archaeological Work on the Tanganyika Coast." *Man* 58: 106–11.

——. 1960. "Historiography of the East African Coast." *Tanganyika Notes and Records* 55: 279–89.

——. 1962. *The East African Coast: Select Documents from the First to the Earlier Nineteenth Century.* Oxford: Oxford University Press.

——. 1965. *The French at Kilwa Island: An Episode in Eighteenth-Century East African History.* Oxford: Clarendon Press.

——. 1973. *Chronology of African History.* Oxford: Oxford University Press.

Fritz, J. 1986. "Vijayanagara: Authority and Meaning of a South Indian Imperial Capital." *American Anthropologist* 88: 44–55.

Funari, P. P. A. 1995a. "The Archaeology of Palmares and Its Contribution to the Understanding of the History of African American Culture." *Historical Archaeology in Latin America* 7: 1–41.

——. 1995b. "A Cultural Material e a Construção de Mitologia Bandeirante: Problemas da Dentidade Nacional Brasileira." *Idéias* 2: 29–48.

——. 1999. "Maroon, Race, and Gender: Palmares Material Culture and Social Relations in a Runaway Settlement." In P. P. A Funari, M. Hall, and S. Jones, eds., *Historical Archaeology, Back from the Edge*, 308–27. London: Routledge.

——. 2002. "Class Interests in Brazilian Archaeology." *International Journal of Historical Archaeology* 6: 209–16.

Funari, P. P. A., and A. V. Carvalho. 2005. *Palmares, Ontem, e Hoje.* Rio de Janeiro: Jorge Zahar.

Furtado, C. 1965. *The Economic Growth of Brazil.* Berkeley: University of California Press.

Gaines, Kevin. 1999. "African American Expatriates in Ghana and the Black Radical Tradition." *Souls* 1 (4): 64–71.

Galke, L. J. 2000. "Did the Gods of Africa Die? A Reexamination of a Carroll House Crystal Assemblage." *North American Archaeologist* 21 (1): 19–33.

Gallaher, A. 1951. "A Survey of the Seminole Freedmen." M.A. thesis, University of Oklahoma, Norman.

Gallardo, J. E. n.d. *Un testimonio sobre la esclavitud en Montevideo, la memoria de Lino Suárez Peña.* Buenos Aires: Idea Viva.

Garlake, P. 1966. *Islamic Architecture on the East African Coast.* British Institute in Eastern Africa, Nairobi.

———. 1977. "Excavations on the Woye Asiri Family Land, Ile-Ife." *West African Journal of Archaeology* 7: 57–95.

———. 1978. "Pastoralism and Zimbabwe." *Journal of African History* 19 (4): 479–93.

Garman, J. C. 1998. "Rethinking 'Resistant Accommodation': Toward an Archaeology of African American Lives in Southern New England, 1638–1800." *International Journal of Historical Archaeology* 2 (2): 133–60.

Garrard, T. F. 1980. *Akan Weights and the Gold Trade.* London: Longman.

———. 1982. "Myth and Metrology: The Early Trans-Saharan Gold Trade." *Journal of African History* 23: 443–61.

Garren-Marrot, L. 1995. "Le Commerce Médieval du Cuivre: La Situation dans la Moyenne Vallée du Sénégal d'après les Données Archéologiques et Historiques." *Journal des Africanistes* 2: 43–56.

Gates, H. L., Jr. 1999. *Wonders of the African World.* New York: Knopf.

Geertz, C. 1973. *The Interpretation of Cultures.* New York: Basic Books.

Geggus, D. 1982. *Slave Resistance Studies and the St. Domingue Slave Revolt.* Occasional Papers Series, Winter, no. 4. Latin American and Caribbean Center of Florida International University, Miami.

———. 2001. "The French Slave Trade: An Overview." *William and Mary Quarterly,* 3rd ser., 58 (1): 119–38.

Gemery, H. A., and J. S. Hogendorn. 1978. "Technological Change, Slavery, and the Slave Trade." In C. Dewey and A. G. Hopkins, eds., *The Imperial Impact: Studies in the Economic History of Africa and India,* 243–69. London: Athlone.

———, eds. 1979. *The Uncommon Market: Essays in the Economic History of the Atlantic Slave Trade.* New York: Academic Press.

Genovese, E. D. 1976. *Roll, Jordan, Roll: The World the Slaves Made.* New York: Vintage Books.

———. 1979. *From Rebellion to Revolution: Afro-American Slave Revolts in the Making of the Modern World.* Baton Rouge: Louisiana State University Press.

Gershenhorn, J. 2004. *Melville J. Herskovits and the Racial Politics of Knowledge.* Lincoln: University of Nebraska Press.

Gibb, J. G. 1997. "Necessary but Insufficient: Plantation Archaeology Reports and Community Action." *Historical Archaeology* 31 (3): 18–26.

Gibbins, D., and J. Adams. 2001. "Shipwrecks and Maritime Archaeology." *World Archaeology* 32 (3): 279–91.

Gibson, A., and A. Woods. 1990. *Prehistoric Pottery for the Archaeologist.* Leicester: Leicester University Press.

Giddens, A. 1979. *Central Problems in Social Theory: Action, Structure, and Contradiction in Social Analysis.* Berkeley: University of California Press.

Gillespie, S. 2000. "Maya 'Nested Houses': The Ritual Construction of Place." In R. A. Joyce and S. Gillespie, eds., *Beyond Kinship: Social and Material Reproduction in House Societies,* 135–60. Philadelphia: University of Pennsylvania Press.

Gillman, C. 1944. "An Annotated List of Ancient and Modern Indigenous Structures in Eastern Africa." *Tanganyika Notes and Records* 17: 44–55.

Gilroy, P. 1993. *The Black Atlantic: Double Consciousness and Modernity.* Cambridge: Harvard University Press.

Girouard, M. 1980. *Life in the English Country House: A Social and Architectural History.* Harmondsworth: Penguin Books.

Glassie, H. 1975. *Folk Housing in Middle Virginia.* Knoxville: University of Tennessee Press.

Glassman, J. 1991. "The Bondsman's New Clothes: The Contradictory Consciousness of Slave Resistance on the Swahili Coast." *Journal of African History* 32: 277–312.

Gleave, M. 1963. "Hill Settlements and Their Abandonment in Western Yorubaland." *Africa* 33: 343–52.

Goggin, J. M. 1951. "Beaded Shoulder Pouches of the Florida Seminole." *Florida Anthropologist* 4: 3–17.

———. 1958. "Seminole Pottery." In James B. Griffin, ed., *Prehistoric Pottery of the Eastern United States,* 200–202. Ann Arbor: Museum of Anthropology, University of Michigan.

Gois, A. 2001. "Grupos Raciais na Universidade Brasileira." *Folha de São Paulo,* January 14, 2001: C1.

Goldberg, M. 1976. "La Población negra y mulata de la ciudad de Buenos Aires, 1810–1840." *Desarrollo Económico* 16 (April–June): 75–99.

———. 1994. "Mujer Negra Rioplatense." In L. Knecher and M. Panaia, eds., *La Mitad del País: La Mujer en la Sociedad Argentina,* 67–95. Buenos Aires: Centro Editor de América Latina.

———. 1997. "Negras y Mulatas de Buenos Aires, 1750–1880." *Actas del XI Congreso Nacional de Arqueología Argentina* 1: 415–20.

———. 2000. "Las Africanargentinas, 1720–1880." In *Historia de las Mujeres en la Argentina,* 1: 67–86. Buenos Aires: Editorial Taurus.

Goldstein, D. 1999. "'Interracial' Sex and Racial Democracy in Brazil: Twin Concepts?" *American Anthropologist* 101: 563–78.

Gomez, M. 1998. *Exchanging Our Country Marks: The Transformation of African Identities in the Colonial and Antebellum South.* Chapel Hill: University of North Carolina Press, 1998.

———. 2006. "Introduction—Diasporic Africa: A View from History." In M. Gomez, ed., *Diasporic Africa,* 1–23. New York: New York University Press.

Gonzalez, N. 1988. *Sojourners of the Caribbean: Ethnogenesis and Ethnohistory of the Garifuna.* Urbana: University of Illinois Press.

Goody, J. R. 1971. *Technology, Tradition, and State in Africa.* London: Oxford University Press.

Gosden, C. 1994. *Social Being and Time.* London: Blackwell.

Gosden, C., and Y. Marshall. 1999. "The Cultural Biography of Objects." *World Archaeology* 31 (2): 169–78.

Goucher, C. 1981. "Iron Is Iron till It's Rust: Trade and Technology in the Decline of West African Iron Smelting." *Journal of African History* 22 (2): 179–89.

———. 1984. "The Iron Industry of Bassar, Togo: An Interdisciplinary Investigation of African Technological History." PhD diss., UCLA.

———. 1990. "African Hammer, European Anvil: West African Iron Making in the Atlantic Trade Era." *West African Journal of Archaeology* 20: 200–208.

———. 1991. "John Reeder's Foundry: A Study of Eighteenth-Century African-Caribbean Technology." *Jamaica Journal* 23 (1): 39–43.

———. 1999. "African-Caribbean Metal Technology: Forging Cultural Survivals in the Atlantic World." In J. B. Haviser, ed., *African Sites Archaeology in the Caribbean*, 143–56. Princeton: Markus Weiner.

Graham, R. 1979. *Escravidão, reforma e imperialismo.* São Paulo: Perspectiva.

Gravrand, H. 1983. *La Civilisation Sereer: Cosaan, les Origines.* Dakar: Nouvelles Editions Africaines.

———. 1990. *La Civilisation Sereer: Pangol, le Génie Réligieux.* Dakar: Nouvelles Editions Africaines.

Gray, J. M. 1947. "Rezende's Description of East Africa in 1634." *Tanganyika Notes and Records* 23: 2–29.

———. 1954. "Nairuzi or Siku ya Mwaka." *Tanganyika Notes and Records* 38: 1–22.

———. 1957. "Trading Expeditions from the Coast to Lakes Tanganyika and Victoria before 1857." *Tanganyika Notes and Records* 49: 226–46.

Greene, L. J. 1942. *The Negro in Colonial New England, 1620–1776.* Port Washington, N.Y.: Kennikat Press. Reprinted 1966.

———. 1944. "The New England Negro as Seen in Advertisements for Runaway Slaves." *Journal of Negro History* 29 (2): 125–46.

Greene, S. 2000. "Cultural Zones in the Era of the Slave Trade: Exploring the Yoruba Connection with the Anlo-Ewe." In P. Lovejoy, ed., *Identity in the Shadow of Slavery*, 86–101. London: Continuum.

Greenlee, R. F. 1952. "Aspects of Social Organization and Material Culture of the Seminole of Big Cypress Swamp." *Florida Anthropologist* 5 (3/4): 25–32.

Greenwood, D. 1977. "Culture by the Pound: An Anthropological Perspective on Tourism as Cultural Commoditization." In V. Smith, *Hosts and Guests: The Anthropology of Tourism*, 129–38. Philadelphia: University of Pennsylvania Press.

Gregory, C. A. 1996. "Cowries and Conquest: Towards a Subalternate Quality Theory of Money." *Comparative Studies in Society and History* 38 (2): 195–217.

Griffin, J. W. 1950. "An Archaeologist at Fort Gadsden." *Florida Historical Quarterly* 28 (4): 255–61.

Guèye, N. S. 1991. *L'Étude de la Céramique Subactuelle et de ses Rapports avec la Céramique de Cubalel.* Mémoire de Maitrise. Université de Dakar.

———. 1993. "Les Pipes de la Moyenne Vallée du Fleuve Sénégal: Rapports des deux Premières Missions." Article de DEA, Université Paris X Nanterre.

———. 1998. "Poteries et Peuplement de la Moyenne Vallée du Fleuve Sénégal du XVIeme au XXeme Siècle: Approches Ethnoarchéologique et Ethnohistorique." Thèse Doctorat es lettres, Université de Parix X, Nanterre.

Guimarães, C. M. 1992. "Esclavage, Quilombos et Archéologie." *Les Dossiers d'Archéologie* 169: 67.

Gundaker, G. 1993. "Tradition and Innovation in African American Yards." *African Arts* 26: 58–71.

———. 1998. *Signs of Diaspora, Diaspora of Signs: Literacies, Creolization, and Vernacular Practices in African America.* New York: Oxford University Press.

———. 2000. "Creolization, Complexity, and Time." *Historical Archaeology* 34 (3): 124–33.

Guyer, J. 1993. "Wealth in People and Self-Realization in Equatorial Africa." *Man,* n.s., 28: 257.

———. 2004. *Marginal Gains: Monetary Transactions in Atlantic Africa.* Chicago: University of Chicago Press.

Guyer, J., and S. M. E. Belinga. 1995. "Wealth in People as Wealth in Knowledge: Accumulation and Composition in Equatorial Africa." *Journal of African History* 36: 91–120.

Gwynn, S. 1935. *Mungo Park and the Quest of the Niger.* New York: G. P. Putnam's Sons.

Haas, J. 2000. "Cultural Evolution and Political Centralization." In J. Haas, ed., *From Leaders to Rulers,* 3–18. New York: Kluwer Academic.

Haas, J., and W. Creamer. 1993. *Stress and Warfare among the Kayenta Anasazi of the Thirteenth Century AD.* Fieldiana Anthropology, n.s., 21. Field Museum of Natural History, Chicago.

Hale, C. A. 1989. "Political and Social Ideas." In L. Bethel, ed., *Latin America Economy and Society, 1870–1930,* 225–300. Cambridge: Cambridge University Press.

Haley, A. 1976. *Roots.* New York: Doubleday.

Hall, D. 1999. *In Miserable Slavery: Thomas Thistlewood in Jamaica.* Kingston: University of the West Indies Press.

Hall, G. 1992. *Africans in Colonial Louisiana: The Development of Afro-Creole Culture in the Eighteenth Century.* Baton Rouge: Louisiana State University Press.

———. 2005. *Slavery and African Ethnicities in the Americas: Restoring the Links.* Chapel Hill: University of North Carolina Press.

Hall, M. 1992. "Small Things and the Mobile Conflictual Fusion of Power, Fear, and Desire." In Anne E. Yentsch and M. C. Beaudry, eds., *The Art and Mystery of Historical Archaeology,* 373–99. Boca Raton, Fla.: CRC Press.

———. 1993. "The Archaeology of Colonial Settlement in Southern Africa." *Annual Review of Anthropology* 22: 177–200.

———. 1997. "Patriarchal Facades: The Ambivalences of Gender in the Archaeology of Colonialism." In L. Wadley, ed., *Our Gendered Past: Archaeological Studies of Gender in Southern Africa,* 221–36. Johannesburg: Witwatersrand University Press.

———. 2000. *Archaeology and the Modern World: Colonial Transcripts in South Africa and the Chesapeake.* London: Routledge.

Hamilton, D. 1992. "Simon Benning, Pewterer of Port Royal." In B. J. Little, ed., *Text-Aided Archaeology,* 39–53. Boca Raton, Fla.: CRC Press.

Hamilton, D. L., and R. Woodward. 1984. "A Sunken Seventeenth-Century City: Port Royal, Jamaica." *Archaeology* 37 (1): 38–45.

Hammond, D., and A. Jablow. 1970. *The Africa That Never Was: Four Centuries of British Writing about Africa.* Prospect Heights, Ill.: Waveland.

Hancock, I. 1980. *The Texas Seminoles and Their Language.* Austin: University of Texas, African and Afro-American Studies and Research Center.

Handelmann, H. 1987. *Geschichte von Brasilien.* Zurich: Manesse.

Handler, J. 1963. "Pottery Making in Rural Barbados." *Southwestern Journal of Anthropology* 19: 314–34.

———. 1964. "Notes on Pottery Making in Antigua." *Man* 64: 184–85.

———. 1982. "Slave Revolts and Conspiracies in Seventeenth-Century Barbados." *Niewe West-Indische Gids* 56: 5–42.

———. 1997. "An African-Type Healer and His Grave Goods: A Burial from a Plantation Slave Cemetery in Barbados, West Indies." *International Journal of Historical Archaeology* 1: 91–130.

Handler, J. S., and F. W. Lange. 1978. *Plantation Slavery in Barbados.* Cambridge: Harvard University Press.

Handler, R. 1994. "Is 'Identity' a Useful Cross-cultural Concept?" In J. R. Gillis, ed., *Commemorations: The Politics of National Identity*, 27–40. Princeton: Princeton University Press.

Handsman, R. G., and M. P. Leone. 1989. "Living History and Critical Archaeology in the Reconstruction of the Past." In V. Pinsky and A. Vylie, eds., *Critical Traditions in Contemporary Archaeology*, 117–35. Cambridge: Cambridge University Press.

Haraway, D. 1988. "Situated Knowledges: The Science Question in Feminism and the Privilege of Partial Perspective." *Feminist Studies* 14 (3): 575–99.

Harding, V. 1997. "Religion and Resistance among Antebellum Slaves, 1800–1860." In T. Fulop and A. J. Raboteau, eds., *African American Religion: Interpretive Essays in History and Culture*, 108–30. New York: Routledge.

Harlan, J. R. 1971. "Agricultural Origins." *Science* 174: 468–74.

Harlan, J. R., J. M. J. de Wet, and A. B. L. Stemler, eds. 1976. *Origins of African Plant Domestication.* The Hague: Mouton.

Harrington, J. C. 1978. "Dating Stem Fragments of Seventeenth- and Eighteenth-Century Clay Tobacco Pipes." In R. L. Schuyler, ed., *Historical Archaeology: A Guide to Substantive Contributions*, 63–65. Farmingdale, N.Y.: Baywood.

Harrington, S. 1996. "An African Cemetery in Manhattan." In B. Fagan, ed., *Eyewitness to Discovery: First Person Accounts of More Than Fifty of the World's Greatest Archaeological Discoveries*, 324–33. New York: Oxford University Press.

Harris, C. L. G. 1994. "The True Traditions of My Ancestors." In E. K. Agorsah, ed., *Maroon Heritage: Archaeological, Ethnographic, and Historical Perspectives.* Kingston: Canoe Press.

Harris, J. 1993. *Global Dimensions of the African Diaspora.* 2nd ed. Washington, D.C.: Howard University Press.

Harris, M. 1972. "Portugal's Contribution to the Underdevelopment of Africa and Brazil." In R. H. Chilcote, ed., *Protest and Resistance in Angola and Brazil*, 209–23. Berkeley: University of California Press.

Hart, R. 1985. *Slaves Who Abolished Slavery*, vol. 2, *Blacks in Rebellion.* Mona: Institute of Social and Economic Research.

Haslip-Viera, G., B. Ortiz de Montellano, and W. Barbour. 1997. "Robbing Native American Cultures: Van Sertima's Afrocentricity and the Olmecs." *Current Anthropology* 38 (3): 419–41.

Hassan, F. A. 1996. "Abrupt Holocene Climatic Events in Africa." In G. Pwiti and R. Soper, eds., *Aspects of African Archaeology*, 83–89. Harare: University of Zimbabwe Press.

———. 1997. "Holocene Paleoclimates of Africa." *African Archaeological Review* 14 (4): 213–30.

——. 2000. "Climate and Cattle in North Africa: A First Approximation." In R. M. Blench and K. C. MacDonald, eds., *The Origins and Development of African Livestock: Archaeology, Genetics, Linguistics, and Ethnography*, 61–86. London: UCL Press.

Hassan, Y. 1967. *The Arabs and the Sudan: From the Seventh to the Early Sixteenth Century.* Edinburgh: Edinburg University Press.

Hauser, M. W. 2001. "Peddling Pots: Determining the Extent of Market Exchange in Eighteenth-Century Jamaica through the Analysis of Local Coarse Earthenware." PhD diss., Syracuse University.

——. 2006. "Hawking Your Wares: Determining Scale of Informal Economy through the Distribution of Local Coarse Earthenware in Eighteenth-Century Jamaica." In J. B. Haviser and K. C. MacDonald, eds., *African Re-Genesis: Confronting Social Issues in the Diaspora*, 160–75. London: University College London Press.

Hauser, M. W., and D. Armstrong. 1999. "Embedded Identities: Piecing Together Relationships through Compositional Analysis of Low-Fired Eathenwares." In J. B. Haviser, ed., *African Sites Archaeology in the Caribbean*, 65–93. Princeton, N.J.: Markus Weiner.

Haviser, J. B., ed. 1999. *African Sites Archaeology in the Caribbean.* Princeton, N.J.: Markus Wiener.

—— 2001. "Historical Archaeology in the Netherlands Antilles and Aruba." In P. Farnsworth, ed., *Island Lives: Historical Archaeologies of the Caribbean*, 60–81. Tuscaloosa: University of Alabama Press.

Hayden, R. C. 1987. *The African Meeting House in Boston: A Celebration of History.* Boston: Companion Press Book.

Hayden, R. C., and K. E. Hayden. 1999. *African Americans on Martha's Vineyard and Nantucket: A History of People, Places, and Events.* Boston: Select Publications.

Heath, B. 1999a. "'Your Humble Servant': Free Artisans in the Monticello Community." In T. A. Singleton, ed., *"I, Too, Am America": Archaeological Studies of African American Life*, 193–217. Charlottesville: University Press of Virginia.

——. 1999b. "Yabbas, Monkeys, Jugs, and Jars: An Historical Context for African-Caribbean Pottery on St. Eustatius." In J. B. Haviser, ed., *African Sites Archaeology in the Caribbean*, 196–220. Princeton, N.J.: Markus Weiner.

——. 1999c. "Buttons, Beads, and Buckles: Contextualizing Adornment within the Bounds of Slavery." In Maria Franklin and Garrett Fesler, eds., *Historical Archaeology, Identity Formation, and the Interpretation of Ethnicity*, 47–69. Richmond, Va.: Dietz Press.

Heath, B., and A. Bennett. 2000. "'The Little Spots Allow'd Them': The Archaeological Study of African American Yards." *Historical Archaeology* 34 (2): 38–55.

Hegmon, M. 1992. "Archaeological Research on Style." *Annual Review of Anthropology* 21: 517–36.

Herbert, E., and C. Goucher. 1987. *The Blooms of Banjeli: Technology and Gender in West African Ironmaking.* Watertown, Mass.: Documentary Educational Resources.

Herlehy, T. J. 1984. "Ties That Bind." *International Journal of African Historical Studies* 17 (2): 285–308.

Herman, B. L. 1999. "Slave and Servant Housing in Charleston, 1770–1820." *Historical Archaeology* 33 (3): 88–101.

Hermon-Hodge, H. B. 1929. *Gazetteer of Ilorin Province.* London: Frank Cass.

Herron, J. 1994. "Black Seminole Settlement Pattern." M.A. thesis, University of South Carolina, Columbia.

Herskovits, M. J. 1958 (1941). *The Myth of the Negro Past*. Boston: Beacon Press.

Herskovits, M., and F. Herskovits. 1958. *Dahomean Narrative: A Cross-Cultural Analysis*. Evanston: Northwestern University Press.

Higgins, N. I. 1991. "The Deforming Mirror of Truth: Slavery and the Master Narrative of American History." *Radical History Review* 49: 25–48.

Higman, B. W. 1976. *Slave Population and Economy in Jamaica, 1807–1834*. Cambridge: Cambridge University Press.

——. 1986. "Plantation Maps as Sources for the Study of West Indian Ethnohistory." In Dennis Wiedman, ed., *Ethnohistory: A Researcher's Guide*, no. 35. Williamsburg, Va.: College of William and Mary, Department of Anthropology.

——. 1996. "Patterns of Exchange within a Plantation Economy: Jamaica at the Time of Emancipation." In R. McDonald, ed., *West Indies Accounts: Essays on the History of the British Caribbean and the Atlantic Economy*, 211–31. Kingston: University of the West Indies Press.

——. 1998. *Montpelier, Jamaica*. Kingston: University of the West Indies Press.

Hildebrand, K.-G. 1958. "Foreign Markets for Swedish Iron in the Eighteenth Century." *Scandinavian Economic History Review* 6: 3–52.

Hill, M. 1976. "Archaeological Smoking Pipes from Central Sierra-Leone." *West African Journal of Archaeology* 6: 109–19.

Hill, M. H. 1987. "Ethnicity Lost? Ethnicity Gained? Information Functions of 'African Ceramics' in West Africa and North America." In M. Glass, S. MacEachern, and P. McCartney, eds., *Ethnicity and Culture*, 135–39. Calgary: Archaeological Association, University of Calgary.

Hilliard, A. G. 1995. *The Maroon within Us: Selected Essays on African American Community Socialization*. Baltimore: Black Classic Press.

Hillier, W., and J. Hanson. 1984. *The Social Logic of Space*. Cambridge: Cambridge University Press.

Hilton, A. 1985. *The Kingdom of Kongo*. Oxford: Clarendon Press.

Hodder, B. W., and U. I. Ukwu. 1969. *Markets in West Africa*. Ibadan: Ibadan University Press.

Hodder, I. 1991. "Interpretive Archaeology and Its Role." *American Antiquity* 56: 7–18.

Hodges, G. R. 1997 (1827). Introduction to Robert Roberts, *The House Servant's Directory; or, A Monitor for Private Families: Comprising Hints on the Arrangement and Performance of Servants' Work*, xi–xlii. Armonk, N.Y.: M. E. Sharpe.

Hogendorn, J., and M. Johnson. 1986. *The Shell Money of the Slave Trade*. Cambridge: Cambridge University Press.

Holloway, J. E. 1990. "The Origins of African American Culture." In J. E. Holloway, ed., *Africanisms in American Culture*, 1–18. Bloomington: Indiana University Press.

Hoogbergen, W. 1990. "The History of Suriname Maroons." In V. H. Sutlive, M. D. Zamora, V. Kerns, and T. Hamada, eds., *Resistance and Rebellion in Suriname: Old and New, Studies in Third World Societies*, 65–102. Williamsburg, College of William and Mary.

hooks, b. 1990. *Yearning: Race, Gender, and Cultural Politics*. Boston: South End Press.

Hoover, G. N. 1974. *The Elegant Royalls of New England*. New York: Vantage Press.

Horton, M. 1984. "The Early Settlement of the Northern Kenya Coast." PhD diss., Cambridge University.

——. 1996. *Shanga: A Muslim Trading Community on the East African Coast.* British Institute in Eastern Africa, Nairobi.

Horton, R. 1992. The Economy of Ife from c. A.D. 900–A.D. 1700. In A. A. Akinjogbin, ed., *The Cradle of a Race: Ife from the Beginning to 1980*, 122–47. Lagos: Sunray Publications.

Howard, R. 2002. *Black Seminoles in the Bahamas.* Gainesville: University Press of Florida.

Howson, J. E. 1990. "Social Relations and Material Culture: A Critique of the Archaeology of Plantation Slavery." *Historical Archaeology* 24 (4): 78–91.

Hudgins, C. 1990. "Robert 'King' Carter and the Landscape of Tidewater Virginia in the Eighteenth Century." In W. Kelso and R. Most, eds., *Earth Patterns*, 59–70. Charlottesville: University Press of Virginia.

Huffman, T. N. 1996. *Snakes and Crocodiles: Power and Symbolism in Ancient Zimbabwe.* Johannesburg: Witwatersrand University Press.

Hughes, R. 1999. "$3 Million for a Foreign Slave-owner." In *Action*, 11. Bridgetown.

Hull, R. W. 1976. *African Cities and Towns before the European Conquest.* New York: Norton.

Hunwick, J. 1992. "Black Slaves in the Mediterranean World: Introduction to a Neglected Aspect of the African Diaspora." In E. Savage, ed., *The Human Commodity: Perspectives on the Trans-Saharan Slave Trade*, 5–38. London: Frank Cass.

Hunwick, J., and P. Trout. 2002. *The African Diaspora in the Mediterranean Lands of Islam.* Princeton, N.J.: Markus Wiener.

Hyatt, V. 1997. *Ghana: The Chronicle of a Museum Development Project in the Central Region.* Washington, D.C.: Smithsonian Institution.

Hyde, C. K. 1977. *Technological Change and the British Iron Industry, 1700–1870.* Princeton: Princeton University Press.

Hyland, A. 1995. "Monuments Conservation Practice in Ghana: Issues of Policy and Management." *Journal of Architectural Conservation* 2: 45–62.

Hymes, D., ed. 1971. *Pidginization and Creolization of Languages.* London: Cambridge University Press.

Inikori, J. E. 1976. "Measuring the Atlantic Slave Trade: An Assessment of Curtin and Anstey." *Journal of African History* 17 (2): 197–223.

——. 1977. "The Import of Firearms into West Africa, 1750–1807: A Quantitative Analysis." *Journal of African History* 18: 339–68.

——. 1982. *Forced Migration: The Impact of the Export Slave Trade on African Societies.* New York: Africana.

——. 2001. "Africans and Economic Development in the Atlantic World, 1500–1870." In S. S. Walker, ed., *African Roots/American Culture: Africa in the Creation of the Americas.* New York: Rowman and Littlefield.

——. 2002. *Africans and the Industrial Revolution in England: A Study in International Trade and Economic Development.* Cambridge: Cambridge University Press.

——. 2003. "The Struggle against the Transatlantic Slave Trade: The Role of the State." In S. Diouf, ed., *Fighting the Slave Trade: West African Strategies*, 170–98. Athens: Ohio University Press; Oxford: James Currey.

Inikori, J., and S. Engerman. 1992. Introduction to J. Inikori and S. Engerman, eds., *The Atlantic Slave Trade: Effects on Economies, Societies, Peoples in Africa, the Americas, and Europe*. Durham: Duke University Press.

Insoll, T. 1995. "A Cache of Hippopotamus Ivory at Gao, Mali, and a Hypothesis of Its Use." *Antiquity* 69: 327–36.

———. 1996. "The Archeology of Islam in Sub-Saharan Africa: A Review." *Journal of World Prehistory* 10 (4): 439–504.

Iroko, F. A. 1989. "Vestiges d'une Ancienne Industrie de Métallurgie du fer dans le Region d'Abomey." *West African Journal of Archaeology* 19: 1–20.

Isaac, Rhys. 1982. *The Transformation of Virginia, 1740–1790*. Chapel Hill: University of North Carolina Press.

Jain, V. K. 1990. *Trade and Traders in Western India*. New Delhi: Munshiram Manoharlal.

Jackson, R. T. 1907. *History of the Oliver, Vassall, and Royall Houses in Dorchester, Cambridge, and Medford*. Boston: Privately published.

Jacobson-Widding, A. 1979. *Red-White-Black as a Mode of Thought: A Study of Triadic Classification by Colours in the Ritual Symbolism and Cognitive Thought of the Peoples of the Lower Congo*. Stockholm: Uppsala University and Almquist and Wiksell.

———. 1991. "The Encounter with the Water Mirror." In A. Jacobson-Widding, ed., *Body and Space: Symbolic Models of Unity and Division in African Cosmology and Experience*, 177–216. Stockholm: Uppsala University and Almquist and Wiksell.

James, C. L. R. 1963. *The Black Jacobins: Toussaint L'Ouverture and the San Domingo Revolution*. New York: Vintage Books.

Jamieson, R. W. 1995. "Material Culture and Social Death: African American Burial Practices." *Historical Archaeology* 29 (4): 39–58.

Jansen, R. 2000. "93% têm preconceito, revela Pesquisa." *O Estado de São Paulo*, May 12, 2000: A4.

Janzen, J. M. 1977. "The Tradition of Renewal in Kongo Religion." In N. S. Booth Jr., ed., *African Religions: A Symposium*, 69–116. New York: NOK.

———. 1985. "The Consequences of Literacy in African Religion: The Kongo Case." In W. van Binsbergen and M. Schoffeleers, eds., *Theoretical Explorations in African Religion*, 225–52. London: KPI Limited.

Janzen, J. M., and W. MacGaffey. 1974. *An Anthology of Kongo Religion: Primary Texts from Lower Zaire*. Publications in Anthropology no. 5. Lawrence: University of Kansas.

Jarratt, Reverend D. 1806. *The Life of the Reverend Devereux Jarratt*. Baltimore: Warner and Hannah; reprint, 1969, New York: Arno Press.

Johnson, A. W., and T. Earle. 2000. *The Evolution of Human Societies: From Foraging Group to Agrarian State*. Stanford: Stanford University Press.

Johnson, M. 1978a. "By Ship or by Camel: The Struggle for the Cameroons Ivory Trade in the Nineteenth Century." *Journal of African History* 19: 539–49.

———. 1978b. "Technology, Competition, and African Crafts." In C. Dewey and A. G. Hopkins, eds., *The Imperial Impact: Studies in the Economic History of Africa and India*, 259–69. London: Athlone Press.

———. 1996. *The Archaeology of Capitalism*. Oxford: Basil Blackwell.

Johnson, S. 1921. *The History of the Yorubas*. Lagos: CSS Bookshop.

Jones, L. 2000. "Crystals and Conjuring at the Charles Carroll House, Annapolis, Maryland." *African American Archaeology* 27: 1–2.

Jones, N. T., Jr. 1990. *Born a Child of Freedom, Yet a Slave: Mechanisms of Control and Strategies of Resistance in Antebellum South Carolina.* Hanover, N.H.: Wesleyan University Press.

Jones, R. 2002. *The First Hermitage Historic Structure Report.* On file at the Hermitage Museum.

Joyner, C. 1984. *Down by the Riverside.* Urbana: University of Illinois Press.

Juwayeyi, Y. M. 1993. "Iron Age Settlement and Subsistence Patterns in Southern Malawi." In T. Shaw, P. Sinclair, B. Andah, and A. Okpoko, eds., *The Archaeology of Africa,* 391–98. New York: Routledge.

Kane, O. 1970. "Samba Gelajo-Jegi." *Bulletin de l'IFAN* series B, 32 (4): 911–26.

——. 1973. "Les unités territoriales du Futa Toro." *Bulletin de l'IFAN* series B, 35 (3): 614–31.

——. 1974. "Les Maures et le Fuuta Toro au 18eme siècle." *Cahiers d'Etudes Africaines* 54: 237–52.

——. 1986. "Le Fuuta Tooro des Satigi aux Almaami." Thèse d'Etat, Université Cheikh Anta Diop.

Kankpeyeng, B. W., and C. R. DeCorse. 2004. "Ghana's Vanishing Past: Development, Antiquities, and the Destruction of the Archaeological Record." *African Archaeological Review* 21 (2): 89–128.

Kapchan, D. A., and P. T. Strong. 1999. "The Metaphor of Hybridity." *Journal of American Folklore* 112 (445): 239–53.

Karasch, M. C. 1987. *Slave Life in Rio de Janeiro, 1808–1850.* Princeton: Princeton University Press.

Karenga, M. 1982. *Introduction to Black Studies.* Inglewood, Calif.: Kawaida.

Karttunen, F. 2003a. "The Village of New Guinea in the Nation of Nantucket: A History of the Five Corners Neighborhood." Annual conference of the Nantucket Preservation Trust, Nantucket, Mass.

——. 2003b. "The Other Islanders" (http://www.nha.org/newexploreshome.htm), accessed August 19, 2003. Nantucket, Mass.: Nantucket Historical Association.

Katz, W. L. 1986. *Black Indians: A Hidden Heritage.* New York: Ethrac.

Katzin, M. F. 1959. "Partners: An Informal Savings Institution in Jamaica." *Social and Economic Studies* 8 (4): 436–40.

——. 1971. "The Business of Higglering in Jamaica." In M. Horowitz, ed., *Peoples and Cultures of the Caribbean,* 340–81. New York: Natural History Press.

Kaur, R., and J. Hutnyk, eds. 1999. *Travel Worlds: Journeys in Contemporary Cultural Politics.* London: Zed Books.

Kea, R. 1971. "Firearms and Warfare on the Gold and Slave Coasts from the Sixteenth to the Nineteenth Centuries." *Journal of African History* 12: 185–213.

Keegan, W., A. V. Stokes, and L. A. Newson. 1990. *Bibliography of Caribbean Archaeology.* 2 vols. Gainesville: Bullen Research Library, University of Florida.

Kelly, K. G. 1995. "Transformation and Continuity in Savi, a West African Trade Town: An Archaeological Investigation of Culture Change on the Coast of Bénin during the Seventeenth and Eighteenth Centuries." PhD diss., UCLA.

——. 1996. "Trade Contacts and Social Change: The Archaeology of the Hueda Kingdom, Republic of Benin." In G. Pwiti and R. Soper, eds., *Aspects of African Archaeology: Papers from the Tenth Congress of the Pan-African Association for Prehistory and Related Studies,* 687–91. Harare: University of Zimbabwe Publications.

———. 1997a. "The Archaeology of African-European Interaction: Investigating the Social Roles of Trade, Traders, and the Use of Space in the Seventeenth- and Eighteenth-Century Hueda Kingdom, Republic of Benin." *World Archaeology* 28 (3): 77–95.

———. 1997b. "Using Historically Informed Archaeology: Seventeenth- and Eighteenth-Century Hueda-Europe Interaction on the Coast of Bénin." *Journal of Archaeological Method and Theory* 4 (3/4): 353–66.

———. 2001. "Change and Continuity in Coastal Benin." In C. DeCorse, ed., *West Africa during the Atlantic Trade: Archaeological Perspectives*, 81–100. Leicester: Leicester University Press.

———. 2002. "Indigenous Responses to Colonial Encounters on the West African Coast: Hueda and Dahomey from the Seventeenth through Nineteenth Century." In C. Lyons and J. Papodopoulos, eds., *The Archaeology of Colonialism.* Los Angeles: Getty Trust Publications.

———. 2004. "The African Diaspora Starts Here: Historical Archaeology of Coastal West Africa." In A. Reid and P. Lane, eds., *African Historical Archaeologies*, 219–41. New York: Kluwer Academic/Plenum.

Kelso, W. M., and R. Most, eds. 1990. *Earth Patterns: Essays in Landscape Archaeology.* Charlottesville: University Press of Virginia.

Kent, S. 1984. *Analyzing Activity Areas: An Ethnoarchaeological Study of the Use of Space.* Albuquerque: University of New Mexico Press.

———. 1990. "A Cross-Cultural Study of Segmentation, Architecture, and the Use of Space." In S. Kent, ed., *Domestic Architecture and the Use of Space: An Interdisciplinary Cross-Cultural Study*, 127–52. Cambridge: Cambridge University Press.

———. 1998. "Gender and Prehistory in Africa." In S. Kent, ed., *Gender in African Prehistory.* Walnut Creek, Calif.: AltaMira Press.

Kirkman, J. S. 1954. *The Arab City of Gedi: Excavations at the Great Mosque, Architecture, and Finds.* Oxford: Oxford University Press.

———. 1956. "The Culture of the Kenya Coast in the Later Middle Ages." *South African Archaeological Bulletin* 11: 89–99.

———. 1957. "The Mosque of the Pillar." *Ars Orientalis* 2: 174–82.

———. 1959. "Mnarani of Kilifi: The Mosques and Tombs." *Ars Orientalis* 3: 95–112.

———. 1964. *Men and Monuments on the East African Coast.* London: Lutterworth Press.

———. 1966. *Ungwana on the Tana.* The Hague: Mouton.

Kiyaga-Mulindwa, D. 1993. "The Iron Age Peoples of East-Central Botswana." In T. Shaw, P. Sinclair, B. Andah, and Al Okpoko, eds., *African Archaeology: Food, Metals, and Towns*, 386–90. New York: Routledge.

Klein, H. S. 1978. *The Middle Passage: Comparative Studies in the Atlantic Slave Trade.* Princeton: Princeton University Press.

Klein, L. 1993. "Conversations with." *Current Anthropology* 34: 723–35.

Klein, M. A. 1994. "Slavery, the International Labour Market, and the Emancipation of Slaves in the Nineteenth Century." In Paul Lovejoy and Nicholas Rogers, eds., *Unfree Labour in the Development of the Atlantic World*, 201. London: Frank Cass.

Klose, H. 1899. *Togo unter Deutscher Flagge.* Berlin: Dietrich Riemer.

Kopytoff, I. 1986. "The Cultural Biography of Things: Commoditization as Process." In A. Appadurai, ed., *The Social Life of Things: Commodities in Cultural Perspective*, 64–91. Cambridge: Cambridge University Press.

———. 1987. "The Internal African Frontier." In I. Kopytoff, ed., *The African Frontier: The Reproduction of Traditional African Societies*, 3–84. Bloomington: Indiana University Press.

———. 1999. "Permutations in Patrimonialism and Populism: The Aghem Chiefdoms of Western Cameroon." In S. K. McIntosh, ed., *Beyond Chiefdoms: Pathways to Complexity in Africa*, 88–96. Cambridge: Cambridge University Press.

Kozlowski, J. K. 1974. *Pre-ceramic Cultures in the Caribbean.* Zespyty Naukowe, Universytute Jagiellonskiego 386, Prace archaeologiczne Ze no. 20.

Kraph, J. L. 1860. *Travels, Researches, and Missionary Labours during an Eighteen Years' Residence in Eastern Africa.* Boston: Ticknor and Fields.

Kriger, C. 2005. "The Conundrun of Culture in Atlantic History." In J. Curto and R. Soulodre-LaFrance, eds., *Africa and the Americas: Interconnections during the Slave Trade.* Trenton, N.J.: Africa World Press.

Krishna, B. 1974. *Commercial Relations between India and England, 1601–1727.* London: Routledge.

Kusimba, C. M. 1993. "The Archaeology and Ethnography of Iron Metallurgy of the Kenya Coast." PhD diss., Bryn Mawr College.

———. 1999a. *The Rise and Fall of Swahili States.* Walnut Creek, Calif.: AltaMira Press.

———. 1999b. "The Rise of Elites among the Precolonial Swahili of the East African Coast." In J. Robb, ed., *Material Symbols in Prehistory*, 318–41. Carbondale: Southern Illinois University Press.

———. 2004. "The Archaeology of Slavery in East Africa." *African Archaeological Review* 21 (2): 59–88.

Kusimba, C. M., and S. B. Kusimba. 1999. "Regional Trains toward Social Complexity in Eastern and Southern Africa." Annual meeting of the Society for American Archaeology, Chicago.

———. 2004. "East Africa." In A. B. Stahl, ed., *African Archaeology: A Critical Introduction.* Malden, Mass.: Blackwell.

Kusimba, S. B., and C. M. Kusimba. 2000. *Archaeology of Urban Hinterlands in the Tsavo National Park.* Presented at annual meeting of the Society for Africanist Archaeology, Cambridge, UK.

Lago, P. C. 2001. *Iconografia Brasileira.* São Paulo: Itaú Cultural.

Laguerre, M. S. 1980. *Voodoo Heritage.* Beverly Hills, Calif.: Sage.

———. 1989. *Voodoo and Politics in Haiti.* New York: St. Martin's Press.

Laman, K. E. 1953. *The Kongo I.* Studies Ethnographica Upsaliensia IV. Uppsala, Sweden: Almqvist and Wiksells.

———. 1957. *The Kongo II.* Studies Ethnographica Upsaliensia IV. Uppsala, Sweden: Almqvist and Wiksells.

———. 1962. *The Kongo III.* Studies Ethnographica Upsaliensia IV. Uppsala, Sweden: Almqvist and Wiksells.

———. 1968. *The Kongo IV.* Studies Ethnographica Upsaliensia IV. Uppsala, Sweden: Almqvist and Wiksells.

Lancaster, P. A., J. S. Ingram, M. Y. Lim, and D. G. Coursey. 1982. "Traditional Cassava-Based Foods: Survey of Processing Techniques." *Economic Botany* 36: 12–45.

Lander, R. 1830. *Records of Captain Clapperton's Last Expedition to Africa.* 2 vols. London: Colburn and Bentley.

Lander, R., and J. Lander. 1832. *Journal of an Expedition to Explore the Course and Termination of the Niger.* 2 vols. New York: Harper.

Landers, J. 1990. "Gracia Real de Santa Teresa de Mose: A Free Black Town in Spanish Colonial Florida." *American Historical Review* 95 (1): 9–30.

———. 1999. *Black Society in Spanish Florida.* Urbana: University of Illinois Press.

Landolphe, J. F. 1975 (1823). *Memoirs du Capitaine Landolphe, Contenant l'Histoire de ses Voyages.* Vol. 2. Ed. J. S. Quesne. Paris: Hachette, Bibliothèque Nationale.

Lane, P. 1999. "Archaeology, Nonconformist Missions, and the 'Colonisation of Consciousness' in Southern Africa, c. 1820–1900." In T. Insoll, ed., *Case Studies in Archaeology of World Religions,* 153–65. Oxford: Archaeopress, BAR S755.

Lanuza, J. L. 1946. *Morenada.* Buenos Aires: Emecé Editores.

Larkin, J. 1988. *The Reshaping of Everyday Life, 1790–1840.* New York: Harper and Row.

LaRoche, C. J., and M. L. Blakey. 1997. "Seizing Intellectual Power: The Dialogue at the New York African Burial Ground." *Historical Archaeology* 31 (3): 84–106.

LaViolette, A., and J. Fleisher. 2005. "The Archaeology of Sub-Saharan Urbanism: Cities and Their Countrysides." In A. B. Stahl, ed., *African Archaeology: A Critical Introduction,* 327–52. Oxford: Blackwell.

Law, R. C. 1974. "The Constitutional Troubles of Oyo in the Eighteenth Century." *Journal of African History* 19 (1): 25–44.

———. 1977. *The Oyo Empire c. 1600–c. 1836: A West African Imperialism in the Era of the Atlantic Slave Trade.* Oxford: Oxford University Press.

———. 1978. "Slaves, Trade, and Taxes: The Material Basis of Political Power in Precolonial West Africa." *Research in Economic Anthropology* 1: 37–52.

———. 1980. *The Horse in West African History.* Oxford: Oxford University Press.

———. 1986. "Dahomey and the Slave Trade: Reflections on the Historiography of the Rise of Dahomey." *Journal of African History* 27 (2): 237–67.

———. 1987a. "Problems of Plagiarism, Harmonization and Misunderstanding in Contemporary European Sources: Early (Pre-1680s) Sources for the 'Slave Coast' of West Africa." *Paideuma* 33: 337–58.

———. 1987b. "Ideologies of Royal Power: The Dissolution and Reconstruction of Political Authority on the 'Slave Coast,' 1680–1750." *Africa* 57 (3): 321–44.

———. 1989a. "'My Head Belongs to the King': On the Political and Ritual Significance of Decapitation in Pre-Colonial Dahomey." *Journal of African History* 30 (3): 399–415.

———. 1989b. "Slave-Raiders and Middlemen, Monopolists and Free-Traders: The Supply of Slaves for the Atlantic Trade in Dahomey c. 1715–1850." *Journal of African History* 30 (1): 45–68.

———. 1991. *The Slave Coast of West Africa, 1550–1750: The Impact of the Atlantic Slave Trade on an African Society.* Oxford: Oxford University Press.

———. 1992. "Warfare on the West African Coast, 1650–1850." In R. B. Ferguson and N. L. Whitehead, eds., *War in the Tribal Zone: Expanding States and Indigenous Warfare,* 103–26. Santa Fe, N.M.: School of American Research Press.

———. 1997. *The Kingdom of Allada.* Leiden: Research School CNWS.

Law, R. C., and P. Lovejoy. 1997. "The Changing Dimensions of African History: Reappropriating the Diaspora." In S. McGrath, C. Jedrej, K. King, and J. Thompson, eds., *Rethinking African History,* 181–200. Edinburgh: Centre of African Studies, Edinburgh University.

———, eds. 2001. *Biography of Mahommah G. Baquaqua*. Princeton, N.J.: Markus Weiner.

Law, R. C., and K. Mann. 1999. "West Africa in the Atlantic Community: The Case of the Slave Coast." *William and Mary Quarterly* 56 (2): 307–34.

Lawrence, A. W. 1963. *Trade Castles and Forts of West Africa*. London: Jonathan Cape.

Lawuyi, O. B. 1988. "Ogun: Diffusion across Boundaries and Identity Constructions." *African Studies Review* 31: 127–39.

LeBlanc, S. 1999. *Prehistoric Warfare in the American Southwest*. Salt Lake City: University of Utah Press.

Le Herissé, A. 1911. *L'Ancien Royaume du Dahomey: Moeurs, Religion, Histoire*. Paris: E. Larose.

Leone, M. 1984. "Interpreting Ideology in Historical Archaeology: The William Paca Garden in Annapolis, Maryland." In D. Miller and C. Tilley, eds., *Ideology, Power, and Prehistory*, 25–35. Cambridge: Cambridge University Press.

———. 1988. "The Georgian Order as the Order of Merchant Capitalism in Annapolis, Maryland." In M. Leone and P. Potter, eds., *The Recovery of Meaning: Historical Archaeology in the Eastern United States*, 235–61. Washington, D.C.: Smithsonian Institution.

———. 2005. *The Archaeology of Liberty in an American Capital: Excavations in Annapolis*. Berkeley: University of California Press.

Leone, M., and G. Fry. 1999. "Conjuring in the Big House Kitchen: An Interpretation of African American Belief Systems Based on the Uses of Archaeology and Folklore Sources." *Journal of American Folklore* 112 (445): 372–403.

———. 2001. "Spirit Management among Americans of African Descent." In C. E. Orser Jr., ed., *Race and the Archaeology of Identity*, 143–57. Salt Lake City: University of Utah Press.

Leone, M., and R. W. Preucel. 1992. "Archaeology in a Democratic Society: A Critical Theory Perspective." In L. Wandsnider, ed., *Quandaries and Quests: Visions of Archaeology's Future*, 115–35. Carbondale: Southern Illinois University Center for Archaeological Investigations.

Lericollais, A. 1975. "Peuplement et Migrations dans la Vallée du Sénégal." *Cahiers de l'ORSTOM Série Sciences Humaines* 12 (2): 123–35.

Leslie, C. 1739. *A New and Exact Account of Jamaica*. Edinburgh: R. Fleming.

Levine, L. W. 1977. "Black Culture and Black Consciousness: Afro-American Folk Thought from Slavery to Freedom." New York: Oxford University Press.

Levtzion, N. 1968: *Muslims and Chiefs in West Africa*. Oxford: Clarendon Press.

———. 1988. "Islam and State Formation in West Africa." In S. N. Eisenstadt, M. Abitbol, and N. Chazan, eds., *The Early State in African Perspective*, 98–108. Leiden: E. J. Brill.

———. 1994. *Islam in West Africa: Religion, Society, and Politics to 1800*. Aldershot: Ashgate.

Levtzion, N., and J. F. P. Hopkins. 2000. *Corpus of Early Arabic Sources for West African History*. Princeton, N.J.: Markus Wiener.

Lewis, D. 1999. "Ghana, 1963: A Memoir." *American Scholar* 68 (1): 39–60.

Libretto, H. R. M. 1990. "The Maroon in Cuban and Jamaican Literature." In J. Pereira, ed., *Caribbean Literature in Comparison*, 9–30. University of the West Indies, Institute of Caribbean Studies, series 1.

Lightfoot, K. G. 1995. "Culture Contact Studies: Redefining the Relationship between Prehistoric and Historic Archaeology." *American Antiquity* 60 (2): 199–217.

Linebaugh, B. 1978. *The African School and the Integration of Nantucket Public Schools, 1825–1847.* Boston: Center for African Studies, Boston University.

Little, B. J. 1994. "People with History: An Update on Historical Archaeology in the United States." *Journal of Archaeological Method and Theory* 1 (1): 5–40.

Little, E. A. 1980. "Probate Records of Nantucket Indians." *Nantucket Algonquian Studies* 2. Nantucket, Mass.: Nantucket Historical Association.

——. 1981a. "The Writings of Nantucket Indians." *Nantucket Algonquian Studies* 3. Nantucket, Mass.: Nantucket Historical Association.

——. 1981b. "The Indian Contribution to Along-Shore Whaling at Nantucket." *Nantucket Algonquian Studies* 8. Nantucket, Mass.: Nantucket Historical Association.

——. 1983. "Indian Place Names at Nantucket Island." In W. Cowan, ed., *Proceedings of the 15th Algonquian Conference, October 28–30, 1983,* 345–62. Ottawa: Carleton University Press.

——. 1990. "Indian Horse Commons at Nantucket Island, 1660–1760." *Nantucket Algonquian Studies* 9. Nantucket, Mass.: Nantucket Historical Association.

——. 1996. "Daniel Spotso: A Sachem at Nantucket Island, Massachusetts, circa 1691–1741." In R. S. Grumet, ed., *Northeastern Indian Lives, 1632–1816,* 193–207. Amherst: University of Massachusetts Press.

Littlefield, D. F., Jr. 1977. *Africans and Seminoles: From Removal to Emancipation.* Westport, Conn.: Greenwood Press.

Livingstone, D. 1874. *The Last Journals of David Livingstone in Central Africa from 1865 to His Death.* London: John Murray.

Loewen, J. W. 1988. *The Mississippi Chinese: Between Black and White.* Long Grove, Ill.: Waveland Press.

Logan, G. C. 1995. "African Religion in America." In M. P. Leone and N. A. Silberman, eds., *Invisible America: Unearthing Our Hidden History,* 154–55. New York: Henry Holt.

Long, C. H. 1997. "Perspectives for a Study of African American Religion in the United States." In T. E. Fulop and A. J. Raboteau, eds., *African American Religion: Interpretive Essays in History and Culture,* 22–35. New York: Routledge.

Long, E. 1774. *History of Jamaica.* 3 vols. London: T. Lowndes.

Lopez, I. 1999. "A cor da Pobreza." *Problemas Brasileiros,* March/April 1999, 14–18.

Lovejoy, P. E. 1974. "Interregional Monetary Flows in the Pre-Colonial Trade of Nigeria." *Journal of African History* 15: 563–85.

——. 1982. "The Volume of the Atlantic Slave Trade: A Synthesis." *Journal of African History* 23: 473–501.

——. 1983. *Transformations in Slavery: A History of Slavery in Africa.* Cambridge: Cambridge University Press.

——. 1989. "The Impact of the Atlantic Slave Trade on Africa: A Review of the Literature." *Journal of African History* 30: 365–94.

——. 1994. "Background to Rebellion: The Origins of Muslim Slaves in Bahia." *Slavery and Abolition* 15: 151–80.

——. 1997. "The African Diaspora: Revisionist Interpretations of Ethnicity, Culture, and Religion under Slavery." *Studies in the World History of Slavery, Abolition, and Emancipation* 1: 1–23.

———. 2000. *Transformations in Slavery: A History of Slavery in Africa.* 2nd ed. Cambridge: Cambridge University Press.

Lovejoy, P. E., and D. Richardson. 1999. "Trust, Pawnship, and Atlantic History: The Institutional Foundations of the Old Calabar Slave Trade." *American Historical Review* 104 (2): 333–55.

Lovell, P. A. 1999. "Development and the Persistence of Racial Inequality in Brazil, 1950–1991." *Journal of Developing Areas* 33: 395–418.

Lubar, S., and W. D. Kingery, eds. 1993. *History from Things: Essays on Material Culture.* Washington, D.C.: Smithsonian Institution Press.

Luccketti, N. 1990. "Archaeological Excavations at Bacon's Castle, Surry County, Virginia." In W. Kelso and R. Most, eds., *Earth Patterns*, 23–42. Charlottesville: University Press of Virginia.

Lupton, K. 1979. *Mungo Park, the African Traveler.* New York: Oxford University Press.

MacEachern, S. 1996. "Foreign Countries: The Development of Ethnoarchaeology in Sub-Saharan Africa." *Journal of World Prehistory* 10 (3): 243–304.

———. 2001. "State Formation and Enslavement in Northern Cameroon and Northeastern Nigeria." In C. DeCorse, ed., *West Africa during the Slave Trade: Archaeological and Historical Perspectives*, 131–51. Leicester: Leicester University Press.

———. 2005. "Two Thousand Years of West African History." In A. B. Stahl, ed., *African Archaeology: A Critical Introduction*, 441–66. Oxford: Blackwell.

MacGaffey, W. 1986. *Religion and Society in Central Africa: The BaKongo of Lower Zaire.* Chicago: University of Chicago Press.

———. 1987. "Art and Healing of the BaKongo Commented by Themselves: Minkisi from the Laman Collection." Estocolmo: Folkens Museum-Etnografiska.

———. 1988a. "Complexity, Astonishment, and Power: The Visual Vocabulary of Kongo Minkisi." *Journal of Southern African Studies.* 14 (2): 188–203.

———. 1988b. "BaKongo Cosmology." *World and I*, September 1988, 512–21.

———. 1991. *Art and Healing of the BaKongo, Commented by Themselves: Minkisi from the Laman Collection.* Stockholm: Folkens Museum-Etnografiska.

———. 1993. "The Eyes of Understanding: Kongo Minkisi." In S. H. Williams and D. C. Driskell, eds., *Astonishment and Power*, 21–106. Washington, D.C.: Smithsonian Institution Press.

———. 2000a. "Art and Spirituality." In J. K. Olupona, ed., *African Spirituality: Forms, Meanings, and Expressions*, 223–56. New York: Crossroad.

———. 2000b. *Kongo Political Culture: The Conceptual Challenge of the Particular.* Bloomington: Indiana University Press.

———. 2000c. "The Kongo Peoples." In F. Herreman, ed., *In the Presence of Spirits: African Art from the National Museum of Ethnology, Lisbon*, 35–59. New York: Museum for African Art; Gent, Belgium: Snoek-Ducaju and Zoon.

———. 2002. "Twins, Simbi Spirits, and Lwas in Kongo and Haiti." In L. M. Heywood, ed., *Central Africans and Cultural Transformations in the American Diaspora*, 211–26. Cambridge: Cambridge University Press.

Mack, M., and M. Blakey. 2004. "The New York African Burial Ground Project: Past Biases, Current Dilemmas, and Future Research Opportunities." *Historical Archaeology* 38 (1): 10–17.

Maestri, M. 2001. *O sobrado e o cativo. A Arquitetura urbana erudita no Brasil escravista. O caso gaúcho.* Passo Fundo: Editora da UPF.

Magnavita, S. 2003. "The Beads of Kissi, Burkina Faso." *Journal of African Archaeology* 1: 127–38.

Mahon, J. K. 1967. *History of the Second Seminole War.* Gainesville: University of Florida Press.

Mallo, S. 1991. "La libertad en el discurso del estado, de amos y esclavos." *Revista de Historia de América* 112: 121–46.

———. 1997. "Los Africanporteños: del peculio al patrimonio y la propiedad." *XI Congreso Nacional de Arqueología Argentina* (La Plata) 1: 434–39.

Malone, A. 1992. *Sweet Chariot: Slave Family and Household Structure in Nineteenth-Century Louisiana.* Chapel Hill: University of North Carolina Press.

Mann, K., and Edna G. Bay, eds. 2001. *Rethinking the African Diaspora: The Making of a Black Atlantic World in the Bight of Benin and Brazil.* London: Frank Cass.

Manning, P. 1981. "The Enslavement of Africans: A Demographic Model." *Canadian Journal of African Studies* 15 (3): 499–526.

———. 1982. *Slavery, Colonialism, and Economic Growth in Dahomey, 1640–1960.* Cambridge: Cambridge University Press.

———. 1990. *Slavery and African Life: Occidental, Oriental, and African Slave Trades.* Cambridge: Cambridge University Press.

Marmon, S. E., ed. 1999. *Slavery in the Islamic Middle East.* Princeton: Markus Wiener.

Marsters, K. F., ed. 2000. *Travels in the Interior Districts of Africa: Performed under the Direction of the African Association in the Years 1795, 1796, 1797 by Mungo Park.* Durham, N.C.: Duke University Press.

Martin, S. 1745. *An Essay upon Plantership Humbly Inscribed to His Excellency George Thomas, Esq., Chief Governor of All the Leeward Islands, as a Monument to Ancient Friendship.* Antigua: Samuel Clapham; reprint, London: A. Millar, 1765.

Marx, K. 1967. *Capital.* Vol. 1. New York: International.

Mathewson, R. D. 1968. "The Painted Pottery Sequence in the Volta Basin." *West African Archaeological Newsletter* 8: 24–31.

———. 1972a. "History from the Earth: Archaeological Excavations at Old King's House." *Jamaica Journal* 6: 3–11.

———. 1972b. "Jamaican Ceramics: An Introduction to Eighteenth-Century Folk Pottery in West African Tradition." *Jamaica Journal* 6: 54–56.

Maugham, R. F. C. 1906. *Portuguese East Africa.* London: John Murray.

Maultsby, P. K. 1990. "Africanisms in African American Culture." In J. E. Holloway, ed., *Africanisms in American Culture,* 185–210. Bloomington: Indiana University Press.

Mauny, R. 1961: *Tableau géographique de l'ouest africain au Moyen Age d'après les sources écrites, la tradition et l'archéologie.* Mémoire de l'IFAN N° 61.

May, D. J. 1860. "Journey in the Yoruba and Nupe Countries in 1858." *Journal of the Royal Geographical Society* 30: 226.

Mbiti, J. 1970. *Concepts of God in Africa.* London: SPCK Press.

———. 1990. *African Religions and Philosophy.* Oxford: Heinemann Press.

Mbuia-Joao, T. N. 1990. "The Revolt of Dom Jeronimo Chingulia of Mombasa, 1590–1637: An African Episode in the Portuguese Century of Decline." PhD diss., Catholic University of America, Washington, D.C.

McCall, G. A. 1974 (1868). *Letters from the Frontiers.* Gainesville: University Presses of Florida.

McCaskie, T. C. 1983. "Accumulation, Wealth, and Belief in Asante History. I. To the Close of the Nineteenth Century." *Africa* 53 (1): 23–43.

McDavid, C. 1997. "Descendants, Decisions, and Power: The Public Interpretation of the Archaeology of the Levi Jordan Plantation." *Historical Archaeology* 31 (3): 114–31.

———. 2002. "Archaeologies That Hurt, Descendants That Matter: A Pragmatic Approach to Collaboration in the Public Interpretation of African American Archaeology." *World Archaeology* 34 (2): 303–14.

McDavid, C., and D. W. Babson, eds. 1997. "In the Realm of Politics: Prospects for Public Participation in African American and Plantation Archaeology." *Historical Archaeology* 31 (3).

McGhee, F. L. 2000. "The Black Crop: Slavery and Slave Trading in Nineteenth-Century Texas." PhD diss., University of Texas at Austin.

McGhee, F. L., and V. Curtis. 2002. "Archaeological Monitoring in Support of Transformer Replacement, Fort Kamehameha Historic District." On file at the Historic Preservation Office, Hickam Air Force Base, Hawaii, and the Hawaii State Historic Preservation Office.

McGowan, W. 1990. "African Resistance to the Atlantic Slave Trade in West Africa." *Slavery and Abolition* 11 (1): 5–29.

McGuire, R. H. 1991. "Building Power in the Cultural Landscape of Broome County, New York, 1880–1940." In R. H. McGuire and R. Paynter, eds., *The Archaeology of Inequality*, 102–24. Cambridge: Blackwell.

———. 1992. "Archaeology and the First Americas." *American Anthropologist* 94: 816–36.

———, ed. 1999. *Beyond Chiefdoms: Pathways to Complexity in Africa.* Cambridge: Cambridge University Press.

McIntosh, S. K., ed. 1999a. Beyond Chiefdoms: Pathways to Complexity in Africa. Cambridge: Cambridge University Press.

———. 1999b. "Floodplains and the Development of Complex Society: Comparative Perspectives from the West African Semi-Arid Tropics." In A. Bacus and L. Lucero, eds., Complex Polities in the Ancient Tropical World, 151–65. Arlington, Va.: American Anthropological Association.

———. 1999c. "Pathways to Complexity: An African Perspective." In S. K. McIntosh, ed., *Beyond Chiefdoms: Pathways to Complexity in Africa*, 1–30. Cambridge: Cambridge University Press.

McIntosh, S. K, and H. Bocoum. 2000. "New Perspectives on Sincu Bara: A First Millennium Site in the Senegal Valley." *African Archaeological Review* 17 (1): 1–41.

McIntosh, S. K., D. Gallagher, and R. J. McIntosh. 2003. "Tobacco Pipes from Excavations at the Museum Site, Jenne, Mali." *Journal of African Archaeology* 1: 171–99.

McIntosh, S. K., R. J. McIntosh, and H. Bocoum. 1992. "The Middle Senegal Valley Project: Preliminary Results from the 1990–1991 Field Season." *Nyame Akuma* 38: 47–61.

McKee, L. 1992. "The Ideals and Realities behind the Design and Use of Nineteenth-Century Virginia Slave Cabins." In Anne E. Yentsch and M. C. Beaudry, eds.,

The Art and Mystery of Historical Archaeology, 195–214. Boca Raton, Fla.: CRC Press.

———. 1994. "Is It Futile to Try and Be Useful? Historical Archaeology and the African American Experience." *Northeast Historical Archaeology* 23: 1–7.

———. 1995. "The Earth Is Their Witness." *Sciences* 35 (2): 36–41.

———. 1999. "Food Supply and Plantation Social Order: An Archaeological Perspective." In T. A. Singleton, ed., *"I, Too, Am America": Archaeological Studies of African American Life*, 218–39. Charlottesville: University Press of Virginia.

McWhorter, J. H. 1997. *Towards a New Model of Creole Genesis*. New York: Peter Lang.

Mead, L. A. 1995. Draft report, "Intensive Archaeological Survey at the Smith School House at Boston African American National Historic Site." Massachusetts Historical Commission, Boston.

Meillassoux, C. 1991. *The Anthropology of Slavery: The Womb of Iron and Gold*. Chicago: University of Chicago Press.

Meneses, U. T. B. 1965. "Sentido e função de um Museu de Arqueologia." *Dédalo* 1: 19–26.

Merritt, E. H. 1975. "A History of the Taita of Kenya to 1900." PhD diss., Indiana University.

Meskell, L. 1998. *Archaeology under Fire: Nationalism, Politics, and Heritage in the Eastern Mediterranean and Middle East*. New York: Routledge.

Metiboba, S. O. 2003. "The Changing Roles of the Family in Socialization Process: The Case of the O-Kun Yoruba." In A. Olukoju, Z. O. Apata, and O. Akinwumi, eds., *Northeast Yorubaland: Studies in the History and Culture of a Frontier Zone*, 124–33. Ibadan: Rex Charles.

Metraux, A. 1972. *Voodoo in Haiti*. New York: Schocken Books.

Michel, P. 1973. *Les Bassins des Fleuves Sénégal et Gambie: Étude Géomorphologique*. Mémoire ORSTOM no. 63, Paris.

Middleton, J. 1992. *The World of the Swahili: An African Mercantile Civilization*. New Haven: Yale University Press.

Midwest Universities Consortium for International Activities (MUCIA). 1991. Natural Resource Conservation and Historic Preservation: A Technical Assistance Funding Proposal for Central Region Integrated Development Project, Cape Coast, Ghana. Submitted to the U.S. Agency for International Development.

Miers, S., and I. Kopytoff, eds. 1977. *Slavery in Africa: Historical and Anthropological Perspectives*. Madison: University of Wisconsin Press.

Miller, D. 1995. "Consumption and Commodities." *Annual Review of Anthropology* 24: 141–61.

Miller, I. 2004. "The Formation of African Identities in the Americas: Spiritual 'Ethnicity.'" *Contours* 2 (2): 193–222.

Miller, J. C. 1982. "The Significance of Drought, Disease, and Famine in the Agriculturally Marginal Zones of West-Central Africa." *Journal of African History* 23: 17–61.

———. 1988. *Way of Death: Merchant Capitalism and the Angolan Slave Trade, 1730–1830*. Madison: University of Wisconsin Press.

Mills, B. 1999. "Ceramics and Social Context of Food Consumption in the Northern Southwest." In J. Skibo and G. Feinman, eds., *Pottery and People: A Dynamic Interaction*, 59–80. Salt Lake City: University of Utah Press.

Minter, W. 2000. "America and Africa: Beyond the Double Standard." *Current History* 99: 200–210.

Mintz, S. 1955. "The Jamaican Internal Marketing Pattern." *Social and Economic Studies* 4: 95–103.

———. 1974. *Caribbean Transformations.* Baltimore: Johns Hopkins University Press.

———. 1984. "Africa in Latin America: An Unguarded Reflection." In M. Fraginals, ed., *Africa in Latin America,* 286–305. New York: Holmes and Meier.

———. 1985. *Sweetness and Power: The Place of Sugar in Modern History.* New York: Viking.

Mintz, S., and D. Hall. 1991. "The Origin of the Jamaican Internal Market System." In H. Beckles and V. Shepherd, eds., *Caribbean Slave Society and Economy: A Student Reader.* Kingston: IRP.

Mintz, S., and R. Price. 1976. *An Anthropological Approach to the Afro-American Past: A Caribbean Perspective.* ISHI Occasional Papers in Social Change, vol. 2. Philadelphia: Institute for the Study of Human Issues.

———. 1992. *The Birth of African American Culture: An Anthropological Perspective.* Boston: Beacon Press.

Miracle, M. P. 1966. *Maize in Tropical Africa.* Madison: University of Wisconsin Press.

Mogobe, R. 1988. "The Ontology of Invisible Beings, Boleswa." *African Spirituality* 1 (2): 1–24.

Molinari, D. L. 1944. "La Trata de Negros: Datos para su Estudio en el Río de la Plata." Buenos Aires: Facultad de Ciencias Económicas.

Monroe, J. C. 2003. "The Dynamics of State Formation: The Archaeology and Ethnohistory of Pre-Colonial Dahomey." PhD diss., UCLA.

———. 2004. "The Abomey Plateau Archaeological Project: Preliminary Results of the 2000, 2001, and 2002 Seasons." *Nyame Akuma* 62: 2–10.

———. 2005. "American Archaeology in the Republic of Bénin: Recent Achievements and Future Prospects." *Antiquity* 79: 305 (http://antiquity.ac.uk/projgall/monroe).

Monroe, J. C., and S. Mallois. 2004. "A Seventeenth-Century Chesapeake Cottage Industry: New Evidence and a Dating Formula for Colono Tobacco Pipes." *Historical Archaeology* 38 (2): 68–82.

Moore, J. 1972. "Slave Castles by the Sea." *Colorado Quarterly* 21 (2): 163–74.

Moore, J. D. 1992. "Pattern and Meaning in Prehistoric Peruvian Architecture: The Architecture of Social Control in the Chimu State." *Latin American Antiquity* 3 (2): 95–113.

Moosvi, S. 1987. *The Economy of the Mughal Empire, c. 1595: A Statistical Study.* Oxford: Oxford University Press.

Morales, W. 2002. *Índios e africanos na Jundiaí colonial.* Jundiaí: Secretaria Municipal de Planejamento e Meio Ambiente.

Morgan, P. D. 1998. *Slave Counterpoint: Black Culture in the Eighteenth-Century Chesapeake and Lowcountry.* Chapel Hill: University of North Carolina Press.

Morner, M. 1992. "Social and Political Legacies of Emancipation of Slavery in the Americas." *Ibero-Americana, Nordic Journal of Latin American Studies* 22: 3–30.

Morris, B. 1994. *Anthropology of the Self: The Individual in Cultural Perspective.* London: Pluto Press.

Morrison, T. 1987. *Beloved.* New York: Penguin Books.

Morton-Williams, P. 1964. "The Oyo Yoruba and the Atlantic Trade, 1670–1830." *Journal of Historical Society of Nigeria* 3 (1): 25–45.

Mouer, L., M. Hodges, S. Potter, S. Renaud, I. Noel Hume, D. Pogue, M. McCartney, and T. Davidson. 1999. "Colonoware Pottery, Chesapeake Pipes, and 'Uncritical Assumptions.'" In T. A. Singleton, ed., *"I, Too, Am America": Studies in African American Archaeology,* 83–115. Charlottesville: University Press of Virginia.

Moutoukias, Z. 1989. *Contrabando y Control Colonial en el Siglo XVIII.* Buenos Aires: Centro Editor de América Latina.

Moynihan, D. P. 1965. *The Negro Family: The Case for National Action.* Washington, D.C.: Office of Policy Planning and Research, U.S. Department of Labor.

Mrozowski, S. A. 1991. "Landscapes of Inequality." In R. McGuire and R. Paynter, eds., *The Archaeology of Inequality,* 79–101. Cambridge: Basil Blackwell.

Mrozowski, S. A., and M. C. Beaudry. 1990. "Archaeology and the Landscape of Corporate Ideology." In W. Kelso and R. Most, eds., *Earth Patterns,* 189–208. Charlottesville: University Press of Virginia.

Mudimbe, V. Y. 1988. *The Invention of Africa: Gnosis, Philosophy, and the Order of Knowledge.* Bloomington: Indiana University Press.

——. 1994. *The Idea of Africa: Changing Perspectives on a Changing Scene.* Charlottesville: University of Virginia Press.

Mukhopadhyay, C. C., and Y. T. Moses. 1997. "Reestablishing 'Race' in Anthropological Discourse." *American Anthropologist* 99 (3): 517–33.

Mulira, J. G. 1990. "The Case of Voodoo in New Orleans." In J. E. Holloway, ed., *Africanisms in American Culture,* 34–68. Bloomington: Indiana University Press.

Mullins, P. 1999. *Race and Affluence: An Archaeology of African American and Consumer Culture.* New York: Kluwer Academic/Plenum Press.

Mulroy, K. 1993. *Freedom on the Border: The Seminole Maroons in Florida, the Indian Territory, Coahuila, and Texas.* Lubbock: Texas Technology University Press.

——. 2004. "Seminole Maroons." In *Handbook of North American Indians: Southeast,* 465–77. Washington, D.C.: Smithsonian Institution Press.

Murdock, G. P. 1959. *Africa: Its Peoples and Their Culture History.* New York: McGraw-Hill.

Mutoro, H. 1979. "A Contribution to the Study of Cultural and Economic Dynamics of Historical Settlements of the East African Coast with Particular Reference to the Ruins of Takwa." M.A. thesis, University of Nairobi.

——. 1987. "An Archaeological Study of the Mijikenda Kaya Settlements on the Hinterland Kenya Coast." PhD diss., UCLA.

——. 1998. "Precolonial Trading Systems of the East African Interior." In G. Connah, ed., *Transformations in Africa: Essays on Africa's Later Past,* 204–18. Leicester: Leicester University Press.

Nadel, S. F. 1942. *A Black Byzantium: The Kingdom of Nupe in Nigeria.* London: Oxford University Press.

Naqar, U. A. 1969. "Takrur: The Origin of a Name." *Journal of African History* 10 (3): 365–74.

Naqvi, H. K. 1972. *Urbanization and Urban Centres under the Great Mughals, 1556–1707.* Vol. 1. Shimla: Indian Institute of Advanced Study.

Nascimento, A. 1980. *O quilombismo, documentos de uma militância panafricanista.* Petrópolis: Vozes.

——. 1995. "O quilombismo." *Carta* 7: 19–30.

Nash, C. 2000. "Historical Geographies of Modernity." In B. Graham and C. Nash, eds., *Modern Historical Geographies,* 13–40. Upper Saddle River, N.J.: Prentice Hall.

Nassaney, M. 1989. "An Epistemological Enquiry into Some Archaeological and Historical Interpretations of Seventeenth-Century Native American–European Relations." In S. J. Shennan, ed., *Archaeological Approaches to Cultural Identity*, 76–93. London: Unwin Hyman.

Nast, H. J. 1996. "Islam, Gender, and Slavery in West Africa circa 1500: A Spatial Archaeology of the Kano Palace, Northern Nigeria." *Annals of the Association of American Geographers* 86 (1): 44–77.

National Commission on Culture. 1994. Report on the proceedings of the conference on preservation of Elmina and Cape Coast Castles and Fort St. Jago in the Central Region held in the Cape Coast Castle, May 11–12, 1994.

Ndiaye, M. 1975. "Histoire du Boundoun par Cheikh Moussa Kamara." *Bulletin de l'IFAN* series B, 37 (4): 784–816.

Neff, H., and M. D. Glascock. 1997. "Compositional Analysis of Ceramics from the Banda Area, Ghana (update)." Manuscript on file with author.

Neill, W. T. 1977. "Knapping in Florida during the Historic Period." *Florida Anthropologist* 30 (1): 15–17.

Neiman, F. D. 1997. "Sub-Floor Pits and Slavery in Eighteenth- and Early-Nineteenth-Century Virginia." Presented at annual meeting of the Society for Historical Archaeology, Cincinnati.

Neuwirth, J. L., and M. Cochran. 2000. "Archaeology in the East Wing of the Brice House, Annapolis, Maryland." Report on file with Department of Anthropology, University of Maryland, College Park.

Newitt, M. D. D. 1987. "East Africa and the Indian Ocean Trade." In A. D. Gupta and M. N. Pearson, eds., *India and the Indian Ocean*, 201–23. Oxford: Oxford University Press.

Ngaido, T. 1993. "Land Tenure and Social Structure of the Halaybe." In T. Park, ed., *Risk and Tenure in Arid Lands: The Political Ecology of Development in the Senegal River Basin*, 145–82. Tucson: University of Arizona Press.

Niang, M. 1975. "Reflexions sur le régime des terres au Sénégal." *Bulletin de l'IFAN*, series B, 37 (1): 137–53.

Nichols, E. 1988. "No Easy Run to Freedom: Maroons in the Great Dismal Swamp of North Carolina and Virginia, 1677–1850." M.A. thesis, University of South Carolina.

Nicholls, C. S. 1971. *The Swahili Coast: Politics, Diplomacy, and Trade on the African Littoral (1798–1856)*. London: George Allen and Unwin.

Nightingale, P. 1970. *Trade and Empire in Western India, 1784–1806*. Cambridge: Cambridge University Press.

Noel Hume, I. 1964. "Handmaiden to History." *North Carolina Historical Review* 41 (2): 215–25.

Nora, P. 1989. "Between Memory and History: Les Lieux de Memoire." *Representations* (special issue) 26: 7–24.

Norkunas, M. 1993. *The Politics of Public Memory: Tourism, History, and Ethnicity in Monterey, California*. Albany: SUNY Press.

Norman, N. 2000. *Through the Medium of the Vessel: An Ethnoarchaeological Investigation of Ritual Earthenwares in Southern Bénin, West Africa*. M.A. thesis, University of Virginia.

Norman, N., and K. Kelly. 2004. "Landscape Politics: The Serpent Ditch and the Rainbow in West Africa." *American Anthropologist* 106: 98–110.

Norris, R. 1789. *Memoirs of the Reign of Bossa Ahádee, King of Dahomy, an Inland Country of Guiney, to Which Are Added the Author's Journey to Abomey, the Capital, and a Short Account of the African Slave Trade.* London: Frank Cass.

Northrup, D. 2002. *Africa's Discovery of Europe.* New York: Oxford University Press.

Nurse, D. 1978. *The Taita-Chaga Connection: Linguistic Evidence.* Institute of African Studies, University of Nairobi.

Nurse, D., and T. Spear. 1985. *The Swahili: Reconstructing the History and Language of an African Society, 800–1500.* Philadelphia: University of Pennsylvania Press.

Obayemi, A. 1972. *Yoruba Genesis: A 1972 Review.* Nsukka: Annual Congress of the Historical Society of Nigeria.

———. 1976. "The Yoruba and Edo-Speaking Peoples and Their Neighbors before 1600." In J. F. A. Ajayi and M. Crowder, eds., *History of West Africa,* 1:196–263. New York: Columbia University Press.

———. 1980. "States and Peoples of the Niger-Benue Confluence Area." In O. Ikime, ed., *Groundwork of Nigerian History,* 144–64. Ibadan: Heinemann.

Ogbomo, O. 1997. *When Men and Women Mattered: A History of Gender Relations among the Owan of Nigeria.* Rochester: University of Rochester Press.

Ogedengbe, A. Y. 1998. "An Historical Archaeology of Zungeru Colonial Settlement: A Case Study." In K. Wesler, ed., *Historical Archaeology in Nigeria,* 273–310. Trenton, N.J.: Africa World Press.

Ogundiran, A. 1991. "The Owari Palace at Ipole Ijesa, Southwest Nigeria." *Humanitas* 7: 22–30.

———. 2001a. "Factional Competition, Sociopolitical Development, and Settlement Cycling in Ilare District (ca. 1200–1900): Oral Traditions of Historical Experience in a Yoruba Community." *History in Africa* 28: 20–40.

———. 2001b. "Ceramic Spheres and Historical Process of Regional Networks in Yoruba-Edo Region, Nigeria, AC Thirteenth–Nineteenth Centuries." *Journal of Field Archaeology* 28 (1): 1–17.

———. 2002a. *Archaeology and History in Ilare District (Central Yorubaland), AC 1200–1900.* Cambridge Monographs in African Archaeology, no. 55 (British Archaeological Reports International Series 1090). London: Archaeopress.

———. 2002b. "Archaeology, Historiographic Traditions, and Institutional Discourse of Development." In Toyin Falola, ed., *Nigeria in the Twentieth Century,* 13–35. Durham, N.C.: Carolina Academic Press.

———. 2002c. "Of Small Things Remembered: Beads, Cowries, and Cultural Translations of the Atlantic Experience in Yorubaland." *International Journal of African Historical Studies* 35 (2/3): 427–57.

———. 2002d. "Filling a Gap in Ife-Benin Interaction Field (AD Thirteenth–Sixteenth Centuries): Excavations and Material Culture in Iloyi Settlement, Ijesaland." *African Archaeological Review* 19 (1): 2–59.

———. 2003. "Chronology, Material Culture, and Pathways to the Cultural History of Yoruba-Edo Region, Nigeria, 500 BC–AD 1800." In T. Falola and C. Jennings, eds., *Sources and Methods in African History: Spoken, Written, Unearthed,* 33–79. Rochester, N.Y.: University of Rochester Press.

Ogunleye, T. 1996. "The Self-Emancipated Africans of Florida: Pan-African Nationalists in the 'New World.'" *Journal of Black Studies* 27 (1): 24–38.

Ohadike, D. C. 1981. "The Influenza Pandemic of 1918–19 and the Spread of Cassava Cultivation in the Lower Niger: A Study in Historical Linkages." *Journal of African History* 22: 379–91.

O'Hear, A. 1997. *Power Relations in Nigeria: Ilorin Slaves and Their Successors.* Rochester, N.Y.: University of Rochester Press.

Ojo, G. J. A. 1966. *Yoruba Palaces: A Study of Afins of Yorubaland.* London: University of London Press.

———. 1967. *Yoruba Culture: A Geographical Analysis.* London: University of London Press.

———. 1968. "Traditional Yoruba Architecture." *African Arts* 1 (3): 14–17, 70–72.

Okpewho, I. 2001. Introduction to I. Okpewho, C. B. Davies, and A. A. Mazrui, eds., *The African Diaspora: African Origins and New World Identities,* xi–xxviii. Bloomington: Indiana University Press.

Okpoko, P. U., and P. Obi-Ani. 2005. "The Making of an Oligarchy in the Bight of Biafra: Perspectives on the Aro Ascendancy." In A. Ogundiran, ed., *Precolonial Nigeria: Essays in Honor of Toyin Falola,* 425–46. Trenton, N.J.: Africa World Press.

Oliveira, Eduardo de Oliveira e. 1984. "Intervenção." In *Trabalho Escravo, Economia e Sociedade,* 69–72. Rio de Janeiro: Paz e Terra.

Olsen, B. J. 1991. "Metropolises and Satellites in Archaeology: On Power and Asymmetry in Global Archaeological Discourse." In R. W. Preucel, ed., *Processual and Postprocessual Archaeologies: Multiple Ways of Knowing the Past,* 211–24. Carbondale: Southern Illinois University Press.

Olwell, R. 1996. "Loose, Idle, and Disorderly: Slave Women in the Eighteenth-Century Charleston Marketplace." In D. Gaspar and D. Hine, eds., *More Than Chattel: Black Women and Slavery in the Americas,* 97–110. Bloomington: Indiana University Press.

Olwig, K. 1977. "Households, Exchange, and Social Reproduction: The Development of a Caribbean Society." PhD diss., University of Minnesota.

———. 1985. *Cultural Adaptation and Resistance on St. John: Three Centuries of Afro-Caribbean Life.* Gainesville: University of Florida Press.

Omi, M., and H. Winant. 1986. *Racial Formation in the United States: From the 1960s to the 1980s.* New York: Routledge.

Omoniyi, J. O. 2003. "Literary and Historical Reflections on the Yagba Protest Movement against Nupe Hegemony before 1939." In A. Olukoju, Z. O. Apata, and O. Akinwumi, eds., *Northeast Yorubaland: Studies in the History and Culture of a Frontier Zone,* 16–24. Ibadan: Rex Charles.

Orser, C. E., Jr. 1985. "Artifacts, Documents, and Memories of the Black Tenant Farmer." *Archaeology* 38 (4): 48–53.

———. 1988a. "The Archaeological Analysis of Plantation Society: Replacing Status and Caste with Economics and Power." *American Antiquity* 53: 735–51.

———. 1988b. "Toward a Theory of Power for Historical Archaeology: Plantations and Space." In M. Leone and P. B. Potter Jr., eds., *The Recovery of Meaning,* 313–43. Washington, D.C.: Smithsonian Institution Press.

———. 1991. "The Continued Pattern of Dominance: Landlord and Tenant on the Postbellum Cotton Plantation." In R. H. McGuire and R. Paynter, eds., *The Archaeology of Inequality,* 40–54. Oxford: Blackwell.

———. 1992. *In Search of Zumbi: Preliminary Archaeological Research at Serra da Bariga Site of Alagoa, Brazil.* Midwestern Archaeological Research Center, Illinois State University, Normal.

——. 1994a. "The Archaeology of African American Slave Religion in the Antebellum South." *Cambridge Archaeological Journal* 4: 33–45.

——. 1994b. "Toward a Global Historical Archaeology: An Example from Brazil." *Historical Archaeology* 28: 5–22.

——. 1996. *A Historical Archaeology of the Modern World.* New York: Plenum Press.

——. 1998. "The Archaeology of the African Diaspora." *Annual Review of Anthropology* 27: 63–82.

——, ed. 2001. *Race and the Archaeology of Identity.* Salt Lake City: University of Utah Press.

Orser, C. E., Jr., and B. Fagan 1995. *Historical Archaeology.* New York: HarperCollins.

Orser, C. E., Jr., and P. P. A. Funari. 1992. "Pesquisa Arqueologica Inicial em Palmares." *Estudo Ibero Americanos* 18: 53–69.

——. 2001. "Archaeology and Slave Resistance and Rebellion." *World Archaeology* 33 (1): 61–72.

Ortiz Oderigo, N. 1974. *Aspectos de la cultura africana en el Río de la Plata.* Buenos Aires: Plus Ultra.

Ortner, S. B. 1973. "On Key Symbols." *American Anthropologist* 75 (5): 1338–46.

——. 1984. "Theory in Anthropology since the Sixties." *Comparative Studies in Society and History* 26: 126–66.

Osei-Tutu, B. 2002. "The African American Factor in the Commodification of Ghana's Slave Castles." *Transactions of the Historical Society of Ghana,* n.s., 6: 115–33.

——. 2003. "Contested Monuments: Research in Ghana." *West African Research Association Newsletter,* 16–17.

——. 2004. "African American Reactions to the Restoration of Ghana's 'Slave Castles.'" *Public Archaeology* 3: 195–204.

Osiruemu, E. 2005. "Water Transportation in the Niger Delta, c. 1500–1900." In A. Ogundiran, ed., *Precolonial Nigeria: Essays in Honor of Toyin Falola,* 411–24. Trenton, N.J.: Africa World Press.

Ottenheimer, M. 1976. "Multiethnicity and Trade in the Western Indian Ocean." In W. Arens, ed., *A Century of Change in Eastern Africa,* 229–38. The Hague: Mouton.

Otto, J. 1984. *Cannon's Point Plantation, 1794–1850: Living Conditions and Status Pattern in the Old South.* New York: Academic Press.

Oyebade, B. 1990. "African Studies and the Africentric Paradigm: A Critique." *Journal of Black Studies* 21 (2): 233–38.

Oyelaran, P. A. 1998. "Early Settlement and Archaeological Sequence of Northeast Yorubaland." *African Archaeological Review* 15 (1): 65–79.

Ozanne, P. 1962. "Notes on the Early Historic Archaeology of Accra." *Transactions of the Historical Society of Ghana* 6: 51–70.

Palmer, C. A. 1995. "From Africa to the Americas: Ethnicity in the Early Black Communities of the Americas." *Journal of World History* 6 (2): 223–36.

——. 1998a. "Defining and Studying the Modern African Diaspora." *Perspectives* 36 (6): 21–25.

——. 1998b. "From Theory to Practice: Experiencing the Nation in Everyday Life." *Journal of Material Culture* 3 (2): 175–99.

Paris, P. J. 1995. *The Spirituality of African Peoples: The Search for a Common Moral Discourse.* Minneapolis: Fortress Press.

Park, M. 1799. *Travels in the Interior Districts of Africa: Performed under the Direction and Patronage of the African Association, in the Years 1795, 1796, and 1797; by*

Mungo Park, Surgeon: with an Appendix, Containing Geographical Illustrations of Africa: by Major Rennell. 2nd ed. London: Bulmer.

Park, T. K. 1992. "Early Trends towards Class Stratification: Chaos, Common Property, and Flood Recession Agriculture." *American Anthropologist* 94: 91–117.

———. 1993. *Risk and Tenure in Arid Lands: The Political Ecology of Development in the Senegal River Basin.* Tucson: University of Arizona Press.

Parris, S. V. 1983. "Alliance and Competition: Four Case Studies of Maroon-European Relations." *Nieuwe West-Indische Gids* 5 (3): 174–222.

Parry, J., and M. Bloch, eds. 1989. *Money and the Morality of Exchange.* Cambridge: Cambridge University Press.

Parry, J. H., and P. M. Sherlock. 1956. *A Short History of the West Indies.* London: Macmillan.

Patten, D. 1992. "Mankala and Minkisi: Possible Evidence of African American Folk Beliefs and Practices." *African American Archaeology* 6: 5–7.

Pauketat, T., ed. 2001. *The Archaeology of Traditions: Agency and History before and after Columbus.* Gainesville: University Press of Florida.

Paynter, R. 1990. "Afro-Americans in the Massachusetts Historical Landscape." In P. Gathercole and D. Lowenthal, eds., *The Politics of the Past,* 49–62. London: Unwin Hyman.

———. 2000a. "Historical and Anthropological Archaeology: Forging Alliances." *Journal of Archaeological Research* 8: 1–37.

———. 2000b. "Historical Archaeology and the Post-Columbian World of North America." *Journal of Archaeological Research* 8: 169–217.

Paynter, R., and R. McGuire. 1991. "The Archaeology of Inequality: Material Culture, Domination, and Resistance." In R. McGuire and R. Paynter, eds., *The Archaeology of Inequality,* 1–27. Cambridge: Basil Blackwell.

Pearce, C. 1842. *A Brief Memoir of the Life and Religious Experience of Cato Pearce, a Man of Color: Taken Verbatim from His Lips and Published for His Benefit.* Pawtucket, R.I.

Pearce, G. 1963. *Of Emirs and Pagans: A View of Northern Nigeria.* London: Cassell.

Pearsall, D. 1989. *Paleoethnobotany: A Handbook of Procedures.* New York: Academic Press.

Pearson, M. N. 1987. *Cafilas and Cartazes: Essays in Indian Medieval History.* Ed. S. Chandra. New Delhi: Indian History Congress Golden Jubilee Year Publications Series, vol. 3.

———. 1998. *Port Cities and Intruders: The Swahili Coast, India, and Portugal in the Early Modern Era.* Baltimore: Johns Hopkins University Press.

Peel, J. D. Y. 1983. *The Ijeshas and Nigerians: The Incorporation of a Yoruba Kingdom, 1890s–1970s.* Cambridge: Cambridge University Press.

Pellow, D., and N. Chazan. 1986. *Ghana: Coping with Uncertainty.* London: Westview Press.

Pemberton, J., and F. Afolayan. 1996. *Yoruba Sacred Kingship.* London: Smithsonian Institution Press.

Perdue, Charles L., Jr., T. E. Barden, and R. K. Phillips, eds. 1976. *Weevils in the Wheat: Interviews with Virginia Ex-Slaves.* Charlottesville: University Press of Virginia.

Pereira, J., ed. 1990. *Caribbean Literature in Comparison.* University of the West Indies, Institute of Caribbean Studies, ser. 1.

———. 1994. "Maroon Heritage in Mexico." In E. K. Agorsah, ed., *Maroon Heritage: Archaeological, Ethnographic, and Historical Perspectives*, 94–108. Kingston: Canoe Press.

Perry, W. 1999. *Landscape Transformation and the Archaeology of Impact: Social Disruption and State Formation in Southern Africa*. New York: Plenum.

Perry, W., and R. Paynter. 1999. "Artifacts, Ethnicity, and the Archaeology of African Americans." In T. A. Singleton, ed., *"I, Too, Am America": Archaeological Studies of African American Life*, 299–310. Charlottesville: University Press of Virginia.

Petchenkine, Y. 1993. *Ghana: In Search of Stability, 1957–1992*. London: Praeger.

Peukert, W. 1978. *Der Atlantische Sklavenhandel von Dahomey (1740–1797): Wirtschaftsanthropologie u. Sozialgeschichte*. Wiesbaden: Steiner.

Philips, J. E. 1983. "African Smoking and Pipes." *Journal of African History* 24 (3): 303–19.

———. 2005. "The African Heritage of White America." In J. Holloway, ed., *Africanisms in American Culture*, 372–96. Bloomington: Indiana University Press.

Phillippo, J. 1843. *Jamaica: Its Past and Present State*. London: John Snow.

Phillips, T. 1732. "Journal of a Voyage Made in the Hannibal of London." *Collections of Voyages and Travels*. Vol. 6. Ed. Awnsham and John Churchill. London: J. Walthoe.

Picotti, D. V. 1998. *La presencia africana en nuestra identidad*. Buenos Aires: Ediciones del Sol.

Piersen, W. D. 1988. *Black Yankees: The Development of an Afro-American Subculture in Eighteenth-Century New England*. Amherst: University of Massachusetts Press.

Pikirayi, I. 1993. *The Archaeological Identity of the Mutapa State: Towards an Historical Archaeology of Northern Zimbabwe*. Uppsala: Societas Archaeologica Upsaliensis.

Piot, C. 1999. *Remotely Global: Village Modernity in West Africa*. Chicago: University of Chicago Press.

Poe, S. 1963. "Archaeological Excavations at Fort Gadsden, Florida." *Notes in Anthropology* 8: 1–35.

Polanyi, K. 1966. *Dahomey and the Slave Trade: An Analysis of an Archaic Economy*. Seattle: University of Washington Press.

Pole, L. M. 1982. "Decline or Survival? Iron Production in West Africa from the Seventeenth to the Twentieth Centuries." *Journal of African History* 23 (4): 503–13.

Pollis, E. 1974. "An Analysis of the Pre-Colonial Polity of Dahomey, West Africa." *Papers in Anthropology* 15 (1): 1–22.

Polomé, E. 1980. "Creolization Processes and Diachronic Linguistics." In A. Valdman and A. Highfield, eds., *Theoretical Orientations in Creole Studies*, 185–202. New York: Academic Press.

Porter, K. W. n.d. "Freedom over Me." Manuscript on file in the Kenneth Wiggins Porter Papers, Schomburg Center for Research in Black Culture, New York Public Library.

———. 1943. "Florida Slaves and Free Negroes in the Seminole War, 1835–1842." *Journal of Negro History* 28 (4): 390–421.

———. 1996. *The Black Seminoles*. Rev. and ed. A. M. Amos and T. P. Senter. Gainesville: University Press of Florida.

Posnansky, M. 1972. "Archaeology, Ritual, and Religion." In T. O. Ranger and I. N. Kimambo, eds., *The Historical Study of African Religion*, 29–44. London: Heinemann.

———. 1976. "Archaeology and the Origins of the Akan Society in Ghana." In G. Sieveking et al., eds., *Problems in Economic and Social Archaeology*, 49–59. London: Duckworth.

———. 1979. "Archaeological Aspects of the Brong-Ahafo Region." In K. Arhin, ed., *A Profile of Brong Kyempim: Essays on the Archaeology, History, Language, and Politics of the Brong Peoples of Ghana*, 22–35. Accra: Afram Publications.

———. 1984. "Towards an Archaeology of the Black Diaspora." *Journal of Black Studies* 15: 195–205.

———. 1987. "Prelude to Akan Civilization." In E. Schildkrout, ed., *The Golden Stool: Studies of the Asante Center and Periphery*, Anthropological Papers of the American Museum of Natural History, vol. 65, pt. 1, 14–22. New York: American Museum of Natural History.

———. 1999. "West Africanist Reflections on African American Archaeology." In T. A. Singleton, ed., *"I, Too, Am America": Archaeological Studies of African American Life*, 21–37. Charlottesville: University Press of Virginia.

Posnansky, M., and C. R. DeCorse. 1986. "Historical Archaeology in Sub-Saharan Africa: A Review." *Historical Archaeology* 20 (1): 1–14.

Posnansky, M., and R. McIntosh. 1976. "New Radiocarbon Dates for Northern and Western Africa." *Journal of African History* 17: 161–95.

Posnanksy, M., and A. Van Dantzig. 1976. "Fort Ruychaver Rediscovered." *Sankofa* 2: 7–18.

Postma, J. M. 1990. *The Dutch in the Atlantic Slave Trade, 1600–1815*. Cambridge: Cambridge University Press.

Potter, P. B., Jr. 1991. "What Is the Use of Plantation Archaeology?" *Historical Archaeology* 25 (3): 94–107.

Pouwels, R. L. 1987. *The Horn and the Crescent: Cultural Change and Traditional Islam on the East African Coast, 800–1990*. Cambridge: Cambridge University Press.

———. 2000. "The East African Coast, c. 780 to 1900 CE." In N. Levtzion and R. L. Pouwels, eds., *The History of Islam in Africa*, 251–72. Athens: Ohio University Press.

Price, R. S. 1973. *Maroon Societies: Analysis of a Maroon Society in Suriname*. Institute of Caribbean Studies, University of Puerto Rico.

———. 1976. *The Guiana Maroons: A Historical and Bibliographical Introduction*. Baltimore: Johns Hopkins University Press.

———. 1979. *Maroon Societies: Rebel Slave Communities in the Americas*. New York: Anchor Books.

———. 1998. "Scrapping Maroon History: Brazil's Promise, Suriname's Shame." *New West Indian Guide* 72: 233–55.

Price, T. D., and G. M. Feinman, eds. 1995. *Foundations of Social Inequality*. New York: Plenum Press.

Prins, A. H. J. 1961. *The Swahili-Speaking Peoples of Zanzibar and the East African Coast*. London: International African Institute.

Puckett, N. N. 1926. *Folk Beliefs of the Southern Negro*. New York: Negro Universities Press.

Pulsipher, L., and C. M. Goodwin. 1999. "Here Where the Old Time People Be: Reconstructing the Landscapes of the Slavery and Post-Slavery Era in Montserrat, West Indies." In J. B. Haviser, ed., *African Sites Archaeology in the Caribbean*, 9–37. Princeton, N.J.: Markus Weiner.

Pwiti, G. 1996. "Continuity and Change: An Archaeological Study of Farming Communities in Northern Zimbabwe, AD 500–1700." *Studies in African Archaeology* 13. Uppsala: Uppsala University.

Quartim de Moraes, M. L. 1999. "West India: Iconographic Documents from the Seventeenth and Nineteenth Centuries in Brazil." In P. P. A. Funari, M. Hall, and S. Jones, eds., *Historical Archaeology: Back from the Edge*, 180–92. London: Routledge.

Quatrin, Z. 2000–2001. Los archivos del suelo: Plaza Roberto Arlt, informe primera etapa, informe inédito. Centro de Arqueología Urbana, Buenos Aires.

Raboteau, A. J. 1980. *Slave Religion: The "Invisible Institution" in the Antebellum South*. Oxford: Oxford University Press.

Radimilahy, C. 1998. "Mahilaka: An Archaeological Investigation of an Early Town in Northwestern Madagascar." *Studies in African Archaeology* 15. Uppsala: Uppsala University.

Randsborg, K. 1998. "Subterranean Structures: Archaeology in Bénin, West Africa." *Acta Archaeologica* 69: 209–27.

Rapoport, A. 1969. *House Form and Culture*. Englewood Cliffs, N.J.: Prentice-Hall.

Rashid, I. 2003. "'A Devotion to the Idea of Liberty at Any Price': Rebellion and Antislavery in the Upper Guinea Coast in the Eighteenth and Nineteenth Century." In S. Diouf, ed., *Fighting the Slave Trade: West African Strategies*, 132–51. Athens: Ohio University Press.

Rathbone, R. 1986. "Some Thoughts on Resistance to Enslavement in West Africa." *Slavery and Abolition* 6: 11–22.

Ravenstein, E. G. 1898. *A Journal of the First Voyage of Vasco da Gama, 1497–1499*. London: Hakluyt Society.

Ravignani, E. 1919. "Crecimiento de la población de Buenos Aires y su campaña 1776–1810." *Anales de la Facultad de Ciencias Exactas* 1: 405–16.

Rawick, G. P., ed. 1976. *The American Slave: A Composite Autobiography*, vol. 17, *Florida Narratives*. Westport, Conn.: Greenwood Press.

———. 1978. "Some Notes on a Social Analysis of Slavery: A Critique and Assessment of 'the Slave Community.'" In A. Gilmore, ed., *Revisiting Blassingame's "The Slave Community": The Scholars Respond*, 17–26. Westport, Conn.: Greenwood Press.

Reeves, Mathew B. 1997. "By Their Own Labour: Enslaved Africans' Survival Strategies on Two Jamaican Plantations." PhD diss., Syracuse University.

———. 2004. "Asking the 'Right' Questions: Archaeologists and Descendant Communities." In Paul A. Shackel and E. Chambers, eds., *Places in Mind: Archaeology as Applied Anthropology*. New York: Routledge.

Reis, J. J. 1992. "Différences et résistances: Les noirs à Bahia sous l'esclavage." *Cahiers d'Etudes Africaines* 125 (37): 15–34.

———. 1993. *Slave Rebellion in Brazil: The Muslim Uprising of 1835 in Bahia*. Baltimore: Johns Hopkins University Press.

Remini, R. V. 1977. *Andrew Jackson*, vol. 1, *The Course of American Empire, 1767–1821*. Baltimore: Johns Hopkins University Press.

Revello, J. T. 1979. *Crónicas de Buenos Aires Colonial.* Buenos Aires: Ediciones Bajel.

Rice, A. 2003. *Radical Narratives of Black Atlantic.* London: Continuum.

Richardson, D. 1979. "West African Consumption Patterns and Their Influence on the Eighteenth-Century English Slave Trade." In H. Gemery and J. Hogendorn, eds., *The Uncommon Market: Essays in the Economic History of the Atlantic Slave Trade,* 303–29. New York: Academic Press.

———. 1989. "Slave Exports from West and West-Central Africa, 1700–1810: New Estimates of Volume and Distribution." *Journal of African History* 30: 1–22.

Rickford, J. 1987. "Dimensions of a Creole Continuum: History, Texts, and Linguistic Analysis of Guyanese Creole." Palo Alto: Stanford University Press.

Rigaud, M. 1985. *Secrets of Voodoo.* Trans. R. B. Cross. San Francisco: City Lights Books.

Rivers, L. E. 2000. *Slavery in Florida: Territorial Days to Emancipation.* Gainesville: University Press of Florida.

Robb, J. 1998. "The Archaeology of Symbols." *Annual Review of Anthropology* 27: 329–46.

Robert-Chaleix, D. 1970. "Les fouilles de Teghdaoust." *Journal of African History* 11 (4): 471–93.

——— . 1991. "Sel, coquillages et jarosite: A propos de la saline médiévale d'Awil." *Journal des Africanistes* 61 (2): 169–85.

Robertshaw, P., M. D. Glascock, M. Wood, and R. S. Popelka. 2003. "Chemical Analysis of Ancient African Glass Beads: A Very Preliminary Report." *Journal of African Archaeology* 1: 139–46.

Robertson, C. 1996. "Africa into the Americas? Slavery and Women, the Family, and the Gender Division of Labor." In D. B. Gaspar and D. C. Hine, eds., *More Than Chattel: Black Women and Slavery in the Americas,* 3–40. Bloomington: Indiana University Press.

———. 1997. "Gender and Trade Relations in Central Kenya in the Late Nineteenth Century." *International Journal of African Historical Studies* 30 (1): 23–47.

Robinson, D. 1975. "The Islamic Revolution of Futa Toro." *International Journal of African Historical Studies* 8 (2): 185–221.

Robinson, D., P. Curtin, and J. Johnson. 1972. "A Tentative Chronology of Futa Tooro from the Sixteenth through the Nineteenth Centuries." *Cahiers d'Etudes Africaines* 48: 555–92.

Robinson, I. V. 1994a. "Ghana–Don't Whitewash the Slave Trade." *New African* 324: 4.

———. 1994b. "Is the Black Man's History Being Whitewashed?" *Uhuru* 9: 48–50.

Rochette, C. 1974. *Le bassin du fleuve Sénégal: Monographie Hydrologique.* Paris: ORSTOM no. 1.

Rodman, M. C. 1992. "Empowering Place: Multilocality and Multivocality." *American Anthropologist* 94 (3): 640–56.

Rodney, W. 1966. "African Slavery and Other Forms of Social Oppression on the Upper Guinea Coast in the Context of the Atlantic Slave Trade." *JAH* 7 (3): 431–43.

———. 1970. *A History of the Upper Guinea Coast, 1545–1800.* Oxford: Clarendon Press.

———. 1981 (1972). *How Europe Underdeveloped Africa.* Washington, D.C.: Howard University Press.

Rodríguez Molas, R. 1955. "El primer libro de entrada de esclavos negros a Buenos Aires." *Revista de la Universidad de La Plata* 2: 139–43.

——. 1958. "Algunos aspectos del negro en la sociedad rioplatense del siglo XVIII." *Anuario del Instituto de Investigaciones Históricas* 3: 81–109.

——. 1959. "El negro en la sociedad porteña después de Caseros." *Comentario* 22: 45–55.

——. 1961. "Negros libres rioplatenses." *Humanidades* 1: 99–126.

——. 1962. "Condición social de los últimos descendientes de los esclavos rioplatenses 1852–1900." *Cuadernos Americanos* 123: 133–70.

——. 1969. "El negro en el Río de la Plata." *Polémica* 2: 38–56.

——. 1993. "Aspectos ocultos de la identidad nacional: los Africanamericanos y el origen del tango." *Ciclos* 3–5: 147–61.

Ronen, D. 1971. "On the African Role in the Trans-Atlantic Slave Trade in Dahomey." *Cahiers d'études Africaines* 11: 5–13.

Rosal, M. A. 1978. "Algunas consideraciones sobre las creencias religiosas de los africanos porteños, 1750–1820." *Investigaciones y ensayos* 31: 369–82.

——. 1982. "Artesanos de color en Buenos Aires, 1750–1850." *Boletín del Instituto de Historia Argentina y Americana* 27: 331–54.

——. 1988. "El tráfico esclavista y el estado sanitario de la ciudad de Buenos Aires 1750–1810." *Jornadas de Historia de la Ciudad de Buenos Aires* 2: 231–40.

——. 1996. "Diversos aspectos relacionados con la esclavitud en el Río de la Plata a través del estudio de testamentos de Africanporteños." *Revista de Indias* 56: 219–35.

Rosaldo, R., S. Lavie, and K. Narayan. 1993. "Introduction: Creativity in Anthropology." In S. Lavie, K. Narayan, and R. Rosaldo, eds., *Creativity/Anthropology*, 1–8. Ithaca: Cornell University Press.

Ross, D. 1987. "Dahomean Middleman System, 1727–c.1818." *Journal of African History* 28 (3): 357–75.

Rossi, V. 1925. *Cosas de Negros*. Buenos Aires: Hachette.

Rouse, I., and L. Allaire. 1978. "The Caribbean." In R. Taylor and C. Meighan, eds., *Chronologies in New World Archaeology*, 431–81. New York: Academic Press.

Rowlands, M. J. 1982. "Processual Archaeology as Historical Social Science." In C. Renfrew, ed., *Theory and Explanation in Archaeology*, 155–74. London: Elsevier Science and Technology Books.

——. 1999. "Black Identity and Sense of Past in Brazilian National Culture." In P. P. A. Funari, M. Hall, and S. Jones, eds., *Historical Archaeology: Back from the Edge*, 328–44. London: Routledge.

Rubertone, P. 2000. "The Historical Archaeology of Native Americans." *Annual Reviews of Anthropology* 29: 425–46.

Ruffins, F. D. 1992. "Mythos, Memory, and History: African American Preservation Efforts, 1820–1990." In I. Karp, C. Mullen, and S. Lavine, eds., *Museums and Communities: The Politics of Public Culture*, 506–611. Washington, D.C.: Smithsonian Institution Press.

Russell, A. E. 1997. "Material Culture and African American Spirituality at the Hermitage." *Historical Archaeology* 31 (2): 63–80.

Russel-Wood, A. J. R. 1974. "Black and Mulatto Brotherhoods in Colonial Brazil: A Study in Collective Behaviour." *Hispanic American Historical Review* 54: 567–602.

Ryder, A. F. C. 1965. "Dutch Trade on the Nigerian Coast during the Seventeenth Century." *Journal of Historical Society of Nigeria* 3 (2): 195–210.

——. 1969. *Benin and the Europeans, 1485–1897*. London: Longmans.

Sacks, S. 1979. *On Metaphor.* Chicago: University of Chicago Press.

Safran, William. 1991. "Diasporas in Modern Societies: Myths of Homeland and Return." *Diaspora* 1 (1): 83–99.

Sahlins, M. 1981. *Historical Metaphors and Mythical Realities: Structure in the Early History of the Sandwich Islands Kingdom.* Ann Arbor: University of Michigan Press.

Sale, M. 1997. *The Slumbering Volcano: American Slave Ship Revolts and the Production of Rebellious Masculinity.* Durham, N.C.: Duke University Press.

Samb, A. 1974. *L'Islam et l'histoire du Sénégal.* Dakar: Hilal.

Samford, P. 1996. "The Archaeology of African American Slavery and Material Culture." *William and Mary Quarterly* 53 (1): 87–114.

Samuels, I. E. 1980. "The Metallography of Cast-Iron Relics from the Bark *Endeavor.*" *Metallography* 13: 345–55.

Santos, J. R. dos. 1995. "Memorial Zumbi." Carta 7: 65–72.

Saraiva, J. F. S. 1993. "Silencio y ambivalencia: el mundo de los negros en Brasil." *America Negra* 6: 37–49.

Sattler, R. 1996. "Remnants, Renegades, and Runaways: Seminole Ethnogenesis Reconsidered." In J. Hill, ed., *History, Power, and Identity: Ethnogenesis in the Americas, 1492–1992,* 36–39. Iowa City: University of Iowa Press.

Saunt, C. 1998. "'The English Has Now a Mind to Make Slaves of Them All': Creeks, Seminole, and the Problem of Slavery" (Indian-Black Relations in Historical and Anthropological Perspective). *American Indian Quarterly* 157 (1): 157–80.

Schaedler, K.-F. 1997. *Earth and Ore: 2,500 Years of African Art in Terra-Cotta and Metal.* Munich: Panterra.

Schafer, D. L. 2000. "Zephaniah Kingsley's Laurel Grove Plantation, 1803–1813." In J. Landers, ed., *Colonial Plantations and Economy in Florida.* Gainesville: University Press of Florida.

Schávelzon, D. 2000a. *Historical Archaeology of Buenos Aires: A City at the End of the World.* New York: Kluwer.

———. 2000b. *Historias del comer y del beber en Buenos Aires.* Buenos Aires: Editorial Aguilar.

———. 2003. *Buenos Aires negra: arqueología histórica de una cudad silenciada.* Buenos Aires: Editorial Emecé.

Schávelzon, D., and M. Silveira. 1998. *Arqueología histórica de Buenos Aires,* vol. 4, *Excavaciones en Michelangelo.* Buenos Aires: Editorial Corregidor.

Schildkrout, E. 1996. "Kingdom of Gold." *Natural History* 105 (2): 36–47.

Schmidt, P. 1995. "Using Archaeology to Remake History in Africa." In P. Schmidt and T. C. Patterson, eds., *Making Alternative Histories,* 119–47. Santa Fe, N.M.: School of American Research Press.

Schmidt, P., N. J. Karoma, A. LaViolette, W. Fawcett, A. Mabulla, L. Rutabanzibwa, and C. Sanane. 1992. *Archaeological Investigations in the Vicinity of Mkiu, Kisarawe District, Tanzania.* Archaeological Contributions of the University of Dar es Salaam, Occasional Paper no. 1. Dar es Salaam.

Schmidt, P., and T. Patterson. 1995. Introduction to P. Schmidt and T. Patterson, eds., *Making Alternative Histories: The Practice of Archaeology and History in Non-Western Settings.* Santa Fe, N.M.: School of American Research Press.

Schmitz, J. 1986. "L'Etat géomètre: les leydi des peuls du Fuuta Tooro (Sénégal) et du Maasina (Mali)." *Cahiers d'études Africaines* 26 (103): 349–94.

479

———. 1994. "Cités Noires: Les Républiques Villageoises du Fuuta Tooro (vallée du fleuve Sénégal)." *Cahiers d'études Africaines* 34 (133–35): 419–60.

Schneider, C. M. 1980. *American Kinship: A Cultural Account.* Chicago: University of Chicago Press.

Schreiber, K. 1987. "Conquest and Consolidation: A Comparison of the Wari and Inka Occupations of a Highland Peruvian Valley." *American Antiquity* 52 (3): 110–24.

Schrire, C. 1995. *Digging through Darkness: Chronicles of an Archaeologist.* Charlottesville: University of Virginia Press.

Schuler, Monica. 1970. "Akan Slave Rebellions in the British Caribbean." *Savacou* 1: 373–86.

———. 1980. *"Alas, Alas, Kongo": A Social History of Indentured African Immigration into Jamaica, 1841–1865.* Baltimore: Johns Hopkins University Press.

Schurhammer, G., and J. Wicki. 1944–45. *Epistolae S. Francisci Xaverii Aliaque eius Scripta: Francisco Xavier, Saint, 1506–1552.* Monumenta Historica Soc. Iesu. Apud, Romae.

Schuyler, R. L., ed. 1980. *Archaeological Perspectives on Ethnicity in America: Afro-American and Asian American Cultural History.* Farmingdale, N.Y.: Baywood.

———. 1999. Book review of *Between Artifacts and Texts: Historical Archaeology in Global Perspective* by Anders Andrén. *American Anthropologist* 101 (4): 845–46.

Schwartz, S. B. 1977. "Resistance and Accommodation in Eighteenth-Century Brazil: The Slaves' View of Slavery." *Hispanic American Historical Review* 57: 69–81.

Scott, E., ed. 1994. *Those of Little Note: Gender, Race, and Class in Historical Archaeology.* Tucson: University of Arizona Press.

Seaburg, C., and A. Seaburg. 1980. *Medford on the Mystic.* Medford, Mass.: Camera Stat Associates.

Seguis, L. 1990. *Note sur la propagation de la crue le long de l'Ile a Morphil et sur les Innondations 1986–1988.* Dakar: ORSTOM.

Seró Mantero, G. 2000. *La Casa de María Josefa Ezcurra, Una de Viviendas mas Antiguas de Buenos Aires.* Buenos Aires: Secretaría de Cultura, Gobierno de la Ciudad.

Serra, O. 1984. "Questões de identidade cultural." In A. A. Arantes, ed., *Produzindo o Passado,* 97–123. São Paulo: Brasiliense.

Sertima, Ivan van. 1976. *They Came before Columbus: The African Presence in Ancient America.* New York: Random House.

Shanks, M., and C. Tilley. 1987. *Re-construction Archaeology.* Cambridge: Cambridge University Press.

Sharma, R. S. 1987. *Urban Decay in India (c. ad 300–1000).* New Delhi: Munshiram Manoharlal.

Shaw, R. 2002. *Memories of the Slave Trade: Ritual and the Historical Imagination in Sierra Leone.* Chicago: University of Chicago Press.

Shaw, R., and C. Stewart. 1994. "Introduction: Problematizing Syncretism." In R. Shaw and C. Stewart, eds., *Syncretism/Anti-Syncretism: The Politics of Religious Synthesis,* 1–26. London: Routledge.

Shaw, T. 1960. "Early Smoking Pipes in Africa, Europe, and America." *Journal of the Royal Anthropological Institute* 90: 272–305.

——. 1961. *Excavation at Dawu.* London: Thomas Nelson and Sons.

Shepherd, G. 1982. "The Making of the Swahili: A View from the Southern End of the East African Coast." *Paideuma* 28: 129–48.

Shepherd, N. 2002. "The Politics of Archaeology in Africa." *Annual Review of Anthropology* 31: 189–209.

Shepperson, G. 1993. "African Diaspora: Concept and Context." In J. Harris, ed., *Global Dimensions of the African Diaspora*, 2nd ed., 41–49. Washington, D.C.: Howard University Press.

Sherif, A. M. H. 1987. *Slaves, Spices, and Ivory in Zanzibar.* Athens: Ohio University Press.

Shinnie, P., and P. Ozanne. 1962. "Excavations at Yendi Dabari." *Transactions of the Historical Society of Ghana* 6: 94–106.

Simmond, L. 1987. "Slave Higglering in Jamaica, 1780–1834." *Jamaica Journal* 20: 31–38.

Simmons, W. H. 1973 (1822). *Notices of East Florida with an Account of the Seminole Nation of Indians.* Charleston, S.C.: A. E. Miller.

Singleton, T. A., ed. 1985. *The Archaeology of Slavery and Plantation Life.* New York: Academic Press.

——. 1990. "The Archaeology of the Plantation South: A Review of Approaches and Goals." *Historical Archaeology* 24 (4): 70–77.

——. 1991. "The Archaeology of Slave Life." In C. E. Orser Jr., ed., *Images of the Recent Past: Readings in Historical Archaeology*, 141–65. Walnut Creek, Calif.: AltaMira Press.

——. 1995. "The Archaeology of Slavery in North America." *Annual Review of Anthropology* 24: 119–40.

——. 1999a. "An Introduction to African American Archaeology." In T. Singleton, ed., *"I, Too, Am America": Archaeological Studies of African American Life*, 1–17. Charlottesville: University Press of Virginia.

——. 1999b. "The Slave Trade Remembered on the Former Gold and Slave Coasts." *Slavery and Abolition* 20 (1): 150–69.

——. 2001a. "An Americanist Perspective on African Archaeology: Toward an Archaeology of the Black Atlantic." In C. R. DeCorse, ed., *West Africa during the Atlantic Slave Trade: Archaeological Perspectives*, 179–84. Leicester: Leicester University Press.

——. 2001b. "Slavery and Spatial Dialectics on a Cuban Coffee Plantation." *World Archaeology* 33 (1): 98–114.

——. 2001c. "Class, Race, and Identity among Free Blacks in the Antebellum South." In C. E. Orser Jr., ed., *Race and the Archaeology of Identity*, 196–207. Salt Lake City: University of Utah Press.

Singleton, T. A., and M. D. Bograd. 1995. *The Archaeology of the African Diaspora in the Americas.* Guides to the Archaeological Literature of the Immigrant Experience in America no. 2. Tucson: Society for Historical Archaeology.

——. 2000. "Breaking Typological Barriers: Looking for the Colono in Colonoware." In J. A. Delle, S. A. Mrozowski, and R. Paynter, eds., *Lines That Divide: Historical Archaeologies of Race, Class, and Gender*, 3–21. Knoxville: University of Tennessee Press.

Sinopoli, C. 1991. *Approaches to Archaeological Ceramics.* New York: Plenum Press.

Skertchly, J. A. 1874. *Dahomey as It Is: Being A Narrative of Eight Months' Residence in That Country.* London: Chapman and Hall.

111

111111

Skidmore, T. E. 1993. "Bi-Racial USA vs. Multi-Racial Brazil: Is the Contrast Still Valid?" *Journal of Latin American Studies* 25: 373–86.

———. 1994. *O Brasil visto de fora.* Rio de Janeiro: Paz e Terra.

———. 2000. Review of *História da Vida Privada no Brasil. Latin American Historical Review* 80: 569–73.

Skinner, E. 1993. "The Dialectic between Diasporas and Homelands." In J. Harris, ed., *Global Dimensions of the African Diaspora*, 2nd ed., 11–40. Washington, D.C.: Howard University Press.

Sloane, H. 1707. A *Voyage to the Islands Madera, Barbados, Nieves, S. Christophers, and Jamaica: With the natural history of the herbs and trees, four-footed beasts, fishes, birds, insects, reptiles, andc. of the last of those islands; to which is prefix'd an introduction, wherein is an account of the inhabitants, air, waters, diseases, trade, andc. of that place, with some relations concerning the neighbouring continent, and islands of America. Illustrated with figures of the things described, which have not been heretofore engraved; in large copper-plates as big as the life.* London: Published by author. Kroch Library and Rare Manuscripts, Cornell University, New York.

Smith, C. G. 1995. "Indians and Africans at Puerto Real: The Ceramic Evidence." In K. Deagan, ed., *Puerto Real: The Archaeology of a Sixteenth-Century Spanish Town in Hispaniola*, 135–372. Gainesville: University Press of Florida.

Smith, E., J. Stewart, and M. E. Kyger. 1964. *The Pennsylvania Germans of the Shenandoah Valley.* Allentown, Pa.: Schlecter's Printing.

Smith, L. 2007. "Archaeological Survey of Settlement Patterns in the Banda Region of West Central Ghana: Exploring External Influences and Internal Responses in the West African Frontier." PhD diss., Syracuse University.

Smith, R. S. 1969. *Kingdoms of the Yoruba.* London: Methuen.

———. 1970. "The Canoe in West African History." *Journal of African History* 11 (4): 515–33.

———. 1973. "Yoruba Warfare and Weapons." In S. O. Biobaku, ed., *Sources of Yoruba History*, 224–49. London: Clarendon Press.

———. 1989. *Warfare and Diplomacy in Pre-colonial West Africa.* London: James Currey.

Smith, W. 2002. *Consumption and the Making of Respectability, 1600–1800.* New York: Routledge.

Snelgrave, W. 1971 (1734). A *New Account of Some Parts of Guinea and the Slave-Trade.* London: Frank Cass.

Soares, L. C. 1991. "From Slavery to Dependence: A Historiographical Perspective." In R. Graham, ed., *Brazil and the World System*, 89–108. Austin: University of Texas Press.

Sobel, M. 1987. *The World They Made Together: Black and White Values in Eighteenth-Century Virginia.* Princeton: Princeton University Press.

Soh, S. A. 1913. *Chroniques du Fouta Sénégalais. Traduction de Manuscrits Inédits de Siré Abbas Soh*, par M. Delafosse et H. Gaden. Paris: Leroux.

Solow, B. 2001. "The Transatlantic Slave Trade: A New Census." *William and Mary Quarterly* 58 (1): 9–16.

Spear, T. 1978. *The Kaya Complex: A History of the Mijikenda Peoples of the Kenya Coast to 1900.* Nairobi: Kenya Literature Bureau.

———. 1982. *Traditions of Origin and Their Interpretation: The Mijikenda of Kenya.* Athens: Ohio University Center for International Studies Africa Program.

482

Sperling, D. C., and J. Kagabo. 2000. "The Coastal Hinterlands and the Interior of East Africa." In N. Levtzion and R. L. Pouwels, eds., *The History of Islam in Africa*, 273–302. Athens: Ohio University Press.

Stack, C. 1974. *All Our Kin: Strategies for Survival in a Black Community*. New York: Harper and Row.

Stahl, A. B. 1985. "The Kintampo Culture: Subsistence and Settlement in Ghana during the Mid-Second Millennium BC." PhD diss., University of California, Berkeley.

———. 1991. "Ethnic Style and Ethnic Boundaries: A Diachronic Case Study from West Central Ghana." *Ethnohistory* 38: 250–75.

———. 1993. "Concepts of Time and Approaches to Analogical Reasoning in Historical Perspective." *American Antiquity* 58 (2): 235–60.

———. 1994a. "Change and Continuity in the Banda Area, Ghana: The Direct Historical Approach." *Journal of Field Archaeology* 21: 181–203.

———. 1994b. "Innovation, Diffusion, and Culture Contact: The Holocene Archaeology of Ghana." *Journal of World Prehistory* 8: 51–112.

———. 1999. "The Archaeology of Global Encounters Viewed from Banda, Ghana." *African Archaeological Review* 16: 5–81.

———. 2001a. *Making History in Banda: Anthropological Visions of Africa's Pasts.* Cambridge: Cambridge University Press

———. 2001b. "Historical Process and the Impact of the Atlantic Trade on Banda, Ghana, 1800–1920." In C. R. DeCorse, ed., *West Africa during the Atlantic Slave Trade: Archaeological Perspectives*, 38–58. Leicester: Leicester University Press.

———. 2002. "Colonial Entanglements and the Practices of Taste: An Alternative to Logocentric Approaches." *American Anthropologist* 104: 827–45.

———. 2004a. "Making History in Banda: Reflections on the Construction of Africa's Past." *Historical Archaeology* 38 (1): 50–65.

———. 2004b. "Political Economic Mosaics: Archaeology of the Last Two Millennia in Tropical Sub-Saharan Africa." *Annual Review of Anthropology* 33: 145–72.

———. 2007. "Dogs, Pythons, Pots, and Beads: The Dynamics of Shrines and Sacrificial Practices in Banda, Ghana, AD 1400–1900." In *Memory Work: The Materiality of Depositional Practice*, ed. Barbara Mills and William Walker. Sante Fe, N.M.: School of American Research Press.

Stahl, A. B., and M. D. Cruz. 1998. "Men and Women in a Market Economy: Gender and Craft Production in West Central Ghana, c. 1775–1995." In S. Kent, ed., *Gender in African Prehistory*, 205–26. Walnut Creek, Calif.: AltaMira.

Stahl, A. B., and L. Smith. n.d. Report on the Banda Research Project, 2000–01 Regional Testing Program.

Stahl, A. B., and P. W. Stahl. 2004. "Ivory Production and Consumption in Ghana in the Early Second Millennium AD." *Antiquity* 78: 86–101.

Stanish, C. 1997. "Nonmarket Imperialism in a Prehispanic Context: The Inca Occupation of the Titicaca Basin." *Latin American Antiquity* 8 (3): 1–18.

Stanton, W. R., and F. Willet. 1963. "Archaeological Evidence for Changes in Maize Type in West Africa: An Experiment in Technique." *Man* 63: 150.

Staples, B. 2002. "The Seminole Tribe: Running from History." *New York Times*, April 21.

Steady, C. F. 1993. "Women of Africa and the African Diaspora: Linkages and Influences." In J. Harris, ed., *Global Dimensions of the African Diaspora*, 167–88. Washington, D.C.: Howard University Press.

Steere, E. 1870. *Swahili Tales.* London: Bell and Daldy.

Stein, R. L. 1978. "Measuring the French Slave Trade, 1713–1792/3." *Journal of African History* 29: 515–21.

Steinberg, J. 2002. "Last Voyage of the Slave Ship Henrietta Marie." *National Geographic*, August 2002, 46–61.

Steiner, C. B. 1985. "Another Image of Africa: Toward an Ethnohistory of European Cloth Marketed in West Africa, 1873–1960." *Ethnohistory* 32: 91–110.

Stevens, P. 1978. *The Stone Images of Esie, Nigeria.* New York: Africana.

Steward, J. H. 1942. "The Direct Historical Approach in Archaeology." *American Antiquity* 7 (4): 337–43.

Stewart, J. 1808. *An Account of Jamaica and Its Inhabitants.* London.

St. George, R. B. 1998. *Conversing by Signs: Poetics of Implication in New England Culture.* Chapel Hill: University of North Carolina Press.

Stigand, C. H. 1913. *The Land of Zinj: Being an Account of the British East Africa, Its Ancient History and Present Inhabitants.* London: Constable.

Stine, L. F., M. A. Cabak, and M. D. Groover. 1996. "Blue Beads as African American Cultural Symbols." *Historical Archaeology* 30 (3): 49–75.

Stoltman, J. 1989. "A Quantitative Approach to the Petrographic Analysis of Ceramic Thin-Sections." *American Antiquity* 54 (1): 147–60.

———. 1999. "The Chaco-Chuska Connection: In Defense of Anna Sheppard." In J. Feinman, ed., *Pottery and People: A Dynamic Interaction,* 9–24. Salt Lake City: University of Utah Press.

Stoner, J. J. 1881. *Bird's-Eye View of Nantucket.* Boston: State Library, Massachusetts State House.

Stuckey, S. 1987. *Slave Culture: Nationalist Theory and the Foundations of Black America.* New York: Oxford University Press.

Studer, E. S. F. de. 1958. *La trata de negros en el río de la Plata durante el siglo XVIII.* Buenos Aires: Universidad de Buenos Aires.

Sturm, F. G. 1977. "Afro-Brazilian Cults." In N. S. Booth, ed., *African Religions: A Symposium,* 217–39. New York: NOK.

Sturtevant, W. C. 1971. "Creek into Seminole." In E. B. Leacock and N. O. Lurie, eds., *North American Indians in Historical Perspective,* 92–128. New York: Random House.

Sundstrom, L. 1974. *The Exchange Economy of Pre-Colonial Tropical Africa.* New York: St. Martin's Press.

Sutherland, P. 1999. "In Memory of the Slaves: An African View of the Diaspora in the Americas." In J. Rahier, ed., *Representations of Blackness and the Performance of Identities,* 195–211. Westport, Conn.: Bergin and Garvey.

Sutton, J. E. G. 1990. *A Thousand Years of East Africa.* Nairobi: British Institute in East Africa.

Swanepoel, N. 2003. "Defensive Geographies: Local Responses to Slave Warfare in Nineteenth-Century Sisaland, Northern Ghana." Presented at annual meeting of African Studies Association, Boston.

Tadman, Michael. 1996. *Speculators and Slaves: Masters, Traders, and Slaves in the Old South.* Madison: University of Wisconsin Press.

Tainter, J. A. 1988. *The Collapse of Complex Societies.* New Studies in Archaeology. Cambridge: Cambridge University Press.

Tate, T., Jr. 1965. *The Negro in Eighteenth-Century Williamsburg.* Charlottesville: University Press of Virginia.

Techenski, M. F. 2003. "Restos óseos en la plaza (trabajo preliminar)." In R. Arlt, ed., *Arqueología Histórica Argentina, Actas del 1er. Congreso Nacional de Arqueología Histórica*, 733–39. Buenos Aires: Editorial Corregidor.

Temple, C. L. 1965. *Notes on the Tribes, Provinces, Emirates, and States of the Northern Provinces of Nigeria.* 2nd ed. London: Frank Cass.

Teulon, A. E. 1967. "Report on the Expedition to Nanny Town." Institute of Jamaica, mimeographed pamphlet, July.

Thiam, M. 1991. *La Céramique au Sénégal: Archéologie, et Histoire.* Thèse de doctorat 3ème cycle, Paris I Sorbonne.

Thiaw, I. 1999. "Archaeological Investigation of Long-Term Culture Change in the Lower Faleme (Upper Senegal Region) AD 500–1900." PhD diss., Rice University.

Thilmans, G., and A. Ravisé. 1980. *Protohistoire du Sénégal: Sinthiou Bara et les sites du Fleuve.* Mémoires de l'IFAN no. 91, Dakar.

Thomas, B. W. 1995. "Source Criticism and the Interpretation of African American Sites." *Southeastern Archaeology* 14 (2): 149–57.

Thomas, J. 2001. "Archaeologies of Place and Landscape." In I. Hodder, ed., *Archaeological Theory Today*, 165–86. Cambridge: Polity Press.

Thomas, R. P., and R. N. Bean. 1974. "The Fishers of Men: The Profits of the Slave Trade." *Journal of Economic History* 34: 885–914.

Thompson, E. P. 1963. *The Making of the English Working Class.* New York: Pantheon.

Thompson, R. F. 1983. *Flash of the Spirit: African and Afro-American Art and Philosophy.* New York: Random House.

———. 1990. "Kongo Influences on African American Artistic Culture." In J. E. Holloway, ed., *Africanisms in American Culture*, 148–84. Bloomington: Indiana University Press.

———. 1993. *Face of the Gods: Art and Altars of Africa and African Americas.* New York: Museum for African Art.

———. 1997. "Translating the World into Generousness." *Res* 32 (Autumn): 19–36.

Thompson, R. F., and J. Cornet. 1981. *The Four Moments of the Sun: Kongo Art in Two Worlds.* Washington: National Gallery of Art.

Thorbahn, P. F. 1979. "Precolonial Ivory Trade of East Africa: Reconstruction of a Human-Elephant Ecosystem." PhD diss., University of Massachusetts.

Thornton, J. K. 1977. "Demography and History in the Kingdom of the Kongo, 1550–1750." *Journal of African History* 18 (4): 507–30.

———. 1981. "Early Kongo-Portuguese Relations: A New Interpretation." *History in Africa* 8: 183–202.

———. 1983. *The Kingdom of the Kongo: Civil War and Transition, 1641–1718.* Madison: University of Wisconsin Press.

———. 1992. *Africa and Africans in the Making of the Atlantic World.* Cambridge: Cambridge University Press.

———. 1993. "'I Am the Subject of the King of Congo': African Political Ideology and the Haitian Revolution." *Journal of World History* 4 (2): 181–214.

———. 1998. *Africa and Africans in the Making of the Atlantic World, 1400–1800.* 2nd ed. Cambridge: Cambridge University Press.

———. 2002. "Religious and Ceremonial Life in the Kongo and Mbundu Areas, 1500–1700." In L. M. Heywood, ed., *Central Africans and Cultural Transformations in the American Diaspora*, 71–90. Cambridge: Cambridge University Press.

Thorpe, S. A. 1991. *African Traditional Religions*. Pretoria: University of South Africa.

Thybony, S. 1991. "Black Seminoles: A Tradition of Courage." *Smithsonian* 22 (5).

Tilley, C. 1999. *Metaphor and Material Culture*. Oxford: Blackwell.

Tolmacheva, M. 1993. *The Pate Chronicle*. East Lansing: Michigan State University Press.

Touré, F. T. 1999. *Rites Funéraires et Coutumes d'inhumation en Pays Seereer du Siin*. Mémoire de Maitrise, Université Cheikh Anta Diop.

Trigger, B. G. 1989. "Hyperrelativism, Responsibility, and the Social Sciences." *Canadian Review of Sociology and Anthropology* 26: 776–97.

———. 1992. "Brown Athena: A Postprocessual Goddess?" *Current Anthropology* 33 (1): 121–23.

———. 1995. "Expanding Middle-Range Theory." *Antiquity* 69: 449–58.

Trimingham, J. S. 1962. *A History of Islam in West Africa*. London: Oxford University Press.

———. 1964. *Islam in East Africa*. Oxford: Clarendon Press.

———. 1980a. *The Influence of Islam upon Africa*. London: Librairie du Liban.

———. 1980b. *Islam in West Africa*. Oxford: Clarendon Press.

Turner, V. 1967. *The Forest of Symbols: Aspects of Ndembu Ritual*. Ithaca: Cornell University Press.

———. 1973. "Symbols in African Ritual." *Science*, March 16, 1973, 1100–1105.

Twombly, R. 1973. "Black Resistance to Slavery in Massachusetts." In W. L. O'Neill, ed., *Insights and Parallels*, 11–56. Minneapolis: Burgess.

Twombly, R., and R. Moore. 1982. "Black Puritan: The Negro in Seventeenth-Century Massachusetts." In Bruce Glasrud and Alan Smith, eds., *Race Relations in British North America, 1607–1783*, 145–63. Chicago: Nelson-Hall.

Twyman, B. E. 1999. *The Black Seminole Legacy and North American Politics, 1693–1845*. Washington, D.C.: Howard University Press.

Tyehimba, C. 1998. "Scarred Walls of Stone." *American Legacy* 4 (2): 22–30.

Ucko, P. 1989. Foreword to S. Shennan, ed., *Archaeological Approaches to Cultural Identity*, ix–xx. London: Unwin Hyman.

Ulin, E. 2001. *Understanding Cultures: Perspectives in Anthropology and Social Theory*. 2nd ed. Boston: Blackwell.

Upton, D. 1988. "White and Black Landscapes in Eighteenth-Century Virginia." In R. B. St. George, ed., *Material Life in America, 1600–1860*, 357–69. Evanston: Northeastern University Press.

———. 1990. "Imagining the Early Virginia Landscape." In W. Kelso and R. Most, eds., *Earth Patterns: Essays in Landscape Archaeology*, 71–86. Charlottesville: University Press of Virginia.

———. 2001. "'Authentic' Anxieties." In N. Alsayyad, ed., *Consuming Tradition, Manufacturing Heritage: Global Norms and Urban Forms in the Age of Tourism*, 298–306. London: Routledge.

Urban, G. 2001. *Metaculture: How Culture Moves through the World*. Minneapolis: University of Minnesota Press.

Usman, A. 2000. "A View from the Periphery: Northern Yoruba Villages during the Old Oyo Empire, Nigeria." *Journal of Field Archaeology* 27 (1): 43–61.

———. 2001. *State-Periphery Relations and Sociopolitical Development in Igbominaland, North-Central Yoruba, Nigeria*. B.A.R. International Series 993. London: John and Erica Hedges.

——. 2003. "The Ethnohistory and Archaeology of Warfare in Northern Yoruba." *Journal of African Archaeology* 1 (2): 201–14.

Vanacker, C. 1983. "Cuivre et Métallurgie du Cuivre à Tegdaoust (Mauritanie Orientale): Découvertes et Problèmes." *Mémoire de la Société des Africanistes* 9: 89–107.

van Dantzig, Albert. 1980. *Forts and Castles of Ghana.* Accra, Ghana: Sedco.

——. 1982. "Effects of the Atlantic Slave Trade on Some West African Societies." In J. E. Inikori, ed., *Forced Migration: The Impact of the Export Slave Trade on African Societies,* 187–201. New York: Africana.

van de Merwe, N. J. 1980. "The Advent of Iron in Africa." In T. A. Wertime and J. D. Muhly, eds., *The Coming of the Age of Iron,* 463–506. New Haven: Yale University Press.

van de Merwe, N. J., and D. H. Avery. 1982. "Pathways to Steel." *American Scientist* 70: 146–55.

Vansina, J. 1966. *Kingdoms of the Savanna.* Madison: University of Wisconsin Press.

Van Wing, J. 1941. "Bakongo Magic." *Journal of the Royal Anthropological Institute of Great Britain and Ireland* 71 (1): 85–98.

Vasconcellos, C. A. 2004. "And a Child Shall Lead Them? Slavery, Childhood, and African Cultural Identity in Jamaica, 1750–1838." PhD diss., Florida International University, Miami.

Verin, P. 1986. *The History of Civilization in North Madagascar.* Rotterdam: A. A. Balkema.

Vickers, D. 1983. "The First Whalemen of Nantucket." *William and Mary Quarterly* 40 (4): 560–83.

——. 1985. "Nantucket Whalemen in the Deep-Sea Fishery: The Changing Anatomy of an Early American Labor Force." *Journal of American History* 72 (2): 277–96.

Vieira, J. L. 2000. "O Brasil da Susi Olodum." *Época,* March 20, 2000, 72–75.

Vlach, J. M. 1976. "Affecting Architecture of the Yoruba." *African Arts* 10 (1): 48–53, 99.

——. 1990. *The Afro-American Tradition in Decorative Arts.* Cleveland: Cleveland Museum of Arts.

——. 1991. "Plantation Landscapes of the Antebellum South." In Museum of the Confederacy, ed., *Before Freedom Came: African American Life in the Antebellum South,* 21–47. Richmond: Carter Printing Company.

——. 1993. *Back of the Big House: The Architecture of Plantation Slavery.* Chapel Hill: University of North Carolina Press.

Wade, P. 1993. "Race, Nature and Culture." *Man,* n.s., 28: 17–34.

Wagner, R. 1975. *The Invention of Culture.* Chicago: University of Chicago Press.

——. 1986. *Symbols That Stand for Themselves.* Chicago: University of Chicago Press.

Walker, J. 1998. *The History of Black Business in America: Capitalism, Race, Entrepreneurship.* New York: Macmillan.

Wallerstein, I. 1974. *The Modern World System.* Vol. 1. New York: Academic Press.

——. 1980. *The Modern World System.* Vol. 2. New York: Academic Press.

——. 1986. *Africa and the Modern World.* Trenton, N.J.: Africa World Press.

Walsh, Lorena S. 1997. *From Calabar to Carter's Grove: The History of a Virginia Slave Community.* Charlottesville: University Press of Virginia.

——. 2001. "The Chesapeake Slave Trade: Regional Patterns, African Origins, and Some Implications." *William and Mary Quarterly* 3rd ser., 58 (1): 139–70.

Walter, E. V. 1988. *Placeways: A Theory of Human Environment*. Chapel Hill: University of North Carolina Press.

Wane, B. 1981. "Le Fuuta Tooro de Cernoo Suleymaan Baal à la fin de l'Almamiyat." *Revue Sénégalaise d'Histoire* 1 (2): 38–50.

Wane, Y. 1969. *Les Toucouleurs du Fouta Tooro (Sénégal): Stratification Sociale et Structure Familiale*. IFAN, Initiations et Etudes Africaines no. 25.

Ward, W. E. F. 1958. *A History of Ghana*. London: George Allen and Unwin.

Warner, Mark S. 1995. "From the Market and from the Water: An African American Household's Changing Responses to a Commercial Marketplace." Presented at 28th annual meeting of the Society for Historical Archaeology, Washington, D.C.

Waselkov, G., and M. Smith. 2001. "Upper Creek Archaeology." In B. McEwan, ed., *Indians of the Greater Southeast: Historical Archaeology and Ethnohistory*, 242–64. Gainesville: University Press of Florida.

Webb, J. L. A. 1985. "The Trade in Gum Arabic: Prelude to French Conquest in Senegal." *Journal of African History* 26: 149–68.

———. 1993. "The Horse and Slave Trade between the Western Sahara and Senegambia." *Journal of African History* 34: 221–46.

Weik, T. 1997. "The Archaeology of Maroon Societies in the Americas: Resistance, Cultural Continuity, and Transformation in the African Diaspora." *Historical Archaeology* 31 (2): 81–92.

———. 2002. "A Historical Archaeology of Black Seminole Maroons in Florida, Ethnogenesis and Culture Contact at Pilaklikaha." PhD diss., University of Florida.

———. 2004. "Archaeology of the African Diaspora in Latin America." *Historical Archaeology* 38 (1): 32–49.

Weisman, B. R. 1989. *Like Beads on a String: A Culture History of the Seminole in North Florida*. Tuscaloosa: University of Alabama Press.

———. 1999. *Unconquered People: Florida's Seminole and Miccosukee Indians*. Gainesville: University of Florida Press.

Wendorf, F., A. E. Close, and R. Schild. 1987. "Early Domestic Cattle in the Eastern Sahara." *Paleoecology of Africa* 18: 441–48.

Wendorf, F., and R. Schild. 1994. "Are the Early Holocene Cattle in the Eastern Sahara Domestic or Wild?" *Evolutionary Anthropology* 3: 118–28.

Werner, A. L. 1915. "A Swahili History of Pate." *Journal of the Royal Asiatic Society* 14: 280–89.

Wertime, T. A. 1962. *The Coming of the Age of Steel*. Chicago: University of Chicago Press.

Westmacott, R. 1992. *African American Gardens and Yards in the Rural South*. Knoxville: University of Tennessee Press.

Wheaton, T., and P. Garrow. 1985. "Acculturation and the Archaeological Record in the Carolina Lowcountry." In T. Singleton, ed., *The Archaeology of Slavery and Plantation Life*, 239–59. Orlando: Academic Press.

White, D. G. 1999. *Ar'n't I a Woman? Female Slaves in the Plantation South*. New York: W. W. Norton.

White, S., and G. White. 1995. "Slave Clothing and African American Culture in the Eighteenth and Nineteenth Centuries." *Past and Present* 148: 149–86.

———. 1998. *Stylin': African American Expressive Culture from Its Beginnings to the Zoot Suit*. Ithaca: Cornell University Press.

Whitten, N. E., Jr. 1962. "Contemporary Patterns of Malign Occultism among Negroes in North Carolina." *Journal of American Folklore* 75: 311–25.

Wilding, R. F. 1980. "The Ceramics of the North Kenya Coast." PhD diss., University of Nairobi, Kenya.

Wilk, R. R. 1985. "The Ancient Maya and the Political Present." *Journal of Anthropological Research* 41: 307–26.

Wilkie, L. A. 1995. "Magic and Empowerment on the Plantation: An Archaeological Consideration of African American World View." *Southeastern Archaeology* 14 (2): 136–48.

———. 1996. "Glass-Knapping at a Louisiana Plantation: African American Tools." *Historical Archaeology* 30 (4): 37–49.

———. 1997. "Secret and Sacred: Contextualizing the Artifacts of African American Magic and Religion." *Historical Archaeology* 31 (4): 81–106.

———. 1999. "Evidence of African Continuities in the Material Culture of Clifton Plantation, Bahamas." In J. B. Haviser, ed., *African Sites Archaeology in the Caribbean*, 264–75. Princeton, N.J.: Markus Weiner.

———. 2000. *Creating Freedom: Material Culture and African American Identity at Oakley Plantation, Louisiana, 1840–1950.* Baton Rouge: Louisiana State University Press.

———. 2001. "Communicative Bridges Linking Actors through Time: Archaeology and the Construction of Emancipatory Narratives at a Bahamian Plantation." *Journal of Social Archaeology* 1 (2): 225–43.

———. 2003. *The Archaeology of Mothering: An African American Midwife's Tale.* New York: Routledge.

———. 2004. "Considering the Future of African American Archaeology." *Historical Archaeology* 38 (1): 109–23.

Wilkie, L. A., and G. W. Shorter Jr. 2001. *Lucrecia's Well: An Archaeological Glimpse of an African American Midwife's Household.* Mobile: University of South Alabama, Center for Archaeological Studies.

Wilks, I. 1975. *Asante in the Nineteenth Century: The Structure and Evolution of a Political Order.* Cambridge: Cambridge University Press.

———. 1993. *Forests of Gold: Essays on the Akan and the Kingdom of Asante.* Athens: Ohio University Press.

Willett, F. 1962. "The Introduction of Maize into West Africa: An Assessment of Recent Evidence." *Africa* 32 (1): 1–13.

———. 1967. *Ife in the History of West African Sculpture.* London: Thames and Hudson.

Williams, B. F. 1992. "Of Straightening Combs, Sodium Hydroxide, and Potassium Hydroxide in Archaeological and Cultural-Anthropological Analyses of Ethnogenesis." *American Antiquity* 57 (4): 608–12.

Williams, D. 1974. *Icon and Image: A Study of Sacred and Secular Forms of African Classical Art.* London: Allen Lane.

Williams, E. 1944. *Capitalism and Slavery.* New York: Chapel Hill.

Williams, R. 1972. *The Country and the City.* New York: Oxford University Press.

Willis, W. S. 1963. "Divide and Rule: Red, White, and Black in the Southeast." *Journal of Negro History* 48 (3): 157–76.

Wilson, T. H. 1978. *The Monumental Architecture and Archaeology North of the Tana River.* Nairobi: National Museums of Kenya.

——. 1980. *The Monumental Architecture and Archaeology of the Central and South-ern Kenya Coast.* Nairobi: National Museums of Kenya.

——. 1982. "Spatial Analysis and Settlement Patterns on the East African Coast." *Paideuma* 28: 201–19.

Wobst, H. 1977. "Stylistic Behavior and Information Exchange." In C. Cleland, ed., *For the Director: Research Essays in Honor of James B. Griffin,* 317–42. Ann Arbor: Museum of Anthropology, University of Michigan.

Wolf, Eric R. 1972. "The Virgin of Guadalupe: A Mexican National Symbol." In W. A. Lessa and E. Z. Vogt, eds., *Reader in Comparative Religion: An Anthropological Approach,* 149–53. New York: Harper and Row.

——. 1982. *Europe and the People without History.* Berkeley: University of California Press.

——. 2001. *Pathways of Power.* Berkeley: University of California Press.

Wondji, C. 1992. "The States and Cultures of the Upper Guinean Coast." In B. A. Ogot, ed., *General History of Africa,* vol. 5, *Africa from the Sixteenth to the Eight-eenth Century,* 368–98. Berkeley: University of California Press.

Wood, J. J., and S. Powell. 1993. "An Ethos for Archaeological Practice." *Human Organization* 52: 405–13.

Wood, W. R. 1967. "An Archaeological Appraisal of Early European Settlements in the Senegambia." *Journal of African History* 8 (1): 39–64.

Woodson, C. G. 1936. *The African Background Outlined.* Washington, D.C.: Associa-tion for the Study of Negro Life and History.

Worth, H. B. 1906. *Nantucket Lands and Landowners.* Nantucket, Mass.: Nantucket Historical Association.

Wright, D. R. 1975. "On Tour in the Gold Coast." In J. Drachler, ed., *Black Home-land, Black Diaspora: Cross-Currents of the African Relationship,* 87–96. London: National University Publications Press.

Wright, J. L. 1986. *Creeks and Seminoles.* Lincoln: University of Nebraska Press.

Wurst, L. 1991. "Employees Must Be of Moral and Temperate Habits: Rural and Urban Elite Ideologies." In R. McGuire and R. Paynter, eds., *The Archaeology of Inequality,* 125–49. Oxford: Basil Blackwell.

Wylie, A. 1985. "The Reaction against Analogy." In M. B. Schiffer, ed., *Advances in Archaeological Method and Theory,* 8:63–111. New York: Academic Press.

Yai, O. B. 2001. "Survivals and Dynamism of African Cultures in the Americas." In D. Diene, ed., *From Chains to Bonds: The Slave Trade Revisited,* 344–56. Paris: UNESCO; New York: Berghahn Books.

Yarak, L. W. 1979. "Dating Asantehene Osei Kwadwo's Campaign against the Banna." *Asantesem* 10: 58.

Yellin, J. F. 1987. *Incidents in the Life of a Slave Girl, Written by Herself.* Cambridge: Harvard University Press.

Yentsch, A. E. 1991. "A Note on a Nineteenth-Century Description of Below-Ground 'Storage Cellars' among the Ibo." *African American Archaeology* 4: 3–4.

——. 1994. *A Chesapeake Family and Their Slaves: A Study in Historical Archaeology.* Cambridge: Cambridge University Press.

——. 1995. "Beads as Silent Witness of an African American Past: Social Identity and the Artifacts of Slavery in Annapolis, Maryland." In M. E. D'Agostino, E. Prine, E. Casella, and M. Winer, eds., *The Written and the Wrought: Complementary Sources in Historical Anthropology,* 44–60. Kroeber Anthropological Society Papers no. 79.

Yinger, J. M. 1994. *Ethnicity: Source of Strength? Source of Conflict?* Albany: State University of New York Press.

Yoffee, N. N., and G. L. Cowgill, eds. 1988. *The Collapse of Ancient States and Civilizations.* Tucson: University of Arizona Press.

York, R. N. 1972. "Cowries as Type-Fossils in Ghanaian Archaeology." *West African Journal of Archaeology* 2: 93–101.

———. 1973. "Excavations at New Buipe." *West African Journal of Archaeology* 3: 1–189.

Young, A. L. 1996. "Archaeological Evidence of African-Style Ritual and Healing Practices in the Upland South." *Tennessee Anthropologist* 21 (2): 139–55.

———. 1997. "Risk Management Strategies among African American Slaves at Locust Grove Plantation." *International Journal of Historical Archaeology* 1 (1): 5–37.

Young, H. 1953. "A Topographical Memoir on East and West Florida with Itineraries of General Jackson's Army, 1818." *Florida Historical Quarterly* 13: 16–164.

Zanettini, P. E. 1996. "Por uma arqueologia de Canudos e dos Brasileiros iletrados." *Revista Canudos* 1 (1): 167–71.

———. 2002. *Arqueologia e reconstituição monumental do Parque Estadual de Canudos.* Salvador: Universidade do Estado da Bahia.

Zeder, M. A. 1997. *The American Archaeologist.* Walnut Creek, Calif.: AltaMira Press.

Contributors

Anna S. Agbe-Davies (PhD, University of Pennsylvania) is assistant professor of anthropology at DePaul University. She has undertaken research that compares colonialism and slavery across several British colonies, including Virginia, Bermuda, and Barbados. She has also studied the transition from indentured servitude to slavery in the Virginia plantation economy. Her current research agenda examines the lives of African Americans in Chicago in the late nineteenth century and early twentieth century.

E. Kofi Agorsah (PhD, UCLA) is professor of black studies and international studies at Portland State University. He was formerly keeper of the Ghana Museums and Monuments Board (1973–78) and served as lecturer and senior lecturer at the University of Ghana (1983–87). He was also the Edward Moulton Barrett Lecturer in Archaeology at the University of the West Indies in Jamaica (1987–92). Dr. Agorsah serves as vice president of the International Association for Caribbean Archaeology and as a board member of the African Burial Ground Project of the City of New York, and he is the leading authority on the archaeology of Maroon heritage. He edited *Maroon Heritage: Archaeological, Ethnographic, and Historical Perspectives* and coauthored *Africa and the African Diaspora: Cultural Adaptation and Resistance* with G. Tucker Childs. He is the author of *An Ethnoarchaeological Analysis of Human Functional Dynamics in the Volta Basin of Ghana: Before and after the Akosombo Dam.*

Whitney L. Battle-Baptiste (PhD, University of Texas at Austin) is a postdoctoral fellow in Africana studies at Cornell University. Her research is on the formation of African American cultural identities with emphasis on African Diasporic material cultures and gender. She is the author of "A Space of Our Own: Redefining the Enslaved Household at Andrew Jackson's Hermitage Plantation," in *Household Chores and Household Choices: Theorizing the Domestic Sphere in Historical Archaeology,* edited by Kerri Barile and Jamie C. Brandon (University of Alabama Press, 2004).

Mary C. Beaudry (PhD, Brown University) is professor of archaeology and anthropology at Boston University. Her chief areas of expertise are historical and industrial archaeology of the Americas. She has been the recipient of three grants from the National Endowment for the Humanities for historical archaeological research in Massachusetts. In 1994 and again in 2001 she was an NEH Fellow at the Center for Advanced Studies at the Winterthur Museum and Library in Winterthur, Delaware. She was editor of *Northeast Historical Archaeology*, the journal of the Council for Northeast Historical Archaeology, from 1984 to 2001. She edited *Documentary Archaeology in the New World* (Cambridge University Press, 1992), coauthored *"Living on the Boott": Historical Archaeology at the Boott Mills Boardinghouses, Lowell, Massachusetts* (University of Massachusetts Press, 1996), and coedited *The Art and Mystery of Historical Archaeology: Essays in Honor of James Deetz* (CRC Press, 1992). She is the author of *Findings: The Material Culture of Needlework and Sewing* (Yale University Press, 2007).

Ellen P. Berkland (MA, Boston University) is the city archaeologist for Boston. Before that, she was employed as a staff archaeologist for the Office of Public Archaeology, a large management company associated with Boston University. Ellen has worked all over New England on both ancient (Native American sites) and historic sites including the Nantucket African Baptist Society Meeting House.

Alexandra A. Chan (PhD, Boston University) is project archaeologist at Independent Archaeological Consulting, LLC, a small woman-owned CRM firm based out of Portsmouth, N.H. She has also taught at Vassar College. She has studied the experiences of early African and African American bondsmen and the nature of master-slave relations in colonial Massachusetts, as seen through landscape, architecture, and artifact. A monograph based on that research is to be published by the University of Tennessee Press in 2007. Research interests include class and counterculture formation among nineteenth-century working-class immigrant neighborhoods of Manchester, N.H.

Alioune Déme (PhD, Rice University) is adjunct professor of anthropology and African history at Texas Southern University. His research is on paleoclimate change, emerging social complexity, and state formation in West Africa, specifically in the Middle Senegal Valley.

Toyin Falola (PhD, Ile-Ife) is University Distinguished Teaching Professor and the Frances Higginbothom Nalle Centennial Professor at University of Texas, Austin. He is the author of several books, including *The Power of African Cultures* (University of Rochester Press, 2003).

Christopher C. Fennell (JD, Georgetown University; PhD, University of Virginia) is assistant professor of anthropology, specializing in historical archaeology, at the University of Illinois at Urbana-Champaign. His research projects address aspects of African American cultural heritage and the dynamics of social group affiliations among European American immigrants in the eighteenth and nineteenth centuries. These research efforts include the development of interpretative frameworks focusing on regional systems theories, diaspora studies, theories concerning ethnicities and racialization, stylistic and symbolic analysis of material culture, and the significance of consumption patterns. He has published several articles on archaeology and African diaspora subjects in peer-review journals, including the *International Journal of Historical Archaeology*.

Pedro P. Funari (PhD, São Paulo State University, Brazil) is professor of ancient history and historical archaeology at the Campinas State University, Brazil. His research focuses on material culture in Europe and the Americas in historical contexts, with particular attention paid to ethnicity and the politics of archaeological knowledge. He is coeditor of *Historical Archaeology: Back from the Edge* (Routledge, 1999) and *Global Archaeological Theory* (Kluwer, 2005).

Candice L. Goucher (PhD, UCLA) is professor of history and director of the College of Liberal Arts at Washington State University, Vancouver. She has conducted archaeological and historical research in West Africa, the Caribbean, and Mauritius. Among her publications and films are the coauthored volume *In the Balance: Themes in Global History* (McGraw-Hill, 1998) and the video *The Blooms of Banjeli: Technology and Gender in West African Ironmaking* (Documentary Educational Resources, 1986), which won the Society for Visual Anthropology Award of Excellence. She is one of two lead scholars for *Bridging World History* (funded by a $2.28-million grant from Annenberg/Corporation for Public Broadcasting), a 26-part video series and multimedia world history curriculum for high school teachers and college students. She is currently the general editor of the *Encyclopedia of Women in World History* (Facts on File).

Ndèye Sokhna Guèye (PhD, French University of Nanterre) is the SEPHIS administrator at the CODESRIA, Senegal. Her research is on ethnoarchaeology in the Middle Senegal Valley from the fifteenth century through the nineteenth century. Dr. Guèye's interests include ceramic, subsistence strategy, technological innovation, gender issues, and precolonial and colonial culture contacts.

Mark W. Hauser (PhD, Syracuse University) is a visiting assistant professor of anthropology at the University of Notre Dame. His research has concentrated on political economy (informal economic systems) and ceramics of the African Diaspora. He has contributed several articles in peer-review journals, including *International Journal of Historical Archaeology* and *Historical Archaeology*.

Chapurukha M. Kusimba (PhD, Bryn Mawr College) worked for seven years as a research scientist at the National Museums of Kenya. He has been curator of African archaeology and ethnology at the Field Museum in Chicago since 1994. His research interests are in the later prehistory of Africa. For the last seventeen years, he has conducted archaeological and anthropological research on the East African coast with the aim of understanding the extraordinarily rapid rise, decline, and resilience of urban societies that coalesced into what is known as the Swahili states. He is the author of *The Rise and Fall of Swahili States* (Altamira Press, 1999) and coeditor of *East African Archaeology* (University of Pennsylvania Press, 2003) and *Unwrapping the Textile Traditions of Madagascar* (Fowler Museums of Cultural History, 2004).

Fred L. McGhee (PhD, University of Texas at Austin) is president and principal investigator of a cultural resources management firm based in Texas and Hawaii. Before joining the private sector, he was chief archaeologist at Hickam Air Force Base in Hawaii, and he managed historic resources associated with the Japanese attack on Pearl Harbor as well as the famous "O-18" site, one of the most important sites in Hawaiian archaeology. A former navy deep sea diving officer, his research interests focus on the African American maritime experience.

J. Cameron Monroe (PhD, UCLA) is assistant professor of anthropology at the University of California, Santa Cruz. He has conducted archaeological research on the nature of African American ethnic identity in seventeenth-century Virginia. He is directing a research project in the Republic of Bénin, West Africa. This project focuses on the relationship between the transatlantic slave trade and political transformation in the precolonial kingdom of Dahomey.

Akinwumi Ogundiran (PhD, Boston University) is associate professor of history and director of African–New World Studies at Florida International University, Miami. His research interests cover the cultural history, material culture, and historical archaeology of the Bight of Benin hinterlands of West Africa. He is the author of *Archaeology and History in Ilare District, Central Yorubaland (1200–1900)* in the Cambridge Monograph in African Archaeology series (Archaeopress, 2002) and editor of *Precolonial Nigeria: Essays in Honor of Toyin Falola* (Africa World Press, 2005). His articles have appeared in *African Archaeological Review, Journal of Field Archaeology, International Journal of African Historical Studies, History in Africa,* and *Journal of World Prehistory,* among others.

Brempong Osei-Tutu is senior lecturer in archaeology at the University of Ghana, Legon. He is on study leave as a doctoral candidate in the Department of Anthropology, Syracuse University, with research interests in archaeological heritage management, public policy archaeology, cultural commodification, and the African Diaspora. His early research focused on the archaeology and culture history of southern Ghana. His most recent publication is "African American Reactions to the Restoration of Ghana's 'Slave Castles'" (*Public Archaeology,* 2004).

Daniel Schávelzon (PhD, University of Mexico) is director of the Center of Urban Archaeology at the University of Buenos Aires. He is the author of more than thirty books, including *The Historical Archaeology of Buenos Aires: A City at the End of the World* (Kluwer-Plenum-Academic Press, 2000), *Buenos Aires Negra* (Emece4 Editores, 2003), and *Arqueología de Buenos Aires* (Emece4 Editores, 1999).

Ann Brower Stahl (PhD, University of California at Berkeley) is professor of anthropology at the State University of New York, Binghamton. Her early research focused on sedentism and subsistence in ceramic Late Stone Age contexts in Ghana (Kintampo Complex), while her more recent research has centered on the effects of global entanglements along the savanna-woodland/forest margins in Ghana. She is the author of *Making History in Banda: Anthropological Visions of Africa's Past* (Cambridge University Press, 2001) and the editor of *African Archaeology* (Blackwell, 2005).

Aribidesi Usman (PhD, Arizona State University) is assistant professor of African and African American Studies at Arizona State University. Since the 1990s, his research has been aimed at understanding and documenting northern Yoruba village activities during the Old Oyo period and the sociopolitical relationship with large centers of power. His current research has focused on understanding how and under what circumstances precolonial urbanism developed in Africa and how trade influenced cultural and ecological transformations in Africa. His publications include a BAR monograph (Archeopress, 2001) and several articles in anthologies and journals.

Terrance Weik (PhD, University of Florida) is assistant professor of anthropology at the University of South Carolina, Columbia. His general interests in anthropology include the cultural origins, social formations, and transformations that have shaped people of African descent. He examined the sociocultural genesis and identity of the Black Seminole and the interchanges between Africans and Native Americans at Pilaklikaha in central Florida. Weik expanded the scope of his research to include both freedom and slavery in the African Diaspora of the Americas. In the last three years he has explored an urban slavery site in South Carolina, a Mississippi plantation/tenant farm, and a Mexican Cimarron site. His publications include "The Archaeology of Maroon Societies in the Americas: Resistance, Cultural Continuity, and Transformation in the African Diaspora" (*Historical Archaeology*, 1997) and "Archaeology of the African Diaspora in Latin America" (*Historical Archaeology*, 2004).

Index

abolition movement, 32; Africa and, 38
Abomey, 101–20. *See also* Abomey
   Pleateau Archaeological Project
Abomey Pleateau Archaeological
   Project, 107–12
adornments, 409–11. *See also* beads
Afrasian world system, 177–79. *See also*
   Indian Ocean trade
Africa, imaginings of, 49–50
African American Society to Preserve
   Cape Coast Castle, 186
African Americans, 192–93; slave castles
   and, 189–90; social memory and, 190
African Baptist Meeting House, 7,
   37, 395, 400–401, 406, 411–12;
   archaeology of, 403–404, 411–12;
   artifacts and, 406–11; function of,
   401–402; landscaping of, 405–406;
   school and, 403
African Burial Ground, 421
African Descendants Association
   Foundation of Ghana, 186
African Diaspora: African Seminoles
   and, 311–31; Bakongo and,
   199–232; Brazil and, 355–71; Buenos
   Aries, 372–83; demography of, 6;
   empowering of, 40–41; identity

and, 17–24, 384, 385; landscapes
   and, 249–76; maritime aspects of,
   34–36, 384–94; metallurgy and,
   277–91. *See also* Diasporic cultural
   change, Bakongo and; Diasporic
   cultural continuity; identity
   construction; metallurgy; *specific
   countries*
African–Native American contact, 24,
   311–13, 316–19, 321, 324, 330–31,
   363. *See also* "African Seminole";
   maroons; Seminole Maroons
"African Seminole," 314–17, 317–19,
   321; ethnogenesis of, 323–31. *See also*
   Seminole Maroons
Africanism, 17–19, 22, 23, 29, 414–15.
   See also Herskovits, Melville
Afro-Brazilian Studies Center, 362
Agaja, King, 103, 111
Agbe-Davies, Anna, 22, 40, 413
Agorsah, Kofi, 33, 34, 332
agriculturalists, 126, 134; East Africa
   and, 166
Aja, 102
Akinjogbin, Adeagbo, 104
Al Bakri, 128, 129, 134
al Idrissi, 128, 134

"displaced geographies," 389–91
divination, 377, 379
division of labor, 27; gender and, 26.
    See also class system; power
    relations
Dom Manuel I, King, 174
"dominant ideology thesis," 251
Drake, S. A., 262–63
drought, 11, 170
Du Bois, W. E. B., 385, 401–402, 419
Durant-Gonzalez, Victoria, 308
Durrans, Brian, 358
Dutch, 338

East Africa, 5, 9, 160–83; structures
    and, 164. *See also* Swahili city-states;
    Swahili culture
"Ebi social theory," 104
Edo, 30–31
Edwards-Ingram, Y., 244
Ekitiparapo, 148
Elmina, 22, 100. *See also* Elmina
    castles
Elmina castles, 185, 189, 190–91, 193,
    194, 195
emancipation, 36, 37, 415; Brazil and,
    356; Buenos Aries and, 376
Enlightenment ideas, 32. *See also*
    abolition movement
entrepreneurs, 168–70
environmental change, 170–71
Escalante, Aquiles, 360
ethnic identity, Brazil and, 357–59,
    360–61. *See also* identity
    construction
ethnohistorical analogy, 208–11
excavations, 13, 22, 59, 69, 72; African
    Baptist Meeting House and,
    403–11; Brazil and, 364; Elmina,
    100; Fort Ruychaver, 100; Hermitage
    Plantation, 237–40; Jamaican
    maroons and, 344–51; North America
    and, 199, 206–208; Okun and, 79–92;
    Swahili city-states, 164–70; yardspace
    and, 27, 28. *See also* archaeology;
    artifacts, African; artifacts, African
    American; Banda Research Project
exchange economies, 25, 296

Father Maclaro, 179
faunal remains, 70, 74, 90, 241
Fennell, Christopher, 23, 24, 199
firearms, 146
fishermen, 126
Florida, 311, 316, 324–25, 326, 337.
    See also "African Seminole";
    Seminole Indians; Seminole
    Maroons; "Seminole Wars"
Florida Armed Occupation Act, 316
food crops, 71, 74, 156; American, 11.
    See also maize
Fort Saint Louis, 131, 132
forts, European, 131–32
Foster, Laurence, 320
Foster, Lucy, 413
France, 71, 116, 131–32, 133
Frazier, Franklin E., 17–18
Frederiksgave plantation, 13
free blacks, 30, 273; Jamaica and, 292;
    New England and, 36–37, 397;
    Seminole Maroons and, 313, 315. *See
    also* African Baptist Meeting House
Freeman, Thomas, 111
fugitive slaves: Brazil and, 362–63, 367,
    370; Caribbean and, 333–34; North
    American and, 260, 315, 316–17,
    323–24. *See also* maroons; Palmares;
    Seminole Maroons
Fulani, 146, 147; jihad and, 148
Funari, Pedro, 34
Fyffe, Dudley, 286–87

Garman, J. C., 275
Garvey, Marcus, 352
Gele, King, 111, 114
gender roles, 26, 28, 234. *See also*
    division of labor
Gezo, King, 111, 114
Ghana, 9, 38, 50, 100, 187, 192–93;
    African American connection to,
    185–86. *See also* Banda; Gold Coast
Gilroy, Paul, 384, 389
Girouard, M., 263
Glassman, J., 360
Goiás, 368, 370
gold, 62–63, 131
Gold Coast, 9, 13. *See also* Ghana

kilns, 296
Kilwa, 168, 171, 173, 174, 178
King Ibrahim, 174–75
Kusimba, Chapurukha, 17, 160
Kuulo Kataa, 62–64, 66
Kwaku I, Nana Okofo Iture, 191

Lamlam, 134–35
Lamu, 171, 175
landscape studies, 251–52. See also Isaac
    Royall House; Medford landscape
Law, Robin, 105
LeHerissé, A., 114
leydi, 126, 128
Liguanea, 292, 303
Lima, 374
Lisbon, 178, 179
Lovejoy, Paul, 6–7
Lucayanos, 332

Ma Lou (Fanny Johnson), 295, 296
Mahilaka, 171
maize, 64, 66, 154
Mali Empire, 130
Malindi, 168, 171, 175, 179, 183
Manning, Patrick, 123
marine archaeology, 386
maritime archaeology. See archaeology;
    Atlantic slave trade
market towns. See trade centers
Maroon Heritage Research Project, 340,
    351, 354
maroons, 24, 27, 30, 33–34, 335;
    academic study and, 33–34, 312–13,
    317–18, 320–21; Caribbean and,
    332–36; Jamaica and, 283, 291, 329,
    336, 340–43, 343–51; migration
    and, 336, 342; North America and,
    311–31, 334–35, 336; resistance and,
    32, 336, 342, 348, 349, 351, 352–53,
    363–64, 366–67. See also Maroon
    Heritage Research Project; Nanny
    Town; Palmares; Seaman's Valley;
    Seminole Maroons
Maryland, 206, 207, 209–10, 220, 226
Masaba, Emir, 148
Masai, 171
master-slave relations, 267

material life, 41–44; Banda and, 59, 62,
    63, 69, 72–73, 74–75; Brazil and, 358,
    359–60, 364, 370–71; Buenos Aires
    and, 373–74; Diaspora and, 206–208,
    252–62, 398; Middle Senegal Valley
    and, 136; Yoruba and, 155–56;
    Yoruba-Edo and, 83–86, 89, 90–92,
    95–96, 97–98. See also archaeology;
    artifacts, African; artifacts, African
    American; commodities; excavations;
    symbolic expression
Mayhew, Thomas, Sr., 396–97
Mbuia-Joao, 178–79
McGhee, Fred, 34–35, 384
Medford, 29–30, 253; demography
    of, 258. See also Medford
    landscape
Medford landscape, 252–53; material
    culture and, 253–62. See also Isaac
    Royall House
metal, 277, 279–80. See also copper;
    iron; metallurgy
metallurgists. See blacksmiths
metallurgy, 26, 69, 97, 142, 155–56;
    academic study and, 277–78;
    Caribbean and, 276, 281–91; East
    Africa and, 166, 178; fuel and,
    280–81; markets for, 283–84.
    See also blacksmiths; copper; iron;
    Ogun; Reeder's Pen
metaphors, religious: Bakongo and,
    201–202, 203, 204, 213–16; Diaspora
    and, 217–18; maritime environment
    and, 385; water and, 204–205, 216,
    220, 384
Mexico Maroons, 240
Middle Passage, 5, 21, 35, 387
Middle Senegal Valley, 9, 122–24,
    134–35, 137–39; Atlantic trade and,
    130–34, 137; geography of, 124–28;
    trans-Saharan trade and, 128–30,
    135–37. See also Middle Senegal
    Valley Project; Senegambia
Middle Senegal Valley Project, 125.
    See also Middle Senegal Valley
Minas Gerais, 368, 370
minkisi, 214, 215, 217–18, 220, 221.
    See also Nkondi